POETRY
for Students

Advisors

Jayne M. Burton is a teacher of secondary English and an adjunct professor for Northwest Vista College in San Antonio, TX.

Klaudia Janek is the school librarian at the International Academy in Bloomfield Hills, Michigan. She holds an MLIS degree from Wayne State University, a teaching degree from Rio Salado College, and a bachelor of arts degree in international relations from Saint Joseph's College. She is the IB Extended Essay Coordinator and NCA AdvancEd co-chair at her school. She is an IB workshop leader for International Baccalaureate North America, leading teacher training for IB school librarians and extended essay coordinators. She has been happy to serve the Michigan Association for Media in Education as a board member and past president at the regional level, advocating for libraries in Michigan schools.

Greg Bartley is an English teacher in Virginia. He holds an M.A.Ed. in English Education from Wake Forest University and a B.S. in Integrated Language Arts Education from Miami University.

Sarah Clancy teaches IB English at the International Academy in Bloomfield Hills, Michigan. She is a member of the National Council of Teachers of English and Michigan Speech Coaches, Inc. Sarah earned her undergraduate degree from Kalamazoo College and her Master's of Education from Florida Southern College. She coaches the high-ranking forensics team and is the staff adviser of the school newspaper, *Overachiever*.

Karen Dobson is a teen/adult librarian at Plymouth District Library in Plymouth, Michigan. She holds a Bachelor of Science degree from Oakland University and an MLIS from Wayne State University and has served on many committees through the Michigan Library Association.

Tom Shilts is the youth librarian at the Okemos branch of Capital Area District Library in Okemos, Michigan. He holds an MSLS degree from Clarion University of Pennsylvania and an MA in U.S. History from the University of North Dakota.

POETRY
for Students

Presenting Analysis, Context, and Criticism
on Commonly Studied Poetry

VOLUME 56

Kristin B. Mallegg, Project Editor

Foreword by David J. Kelly

GALE
CENGAGE Learning

Farmington Hills, Mich • San Francisco • New York • Waterville, Maine
Meriden, Conn • Mason, Ohio • Chicago

GALE
CENGAGE Learning·

Poetry for Students, Volume 56

Project Editor: Kristin B. Mallegg

Rights Acquisition and Management:
  Ashley Maynard, Carissa Poweleit

Composition: Evi Abou-El-Seoud

Manufacturing: Rita Wimberley

Imaging: John Watkins

For product information and technology assistance, contact us at
Gale Customer Support, 1-800-877-4253.
For permission to use material from this text or product,
submit all requests online at **www.cengage.com/permissions.**
Further permissions questions can be emailed to
permissionrequest@cengage.com

While every effort has been made to ensure the reliability of the information presented in this publication, Gale, a part of Cengage Learning, does not guarantee the accuracy of the data contained herein. Gale accepts no payment for listing; and inclusion in the publication of any organization, agency, institution, publication, service, or individual does not imply endorsement of the editors or publisher. Errors brought to the attention of the publisher and verified to the satisfaction of the publisher will be corrected in future editions.

Gale
27500 Drake Rd.
Farmington Hills, MI, 48331-3535

ISBN-13: 978-1-4103-2848-9
ISSN 1094-7019

This title is also available as an e-book.
ISBN-13: 978-1-4103-2853-3
Contact your Gale, a part of Cengage Learning sales representative for ordering information.

Printed in Mexico
1 2 3 4 5 6 7 21 20 19 18 17

Table of Contents

Just a Few Lines on a Page

I have often thought that poets have the easiest job in the world. A poem, after all, is just a few lines on a page, usually not even extending margin to margin—how long would that take to write, about five minutes? Maybe ten at the most, if you wanted it to rhyme or have a repeating meter. Why, I could start in the morning and produce a book of poetry by dinnertime. But we all know that it isn't that easy. Anyone can come up with enough words, but the poet's job is about writing the *right* ones. The right words will change lives, making people see the world somewhat differently than they saw it just a few minutes earlier. The right words can make a reader who relies on the dictionary for meanings take a greater responsibility for his or her own personal understanding. A poem that is put on the page correctly can bear any amount of analysis, probing, defining, explaining, and interrogating, and something about it will still feel new the next time you read it.

It would be fine with me if I could talk about poetry without using the word "magical," because that word is overused these days to imply "a really good time," often with a certain sweetness about it, and a lot of poetry is neither of these. But if you stop and think about magic—whether it brings to mind sorcery, witchcraft, or bunnies pulled from top hats—it always seems to involve stretching reality to produce a result greater than the sum of its parts and pulling unexpected results out of thin air. This book provides ample cases where a few simple words conjure up whole worlds. We do not actually travel to different times and different cultures, but the poems get into our minds, they find what little we know about the places they are talking about, and then they make that little bit blossom into a bouquet of someone else's life. Poets make us think we are following simple, specific events, but then they leave ideas in our heads that cannot be found on the printed page. Abracadabra.

Sometimes when you finish a poem it doesn't feel as if it has left any supernatural effect on you, like it did not have any more to say beyond the actual words that it used. This happens to everybody, but most often to inexperienced readers: regardless of what is often said about young people's infinite capacity to be amazed, you have to understand what usually does happen, and what could have happened instead, if you are going to be moved by what someone has accomplished. In those cases in which you finish a poem with a "So what?" attitude, the information provided in *Poetry for Students* comes in handy. Readers can feel assured that the poems included here actually are potent magic, not just because a few (or a hundred or ten thousand) professors of literature say they are: they're significant because they can withstand close inspection and still amaze the very same people who have just finished taking them apart and seeing how they work. Turn them inside out, and they will still be able to come alive, again and again. *Poetry for Students* gives readers of any age good practice in feeling the ways poems relate to both the reality of the time and place the poet lived in and the reality of our emotions. Practice is just another word for being a student. The information given here helps you understand the way to read poetry; what to look for, what to expect.

With all of this in mind, I really don't think I would actually like to have a poet's job at all. There are too many skills involved, including precision, honesty, taste, courage, linguistics, passion, compassion, and the ability to keep all sorts of people entertained at once. And that is just what they do with one hand, while the other hand pulls some sort of trick that most of us will never fully understand. I can't even pack all that I need for a weekend into one suitcase, so what would be my chances of stuffing so much life into a few lines? With all that *Poetry for Students* tells us about each poem, I am impressed that any poet can finish three or four poems a year. Read the inside stories of these poems, and you won't be able to approach any poem in the same way you did before.

David J. Kelly
College of Lake County

Introduction

Purpose of the Book

The purpose of *Poetry for Students* (*PfS*) is to provide readers with a guide to understanding, enjoying, and studying poems by giving them easy access to information about the work. Part of Gale's "For Students" Literature line, *PfS* is specifically designed to meet the curricular needs of high school and undergraduate college students and their teachers, as well as the interests of general readers and researchers considering specific poems. While each volume contains entries on "classic" poems frequently studied in classrooms, there are also entries containing hard-to-find information on contemporary poems, including works by multicultural, international, and women poets.

The information covered in each entry includes an introduction to the poem and the poem's author; the actual poem text (if possible); a poem summary, to help readers unravel and understand the meaning of the poem; analysis of important themes in the poem; and an explanation of important literary techniques and movements as they are demonstrated in the poem.

In addition to this material, which helps the readers analyze the poem itself, students are also provided with important information on the literary and historical background informing each work. This includes a historical context essay, a box comparing the time or place the poem was written to modern Western culture, a critical

overview essay, and excerpts from critical essays on the poem. A unique feature of *PfS* is a specially commissioned critical essay on each poem, targeted toward the student reader.

To further help today's student in studying and enjoying each poem, information on audio recordings and other media adaptations is provided (if available), as well as reading suggestions for works of fiction and nonfiction on similar themes and topics. Classroom aids include ideas for research papers and lists of critical and reference sources that provide additional material on the poem.

Selection Criteria

The titles for each volume of *PfS* are selected by surveying numerous sources on notable literary works and analyzing course curricula for various schools, school districts, and states. Some of the sources surveyed include: high school and undergraduate literature anthologies and textbooks; lists of award-winners, and recommended titles, including the Young Adult Library Services Association (YALSA) list of best books for young adults.

Input solicited from our expert advisory board—consisting of educators and librarians—guides us to maintain a mix of "classic" and contemporary literary works, a mix of challenging and engaging works (including genre titles that are commonly studied) appropriate for different age levels, and a mix of international, multicultural and women authors. These advisors also consult on each volume's entry list, advising on which titles are most studied, most appropriate, and meet the broadest interests across secondary (grades 7–12) curricula and undergraduate literature studies.

How Each Entry Is Organized

Each entry, or chapter, in *PfS* focuses on one poem. Each entry heading lists the full name of the poem, the author's name, and the date of the poem's publication. The following elements are contained in each entry:

Introduction: a brief overview of the poem which provides information about its first appearance, its literary standing, any controversies surrounding the work, and major conflicts or themes within the work.

Author Biography: this section includes basic facts about the poet's life, and focuses on events and times in the author's life that inspired the poem in question.

Poem Text: when permission has been granted, the poem is reprinted, allowing for quick reference when reading the explication of the following section.

Poem Summary: a description of the major events in the poem. Summaries are broken down with subheads that indicate the lines being discussed.

Themes: a thorough overview of how the major topics, themes, and issues are addressed within the poem. Each theme discussed appears in a separate subhead.

Style: this section addresses important style elements of the poem, such as form, meter, and rhyme scheme; important literary devices used, such as imagery, foreshadowing, and symbolism; and, if applicable, genres to which the work might have belonged, such as Gothicism or Romanticism. Literary terms are explained within the entry, but can also be found in the Glossary.

Historical Context: this section outlines the social, political, and cultural climate in which the author lived and the poem was created. This section may include descriptions of related historical events, pertinent aspects of daily life in the culture, and the artistic and literary sensibilities of the time in which the work was written. If the poem is a historical work, information regarding the time in which the poem is set is also included. Each section is broken down with helpful subheads.

Critical Overview: this section provides background on the critical reputation of the poem, including bannings or any other public controversies surrounding the work. For older works, this section includes a history of how the poem was first received and how perceptions of it may have changed over the years; for more recent poems, direct quotes from early reviews may also be included.

Criticism: an essay commissioned by *PfS* which specifically deals with the poem and is written specifically for the student audience, as well as excerpts from previously published criticism on the work (if available).

Sources: an alphabetical list of critical material quoted in the entry, with full bibliographical information.

Further Reading: an alphabetical list of other critical sources which may prove useful for the student. Includes full bibliographical information and a brief annotation.

Suggested Search Terms: a list of search terms and phrases to jumpstart students' further information seeking. Terms include not just titles and author names but also terms and topics related to the historical and literary context of the works.

In addition, each entry contains the following highlighted sections, set apart from the main text as sidebars:

Media Adaptations: if available, a list of audio recordings as well as any film or television adaptations of the poem, including source information.

Topics for Further Study: a list of potential study questions or research topics dealing with the poem. This section includes questions related to other disciplines the student may be studying, such as American history, world history, science, math, government, business, geography, economics, psychology, etc.

Compare & Contrast: an "at-a-glance" comparison of the cultural and historical differences between the author's time and culture and late twentieth century or early twenty-first century Western culture. This box includes pertinent parallels between the major scientific, political, and cultural movements of the time or place the poem was written, the time or place the poem was set (if a historical work), and modern Western culture. Works written after 1990 may not have this box.

What Do I Read Next?: a list of works that might give a reader points of entry into a classic work (e.g., YA or multicultural titles) and/or complement the featured poem or serve as a contrast to it. This includes works by the same author and others, works from various genres, YA works, and works from various cultures and eras.

Other Features

PfS includes "Just a Few Lines on a Page," a foreword by David J. Kelly, an adjunct professor of English, College of Lake County, Illinois. This essay provides a straightforward, unpretentious explanation of why poetry should be marveled at and how *PfS* can help teachers show students how to enrich their own reading experiences.

A Cumulative Author/Title Index lists the authors and titles covered in each volume of the *PfS* series.

A Cumulative Nationality/Ethnicity Index breaks down the authors and titles covered in each volume of the *PfS* series by nationality and ethnicity.

A Subject/Theme Index, specific to each volume, provides easy reference for users who may be studying a particular subject or theme rather than a single work. Significant subjects from events to broad themes are included.

A Cumulative Index of First Lines (beginning in Vol. 10) provides easy reference for users who may be familiar with the first line of a poem but may not remember the actual title.

A Cumulative Index of Last Lines (beginning in Vol. 10) provides easy reference for users who may be familiar with the last line of a poem but may not remember the actual title.

Each entry may include illustrations, including photo of the author and other graphics related to the poem.

Citing Poetry for Students

When writing papers, students who quote directly from any volume of *PfS* may use the following general forms. These examples are based on MLA style; teachers may request that students adhere to a different style, so the following examples may be adapted as needed.

When citing text from *PfS* that is not attributed to a particular author (i.e., the Themes, Style, Historical Context sections, etc.), the following format should be used in the bibliography section:

> "Grace." *Poetry for Students*. Ed. Sara Constantakis. Vol. 44. Detroit: Gale, Cengage Learning, 2013. 66–86. Print.

When quoting the specially commissioned essay from *PfS* (usually the first piece under the "Criticism" subhead), the following format should be used:

> Andersen, Susan. Critical Essay on "Grace." *Poetry for Students*. Ed. Sara Constantakis. Vol. 44. Detroit: Gale, Cengage Learning, 2013. 77–80. Print.

When quoting a journal or newspaper essay that is reprinted in a volume of *PfS,* the following form may be used:

> Molesworth, Charles. "Proving Irony by Compassion: The Poetry of Robert Pinsky." *Hollins Critic* 21.5 (1984): 1–18. Rpt. in *Poetry for Students*. Ed. Sara Constantakis. Vol. 44. Detroit: Gale, Cengage Learning, 2013. 189–92. Print.

When quoting material reprinted from a book that appears in a volume of *PfS,* the following form may be used:

> Flora, Joseph M. "W. E. Henley, Poet." *William Ernest Henley*. New York: Twayne, 1970. 119–41. Rpt. in *Poetry for Students*. Ed. Sara Constantakis. Vol. 43. Detroit: Gale, 213. 150–52. Print.

We Welcome Your Suggestions

The editorial staff of *Poetry for Students* welcomes your comments and ideas. Readers who wish to suggest poems to appear in future volumes, or who have other suggestions, are cordially invited to contact the editor. You may contact the editor via E-mail at: **ForStudentsEditors@cengage.com.** Or write to the editor at:

Editor, *Poetry for Students*
Gale
27500 Drake Road
Farmington Hills, MI 48331-3535

Literary Chronology

1503: Thomas Wyatt is born near Maidstone, Kent, England.

1542: Thomas Wyatt dies on October 11 in Sherborne, Dorset.

1557: Thomas Wyatt's "They Flee from Me" is published in *Tottel's Miscellany*.

1840: Thomas Hardy is born on June 2 in Upper Bockhampton, Dorsetshire.

1874: Amy Lowell is born on February 9 in Brookline, Massachusetts.

1894: E.E. Cummings is born on October 14 in Cambridge, Massachusetts.

1899: Hart Crane is born on July 21 in Garrettsville, Ohio.

1901: Thomas Hardy's "The Ruined Maid" is published in *Poems of the Past and Present*.

1915: Amy Lowell's "Patterns" is published in the *Little Review*.

1923: Mitsuye Yamada is born on July 5 in Fukuoka, Japan.

1925: Maxine Kumin is born on June 6 in Philadelphia, Pennsylvania.

1925: Amy Lowell dies of a stroke on May 12 in Brookline, Massachusetts.

1926: Amy Lowell is posthumously awarded the Pulitzer Prize for Poetry for *What's O'Clock*.

1928: Thomas Hardy dies of a heart attack on January 11 in Dorset, England.

1932: Hart Crane's "The Broken Tower" is published in *New Republic*.

1932: Hart Crane dies of suicide by drowning on April 27 in the Gulf of Mexico.

1940: Kelly Cherry is born on December 21 in Baton Rouge, Louisiana.

1941: Janice Mirikitani is born on February 4 in Stockton, California.

1942: Sharon Olds is born on November 19 in San Francisco, California.

1943: Michael Ondaatje is born on September 12 in Colombo, Ceylon.

1951: Joy Harjo is born on May 9 in Tulsa, Oklahoma.

1954: Luis J. Rodríguez is born on July 9 in El Paso, Texas.

1955: Patricia Smith is born on June 25 in Chicago, Illinois.

1956: Chirtra Banerjee Divakaruni is born on July 29 in Kolkata, India.

1957: Li-Young Lee is born on August 19 in Jakarta, Indonesia.

1958: E.E. Cummings's "a total stranger one black day" is published in *95 Poems*.

1962: E.E. Cummings dies of a stroke on September 3 in North Conway, New Hampshire.

1972: Maxine Kumin's "Woodchucks" is published in *Up Country: Poems of New England*.

1973: Maxine Kumin is awarded the Pulitzer Prize for Poetry for *Up Country*.

1976: Mitsuye Yamada's "To the Lady" is published in *Camp Notes and Other Poems*.

1981: Li-Young Lee's "Persimmons" is published in *American Poetry Review*.

1984: Michael Ondaatje's "Inner Tube" is published in *Secular Love*.

1984: Sharon Old's "Rite of Passage" is published in *The Dead and the Living*.

1990: Joy Harjo's "Eagle Poem" is published in *In Mad Love and War*.

1991: Luis J. Rodríguez's "The Concrete River" is published in *The Concrete River*.

1992: Patricia Smith's "Blonde White Women" is published in *Big Towns, Big Talk*.

1992: Michael Ondaatje is awarded the Booker Prize for *The English Patient*.

1997: Kelly Cherry's "Alzheimer's" is published in *Death and Transfiguration*.

1997: Chitra Banerjee Divakaruni's "Indigo" is published in *Leaving Yuba City*.

2002: Janice Mirikitani's "For a Daughter Who Leaves" is published in *Love Works*.

2013: Sharon Olds is awarded the Pulitzer Prize for Poetry for *Stag's Leap*.

2014: Maxine Kumin dies of natural causes on February 6 in Warner, New Hampshire.

Acknowledgements

The editors wish to thank the copyright holders of the excerpted criticism included in this volume and the permission managers of many book and magazine publishing companies for assisting us in securing reproduction rights. We are also grateful to the staffs of the Detroit Public Library, the Library of Congress, the University of Detroit Mercy Library, Wayne State University Purdy/Kresge Library Complex, and the University of Michigan Libraries for making their resources available to us. Following is a list of the copyright holders who have granted us permission to reproduce material in this volume of *PfS*. Every effort has been made to trace copyright, but if omissions have been made, please let us know.

COPYRIGHTED EXCERPTS IN PfS, VOLUME 56, WERE REPRODUCED FROM THE FOLLOWING PERIODICALS:

Booklist, Vol. 101 (22), August, 2005. Copyright © 2005 Courtesy of American Library Association. —*America Magazine*, Vol. 197 (17), November 26, 2007, p. 27. Copyright © 2007 America Magazine. —*America Magazine*, Vol. 211 (3), August 04, 2014, p. 33. Copyright © 2014 *America Magazine*. —*Ascent Aspiration*, Vol. 18 (11-12), November/December, 2014. Copyright © 2014 Courtesy of *Ascent Aspiration*. —*Concentric: Literary and Cultural Studies*, Vol. 39 (2), September, 2013. Copyright © 2013 *Concentric: Literary and Cultural Studies*. —*Los Angeles Times*, June 05, 1985. Courtesy of *Los Angeles Times*. —*Los Angeles Weekly*, October 09, 2014. Copyright © 2014 Courtesy of *Los Angeles Weekly*. —*PIF Magazine*, October 01, 2010. Copyright © 2010 *PIF Magazine*. —*The Poet's Forum*, 2016. Copyright © 2016 *The Poet's Forum*. —*Publishers Weekly*, 2016. Copyright © 2016 Courtesy of PWXYZ, LLC. —*The Rumpus*, February 20, 2013. Copyright © 2013 *The Rumpus*. —*San Francisco Chronicle*, February 25, 1996. Copyright © 1996 *San Francisco Chronicle*.

COPYRIGHTED EXCERPTS IN PfS, VOLUME 56, WERE REPRODUCED FROM THE FOLLOWING BOOKS:

Barbour, Douglas. From *Michael Ondaatje*. The Gale Group, 1993. Copyright © 1993, Courtesy of The Gale Group.—Benvenuto, Richard. From *Amy Lowell*. The Gale Group, 1985. Copyright © 1985, Courtesy of The Gale Group. —Carabi, Angels. From *Truthtellers of the Times: Interviews with Contemporary Women Poets*. University of Michigan Press, 1998. Copyright © 1998 University of Michigan Press. Reprinted with permission of University of Michigan Press. Permission conveyed through Copyright Clearance Center, Inc. —Crane, Hart. From *My Grandmother's Love Letters*. The Gale Group, 1920. Courtesy of The Gale Group. —*Contemporary Women's Writing in India*. Rowman 2014.Used by permission of Rowman Davie, Donald. From *Thomas Hardy and British Poetry*. Oxford University Press. Copyright © 1972, Oxford University Press. —Hardy, Thomas. *Poems of the Past and the Present*.

HarperCollins, 2016. Copyright © 2016, Courtesy of HarperCollins. —Harjo, Joy. From *In Mad Love and War*. WesleyanUniversity Press, 1990. Copyright © 1990, Joy Harjo. Used by permission. —Kennedy, Richard S. From *E.E. Cummings Revisited*. The Gale Group, 1994. Copyright ©1998, The Gale Group. —Kumin, Maxine. From *To Make a Prairie: Essays on Poets, Poetry, and Country Living*. University of Michigan Press, 1979. Copyright © 1979 University of Michigan Press. Reprinted with permission of University of Michigan Press. Permission conveyed through Copyright Clearence Center, Inc. —Landles, Iain. From *The Case for Cummings: A Reaction to the Critical Misreading of E.E. Cummings*. OmniScriptum, 2008. Copyright © 2008 OmniScriptum. —Lowell, Amy. From *For Men, Women and Ghosts*. Eureka Press, 2007. Copyright © 2007, Courtesy of Eureka Press. —Mirikitani, Janice. From *Love Works*. City Lights Publishers, 2003. Copyright © 2003, Janice Mirikitani. Reprinted with the permission of The Permissions Company, Inc., on behalf of City Lights Publishers, www.citylights.com. —Munich, Adrienne and Melissa Bradshaw, eds. From *Amy Lowell: American Modern*. Rutgers University Press, 2004. Copyright © 2004 by Mitsuye Yamada. Reprinted by permission of Rutgers, theState University. —Quinn, Vincent. From *Hart Crane*. Twayne Publishers, 1963. Copyright © 1963, Courtesy of Twayne Publishers. —Smith, Patricia. From *Big Towns, Big Talk*. Copyright © 1992 Patricia Smith. —Szalay, Krisztina. From *The Obstinate Muse of Freedom: On the Poetry of Sir Thomas Wyatt*. AkadÕmiai Kiadœ, 2000. Copyright © 2000 AkadÕmiai Kiadœ. —Widdowson, Peter. From *Thomas Hardy*. Northcote House, 1996. Copyright © 1996 Northcote House. —Wyatt, Sir Thomas. From *The Norton Anthology of English Literature*. W.W. Norton 2016, Courtesy of W.W. Norton Yamada, Mitsuye. From *In Camp Notes and Other Writings*. Rutgers UniversityPress, 1998. Copyright ©1998, Mitsuye Yamada. Reprinted by permission of Rutgers University Press.

Contributors

Susan K. Andersen: Andersen is a teacher and writer with a PhD in English. Entry on "Eagle Poem." Original essay on "Eagle Poem."

Bryan Aubrey: Aubrey holds a PhD in English. Entry on "They Flee from Me." Original essay on "They Flee from Me."

Rita M. Brown: Brown is an English professor. Entry on "The Ruined Maid." Original essay on "The Ruined Maid."

Klay Dyer: Dyer is a freelance writer specializing in topics relating to literature, popular culture, and the relationship between creativity and technology. Entry on "a total stranger one black day." Original essay on "a total stranger one black day."

Charlotte M. Freeman: Freeman is a writer, editor, and former academic living in small-town Montana. Entry on "Persimmons." Original essay on "Persimmons."

Kristen Sarlin Greenberg: Greenberg is a freelance writer and editor with a background in literature and philosophy. Entry on "Alzheimer's." Original essay on "Alzheimer's."

Michael Allen Holmes: Holmes is a writer with existential interests. Entries on "Blonde White Women," "The Concrete River," and "Inner Tube." Original essays on "Blonde White Women," "The Concrete River," and "Inner Tube."

Amy L. Miller: Miller is a graduate of the University of Cincinnati. Entries on "Indigo" and "To the Lady." Original essays on "Indigo" and "To the Lady."

Michael J. O'Neal: O'Neal holds a PhD in English. Entries on "The Broken Tower" and "Patterns." Original essays on "The Broken Tower" and "Patterns."

Jeffrey Eugene Palmer: Palmer is a scholar, freelance writer, and teacher of high school English. Entry on "For a Daughter Who Leaves." Original essay on "For a Daughter Who Leaves."

Bradley A. Skeen: Skeen is a classicist. Entry on "Woodchucks." Original essay on "Woodchucks."

Sara Noelle Stancliffe: Stancliffe is a freelance writer and practicing poet. Entry on "Rite of Passage." Original essay on "Rite of Passage."

Alzheimer's

KELLY CHERRY

1997

Writer Kelly Cherry knows that a lot of literature "begins in autobiography, though the connection may remain hidden from the reader," as she related in an interview with Pam Kingsbury. Cherry went on to joke about the assumptions readers make after reading her work. At various points in her career, people have asked questions based on the experiences of characters in her fiction and events in her poems, assuming them to be autobiographically inspired:

> Readers... have asked me what arrangements I make for my daughter when I travel to give readings...; why I went to med school if I'm not practicing...; if they can tell me about their own recollections of my ex-husband's father...; if I enjoyed my time in Bolivia.... When *My Life and Dr. Joyce Brothers* came out, old friends of my brother called me to say they were sorry to learn he had died.

Cherry then told Kingsbury,

> No daughter. Couldn't cut up a frog, much less a person. Never met my ex-husband's father. Have never been to Bolivia. And I'm happy to note for the record that my brother is alive and well and living in Houston.

So while life feeds art, there is not always a directional relationship between a writer's life and work. In Cherry's 1997 collection *Death and Transfiguration*, however, a page following the table of contents brings a stark reality to the collection with a list of birth and date dates for her father, mother, and ex-husband. As she was

The random collection of items in the man's suitcase, such as the piggy bank, is the first sign of his mental confusion (©Brooke Becker | Shutterstock.com)

composing the poems in the collection, these three important figures in her life story passed away. The collection therefore explores themes of loss and grief, including a kind of loss caused by something other than death: a father's struggle with dementia, as shown in the poem "Alzheimer's."

AUTHOR BIOGRAPHY

Cherry was born in Baton Rouge, Louisiana, on December 21, 1940. She was the second of three children born to musician parents. Cherry's mother and father both played the violin, and the family moved to Ithaca, New York, to stay with the string quartet in which they played. When Cherry was nine, her father attained a teaching position at Richmond Professional Institute, so the family moved again, settling in Chesterfield County, Virginia. Both parents continued to perform.

In 1961, Cherry earned a bachelor's degree in mathematics and philosophy from Mary Washington College. She continued her studies in philosophy at the University of Virginia before transferring to the University of North Carolina at Greensboro, where she completed her master of fine arts degree. While at the University of North Carolina, Cherry met Jonathan Silver, her first husband. The couple moved to New York City, where Cherry held various jobs in publishing. Her marriage to Silver ended in divorce in 1969. Cherry taught at numerous colleges around the country until in 1977 she secured a position at the University of Wisconsin–Madison. She retired from teaching in 1999 with the positions of Eudora Welty Professor Emerita of English and Evjue-Bascom Professor Emerita in the Humanities. As of 2016, Cherry was living in a farmhouse in Virginia with her husband, writer Burke Davis III, whom she married in 2000. She still occasionally gives readings and is still writing.

During her long career, Cherry published more than twenty books of poetry, memoirs, essays, translations, and fiction—both novels and short stories. Her poetry collections include *Songs for a Soviet Composer* (1980); *God's Loud Hand* (1993); *Death and Transfiguration* (1997), which includes "Alzheimer's"; *Rising Venus* (2002); *Hazard and Prospect: New and Selected Poems* (2007); and *The Retreats of Thought* (2009). Cherry was appointed the poet laureate of Virginia in 2010 and has received several prestigious fellowships, such as from the National Endowment for the Arts and the Rockefeller Foundation. She has received dozens of awards for her work, including three PEN/Syndicated Fiction Awards, a Dictionary of Literary Biography Award for the best volume of short stories, the Hanes Poetry Prize given by the Fellowship of Southern Writers for a body of work, the Bradley Major Achievement (Lifetime) Award, the Taramuto Prize, the Carole Weinstein Prize for Poetry, and the L. E. Phillabaum Poetry Award.

POEM SUMMARY

The text used for this summary is from *Death and Transfiguration*, Louisiana State University Press, 1997, p. 13. Versions of the poem can be found on the following web pages: http://trauma.blog.yorku.ca/2014/11/alzheimers/ and http://www.zarcrom.com/users/yeartorem/ADpoetry/KCAlzheimers.html.

"Alzheimer's" opens with an older man hesitating at the entrance to a house. He has just returned from a stay in a hospital and carries his suitcase, which contains an assortment of objects. Some of the items in the suitcase might be useful, such as the shaving cream or the change in a piggy bank, and of course his clothing, but overall he seems to carry little of importance. He has a book with him, but line 5 makes it clear that he only feigns reading; perhaps he does not enjoy the book or even understand what he is looking at on the page.

Lines 8 and 9 set the poem at a house in England in the late afternoon. It has recently rained, but the sun is now shining. The man notes the flowers growing against the wall beside him, vying for space and fighting for a grip between the bricks. The poet compares the way the sun hits the ironwork trim of the house to a blacksmith's activity at his forge, with the stray rays of light in the surrounding plants like burning cinders from the forge's fire.

MEDIA ADAPTATIONS

- A video of Cherry at the National Book Festival in 2011, produced by the Library of Congress, is available online (https://www.youtube.com/watch?v = PfOT16EtclA&index = 7&list = PLaYPMBLAyZME07kHuv1BvuHtKbWjn1xNw). She reads several of her poems and answers questions from the audience about her work.

The house has white-painted trim outlining its edges, giving clear definition to its shape in the late-afternoon light. The old man realizes that the house in front of him is his home. He recalls planting flowering bushes in the garden, building the path between the house and the garage, and driving the vehicle that was housed there. He can also picture himself living there when he was younger, when he enjoyed music. His life has no room for music now, no time for basking in the sense of how he feels about things.

Because of his Alzheimer's disease, as the poem makes clear, the man struggles to understand the world around him; this is what has become urgent and important. The final lines of the poem stress the importance of the puzzle the man is now trying to figure out. There is a woman greeting him at the door. Like him, she is old, and she seems glad to see him and eager to have him home, but he does not remember who she is. The woman is likely his wife. Therefore the poem ends on a bittersweet note: he is welcomed home and has someone to care for him, but he has no recollection of one of the most important people in his life.

THEMES

Memory
Memory is an important theme in "Alzheimer's." The title gives readers an early clue that the person featured is struggling with his

TOPICS FOR FURTHER STUDY

- Read Linda Vigen Phillips's *Crazy*, a 2014 novel in verse for young adults. The story is set in the 1960s, when protagonist Laura is fifteen years old. While she struggles with the same issues as most teens—school, friends, and romance—she faces the additional problem of her mother's mental illness. After reading the novel, write an essay comparing how Phillips, in *Crazy*, and Cherry, in "Alzheimer's," portray the struggle of watching a parent with mental health issues.

- Using online and print resources, compile a list of resources for those with a family member suffering from Alzheimer's disease. Create a website to collect all of the information you have gathered, providing links to scientific research about the treatment and prevention of Alzheimer's, practical resources for familes about the care of their ailing loved one, support groups for both patients and families, and a list of good reference books.

- Although "Alzheimer's" is written in free verse, most critics consider Cherry a formalist. Research the poetic movement of formalism, and think about the different strategies needed to write poems in free verse and in traditional poetic forms. Write two poems on the same topic: one in a traditional form (sonnet, haiku, villanelle, etc.) and the other in free verse. Then think about the writing process for each poem. Was there a value in forcing your thoughts and words to fit a certain rhyme scheme and meter? Or did you prefer having freedom from those boundaries? Which of your poems do you feel is more successful? Write a reflection piece that addresses these questions.

- Read New Formalist critic and poet Dana Gioia's 1991 essay "Can Poetry Matter?" (http://www.theatlantic.com/past/unbound/poetry/gioia/gioia.htm). Stage a debate in class about whether you agree with Gioia and whether you believe poetry can become part of people's daily lives in modern America.

memory. This is common for many older people, but the very first line of the poem describes the man as *crazy*. He has an illness that makes his memory problems far worse than the average person's. There are lots of indicators in the poem that his memory does not function properly. His mind is compared to a suitcase with random things "rattling" around in it. He seems to have forgotten how to read—or perhaps he cannot remember enough of the text from one line to the next—and therefore can only imitate what he sees others doing with books. Lines 15–18 show the man's thoughts as he looks at his house. It takes him a long while to consider the details before he recognizes his home, which is true to life: many people with dementia can remember events of years ago better than what happened the day before, and the

poem makes it clear that the man has lived in the house for a long time. The old man can remember a younger version of himself and a car in the garage that he once drove. But his memory has deteriorated so far that he does not remember his wife. He does feel welcomed by her, however, so perhaps some ghost of a memory gives him positive associations when he sees her face.

Alienation

The theme of alienation in "Alzheimer's" is related to the theme of memory. Because the old man in the story cannot easily remember his home and his family, he feels alienated from his own life. He is coming home from a stay in the hospital, but rather than rushing gratefully inside and relaxing, he is shown pausing at the door. Because of the uncertainty of his memory,

The old man's wife is welcoming him home, though he cannot remember her (©bikeriderlondon | Shutterstock.com)

he does not feel at ease in his own home and must study the minute details of the place before entering; his brain needs time to dredge up the memories. His loss of memory has also alienated him from his habits and pastimes. They are no longer second nature: he plays at reading a book and cannot even enjoy listening to music, much less play an instrument himself, a state of affairs that must be especially frustrating for a musician, which lines 21–22 suggest the man has been. His alienation seems to be at its worst at the close of the poem, in that he cannot even remember his own wife. Being alienated from one's immediate family might be the loneliest aspect of Alzheimer's.

STYLE

Free Verse

"Alzheimer's" is written in free verse. *Free verse* is poetry without a consistent arrangement of rhyme or meter (*meter* being the pattern of stressed and unstressed syllables). Cherry often uses traditional poetic forms with regular rhyme

and metrical schemes, but she opted not to use such a form for "Alzheimer's." The choice of free verse is suited to her subject matter. The man described in the poem has lost a lot of the structure in his life—the structure of daily activities, the structure of his marital relationship, and, indeed, the structure in his very mind; therefore a strictly structured poem would be out of place. Instead, the lines of the poem flow more organically, like the thoughts that flit through his head. He notices details of his house in seemingly random order: the flowers in the garden, the ironwork, the white-painted trim. It takes a great effort of mental processing before he comprehends, in line 15, that he has come home. His thoughts have become so disorganized and hard to grasp that he cannot even recognize his own wife. For Cherry's chosen content, a highly structured poem, such as a sonnet, would have attempted to impose order on something that is, by its very nature, disordered.

Metaphor

A *metaphor* is figurative language comparing two otherwise unlike objects. Cherry uses several metaphors in "Alzheimer's," and each one serves a different purpose. For example, lines 10–12 compare the sun's hitting the ironwork on the old man's house to the forge of a blacksmith. The flecks of light in the leaves of the surrounding plants are like sparks. This metaphor is used to give a visual image to the reader, one suggesting intense activity not unlike that inside the old man's mind. Later metaphoric language, in lines 20–22, ties together the ideas of music and emotion: the man has no spare time for playing the violin or *fiddling* around with how he feels because, with Alzheimer's, he is always scrambling to understand on a basic level what is happening around him. This is a particularly poignant comparison if the reader knows that Cherry's father worked as a concert violinist and that music was very important to him.

Metaphor is also used to highlight the topic of the poem: the opening lines compare the man's mind to the suitcase he carries. Just as his mind is filled with random thoughts, the suitcase is filled with random objects, rattling around without structure. The contents of the suitcase are also meaningful. The shaving cream suggests that the old man retains some sense of his masculinity. The piggy bank indicates that he still understands the need for money but also reflects the deterioration of his mind: whatever spare change the piggy bank might hold, it is unlikely to last long, and piggy banks are typically reserved for children, with adults moving on to wallets, purses, and bank accounts. In this sense, the old man has regressed. Finally, the suitcase contains a book, but the poem indicates that the man cannot concentrate long enough to actually read. Instead, he only pretends, giving the reader the feeling that he often pretends to be functioning normally in other aspects of life, when in fact he feels lost.

Enjambment

Enjambment involves a thought or phrase in poetry that continues from one line to the next rather than ending at a break between lines or stanzas. In "Alzheimer's," Cherry uses enjambment several times for different effects. The enjambment between lines 2 and 3 allows the final word in line 2 to do double duty. Upon finishing that line, the word *rattling* lingers in the reader's mind, just as the old man's thoughts rattle around in his head; the enjambment makes the reader pause and consider what it would be like to have one's brain clattering around in

one's head. The word *rattling* also is part of the metaphor in line 3, the importance of which is discussed earlier. Without the line break, the reader's eye would not pause, and likely the first effect would be lost in the overall phrasing of the figurative language.

Highlighting certain words is perhaps the most common effect of enjambment. As described earlier, Cherry uses enjambment to stress the final word in line 2. She also uses the line breaks to draw attention to the first word on the second of a given pair of enjambed lines. For example, if Cherry had broken the sentence in lines 24 and 25 with the punctuation or at the end phrase, the word *consequence* would have been buried in the middle, but as the poem stands, *consequence* gains in importance because it appears at the start of a line. Similarly, the enjambment in lines 19 and 20 adds a dramatic pause to reflect the mix of nostalgia and sadness the man must feel as he suddenly recalls his love for music. Cherry also bookends line 20 with the same word again to further stress its importance.

Enjambment can also be used to set apart an entire phrase, not just a single word, for particular attention. An example of this appears in line 22: Cherry could have contained the sentence in lines 21 and 22 all within one line, but by adding enjambment, Cherry made line 22 one of the shorter lines in the poem. Therefore, in addition to the slight pause for the enjambment, line 22 stands out visually.

Cherry also uses enjambment to mimic the way the old man's mind works. For example, lines 12 and 13 contain repetition. It is as if the old man is gradually remembering: he first thinks of the plant, then recalls the specific kind of plant, and finally in line 17 remembers putting another kind of plant in the garden. As he works to recover his memories, more details surface, and the enjambment in lines 12 and 13, signalled by the dashes (which might be considered the punctuation mark of prose enjambment), reinforces this.

HISTORICAL CONTEXT

Formalism

While Cherry does write in free verse, as in "Alzheimer's," many of her poems are written in traditional poetic forms. Critic Angela O'Donnell,

COMPARE & CONTRAST

- **1990s:** Long-term care insurance, which helps cover the cost of nursing homes, in-home care, and assistance with daily activities, is popular with both consumers and insurance companies. It is perceived as a wise investment, especially for people in their sixties or older, to help ensure that they will have skilled care if they are disabled by age or a serious condition such as Alzheimer's.

  Today: Rising health-care costs and longer life spans have changed the equation for what insurers collect in premiums versus what they pay out in care. Some companies refuse to pay claims or end up going out of business; others raise their prices for new policies. With the average cost of a policy approaching two hundred dollars a month for purchasers in their late fifties, this insurance is too expensive for many Americans to afford.

- **1990s:** Researchers identify the first gene known to indicate a risk for developing Alzheimer's in 1993. Two years later, scientists develop the first mouse model replicating the disease, which allows them to test potential treatments before beginning human trials. An "Alzheimer's vaccine" is tested in mice in 1999, and it prevents animals' brains from developing Alzheimer's-like changes.

  Today: Efforts continue to pinpoint genetic causes of Alzheimer's. A 2013 study reveals eleven genes that contribute to the development of the disease. The identification of such genes might ultimately help in treatment and prevention.

- **1990s:** Tacrine, the first Alzheimer's drug, is approved by the Food and Drug Administration in 1993. The medicine does not cure the disease but helps maintain memory and thinking, lessening the symptoms that compromise patients' quality of life.

  Today: There are now five drugs approved to treat Alzheimer's disease, but they help thinking and memory only temporarily and only work in approximately half of patients. There is still no cure. In 2011, President Barack Obama signs the National Alzheimer's Project Act, which incorporates a plan to coordinate efforts in research and patient care.

---

in *America*, praises Cherry's "superb formal control" and points out that all of the volume's poems, "including those in open form, demonstrate her thorough grounding in English literary tradition." Many critics also applaud the clarity of thought and language in Cherry's work, which also lends even the free-verse poems a kind of structure. Cherry demurs when asked to categorize herself with a particular school of poetry, but her style aligns her with the New Formalist, or Neo-formalist, poets of the late twentieth and early twenty-first centuries.

Formalism was not a coherent, planned movement but rather a trend in poetry toward the inclusion of regular rhyme schemes, regular meter, and symmetry of stanzas. This return to traditional poetic forms was in part a reaction to the relatively unstructured poems of the 1960s and 1970s. The popular style then was more experimental, with many poems written in free verse (poetry that lacks patterns of rhyme and meter). Indeed, many poems had no rhyme at all and contained both lines and stanzas that varied greatly in length. Some readers and critics appreciated the return to traditional forms and the thoughtfulness and attention to detail that contemporary formalist poets dedicated to their work. Others, feeling that the structures imposed by such forms are artificial and restrain honest expression, saw formalism as a step backward and feared that formalism suppresses innovation.

The old man returns home from a hospital visit
(©alphaspirit | Shutterstock.com)

Formalism grew out of a trend in theoretical orientation from the generation before. As early as the close of World War I, a technique for literary interpretation called New Criticism emerged, stressing the value of a work of art as a thing independent from the act of its creation—meaning that the New Critics did not want to involve biographical or historical information when studying a poem. The New Critical approach concentrated on the close analysis of a text. Many of the New Critics—for example, John Crowe Ransom, Allen Tate, and Yvor Winters—were the teachers and mentors of the generation of poets publishing in the mid-twentieth century, specifically those who continued to use traditional forms, such as Howard Nemerov, Anthony Hecht, Mona Van Duyn, and Richard Wilbur.

With these writers the traditional poetic forms were maintained, but many more poets opted for wide-ranging, less formal free verse in the 1960s and 1970s. New Formalism arose in later reaction to this nontraditional, unstructured style. Critically acclaimed poets of the New Formalist movement include Dana Gioia, X. J. Kennedy, Brad Leithauser, Marilyn Hacker, Charles Martin, Molly Peacock, Mark Jarman, Phillis Levin, and Timothy Steele.

CRITICAL OVERVIEW

The numerous fellowships, honorary chairs, and prizes awarded to Cherry are evidence of her popular and critical success. She has tried her hand at several genres and excelled at them all. Her success is likely due in part to what Dennis Vellucci describes in his *America* review of Cherry's short-story collection *A Kind of Dream* as her "insight into human nature." Vellucci credits "Cherry's understanding of how our formative experiences, our connections to others and our knowledge of ourselves play out over time" with giving "her book wisdom and pathos." Though Vellucci is discussing Cherry's fiction, the point applies to her poetry as well, which delves just as deeply into the fine points of human behavior and emotion.

In a review of *Hazard and Prospect: New and Selected Poems*, which compiles several of Cherry's poetry collections in one volume, Angela O'Donnell raves about the work: "Formally engaged and linguistically rich, these are poems that sing, that stop you in your tracks, that make you want to read them to other people and share what has come as a pure gift." O'Donnell does acknowledge that "for all their surface pleasure, Cherry's poems lead us to dark places." However, Cherry's sometimes grim subject matter does not mean that her poems are self-indulgent trips into angst and grief. Patricia A. Gabilondo, reviewing *Death and Transfiguration*, concedes that

> the death of a mother from emphysema, the slow cerebral death of a father suffering from Alzheimer's, the death of a former husband years after the death of a marriage, and the death of an unborn child are occasions for elegy

but also points out that "Cherry avoids the sentimental by a self-conscious, often ironic sounding of the echoes of transfiguration, ... including the transfiguration and resurrection of Christ."

O'Donnell notes that Cherry's technical skills are central to the success of her work. "Though Cherry is not a rigid formalist," O'Donnell writes, her poems, "including those in open form, demonstrate her thorough grounding in English literary tradition." According to O'Donnell, it is Cherry's "superb formal control" that "makes these poems of desolation bearable." With her mastery of poetic form, Cherry "shapes the chaotic experiences of life into art." A *Hollins Critic* review of *Death and Transfiguration* draws attention to another facet of Cherry's success: the thoughtfulness with which she composes her poems. The review summarizes the collection as "a series of meditations and elegies on the ultimate mysteries, personal and cosmic," and declares that the book ends with "a long requiem, as closely and brilliantly reasoned as philosophy, which draws the sonorous strands of the other poems together in a transformative embrace."

CRITICISM

Kristen Sarlin Greenberg

Greenberg is a freelance writer and editor with a background in literature and philosophy. In the following essay, she compares the themes and formal elements in Cherry's poems "Alzheimer's" and "My Mother's Stroke."

There are many elements that contribute to a poem's success. A poet must consider the importance of the content—the message to be delivered and the intended emotional impact on the reader—as well as more technical considerations, such as rhyme and meter (or lack thereof), vocabulary, and typography. Critics agree that American poet Cherry excels at both sides of this delicate balancing act. Angela O'Donnell, in *America*, describes Cherry's poems as "formally engaged and linguistically rich." Other critics agree that Cherry's technical skills are indisputable, and most also mention her talent for examining the human condition. Also writing in *America*, Dennis Vellucci marvels at "Cherry's understanding of how our formative experiences, our connections to others and our knowledge of ourselves play out over time." Cherry explores what happens when these connections are broken in her collection *Death and Transfiguration*, tackling challenging, grim issues such as the death of a former spouse, the extended illness and death of one's parents, and the death of an unborn child.

Despite the unity of theme in the collection, the poems are varied in tone—they are not all grim contemplations of human mortality and loss—and style. By comparing two poems in *Death and Transfiguration* that address similar topics, we can highlight both Cherry's formal poetic skills and her ability to delicately handle difficult subject matter. Two poems that are

ideal for comparison are "Alzheimer's" and "My Mother's Stroke." In the first poem, an old man returns home after a stay in the hospital. He looks around him and gradually remembers aspects of his house, his yard, and his life but still cannot quite recognize his wife, who waits for him at the door. While readers should not assume the content of a poem to be directly autobiographical, it is not far-fetched to assume that this poem was inspired by Cherry's father, who suffered from Alzheimer's before he died in 1986. "My Mother's Stroke" also draws from Cherry's own life, namely her mother's decline before her death in 1988.

From the first glance at the titles, the reader can infer that the poems will have some obvious points of comparison and contrast. Both titles instantly inform the reader about what to expect. Their straightforward reference to debilitating illnesses suggest that Cherry will not pull any punches—she will tell it like it is. However, though "Alzheimer's" gives a clear description of the poem's topic, "My Mother's Stroke" provides additional information: the use of the first-person pronoun makes it more personal. We know the speaker is dealing with a parent with this serious health concern.

This difference in the titles clues the reader in to another major difference in the poems: "Alzheimer's" has what in prose would be a third-person narrator, whereas "My Mother's Stroke" has a first-person narrator. This changes how the reader experiences the events in each poem. With the third-person narration, the reader experiences the return home from the old man's perspective. However, the first-person narration of "My Mother's Stroke" brings the reader one step closer to the emotion of the poem, closer to the intense emotion of a woman struggling to communicate with her

WHAT DO I READ NEXT?

- *History, Passion, Freedom, Death, and Hope: Prose about Poetry* (2005) gathers thirty years' worth of Cherry's thoughtful essays about poetry. Her prose is as clear and as revealing as her verse as she explores the meaning and purposes of poetry.

- Jenny Downham's *Unbecoming* (2016) is a multigenerational young-adult novel. Katie and her mother, Caroline, struggle with their relationship as they work together to care for grandmother Mary, who has dementia.

- In *Animal Dreams* (1990), Barbara Kingsolver enriches the story of sisters Codi and Hallie Noline with mystical dreams and elements of Native American myths. Hallie and Codi are close but follow very different paths in life: Hallie travels to Nicaragua to help poor farmers, while Codi goes home to help their father, who shows the early symptoms of Alzheimer's.

- Cherry's collection *The Retreats of Thought: Poems* (2009) is a philosophical series of sonnets, reflecting Cherry's interest in traditional poetic form. The included poems vary widely both in tone and in subject matter.

- In Camron Wright's *Letters for Emily* (2002), Harry Whitney knows that the effects of Alzheimer's disease will dissipate his clarity of mind. He hopes to pass on the wisdom of his life experience to his granddaughter Emily, so he gathers a book of poems and letters for her, providing clues for the whole family about the kind of man he really was.

- The *Mayo Clinic Guide to Alzheimer's Disease* (2006) is a complete but concise overview of the disease, describing warning signs, the latest research, and tips for caregivers.

ailing mother. Also, Cherry writes some of the lines in "My Mother's Stroke" in the second person (meaning that the subject of the sentences is *you*). It is as if the speaker is directly addressing her mother. This is what literally occurs in the poem's lines, but when the reader sees *you* and *your* repeated several times, the speaker might seem to be talking directly to the reader. This draws the reader in emotionally, potentially making the reader feel vulnerable, wondering if the mother's fate could be her own someday.

The slightly greater feeling of narrative distance in "Alzheimer's" relates to the subject matter. The old man has forgotten a lot about his life. Therefore he feels alienated and is trying to reestablish connections to his home and his family. He has to relearn how he sees and remembers. In contrast, "My Mother's Stroke" depicts more interaction between people: the daughter is talking to her mother, though the mother cannot respond as she used to.

Cherry shows feelings of distance in her use of music in the poems. As explained, it is not always appropriate to impose purely biographical facts on the interpretation of a poem, but both of Cherry's parents worked as professional musicians, and clearly music used to be important to the elderly man in "Alzheimer's." It is easy to imagine that someone who loved music enough to devote his life and career to it would miss it if his illness made it impossible to play an instrument, and Cherry's poem illustrates that feeling. Rather than enjoying music now, the old man can only remember that he *used* to love it. Again, the man in the poem, because of his memory difficulties, must look at the world in terms of how it relates to him. He believes he no longer has time for music because all of his efforts are devoted to figuring out how to function with his disability.

In "My Mother's Stroke," on the other hand, the music is about communication rather than distance. The small gestures that the mother makes—the only communication she is capable of—float to the surface of her underwater world to her daughter, who waits for these messages patiently. The music throughout the poem, then, is tied to imagery of water and fluidity, which is in sharp contrast to the hard images in "Alzheimer's": the objects rattling around in the man's suitcase, the sun striking the house like a blacksmith would, and the sharply defined borders of the house.

Cherry strikes a balance in the reader's engagement with the central characters in part through the poems' formal elements. Both poems are written in free verse, in that neither has a regular rhyme scheme or meter. "My Mother's Stroke," however, includes some of the elements of traditional poetic form. Though it lacks a consistent pattern of rhyme, Cherry uses some end rhyme throughout, and the stanzas contain four lines each, though the line length varies greatly. This regular structure—regular at least in comparison with the structure in "Alzheimer's"—mimics the orderly thoughts of the daughter. In contrast, "Alzheimer's" imitates the disjointed and tangential thoughts of a brain afflicted with Alzheimer's disease: several lines are enjambed, words repeat, and there is no regularity to the structure.

Both of these poems from *Death and Transfiguration* focus on loss. Both poems center on what happens with diseases like Alzheimer's and brain injuries caused by trauma like a stroke. Even before a patient dies, he is not himself, or she is not herself. However, the poems handle their similar issues in different ways. This is true to life: major life events are experiences universal to all yet still unique for each individual. Some incidents in a family, such as the decline of a parent, follow the same overall story arc, but the details and emotional patterns are often very different. This is reflected in Cherry's message and the form she uses to communicate that message in each poem, showing her mastery of poetic elements as well as of the description and understanding of human experience.

While these two poems reflect the overall themes of *Death and Transfiguration*, loss and illness and facing one's mortality, neither leaves the reader with a feeling of hopelessness. When reading "Alzheimer's," of course the reader feels sadness that the man cannot immediately recognize his own wife. Similarly, watching one's mother lying in a bed, almost motionless, unable to see clearly or hear barking dogs, would be heartbreaking, and the reader surely empathizes with the daughter in "My Mother's Stroke." However, both patients have a family member there. The old man's wife is welcoming him home, and the daughter—loving and listening—eagerly awaits any kind of communication from her mother. Rather than being mournful, the poems end on a note that is bittersweet. It is challenging to forge a true connection with another person and even more challenging to confront the inevitable loss of that connection, whether that loss be caused by divorce, distance, or death. However, we

The old man remembers himself when he was younger with flashes of detail, like the tweed hat he used to wear *(©Nejron Photo | Shutterstock.com)*

hunger for that kind of connection, and, if Cherry's poems "Alzheimer's" and "My Mother's Stroke" hold true, there are rewards that make the pain worthwhile.

Source: Kristen Sarlin Greenberg, Critical Essay on "Alzheimer's," in *Poetry for Students*, Gale, Cengage Learning, 2017.

Dennis Vellucci

In the following review, Vellucci praises Cherry's collection of short stories.

In this collection of interrelated, multigenerational stories, *A Kind of Dream*, Kelly Cherry explores themes of family, creativity and mortality. Though it is the third of a trilogy, preceded by *My Life and Dr. Joyce Brothers* and *The Society of Friends: Stories*, *A Kind of Dream* is intended to stand alone and self-contained, as its separate narratives and varied points of view eventually resolve themselves into the consciousness of one character, Nina, a writer of some repute who is facing the end of her life.

What a life it has been! Nina has adopted and raised her 14-year-old niece's daughter, Octavia, who, as a child, suffers trauma when she witnesses a beloved librarian gunned down by a madman but goes on to become a passionate artist and single mother to the precocious, spirited and biracial Callie. The niece, BB, having fled from Wisconsin to California, becomes a celebrated film star married to an equally successful director, but suffers personal tragedy as a desperately longed-for child dies shortly after birth, causing her to seek a reunion with the daughter (Octavia) she had abandoned 26 years earlier. In middle age, Nina marries Palmer, a historian and professor, who gratefully begins a second life when his first wife leaves him for a woman, throwing him into a vortex of self-doubt. Assorted neighbors, acquaintances, forbears and pets drift through these stories to form a composite portrait of this artist, Nina, as she negotiates pancreatic cancer and makes the transition from this world to the next.

If some of these incidents carry a whiff of soap opera, Cherry brings to them a poetic sensibility, a sincerity of purpose and a distinctiveness of vision that strive to transcend the trite and the mawkish. She begins with a prologue, "On Familiar Terms," that in brief and vivid vignettes introduces the many characters that become familiar and more fully developed in the subsequent stories. The prologue may be more accessible, less elusive to those who have read Cherry's earlier volumes, but for those who have not, a judicious strategy might be to reread it after finishing the collection in order to bring Cherry's literary landscape into clearer, sharper focus.

The eight tales and the epilogue that follow vary in style, content and length. (The shortest runs three pages; the longest, 26.) One of the most compelling is "The Only News That Matters," in which Conrad, a character who turns out to be tangential to Nina's experience—he's a neighbor and a colleague of Palmer's—obsessively reads the *New York Times*, watches CNN and MSNBC and keeps a journal, *Harper's Magazine* "Findings"-style, month by month, on the most noteworthy (usually cataclysmic) events. This fixation on the present is his way of suppressing a tragic event in his past, of repressing his grief and taking an odd sort of comfort in news, however awful, of more universal significance. "So many current events, so little comprehension of the self," the narrator comments. Only by confronting his past and giving full expression to sadness and loss can Conrad be fully present to those he loves now.

It is this kind of insight into human nature, Cherry's understanding of how our formative experiences, our connections to others and our knowledge of ourselves play out over time, that gives her book wisdom and pathos. The character BB, for instance, is particularly well rendered; she is drawn with precision and individuality and defies any preconceptions one may have of either teen mothers or Hollywood stars. Far from being sorry for herself or spoiled or entitled, she acknowledges that any success she has had is due to good fortune, and any suffering due to her own bad choices. Her patience, grace and resilience in "The Autobiography of My Mother(s)," in which she returns to Nina and Octavia without apology or self-pity or self-flagellation, lift the story safely out of the pit of melodrama into which the subject matter might have caused it to topple and infuse it instead with admirable, clear-eyed, matter-of-fact authenticity.

Alas, not all the stories manage quite so successfully to avoid sentimentality and contrivance. A vision of being guided into heaven in lively and philosophical conversation with the dogs one has raised in one's lifetime, or a character's definition of love as "two people trying to walk side by side on a busy sidewalk," may put off readers who bristle at any trace of the maudlin. But these touches emerge naturally from the characters' experiences and worldviews. Cherry is true to the people who inhabit her fiction. She treats her characters without condescension, and honors in them even what outsiders might see as limitations.

This is especially true of Nina, who after all is a writer of fiction and who invites the question of fiction as autobiography in "Faith, Hope and Clarity," which examines the process and craft of writing. If the other stories are meant to represent Nina's life work, then questionable stylistic choices like the occasional cliche ("stopped in her tracks," "a dime a dozen"), or the labored metaphor ("Lightning slashed the sky the way Tony Perkins had slashed Janet Leigh in *Psycho*") or the infelicitous stereotype (a Japanese businessman actually says things like, "Velly interesting" and "Ahso") are functions of the character (Nina), not the writer (Cherry).

Indeed, when read as a collection of narratives that the character, Nina, has conjured, *A Kind of Dream* becomes a richer and more complex work than when read otherwise, but because Cherry does not explicitly invoke

" MY WORK BEFORE I BEGAN TO PUBLISH TENDED TOWARD THE INTERIOR. YET, I BELIEVE THAT A WRITER MUST ALSO PAY ATTENTION TO THE EXTERNAL WORLD. I LIKE TO THINK I'VE BECOME BETTER AT THAT. THE WORLD IS WHERE WE MEET AND WHAT WE SHARE."

Nina's point of view until the eighth of the 10 pieces, her intent is unclear. Yet in "Faith, Hope and Clarity," Nina uses her own name as the name of a character, and quotes a writer named Phillip Routh (not Roth, we are cautioned): "The main purpose of one's double was to show you yourself or what you're about to become." Whether or not Nina is Cherrys doppelganger or avatar, what is clear is the kinship Cherry feels with her, even as Nina contemplates death. "The dead are not all dead," Nina writes. "They are alive and well and having a riotous time in your own mind." So, it seems, are the imaginary figures that populate *A Kind of Dream*.

Source: Dennis Vellucci, "Meeting One's Self," in *America*, Vol. 211, No. 3, August 4, 2014, p. 33.

Derek Alger

In the following interview, Cherry talks about her belief that life and literature are closely related.

Derek Alger: Let me start by asking you to elaborate on your belief that, for a writer, beauty and knowledge begin in the same place.

Kelly Cherry: Keats's notion that truth and beauty are the same is, I think, always the case for a writer. Definitions and examples of either are necessarily broad, but both begin in wonder (as does philosophy) and evolve from there. It's especially easy to see (if not always demonstrate) how language can move into truth and beauty, but I believe the two are twinned in any thoughtful endeavor—visual art, music, science, architecture, mathematics, and so on.

DA: Maybe we can cover your early years by asking about your book, Girl in a Library, *a collection of essays about "life" and "literature."*

KC: The book argues that life and literature are intertwined and goes on to illustrate that with examples from literature and from my own life. There are memoirs about my mother's father, who was a sawyer in Louisiana, my mother, a semester I spent at the University of Tennessee in Knoxville, and so on. Other essays discuss the shape and arc of the writing life, other writers' work, and the nature of writing.

DA: You have written a number of essays on exceptional southern women writers, such as Eudora Welty and Elizabeth Hardwick.

KC: Yes, there are several essays about women writers in the book. I met both Eudora Welty and Elizabeth Hardwick, though the meetings were brief. Bill Stafford once set up as a choice between role models the writers Welty and Katherine Anne Porter and said, "Be like Welty." His point was how to live a literary life, not a dismissal of Porter's work (both of them are great writers). Someday I'd like to write about Porter—and Elizabeth Spencer, another astoundingly terrific female story writer. But first I have to finish more of my own work.

DA: Would it be fair to say you were somewhat rebellious during your college years?

KC: Of course. Though I didn't think of myself as rebellious, not at all. I was asking questions, and it turned out that at that time and place asking questions was incendiary.

DA: You published your first work of fiction, Sick And Full Of Burning, *followed the next year with publication of a collection of poetry,* Lovers And Agnostics.

KC: I was always interested in language and character, which meant poetry and fiction. I did at first think of playwriting and wrote a couple of verse plays but I didn't have the temperament or patience for collaboration, and play usually involves collaboration. I never thought it was strange to do both poetry and fiction; many Southern writers do both, and my teachers did both. Nonfiction came later for me, because I felt that it required a habit of authority that I didn't have. But now I love writing nonfiction too.

Lovers And Agnostics was, I now see, a book in which I knocked on various doors, wondering where I, as a woman, could enter the poetic tradition. I think I handled novel structure in my first novel pretty well, but it was my second book of poems, *Relativity: A Point Of View*; that gave me my prose sentence.

I said "language and character" above, but I often thought of both of those in terms of music. I doubt I can explain what I mean. I guess I'll just mention that two early influences on me were Shakespeare and Beethoven. As string quartet violinists, my parents liked best to play the late Beethoven quartets, and my somewhat older brother had read Shakespeare even before I was born and, not yet eight, was given to quoting some of the fiercer lines when he wanted to express dissatisfaction or frustration.

DA: You were fortunate to run across some noted and generous writers as teachers when you earned an MFA at the University of North Carolina at Greensboro.

KC: Fred Chappell was there. Robert Watson. Allen Tate. I had Tate for literary criticism and a poetry workshop. Guy Owen. Randall Jarrell. Peter Taylor. I was too shy to sign up for Taylor's fiction workshop, but I gave my little stories to Fred and he took them to Peter, who always made a comment that Fred always relayed to me. Not at UNCG, but more or less present anyway, were George Garrett, Henry Taylor, and R.H.W. Dillard, all of whom I had met while doing graduate work in philosophy. Poets William Pitt Root and Harry Humes were in my class. The poet Gibbons Ruark was a young instructor. Eudora Welty, Carolyn Kizer, X.J. Kennedy were among the visiting writers. It was a lovely time to be there. Everything was just getting going. We knew nothing about contracts or agents, and in our ignorance felt free to aim as high as we wanted. Lawrence Judson Reynolds started the *Greensboro Review* with Bob Watson's guidance.

DA: Perhaps you can comment a bit on The Exiled Heart: A Meditative Autobiography.

KC: In January, 1965, I went to the Soviet Union, prompted by my love of Tolstoy, Dostoevsky, Chekhov, Turgenev, Pasternak, and Gogol. What I found, obviously, was a very different world. In a coffee shop in a hotel in Moscow, I struck up a friendship with a Latvian composer. I scribbled some of my lines on a paper napkin for him, and he played a tape of his first symphony for me. We wanted to get married but had no idea how to make it happen. I returned to the states and went to UNCG. Time elapsed. Our friendship began to seem like a daydream. I met a young artist and

married him. My Latvian friend married. Ten years later we were free to resume our correspondence and I returned to the Soviet Union to visit him. He informed the chief of the Musicians' Union that he planned to marry me. Spies came out of the woods. He was threatened. I received scary phone calls in the middle of the night. When I left there, for England, our correspondence was censored. He was interrogated repeatedly. Senator Mondale wrote me a letter that was instrumental in the progression of our friendship. All this is in *The Exiled Heart*. What I also tried to do in *The Exiled Heart* was ask questions: What does it mean to love someone? What is the individual's relationship to the state? What is the best relationship between state and art? What is justice? I think somewhere in the book I called it a "moral travelogue," and that's pretty much what it is.

DA: Although you have never written a travel essay, the essays in Writing The World *are very much about the importance of place in a person's life.*

KC: Well for one reason and another I've traveled a fair amount, not on anybody's expense account; just for personal reasons. Traveling is a form of self-interrogation and also requires constant repositioning of one's ideas about the world. Something new comes at you—or you go to it—and you're obliged to reconcile the new information with your former view of the world.

My work before I began to publish tended toward the interior. Yet, I believe that a writer must also pay attention to the external world. I like to think I've become better at that. The world is where we meet and what we share. I am fairly often experimental, but I am not postmodern; I don't believe we change our personalities and perspectives every minute of every day, though we all know well that changes accrue over time. Time, as Thomas Mann said, is what the novel is about. We have to be in the world to experience space and time.

DA: You sort of stumbled into teaching writing.

KC: For some reason I assumed: (a) I couldn't teach without a Ph.D., and (b) I also couldn't teach because I was too shy. There were hardly any writing programs at the time, so I must have thought that to teach meant to teach an academic discipline, and I hadn't finished the Ph.D. program in philosophy at the University of Virginia. As for the shyness, it dissipated, but not until I was pushing forty.

DA: What did you do to earn your keep?

KC: I worked in Richmond at the Presbyterian Board of Education and as a letter writer for the Christian Children's fund, which was, perhaps, not so Christian, and in New York City as writer or copy editor or managing editor at Behrman House, a publisher of Judaica, Harper & Row, Dutton, and Scribner's. At the trade houses, I was in Children's Books—as a result of the first job I took—which meant I didn't typically meet publishing folk who could help me get started as a writer, although the writer Abraham Rothberg used an office at Behrman House and directed me to send a story I'd written to *Commentary*, which took it. My literary relationship with *Commentary* has been one of the blessings of my life. Also in New Yolk, I taught emotionally disturbed middle-school and high-school children at a small private school for the same. And I tutored. My first college teaching post was at Southwest Minnesota State College (now University), a lovely place where able-bodied kids received funds for helping disabled or differently-abled kids. It gave a wonderful flavor of kindness to the whole place.

DA: How did you end up at the University of Wisconsin?

KC: I was living in England with my parents, who had chosen to retire there. I was a citizen of one country, living in a second country, trying to get a visa to a third country to get married. I had only a little bit of money left from the paperback sale of my first novel and needed a job. I applied to Cottrell, Austin, and Wisconsin. They all required an interview at the MLA. I didn't have the dough to fly over and back and, maybe, back again so I had to pass by those opportunities. Then one day I received a call from the University of Wisconsin asking if I'd come for a year as a visitor. 1 said yes. Later I learned that, like Cornell and Austin, they had scratched me off the list because I wasn't available to interview, but then the dean dragged his feet about funding. By the time funding came through, all the other candidates had been hired elsewhere. Ron Wallace said to the department, if we're hiring blind, why not hire our original first choice? So I wound up in Wisconsin. The University was not a happy place, and not a good one to be in, either, but Ron was a great colleague, and together we started the writing program.

DA: I suspect you've had many positive experiences in what you have referred to as "The American Literary Soft-Shoe Shuffle."

KC: Some very lovely ones, though when I used that phrase I was referring to the teaching-grant-colony-agent-publisher-blurb merry-go-round that can be exhausting and debilitating. But yes, absolutely, there are always wonderful writing friends ready to help someone out, and publishers and agents who are insightful and caring, and jobs and grants and colonies that reward writers in their various ways. For example, I think of my longtime association with Louisiana State University Press, which has been nothing short of a lifesaver. I think of Ben Furnish, the editor of *Girl In A Library*, who devoted time and attention to the book and a happy and positive attitude to the author. I think of friends like William Jay Smith, Fred Chappell, R.H.W. Dillard, Henry Taylor, David R. Slavin, Abraham Rothberg, and the late great George Garrett, one of the liveliest men who ever lived. One tries to pay back by helping other writers however one may.

DA: You recently spent some quality time doing research for a project in which you are excitedly involved.

KC: I was at the Institute for Advanced Study in Princeton this summer, working on a long poem and doing research. It was amazing. They gave me an apartment, and with free fruit and cookies every weekday afternoon. I hardly had to spend anything on food. The apartment came with a small study with windows that took up most of two walls. The windows looked out on a green ocean of trees. I had access to the library and the Archives. And everywhere were these incredibly beautiful, often exotic, small children, all with perfect teeth and, I don't doubt, astronomical IQs.

With whole days free—sequences of whole days—I was able to concentrate intensely. This is a long poem that, like most American long poems, is made up of smaller poems. Right now most of the poems act like placeholders. It will take me another year or two to revise them into, I hope, real poetry. Meanwhile I have other books underway. I work on one manuscript for awhile, set it aside to simmer, work on another, set that aside to simmer, then return to the first. "Simmer" is purely a metaphorical term; I don't cook.

This was not a method I devised; it just happened, I think because I need a lot of time to recognize and realize all the potential of a book. The nice thing about the method is that after one's been doing it for several years, it turns out that something is almost always nearing completion.

Source: Derek Alger and Kelly Cherry, "Kelly Cherry," in *pif Magazine*, October 1, 2010.

Angela O'Donnell

In the following review, O'Donnell points out that Cherry's poems are evidence of her "thorough grounding in English literary tradition."

For the reader whose misfortune it is not to have yet discovered Kelly Cherry's poems, this is your lucky day. Cherry's new book, *Hazard and Prospect: New and Selected Poems*, offers a generous sampling of the poet's work, culled from six previous volumes, and features a dozen previously uncollected poems that explore new literary terrain. Formally engaged and linguistically rich, these are poems that sing, that stop you in your tracks, that make you want to read them to other people and share what has come as a pure gift.

And yet, for all their surface pleasure, Cherry's poems lead us to dark places. To read the collection chronologically is to accompany the poet on a painful journey. As the narrative unfolds, we witness the slow erasure of memory and identity as the speaker's parents age and die, the dissolution of a marriage, the death of an estranged husband and a descent into madness. Indeed, the latter experience marks the nadir of the speaker's interior drama, a dark night of the mind and soul wherein she cries for help and declares her despair: "There is blood everywhere / and I am lost in it. Doctor, I breathe blood, not air."

What makes these poems of desolation bearable is a superb formal control through which the poet shapes the chaotic experiences of life into art. For all its agony, "Lady Macbeth on the Psych Ward" (quoted above) is a tour de force of formal wit. Its nine lines, arranged symmetrically in three tercets, employ rhymes that often do not look like rhymes (nowhere, nightmare, hair). The disjunction between orthography and sound, as well as the obsessive repetition we associate both with madness in general and with Lady Macbeth's particular manifestation of it, are embodied in this unsettling, relentless rhyming. Madness is often characterized by

hyper-rationality as well as irrationality, and the former is eerily evident in the speaker's tightly controlled expression of her uncontrollable thoughts. Here the use of form and musical language elicit in the reader both terror and pleasure simultaneously.

Though Cherry is not a rigid formalist, all of these poems, including those in open form, demonstrate her thorough grounding in English literary tradition. *Hazard and Prospect* offers the reader skillful variations on the villanelle, the ballad, the sestina and, most prominently, the sonnet. In each of these poems, form participates in conveying meaning, so much so that the formal structure seems to have come about organically at the poem's inception rather than having been imposed later upon an already existing arrangement of words or lines.

In addition to the pleasures of craft, the other element that redeems the desolation of the early poems is the consolation offered in the later ones. In the course of her journey, the speaker gathers strength and recovers a sense of her own worthiness, as well as the ability to love. In a celebratory poem dedicated to an unnamed young woman on her graduation from college, the speaker turns her attention away from herself and towards another human being for whom she has great affection and pronounces this benediction: "I tell you, there is an economy in this, / the way love returns."

The healing power of love leads the speaker to contemplate ultimate "Questions and Answers" in the section of the volume bearing that title. These poems, among the finest in the book, are meditations on the Annunciation, the "Virgin and Child," on "Galilee" and "Golgotha," wherein she places herself in the presence of the divine in an attempt to understand the relationship between suffering and love. Tried by personal tragedy and by the experience of living in a culture that privileges the seeming certainties of science over the revelations of faith, she emerges from this baptism by fire physically, psychologically and spiritually whole, a resurrection made manifest most clearly in the quality of joy evident in the remaining poems of the volume.

Among these final offerings is "Byrd's Survey of the Boundary: An Abridgment," a found poem consisting of excerpts from William Byrd II's *History of the Dividing Line Between Virginia and North Carolina*. Alternating between his reports (written in gracious 18th-century English prose) on the "Hazards" and "Prospect" discovered in this brave new world, Byrd's charming meditation likely influenced Cherry's book title and sounds the keynote of the collection: there can be no prospect without hazard, no joy without sorrow, no resurrection without crucifixion. Kelly Cherry's poems bring us, finally, to this wisdom.

As she nears the end of her journey, having laid claim to her home, her faith and a husband she loves, the speaker discovers that what finally endures is "Joy": "You could be doing anything, / arranging dahlias in a vase . . . driving a truck . . . having a baby . . . / you could be anywhere, at home / . . . walking through woods or sitting on/ a screened-in porch, writing a poem— / and there you are, surprised by it." The final line of the poem, an echo of Wordsworth's poignant sonnet on his recovery from the death of his young daughter, "Surprised by Joy," places poet and reader in the company of those who have come before us, have suffered greatly and have left behind eloquent testimony to the astonishing resilience of the spirit and the power of poetry to speak of it.

Source: Angela O'Donnell, "Surprised by Joy," in *America*, Vol. 197, No. 17, November 26, 2007, p. 27.

SOURCES

"Books by Our Editors," in *Hollins Critic*, Vol. 34, No. 5, December 1997, p. 19.

"A Brief Guide to New Formalism," Poets.org, February 21, 2014, https://www.poets.org/poetsorg/text/brief-guide-new-formalism (accessed September 17, 2016).

Cherry, Kelly, "Alzheimer's," in *Death and Transfiguration: Poems*, Louisiana State University Press, 1997, p. 13.

———, "My Mother's Stroke," in *Death and Transfiguration: Poems*, Louisiana State University Press, 1997, p. 6.

Gabilondo, Patricia A., Review of *Death and Transfiguration*, in *Anglican Theological Review*, Vol. 82, No. 1, Winter 2000, https://www.questia.com/library/journal/1P3-51035011/death-and-transfiguration (accessed September 14, 2016).

Hagelman, Jr., Ronald R., Denise Liston, and Monica E. Rutkowski, "SOA '10 Health Meeting June 28–30, 2010, Session 48 PD: The Future for LTC Insurance," Society of Actuaries, 2010.

"The History of Long Term Care Insurance," FreeAdvice website, http://law.freeadvice.com/insurance_law/long_term_care/history-of-long-term-care.htm (accessed September 17, 2016).

"Kelly Cherry," Poetry Foundation website, https://www.poetryfoundation.org/poems-and-poets/poets/detail/kelly-cherry (accessed September 14, 2016).

"Kelly Cherry," University of Wisconsin–Madison website, https://english.wisc.edu/emeritus-cherry.htm (accessed September 14, 2016).

"Kelly Cherry," Wisconsin Literary Map, http://www.wisconsinlitmap.com/kelly-cherry.html (accessed September 14, 2016).

Kingsbury, Pam, "'Words Will Take You Anywhere': An Interview with Kelly Cherry," in *Southern Scribe*, 2002, http://www.southernscribe.com/zine/authors/Cherry2_Kelly.htm (accessed September 18, 2016).

Lambert, Jean-Charles, et al., "Meta-analysis of 74,046 Individuals Identifies 11 New Susceptibility Loci for Alzheimer's Disease," in *Nature Genetics*, Vol. 45, 2013, pp. 1452–58.

"Long-Term Care in the United States: A Timeline," Henry J. Kaiser Family Foundation website, August 31, 2015, http://kff.org/medicaid/timeline/long-term-care-in-the-united-states-a-timeline/ (accessed September 17, 2016).

"Major Milestones in Alzheimer's and Brain Research," Alzheimer's Association website, http://www.alz.org/research/science/major_milestones_in_alzheimers.asp (accessed September 17, 2016).

"New Criticism: Anglo-American Literary Criticism," in *Encyclopædia Britannica*, https://www.britannica.com/art/New-Criticism (accessed September 22, 2016).

"New Formalism," Poetry Foundation website, https://www.poetryfoundation.org/resources/learning/glossary-terms/detail/new-formalism (accessed September 17, 2016).

O'Donnell, Angela, "Surprised by Joy," in *America*, Vol. 197, No. 17, November 26, 2007, p. 27.

Sauer, Alissa, "History of Alzheimer's: Major Milestones," Alzheimers.net, December 30, 2013, http://www.alzheimers.net/2013-12-30/history-of-alzheimers/ (accessed September 17, 2016).

———, "Study Shows Double the Number of Alzheimer's Risk Genes," Alzheimers.net, October 30, 2013, http://www.alzheimers.net/2013-10-30/11-risk-genes-discovered/ (accessed September 17, 2016).

"Treatment Horizon," Alzheimer's Association website, http://www.alz.org/research/science/alzheimers_treatment_horizon.asp (accessed September 17, 2016).

Vellucci, Dennis, "Meeting One's Self," in *America*, Vol. 211, No. 3, August 4, 2014, p. 33.

Weaks, Mary Louise, "Kelly Cherry (1940–)," in *Southern Writers: A New Biographical Dictionary*, edited by

Joseph M. Flora and Amber Vogel, Louisiana State University Press, 2006, pp. 67–68.

"What We Know Today about Alzheimer's Disease," Alzheimer's Association website, http://www.alz.org/research/science/alzheimers_disease_causes.asp (accessed September 17, 2016).

FURTHER READING

Cherry, Kelly, *God's Loud Hand: Poems*, Louisiana State University Press, 1993.
> As the title suggests, many of the poems in this collection examine religious themes. They are more philosophical than devotional, showing the clarity and honesty central to Cherry's work.

Geist, Mary Ellen, *Measure of the Heart: A Father's Alzheimer's, a Daughter's Return*, Springboard Press, 2008.
> Geist left a prestigious job as a radio anchor to help her mother care for her aging father, who suffered from Alzheimer's. In this memoir, Geist reveals the love and heartbreak of a daughter seeing a parent's health and mind fade but balances the emotion with the objectivity of a professional journalist.

Gioia, Dana, *Can Poetry Matter? Essays on Poetry and American Culture*, Graywolf Press, 1992.
> This celebrated volume was a finalist for the National Book Critics Circle Award in Criticism. In addition to Gioia's much-discussed essay "Can Poetry Matter?," the book includes a number of thoughtful essays discussing the place of poetry in modern American mainstream culture.

Leavitt, Sarah, *Tangles: A Story about Alzheimer's, My Mother, and Me*, Skyhorse Publishing, 2012.
> Leavitt's memoir combines candid personal reflection with black-and-white drawings. The book recounts the author's experience of seeing her mother transformed by her disease and how it affected the family dynamic, both for ill and for good.

SUGGESTED SEARCH TERMS

Kelly Cherry AND "Alzheimer's"

Kelly Cherry AND Death and Transfiguration

Kelly Cherry AND interview

Kelly Cherry AND novels

Kelly Cherry AND memoir

Kelly Cherry AND poet laureate

symptoms of Alzheimer's

effects of Alzheimer's on family members

Blonde White Women

PATRICIA SMITH

1992

The renowned slam poet Patricia Smith included in her 1992 collection *Big Towns, Big Talk* a poem titled "Blonde White Women." The people specified in the title of the poem are probably not the target audience. The first line likens women of the physical description in question to blizzards that do little more than make it difficult for city dwellers to get through their days. This is a provocative description, one that some readers—such as blonde, white, female readers—may object to as an unfair overgeneralization. But the poem proceeds to suggest that Smith is not just propagating a stereotype; she is responding to circumstances that she has personally experienced, past and present alike.

The poem continued to be relevant decades after its publication, as race came to the forefront of the American consciousness with the election of President Barack Obama in 2008. And in the mid-2010s, racial tension ran high, as in cases in which police officers used lethal force against black suspects who were neither armed nor dangerous. *Big Towns, Big Talk* won the Carl Sandburg Literary Award upon publication.

AUTHOR BIOGRAPHY

Smith was born on June 25, 1955, in Chicago, Illinois. She was raised there and upon reaching college age completed coursework at Southern

The poem's speaker counts the white women on the train (©*Matej Kastelic | Shutterstock.com*)

Illinois University and Northwest University. She began working for the *Chicago Daily News* as a typist and in time became a music and entertainment reviewer there and at the *Chicago Sun-Times*. A pivotal moment came when the *Sun-Times* assigned her to cover the Neutral Turf Poetry Festival, which introduced her to slam poetry. By the late 1980s, Smith was a seminal figure in the burgeoning slam movement, Chicago being, as the scholar Kurt Heintz called it, the true ground zero of the form. Smith garnered kudos for her representations of urban life and the energy she brought to readings, an energy impossible to fully communicate on the lifeless page. She became a five-time champion of Chicago's Uptown Poetry Slam and four-time champion of the National Poetry Slam, participated in the Taos Poetry Circus in New Mexico, and was featured on a number of video and audio slam poetry recordings.

In 1990 Smith took a position at the *Boston Globe*, becoming a reporter and regular columnist, the first African American woman to do so with the prestigious paper. In this decade she began publishing her poetry in volumes, beginning with *Life according to Motown* in 1991 and *Big Towns, Big Talk*, which includes "Blonde White Women," in 1992. She also brought slam poetry to New England with the help of her then husband, Michael Brown, leading to its becoming a national phenomenon. Smith was nominated for the Pulitzer Prize for investigative reporting in 1981 and for commentary in 1998. Also in 1998, however, she was relieved of her position at the *Globe* when she was unable to substantiate some of the sources and quotes included in her articles. Although she conceded that her efforts amounted to fabrications, she affirmed that she executed them not to deceive but to give the realest possible representation of circumstances.

Smith returned to poetry, literature, and performance. She wrote the children's book *Janna and the Kings* in 2003. Her 2008 volume of poetry *Blood Dazzler* was a finalist for the National Book Award, and her 2012 title *Shoulda Been Jimi Savannah* won the Lenore Marshall Poetry Prize, awarded by the Academy of American Poets for the year's best collection. She also wrote and starred in several one-woman plays, drawing on her personal and career experiences. She served as a faculty member for the poetry collective Cave Canem and as an instructor in the MFA program at Sierra Nevada College, in Nevada. In 2016 she was a professor of creative writing at the College of Staten Island, City University of New York, and living in Howell, New Jersey.

POEM TEXT

They choke cities like snowstorms.

On the morning train, I flip through my *Ebony*,
marveling at the bargain basement prices
for reams of straightened hair
and bleaches for the skin. Next to me,   5
skinny pink fingers rest upon a briefcase,
shiver a bit under my scrutiny.
Leaving the tunnel, we hurtle into hurting sun.
An icy brush paints the buildings
with shine, fat spirals of snow   10
become blankets, and Boston stops breathing.

It is my habit to count them. So I search
the damp, chilled length of the train car
and look for their candle flames of hair,
the circles of blood at their cheeks,   15
that curt dismissing glare
reserved for the common, the wrinkled, the
     black.

I remember striving for that breathlessness,
toddling my five-year-old black butt around
with a dull gray mophead covering my   20
nappy hair, wishing myself golden.
Pressing down hard with my
carnation pink crayola, I filled faces
in coloring books, rubbed the waxy stick
across the back of my hand until the skin broke. 25

When my mop hair became an annoyance
to my mother, who always seemed to be
     mopping,
I hid beneath my father's white shirt,
the sleeves hanging down on either side of my
     head,
the coolest white light pigtails.   30
I practiced kissing, because to be blonde and
     white
meant to be kissed, and my fat lips slimmed
around words like "delightful" and "darling."
I hurt myself with my own beauty.
When I was white, my name was Donna.   35
My teeth were perfect; I was always out of
     breath.

In first grade, my blonde teacher
hugged me to her because I was the first
in my class to read, and I thought the rush
would kill me. I wanted her to swallow   40

me, to be my mother, to be the first fire
moving in my breast. But when she pried
me away, her cool blue eyes shining with
righteousness and too much touch
I saw how much she wanted to wash.   45

She was not my mother,
the singing Alabama woman
who shook me to sleep
and fed me from her fingers.
I could not have been blacker   50
than I was at that moment.
My name is Patricia Ann.

Even crayons fail me now—
I can find no color darker,
more beautiful, than I am.   55
This train car grows tense with me.
I pulse, steady my eyes,
shake the snow from my short black hair,
and suddenly I am surrounded by snarling
     madonnas
demanding that I explain   60
my treachery.

POEM SUMMARY

The text used for this summary is from *Big Towns, Big Talk*, Zoland Books, 1992, pp. 21–23. A version of the poem can be found on the following web page: http://coursesite.uhcl.edu/HSH/Whitec/texts/AfAm/afampoetry/SmithPBlondeWW.htm.

The version of the poem in *Big Towns, Big Talk* consists of sixty-one lines in ten stanzas of unequal length, the first and last being the shortest.

Line 1

After the bold title, the poem opens with a single-line stanza declaring that an unspecified *they*—probably the women of the title—congest cities much in the way snowstorms do.

Lines 2–11

The speaker establishes a setting, a morning ride on a subway train and her location on the train, where she reads *Ebony* magazine. She takes particular note of the low prices for bundles of straightened hair (to be attached to existing hair) and products designed to lighten the skin color of people of African descent. The cause of her amazement seems to be that the products are popular enough that they can be sold at very low prices. It is also possible, however, that the bargain prices indicate that the products have been

MEDIA ADAPTATIONS

- Smith has been featured reading her poetry on the HBO series *Def Poetry Jam* and in the film *SlamNation* (1998). She also appears on the CDs *Grand Slam! Best of the National Poetry Slam*, Vol. 1 (1996); *A Snake in the Heart: Poems and Music by Chicago Spoken-Word Performers* (1995); and *Lip: The CD with a Big Mouth* (1994).

selling so poorly that people are not expected to purchase them at all unless prices are dramatically reduced.

As she reads, the poet notices that a neighbor's thin white fingers resting on a briefcase appear to tremble under her gaze. As the train exits the tunnel and emerges above ground, sunlight glares into the train car and causes pain— presumably just the momentary pain of bright light on eyes adjusted to darkness. The description in lines 9–11 indicates that the snowstorm mentioned in line 1 is not exclusively metaphorical: the buildings are painted with ice, and snow tumbling down in large spirals forms layers that blanket the ground. (The snow would make the sunlight extra bright and more hurtful to the eyes.) The city of Boston (the setting) is said to cease its respiration, its ordinary pulsing activity, owing to the snow.

Lines 12–17

The speaker's usual practice during her commute is to count the people referred to in line 1. The inside of the train feels cold and wet from snow melting off people's boots and jackets. The speaker identifies the people in question as having hair like candle flames (which can suggest orange but in the context means yellow), glowing or emitting its own light, and cheeks flushed red from the cold. The tendency or typical behavior of these women is to glance with a measure of condescension or even disdain at people whom

they judge inferior to themselves, whether owing to low status, advanced age, or black skin.

Lines 18–25

The speaker signals a shift in tone in announcing a remembrance, and this shift extends through several stanzas. In her past, the speaker has sought to achieve the sort of breathlessness that blonde white women seem to have, whether entering a subway train out of the cold or just walking through a crowded room—as if their lives are so full of self-centered excitement that they are left constantly short of breath. Even at the age of five the speaker was conscious of this common quality. Back then, she would place a gray mop head atop her own head to cover up her characteristically African hair, wishing herself to be blonde. With a pink crayon, she would color face after face in coloring books and even try to change the color of the back of her hand, to the point of breaking through the skin.

Lines 26–34

The speaker's mother, who always needed the mop head, eventually ended her daughter's use of it. The speaker then started concealing herself within a white shirt of her father's, the sleeves of which would trail down like bright and agreeable pigtails. To further fill out her role as a white person, the speaker would prepare for desirability later in life by developing her manner of kissing, perhaps using dolls. She would compress her full lips to give them a more slender appearance as she uttered with breathy sophistication words she held to be commonly used by blonde white women. The fact of her resulting beauty— the beauty she achieved by altering her image to better resemble that of a white person—was painful, like a self-inflicted wound.

Lines 35–36

Whenever she playacted as white, the speaker called herself Donna, a name that resonates with the madonnas of line 59—and with the blonde white pop star whose career was thriving when Smith wrote the poem. The speaker had (or imagined herself to have) impeccable teeth, and she was, as she saw it, constantly short of breath.

Lines 37–45

One time, the speaker relates, in first grade, she was given a hug by a blonde teacher when she was the first person in her class to successfully read. The experience was exhilarating, leaving the speaker wanting to be absorbed into the teacher's being, to be swallowed up by her as if to enter her body (particularly her womb) and become the teacher's own daughter. In a related but inverse image, she wanted the teacher to be the original spark of warmth or life in her own body. The exhilaration ends, however, when the teacher lets go. The look in her eyes reflects not only her egotistic sense that she is doing good for the world and proving herself a superior person by stooping to hug this African American child but also her impulsive desire to wash herself after the physical contact.

Lines 46–52

The teacher, the speaker notes, is not her mother, a woman from Alabama who helped her daughter sleep by gently shaking her and who used her own fingers, not necessarily a spoon, to feed the girl. In the moment after the teacher hugs her but then appears repulsed by her, the speaker feels as black as she possibly could. The speaker at this point reveals her actual name, Patricia Ann.

Lines 53–59

In the speaker's present life, crayons are somehow insufficient for her—that is, they fail to represent how dark and beautiful she feels she is. Back on the train, the speaker relates that the people in the car grow tense along with her, presumably as she responds in kind to the vibes being put out by the disdainful white people. She *pulses* (perhaps suggesting that she feels an especially strong and suffusive heartbeat in a moment of deliberate pause), holds her gaze steady, and shakes the snow out of her short, black hair. At this, the madonnas, or morally pure and chaste women, though the term also invokes the Virgin Mary, surround the speaker and issue reserved yet threatening leers and noises.

Lines 60–61

The surrounding women insist that the speaker explain her purportedly treacherous act.

THEMES

Prejudice

If the reader is not already familiar with Smith's identity as a black woman, it becomes apparent from the combination of the title and the first

TOPICS FOR FURTHER STUDY

- Write a poem based on personal experience in which you are confronted—whether subtly or straightforwardly—by a group of people who antagonize you. In the poem, flash back to scenes that explain the antagonism. Feel free to use the poem as a means of catharsis, a way to give a figurative shake of the head and loose yourself from negative conceptions and emotions, but be careful about unfairly demeaning the group in question and about propagating stereotypes.

- Read the poem "Life Doesn't Frighten Me at All," which can be found in the Poetry for Young People series volume *Maya Angelou* (2007), edited by Edwin Graves Wilson, and online. Angelou's speaker and Smith's seem to have similar concerns with society but different temperaments and means of achieving resolution and tranquility. In an essay, elucidate the various points of comparison and contrast between the two poems.

- Read the essay posted at the blog *Race and Technology* titled "'Whitewashing' in Mass Media: Exploring Colorism and the Damaging Effects of Beauty Hierarchies," dated December 10, 2014. In response, write your own post or essay in which you provide an in-depth personal reaction to the content of the article. Consider ways in which its revelations are relevant to you, and comment on Smith's poem in view of the article.

- Research the history of *Ebony* magazine and either write a conventional research paper or prepare a multimedia presentation to provide in-depth treatment of the magazine's cultural significance over the decades, including discussion of contributors, trends, and challenges. One topic worth considering is the art exhibition and book *Speaking of People:* Ebony, Jet *and Contemporary Art* (2014).

line. That an oppositional stance is being presented, one that positions blonde white women
as something of a menace to society, naturally
suggests that the poet has an African American
identity. This is confirmed by the second line and
its reference to the speaker's reading a magazine
aimed at black people. The inspiration for the
poet's oppositional stance becomes clear as the
poem unfolds: she has been subject to experiences
of distinct prejudice on the part of white people
and is subjected to them on a regular basis.

The signs are subtle enough; that is, it would
be hard to suggest that they represent outright
discrimination or even racism, concepts that
generally suggest decisive action, conscious conviction, or both. On the subway train, the
speaker notices only the slight shaking of someone's hand in what appears to be a fearful,
racially motivated response to her presence and
pointed glances with hints of both condescension
and animosity directed her way. What is communicated in a look can be debatable; these
white women may not even be conscious of the
impression they are producing with the expressions on their faces as they scan the train. But a
person who pays regular attention to such
looks—a person who has felt the sense carried
by those looks in having them directed at her—
can better recognize precise, concealed emotions. These people, along with the speaker's
first-grade teacher, may not commit any clear-
cut act that discriminates against the speaker,
but their prejudice against people of African
heritage is all too evident in their facial expressions and body language.

Childhood

The speaker begins with a scenario in which she
experiences apparent prejudice in the present
day, and she has a charged response to that
prejudice. To put that response in context, the
speaker takes care to turn back in time to experiences that shape her outlook during her formative years. As they grow, children have to learn
everything about how the world functions; little
is self-evident in the way people act and communicate with each other, and it is only through
interaction that children can learn to participate
in the world. One extension of this is a heightened sensitivity to other people (unless that sensitivity is blunted, as by constant exposure to
television or violence). As parents dominate
their children's lives, the children become highly
attuned to what is expected of them, and as they

make friends, they become highly attuned to
other people's feelings toward them, developing
interpersonal skills that are crucial to maintaining healthy relationships.

In "Blonde White Women," the speaker
does not specify exactly how she comes to ideal-
ize the figure of the blonde white girl, but it is not
hard to imagine. In the early 1990s, the mainstream media (excluding MTV) were still saturated with white people. Disney princesses were
exclusively white, and children in commercials
were white. One (wrongly) learns from such
overexposure to images glorifying white beauty
that being white is beautiful and that by implication, in the absence of alternative affirmative
images, black is not. Even more powerful can be
personal experiences. If a child learns from an
otherwise admired teacher that a black student is
best kept at arm's length, it is impossible to say
how thoroughly this will resonate through the
child's mind. It is not a stretch to imagine that,
from then on, however much she may admire a
white person, she will be reluctant to approach
close enough for an embrace out of fear of that
same feeling of rejection. In other words, she will
enact the prejudice she has been exposed to by
rendering herself subservient to the presence of
white women.

Self-Image

The speaker, in light of her exposure to images
glorifying whiteness, comes to fantasize that she,
too, can be white and beautiful. Donning a mop
head is only playacting at heart, but it represents
a serious deficit in the girl's racialized self-image:
the satisfaction that she gets from the playacting
attests to her desire to transcend her true racial
identity to achieve what society has taught her
would be a better one. That she would rub the
crayon on her hand so hard as to break the skin
calls to mind more serious issues that may arise
later in life, as some individuals take to cutting,
deliberately injuring themselves as a means of
enhancing or transcending what feels at the
time like an unsatisfactory existence. This sort
of self-destruction is close to the self-annihila-
tion represented by suicide.

The speaker understands that her habits
were self-destructive, not just physically but psy-
chically. She understands that she was literally
causing herself pain, emotional and psychic
pain, in trying to fulfill a sense of beauty based
entirely on white ideals and attributes. When, in

The speaker turns from coloring on paper to trying to change the color of her own skin
(©karelnoppe / Shutterstock.com)

sharp contrast to her playacting as white, the poet as a girl endures the experience of her teacher's repulsion, she feels as black as she possibly could. Sometime between the speaker's childhood and her ride on the train in the present day, the reader hopes, the speaker's self-image has recuperated.

Acceptance

With all the psychic pain represented in the poem, it comes as a great relief when in line 52 the poem suddenly assumes a tone of acceptance. Immediately after commenting on her enhanced sense of her own blackness after the teacher's unfortunate embrace, the speaker declares her name. It may not be immediately clear why she is moved to declare it. But as one recalls how the speaker, as a girl, went by another name, Donna, when she playacted white, her true name takes on the significance of an affirmation of her black identity. It is as if recalling the moment in which she was supremely conscious of her blackness has the effect of making the speaker pause in

thought—but so momentarily as to not even call for a new stanza. Suddenly she realizes that she wants to proclaim her true name, and she at once does so. The next stanza furthers this sense of self-acceptance as the speaker specifically affirms the beauty of her blackness and acts out that beauty by boldly shaking her hair in the midst of the white women on the train. This hardly leads to the speaker's being accepted by these women—to the contrary, it ignites their indignity, over how the speaker has effectively, in her assertively feminine act, made a public affirmation of her beauty as being equal, perhaps even superior, to that of the blonde women. This is blasphemy in their eyes, but victory in the speaker's.

STYLE

Free Verse

The poem is written in free verse, that is, it has no consistent rhyme or meter. The stanzas are of unequal numbers of lines, though the lines themselves are generally similar lengths. The exceptions are the stanza consisting of lines 46–52, which are rather short, perhaps suggesting the speaker's nearing an epiphany, as reached in line 52, and the last stanza, which consists of two short lines that bring the poem to a definitive and majestic close.

Smith uses some noticeable poetic language, as one can expect from a slam poet highly conscious of the aural effects of sequences of words. She uses alliteration—*s* in line 10 and *b* in line 11—and consonance in lines 12–17, which have an abundance of hard *c* and *k* sounds. Other examples are present throughout. The *s* sounds in lines 57–59 are especially resonant. This may be seen to suggest snakes (a word not far removed from *shake* in line 58) with their hissing and to amplify the sense of the speaker's shaking out her black hair by suggesting she is an image of Medusa. But Smith inverts the sense of the image in having herself be the sympathetic heroine while the blonde women surrounding her are the ones snarling with grotesque antagonism.

Personal Narrative

The poem takes the form of a personal narrative, using as a framework a situation experienced in the present day and in the middle delving into key remembrances from earlier in the speaker's life. In presenting such a plot-driven story, Smith has taken care to avoid ambiguity, which would threaten the reader's understanding of the circumstances. For example, the poem would have been much more subtle if the *they* were never specified, as they are by the title. But Smith has a specific point to make, and she is using the title and the labeling of the group of perceived oppressors to ensure that the point is made. Within the poem, similarly, instead of simply mentioning that her white neighbor's hands are trembling on the train, she specifies that they do so under her gaze. The directness with which the speaker communicates her line of thought solidifies the sense of the narrative and the power of the poem.

HISTORICAL CONTEXT

African American Self-Perception and the Media

The long-term relation between the African American mind-set and the white-majority Western culture in which it has developed is succinctly presented by the historian Asa G. Hilliard:

> For nearly four hundred years, the slave trade, colonization, segregation, and racism—highly sophisticated systematic strategies of oppression—have been the massive political and economic forces operating on African people. These forces have affected the culture, the socialization processes, and the very consciousness of African people.

White Europeans and Americans took advantage of their culture's being advanced in materialist terms—to say nothing of spiritual or existential terms—to look down on not only African cultures but also Africans themselves from the beginning of extensive cross-continental contact in the late fifteenth through seventeenth centuries. Richard L. Allen, in *The Concept of Self: A Study of Black Identity and Self-Esteem*, cited several philosophers and statesmen, including David Hume, Georg Wilhelm Friedrich Hegel, Abraham Lincoln, and Thomas Jefferson, who made bald assertions about black racial inferiority based on the one-sided relations between blacks and whites up to their times. Slaves were directly instructed as to their inferiority and made to exemplify it at all times merely to survive. The slaves who showed too much pride in any form, those who refused to believe in their inferiority, were liable to be whipped or otherwise punished—often lethally—to set an example to keep the other slaves under the yoke of their oppression.

Times changed with emancipation, but especially in the South, this simply made the mechanisms of oppression less overt. If whites could not keep blacks in line through the profoundly unbalanced master-slave relationship, they could discount and inconvenience blacks in whatever other ways possible, through casual discrimination, Jim Crow laws, and segregation at every level of society. Meanwhile, white-controlled media constantly reinforced conceptions of blacks as inferior beings. Even late in the nineteenth century and into the twentieth, well beyond the days of slavery, minstrel shows in which white performers in blackface lampooned stereotyped black personae were common. With the advent of film, such stereotyped characters—sometimes played by black actors, but universally presented by white directors for white-owned film companies—reached larger audiences and became further exaggerated for comic effect on the screen. In the absence of

COMPARE & CONTRAST

- **1990s:** People are generally exposed to media images, typically dominated by white actors, models, and other celebrities, through film, television, magazines, and newspapers. The Internet is just coming into popular use.

  Today: Media have expanded to allow Internet access through not only home computers but also portable devices, such as laptop computers, tablets, and cellular telephones, increasing the opportunities for people to be exposed to images and advertisements. Corporations and advertisers realize that they need to reach out to all demographics to successfully project an inclusive sensibility.

- **1990s:** The circulation of *Ebony* is approximately 1.9 million readers.

- **Today:** The circulations of magazines of all types have decreased. *Ebony* is the leading African American magazine, with a circulation of just over 1.2 million readers, but *Essence* is gaining in relative popularity, holding steady at just under 1.1 million.

- **1990s:** A storm drops over twenty inches of snow on Boston in 1997.

  Today: With global warming changing climate and weather patterns worldwide, harbor cities like Boston see rising tides and intensified storm patterns. Four of Boston's seven largest storms over the last eighty years occur between 2003 and 2015.

---

soundtracks, early films demanded particular emphasis of physical acts and gestures.

The earliest means by which African American populations countered demeaning conceptions of the character of African peoples was through newspapers such as the *Chicago Defender*, established in 1905, and the NAACP *Crisis*, in 1910. This advancement in journalism led into the Harlem Renaissance, in which blacks made clear that their intellectual and artistic capacities were in no way inferior to whites'. Although the Great Depression slowed cultural development in all quarters, the 1940s saw significant advances in black publishing, as with the founding of the African American–owned and –oriented magazines *Negro Digest* in 1942 and *Ebony* in 1945, both founded by the entrepreneur John H. Johnson. *Ebony*, modeled on *Life*, emphasized black cultural achievements, interests, news, and topics of note. Attesting to its dedication to cultural, societal, and political concerns, Martin Luther King Jr. contributed a column, "Advice for Living By," in the 1950s, and *Ebony* was in the intellectual vanguard and on the scene of the civil rights movement. Still, as media evolved, African Americans were

consistently left a step behind. The new medium of television in mid-century was overwhelmingly dominated by white interests, and even after the civil rights era, black interests only occasionally squeezed into the mainstream programming market that the major networks dominated.

The famed black intellectual W. E. B. DuBois coined the term *double consciousness* to describe the way in which black Americans were historically forced to look past the negative perceptions inflicted upon them by society—often communicated in such simple forms as gestures of prejudicial wariness or eye contact with notes of condescension or aggression—in order to achieve a counterbalancing sense of pride. The sense of *double consciousness* is on display in Smith's poem. The speaker, an African American, has an acquired sense of how white people perceive her, and she in turn perceives that mode of perception in (perhaps even projects it onto) nearly every blonde white woman she meets, as if that class of people in particular has a reason for sustaining psychological oppression of a black woman (fear of romantic competition or fear of a shift in conceptions of female beauty?). That the speaker is able to push through the negative

Although the woman now appreciates her own beauty, she feels the animosity of the white women around her (©Piotr Marcinski | Shutterstock.com)

white-inflicted consciousness—in this particular case, that white is no more attractive than black—to achieve a double consciousness encompassing African-affirmative self-esteem and pride is a victory. The downside to the concept of double consciousness is that the white-inflicted share cannot necessarily be erased, especially when it is yet reinforced on a daily basis even in the modern world. Figures like Smith have continued to even the score for white-inflicted deficits in black consciousness. As Allen, citing the work of Herman Gray, notes with regard to popular culture since the 1980s, "African American cultural purveyors—writers, filmmakers, hiphop and rap artists, musicians and painters—introduced many powerful conceptions of the world and African Americans' place in it."

CRITICAL OVERVIEW

Reviewers have generally responded well to the live energy conveyed in Smith's poetry collections. Considering *Big Towns, Big Talk* in *Library Journal*, Lenard D. Moore affirms that in Smith's "glimmering poems, the language itself comes alive and touches the soul," attesting to her popularity as a performer. Moore deems Smith "a master at overlaying vivid scenes with compassionate concern," allowing important insight into the lives of ordinary people. Writing for *Booklist*, Pat Monaghan declares that *Big Towns, Big Talk* is a volume that "fiercely proclaim[s] that poetry is alive and well" in both the African American and broader American communities. Monaghan writes that in a voice that is "direct and colloquial," Smith displays "a vigorous, impressive talent."

Responding to Smith's statement on the back cover of the 1992 Zoland Books edition of *Big Towns, Big Talk* that the collection's poems "beg to be read aloud. If I could visit everyone to read them personally I would," Eric Murphy Selinger, in an article in *Parnassus*, notes that the kind offer is unnecessary, because the poems' "snap and swagger and authority come through." Selinger sees the volume as amply demonstrating Smith's strengths as a poet, as "her personae stay in character, her sexy stuff stays on key, heading off melodrama with its innocence, wit, and momentum." Where the poems tip toward the bombastic slam style, such as "when she hammers out a brag, she frames the lines with a saving flash of humor or complication." Selinger perceives that although the collection lends itself to classification as a genre book—specifically a slam poetry book—this "may mean, in short, both that it plays by the rules and that it wins—it's a winning book."

In an assessment of Smith posted online for *Modern American Poetry*, Kurt Heintz offers effusive praise, declaring,

> Smith coined a kind of performance poetry which defined slam.... She throws fierce charisma. She always has. And while she writes from the "I," she writes selflessly so. The audience is free to step into her shoes as they will, trying on her point of view as her writing slips into the identities of others. In all of this, there is an enlightened, worldly political conscience.

Heintz concludes, with regard to Smith's poetry readings, that "her ensemble of energies is infectious, delicious to the eye and ear, full and provocative to the mind." And with regard to her historical significance, he affirms, "More than any other artist, Patricia Smith sounds slam poetry's keynote.... In many regards, the slam movement followed in her wake as much as she did in its."

CRITICISM

Michael Allen Holmes

Holmes is a writer with existential interests. In the following essay, he considers whether "Blonde White Women" represents reverse racism, that is, a response to racism that is itself racist.

Smith is known as a naturally outspoken writer, one whose modus operandi is to speak truth to power in true slam poet form using rhythmic and sonorous language, bold declarations, humorous asides, and provocative twists. All of these qualities are present in the opening line of "Blonde White Women." Regarding the language, five stressed syllables sound out in regular succession (with only the unstressed second syllable of *cities* slipping quickly between them), and assonance is found in the several long *o* sounds. In terms of boldness, the line suggests an antagonistic role for a group of

> COUNTING PEOPLE OF A CERTAIN
>
> APPEARANCE ON A SUBWAY TRAIN AMOUNTS
>
> TO A HOSTILE ACT."

people who are stereotypically referred to as having more fun, an inclination that is usually considered protagonistic. However resentful the speaker may actually be, there is a note of comedy in the line in that it is rather absurd to think of any group of people as being as irritatingly congestive as a city snowstorm. The claim represents a humorous expansion or exaggeration of the true circumstances.

For many readers, however, the provocation is what stands out the strongest. The claim about blonde women is not only bold but also sweeping, generalizing, and even stereotypical. It suggests to the listener or reader that for any person whose hair is blonde, whose skin is white, and whose gender is female, the description applies. These people, writ large, are a societal nuisance, gumming up the works. But what should the many intelligent and conscientious blonde women in the world glean from such a poem? Is their character being defamed? Is their race being genuinely maligned? Is this a fair statement for a poet, no matter his or her race, to make? In a word, is the characterization racist—does it indicate a belief that one race is inferior (in this case morally) to another to the extent that one can judge people's qualities on the basis of their race? It seems that the poem may cross the thin line from the realm of emotional reparation into vindictive retribution.

One can perhaps imagine how Smith would read that opening line: with impressive gravitas, meaning every word, apparently perfectly serious and yet with a note in her voice revealing a certain playfulness, a sense that she precisely intends for the reader to take her seriously and thus, quite possibly, take offense. Reading with just the right pitch, Smith would likely get a smile out of most of the African Americans and other minorities in the room, along with any white people—dark-haired, perhaps—who have their own concerns about the attitudes of (some of the) blonde women they have met. She

WHAT DO I READ NEXT?

- Soon after issuing *Big Towns, Big Talk*, Smith published *Close to Death* (1993), considered by some the best of her three books up to that point. Treating the positions of a range of black men in American society—from the famous to the homeless, from the cultured to the streetwise—the collection lends historical perspective to the concerns over race relations in the mid-2010s.

- Having emerged during the civil rights era to become a leading figure in the black arts movement and a most admired literary and political voice, Gwendolyn Brooks is one of the most important American poets of the late twentieth century. She won the Pulitzer Prize for poetry with her second collection, *Annie Allen* (1949), which follows a black girl as she matures into a woman while facing society's challenges.

- Much as Smith delves into the everyday world of Chicago with the poetry in her 1992 collection, Yusef Komunyakaa delves into the everyday world of Louisiana's bayou country in his contemporary collection *Magic City* (1992), which uses bold language reminiscent of that of slam poets.

- In her novel *The Bluest Eye* (1970), the Nobel Prize winner Toni Morrison takes on the topic of how a young black girl can be affected by the idealization of white beauty. Although the main character is young, the novel includes subject matter best suited to mature readers

- *Aloud: Voices from the Nuyorican Poets Cafe* (1994) is a collection featuring diverse voices—especially those of New Yorkers of Puerto Rican descent, known as Nuyoricans—culled from a scene where poetry readings are an important part of the culture. Two of Smith's poem are included.

- In a style reminiscent of slam poetry but distinguished in the introduction as jam poetry, the verse in *Bum Rush the Page: A Def Poetry Jam* (2001), edited by Tony Medina and Louis Reyes Rivera, with a foreword by Sonia Sanchez—another key figure in the black arts movement—is oriented toward young adults and through the language and imagery is considered to hold especial appeal to conscientious urban students.

---

also might win over most of the blonde people as well. Yet there remains room for the serious objection that she is not only proclaiming but also propagating a stereotypical viewpoint. She at once demonstrates that issues of appearance are of particular concern for her as she takes note of the skin bleaches and straightened hair being advertised in *Ebony*. Some African Americans might suggest that such products should be banned from the pages of a black publication of such historic significance.

Exactly why the prices of the products are so low is beside the point. They are there, in the magazine, one way or another, and why? Because American society has for so long pushed

the opinion that lighter is better, especially when it comes to skin and hair. And the paragon of that ideal of beauty is blonde white women. Of course, this is not to say that any individual blonde woman bears responsibility for the beauty ideals that have been developing for thousands of years of civilization. In fact, the blonde people themselves have the least control over how other people perceive them. If one were going to take issue with a group of people over the American female beauty ideal, it should be not the women who exemplify it but the individuals who run mass media—men, by and large—and in so doing consistently position blonde women at the top of the hierarchy. Consider, for example, the frequency with which light-haired white women grace the cover of the *Sports Illustrated* swimsuit issue.

Smith's speaker, on a train during her morning commute, is probably not in the presence of any such men, and moreover, despite the early emphasis on the products for sale in *Ebony*, she has more in mind than the beauty ideals themselves. White people, in her experience, are not only innocent bystanders but also purveyors of prejudicial notions and racist attitudes. Take the person with his or her thin fingers trembling on a briefcase. This person, as the speaker sees things, is revealing fear of the speaker, of people like her, based on her skin color. If this is the situation, indeed, this is prejudicial and perhaps, depending on the person's level of consciousness about the matter, racist. And yet the speaker may be taking the trembling out of context. Perhaps the person simply feels a chill due to the winter cold, is older, or has a medical condition that causes tremors. It seems possible that the speaker is jumping to conclusions. Whether she is or not, that she may be leaves the door open for an assessment of the speaker herself as prejudiced. Is she prejudging that because this person's skin is white, a trembling hand can be accounted for only by racially inspired fear? If she is just looking up and around after being appalled by the products on sale in *Ebony*, she may have been predisposed to reading racism into any ambiguous activity.

The speaker may not improve her standing in the reader's eyes in relating that, as a habit, she counts the blonde people on the train. By now the reader gathers that the African American speaker, conscious of the psychological oppression of black Americans that simply will not go away, is to a degree resentful of white America and, indeed, of white Americans. Counting people of a certain appearance on a subway train amounts to a hostile act, reckoning the people in question not as individual human beings but as mere figures or statistics, mere quantities in the counter's scheme of things. If one imagines the reverse situation, a white person on a subway train counting black people, one likely imagines a bigoted descendant of the Confederacy, perhaps a member of the Ku Klux Klan, taking mental notes about how black people want to take over society and perhaps even preparing to deliver some absurd public declaration about how much roomier the subway car would be

for the true Americans, the white people, if the black people were not there. Smith's speaker, to be sure, does not make herself out to be nearly so racist, if racist at all, but she does provide a context in which racism can easily be read into her line of thought.

More ambiguity arises later in the stanza, lines 12–17, as the narrator takes note of the brusque, dismissive looks that the blonde women give her. One likely takes the speaker's word for what is going on in the situation. She is in control of the poem; she has suggested herself to be highly socially conscious and aware, and, with the first-person narration, the reader is placed inside her perspective. It seems reasonable and makes sense. Yet again, it is hard to say how much a person's momentary glance can be read into. If the speaker is visibly counting the blonde women, and if the look on her face reflects the sort of interracial animosity communicated from line 1 on, it is possible that the blonde women are actually responding defensively to the look on the speaker's own face. The speaker has probably legitimately read such sentiments as disdain, indifference, and fear in the countenances of blonde women who have regarded her. Yet the problem is that she is suggesting, by way of universalized language, that it is fair to conclude that all blonde women harbor these feelings toward black people.

As the poem continues, the speaker delves into experiences in her past that have shaped her present attitude. She explains whether her current position with respect to blonde white women is feasible. The discussion of how she wished herself white as a very young child reveals the psychological depth of the issue. Perhaps before she had ever even met a blonde white woman who could personify the American beauty ideal, she was, one imagines, so thoroughly exposed to it via television, movies, and magazines as to simply believe that white beauty is superior to black. The inculcation of such an attitude so early in life is not easily rectified.

The inculcation worsens when a blonde white woman does step up not only to personify the beauty ideal but also to negatively define the relationship between one who holds the ideal and one who does not. There is no reason to assume that the speaker is any less clean than the other children in her class. When she points out how the teacher who hugs her immediately afterward conveys a desire to wash herself, the

Although the speaker idolized her first-grade teacher, she sees the distance between them
(©ESB Professional | Shutterstock.com)

sense should be read as indicating that the speaker's skin itself is what the teacher interprets as unclean. (One may, with a sense of humor, believe that the teacher may have been caught off guard by the smell of mop water on the speaker's head, but even if that is the case, it only symbolically shows how the speaker's very desire to be white is what leaves her unclean, much as her acting out white beauty is a manner of injuring herself, specifically her self-conception.) The teacher seems to conceive of the young speaker as unclean precisely to fit the conception that leaves her righteous, the conception that she is humbling herself by stooping to the level of *these people*, unclean as they are, to do societal good.

The significance of such a moment in the life of a young person, a girl of six or seven, cannot be understated. At precisely the moment when her inner worship of the blonde ideal is consummated in the experience of a white maternal embrace, her foundation for worship is exploded. This mother figure does not truly

love her, and she does not even really want to touch her. What, then, can a young person's mind do with that feeling of worship when the object of worship has been removed? There is little psychological choice but to cease to worship and to deplore the individual who has betrayed her and the group she represents: blonde white women. The speaker's mentally drifting back to the presence of her Alabama mother makes clear that however much the poem's title may lend fame—or notoriety—to a particular group of people that does not include the speaker, the poem is about the speaker herself, about the relations between societal ideals and the reality of her own body, between the people who exemplify those ideals and the speaker's state of mind. To be sure, the importance lies not in the relationship between the blonde women and the speaker but in the relationship between the blonde women and the speaker's state of mind. From a very young age, she has had a complicated reaction to the images and presence of blonde women, owing to the ways they have been inflicted on her, and that reaction, far more than the women, is what the poem is about.

In lines 53–59, the speaker's tack of provocation has a different feel to it. Rather than complaining, however much the blondes' looks may superficially irritate her, the speaker is seeking to work through precisely the profound antagonistic reaction that blonde women inspire in her. It is a feeling that means something to her and that seems to need resolution. As she notes in line 56, she has grown tense. With the looks, counterlooks, counting, and preconceiving, the entire train car has grown tense. What, then, might she do? Denounce or insult the people around her? Lash out at them? Perpetrate some mischievous or violent act? If she truly were a racist, she just might do some such thing, but she clearly is not, given what she does do. Ultimately her concern with the blonde women lies with what she finds within herself in their presence, what is constrained within herself. The best way to resolve that tension proves to be a very simple gesture: a shake of the head, functional in removing the snow from her hair but also symbolic in showing that even if she lacks the blonde locks that society prefers, she can draw attention to her hair with pride, releasing her inner sense of beauty to match and amplify her outer sense. This is the gesture not of a racist but of one who is doing what she can to shed the burden that a lifetime of incidental racism has left upon her. By the time she closes the poem with one last image of the snarling blonde antagonists, it seems clear that her playfulness and exaggeration alike have been conscientiously put on display and that she has earned a right to a creative re-visioning of ideal beauty.

Source: Michael Allen Holmes, Critical Essay on "Blonde White Women," in *Poetry for Students*, Gale, Cengage Learning, 2017.

SOURCES

Allen, Richard L., *The Concept of Self: A Study of Black Identity and Self-Esteem*, Wayne State University Press, 2001, pp. 17–43.

Bauer, Eric, "Boston's 10 Biggest Snowstorms," in *Boston Globe*, February 9, 2013, https://www.bostonglobe.com/metro/2013/02/09/boston-biggest-snowstorms/DzY KmJfGEdy7C9Wd7uKmXM/story.html (accessed September 11, 2016).

"*Ebony, Jet* and *Essence* Making History on Their Own," in *New York Post*, February 2, 2014, http://nypost.com/2014/02/02/ebony-jet-and-essence-making-history-on-their-own (accessed September 9, 2016).

Glasrud, Bruce, "*Ebony* Magazine," in *BlackPast.org*, http://www.blackpast.org/aah/ebony-magazine (accessed September 9, 2016).

Gray, Herman, *Watching Race: Television and the Struggle for "Blackness,"* University of Minnesota Press, 1995.

Guskin, Emily, Paul Moore, and Amy Mitchell, "African American Media: Evolving in the New Era," in *State of the News Media 2011*, http://www.stateofthemedia.org/2011/african-american (accessed September 11, 2016).

Heintz, Kurt, Introduction to "About Patricia Smith," in *Modern American Poetry*, http://www.english.illinois.edu/maps/poets/s_z/p_smith/about.htm (accessed September 9, 2016).

Hilliard, Asa G., Introduction to *The Maroon within Us: Selected Essays on African American Community Socialization*, Black Classic Press, 1995, pp. 7–12.

"Journalism," in *Encyclopedia of African American Society*, edited by Gerald D. Jaynes, Sage Publications, 2005, p. 478.

Monaghan, Pat, Review of *Big Towns, Big Talk*, in *Booklist*, October 1, 1992, p. 231.

Moore, Lenard D., Review of *Big Towns, Big Talk*, in *Library Journal*, Vol. 117, No. 18, November 1, 1992, p. 91.

Selinger, Eric Murphy, "Trash, Art, and Performance Poetry," in *Parnassus: Poetry in Review*, Vol. 23, Nos. 1/2, 1998, pp. 356–81.

FURTHER READING

Fraser, Benjamin, and Steven D. Spalding, eds., *Trains, Culture, and Mobility: Riding the Rails*, Lexington Books, 2012.

> This collection of essays on the cultural theory of the urban space of subway and metro trains explores an array of aspects of the experience of modern-day commuting via mass transit.

Harmel, Kristin, *The Blonde Theory*, Grand Central Publishing, 2007.

> In this fictional exploration of the significance of appearance, a blonde corporate attorney in Manhattan has difficulty finding a date; men seem to lose interest as soon as they discover how intelligent she is. When she goes undercover as a less-educated blonde, she realizes just how superficial people can be and learns much about herself in the process.

Jacob, Iris, ed., *My Sisters' Voices: Teenage Girls of Color Speak Out*, H. Holt, 2002.

> Presenting verse written by teenagers of a range of ethnicities, including Native American, Hispanic, Asian American, and African American, Jacob's collection gives insight into the experiences that many teens go through and can inspire readers to face their challenges, perhaps through art of their own.

Norwood, Kimberly, *Color Matters: Skin Tone Bias and the Myth of a Post-racial America*, Routledge, 2014.

> The essays in this volume seek to dispel the myth that America has reached a postracial phase, in which discrimination based on ethnicity is a thing of the past. At both the conscious and the subconscious levels, racial prejudice continues to operate in myriad forms.

SUGGESTED SEARCH TERMS

Patricia Smith AND "Blonde White Women"

Patricia Smith AND Big Towns, Big Talk

Patricia Smith AND slam poetry

skin color AND bias OR prejudice

hair color AND bias OR prejudice

African Americans AND skin bleach OR straightened hair

African Americans AND self-esteem OR self-hatred

black power AND self-esteem

black is beautiful

blonde white women

The Broken Tower

HART CRANE

1932

"The Broken Tower" is the last poem written by the American author Harold Hart Crane, known as Hart Crane. Crane wrote the poem in the weeks before his death in April 1932. It was not published during his lifetime, but Crane had sent the poem to Malcolm Cowley, an editor at the *New Republic*, who published it in the magazine's June 8, 1932, issue. It was later included in *The Collected Poems of Hart Crane*, first published by Liveright in 1933. It is also available in *Hart Crane*, edited by Maurice Riordan, Faber and Faber, 2008.

Crane's life was short, and he published only two collections of poetry. Nevertheless, he is regarded as holding a place in or near the top tier of American poets in the 1920s. Many critics regard "The Broken Tower" as among his finest achievements. The poem defies easy summary. A love poem constructed around the symbol of a bell tower, the poem traces the speaker's ascent from despair and hopelessness to an affirmation of human triumph and transcendence as a result of his relationship with a woman. It ends by affirming an optimistic view that each person has within himself or herself a creative force that can lead to transcendence.

AUTHOR BIOGRAPHY

Crane was born on July 21, 1899, in Garrettsville, a small town in northeastern Ohio. Much of his early life was spent with his grandparents

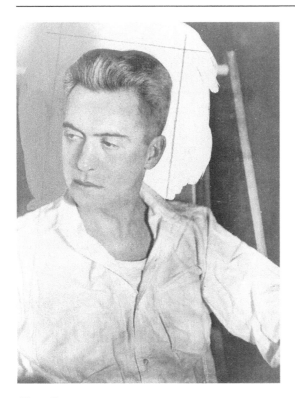

Hart Crane (©*Library of Congress, Prints & Photographs Division, Reproduction number LC-USZ62-122934*)

in an effort to escape the bitter quarreling of his parents. His father, Clarence, was a successful businessman, a candy manufacturer who invented Life Savers candies. His mother was Grace Edna Hart, a domineering, strong-willed woman of artistic leanings. Crane disappointed both of his parents. His father wanted the young poet to pursue a career in business, and his mother tried to impose her intense Christian Science religiosity on a son who turned out to be gay. The parents divorced in 1917.

While the divorce proceedings were under way, Crane dropped out of high school in the middle of his junior year and headed for New York City, where he worked as a copywriter. For several years he moved back and forth between New York and Cleveland, supporting himself as an advertising writer and, during the remainder of World War I, working in a munitions factory in Cleveland. After the war, he worked in his father's business, but his relationship with his father was always strained. During this period, he also published poetry in literary magazines.

In 1923, Crane settled in New York, where he was caught up in a vortex of excess and

prodigality that was punctuated by bursts of hectic creativity. His first major work was *White Buildings*, a collection of poems published in 1926. The volume includes a sequence of erotic poems, "Voyages," arising from his passion for Emil Opffer, a Danish ship's purser. It also includes "For the Marriage of Faustus and Helen," a poem Crane regarded as a response to what he saw as the corrosive and unwarranted cultural pessimism of T. S. Eliot's *The Waste Land*. The collection met with mixed reviews, sending the poet into a depression. After a bitter quarrel with his mother, Crane fled to Europe, but he returned to New York City in 1928.

Over the next two years, Crane cobbled together a living from temporary copywriting jobs, unemployment benefits, the generosity of friends, and support from his father. He returned to Europe in 1929, where he attempted to focus on his next collection, *The Bridge*, but his heavy drinking led to a bar brawl, his arrest, and six days in jail. Back in New York, he finished *The Bridge*, a collection of fifteen poems published in 1930 by Black Sun Press, which brought the works of a number of modernist poets to the reading public. The collection was inspired by his view of the Brooklyn Bridge in New York, which he saw as symbolic of human creative power. Although critics found Crane's attempt to compose an epic of the American experience along the lines of Walt Whitman's *Leaves of Grass* to be a partial failure, they regarded some of the individual poems in *The Bridge* as among the author's best. At the time, however, the collection was poorly received, again sending the poet into a downward cycle of despair and to the conclusion that he was a failure.

Crane led a tumultuous, chaotic life. He was highly neurotic and drank heavily. His bohemian, unorthodox lifestyle and dissipations seemed to confirm the stereotype of the avant-garde poet. Nevertheless, in 1931 he was awarded a Guggenheim fellowship, which enabled him to travel to Mexico City, where his intention, never realized, was to write an epic poem about Aztec civilization. In Mexico, he was joined by Peggy Baird Cowley, the estranged wife of the novelist, poet, and critic Malcolm Cowley. Peggy Cowley was an avant-garde artist and feminist activist who had lived among Greenwich Village radicals before her marriage and who was notorious for her sexual freedom.

She and Crane consummated their relationship on Christmas night 1931 in Taxco, Mexico, to the sound of church bells that rang throughout the night, producing in the poet an unwonted sense of elation. "The Broken Tower" was written to commemorate this relationship, which is thought to have been his only heterosexual one. Later, on January 27, 1932, Crane accompanied a local bell ringer to the tower in Taxco and helped ring the bells himself.

On March 27, 1932, Crane sent "The Broken Tower" to the editor of *Poetry* magazine for publication and to (of all people) Malcolm Cowley, an editor at *New Republic*, for comment. By the time he boarded the USS *Orizaba* in Veracruz on April 24, 1932, for the voyage home, Crane had received no responses, leading him to conclude that what he regarded as the best poem he had written in two years was without merit. The editor of *Poetry* later claimed that the poem and accompanying letter must have been lost in the mail, for they never arrived. Cowley published the poem in the June 8, 1932, issue of the *New Republic*.

On board the *Orizaba*, Crane was roughed up after making sexual advances to a male crew member. On the morning of April 27, he hurled himself overboard from the stern of the ship and drowned in the Gulf of Mexico. No suicide note was found, and his body was never recovered. The almost universally accepted view is that his death was a suicide, but the slight possibility remains that Crane, after a night of heavy drinking, was making a flamboyant gesture and expected that he would be rescued.

POEM SUMMARY

The text used for this summary is from *Hart Crane*, Faber and Faber, 2008, p. 89. A version of the poem can be found on the following web page: https://allpoetry.com/The-Broken-Tower.

"The Broken Tower" consists of ten four-line stanzas that can be grouped into three sections.

Stanzas 1–4

In stanza 1, the speaker imagines a bell rope used to issue a call to God at dawn. For the speaker, however, the call is more in the nature of a knell, suggesting death or the end of a day. He then describes wandering from a pit to a crucifix over the lawn of a cathedral on steps from the depths

MEDIA ADAPTATIONS

- Caedmon released a vinyl LP of playwright Tennessee Williams's readings of Crane's poetry, including "The Broken Tower," in 1960. The readings were re-released on cassette by Caedmon Audio in 1985. Harper Audio released an audio cassette of the readings in 1977.

- For his master's thesis in film studies at New York University, James Franco, wrote, directed, and starred in *The Broken Tower*, based on a 1999 biography of Crane by Paul Mariani. The black-and-white film was released on DVD in 2011 and is available from Amazon Video. The running time is one hour, thirty-nine minutes.

of hell. Stanza 2 consists of a question: the speaker asks the reader to envision the movement of the bells in a tower as they sway with the movement of the bell ringers' shoulders. This movement creates sounds that are like those of a carillon, that is, chromatically tuned bells in a bell tower. As dawn approaches, the speaker imagines the points of light of the stars being gathered, like bees in a hive, to produce the light of day at dawn.

In stanza 3, the speaker sees the bells as breaking down the tower that holds them. He does not know, then, where they are swinging, and the image suggests that the bells have broken free. He then imagines the clappers of the bells engraving themselves on his marrow, suggesting that he is infused with the sounds of the bells. He associates the ringing of the bells with his own creativity, comparing his poems to a musical score that has been scattered and that consists of the intervals of music, that is, to the pitch between tones, suggesting at the same time the poet's intermittent bursts of creativity. The speaker envisions himself as a sexton, or bell ringer, enslaved to the bells. In stanza 4, the speaker creates images of the sounds of the bells as they die away in the distance. The sounds carry a religious message, like a papal encyclical (a letter from the pope to bishops), but the message can be blocked or remain piled up on a plain. He imagines a contrast between vertical structures, such as pagodas and campaniles (another word for bell towers), and the flat plains on which the echoes of his sounds lie prostrate.

Stanzas 5–6

In stanza 5, the speaker says that he has now entered a broken world, thus comparing himself and his poetry to the sounds from the bell tower. He has entered the world of reality, but he has found the company of love. His poetry is like the wind that for a moment broadcasts the power of love but then is fleeting, much like moments of poetic inspiration. The speaker refers to the desperate choices he makes in his love affairs, perhaps suggesting failed gay relationships. Stanza 6 creates sexual images as the speaker imagines his words pouring forth but asking whether they are consistent with the creative power of the rising sun god whose light makes the earth bronze.

Stanzas 7–10

Stanza 7 also poses a question. The speaker asks whether his instincts, represented by blood, and the way that those instincts can overwhelm the individual can allow some higher principle, represented by the rising sun, to inspire his poetry. He expresses his uncertainty about whether his instincts enable him to come near to the divine. At the moment he feels creative, imaginative power, but he is uncertain whether that power has come from the divine or has been stirred by the woman he has been with and the new form of love he has experienced.

In stanza 8, the speaker mentions the beating of the woman's pulse, seeing the blood in his own veins coursing in harmony with hers, as though he were a second bell. That ringing is an Angelus, that is, a devotion commemorating the Incarnation (referring to the Christian belief in the Incarnation of Christ, that is, the belief that Christ took on human form). This devotion is usually accompanied by the Angelus bell, which peals in the morning, at noon, and at sundown. He sees himself as having been healed of his wounds by the woman he loves; he has been reborn and made pure.

In stanza, 9 the speaker describes how the woman creates in him a new tower of human connectedness. This tower is not made of stone, as a church might be, for a union with the divine cannot be made through stone. This union is more in the nature of pebbles, or moments of joy or perhaps of insight, that slide into a blue lake, creating ever-widening circles, or ripples. Such a tower, further, cannot be built purely on instinct or blood; it must be constructed by the spiritual and physical love of the man and the woman. The azure lake reflects the blue sky, where the visible wings of silence suggest the apex of human aspiration. Poetry can be created only in silence.

In stanza 10, which flows from the preceding one without punctuation, the speaker sees the widening circles of insight as an integrated matrix that turns the lake into a shrine and that raises a tower. The wide-open sky, then, unseals the earth and raises love.

THEMES

Love

At bottom, "The Broken Tower" can be described as a love poem, although such a description fails to do justice to its complexity. Throughout his life, Crane struggled with his homosexuality. In this regard, he was not alone, for the culture of the time told him that as a gay man he was at best mentally ill and at worst morally corrupt. However, after he won a Guggenheim fellowship that allowed him to work in Mexico City, he was joined there by Peggy Baird Cowley. Cowley, an ardent feminist, believed that it was imperative for the barriers between men and women to be broken down through sexual relationships. She and Crane consummated their relationship to the sound of bells pealing on Christmas night in 1931. "The Broken Tower" was written largely in response to Crane's welter of elation, confusion, joy, and uncertainty in having found a new mode of sexual expression that he believed held the potential to unleash his poetic powers. In the first four stanzas, he envisions a broken world, symbolized by the broken tower, which is broken as his words try to burst their boundaries and pour forth. In the poem's second movement, stanzas 5 and 6, he sees himself as entering that broken world, the world of reality, and wonders whether his words will have any effect. It is in

TOPICS FOR FURTHER STUDY

- Liveright published *Complete Poems of Hart Crane* in 1932 immediately after the poet's death. Until 1931, the company's name was Boni & Liveright, and the company gained fame as the publisher of the work of a who's who of modernist poets and fiction writers and for challenging censorship and obscenity laws. Conduct research into the firm. Which authors did it publish? How did it challenge such organizations as the New York Society for the Suppression of Vice? Why was the firm important in the history of modern American literature? As an alternative, consider the same or similar questions in reference to *Poetry* magazine, the periodical to which Crane sent "The Broken Tower." After narrowing down your topic, present the results of your findings in a written report. Be sure to include examples of authors and their works.

- Produce a painting or sketch of a bell tower such as the one Crane rang in Taxco, Mexico, and in part inspired him to write "The Broken Tower."

- Crane was a student of French poetry. "The Broken Tower" owes a great deal to "The Bell Ringer" (1862, in French, "Le sonneur"), a sonnet by Stéphane Mallarmé. The poem is available in a parallel French-English edition, *Stéphane Mallarmé: Collected Poems*, edited and translated by Henry Weinfield (University of California Press, 1994). Locate the poem, then give a reading of it to your classmates, inviting them to comment on similarities they see between Mallarmé's poem and Crane's.

- A key figure in American literature in the years before and after 1932 was the expatriate author Gertrude Stein. In 1932, the year of Crane's death, she wrote a sequence of poems under the title *Stanzas in Meditation* (in *Stanzas in Meditation and Other Poems*, Sun and Moon Press, 1994). Each of the stanzas, that is, the poems, can be read individually. Select one of the poems, and in a written report trace similarities and differences between Stein's poetic techniques and Crane's.

- In the February 1927 issue of *Harper's* magazine, Countee Cullen, a leading poet of the Harlem Renaissance, published "To Lovers of Earth: Fair Warning." The poem was included in a 1927 collection he edited titled *Caroling Dusk: An Anthology of Verse by Negro Poets* (Citadel, 1998). Read the poem, then recreate a dialogue between Cullen and Crane about love and its impact on the creative process. Post the dialogue on your social networking site and invite your classmates to comment.

- Crane's work is often seen as a response to the cultural pessimism expressed by the leading modernist poet of the early twentieth century, T. S. Eliot, particularly in his long poem *The Waste Land* (1922, edited by Michael North, Norton, 2000). Read selections from Eliot's poem, then write a review of the poem as you imagine Crane might have responded to it.

- Locate a copy of *Paint Me like I Am: Teen Poems from WritersCorps* (HarperTeen, 2003), which includes an introduction by Nikki Giovanni. This collection includes work written by teen participants in writing programs run by a national nonprofit organization called WritersCorps. Using their work along with "The Broken Tower" for inspiration, write your own poem using a landmark in your town (a tower, a bridge, a statue, a steeple, a historic building) as the central image or symbol.

---

the third movement of the poem, stanzas 7 through 10, that he celebrates love, indicating that the woman he loves has stirred his creative powers, enabling him to build a new tower, one made not of stone but of words that ripple and soar through the world and bring about positive change.

Creativity

If "The Broken Tower" is a poem about the transcendent effects of love, specifically sexual love, it is also a poem about creativity and creative forces. To this end, the poem relies on metaphors and images of creation. The bell tower creates sound that reverberates and spreads. The antiphons of a carillon are heard after they have been launched on the world. (An antiphon is a verse, psalm, or anthem that is sung as a liturgical response.) Most important, though, Crane celebrates a renewed sense of creative power as a result of his relationship with a woman. The woman is seen as stirring within him a creative power that had been lacking in his life—or at least that manifested itself only intermittently, in broken intervals. He feels her pulse as her blood courses. His own veins answer and respond to the pulsing of hers, allowing him to achieve a kind of purity and to build a new tower, an edifice of poetic creation that is not made of stone but is more like the ripples in a pond that are created when pebbles are dropped in. The new tower created swells into the heavens and lifts the poet and his creative vision aloft with it.

Christian Symbolism

Crane was raised in a household ruled by a dominant woman who practiced the religion of Christian Science, so the author in his early years was surrounded by the language and iconography of Christianity. It comes as no surprise, therefore, that "The Broken Tower," and his other poems, makes extensive use of the symbolism of Christianity and that the Christian Science belief that the material world is illusory (in contrast to the reality of the spiritual world) seeped into his work. The bell tower is housed in the steeple of a cathedral. The bell rope gathers God first thing in the morning. The poet approaches the cathedral on steps from hell, suggesting a Dante-like ascent from the inferno to paradise. Reference is made to antiphonal carillons, emphasizing the role of the bells in religious worship. He refers to the bells as oval encyclicals; the bells are oval-shaped, and their function is similar to that of an encyclical. (An encyclical is an official letter written by the pope to bishops, generally outlining and enforcing a point of church doctrine.) Use of the word *word*

The tower is composed of pebbles rather than mighty stones (©Wendy Walkin / Shutterstock.com)

recalls the biblical concept of Christ as word made flesh—that is, the instantiation of the divine in the human world. Later, the poet refers to the Angelus, which, often accompanied by the Angelus bell, is a devotion that commemorates the Incarnation of Christ, referring to the belief that Christ took on human form. This religious theme underlines the sense that the poet has achieved a kind of apotheosis, salvation, or beatification: human love has infused him with creative potential.

STYLE

Diction

Diction refers to the selection of words in a literary work. The thematic concerns of an author can frequently dictate, perhaps unconsciously, a pattern of word choices that buttress his or her treatment of the theme. In "The Broken Tower" (and others of his poems), Crane shows a predilection for the word *lift*, a good example of the overall simplicity of his diction.

The word and others that suggest rising, raising, soaring, flight, and the like are frequently used in contexts that suggest that the poet is struggling to find some sort of transcendence or is feeling an urge to be elevated above the fetters and fogs of earthly existence. Frequently, this urge takes the form of an impulse to be linked to the divine—which emerges in the poem in part through numerous words with religious connotations. The lexical emphasis on lifting and raising is further created through diction having to do with wings (with implications of flight), as well as with the symbol of the tower. A counterpoint to lifting is lowering and falling. In stanza 1, the poet speaker says that he dropped down, and the wings of stanza 9 dip. In the end, however, a tower is raised, and the speaker is able to slip the bonds of the earth.

Imagery

Closely related to diction is imagery, that is, the representation of sensory experience. Although the term suggests visual experience, imagery broadly refers to any of the senses, including hearing, touch, smell, taste, and even sensations such as texture and temperature. Crane believed that images had to be indefinite; only in this way could they provide multiple layers of suggestion while achieving poetic condensation. A good example of Crane's rich use of imagery can be found in stanza 2, in which he unites images of sound (antiphons, carillons), shadows and light, the rising of the sun and the fading of the stars at dawn, and tactile images suggesting that the stars are caught and hived—that is, gathered. These and other image patterns create a rich suggestibility that requires from the reader a willingness to derive meaning from the poem not through rational denotation but through physical, sensory experience and the illogicality of connotation.

Stanza

At first glance, "The Broken Tower" appears to use a highly conventional stanzaic form. The poem consists of ten quatrains—that is, four-line stanzas. Each stanza has a traditional rhyme scheme, conventionally indicated by *abab*. This traditional stanzaic form tussles with the theme of the poem as the poet struggles to break free of earthly restrictions and limitations and strives to achieve a poetic state of grace—to erect a tower of language and art on the ruins of a broken tower, a broken world, and

the poet's own doubts and intimations of inadequacy. Thus, it is noteworthy that Crane makes promiscuous use of enjambment—that is, the running of a thought from one line to the next or from one stanza to the next without any kind of break or punctuation. *End-stopped* refers to the opposite, to lines or stanzas that correspond with syntactic units and are brought to an end by a pause or by punctuation. The first movement of the poem (stanzas 1 through 4) makes use of several end-stopped lines as the poet raises questions and struggles with the notion that something is broken. His thoughts and questions are fragmented and jagged. In the second movement (stanzas 5 and 6), the poet inches closer to insight; each of these stanzas is a complete sentence. Each concludes with end punctuation, but the lines within the stanzas are enjambed. After another question contained in stanza 7, stanzas 8 through 10 consist of a single sentence as the poet grows convinced that he can create through his own powers a poetry that is based on imaginative truth and human love. The enjambed lines thus sweep and soar and swell as the poet gains confidence that he can create on the ruins of the broken tower. In sum, the stanzaic form and the use of end-stopped and then enjambed lines mirror the movement from doubt and hesitation to mounting and onrushing confidence and exaltation.

HISTORICAL CONTEXT

The Roaring Twenties

"The Broken Tower" makes no specific reference to historical events, but it was written in the context of significant cultural and economic developments in the United States. The 1920s—during which Crane came of age and published virtually all of his poetry—is widely referred to as the Roaring Twenties. The nation was carefree and at peace. Standards of living were on the upswing. Colorful figures like big-city gangsters defied Prohibition by selling bootleg liquor in urban speakeasies—the kinds of nightspots Crane frequented during his New York City days. Industrial giants such as Henry Ford, developer of the assembly line and the Model T automobile, were amassing fortunes that were matched by those of the Rockefellers, the Vanderbilts, and other prominent members of the social elite, including the Guggenheims,

COMPARE
&
CONTRAST

- **1932:** The United States and much of the world are mired in a devastating economic depression with widespread bank and business failures and an unemployment rate of nearly 25 percent.

  Today: The American economy in 2016 is emerging from a prolonged economic recession, although wages remain stagnant and the growth of the American economy is slow.

- **1932:** The Harlem Renaissance—an explosion of literary, artistic, and intellectual activity in the African American community centered in Harlem, New York—has been a cultural force for more than a decade.

  Today: Heightened interest in diversity and multiculturalism fosters attention to writers and artists from a multiplicity of cultural traditions, including African American and Hispanic.

- **1932:** Homosexuality is illegal and regarded by the psychiatric community as a mental disorder. Although attitudes toward gays and lesbians had become somewhat more tolerant during the Roaring Twenties, more conservative views recur during the Great Depression.

  Today: The *Diagnostic and Statistical Manual of Mental Disorders* no longer lists homosexuality. Acceptance of gays, lesbians, bisexuals, transgender people is rapidly widening.

---

whose foundation provided Crane with a fellowship. Flappers were a new, plucky type of woman who defied the conventions of their grandmothers and mothers: they smoked, drank, voted (thanks to the Nineteenth Amendment to the U.S. Constitution), and projected boldness, poise, and freedom in dress and manners—in much the same way Peggy Baird Cowley did in the company of Crane and others.

The first Miss America pageant was held in 1921, and the first sheer stockings, by creating the impression of nude legs, were shocking to many. Jazz was a dominant musical form of the decade. People danced the Charleston and the Lindy hop, a dance named after Charles Lindbergh, who broke boundaries by making the first solo airplane flight across the Atlantic. The excess of the decade was reflected in the popularity of dance marathons, some of which lasted for days or weeks. The film industry was expanding as the demand for entertainment exploded: by the end of the decade, silent films had given way to talkies shown in immense downtown movie palaces, and radios were found in nearly every home that had electricity. The Ziegfeld Follies, which reached the height of its popularity in the 1920s, was a lavish extravaganza featuring music, dance, and comedy. Larger-than-life sports figures, such as baseball's Babe Ruth, boxing's Jack Dempsey, golf's Bobby Jones, and football's Knute Rockne and the Four Horsemen of Notre Dame became household names.

Most important, however, was the fundamental shift taking place in American society. To many observers, the 1920s were the first modern decade. The Protestant values of rural and small-town America were giving way to the more urban, industrial, and technological world of the twentieth century. In 1920, for the first time in American history, more people lived in urban than in rural areas. The nation's cultural elites looked down on rural and small-town America as bigoted and out of date. Further, they tended to regard American culture as a whole as crass and materialistic, prompting many artists, writers, and intellectuals to live and work overseas. Gertrude Stein, for example, was the central figure of an expatriate literary set in Paris, and even Crane felt the need to jump-start his writing with trips to France and Mexico. Writers such as Theodore Dreiser produced work that was sharply critical of the American emphasis on financial success. The bohemian set of Greenwich Village, New York City, mocked convention and traditional restraints, valuing self-expression, sincerity, beauty, and sexual freedom over money and the repressed attitudes of their ancestors. But whereas many of these authors took a gloomy view of America and its future, Crane expressed a more optimistic attitude. Although he shared the belief that American commerce was static and deadening, he also believed that the creative power of the individual was a positive and uplifting force.

The Roaring Twenties was a decade of personal freedom—but also a decade of excess. The stock market, along with women's hemlines, was rising to dizzying heights. In 1929, however, a precipitous stock market crash was the first in a sequence of economic reverses that produced the Great Depression. For more than a decade, until World War II, optimism and the belief in an expansive, unlimited future exploded in the face of poverty, stubbornly high unemployment (and sharply lower wages for those fortunate enough to have jobs), business and bank failures, and low productivity. This was the America that Crane, penniless after the death of his father and the discovery that most of the family assets were gone, was returning to in 1932.

Harlem Renaissance

The Harlem Renaissance was the growth of artistic, literary, and intellectual activity among African Americans centered in the Harlem neighborhood of Manhattan, New York City, primarily in the 1920s and 1930s. Boni & Liveright, which (as Liveright, after Albert Boni sold his share of the business to Horace Liveright) published a collected edition of Crane's poetry in 1933, was a major publishing force behind the Harlem renaissance, bringing the work of such prominent African American writers as Jean Toomer and Jessie Redmon Fauset to a wider audience.

Homosexuality

At a time when homosexuality was illegal and regarded as a form of mental illness, a gay writer such as Crane would have felt some level of unease and self-doubt. Even so, the license and sense of personal freedom of the 1920s, along

After the religious imagery throughout the first stanza, the reader may be surprised that the stairs in the last line do not lead to a cathedral

(©VojtechVlk / Shutterstock.com)

with the partial breaking down of conventional sexual codes, led to some measure of tolerance of gays and lesbians, particularly in the cities. At the time, however, people simply did not talk openly about these matters; gay or straight, discretion in sexual matters was observed.

CRITICAL OVERVIEW

Modern critics are of one mind about "The Broken Tower": that it has earned its place in the top tier of American modernist poetry. Brom Weber, in *Hart Crane: A Biographical and Critical Study*, observes that the poem

> is as personal as any poem could be; it is unquestionably one of Crane's most magnificent pieces; and it reveals both in itself and in

the way in which Crane developed it from an early draft that his powers were at their prime.

R. W. B. Lewis, in *The Poetry of Hart Crane: A Critical Study*, focuses on the style and literary technique of the poem, writing that "in 'The Broken Tower,' every word not only counts, but counts for double and triple; never did the connotations of Crane's language interact to greater ranges of beauty and meaning." Lewis goes on to enthuse:

> It is, I believe, in the deepest sense autobiographical, a retracing of the particular visionary path he had been ardently and desperately following for more than a decade. What is new is the pattern of ingredients—a freshness of idiom, an originality (for Crane) of symbol, a new melodic structure, and as it were a newly contrived dialectic.

John T. Irwin, in *Hart Crane's Poetry*, calls "The Broken Tower" "the best poem Crane wrote between the publication of *The Bridge* in 1930 and his death." Commenting on the genesis of the poem, Irwin writes that after making love with Peggy Cowley on Christmas night in 1931,

> Crane began writing "The Broken Tower" almost immediately, making part of the poem's theme his hope that this (for him) new kind of love had restored his inspiration and creative energy, and part his uncertainty about whether in the long run this relationship would bring a measure of domestic order that would enable him to work more consistently.

Irwin goes on to elucidate the theme of the poem in these terms:

> The speaker says that he entered, via his poems, the broken or fallen world of time and reality, in much the same way that the sound of the bells broadcast on the wind entered the world. In the case of the poet, however, the wind that holds for "an instant" the visionary voice proclaiming the love of ideal, eternal beauty evokes the romantic trope of the wind, the divine breath of in*spira*tion.

Melvin E. Lyon, in an article titled "The Centrality of Hart Crane's 'The Broken Tower'," offers this view of the thematic significance of the bells and the tower:

> The speaker has lost all sense of identification with the Tower of Christianity. But he is still the "slave," though now unwillingly, of the bells of divine inspiration, subject to the agony which their anarchy produces. His poems are only "broken intervals" in the "broken world" of the "broken tower."

Lyon further argues that Crane depicts "a new kind of tower, psychological and spiritual rather than external and material, whose primary function is to unite a man and woman."

Some critics took up the issue of whether "The Broken Tower" was Crane's farewell or even subconsciously a suicide note. In an article titled "Hart Crane's Last Poem," for example, Marius Bewley concludes that

> Crane had learned that the tower of absolute vision was much too high for him to climb in his poetry, and he realized this with peculiar clairvoyance at the close of his life when he seemed to be running down in a frenzy of neurotic debauchery.

M. D. Uroff, in *Hart Crane: The Patterns of His Poetry*, touches on this issue:

> The violence of poetic vision is the subject of the last poem Crane wrote before he committed suicide. Read as his epitaph, "The Broken Tower" has been given elaborate significance. The brokenness of the title and of the major symbol in the poem has been generally regarded as Crane's indictment of the modern world and a summary of the kind of poetry he could write.

For decades, in an era when homosexuality was regarded as immoral, critics tended to downplay or sidestep the issue in Crane's poetry. Under the aegis of so-called queer theory, however, some later critics focused on Crane's prominent position in gay aesthetics. Niall Munro, for example, in *Hart Crane's Queer Modernist Aesthetic*, highlighted images and symbols of "The Broken Tower" that he believed have sexual connotations. Munro concludes:

> The poem provides a record of how Crane has tried to fit his language to his queer "character."... Rather than being a conclusion of his writing career, "The Broken Tower" indicates Crane's desire to continue the search for the right words to describe experience

—a specifically gay (or bisexual) experience.

CRITICISM

Michael J. O'Neal

O'Neal holds a PhD in English. In the following essay, he examines various critical approaches to "The Broken Tower."

When literary scholars dig into a work of literature, they do not simply practice a discipline of criticism. Each practices a particular

> A SIGN OF THE RICHNESS AND COMPLEXITY OF
> 'THE BROKEN TOWER' IS THAT IF ONE WERE TO LINE UP
> A HALF-DOZEN SCHOLARS, ONE WOULD LIKELY SPOT A
> HALF-DOZEN CRITICAL PERSPECTIVES, FOR THE POEM
> PROVIDES THE SCHOLAR WITH A SMORGASBORD OF
> POSSIBILITIES, WHICH PERHAPS EXPLAINS ITS
> POPULARITY."

form or type of criticism, selecting the type on the basis of an assortment of factors: the characteristics of the work at hand, characteristics that pervade the body of the author's work, current fashions in literary criticism, and perhaps simple personal preference.

Some scholars, for example, devote their attention to biographical criticism. They want to know all that they can about the author's life and elucidate ways in which the details of the author's life stretching all the way back to childhood—the tragedies and triumphs, the loves and losses, the heartbreaks and achievements—find their way into the work under examination. Others pursue what can be called cultural criticism. These scholars examine the work in the context of the culture out of which it arises and try to locate where and how the work reflects the zeitgeist surrounding its production. The word *zeitgeist* is from German and means "spirit of the time"; it refers to the dominant set of beliefs and ideals among a people during a certain time and in a certain place.

Still other scholars practice what since the 1930s has been called New Criticism. This approach regards anything outside the boundaries of the work as irrelevant to its interpretation. These critics are interested in irony, metaphor, paradox, diction, metrics, and other features that can be parsed through close reading. They regard a poem as a self-contained, self-referential aesthetic object, and the author's intentions about its meaning and about his or her life are matters separate from what the poem as an artifact actually means. Those who question the New Critical approach, in contrast, emphasize the author's intentions as the governing interpretive yardstick.

Another approach is source criticism, which traces the historical and literary sources of a work. The critics ask questions such as "Where did Shakespeare get the plot for *Hamlet*"? Philological and linguistic criticism examines the language of the text from the standpoint of the history of the language. The questions would be "What contributions to the English language did Shakespeare make, and what are the linguistic roots of his many coinages?" Historical criticism is an attempt to recreate the original meaning of texts, usually ancient texts, as they would have been understood in their original historical context. Reader response criticism is an attempt to unfold the emerging and changing responses of a reader to the work as it is experienced. One strain of genre criticism identifies the features of a work that reflect the archetypal patterns of tragedy, comedy, romance, and satire or irony. Myth criticism examines the work in the context of its debt to fundamental ancient mythologies and truths about a culture's history, customs, beliefs, origins, and behaviors. Textual scholarship is an attempt to establish complete, authoritative texts or to trace the author's processes of revision through successive drafts of a work.

A sign of the richness and complexity of "The Broken Tower" is that if one were to line up a half-dozen scholars, one would likely spot a half-dozen critical perspectives, for the poem provides the scholar with a smorgasbord of possibilities, which perhaps explains its popularity—and the popularity of all of the author's poetry—among many students of modern American literature.

The poem for many critics is clearly autobiographical, and the speaker of the poem can confidently be regarded as Crane himself. Thus, some scholars, seeing the poem as a retrospective of the poet's career, may note that the poem traces the poet's own insecurities about his talent and creative processes, that he felt he was able to create only at broken intervals. They may note that the poem emerged from a night of lovemaking in Mexico with Peggy Cowley, the first and probably only heterosexual relationship of Crane's life. They may even note that this event, which took place on Christmas night 1931, was accompanied by the ringing of bells in a nearby church tower, and they may conclude that this relationship and the elation that it sparked inspired the poet and converted his pessimism and despair about his creative potential into hope and optimism. At the same time, some

WHAT DO I READ NEXT?

- Crane explains what he calls the logic of metaphor in a letter to Harriet Monroe that was reprinted in *Poetry* magazine in October 1926. The passage from the letter can be found in *O My Land, My Friends: The Selected Letters of Hart Crane*, edited by Langdon Hammer and Brom Weber (Four Walls Eight Windows, 1997).

- "To Brooklyn Bridge," another poem by Crane constructed around a towering structure, is the opening section of his 1930 collection, *The Bridge*. It can be found in *Hart Crane*, edited by Maurice Riordan (Faber and Faber, 2008).

- *Love Speaks Its Name: Gay and Lesbian Love Poems*, edited by J. D. McClatchy (Everyman's Library, 2001) is a collection of 144 poems by and about gays and lesbians from the ancient world to modern times.

- Frederick Lewis Allen's *Only Yesterday: An Informal History of the 1920s* (Harper Perennial, 2010), originally published in 1931, is a vivid portrait of the decade during which Crane came of age and published most of his poetry; there is some emphasis on economic events.

- Born in the same year as Crane (1899), the American poet Allen Tate became Crane's friend and correspondent, and the two often traded comments on each other's work. Tate's most famous poem, one considered a major contribution to the modernist movement, is "Ode to the Confederate Dead," included in his 1928 collection *Mr. Pope and Other Poems*. The poem is available in *Collected Poems, 1919–1976* (Farrar, Straus and Giroux, 2007).

- James Weldon Johnson was the editor of *The Book of American Negro Poetry* (Harvest Books, 1969). The collection by important poets of the Harlem Renaissance, whose work in many cases was contemporaneous with Crane's, first appeared in 1922, but a revised edition appeared in 1931.

- Readers interested in a strain of modern American poetry very different from that represented by Crane may enjoy Carl Sandburg's *The Sandburg Treasury: Prose and Poetry for Young People* (Houghton Mifflin Harcourt, 2000).

- The American poet Robert Lowell paid tribute to Crane and his legacy in a 1959 poem titled "Words for Hart Crane," which can be found in *Robert Lowell: Selected Poems* (2nd ed., Farrar, Straus and Giroux, 2007).

---

scholars, noting that this is Crane's last poem and that he committed suicide soon after completing it, may argue that the poem is an elaborate suicide note, or at least a kind of swan song, a final performance before the poet's ostentatious death.

A cultural critic, while granting these facts, would see the poem in a broader context. This critic is likely to see the broken tower as an indictment of the state of the nation's culture. Early on, the poet wanders; his feet are chill; his steps are from hell; the pealing of the bells breaks down the tower, perhaps signifying the power of art to break its boundaries, although art remains trapped and prostrate on the barrenness of a plain. The world itself is described as broken—which in many ways it was, given the depth and pervasiveness of the Great Depression and the poverty and sheer misery it was causing. Within this cultural climate, the poet expresses the belief that human love, specifically sexual love, can lift the artist out of his culture's doldrums and allow a new tower of art to soar into the sky. In this respect, "The Broken Tower," like much of Crane's poetry, challenged a dominant belief among artists

The sound of bells seems ominous to the speaker (©*Ivanov Oleg / Shutterstock.com*)

and intellectuals that the Western world was a rainless wasteland in a state of irrevocable cultural decline.

Because of its density and complexity, much modernist poetry, including "The Broken Tower," invites a New Criticism approach, that is, a line-by-line explication, or unfolding, of the poem's meaning as imagery, symbol, paradox, irony, and connotation collide and combine, often through contrast and paradox: rising and falling, up and down, leaping and prostration, gathering and dispatching, breaking and building. In his letters, Crane frequently alluded to the illogic of his writing, frankly confessing his desire to be elliptical and nuanced. He rejected the belief, held by some, that he was merely juggling words in an effort to be novel. Rather, he contended that the combinations and interplay of metaphors, symbols, and images can produce new perceptions of reality—can in fact reflect a logic of their own. It is the poet's task to create this alternative form of logic and perception through language.

A scholar of New Criticism would muscle through "The Broken Tower" word by word, image by image, line by line, stanza by stanza. Such a critic would focus on the central symbol of the tower and offer competing theories of what the tower symbolizes. The pealing of the bells becomes part of a set of images having to do with the production of sound and by extension music and thus by extension art, and the sound of the bells as it breaks down the tower seems to symbolize the ability of art to break out of its conventions, restrictions, and limitations. The critic would likely zero in on the religious language of the poem: the references to God, the cathedral, the crucifix, hell, the antiphon, the Angelus, noting perhaps that these references foster a sense of beatification and apotheosis in the speaker—the notion that the speaker has achieved a kind of artistic salvation. This context, then, adds a layer of significance to the wings mentioned late in the poem, suggesting perhaps a visitation by the Holy Spirit, the dove, whose dips and flights spread love and hope to the faithful. This interplay of language elements makes reading a poem like "The Broken Tower" challenging yet ultimately rewarding.

One final critical approach is to examine the poem in terms of its underlying myths. Clearly, the Christian mythology of death and resurrection plays an important role in the poem, with its images of falling then rising in a kind of incarnation. Beyond that, the reader must remember that at the time of the poem's composition, Crane was steeped in the culture of Mexico. In a letter to Caresse Crosby (the widow of Henry Crosby, who founded the firm that published *The Bridge*) dated March 31, 1932, he describes in vivid terms his enthusiasm for that culture:

> Mexico with its volcanoes, endless ranges, countless flowers, dances, villages … and constant sunlight—it enthralls me more than any other spot I've ever known.… But it would take volumes to even hint at all I have seen and felt. Have rung bells and beaten pre-Conquistadorial drums in firelit circles at ancient ceremonies, while rockets went zooming up into the dawn over Tepoztlan.

In this environment, one could read "The Broken Tower," with its emphasis on dawn and the rising of the sun, as deriving in part from Crane's immersion in early Mexican culture, with its pantheon of sun gods of the past. In Aztec mythology—Crane was in Mexico on a Guggenheim Fellowship, intending to write an epic about the Aztecs—there were distinct ages, each ruled by a succession of sun gods, among them Tezcatlipoca, Quetzalcoatl, Tlaloc, Chalchiuhtlicue, Ehecatl, Nanauatl, and Huitzilopochtli. This succession was the result of a process of destruction and creation, as each of the gods wreaked destruction on the earth and was replaced by the next in line, who created the earth anew. This mythology can be seen as informing Crane's concept of a broken world that is reconstructed under the influence of a new rising sun, the monarch that gathers and creates anew and that colors the earth bronze.

Each critic makes a set of assumptions about literature: how it is created, how it functions, how it achieves its effects, how readers respond to it. That so much can be taken from "The Broken Tower" is testament to the abundance that Crane poured into it.

Source: Michael J. O'Neal, Critical Essay on "The Broken Tower," in *Poetry for Students*, Gale, Cengage Learning, 2017.

> CRANE'S REFERENCES TO SOCIETY REFLECT THE SAME UNHAPPY STRAIN. DISAPPOINTED BY FAMILY AND FRIENDS, HE IS REPELLED BY THE HARSH, MATERIALISTIC WAYS OF HIS ERA."

Vincent Quinn

In the following excerpt, Quinn discusses a few of the major themes that recur in Crane's work.

As already indicated, unhappiness is at the core of Crane's themes. A vein of misery runs from his earliest poems to his last. His disposition is fearful; his relationships with family and friends, melancholy; his attitude toward society, hostile.

Several poems suggest a generally troubled, anxious temperament. In an early one, "In Shadow," the lover is relieved by the presence of his beloved because, in the growing dusk of the garden, it is "too late / To risk alone the light's decline." In "Repose of Rivers," the poet recalls from his youth "the pond I entered once and quickly fled." "Paraphrase" is a morbid fantasy of dying in one's sleep and being found "already / Hollowed by air," "a white paraphrase" of oneself "among bruised roses on the papered wall."

Anxiety is expressed more successfully in "Poster," written in 1922 and later published as "Voyages I." The weakness of his other poems on this theme is that they suggest merely a personal, childish terror. In "Poster" a universal relevance is attained by his use of the sea to symbolize the unavoidable painfulness of life. The poem is also strengthened by his dramatic invention: the poet, whose innocence has been lost, utters a warning to "bright striped urchins," who, "gaily digging and scattering" sand and shells at the shore, are unaware of any danger.…

At the same time he knows that such a warning is never heeded. As he wistfully regards their still unspoiled joy, he suffers the foreknowledge of their inevitable discovery of suffering.

In choosing the sea as a symbol of the apparent benevolence masking the terror of life, Crane was especially fortunate. He used it for the first time in this poem and responded to it richly. It provided him with a metaphor that could bear the heaviest pressure of his own experience without becoming sentimental or eccentric. Its universal significance was quickened by his personal response but not overcome by it. His further exploration of the resilience of this symbol led to the "Voyages" sequence and to some of the best sections of *The Bridge*. It also drew him close to the earlier American writers with whom he was most congenial—Melville and Whitman. He felt this kinship and drew strength from it. Indeed, "Poster" reminds the reader of Melville's repeated contrast in *Moby Dick* between the safe, gentle life of the land and the dangerous, terrifying life of the sea.

Crane's fear of nature is more grimly expressed in two later poems planned for *Key West*—"O Carib Isle!" and "Hurricane." Both poems bespeak his astonishment at the violence of the tropics. In "0 Carib Isle!" he is frightened by the predominance of waste and death. "The tarantula rattling at the lily's foot / Across the feet of the dead" vividly suggests his terror. He also observes that, although death abounds, there is no mourning. Life seems to be reduced to a wanton mingling of fecundity and destruction.

He wonders about the metaphysical implications of this stark drama. "Where is the Captain of the doubloon isle?" he asks. He questions the nature and even the existence of its creator. Ironically he ponders the "Commissioner of the mildew" with his "Carib mathematics"—the "blue's comedian host," "Satan"—and inquires: "Who but catchword crabs / Patrols the dry groins of the underbrush?" He seeks self-definition in terms of this revelation of nature....

Desperately he seeks grounds for rejecting this crippling identification but, as no alternative is discovered, he suffers a vision of his disintegration: "I ... / Congeal by afternoons here, satin and vacant."

"The Hurricane" presents a different but no more comforting view of nature. The violence of a tropical hurricane is evoked in couplets that burst furiously. Although the storm is addressed as God and Lord, it has no personal consciousness. It is absolute, raw power, lacking all awareness and discrimination.

Everything is ripped and swept before it: "Naught stayeth, naught now bideth / But's smithereened apart!" Crane's use of archaic forms to suggest biblical usage—"Lo," "Ay," "Thou," "e'en"—and his reference to "Scripture" are both appropriate and ironic. They suggest the harsh God of the Old Testament, or even the apotheosis of nature itself. It is as though the whirlwind of the Book of Job were not subject to God's control but asserted itself blindly. One might address it as a primitive deity:

> Thou ridest to the door, Lord!
> Thou bidest wall nor floor, Lord!

The storm is saluted as a personal God, but its action belies its consciousness.

Undoubtedly, Crane's anxious forebodings were conditioned by his unhappy family life. His letters document his difficulties; his poems attest to them in that every reference to a family relationship is sad. In the "Van Winkle" section of *The Bridge*, the poet thinks of his youth: ...

He refers with greater bitterness in "Quaker Hill" to his plight as the child of divorced parents. He must "shoulder the curse of sundered parentage, / Wait for the postman driving from Birch Hill / With birthright by blackmail." An early poem, "My Grandmother's Love Letters," describes the poet's attempt to draw closer to his grandmother by sharing in her youthful experience of love. Alone on a rainy evening, he tries to discover his "mother's mother, Elizabeth," in letters that have grown brown and soft over the years. He knows that

> Over the greatness of such space
> Steps must be gentle.
> It is all hung by an invisible white hair.
> It trembles as birth limbs webbing the air.

In becoming aware of how precarious his quest is, he loses confidence. Difficulties become apparent and paralyze his desire. The task of realizing the original force of old letters that were but the echoes of passion seems too large. He feels that he would inevitably impose himself upon his grandmother's experience and thereby distort it.

> And so I stumble. And the rain continues on
>   the roof
> With such a sound of gently pitying laughter.

His ambition has been blocked; the desire for human sympathy seems unable to surmount the barrier of subjectivity. Only the consciousness of failure survives his impulse toward fellowship.

A similar conviction of the unbridgeable gulf in even the most intimate relationship is expressed in "Stark Major." A couple conceives a child in the ecstasy of love, but dawn brings "the lover's death." Not only must the lovers part, but the still unseen child will prevent their complete reunion....

Crane's poems about friendship are equally melancholy. In "Praise for an Urn," one of the most successful elegies in American poetry, he confronts the fact of death with his desire for a lasting relationship. Several impulses incline him to believe in the presence of his deceased friend. There is his affection, of course, but also his recollection of the large spirit of his friend, mingling "the everlasting eyes of Pierrot / And of Gargantua, the laughter." In addition, he recognizes that all his friend's ideas were "inheritances," gifts from other minds, "delicate riders of the storm." Just as men of the past lived on in the consciousness of his friend, so his friend may live on in him. Most of all, there are the experiences they shared....

Tranquil, moon-charged evenings intimated the immortality of the soul to both of them and directed their conversation toward this possibility. Under the spell of nature's serenity and their spiritual intimacy, all reality seemed united and harmonious.

Now the confidence they felt together collapses as the lone survivor faces the fact of death. The funeral with its bold assertion of lifelessness and, even more, the cremation of his friend break the poet's faith. He realizes that even while he and his friend had been speaking of immortality and believing that nature sustained their faith, the clock "perched in the crematory lobby" had been ticking ironically toward that moment of dissolution. The poet's faith in personal immortality cracks under the mechanical flux of matter.

His resolution of this conflict is plaintively uncertain. The funeral and its aftermath of loneliness have dangerously weakened the poet's confidence in a deathless relationship but not destroyed it. Images of his friend return insistently and by their invincibility keep his hope alive....

This slim basis for hope holds the issue in tension, but it is in discouraging contrast to the trust he has felt while his friend was alive. He can only assert his desire; objective support is not available. So the poem ends meekly. "Well-meant

idioms" are all that remain of their earlier "assessments of the soul."...

He fears that the same ashen fate that claimed his friend's body will be suffered—and perhaps deserves more to be suffered—by his poetic tribute to "what the dead keep, living still."

Crane's other poems about friendship speak of infidelity and alienation. The most poignant of these is "Voyages V." As we shall see later, the poet, having "dreamed / Nothing so flagless as this piracy," must endure being abandoned by his friend. This loss occasions his wistful yearning in "Voyages VI" for an "unbetrayable reply / Whose accent no farewell can know."

Crane's references to society reflect the same unhappy strain. Disappointed by family and friends, he is repelled by the harsh, materialistic ways of his era. In two sections of *The Bridge*— "The River" and "The Tunnel"—he expresses his revulsion. "The River" presents a kaleidoscopic nightmare of advertisements seen from a transcontinental railroad:...

In "The Tunnel" chaos is represented by a subway descending beneath the East River. Disconnected tags of vulgar conversation mingle with gongs, hissing doors, and cars screaming around curves. The poet feels "caught like pennies beneath soot and steam," and he identifies his spiritual agony with the torment of Edgar Allan Poe:...

Feeling alien to these conditions, the poet in "Chaplinesque" identifies himself with the lonely, abused tramp of the movies and uses him to symbolize the fate of human values in his time. The familiar cop who always chases Charlie away from some innocent enjoyment represents society. His prohibiting thumb is "inevitable"; he sees life through a "dull squint" and opposes all more liberal views....

Source: Vincent Quinn, "Major Themes," in *Hart Crane*, Twayne Publishers, 1963, pp. 33–39.

SOURCES

"Aztec Sun-God," Aztec-History.com, http://www.aztec-history.com/aztec-sun-god.html (accessed July 25, 2016).

Bewley, Marius, "Hart Crane's Last Poem," in *Hart Crane: A Reference Guide*, edited by Joseph Schwartz,

G. K. Hall, 1983, p. 94; originally published in *Accent*, Vol. 19, Spring 1959.

Brunner, Edward, ed., "Hart Crane: Biographical Sketch," in *Modern American Poetry*, http://www.english.illinois.edu/maps/poets/a_f/crane/bio.htm (accessed July 18, 2016).

"Carl Sandburg," Poetry Foundation website, http://www.poetryfoundation.org/poems-and-poets/poets/detail/carl-sandburg (accessed July 21, 2016).

Crane, Hart, "The Broken Tower," in *Hart Crane*, edited by Maurice Riordan, Faber and Faber, 2008, pp. 66–67.

———, "The Broken Tower," in *New Republic*, June 8, 1932, p. 91.

———, "To Caresse Crosby—31 March, 1932," in *Hart Crane*, edited by Maurice Riordan, Faber and Faber, 2008, p. 89.

"Crane, Hart," in *Merriam-Webster's Encyclopedia of Literature*, Merriam-Webster, 1995, pp. 279–80.

"Divisions: City and Town," in *Becoming Modern: America in the 1920s*, America in Class website, 2012, http://americainclass.org/sources/becomingmodern/divisions/text3/text3.htm (accessed July 22, 2016).

"Hart Crane," in *An Anthology of American Literature*, Vol. 2, *Realism to the Present*, 2nd ed., edited by George McMichael, Macmillan, 1980, pp. 1229–30.

"Hart Crane," Poetry Foundation website, http://www.poetryfoundation.org/poems-and-poets/poets/detail/hart-crane (accessed July 24, 2016).

Holden, Stephen, "Intoxicated by Language, a Poet Is Destroyed by Life: James Franco Is Hart Crane in *The Broken Tower*," in *New York Times*, April 26, 2012, http://www.nytimes.com/2012/04/27/movies/james-franco-is-hart-crane-in-the-broken-tower.html?_r=0 (accessed July 18, 2016).

Irwin, John T. *Hart Crane's Poetry: "Appollinaire Lived in Paris, I Live in Cleveland, Ohio,"* Johns Hopkins University Press, 2011, pp. 371–83.

"Labor: Labor Force (Series D 1-682)," in *Historical Statistics of the United States: Colonial Times to 1970*, U.S. Bureau of the Census, September 1975, p. 135, http://www2.census.gov/library/publications/1975/compendia/hist_stats_colonial-1970/hist_stats_colonial-1970p1-chD.pdf (accessed July 20, 2016).

Lewis, R. W. B., *The Poetry of Hart Crane: A Critical Study*, Princeton University Press, 1967, pp. 410, 413–14.

Lyon, Melvin E., "The Centrality of Hart Crane's 'The Broken Tower'," in *University of Nebraska Studies*, New Series No. 42, University of Nebraska, March 1972, p. 13.

Munro, Niall, *Hart Crane's Queer Modernist Aesthetic*, Palgrave Macmillan, 2015, pp. 146–47.

Uroff, M. D., *Hart Crane: The Patterns of His Poetry*, University of Illinois Press, 1974, p. 38.

Weber, Brom, *Hart Crane: A Biographical and Critical Study*, Russell & Russell, 1948, p. 313.

FURTHER READING

Davis, Alex, and Lee M. Jenkins, eds., *The Cambridge Companion to Modernist Poets*, Cambridge University Press, 2007.

> This collection of essays by various scholars provides a broad overview of modernist poetry. It examines the historical and cultural contexts of modernism and summarizes the reception accorded to modernist poets. It also examines the work of a number of important modernist poets.

Hammer, Langdon, ed., *Hart Crane: Complete Poems and Selected Letters*, Library of America, 2006.

> This volume includes not only Crane's entire poetic output but also a generous selection of his voluminous correspondence. These letters remain important in the history of modernist poetics, for in them he elucidated his goals as an artist.

Howarth, Peter, *The Cambridge Introduction to Modernist Poetry*, Cambridge University Press, 2011.

> Howarth introduces the work of several key modernist poets from Britain and the United States. Beyond that, he undertakes to answer the larger question of why modernist poets wrote verse that is dense and often difficult to read.

Mariani, Paul, *The Broken Tower: The Life of Hart Crane*, Norton, 1999.

> This volume was the first biography of the poet to appear in three decades. Relying heavily on Crane's correspondence, the book focuses on the poet's homosexuality, his complicated relationship with his parents, and his final months in Mexico.

SUGGESTED SEARCH TERMS

Harlem Renaissance

Hart Crane

Hart Crane AND The Bridge

Hart Crane AND "The Broken Tower"

Hart Crane AND logic of metaphor

homosexuality AND 1920s

Modern American poetry

modernism

Peggy Baird Cowley

Roaring Twenties

The Concrete River

LUIS J. RODRÍGUEZ

1991

Luis J. Rodríguez's poem "The Concrete River" offers the reader quite a trip. The title hints at the sort of unique sensory perceptions and associated verbal conceptions that many readers expect from the greatest poets. More than just a whimsical description of a concrete expanse that might be said to stream along like a river, however, the image in question is derived from an urban hallucination brought on by a most unnatural source, the inhaled fumes of a spray can. The poet is, in fact, aware that his habit represents a low point in his life, one that could well prove lethal—a notion about which this poem has much cause to concern itself and much to say.

A Chicano author, Rodríguez has gained renown in part for the revelations of the street life of his youth presented in his memoir *Always Running: La Vida Loca; Gang Days in L.A.* (1993). He largely deals with the same period of his life in his verse collection *The Concrete River* (1991), in which the title poem was first published. "The Concrete River" can also be found in Rodríguez's 2005 collection *My Nature Is Hunger: New and Selected Poems, 1989–2004.*

AUTHOR BIOGRAPHY

Luis Javier Rodríguez was born in El Paso, Texas, on July 9, 1954. He lived the first two years of his life with his family across the border

Luis J. Rodriguez (©ZUMA Press, Inc. / Alamy Stock Photos)

in Ciudad Juárez, Mexico. His father was a school principal, but political enemies had him removed through false accusations of embezzling; he was found innocent at trial, but the job was lost. He responded by immigrating with his family to Los Angeles, California, in 1956, settling in the neighborhood of Watts. Luis's mother took on work as a seamstress and home cleaner, his father worked variously in construction or as a salesman.

Young Luis's impressions about life for immigrants to the United States were not good, owing to the poor treatment and disrespect they received; the memory of a white woman's telling his mother, as she rested on a park bench, that she could not sit there because "this is not your country" would stay with him for years. (The Rodríguez family had immigrated legally.) The children—Luis had three siblings and three half siblings—inherited anger; Rodríguez has recorded times when his older brother pushed him off the roof of a building and dragged him around the yard by a noose. In 1962, the family moved to the San Gabriel Valley, in East Los Angeles, a landscape of barrios, or Latino

neighborhoods, that were often left by municipalities in ghetto conditions.

In such marginalized positions, many of Rodríguez's friends and extended family turned to gang life, which in many ways gave life a meaning that was unavailable elsewhere. Unfortunately, much of this meaning revolved around ethnic rivalry, randomized violence, drug consumption, and perilously early sexual activity. (Rodríguez covers this period of his life in great detail in *Always Running*, which some communities have accordingly sought to ban.) Rodríguez became involved in the local Lomas gang by age eleven. The social conditions proved a vicious cycle, as Anglo (white) discrimination inspired Latino anger, which underwrote Latino violence, which brought forth retributive Anglo violence and heightened discrimination. Rodríguez participated in gang life but with a critical eye; meanwhile, he was in and out of school and jobs, but he never lost a passion for the different sort of escape offered by reading. His nurtured intellect led him toward increasing community involvement and political action, through the ongoing Chicano movement as well as Vietnam War protests. By the end of high school, in 1972, Rodríguez's poetry had earned him a Quinto Sol Literary Award and a trip to Berkeley, California.

After high school, Rodríguez sustained himself in a variety of labor positions, including carpenter, steelworker, furnace operator, truck driver, and refinery mechanic. By 1980, he was writing and also photographing for East Los Angeles newspapers, and in 1982 he was a *San Bernardino Sun* reporter—though the Republican editor would blacklist him for Communist sympathies. Becoming the director of the Los Angeles Latino Writers Association, Rodríguez also started publishing *Chismearte*, a Latino literary journal. His family would include two children born to his first wife in the late 1970s and two more born to his third wife in 1988 and 1994.

Rodríguez moved to Chicago in 1984 to become editor of the *People's Tribune*, a weekly paper with a revolutionary orientation. He would also run poetry workshops in such places as homeless shelters, gang-member gatherings, prisons, and migrant camps. He was the founding director of a publishing house, Tía Chucha Press, which would issue his debut poetry collection *Poems across the Pavement* (1989). He would find a home at Curbstone Press for his next several volumes, putting out the ensuing verse collection *The Concrete River* (1991)—which contains "The Concrete River"—his memoir, more poetry, and children's books. Later publications included social commentary and more autobiography. Returning to Los Angeles, Rodríguez ran for governor as the Green Party nominee in 2014, and that year he was named the second poet laureate of Los Angeles, to hold a two-year term.

POEM SUMMARY

The text used for this summary is from *The Concrete River*, Curbstone Press, 1991, pp. 38–41. Versions of the poem can be found on the following web page: https://www.poets.org/poetsorg/poem/concrete-river.

"The Concrete River" is a poem of 109 lines in fourteen stanzas; in online versions, the line spacing and indentation do not necessarily match the original.

Lines 1–7

In the first stanza, the poet reports dropping onto dust (on the ground) alongside a companion named Baba, with thorny bushes or branches hanging over them. Line 4 creates an image of trees being suffocated by climbing ivy, an image that transitions directly into mention of the narrator and Baba's singing during a ceremonial last ritual of some sort (suggesting death)—a ritual associated with *locura*, which Rodríguez colloquially defines in the glossary of his memoir *Always Running* as "craziness; referring to a state of being, not so much a state of mind, among barrio gangs." The narrator characterizes himself and his friend as *homeboys*, suggesting urban status as streetwise. What they worship, through their present ritual, is God in the form of fumes extracted from aerosol spray cans.

Lines 8–14

The poet and Baba's backs are up against fencing of corrugated steel (molded into repeating ridges) on the waterless bank of a river of concrete; this suggests an aqueduct in the dry season. Sprayed-on graffiti covers nearby walls, lending a sense of total colorful disorder to the viewer.

MEDIA ADAPTATIONS

- University of California Television has posted a recording of Rodríguez recounting stories from his life and reading his poetry as part of the Lunch Poems Reading Series in 2008, available at https://www.youtube.com/watch?v=Fxgyz4P1S4k.

Lines 15–24

Where the two young men are is, in some sense, currently their home. It is well concealed by surrounding weedy overgrowth. The furniture includes visibly used mattresses and standard milk crates, while planks of wood and the overhanging branches function as a makeshift roof. A doorway is suggested by a curtain of ripped fabric, on which the reader is, mockingly, instructed to knock. Again, in line 23 as in line 15, the place is defined as their present home—or in another way of reading the line, the young men are described as presently being at home. That sense of home is compressed in the middle of days that drive one crazy.

Lines 25–30

The poet directly describes their method of inhaling the fumes: they first spray them into paper bags, then suck them out, breathing in deeply. The immediate attainment of a high is suggested by the next line's description of a sky-rending sound, a sound that signals immersion in sensory perception that has been intensified beyond ordinary bounds. (The steely sound itself specifically suggests activity at a nearby construction site.) A third repetition of the fragmented sentence reaffirms the poet's current occupation of *home*, whether his home is the physical place or the drug itself or the mental place to which the drug takes him. The poet's perception now includes muck along the concrete river, the products of urban living, alongside which he and Baba further imbibe, as if gargling a liquid, the electrified colors of the surrounding insanity.

Lines 31–40

The opening line of the fifth stanza focuses the reader's attention back on the setting, the concrete landscape whose status as a *river* is affirmed twice in line 31. The expanse of concrete evolves—under the influence of the fumes, one may presume—into a river-like serpent, or a serpentine river, so hot it steams and bubbles, washing over (and thus submerging or washing away) the nightmares of waking consciousness. A number of birds are seen to suddenly emerge from the river as if poured out of it. The river itself is a clear liquid on a day when not a cloud occupies the sky; by now the image of rippling heat waves over the searing hot concrete is readily seen to contribute to the poet's hallucinatory perception. This river, in its clarity, is unlike the dark stains of oil in which the young men lie (whether literally or figuratively), and unlike the factory-polluted air that they are obliged to breathe; it is also unlike the death embodied in the plastic of the can. (In *Always Running*, Rodríguez describes the inhalant in question as "cans of clear plastic.")

Lines 41–46

Rays from the sun move exuberantly on the surface of the concrete river, while gray fish (perhaps actually individual concrete blocks) can be seen agitating beneath the surface. The young men themselves, to the poet, resemble Mark Twain's classic fictional characters Huckleberry Finn and Tom Sawyer, boys out to live their own adventures. The young men's fishing poles may be the overhanging branches as perceived creatively; some of the branches hang quite low, and the poet can perceive dew dripping from them, as if milk from the earth's own breast.

Lines 47–51

On a plaintive note, the poet slips into a lament about what he and Baba should have been. They should have been explosions of light in their living selves. They should have been barefoot pushing caked mud around with their toes, the skin hardened by usage. They should have been like the petals of flowers, blossoming while playing a ball game of some kind.

Lines 52–61

The images of water and fish and dewdrops all fade into the background as a throbbing whiteness overtakes the poet's senses. He goes into a tunnel marked by circles, moving as if he is swimming toward a profusion of light from multiple sources. He is being beckoned by family and friends—perhaps the spirits of the departed. He wants to reach the place to which they summon him, a world of unending dreams with a soundscape denoted by screams that are somehow perceived as *exquisite*—as refined, perhaps beautiful, and even sensibly enjoyable. The comfort that he can feel coursing through him, in which he is currently immersed, is like an all-engulfing motherly presence that he wants to become more familiar with and fully understand.

Lines 62–81

The series of lines in the ninth stanza, in the original, feature marked indentation after each of the six flush-left lines beginning *I am*. The poet describes himself first as a small but nonetheless brightly burning ember heading into a bright womb. Then he is a ghostly presence floating up out of a body marked by scars. Then he is a clown emerging slyly from a mouth painted in the sky. Then he is the son of his mother, who is addressed directly as "you," a son who is looking for safety in darkness and escape from the tired eyes that nonetheless flare out a deep brown from behind a sewing machine. Then he is the brother to a sibling, who is also directly addressed, who was the one to throw the poet off roofs and ragingly attack him—though the sibling (a brother, one gathers) did also visit the poet when he was in the hospital, injured and stricken. Finally, the poet describes himself as someone who befriends books, is attacked by police officers, and loves the barrio women who sell food at a local burger stand.

Lines 82–85

The poet seems to recognize that he is enshrouded by something heavy, a garment associated with death—but he is pleased to bear it, and he even wants to be buried wrapped in the garment. It will make of him, he imagines, a marble sculpture, the artistry of which would suggest a better craftsman than does the scarred body he currently inhabits (inadequately crafted, one gathers, by God).

Lines 86–89

After a period of time, humming electricity bites into the poet's mind, and he feels grasping, scraping hands encircling him and pulling him out of the mindscape he has just inhabited and back to the reality of the dusty ground and the expanse of concrete.

Lines 90–95

The poet's response to this turn of events is an impassioned appeal (only thought, not spoken) to be released, to be allowed to go back to the entanglement of the peacefulness he had found, however much like a barbed net it might have been. Despite his appeal, a face lingers over his own, apparently in the act of resuscitating the poet by breathing air into his mouth. The air comes to the poet in a rush, and he is aware also of the small rocks and debris beneath him.

Lines 96–100

The poet speaks with difficulty, appealing aloud now for the return of the paper bag, so that he can inhale more fumes. But Baba refuses outright, pointing out, in no uncertain terms, that the poet had died; he was no longer breathing. Nonetheless, the poet insists that he must return to where he was, something he does not imagine that Baba comprehends.

Lines 101–109

The poet attempts to rise, to make contact with the air above him. Once more sounding a plaintive note by opening a line with *Oh*, the poet speaks in fragments about something being, or being done, *for* the surrounding lights and *for* the sun (personified as a prostitute), something that would cause the poet to go blind. This would also lure the poet toward a state of burning. Now speaking as if to his intoxicated state itself, the poet asks for the return of that state. He asks to be allowed to sway, hanging, joyously, even though there would be a recurring bell-like sound with ominous and foreboding tones. As such, he could penetrate the colors that the untouched skies present to him. He would not be where he is now, alongside the river of concrete, but in that other place, where flames would reach out to caress him.

THEMES

Escape

From early in "The Concrete River" it is apparent that the poet is engaging in the self-destructive behavior to which the poem leads up as a means of escape. The scene that the poem paints suggests

poverty, although the fact that the setting is isolated from where the poet actually lives makes it difficult to be sure. Nonetheless, between the graffiti, the concrete, the steel fences, and the makeshift homestead, a state of poverty approaching actual homelessness is suggested, while the fact that the poet and his companion are inhaling chemicals to escape reality indicates both a level of unpleasantness in their lives and a lack of resources with which to more sanely cope with that unpleasantness. In fact, for all its sparseness, the makeshift home itself is an element of the escape: one might look at the shelter's inadequacy for regular domestic functioning (torn cloth for a "door," planks and branches for a "roof") as signifying a pathetic state of existence in which no one could be comfortable, but as the allusion to Huck Finn and Tom Sawyer suggests, making do and getting by with little more than what society has cast away can be an empowering experience. In creating this little world from boards and crates in a neglected corner of urban nature, the young men enable themselves to literally step outside of ordinary money-dependent life in the modern world. This first layer of escape can be seen as a potentially rational means of objecting to and protesting against the modern world, but the second layer of escape, resorting to momentary highs from inhalants, is what nearly ends the poet's life.

Addiction

As is the case with many people who turn to intoxicants to escape from the rigors and trials of their lives, the poet appears to have become addicted. Although he does not come out and state that he has an addiction—which might well have undermined the poem, tilting the tone into the didactic (preachy)—he seems to be conscious, as writer of the poem, that he was, in fact, addicted during the time he is describing. This is suggested by the religious connotations in the first stanza, where the fumes themselves are said to represent or be equivalent to a god, something that the poet and Baba pray to, bow down to—in a word, worship. Few people would consciously assert that sniffing aerosols is a way of connecting with God, and so the description comes across as implying the poet's retrospective recognition of the way his dependence on the practice pushed the bounds of rationality, reaching a dangerous level of belief in the "virtue" of his behavior that blurred its self-destructive nature.

TOPICS FOR FURTHER STUDY

- Write a poem about a time when you sought escape from the world—and perhaps nearly escaped too far. (Note that your teacher will of course treat your material confidentially.) This may have been a time of excessive consumption of alcohol, food, or drugs; prolonged abandonment to technological entertainment; or perhaps simply a long journey out on your own, whether on foot or by vehicle. Try to capture the essence of your mind-set at the time without judgment as to what you were feeling and experiencing or, if you prefer, write in a way that allows you to distance yourself from your act of escape.

- Read the Gary Soto poem "Saturday at the Canal," which can be found in the revised version of his young-adult verse collection *A Fire in My Hands* (2006). Soto, a prolific Chicano author, was raised in the San Joaquin Valley, which, in contrast to Rodríguez's San Gabriel Valley, is a rural locale. Soto's and Rodríguez's poems offer striking contrasts between urban and rural life in California for sons of Mexican immigrants.

Write a dialogue between the two poems' narrators, in whatever context you choose, in which they discuss their differences as well as similarities and reconcile their attitudes with each other's realities.

- Conduct online inquiries to research the science behind and hazards of the practice of sniffing fumes from spray cans, as well as the demographics of populations who have resorted to such inhalants. Discuss your findings in a written report or in a science fair–style presentation, including at least two graphs/charts and two photographs/illustrations regardless of format.

- Imagine that you are a speechwriter for a politician who is involved in the question of the legalization of marijuana. Craft a policy speech either for or against legalization (if your state has already legalized it, step back to a time prior to the event) in which the argument ultimately revolves in some fashion around "The Concrete River" and how it might be read in relation to the political question.

The poet's consciousness of an addiction is further suggested by the references to insanity, in lines 5, 24, and 30. The first, using the word *locura*, for "craziness," indicates most directly that the poet's addiction represents a breach of sanity (although Rodríguez has reported that the word is commonly used as slang for gang life). The second reference, in line 24, adds that the days are responsible for driving the poet mad; his daily life is what makes him crazy. Thus, this usage pushes responsibility for the poet's troubles onto the greater world (which addicts are often inclined to do, to dissociate themselves from responsibility for their problem). But the next use, in line 30, again more directly connotes that the poet's response to life's troubles is itself a sort of immersion in madness, an embrace of

insanity. The worst part of the addiction is that the poet is so blinded by the euphoria he experiences that he is no longer even concerned with his physical well-being; he takes himself right to the brink of death.

Death

The place where the poet is taken by his inhalation of chemicals is at first described as an enhanced sensory experience, one in which noises take on different dimensions and perceptions are twisted. But the high moves beyond this into a state of more intense hallucination in which what he perceives is entirely disconnected from the reality before him. He sees unaccounted-for sources of illumination, and he is called to by family and friends who are not

---

The speaker lives in an urban landscape decorated only by graffiti (©*Fernando Cortes | Shutterstock.com*)

actually present. There is also an emotional component: the experience is marked by a sense of supreme comfort like that in a mother's embrace of a baby. But it turns out the high brings the user quite low in the end, nearly as low as six feet under ground, as the entire hallucination proves a sort of summons to the afterlife—potentially not just a momentary high, but a permanent escape from the trials of living existence. The poet was indeed on death's doorstep, and in the moment, death felt like the place where he wanted to be. Even after his companion summons him back to the world of the living by performing impromptu CPR—the poet has only barely escaped death—he wants to go back, he wants to return to death, through the fumes, and reach again the state of total abandonment into which he momentarily dipped his desperate soul.

Desperation

The last stanza of "The Concrete River" resounds with the profound, even heartbreaking desperation that the poet still feels after his near-death experience. His life was nearly ended; his friend's awareness and devotion alone are what kept him alive. And yet still he wants to go back there, suggesting that life leaves him feeling so overwhelmingly broken, in such a constant state of desperation, that permanent escape is all he wants. Again, there is a later consciousness, on the poet's part, that his mind-set is unbalanced by addiction and the desire for escape, as the lights he reaches out to in the end are not just beckoning him, they are blinding and burning him. The use of language is complicated in this final stanza, making the meaning partly ambiguous, but it seems that both the real sunlight and the light of his hallucination are shown to be damaging him. It is as if the sunlight lures him into again desiring that other blinding, burning light, the light that nearly led him to death. The reader is left, then, to reflect on how a society could so fail a person as to leave him so tantalized by the ending of his existence. The implied positive note is that the poet did not, after all, heed the call to an early and tragic death; he survived to write this poem, perhaps having emerged the stronger for what he put himself through—or perhaps merely lucky to have survived. Either way, that he is grateful to have survived is without question; sooner or later he must have chosen life, and he must know it was the better choice.

STYLE

Anaphora

Rodríguez makes noteworthy use of repetition in "The Concrete River," especially in the form of *anaphora*, the repetition of a phrase at the beginning of multiple lines or clauses. Lines 38–40 all begin with the word *not*, two of them following with *like*, hammering into the reader's mind how the euphoria of the clear river is utterly unlike the reality of the poet's living existence, with the oil stains suggested as both literal—the stains on the mattresses—and figurative, evoking the grimy, neglected lives that he and his family have been mired in, like a proverbial tar pit. In the third of that set of three anaphoric lines, the poet signals his first awareness that his practice of inhaling spray-can fumes could well prove fatal.

A briefer but no less powerful use of anaphora occurs soon after, in lines 48 and 50, where two successive sentences begin with *we should be*, again hammering home the sense of the lines, the repetition like a eulogy for the lives that the poet and his companion might have been living, in a different place or a different time. The poem's most impressive use of anaphora comes with the ninth stanza, where six successive sentences begin with the words *I am*. This echoing and reimagining of the poet's identity expands his very existence in an almost mystical way, rendering himself as a source of light, a ghost, a jester (or trickster), a son, a brother, and someone who believes in the power of ideas, as represented in books, and who loves his fellow humans, in particular the women who provide him with nourishment. He is all these things at once, and to recognize them in sequence overlaps the presence of those identities, bringing to the surface everything that the poet's life signifies. It is like the sum of his life. The downside of this conception of it all is that the poet feels himself ready to close the account, to tally the total and leave it at that—that is, to die. But a strong hint of existential affirmation shines through in the ninth stanza, an affirmation that could be the poet's saving grace.

Chicano Poetry

There is a strong tradition of poetry among Mexican Americans, especially as emerging from the Chicano movement of the 1960s and beyond. An influential work of Chicano verse was *I Am Joaquín* (1967), Rodolfo Gonzales's epic poem of racial and national identity interrogation. Rodríguez's "The Concrete River" distinguishes itself as a work of Chicano literature in two distinct ways. One is the inclusion of a scattering of Spanish words, in usage that both acknowledges the poet's linguistic roots and puts the English-only reader at a (very slight) disadvantage in the comprehension of the poem—turning the tables from the perspective of a poet whose family of Mexican immigrants faced an uphill battle in learning English and adapting to US culture. Although the poem's three words italicized as foreign amount only to a gesture toward Hispanic culture, it is a significant gesture in a country that has at times vilified immigrants who cannot speak English and refused to accommodate Spanish speakers in municipal proceedings (in voting forms, health care and welfare communications, legal documents, and so forth).

"The Concrete River" also features what Bruce-Novoa, in *Chicano Poetry: A Response to Chaos*, identifies as a hallmark of much Chicano verse: an elegiac orientation toward death. (An elegy is a poem of mourning and reflection upon someone who has died, often addressing their significance to the public.) This is not to suggest, Bruce-Novoa clarifies, on a broader scale, that Chicano verse should be understood as amounting to a collective lament for a dying or even dead culture; rather, it suggests that a tragic perspective is often assumed with respect to the trials Mexican Americans have endured, and indeed death is a frequent and common theme. And what is lost is not the culture itself, but the central and foundational elements or principles that hold the Chicano community together, in its dispersion and subjugation in English-speaking, majority Anglo American culture. These elements and principles collectively amount to the axis mundi (axis of the world, in a metaphorical sense) of the Chicano community, the line around which it revolves. Bruce-Novoa quotes Mircea Eliade as noting that the disappearance of a culture's axis mundi is "like 'the end of the world,' a reversion to chaos"—a chaos signaled for the poet of "The Concrete River" in the vivid chaos of colors in the walls of graffiti. Bruce-Novoa goes on to ask, regarding the loss of a community's axis mundi, "How can one survive such a loss? By magic, by the sacred invocation of a transcendent principle...in short, through ritual." These words seem an accurate description of what the poet by the concrete riverside is doing, or trying to do.

COMPARE
&
CONTRAST

- **1970s:** With drug culture having flourished during the sixties, President Richard Nixon first declares the US government's "war on drugs" in June 1971, increasing funding for regulatory federal agencies and stiffening sentences for those convicted of drug-related crimes. Nixon originally designates marijuana a Schedule I drug, maximally restricting its use, and ignores a commission's 1972 recommendation that marijuana be decriminalized for personal use.

  Today: After First Lady Nancy Reagan's spearheading major expansions of the drug war in the 1980s, American jails start filling to overflow capacity with minor drug offenders. In the twenty-first century, efforts are made to reduce and commute the sentences of those given excessive prison time for such offenses, and Colorado, Washington, Oregon, Alaska, and Washington, DC, legalize marijuana use.

- **1970s:** Rodríguez is among those present at the largest Chicano protest gathering to date, a march in East Los Angeles against the Vietnam War—which saw disproportionate numbers of fatalities among Mexican Americans—on August 29, 1970, with about thirty thousand people in attendance. At the event, known as the Chicano Moratorium, the police violently suppress the march.

  Today: With immigration reform a topic of heated debate in 2006, as some Washington politicians seek to strengthen border security and crack down on the employment of illegal immigrants, marches and protests are carried out nationwide. In Los Angeles on March 25, 2006, some five hundred thousand people of various nationalities and ethnicities participate in a peaceful march. Immigration is again a topic of heated rhetoric at the time of the 2016 presidential election.

- **1970s:** In 1972, the National Association for Chicano Studies is founded, setting the stage for the establishment of academic departments devoted to Mexican American history and concerns in universities nationwide, with the Southwest a region of focus.

  Today: While Chicano studies departments have flourished, especially in California, Arizona, and Texas, some departments have seen declining enrollment despite record numbers of Mexican Americans attending college. Some contend that the affirmative term *Chicano* has itself declined in usage, with more youths being inclined to label themselves Mexican American or simply American, reflecting the nation's ever-increasing diversity. Some departments have explicitly expanded their focus to more broadly encompass Hispanic/Latino concerns.

HISTORICAL CONTEXT

The Barrios of East Los Angeles

Parts of Los Angeles were cauldrons of racial unrest for much of the second half of the twentieth century. Prior to the achievement of civil rights legislation in the mid-1960s, African Americans were growing more and more discontented with forms of oppression and discrimination, and riots erupted in Watts in 1965. As the decade progressed and the Chicano civil rights movement gathered steam, Chicano social concerns, focused in East Los Angeles, came to the fore. Political organizations like the Congress of Mexican American Unity and student unions tried to make the best of the turning historical tide to demand recognition in such forms as Chicano studies departments in colleges and increased representation in political office and civic employment sectors, such as police forces.

Even with the Chicano population in the Southwest at 12 percent and climbing as of 1960, by 1968 still only 7.5 percent or less of police officers were of Mexican American descent. Chicanos were deliberately discriminated against in jury selections—a commission concluded that the situation was comparable to jury discrimination against African Americans in the South—leaving vast majorities of white voices to pronounce the public's judgments on Chicanos accused of crimes.

The criminal justice system was a flash point for confrontation, as detailed in testimony given to the US Commission on Civil Rights in 1970. A lack of bilingualism among police frequently led officers to assume the worst of Hispanic citizens, such as when, for example, a young Chicano was trying to minimize tensions among his fellow Spanish speakers but was assumed to be trying to incite a riot and was arrested. A commission report concluded that throughout the Southwest, Anglo juvenile offenders were typically released into the custody of parents without charges being filed, while Chicano juvenile offenders were typically charged, detained, and sent to reformatories. At the street level, police frequently overrode Mexican Americans' constitutional right to assembly, breaking up public gatherings without any legal justification beyond race-based suspicion. As reported by Chicano journalist Ruben Salazar—who, in the midst of reporting on Chicano-police confrontations, was killed in August 1970 when a gas shell was fired into a bar—in his essay "La Ley—The Law," one LA psychiatric social worker, Armando Morales, contended that police aggression seemed to be approved by political higher-ups. Even when accusations of police brutality were filed, the discrimination persisted: as Morales, member of a council that investigated such filings, reported, among twenty-five police brutality cases, only five were referred to the FBI, which in turn referred them to the Justice Department—which simply never acted on them.

The oppressive social infrastructures in places like Los Angeles fostered more aggression than communities and individuals could handle, contributing to the growth and spread of gang life—territorial aggression marked by outright refusal to abide by established laws and rules as well as violence against targets both in rival gangs and among innocent bystanders, in what often amounted to local terrorism. Rodríguez, in

The image of ivy smothering other plants emphasizes the speaker's feeling of being trapped in this life (©FashionStock.com | Shutterstock.com)

Always Running, relates harrowing accounts of his own and fellow gang members' activities, ranging from armed robberies of convenience stores and passing trucks, to racially motivated fights and beatings (at his high school, the annual antagonism between Anglos and Chicanos was known as "The Tradition"), to an attack on the house of a rival gang member with Molotov cocktails. Some people he knew engaged in deliberate sexual violence. He also relates a personal experience of police aggression: plainclothes officers, dressed as surfers, instigated Rodríguez and his companions to violence by repeatedly hurling racial slurs in their direction; once they became aggressive, the police detained them using unnecessary physical cruelty, then found among their belongings recreational drugs that retrospectively (but not legally) justified their tactics. Many gang members variously developed habits in hard drugs, including mescaline, meth, PCP, and heroin.

Fortunately for Rodríguez, his father's insistence that he sustain his education allowed him to touch base with individuals working in the wings of the Chicano movement, such as through local youth-based organizations. In Lomas, the Bienvenidos Community Center hired a man named Chente Ramírez, who avoided gang life in his own East LA barrio upbringing and became a founding member of United Mexican American Students. He also had martial arts expertise. Ramírez would prove a crucial influence on Rodríguez in his path away from gang life and into the world of letters.

CRITICAL OVERVIEW

Rodríguez has been largely praised by those who have regarded his work. In *Publishers Weekly*, a reviewer comments that in *The Concrete River*, Rodríguez "writes eloquently ... of a populace locked out of privilege and prosperity." The reviewer notes that Rodríguez illustrates how societal oppression combined with violence on the part of the police leads to anger and sometimes emotional implosion, such as in the title poem. Nonetheless, Rodríguez finds the beauty in the barrio, such as in the simple cupping of a man's hand on the small of a woman's back. In sum, the reviewer states, "This poetry is of the barrio yet stubbornly refuses to be confined by it—Rodríguez's perceptive gaze and storyteller's gift transport his world across neighborhood boundaries."

Looking at the context of the different sections of *The Concrete River*, Dina G. Castillo, in the *Dictionary of Literary Biography*, notes that the section "Dancing on a Grave," which contains "The Concrete River," hinges on

> the poet's adolescence and dangerous flirtation with death. He is depicted in conflict with the police, his family, and himself as he abandons his life to violence and drugs. In "The Concrete River" he combines reality with fantasy to illustrate what his life had become up to that point.

Castillo comments with regard to the collection as a whole:

> Rodríguez uses the motifs of concrete and pavement to represent all that has limited him in the past but that nevertheless became the source of his literary creativity. In essence, life is produced from a hardened environment. He views poetry as the water that runs through the concrete river, cleansing and restoring life.

In his essay on contemporary Chicano poetry in the *Bilingual Review*, Andrés Rodríguez recognizes Luis J. Rodríguez as "a true spokesperson of our contemporary urban situation; he speaks with eloquence and with the force of his occasions." The scholar describes *The Concrete River* as "a book devoted to its contexts: anger, confusion, loss of connection (familial as well as social), resistance, rebuilding." He writes that "the reality that appears in his poems is often the specific context of an instant's possibility," such as with "the vision of an unfolding self in the title poem." The scholar concludes that Rodríguez

> is one of Chicano literature's most gifted and committed artists today. He is also an activist, whose action, above all, is to strike at our complacency.... His is a refreshing voice—of rebellion and beauty—in an increasingly narrow age of literature's disengagement from the ground of great art and true history.

CRITICISM

Michael Allen Holmes

Holmes is a writer with existential interests. In the following essay, he examines how in "The Concrete River," hallucination brings revelation.

It is not difficult to find artists who have dabbled in drugs, perhaps even become dependent on them. Although mainstream society often prefers to ignore the notion, it is difficult to deny that alcohol and drugs are seen as playing a role in the creative process that some cannot fill in other ways. From writers like Charles Baudelaire, Ernest Hemingway, and Jack Kerouac, to painters and visual artists like Pablo Picasso and Andy Warhol, to musicians like Charlie Parker, Jimi Hendrix, and the Beatles, drug use has often been connected with revolutions in musical perception and artistic style. To be sure, not all drugs have positive creative effects; alcohol is associated with creativity primarily as a relaxant, but is known to have had devastating effects on many an artist's life. Otherwise, hallucinogens alone seem to promote revolutions in perception and give positive impetus to the creative impulse. A conservative reading of Luis J. Rodríguez's poem "The Concrete River" would look upon the narrator's drug use as a failure pure and simple, a low point in his life that offers no benefits and simply reflects poor life choices,

THE POET STILL WANTS TO ESCAPE, BUT
HE ENTIRELY IN HIS CONSCIOUS MIND, THAT
THE PLACE TO WHICH HE WANTS TO ESCAPE IS
THE WRONG PLACE."

perhaps in response to a difficult life. In such a reading, the utter lack of benefits to the drug use is demonstrated in the fact that the poem ends with the poet clinging to that momentary death he experienced; the drug presents such a lure to his senses that it threatens to end his life, and the threat is so powerful that the user does not even care about its being fulfilled. Many a youth's tragic death has come about in just such a nihilistic, if not actually willful, fashion. In "The Concrete River," though, the poet is left literally willing himself back toward death—a devastating conclusion. Perhaps, though, the ending should be interpreted another way. A more liberal reading might dare to suggest that the hallucination itself, despite being attained in such a perilous fashion, leads the poet to a hidden revelation.

The notion that the poem even contains a revelation is open to debate, since, again, the poet is left yet yearning for death; presumably an adequate revelation, about the world and his place in it, would turn the poet away from seeking his death through drug use. But the reader may easily assume that the poet did not meet such a death and moreover flourished in his later life, allowing him to write and publish this exquisite poem describing the experience. In respect to his survival, Rodríguez offers helpful context in his riveting memoir *Always Running*. He describes the same experience in prose, with such similarities of phrasing that one readily gathers that he adapted the language of the poem into the prose. The equivalencies make clear that the poem is almost entirely autobiographical, save one significant alteration: actually present at the time of the experience were two companions, Baba and Wilo. A few scattered details to the experience fill out the reader's sense of the poem (perhaps in ways other than originally imagined). The specific

location of the "makeshift hideout" was the Alhambra Wash; there was, in fact, some water in the waterway, but only a trickle. The steely sounds seem rather to have been coming from a radio playing Led Zeppelin nearby, and the family members envisioned by the poet included those still living.

Also in the prose text, Rodríguez helpfully clarifies, less cryptically than in the poem, just why he turned to sniffing inhalants, as well as his full consciousness of the effects:

> Spray was dangerous; it literally ate your brain. But it was also a great escape. The world became like jello, like clay, something which could be molded and shaped. Sounds became louder, clearer—pulsating. Bodies removed themselves from bodies, floating with the sun. I sought it so desperately. I didn't want to be this thing of bone and skin. With spray I became water.

It is clear, then, that the hallucination of the poem is an engulfing one, not only altering his perceptions but allowing him to mold them himself, as if at will, while also fully immersing him in the present moment—not unlike the way one immerses oneself in the present moment through the far more natural process of Zen meditation. The focus on sensory perceptions is a major component of the escape, bypassing the daily anxieties and concerns that hound his life—the racism, the violence, and the fear. While high he is no longer a person, in a way; he is as formless and feelingless as water. This, too, rings with mystical ideas: one's transcendent consciousness merges with the surrounding world, including nature as well as one's fellow human beings. In his essay *Nature*, Ralph Waldo Emerson—one of the authors who influenced the young Rodríguez—famously describes such a consciousness as that of a "transparent eyeball": "I am nothing; I see all; the currents of the Universal Being circulate through me; I am part or particle of God."

Regarding Rodríguez's memoir, more important than the event itself, in relation to the poem about it, is what the poet describes as happening afterward. At the time, his desperation was undeniable. He writes, about being returned to consciousness by his friend's life-saving effort: "A kind of grief overwhelmed me. I was no longer this dream. I was me again. I wished I did die." Later episodes in his life, however, left the experience in a different light. For

WHAT DO I READ NEXT?

- As quoted by Castillo, Rodríguez once said, "Poetry is the foundation of everything I do.... The written, powerful expressive language of poetry is the springboard for everything that I want to write." His other poetry collections include his debut volume, *Poems across the Pavement* (1989), *Trochemoche: New Poems* (1998), and *My Nature Is Hunger: New and Selected Poems, 1989–2004* (2005).

- An especially bright star in the Chicano poetry world is Jimmy Santiago Baca, who was born two years before Rodríguez and is of both Mexican and Apache descent. Like Rodríguez, Baca was drawn into an edgy, violent lifestyle as a youth, and he ended up in prison, where he learned to read and began writing poetry. His collection *Immigrants in Our Own Land and Selected Early Poems* is available in the original 1979 edition and an expanded 1990 edition.

- Chicana poet Marisela Norte is another strong voice coming out of East Los Angeles, with verse that focuses on the experience of the city. She has honed her voice through powerful spoken-word readings. Her debut collection is *Peeping Tom Tom Girl* (2008).

- A volume that Rodríguez has cited as being an important influence on him is *Down These Mean Streets* (1967), the autobiography of Piri Thomas, a man of Cuban, Puerto Rican, and African descent who was raised in the barrios of New York City and was drawn into gang life.

- Although they mostly met in New York, the Beat poets came to call California home (between wanderings, that is), especially after Allen Ginsberg's spine-tingling, jaw-droppingly momentous reading of his long poem "Howl" in San Francisco in 1955. First published in *Howl and Other Poems* (1956), it deals with the ways that society oppresses the individual, especially creative individuals, and includes reference to mature content, such as regarding the Beats' use of mind-expanding substances.

- The young-adult anthology *Mindscapes: Poetry for the Real World* (1971) was published right around the time of the experience recorded in "The Concrete River," in which the poet's mindscape plays such an important role. Edited by Richard Peck, the collection includes verse by Robert Frost, Lawrence Ferlinghetti, W. H. Auden, and others.

---

one thing, he started dating a girl who shared his appreciation for sniffing, and who in fact enjoyed it so much she started doing it often without him—and suffering consequences: "Sniffing took the best out of her.... Payasa became too much like the walking dead." He broke up with her, she attempted suicide, and she ended up in a rehabilitation hospital.

Payasa's story transitions into Rodríguez's own brush with suicide, carried out far more deliberately than his near-death experience with sniffing. He even touched a blade to his skin, repeatedly—but, as he movingly writes,

each time this song became louder in my head, a song which wouldn't let up, as the melody resonated through me and the emptiness inside compressed into itself. Soon I filled up with a sense of being, of worth, with a clarity that I belonged here on this earth, at this time. Somehow, some way, it all had meaning. *I* made sense. There in the garage. Alone but alive. I barely made it. I almost got to the light. And somehow I knew the light wasn't all the great feeling, hope and desire I thought at the time it would be. I stumbled upon the blackness; I had dared to cross the light, to enter the other side, beyond the barrier, into the shadow. But I had been yanked back just in time.

The passage makes a fitting conclusion to "The Concrete River"; it presents the affirmation of life that the poem is missing. That this affirmation did exist is a great relief, but the question about how the poet reached it is left open. One might turn, then, to the poem, and see what might be read between the lines of the hallucinatory experience.

The opening stanza hints that something at least pseudo-spiritual, perhaps genuinely spiritual, is going on, with the persona of God being infused into the spray fumes themselves. Notably, Buddhist monks acknowledge that the Buddha—meaning, effectively, the divine energy of the universe—is to be found in both the highest and the lowliest things, including rocks, dirt, and even fecal matter. If he is not being ironic, Rodríguez may have a similar notion here. As far as possible transcendence goes, the chaos of the graffiti can be seen as a step in the right direction, as suggested by a line from *The Book of Chuang tzu* that seems to speak directly to the poet by the concrete river: "By the light shining out of chaos, the sage is guided; he does not make use of distinctions but is led on by the light." Still, the setting remains largely ordinary up to the point when the chemicals are inhaled, and line 30 marks the onset of visual hallucination.

Whether the river the poet envisions should be seen as fascinating or frightening is not entirely clear at first. The steaming and bubbling would seem to suggest a dangerous degree of heat. And snakes, among Anglo Americans at least, are often figured as perilous, both physically and morally—thanks in no small part to the serpent embodying evil in the biblical Garden of Eden. But in cultures of the Southwest, snakes are often worshipped as guardians and divine representatives. In the poet's experience, the snakelike river indeed seems to provide a positive service, obscuring the nightmares of ordinary waking life (as the lines seem to mean), issuing flying symbols of freedom (the birds) from its midst, and representing a perfect clarity, not unlike the perfect clarity of the pure blue sky overhead, thus implying purity. Indeed, this envisioned river is completely unlike the darkness and poison on the ground and in the air about them.

The poet's vision of the river, then, is like an embodiment of purest nature—mirroring the sky above—in contrast to the mechanical nature of society, the oil and pollution. As his vision

evolves, the poet sees himself and his companion as the classic characters of Huck Finn and Tom Sawyer, signifying renewed youth and innocence, a capacity to step out into nature and simply be one with it. Nature is immediately presented as a maternal presence, with the dew dripping from the branches like milk from a mother's breast, suggesting how nature itself gives life to and nurtures its many children, animals and humans alike; all ultimately find sustenance from the earth.

With his visual hallucinations having taken him this far, the poet is led to his first impassioned lament—the first clear sign that he has a consciousness outside of the sniffing experience: his conscience, perhaps, looking at his own actions in the present moment. This critical consciousness has been led, apparently by the reflections about nature, to a sudden awareness of what people like him and his friend ought to be doing, as far as the natural order is concerned. They should not be forcing poisonous chemicals into their bodies while overlooking expanses of urban muck and concrete; they should be barefoot along the banks of a real river, toes hardened from a life in the wilderness. They should be like the petals of flowers blossoming as they engage in the age-old practice of play, such as with a ball—perhaps in a game of lacrosse, a sport invented by Native Americans.

The stanzas that follow contain the sort of imagery one might expect from a near-death experience. There are tunnels of light, reunions with loved ones, and even the poet's life flashing before his eyes, in a manner of speaking. The Christian connotation of such imagery, of course, is heaven: the light of heaven is supreme, those who have already died are to be met there, and to be sure one is in the right place, one's sins and good deeds are tallied up at the gates, in a flash. But to get to heaven, as constructed by the religion, one must die. There is no such thing, in a fundamentalist sense, as heaven on earth. The poet seems to realize this: he realizes that to reach this heavenly afterlife, he simply has to die, and that afterlife, he imagines, is one where all his hopes and dreams will finally be fulfilled.

But of course, there is the tallying of sins to be reckoned with—and as a budding gang member, it would suffice to say that Rodríguez was already racking up more demerits than credits. More to the point, he knows, in his soul, that using chemical inhalants to find something that

The speaker is homeless, sleeping on a dirty mattress with an old curtain for a front door (©*Boom Boom Bang Photo | Shutterstock.com*)

resembles inner peace is going in the wrong direction—right to an underground grave, if not all the way to the underworld. It is curious, of course, how in heaven one gets light without the heat of the flames, while in hell one gets a burning darkness; the constructs have managed to separate what in reality cannot be divided, the light from the flame. Rodríguez brings this notion to mind in the dazzling final stanza, with ambiguous wording that leaves the reader uncertain both where the poet is and the direction in which he is going. He wants to rise to the sky—to heaven—but it seems he can only try. As he reports in *Always Running*, "I tried to get up, but fell back to the ground." He is seeking light, but he cannot seem to get it from anywhere but the sun, which burns him; the light of his hallucination, too, seems to both blind him and burn him. He is inclined to think he is looking heavenward, but the corresponding sensation of heat suggests the opposite—he is on his way to hell;

he is being enticed to burn. The mention of swinging can be seen to grimly evoke the image of a self-hanged corpse. The poet still wants to escape, but he can see already, if not entirely in his conscious mind, that the place to which he wants to escape is the wrong place. In that place below, the white light will be dissipated into color, and the poet would be left exposed to flames, set to burn. Even as the poet reaches back toward the death he sought, his envisioning mind, let loose by the hallucination, has recognized that if he wants his soul to go up, he first must be sure that his body does not sink down.

Source: Michael Allen Holmes, Critical Essay on "The Concrete River," in *Poetry for Students*, Gale, Cengage Learning, 2017.

Publishers Weekly

In the following review, the anonymous reviewer writes that Rodríguez's poems are "best read aloud."

Active on the Chicago spoken-word scene, Rodriguez has appeared on a number of CD compilations and a PBS special, is the author of the memoir *Always Running: La Vida Loca, Gang Days in L.A.* and the founder of Tía Chucha press. His third collection, titled after the Spanish expression for "helter-skelter, pell mell; all over the place," takes street-tough rhythms and a flair for self-dramatization, and imbues them with a lyric sensibility, forging lines best read aloud: "I am capitalism's angry Christ, techno Quetzacoatl, toppling the temples/of modern thievery, of surplus value in word-art/—exploited, anointed, and perhaps double-jointed." More prevalent are loose free-verse narratives of Rodriguez's post-barrio life as a poet, father and husband. Getting frisked by the cops, running into "The Animal" from a rival section of East L.A. and worries over the next generation's trials and tribulations are all taken in stride, and offset by a section of imagistic vignettes: "Poems Too Short To Braid." Despite the poet's spoken-word tendencies, many of these tender poems easily hold their own on the page: "Whose Jalisco harangues the Jalisco in my stroll?/who lays across the ruins of Teotihuacan like rainwater;/whose face outlines the bathroom walls of cantinas;/who is the aguardiente that tongues my callused throat?"

Source: Review of *Trochemoche: Poems by Luis Rodriguez*, in *Publishers Weekly*, 2016.

Publishers Weekly

In the following review, The anonymous reviewer praises Rodríguez's talent for telling stories with his poems.

Rodriguez (*Poems Across the Pavement*) writes eloquently of "a severed America," of Mexicans exiled to "the armed camp called East Los Angeles," of laid-off laborers and evicted families—in short, of a populace locked out of privilege and prosperity. Turned away, they turn fury pk and desire inward—and implode. In the title poem, homeboys gather on the cement banks of the L.A. River to inhale aerosol fumes. Their ensuing visions transform "an urban-spawned / Stream of muck" into "a flow of clear liquid / On a cloudless day"—yet end in near suffocation. However, Rodriguez's men and women are more often the victims of the anger of others—especially the police. A moving elegy, "The Best of Us" tells how a few words exchanged by a young Mexican and the police end in the man's murder. But while

violence is always on the verge of eruption, beauty also blossoms in unusual places. As a couple dances in a dive, the poet notes "how a hand opens slightly, / shaped like a seashell, / in the small / of a back." This poetry is of the barrio yet stubbornly refuses to be confined in it—Rodriguez's perceptive gaze and storyteller's gift transport his world across neighborhood boundaries.

Source: Review of *The Concrete River*, in *Publishers Weekly*, 2016.

Jennifer Swann

In the following essay, Swann showcases what Rodríguez hopes to accomplish as the poet laureate of Los Angeles.

Ex-gang member, author, publisher, organizer, activist, lifelong Angeleno and Green Party California gubernatorial candidate Luis J. Rodriguez can officially add yet another hefty title to his resume: Poet Laureate of Los Angeles, as appointed by Mayor Eric Garcetti today at a ceremony at the Central Public Library. Rodriguez is only the second poet to earn the title, following Eloise Klein Healy, who resigned from the inaugural role last year to recover from an illness.

As L.A.'s poet laureate, Rodriguez will serve a two-year term in which he'll act as "the official ambassador of L.A.'s vibrant creative scene," a sort of spokesman for the written word, according to a statement issued by the mayor's office. It's a natural fit for Rodriguez, who's already been filling that role on his own, as the founder of Tia Chucha's Centro Cultural, a nonprofit bookstore and cultural center that fosters art, literary and music workshops in the largely Latino community of Sylmar.

In his new position, the best-selling author of the memoirs *Always Running, La Vida Loca: Gang Days in L.A.* and *It Calls You Back* is expected to host a series of readings, workshops and classes at the L.A. Public Library, which sponsors the poet laureate program, along with the Department of Cultural Affairs. The program is aimed at educating inner-city kids with limited access to poetry.

Rodriguez himself would have likely been the target audience for a program like this when he was a teenager. Growing up in San Gabriel, he was recruited to the Lomas gang at the age of 11, and at the age of 18 faced a six-year prison sentence that was dropped after letters of support flooded in from the community. He eventually found his voice and wrote about his experiences through poems like "The Concrete River": "I am a friend of books, prey of cops / lover of the barrio women / selling hamburgers and tacos / at the P&G Burger Stand."

In our 2012 People issue, Rodriguez talked to us about battling addiction, violence and *la vida loca* in East L.A. In the same issue the following year, Rodriguez's predecessor, Eloise Klein Healy, divulged her aspirations to read poetry at Dodger Stadium. As far as we know, that plan was never realized, but Rodriguez's ambitions are perhaps far more attainable.

In a statement about his appointment as L.A. Poet Laureate, he said: "To me, poetry is deep soul-talk, a powerful means to enlarge one's presence in the world." His goal? Making L.A. "a livable, welcome, and artistically alive city."

Source: Jennifer Swann, "New Poet Laureate Luis J. Rodriquez Wants to Make L.A. an 'Artistically Alive City,'" in *LA Weekly*, October 9, 2014.

Donna Seaman

In the following review, Seaman points out that Rodriguez features both humor and tragedy in his work.

Whether he's writing fiction, essays, children's books, or poetry, Rodriguez, an activist as well as an artist and the son of Mexican immigrants, writes of the anguish and anger, determination and revelation experienced by individuals driven from one world and not welcomed in another, and those who are maligned and marginalized for their ethnicity even in the country of their birth. Following his first novel, *Music of the Mill* (2005), this haunting retrospective volume gathers selections from *Poems across the Pavement* (1989), *The Concrete River* (1991), and *Trochemoche* (1998) and presents more than two-dozen deeply affecting new poems. Beginning with a border-crossing poem, "Running to America," and ending with "The Wanton Life," a wrenching yet empowering poem to the poet's imprisoned son, this potent volume embraces the tough life of the barrio and the transcendent life of the spirit. Rodriguez also writes resoundingly of the lies and tragedy of war, the strength of women, and the beauty of the earth, and he parses the absurdities of life with knowing humor.

Source: Donna Seaman, Review of *My Nature Is Hunger: New & Selected Poems*, in *Booklist*, Vol. 101, No. 22, August 2005, p. 1963.

SOURCES

Acuña, Rodolfo F., *Anything but Mexican: Chicanos in Contemporary Los Angeles*, Verso, 1996, pp. 19–38.

"A Brief History of the Drug War," Drug Policy Alliance website, http://www.drugpolicy.org/facts/new-solutions-drug-policy/brief-history-drug-war-0 (accessed September 27, 2016).

Bruce-Novoa, *Chicano Poetry: A Response to Chaos*, University of Texas Press, 1982, pp. 3–10.

Castillo, Dina G., "Luis J. Rodríguez," in *Dictionary of Literary Biography*, Vol. 209, *Chicano Writers: Third Series*, edited by Francisco A. Lomeli and Carl R. Shirley, The Gale Group, 1999.

Chuang-tzu, *The Book of Chuang Tzu*, translated by Martin Palmer, Elizabeth Breuilly, Chang Wai Ming, and Jay Ramsay, Arkana, 1996, p. 15.

Emerson, Ralph Waldo, *Nature*, in *Selected Writings of Ralph Waldo Emerson*, edited by William H. Gilman, Signet Classic, 1983, p. 193.

Florido, Adrian, "Declining Interest in 'Chicano Studies' Reflects a Latino Identity Shift," KPBS (San Diego, CA) website, March 6, 2013, http://www.kpbs.org/news/2013/mar/06/declining-interest-chicano-studies-reflects-latino/ (accessed September 27, 2016).

"Patt Morrison Asks: L.A.'s Poet Laureate Luis J. Rodríguez," in *Los Angeles Times*, March 30, 2016, http://www.latimes.com/opinion/op-ed/la-le-patt-morrison-asks-poet-laureate-luis-j-rodriguez-20160329-story.html (accessed September 25, 2016).

Review of *The Concrete River*, in *Publishers Weekly*, Vol. 238, No. 22, May 17, 1991, p. 58.

Rodríguez, Andrés, "Contemporary Chicano Poetry: The Work of Michael Sierra, Juan Felipe Herrera, and Luis J. Rodríguez," in *Bilingual Review/La Revista Bilingüe*, Vol. 21, No. 3, September–December 1996, pp. 203–18.

Rodríguez, Luis J., *Always Running: La Vida Loca; Gang Days in L.A.*, Touchstone, 1993, pp. 1–131.

———, "The Concrete River," in *The Concrete River*, Curbstone Press, 1991, pp. 38–41.

Salazar, Ruben, "La Ley—The Law," in *Los Angeles: Biography of a City*, edited by John and Laree Caughey, University of California Press, 1976, pp. 431–33; originally published in *Strangers in One's Land*, US Civil Rights Commission, 1970.

Swann, Jennifer, "New Poet Laureate Luis J. Rodríguez Wants to Make L.A. an 'Artistically Alive City,'" in *LA Weekly*, October 9, 2014, http://www.laweekly.com/arts/new-poet-laureate-luis-j-rodriguez-wants-to-make-la-an-artistically-alive-city-5136665 (accessed September 25, 2016).

Watanabe, Teresa, and Hector Becerra, "500,000 Pack Streets to Protest Immigration Bills," in *Los Angeles Times*, March 26, 2006, http://articles.latimes.com/2006/mar/26/local/me-immig26 (accessed September 27, 2016).

FURTHER READING

Herrera, Juan Felipe, *Half of the World in Light: New and Selected Poems*, University of Arizona Press, 2008.

Named California's poet laureate in 2012 and US poet laureate in 2015, Herrera is among the most decorated of Chicano poets. He was born to migrant workers and raised in various locales up and down California. This collection presents some of his best work from years past, as well as more recent verse.

Palley, Reese, *Concrete: A Seven-Thousand-Year History*, Quantuck Lane Press, 2010.

One might imagine that the topic of concrete would not be weighty enough to merit a volume of over two hundred pages devoted to historical discussions and photographs of its architectural use. This volume, though, provides a look at the history, environmental impact, and potential future of this versatile material.

Rodríguez, Luis J., *The Republic of East L.A.: Stories*, Rayo, 2002.

Although he has favored poetry as well as autobiography, Rodríguez has produced fiction as well, including one novel (*Music of the Mill*) and this short fiction collection, which provides a sweeping portrayal of the various turns life takes for youths in the LA barrios.

Sheff, David, *Clean: Overcoming Addiction and Ending America's Greatest Tragedy*, Houghton Mifflin Harcourt, 2013.

Drawing on the most recent scientific, medical, and psychological research and expert opinions, Sheff provides a straightforward, accessible discussion of how to help oneself or others overcome addiction, especially the sorts of addictions that could prove fatal.

SUGGESTED SEARCH TERMS

Luis Rodríguez AND "The Concrete River"

Luis Rodríguez AND interview

Mexican Americans AND California

Mexican Americans AND Los Angeles

Chicano poetry

poetry AND Los Angeles

poetry AND gang life

gang life AND photography

East Los Angeles AND photography

Luis Rodríguez AND Always Running AND controversy

Eagle Poem

JOY HARJO

1990

Joy Harjo is one of the well-known American Indian poets who appeared during the second wave of the Native American Renaissance in the 1970s. Her book of poems *In Mad Love and War* (1990), in which "Eagle Poem" appears, is divided between poems about war, the war of Indian peoples to survive, and about love. "Eagle Poem" appears in the half about love. In this poem, the speaker and her friends see an eagle flying over the river. In that moment, the speaker is able to pray and explains what prayer is and what it does. Prayer blesses. She feels at one with everything in creation when she prays in this manner.

Harjo is known for the joy and compassion in her poetry, though she speaks with candor about being marginalized as a Native American woman and about the hardships of her people. Now a grandmother and jazz musician as well as a poet, Harjo seems bent on moving toward the impulses of love and forgiveness that have always been present in her work in its deep understanding of human nature. In her latest collection of poetry, *Conflict Resolution for Holy Beings* (2015), Harjo dedicates the volume to poets, workers for justice, dancers, singers, and visionaries, claiming that humans will make it through difficult times despite all odds because there is only love. She turns the pressure of centuries of racial hatred into pearls of great beauty and wisdom in such poems as "Talking with the Sun" and "This Morning I Pray for My

Joy Harjo *(©J. Vespa / WireImage / Getty Images)*

Enemies," in which enemies become friends. She points out the paradox that she is singing a song that can only come from having lost her country, a reference to the Trail of Tears that her Musko-gee ancestors walked from Alabama to Okla-homa under the cruel policy of Indian removal from their ancestral homes. Despite her tribal and personal history of loss, Harjo has a strength and vision that leads out of darkness.

AUTHOR BIOGRAPHY

Joy Foster was born on May 9, 1951, in Tulsa, Oklahoma, to Allen and Wynema Baker Foster. Her father was a full-blooded Muskogee—the main tribe of the Creek confederacy—and her mother was Cherokee, French, and Irish. Her father was a construction worker who died of asbestos lung disease. Her mother waitressed and cooked in truck stops. In 1970, Joy took the surname of her Muskogee grandmother,

Naomi Harjo. She is enrolled as a member of the Muskogee Tribe. Harjo credits her great-aunt Lois Harjo Ball, to whom Harjo dedicated her verse collection *She Had Some Horses*, with teaching her about her Indian identity.

Having won prizes in school for her visual art, Harjo at sixteen enrolled in the Institute of American Indian Arts in Santa Fe, hoping to be a painter, like her Muskogee aunt and grand-mother, and also to escape the domestic tension at home with a stepfather. In an early teen mar-riage, a son, Phil, was born to her at seventeen. She had a daughter, Rainy Dawn, in a marriage with Acoma Pueblo poet Simon J. Ortiz when she was twenty-two. She divorced and became a single mother, raising her children and working as a waitress and nursing assistant while she pursued her education.

Harjo graduated from the University of New Mexico in 1976 with a BA in poetry after she decided to switch from art to writing. She received her MFA in creative writing from the University of Iowa in 1978 and has held teaching positions at the Institute of American Indian Arts, Santa Fe Community College, Arizona State University, the University of Colorado, the University of New Mexico, the University of California at Los Angeles, and the University of Illinois. Important influences on her poetry included Ortiz, Leslie Marmon Silko, Galway Kinnell, Meridel Le Sueur, Audre Lorde, and Pablo Neruda.

Books of her poetry and stories include *The Last Song* (1975); *What Moon Drove Me to This?* (1979); *She Had Some Horses* (1983); *In Mad Love and War* (1990), which includes "Eagle Poem"; *The Woman Who Fell from the Sky* (1994); *A Map to the Next World: Poetry and Tales* (2000); *How We Became Human: New and Selected Poems, 1975–2001* (2004); and *Conflict Resolution for Holy Beings* (2015). With Gloria Bird she edited an important anthology called *Reinventing the Enemy's Language: Contempo-rary Native Women's Writings of North America* (1997). Harjo contributed poetic prose to accom-pany photographs by Stephen Strom in *Secrets from the Center of the World* (1989) and has writ-ten two children's books, *The Good Luck Cat* (2000), and *For a Girl Becoming* (2009). She has been an editor for literary journals and a member of the Native American Public Broadcasting Consortium board of directors, as well as a nar-rator and scriptwriter for educational television.

Harjo plays tenor and soprano saxophone with her band Poetic Justice to accompany readings of her poems on her music CD *Letter from the End of the Twentieth Century* (1997). Other music CDs include *Native Joy for Real* (2004), *She Had Some Horses* (2006), *Winding through the Milky Way* (2008), and *Red Dreams: A Trail beyond Tears* (2010). She published the autobiography *Crazy Brave: A Memoir* in 2012. Selected awards include the American Book Award from the Before Columbus Foundation, the William Carlos Williams Award, the American Indian Distinguished Achievement in the Arts Award, the Lifetime Achievement Award from the Native Writers Circle of the Americas, and the Academy of American Poets' Wallace Stevens Award.

POEM TEXT

To pray you open your whole self
To sky, to earth, to sun, to moon
To one whole voice that is you.
And know there is more
That you can't see, can't hear,   5
Can't know except in moments
Steadily growing, and in languages
That aren't always sound but other
Circles of motion.
Like eagle that Sunday morning   10
Over Salt River. Circled in blue sky
In wind, swept our hearts clean
With sacred wings.
We see you, see ourselves and know
That we must take the utmost care   15
And kindness in all things.
Breathe in, knowing we are made of
All this, and breathe, knowing
We are truly blessed because we
Were born, and die soon within a   20
True circle of motion,
Like eagle rounding out the morning
Inside us.
We pray that it will be done
In beauty.   25
In beauty.

POEM SUMMARY

The text used for the following summary is from *In Mad Love and War*, Wesleyan University Press, 1990, p. 65. A version of the poem can be found on the following web page: https://www.poetryfoundation.org/poems-and-poets/poems/detail/46545.

Lines 1–3

"Eagle Poem" concerns and addresses an eagle that the speaker and her friends saw circling the sky over Salt River in Arizona on a Sunday morning. Inspired by this sight, the speaker begins with the infinitive form of the verb *to pray*. This poem will be about how to pray and will itself be a prayer. The verb is followed by a description of the kind of prayer the eagle inspires: one should be completely open to the whole self and environment in order to pray. This is a surprising beginning because the speaker identifies prayer not with a request to receive something concrete but with a state of being completely oneself, completely open, not only to oneself but also to nature—to sky, earth, sun, and moon. All these together constitute the complete voice of oneself. Thus, in this opening the speaker establishes a state of unity between nature and the self. This must be where prayer starts and ends, a unified state of life rather than a division between a petitioner and a god. Prayer brings everything together. This togetherness is identified as a voice, one's own voice.

The first three lines are roughly iambic tetrameter, with the emphasis on the strong syllables creating drumbeats of self, sky, earth, sun, and moon, making them in a sense equivalent, all the parts of one's own voice and, indeed, of oneself. The direct address to the reader or listener as *you* makes the speaker's voice sound both intimate and authoritative. The speaker's voice gains further authority through the ecstasy created by seeing the eagle and its message. The visionary speaker knows what the eagle is telling her about prayer.

Lines 4–9

The speaker continues in this same ecstatic state of mind to unfold the poem's message. There is more to you than you can see or hear or know except in certain moments. The line break at the end of line 6 creates the space in which one can feel that kind of moment outside of ordinary time, where you can know the part of you beyond the senses, beyond hearing or seeing. The parallel construction to the negations—cannot see, cannot hear, cannot know—makes powerful repetition, putting the listener in another mode of perception. The speaker is affirming something and negating something at the same time.

MEDIA ADAPTATIONS

- Harjo's music CD *Native Joy for Real* contains "Eagle Poem" as "Eagle Song." It was originally published by Mekko Productions in 2004 and later released by CD Baby in 2016. She plays saxophone with her jazz band.

- Harjo reads "Eagle Poem," again as "Eagle Song," in a music video made by Mekko Productions, directed by Lurline Wailana McGregor in 2002 and uploaded to YouTube at https://www.youtube.com/watch?v=y8mEdBmC9Jo on November 5, 2007. Harjo plays saxophone with a group of jazz musicians featured with her, over footage of herself teaching young girls stomp dancing.

- "Poems are Houses for Spirits" is a discussion (twenty-eight minutes long) between Harjo and host Barbara Goldberg on the show *The Writing Life*, sponsored by the Howard County Poetry and Literature Society in Columbia, Maryland. It was filmed in 2008 and uploaded to YouTube at https://www.youtube.com/watch?v=fJJLtJnl8qM on December 14, 2012. Harjo discusses the poetic process, plays flute, and reads four poems: "This Morning I Pray for My Enemies," "I Give You Back," "Emergence," and "My House Is the Red Earth."

- Bill Moyers speaks with Harjo, Garrett Kaoru, and Mary Tall Mountain in a fifty-six-minute show called "Ancestral Voices," on his *Power of the Word* series, recorded on September 29, 1989. On this program, available online at http://billmoyers.com/content/ancestral-voices-2/, Harjo reads "She Had Some Horses."

Line 7 continues the thought from line 6. The moments in which one knows something about oneself beyond the senses grow steadily in strength, and that is why one pays attention. It is a sort of language or communication beyond sound but through circles of motion like the eagle's. The eagle circles several times, and these circles are like circling back on oneself in a silent kind of knowing. The lines themselves recreate a silent circling motion.

Lines 10–13

This silent circling is like the eagle's on that Sunday morning over Salt River. As it circled in the blue sky and wind, it swept their hearts clean with its wings. In many Indian cultures the eagle is a messenger to the Creator and carries prayers. The eagle also carries the energies of courage, wisdom, strength, and truth. The onlookers feel the sweep of the eagle's purifying and strengthening powers. The epithet *sacred wings* lets the reader know that this is not just an ordinary eagle.

Lines 14–16

If the eagle carries prayers to the Creator, it also seems to be a messenger from the Creator. The speaker now addresses the eagle as *you* and explains the message the onlookers are receiving from the eagle. As they see the eagle, they see themselves and know they must do everything with care and kindness. The lesson about care and kindness is spoken in strong spondee metrical feet—two stressed syllables—creating emphasis and slowing down the rhythm.

Lines 17–23

The speaker now addresses the people, advising them to breathe in because they are made of everything that they experience. With one's breath one should know that one is blessed to be born and will die soon, but it is all within the circle of true motion, as the eagle represents that circle of life in its sweep. For Indian peoples, life is not linear but circular. It is like a breath from the Creator that is ultimately given back to the Creator. There is no loss in all this, for life itself

TOPICS FOR FURTHER STUDY

- The Indian removal policy of 1830 and the resulting Trail of Tears, with Indians forced from their lands and marched westward, was, among other things, part of the rising tension between southern states and the federal government leading to the American Civil War. Complete a written paper or an oral report, with visual slides and film cuts if possible, illustrating how race, including the future of both African Americans and Native Americans, became a core issue of the American Civil War.

- Many American Indian poets, such as Sherman Alexie and Harjo, have laid claim to the universal values of African American jazz, incorporating it into their own music and philosophy. Create a blog or wiki on the Indian-African connection through jazz, including audio files and film clips.

- "Eagle Poem" is a prayer. Have members of a group each bring a prayer from a different tradition, religion, or culture and present it, explaining the references and philosophy behind it. Record the prayers and put the spoken prayers along with explanations on a group website dedicated to world religions or upload them to YouTube.

- Harjo's adopted land is Hawaii, where she enjoys outrigger canoeing. The Hawaiian renaissance of the 1970s brought back the sacred knowledge of hula and Hawaiian stories. Read the young-adult novel *One Shark, No Swim* (2013), book 2 in the Niuhi Shark Saga, by Lehua Parker, who grew up on the islands and knows the old tales. In her novel, the boy Zader is allergic to water but is adopted into a family of fishermen. His uncle Kahana is an elder who teaches him. In a discussion of the story, point out native Hawaiian views of nature and compare them to American Indian views. Then write a poem or short story about some incident that illustrates your own connection to nature.

continues. There is repetition in lines 18–20 with the alliteration and consonance of the *b* and *s* sounds.

The circle of life is like the circle of the eagle happening inside of us. It is bringing us a message about ourselves. Nature outside is the same as the nature inside. There is no separation of outer and inner truth. The eagle tells us about our own lives.

Lines 24–26

The speaker and the onlookers pray that their own circling of life will be done in beauty. *In beauty* is repeated twice and recalls the Navajo Beauty Way chant, holding that everything be beautiful before and behind, above and below. For something sacred to be done in beauty means properly in ritual and in harmony with all things. This is what the speaker learns from the eagle. The eagle is sacred and teaches the onlookers what prayer is and what a life well lived means. The eagle is a sacred being emanating the cleansing power of prayer and connection to the sacred. When the witnesses see it they are touched by its circles and participate in a universal prayer with it.

THEMES

Native American Culture

Harjo's poem celebrates the American Indian perception of self as part of nature. Nature is not an external phenomenon to be controlled. The speaker of the poem makes a major event out of seeing an eagle over the river. This is not trivial chance or bird-watching, but a religious experience, for the eagle is a messenger from the

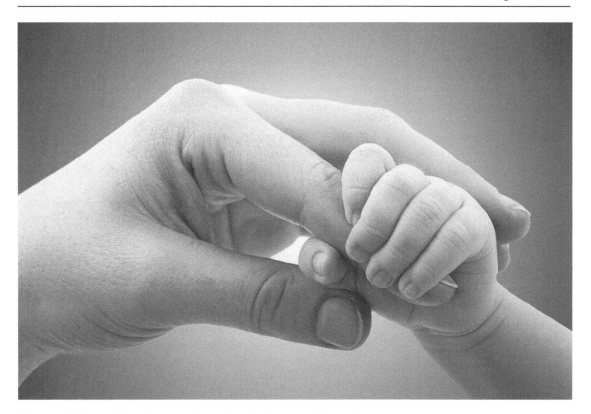

Human births and deaths echo the cycles of the natural world *(©Evgeny Atamanenko / Shutterstock.com)*

Creator and teaches the onlookers about the right way to behave and worship. The eagle is teaching the speaker how to pray. This prayer is not about asking for something but a way to be part of creation. The eagle is endowed with sacred power and can give gifts and wisdom. Native American religions do not see nature as evil or lower than human nature. All of nature is sacred and must be treated with respect. Here, the speaker learns a sense of responsibility from the eagle, to do everything carefully and with beauty and harmony, just as the eagle carefully circles the river. One's life must be lived in conscious harmony with other beings.

Unity

The speaker has a mystical experience of the oneness of all life when seeing the eagle soaring over the river. The eagle's circular flight is the outward visual sight of something that is happening within the speaker's awareness. The circular motion of the bird is like the circular motion within that makes her feel whole. That is the way she conceives of prayer, as an act or perception of wholeness, being and feeling her whole and real self. The eagle is authentic and truthful in his flight, and this cleanses the speaker's heart, taking away what is false and small. The eagle tells her about the part of herself that cannot be seen or known through the senses but is real and exalted like his flight. The eagle opens her to her inmost self, that inner voice that unites everything, perhaps the source of her poetic voice. She mentions that this unity of nature and self is a whole voice of life equivalent to the deepest part of a person. The unity can be experienced simply by breathing in, for we are made of everything we take in. We are the eagle and the river, the earth and the sun. The sense of unity with nature brings with it the feeling of the sacredness of all life.

Transformation

One of Harjo's major themes in her poetry is transformation. Transformation is a process always going on in nature—cleansing, renewing, and evolving. In this poem, the eagle is the agent of transformation for the speaker. The event of seeing his flight over the river becomes a ritual of purification: his wings are sacred and sweep the heart clean. She is inspired to live her life more fully and consciously, with beauty and care, as he reminds her to do in his flight. His soaring over the river is her prayer, the way to pray, and the answer to her prayer. Eagle teaches her to pray by opening her whole self to life. In this way she breathes in the essence of life and unity with the other beings. She wants to surrender to a greater wholeness that is at once nature and herself.

STYLE

Contemporary Native American Poetry

Native American poets, many of whom prefer to be called American Indians, assert their roots in traditional life, but also speak of the challenges for traditional peoples in the contemporary world. They speak and write in English and are educated in universities, yet many Indian writers retain the flavor of oral tribal poetry by performing their poems with music, like Harjo and Simon J. Ortiz do. "Eagle Poem" gives a direct experience without the ironic filters and distancing personae of modernist poets. Figures in American Indian poetry often have mythic qualities, as with Harjo's character Noni Daylight in "Someone Talking." Here, the eagle—who, notably, is referred to not as "the eagle" but simply as "eagle," as if that is his name, not simply the type of animal he is—is not an animal or a symbol of something else, but a sacred personality.

Free Verse

Harjo's poem appears in English as free verse, that is, a poem with rhythm and line breaks and occasional meter but without a certain form, rhyme scheme, or fixed meter. This is the predominant contemporary form of poetry, replacing the older set forms such as the sonnet, the ballad, or blank verse. Having attended the Iowa Writers' Workshop, Harjo is familiar with an array of poetic forms, such as the prose poem, but here she uses the free-verse form to capture the experience of the eagle's flight. Free verse does not have regular meter, but this poem is in underlying iambic, with unstressed followed by stressed syllables, over differing line lengths and with many spondees, two strong beats together, for a stronger rhythm. The shorter lines create emphasis and focus attention. Frequent use of enjambment, or the continuation of a sentence beyond the end of a line and into the next, in this poem re-creates the feel of the eagle's flight of circling without needing to stop. Repetition is part of the rhythm of any poem, regardless of form, but in this poem the repetition of words and sounds also reinforces the heightened feel of a Native ceremony.

Native American Ceremony, Myth, and Song

Native American ceremony is an underlying structure of most modern American Indian poetry because it produces a certain perception and experience of the world. Tribal ceremonies use incantation, song, dance, prayer, visual symbols, and gestures to restore wholeness to the land and community. Oral traditions had the purpose of reminding the community of its links with cosmic forces. The ceremonies, such as the Navajo Night Chant, used for healing, were sacred and performed at specific times and places. "Eagle Poem" is itself a ceremony for reinvigorating the heart and restoring wholeness to the speaker and her friends. As the speaker sees the eagle, she is transported to a sacred perception of him and his power. She participates with him in ceremonial prayer, a sort of union with cosmic forces. Eagle brings his gifts of wisdom, courage, and connection from the Creator, when invoked, as here. The oral tradition is felt in the voice Harjo creates in the poem, a voice of authority and wisdom and vision. It is not the confessional voice of an individual modern poet but is impersonal in identifying with the history of a people and the forces of the land.

HISTORICAL CONTEXT

Trail of Tears

The Trail of Tears is central in Harjo's writing because it is part of her family history. The Trail of Tears was part of a certain episode in Indian removal but is emblematic of the forced relocation of all Indians away from their homelands. The Indian Removal Act of 1830 legitimized the moving of several Native American tribes from the southeastern United States off their traditional lands to reservations in the western territories, beyond the Mississippi River, then deemed uninhabitable land for European Americans.

COMPARE & CONTRAST

- **1990:** Despite the act protecting golden and bald eagles since 1940, bald eagles remain on the endangered species list.

  Today: Bald eagles are off the endangered list but still under protection. Only enrolled members of Native American tribes can legally own eagle feathers and must apply for them.

- **1990:** The Salt River flows through Fort Apache Reservation and supplies much of the water to Phoenix as a result of the Salt River Project, the building of a series of dams to control the river, including Roosevelt Dam, in 1911.

  Today: Whitewater rafting in Salt River Canyon is advertised on Facebook and popular with tourists, who can be seen on inner tubes crowding the river from shore to shore by the hundreds.

- **1990:** Harjo is part of the Native American Renaissance, which includes writers who capture Indian heritage in poems like "Eagle Poem."

  Today: Younger American Indian poets do not stick to remembering Indian ways in verse but branch out into mainstream styles and projects, including music, filmmaking, and satiric novels and stories. Harjo experiments with combining saxophone and poems on CDs.

This act, though vigorously opposed by Indians and Christian missionaries, was passed during the administration of President Andrew Jackson and pushed by white southerners who wanted prime Indian land in Georgia, Tennessee, Alabama, and Florida.

The early American presidents, in particular, George Washington and Thomas Jefferson, had established a policy of Indian acculturation among southeastern tribes, promising they could keep their land if they adopted Western culture and the Christian religion. The five tribes who submitted to this agreement were called the five civilized tribes: the Chicasaw, the Choctaw, the Muskogee-Creek, the Seminole, and the Cherokee. Many in these tribes had become university educated, earning livelihoods as landowners, farmers, Christian ministers, and professionals like lawyers and businessmen—they were leaders of their people. The conflict for the Jackson administration, which sought to trample the policy of acculturation, partly involved the power struggle between the federal government and the southern states, a constitutional problem that would be settled only with the Civil War, when Abraham Lincoln asserted the supremacy of federal law. Southern states believed they had the legal right to remove the Indians and did not believe the Indians could be given sovereignty over land except by the federal government. In that case, in the South's opinion, they would have to move to a federal territory in the West. The southern states thus asserted their own local right to the land, especially after gold was discovered in Georgia in 1829 near Dahlonega, on Cherokee land, resulting in a gold rush.

The Indian Removal Act was passed by Congress and authorized by President Andrew Jackson but was challenged by both Indian and white lawyers. At first the Supreme Court ruled in favor of the state of Georgia in the 1831 case *Cherokee Nation v. Georgia*. In 1832 this was overturned by the Supreme Court under Justice John Marshall in *Worcester v. Georgia*, recognizing the Cherokee as a sovereign nation. The federal court had recognized the right of the Cherokee to their land, but this bypassed the authority of the state of Georgia. Jackson saw this as a crisis that threatened civil war, with Georgia insisting that its own law prevailed over federal law. Georgia ignored the Supreme Court decision and allowed the removal by state

The image of the eagle recalls a Native American myth (©GUDKOV ANDREY / Shutterstock.com)

and local militia, who forcibly drove the Indians from their homes. Throughout the Southeast, Jackson continued pushing tribes to sign treaties and allowing federal and state troops to enforce their removal to land west of the Mississippi, for their own safety, he explained, as he ignored the Supreme Court decision. The Choctaw were removed in 1831, the Seminoles in 1832, the Creeks in 1834, the Chickasaw in 1837, and finally the Cherokee in 1838. The Cherokee were forced on a long march of a thousand miles on foot without warm clothes or supplies, during winter, from Tennessee to Oklahoma. Thousands perished from cold and hardship. Within these few years almost fifty thousand Indians were removed to the West, and twenty-five million acres of land were opened for whites in the Southeast.

The French philosopher Alexis de Tocqueville, who was to write the celebrated study *Democracy in America* (1835), witnessed and wrote about the heart-wrenching march of the Choctaw on what they called their trail of death and tears when he was in Memphis, Tennessee, in 1831. Seminoles resisted removal in the Seminole Wars under Chief Osceola. They had to leave eventually, but one band of Seminoles escaped to the Everglades and never capitulated. The Chickasaws received monetary compensation for their land and were able to take their belongings to Oklahoma Territory, where they merged with the Choctaw nation. In the twenty-first century, many of America's indigenous people are primarily located as cultural nations in California, Arizona, and Oklahoma, owing to the removal policies.

Red Stick War

Harjo's great-great-grandfather was the Muskogee-Creek leader Menawah (ca. 1765–1835). He was a chief and fought in the Red Stick War against the United States as part of the Indian Wars.

The Red Sticks were a faction within the Creek nation who did not want to modernize and take on Western ways. They grew violent, a band of about four thousand warriors who became a serious threat to the United States in the Southeast. The Creek War, or Red Stick War (1813–1814), was one of the campaigns of Major General Andrew Jackson (1767–1845), who became the seventh president and signed the Indian Removal Act. He was known as a successful Indian fighter and appears in Harjo's writings as a villain. Though Menawah survived the Battle of Horseshoe Creek, he died during the tribal march from Alabama to Oklahoma on the Trail of Tears. An image of her ancestors walking to Oklahoma occurs in Harjo's poem "Protocol."

Self-determination

The final attempt to assimilate the Native population came with the planned policy of termination in the 1950s and 1960s. This policy was designed to take all Native Americans off the reservations and relocate them to cities, thus disbanding their tribal groups and taking their lands for their natural resources. It meant the government would no longer recognize tribal sovereignty. With the example of the black civil rights movement of the 1960s, Native American activist groups were formed and fought termination. In 1975 the Indian Self-Determination and Education Assistance Act allowed Native Americans to form their own governing bodies and to keep their reservations. In 1978 the American Indian Freedom of Religion Act was passed.

Native American Renaissance

Harjo had a difficult childhood and could not speak very well. She began to express herself in painting, encouraged by the example of her Muskogee great-aunt, Lois Harjo Ball, and Muskogee grandmother, Naomi Harjo, whose surname she took. Both women were college-educated painters. Joy had an artistic gift and learned about her Indian heritage from her great-aunt Lois. Her path changed, however, because of the Native American Renaissance in the 1960s and 1970s. During this literary flourishing, Harjo discovered poetry and was briefly married to Simon J. Ortiz, the Acoma Pueblo poet of the first generation of this literary movement. He became her mentor, along with Leslie Marmon Silko, a lifelong friend. The main contributions of these artists have been to keep the memory of their peoples alive and to bring the richness of Indian voices into the mainstream of American art.

CRITICAL OVERVIEW

With her earlier book of poems *She Had Some Horses* (1983), Harjo became well known as an important voice for contemporary American Indian culture. The collection *In Mad Love and War* (1990), for which she won an American Book Award from the Before Columbus Foundation, contains the poem "Eagle Poem." This collection became a turning point in positioning her as a major mainstream poet, as she successfully integrated Western literary forms with Native traditions. The book is concerned with politics and the transformational power of poetry. In a review of *In Mad Love and War* called "Nothing to Lose" in the *Women's Review of Books* for 1990, Margaret Randall speaks of the increasing power and wildness of Harjo's poetry and how her "voice most relentlessly bridges the several worlds she inhabits." Randall calls the poetry "bright and courageous and well made."

Leslie Ullman, in a 1991 review called "Solitaries and Storytellers, Magicians and Pagans: Five Poets in the World" for the *Kenyon Review*, notes that Harjo speaks with "great sureness of spirit and the mercurial, expansive imagination of a conjurer" while demonstrating a "warrior-like compassion." Her stories "resurrect memory, myth, and private struggles." In a 1992 review of the book for *Prairie Schooner*, Kathleene West calls the poetry magical, from another dimension. It is an "exploration of the *beyond*," and Harjo's poetry "has the power and beauty of prophecy and all the hope of love poised at its passionate beginning." In a 1992 essay for *World Literature Today* called "Representing Real Worlds: The Evolving Poetry of Joy Harjo," John Scarry speaks of the influence of painting, film, and music in Harjo's poetry, of the "striking and crystalline images found throughout her poetry." He notes the intensity of her tone, the surreal landscapes, and emphasis on transformations.

In a 2011 foreword to *Soul Talk, Soul Language: Conversations with Joy Harjo*, Laura Coltelli mentions that Harjo depicts a geography of the soul in her poetry. This geography is rooted in her Indian heritage, but she has expanded the landscape over the years to include a reshaping of America itself, as she crosses the boundaries of other genres and cultures.

CRITICISM

Susan K. Andersen

Andersen is a teacher and writer with a PhD in English. In the following essay, she considers "Eagle Poem" in terms of American Indian philosophy.

Harjo's "Eagle Poem," like the eagle's motion it describes, circles out from a center to express a spiritual experience that encompasses the speaker and landscape in a unity she calls prayer. This prayer is not a request to a deity. It is not even a request. It is a communication with all living things. To pray, she says, one must open oneself completely to what is all around—the beings, nature, oneself. This wholeness has a voice and is a voice that results in the poem. This wholeness speaks itself through the speaker, the poet, who is inspired by the eagle's circled motion above. This poem announces a moral responsibility that depends on a sacred perception of where one fits into the cosmic order. The sight of this eagle has brought a very deep understanding of life to the speaker. She has been trained to know the language of eagles and of earth, sun, and moon by her upbringing as a Native woman and to be humbled by the gift of the eagle, though others might see it as just an animal in the sky. To her, eagle is a sacred being with a message, and she can hear and speak the message to others in this poem.

The first part of the poem explains what prayer is to the speaker. It is a moment of complete openness and clarity in which all things may enter one's awareness as they truly are. The immediate knowledge that this kind of prayer brings is not specific. It is the understanding that truth is beyond the senses—more than one can hear or see. These moments of revelation grow steadily in the speaker's life and come to her in many languages. The eagle's circles of motion are such a language to her.

First, the eagle circles and sweeps clean the hearts of the onlookers, Harjo and her friends, with its wings. Eagle feathers are often used in Indian ceremonies to take prayers to God, or the Great Spirit. The eagle's wings are not just a

> TO HER, EAGLE IS A SACRED BEING WITH A MESSAGE, AND SHE CAN HEAR AND SPEAK THE MESSAGE TO OTHERS IN THIS POEM."

symbol of prayer, but an instrument of prayer. The heart has to be swept clean before prayer can be effective, so the person can be in a state of innocence and receptivity. As the onlookers open in this innocence, they see the eagle as an aspect of themselves, and they can receive its wisdom. Eagle is known for precision, for courage, for seeing far. Humans too must act this way, with care, kindness, and awareness in their affairs. Eagle is a teacher.

All this is not the same as a romantic poet's use of imagination to portray an eagle as a symbol. Indian poet and scholar Paula Gunn Allen explains in her book *The Sacred Hoop: Recovering the Feminine in American Indian Traditions* that reference to a tree or a mountain in Native ceremony is not symbolic of a concept or of something else. It evokes precisely a tree or mountain, as though calling the name of that particular being to be present. Indian poetry uses symbols in the same sacred or magical way. For the Indian, eagle is a sacred personality and teaches directly through communion with its presence. Eagle speaks to the poet in this poem through its own language, making circles over the river.

The speaker asserts that the humans watching the eagle can get this message because if they breathe in, they breathe in the life they themselves are made of. Breath is spirit. All creatures have a common breath or spirit on the earth. They are not on the outside and isolated from one another but are inside the one living earth. Earth is their body, as it is the eagle's. They are all parts of a living unity. If one sees other beings in this way, not as the "other" but as oneself, it alters behavior and perception. If one truly sees all things around as an aspect of one's own being, one has to behave with care and kindness, as she says the eagle reminds them to do.

Paula Gunn Allen mentions that for Indians space and time are cyclical. They are represented

WHAT DO I READ NEXT?

- *Code Talker: A Novel about the Navajo Marines of World War Two* (2005), by Joseph Bruchac, is a young-adult novel telling the story of a Navajo boy raised in a school where his native tongue is forbidden. When he joins the marines in World War II, he becomes one of the Code Talkers, the Indian team that invented a Navajo code the Nazis and Japanese could not crack.

- Sandra Cisneros's *The House on Mango Street* (1984) is a young-adult coming-of-age book by a Mexican American writer who was Harjo's friend at the Iowa Writers' Workshop. It tells the story of a Latina girl, Esperanza Cordero, growing up in a Chicano neighborhood in Chicago.

- Jerry Ellis's *Walking the Trail: One Man's Journey along the Cherokee Trail of Tears* (1991) is a nonfiction account of walking the entire nine hundred miles of the Cherokee Trail of Tears from Alabama to Oklahoma, by a writer who is of Scottish and Cherokee descent. His ancestors lived in Alabama but escaped removal.

- Louise Erdrich's 1984 novel *Love Medicine* won the National Book Critics Circle Award. She is a Chippewa author who tells stories of love and difficult survival among Chippewa families in North Dakota on their land on Turtle Mountain Reservation.

- Harjo's award-winning collection *The Woman Who Fell from the Sky* (1994)

includes her poetry and tribal mythic stories, including "The Woman Who Fell from the Sky," a creation story retold in a city setting.

- Steve Inskeep's *Jacksonland: President Andrew Jackson, Cherokee Chief John Ross, and a Great American Land Grab* (2015) is a historical thriller about President Andrew Jackson and Cherokee Chief John Ross, who fought over the policy of removal in the 1830s. Ross took the case all the way to the Supreme Court and had allies in Senator Henry Clay, Chief Justice John Marshall, and Davy Crockett but still could not stop the brutal expulsion of Indians from their homelands in the southern states.

- Simon Ortiz's poem "Speaking," found in *A Good Journey* (1984), volume 12 of the Sun Tracks series, edited by Larry Evers, is a poem by Harjo's mentor with a theme similar to that of "Eagle Poem," about the communion and unity of humans with nature. Ortiz, a full-blood Acoma Pueblo, has noted that his people were never the victims of Indian removal but have been the caretakers of their land in New Mexico continuously for the last ten thousand years.

- Leslie Marmon Silko's *Storyteller* (1981) may have inspired the format of *The Woman Who Fell from the Sky*. It is a collection of original poems, autobiography, and retold Indian myths by Harjo's friend from the Pueblo Laguna tribe.

this way on the medicine wheel, or sacred hoop, the ceremonial circle or mandala of life. This circle includes everything and also describes the Native view of life as nonlinear. Humans are born and die within a circle of all beings, and their lives are only good if they have acted with respect and kindness to all, understanding they all share the same cycle of life with other creatures. In a circle,

no one is above another, no one wins over another. All are dependent on each other. This is the Indian way of life on the earth. The eagle shows them this true circular pattern of life, and the speaker's closing prayer that all will be done in beauty, an evocation of the Navajo Beauty Way, is a prayer that they may walk in harmony and balance with all beings.

The poem is therefore a ceremony. Allen mentions that the purpose of Native ceremony is to integrate humans with self, community, and nature: "Ceremonial literature serves to redirect private emotion and integrate the energy generated by emotion within a cosmic framework." Consciousness is expanded. Harjo has mentioned, in a 1987 interview with Joseph Bruchac, that "Eagle Poem" seems to have truly had the force of prayer or ceremony: a woman in the party at Salt River that day, who saw the eagle, liked Harjo's resulting poem and went to the same spot the next day to recite the poem aloud—and the eagle reappeared.

Laura Coltelli, in her introduction to *Joy Harjo: The Spiral of Memory; Interviews* mentions that Harjo's poetry, like a lot of modern Native poetry, is not descriptive poetry. This poem does not describe the sight of an eagle. Her poetry is "evocative." That is, it calls up the presence of creatures, things, and places through names, as this poem calls up the presence of the eagle. Coltelli adds that the key word for the volume *In Mad Love and War*, in which "Eagle Poem" appears, is "transformation." Allen points out that the notion of transformation reflects an old tribal point of view of nature. Objects are not fixed but understood to be undergoing constant metamorphosis. Everything is alive and interconnected, part of one vast and constant transformation of energy and form. The eagle is a power of nature that transforms the landscape and the watchers as it flies over. This emphasis on transformation moves the poem beyond message or meaning. Harjo explains the power of poetry to move the spirit of the listener and the spirit of nature.

In an interview with Bill Moyers, Harjo mentioned that prayer that opens the whole self, like she speaks of in "Eagle Poem," takes us beyond the world of separation and alienation we falsely create. The poet has to see beyond this shadow world to what is real. *In Mad Love and War*, Harjo related in an interview with Sharyn Stever, shows the spiritual and physical to be different vibrations of the same thing. To perceive the metaphysical aspect of the physical world is to see it as it is, she says.

Though most American Indian poets writing today write in English and are well versed in modern Western poetic form and theory, it is not possible to use Western critical methods alone to analyze Indian poetry based deeply in ceremony.

The poem asserts that with a true prayer, one must open up to the world (©Be Good | Shutterstock.com)

Harjo discusses this dilemma along with Gloria Bird in their introduction to their anthology of Native American women poets, *Reinventing the Enemy's Language: Contemporary Native Women's Writings of North America*. Indian poets are writing in English, the language of their European conquerors. Yet, almost paradoxically, Indian poets have become empowered by taking this foreign language and making it their own. Their way of perceiving the world still remains, as "Eagle Poem" testifies. They still use language to make ceremonies of healing, as "Eagle Poem" does. Their language still includes instead of excludes, as "Eagle Poem" takes in everything in a sacred circle.

Source: Susan K. Andersen, Critical Essay on "Eagle Poem," in *Poetry for Students*, Gale, Cengage Learning, 2017.

Julie Morse

In the following interview, Harjo talks about poets who have influenced her work.

" I ALWAYS TELL YOUNGER POETS TO FEED
THE SOURCE OF THE POETRY. TO GIVE HONOR
AND THANKS TO THOSE WHO CAME BEFORE US, AND
TO TAKE CARE OF THOSE WHO ARE FOLLOWING."

...The Rumpus: In your memoir, Crazy
Brave, *you talk about the "knowing." The "knowing" is a clairvoyant inkling that lets you know
when life is going to change course, How does the
"knowing" play a role in your life today?*

Joy Harjo: The "knowing" is a vast field of
intelligence beyond mental clatter and any kind of
dividing line. It can be seen as a being, and it is,
many beings, and it is, a geometric flow, and it is—
it is part of all of us, or, we are part of it. The
intelligence is metaphor to the thousandth-plus
power. It is small and it is large. Creative artists
immerse themselves in this flow. You cannot force
it. I believe you can feed it or turn your back on it;
no matter—it is still dynamically at work.

I listen to the "knowing" more directly and
willingly than I did when I was younger. I tend to
by hyper-analytic, which is useful, especially in
revision, but not when in the creative and/or
listening mode. I'm learning how to shift and
how to trust.

*Rumpus: How has the "knowing" influenced
your writing? Do you feel like your style has
changed as your awareness has grown?*

Harjo: The "knowing" is part of the inherent
person. A person is many streams of events:
persons come together in a coherent structure
(or maybe sometimes not so coherent!).

*Rumpus: You attended high school at the
Institute of American Indian Arts and studied a
myriad of mediums, among them poetry. You say
in* Crazy Brave, *"We began to understand that
poetry did not have to be from England or of an
English that was always lonesome for its homeland in Europe." Do you think academia and the
industry of poetry has becomes less Anglo-
centric? Do you think we're progressing in the
respect that popular poetry is becoming more
diversified? Or no?*

Harjo: As a poet, I was present at the beginning of the multicultural literary movement in
the mid-'70s. There was great resistance in the
academy. There still is. I was told that a voice
against my hire in a major university believed
that multicultural literature was a sham. This
was in 2000. A colleague in my first university
hired in the mid-'80s sauntered into my office
and called me a primitive poet. And anything of
indigenous/aboriginal origin often falls away
into the "disappeared" or "exotic other"
category.

Some of us emerge despite the difficulties.
Poetry is always diversifying. That is the nature
of art. There will always be stalwarts of Euro or
even other classical traditions, who dismiss any
version or branch. This is true in Muscogean
dance traditions, jazz, or any other form.

*Rumpus: I think of your poetry as anything
but primitive. Your poetry always has a very
strong, fresh narrative voice. How did you struggle
against the "disappeared" and "exotic other"
labels in your writing?*

Harjo: I still struggle, or rather I should say,
I am aware that these forces of thinking are still
very present—there's an investment in this country and perhaps all of the Western hemisphere to
disappear indigenous peoples. It's not necessarily a calculated plan. The disappearance happened when physical, mental, and spiritual
violence was used to take over lands, when indigenous peoples and cultures were pronounced
inferior or even demonic. To accept that there
are still indigenous peoples with major cultural
and social accomplishments means that the
story, or the wound, will have to be reopened
and examined. I just have to keep moving and
honor the indigenous presence within myself.
That's not necessarily an easy thing to do in
this American social structure.

Rumpus: You mentioned that Crazy Brave
*took you fourteen years to write. For someone
who ingeniously cranks out new art, music, and
poetry at such a frequent speed, I gather that
writing your memoir must have been a very deep,
visceral undertaking. Can you expound upon the
experience of writing it, and how has its publication affected you?*

Harjo: There were three starts to the memoir. The first was as a collection of memory riffs,
based on songs. That title was *A Love Supreme.*
The second was as a short story collection. That
book, when I stopped that track, was at almost

two hundred pages. The third was a collage of vignettes, stories, dreams, and poems. A year before publication, my editor at Norton, Jill Bialosky, wrote to say that the book was being called in—and I gave up and wrote the memoir that was waiting for me to be brave enough. I thought I was only seven years late, until I read the contract after turning in the final manuscript. I was horrified that I was fourteen years past my delivery date. The first days of publication, I felt stripped down and raw. That feeling is both terrifying and liberating.

Rumpus: You say "poetry came into the world with music" and that "most poetry isn't on the page." Do you think that with the advancement and popularity of technology we are reverting back to the indigenous style of poetry, and veering away from the academic format? Or do we continue to remain stagnant?

Harjo: I believe that we always return to the root, in some manner or other—there's a kind of spiral looping back to keep integrity of form. Even written-down or printed forms are inculcated with elements of orality. Poetry, dance and music came into the world together. The academic can be rigid and dogmatic at worst, and at best, rigorous and demanding in preciseness of form. When I say "academic" here, I mean verse with Euro-Anglo derivations.

Rumpus: Your poetry and music are obviously void of such derivations. Do you think you would be a musician if you hadn't been a poet first?

Harjo: I am a musician . . . I was going to say that if my music hadn't been so stifled in my early teens, I would have been a musician first, but my writing was not safe in my home. It was most likely less threatening to take to a pen than to perform with my voice and a horn. You cannot hide when you are singing by voice or horn.

Rumpus: You say that poetry is "to that place without words." To me, that means poetry is a journey of speaking and it ends with catharsis. Could you go into detail on that statement?

Harjo: The first time I stated this was probably in the mid-'80s, when I was in Denver and spent several nights a week in the jazz clubs, listening. I wasn't praying saxophone yet. I heard where music could go that words could not—words can be more easily bound by culture, language, and other expectations. Music also has parameters of construction and

expectation, but can saturate and move—beyond words.

. . . I don't believe I particularly mean that a poem necessarily must end with catharsis. Words are representations and architectural materials for a structure through which meaning is derived, through which spirit can move. The "without words" is that which cannot be finally captured. It can be experienced. Catharsis can be the initiating impetus or occur many times within the body. Catharsis doesn't have to necessarily be the end event.

Rumpus: With that theory in mind, what poets do you share the stage with (metaphorically)?

Harjo: Robert Sullivan, the Maori poet, comes to mind. Adrienne Rich, Audre Lorde, Jim Morrison, Jayne Cortez (a great inspiration in my journey to return music to poetry in the original traditions of poetry), Ray Young Bear, Patricia Smith . . . I've literally shared the stage with Cornelius Eady and my Arrow Dynamics band for the New Mexico Jazz Workshop's *Jazz Deconstructed* series. We performed our original songs. Both Cornelius and I sang. I played saxophone and flute.

Rumpus: Are those the same poets who influence you?

Harjo: Yes, and no. Charles Bukowski was an influence. Pablo Neruda. One of my utter favorite poets is Mahmoud Darwish, the Palestinian poet. There's Ruben Dario, the Nicaraguan poet. Then there's the poet of saxophone, John Coltrane. I would also include Jim Pepper.

I always tell younger poets to feed the source of the poetry. To give honor and thanks to those who came before us, and to take care of those who are following. You can do this by honoring your mentors with your gift, and literally feeding their spirits. When I taught creative writing classes at the Institute of American Indian Arts in 1979 and 1980, I involved the students in teaching creative writing to Albuquerque Indian School high school students. We are in a dynamic continuum.

Rumpus: That's a great teaching method. How has teaching shaped your poetry?

Harjo: I'm not sure that teaching has shaped my poetry. I have been inspired by teaching, by being in the classroom, which is an active creative space, or can be. The atmosphere of competitiveness and rigidity in academic institutions in this country has set up major tests for me. I have had to learn how to make it work on behalf of my students and myself. Sometimes we even fly a little. This whole earth is a teaching institution.

Source: Julie Morse and Joy Harjo, "The *Rumpus Interview with Joy Harjo*," in *Rumpus*, February 20, 2013, *online*.

SOURCES

Allen, Paula Gunn, *The Sacred Hoop: Recovering the Feminine in American Indian Traditions*, Beacon Press, 1986, pp. 55–56, 69–70, 162.

Bruchac, Joseph, "The Story of All Our Survival," in *Joy Harjo: The Spiral of Memory; Interviews*, edited by Laura Coltelli, University of Michigan Press, 1996, p. 31; originally published in *Survival This Way: Interviews with American Indian Poets*, University of Arizona Press, 1987.

Coltelli, Laura, "Foreword: A Carrier of Memory," in *Soul Talk, Soul Language: Conversations with Joy Harjo*, edited by Joy Harjo and Tanaya Winder, Wesleyan University Press, 2011, p. xv.

———, "Introduction: The Transforming Power of Joy Harjo's Poetry," in *Joy Harjo: The Spiral of Memory; Interviews*, edited by Laura Coltelli, University of Michigan Press, 1996, pp. 4, 8.

Harjo, Joy, *Conflict Resolution for Holy Beings: Poems*, W. W. Norton, 2015, pp. 31, 75.

———, "Eagle Poem," in *In Mad Love and War*, Wesleyan University Press, 1990, p. 65.

Harjo, Joy, and Gloria Bird, eds., Introduction to *Reinventing the Enemy's Language: Contemporary Native Women's Writings of North America*, W. W. Norton, 1997, pp. 19–34.

Moyers, Bill, "Ancestral Voices," in *Joy Harjo: The Spiral of Memory; Interviews*, edited by Laura Coltelli, University of Michigan Press, 1996, p. 40.

Randall, Margaret, "Nothing to Lose," in *Women's Review of Books*, Vol. 7, Nos. 10–11, July 1990, pp. 17–18.

Scarry, John, "Representing Real Worlds: The Evolving Poetry of Joy Harjo," in *World Literature Today*, Vol. 66, No. 2, Spring 1992, pp. 286–91.

Stever, Sharyn, "Landscape and the Place Inside," in *Joy Harjo: The Spiral of Memory; Interviews*, edited by Laura Coltelli, University of Michigan Press, 1996, p. 79; originally published in *Hayden Ferry's Review*, No. 6, Summer 1990.

Ullman, Leslie, "Solitaries and Storytellers, Magicians and Pagans: Five Poets in the World," in *Kenyon Review*, Vol. 13, No. 2, Spring 1991, pp. 179–93.

West, Kathleene, Review of *In Mad Love and War*, in *Prairie Schooner*, Vol. 66, No. 2, Summer 1992, pp. 128–32.

FURTHER READING

Brown, Joseph Epes, with Emily Cousins, *Teaching Spirits: Understanding Native American Traditions*, Oxford University Press, 2001.

> Brown lived with Black Elk, the famed Lakota holy man, for a year before he died. Though himself a white man and college professor of religion with a background in anthropology, Brown became a mentor during the Native American Renaissance, passing on the wisdom of the old traditions to generations of young Indian students who took inspiration from his respect for their ways.

Harjo, Joy, *Crazy Brave: A Memoir*, W. W. Norton, 2012.

> Harjo's autobiographical memories include her mystical experiences that led to her becoming a poet.

Lincoln, Kenneth, *Native American Renaissance*, University of California Press, 1983.

> Lincoln's groundbreaking work helped to establish Native American studies programs in universities nationwide through critical evaluation of the young Indian writers of the 1960s and 1970s. They were the first college-educated generation of bicultural writers to make an impact on mainstream America. He includes in this group Joy Harjo, Simon J. Ortiz, N. Scott Momaday, Leslie Marmon Silko, Louise Erdrich, James Welch, and Paula Gunn Allen, among others.

Pettit, Rhonda, *Joy Harjo*, Western Writer Series, Boise State University, 1998.

> This critical study of Harjo covers her important poetry of the twentieth century that made her well known.

SUGGESTED SEARCH TERMS

Joy Harjo

"Eagle Poem" AND Harjo

In Mad Love and War AND Harjo

Native American Renaissance

Trail of Tears

Red Stick War

Muskogee tribe

Salt River

Iowa Writers' Workshop

Joy Harjo AND saxophone

For a Daughter Who Leaves

JANICE MIRIKITANI

2002

"For a Daughter Who Leaves" is a poem composed in blank verse by Japanese American writer and activist and former San Francisco poet laureate Janice Mirikitani. It was first included in Mirikitani's fourth collection of verse, *Love Works*, which was published in 2002 and hailed as the poet's crowning literary achievement to date. The collection was praised not only for its graceful fusing of intimate and societal themes but also for setting forth Mirikitani's guiding poetic philosophy and cementing her reputation as an advocate for silenced and downtrodden humanity.

Inspired by historical and cultural memory, "For a Daughter Who Leaves" is a poem rich in the imagery of folklore and heavy with the weight of tradition. It is a composition of great sadness as well as beauty, expressing the sorrow of a mother who gives up her daughter to be married and to be given, body and soul, to a husband. In keeping with custom, the daughter must forsake her old family for a new one, never to return to the household of her birth.

AUTHOR BIOGRAPHY

The daughter of first-generation parents of Japanese heritage, referred to as Nisei, Mirikitani was born on February 4, 1941, in the burgeoning metropolis of Stockton, California. Like many

Janice Mirikitani (©David Paul Morris / Getty Images Entertainment / Getty Images)

others of their cultural background, the Mirikitanis became the victims of heightened xenophobia during World War II and were incarcerated in Arkansas's Rohwer War Relocation Center for the duration of the conflict. Following their release, the persecuted family sought refuge from the anti-Japanese sentiments that still prevailed on the West Coast and relocated to Chicago in search of new opportunity. Mirikitani's parents soon divorced, and five-year-old Janice returned with her mother and her mother's new husband to California. The fallen fortunes of the household, Mirikitani's sense of rootlessness and isolation, and her long-lasting abuse by her stepfather all combined to make the following decade the most harrowing of the young poet's life.

A hardworking and distinguished student, Mirikitani graduated from the University of California, Los Angeles and was licensed as a teacher through the University of California, Berkeley. She earned her keep as an educator in a nearby school district and as an administrative assistant at Glide Memorial Church, an institution with which she has maintained a lifelong association. Not long after her entrance into the professional world, Mirikitani was briefly married in 1966 and gave birth to a daughter, Tianne Tsuikiko Miller, the following year.

In the following decade, Mirikitani took up the pursuit of an advanced degree in creative writing at San Francisco State College, where she became involved in activism and emerging literary publications dedicated to advancing the creativity and concerns of Asian Americans. Her poetry was inspired not only by her growing sense of cultural identity but also by her complex relationship with her own mother and grandmother.

Inspired by the fine work included in these publications, Mirikitani herself took up the pen, releasing her first collection of combined poetry and prose, *Awake in the River*, to enthusiastic readership in 1978. Since that time, Mirikitani has released several more volumes of poetry and collaborated on various influential essays and San Francisco–based literary projects. For her growing recognition within the arts, Mirikitani was named San Francisco poet laureate, a position she held from 2000 to 2002, the year she published her most celebrated collection, *Love Works*.

In addition to her many artistic achievements and honorary degrees from prestigious universities, Mirikitani is recognized as one of San Francisco's most prominent philanthropists. Through her association with Glide Memorial Church and with the help of her second husband, the Reverend Cecil Williams, the community activist established the enormously beneficial Glide Foundation, committed to ending cycles of poverty and misery within marginalized, local communities. As of 2016, Mirikitani lives with her husband in San Francisco and remains a cherished pillar of the community and a respected patron of the arts.

POEM TEXT

A woman weaves
her daughter's wedding
slippers that will carry
her steps into a new life.
The mother weeps alone   5
into her jeweled sewing box

slips red thread
around its spool,
the same she used to stitch
her daughter's first silk jacket   10
embroidered with turtles
that would bring luck, long life.
She remembered all the steps
taken by her daughter's
unbound on the stones   15
dancing on the stones
of the yard among yellow
butterflies and white breasted sparrows.
And she grew, legs strong
body long, mind   20
independent.
Now she captures all eyes
with her hair combed smooth
and her hips gently
swaying like bamboo.   25
The woman
spins her thread
from the spool of her heart,
knotted to her daughter's
departing   30
wedding slippers

POEM SUMMARY

The text used for this summary is from *Love Works*, City Lights Foundation, 2002, p. 43. Versions of this poem can be found on the following web pages: https://www.poets.org/poetsorg/poem/daughter-who-leaves and http://www.poemhunter.com/poem/for-a-daughter-who-leaves/comments/.

Prelude

Mirikitani prefaces her own composition by citing an eighth-century Japanese poetess of high birth, Lady Otomo, who expresses the depth of her own love for her daughter. Her love exceeds her admiration of all costly gems and worldly treasures.

Lines 1–4

An unnamed woman makes preparations for her daughter's wedding day, handcrafting the fine silk slippers that will adorn her feet in all the years to come. These tokens of love have practical as well as emotional significance and will allow the bride to take her first, tentative steps in her new life as a married woman.

Lines 5–8

The solitary seamstress weeps unobserved by others, her tears falling into the ornate sewing box and anointing the materials of her craft. She utilizes red thread in the making of the slippers, a color associated with regeneration and childbirth in Japanese culture, which she unwinds with care from its protective spool.

Lines 9–12

She reflects how she once made use of the same thread to commemorate her daughter's birth, embroidering a fine jacket for her infant with designs of turtles signifying long life, luck, and future happiness.

Lines 13–15

The grieving mother recollects the many steps taken by her youthful daughter before this momentous change in her life. As a girl and not yet a woman, the daughter is not yet subjected to foot binding, a discouraged but still sometimes practiced form of mutilation that breaks and reshapes the bones of the feet and severely limits movement. In the mother's imaginings, her daughter's steps are still carefree and agile like those of a little girl.

Lines 16–18

The daughter's feet dance through her mother's memories and across the stones of the outside yard. She is joined in her carefree revelry by yellow butterflies and white-breasted sparrows, graceful, airborne creatures marked by the colors of youth and purity.

Lines 19–21

The girl grows, suddenly no longer a child but a young woman. Her body lengthens, her limbs increase in strength, and her mind becomes independent and ungovernable.

Lines 22–25

In her fully grown form, the daughter is now an object of intense desire and attracts many gazes. Her hair is combed to a smooth and flawless luster, and the shape of her body becomes enticing. The sway of her hips beneath her robes is likened to the movement of bamboo in the wind, a plant famed for its beauty but also strong and unyielding nature.

Lines 26–28

The mother no longer draws out the red thread of the slippers from the spool but from her own heart.

Lines 29–31

The thread is now symbolic as well as literal and connects the mother's heart to the daughter's departing slippers as she nears her wedding night and new life with a husband.

THEMES

Attachment

The depth of emotional attachment between the mother of the poem and her departing daughter is established even before the opening of the poem by an eighth-century poet's expression of her limitless, unearthly love for her offspring. The meat of the poem sustains the spirit and intensity of this theme by its poignant portrayal of a mother's final act of love toward her daughter on the eve of her wedding and a new life away from home. The creation of the slippers takes on a physical as well as an emotional significance, the silk thread used in their making spooling directly from the mother's heart. In this way, each step the daughter takes away from home will be felt in the breast of her pining mother, a guarantee of their connection, both literal and symbolic, across the great expanse of distance and the passing years.

Marriage

The poem is inseparable from the theme of marriage, both as a sacrament of adulthood and continued life and as a source of sorrow. The mother clings to the memory of her soon-to-be-married daughter as a child and laments her imminent adulthood and transition from one stage of life to another. The red string, as a reminder of the cyclical nature of new life and mature female reproduction, connects these two phases of the daughter's existence and traces her growth through the years. In this way, the carefree dance of a child and the mincing, dignified steps of a new wife are portrayed by the poem as but two sides of the same coin.

While the mother is inclined to lament the imminent departure of her cherished offspring and union with a husband, the daughter's implied perspective on the prospect of marriage is tinged with independence and a sense of personal fulfillment. Mirikitani bolsters this interpretation through her portrayal of the growing girl's body as strong, willful, and sexually self-aware. The poem resists associations of dependency, whether on family or a husband, and suggests informed free will in the choosing of a suitable partner and future life. In this way, marriage represents the closing of one chapter and the beginning of another.

Memory

The narrative fluidity of Mirikitani's composition and its melding of the present moment with past recollections elevate the theme of memory to a position of great importance. As she weaves fine red silk into slippers for her daughter's wedding day, the central figure of the poem casts her thoughts to days now long past, observing in an instant the growth of her little girl into a beautiful and strong-minded woman. The compression of years into a single mental image suggests the immateriality of time when framed by memory, an impression strengthened by the quote of the far earlier poetess that begins the composition. Memory is not stagnant, suggests Mirikitani in the arrangement of her verse, but remains unchanging and cyclical throughout the ages.

The mother's recollections coexist seamlessly with the chore at hand and take on an ethereal, dreamlike quality. In these memories, the daughter is joined by stunning and symbolic creatures and likened in beauty to aspects of the land itself. Even at the end of the poem, when the inevitability of her daughter's departure is fully realized, the mother refuses to altogether relinquish this idealized memory of her offspring. By way of the red silk thread attached to her own heart and incorporated into the bride's slippers, she establishes an anchor to the past that spools endlessly into the daughter's future as a married woman.

Youth

"For a Daughter Who Leaves" is both an elegy and a celebration of the beautiful brevity of youth. Childhood is equated to a state of unencumbered joy in Mirikitani's poem, a period of life unfettered by tradition and societal expectations. The freedom of the child from painful initiations into adulthood, like foot binding, as well as the heedlessness of decorum and mature responsibility is also amply reflected by the composition. The dancing of the young girl across a yard of polished stones indicates her freedom from the burden of later cares, both physical and emotional. As opposed to her rapid transformation into womanhood, in which the

TOPICS FOR FURTHER STUDY

- "For a Daughter Who Leaves" weaves a powerful poetic narrative around the significance of a single object, in this case a pair of silk slippers intended as a wedding present. Dig into your own family's history and select a photograph or memento from a particularly important occasion celebrated by your household, such as a wedding, a graduation, a reunion, or even a birthday party. Connect a memory, real or imagined, to the memento and its significance within that occasion. Lastly, craft this memory into a brief narrative to share with your classmates.

- The weeping mother of Mirikitani's poem observes the growth of her daughter from a carefree girl into a beautiful young woman in the space of a single, instantaneous memory. Select a picture of yourself or of another individual roughly your age and upload it to the free online aging program provided by http://cherry.dcs.aber.ac.uk/Transformer/. Saving and printing the prematurely aged photograph for inspiration, craft a brief poem containing some of the observations and feelings evoked by the familiar and yet greatly changed face.

- The poet emphasizes human qualities through her pointed inclusion of symbolic images from the natural world, such as ephemeral butterflies, long-lived tortoises, and supple, strong bamboo. With a partner, brainstorm a list of animals and plants that you feel embody aspects of your spirit and your most prominent positive qualities. Next, perform the quick personality quiz located at www.spiritanimal.info to generate a spirit animal, printing the provided results and in-depth explanations for use in

further discussions. Discuss the outcome of the quiz with your partner, comparing the computer-generated results with the fruits of your initial brainstorming.

- The ancient institution of marriage celebrated in Mirikitani's poem is one shared, albeit in a multitude of forms, by almost every culture around the globe. Choose one culture of special interest or personal significance to you and research its customs and views in regard to the rite of matrimony. In combination with striking visuals, summarize your research for inclusion in an informational poster to be shared with your classmates.

- Yoshiko Uchida's "The Bracelet" is a well-loved short story dealing with the trauma of the very Japanese internment camps that held Mirikitani's family during the dark years of World War II. Read the story and reflect on a time of difficult transition or anxiety in your own life and of the tokens, physical or emotional, that helped you to persevere. Commit this memory to your journal and share it with classmates if you feel comfortable.

- Mirikitani's poetic description of a mother spooling blood-red thread from her grieving heart is an undeniably powerful and unexpected image. Using whatever artistic medium you prefer, create a visual representation of this or some other scene from the poem that you feel accurately represents the complex emotions evoked by the poet's skillful use of language and imagery. Participate in a "gallery showing" by joining your classmates in displaying your creations around the room, inviting feedback and promoting dialogue.

changes of her body mirror sexual maturity and growing self-awareness, the girl does not yet anticipate the need for choice or for change.

The independence inherent in the passing of the years and the waning of childhood is not the death of youth, however, but rather its full

The detailed embroidery reflects the care the mother takes in preparing her daughter for her life to come
(©krutar | Shutterstock.com)

blossoming. The newly realized strength of the young woman's limbs, her mastery over her own body and desires, is amplified by her poetic likening to the pliable strength of bamboo. She is now at the full height of her powers, able and willing to sever her ties from the comforting dependency of childhood and engage in the act of marriage according to her own free will. Her fine mind grows in proportion to her young body, a change that her mother notes with mingled pride and sadness. "For a Daughter Who Leaves," while containing strong elements of nostalgia and remorse, is at its heart a celebration of the passing of childhood into the full realization and promise of young adulthood.

STYLE

Allusion

By way of introducing her own poetic composition, Mirikitani cites the work of a far earlier poet, the eighth-century Lady Otomo of feudal Japan. This creative decision not only serves to

reinforce the themes of maternal love and precious offspring so central to the verse but also situates the comparatively contemporary "For a Daughter Who Leaves" within an ancient literary tradition spanning centuries. At the same time that this allusion connects Mirikitani to her Japanese forbears, however, it also universalizes the emotions evoked by the poem and places them outside considerations of time and nationality. In this way, readers are instantly brought to the realization that a mother's love for her daughter knows no limitations.

Folklore

"For a Daughter Who Leaves" is a poem consciously steeped in the traditions and cultural values so cherished by the Japanese people. The use of traditional symbols supports this aspect of the poem, like the turtle, representing prosperity and long life in the ancestral memory of Mirikitani's ancestors, and even the silk thread employed so artfully by the weavers of ancient Japan. Mirikitani's allusion to bound feet, a popular if controversial practice of a bygone era, serves to deepen the connection of the verse to long-held rites of womanhood in the Far East. Even the overarching theme of marriage contributes to the gravity of tradition established by the poet's composition, acknowledging the sadness as well as the celebration inherent in one of the world's most ancient and sanctified ritual ceremonies.

Imagery

Mirikitani's poem abounds with elemental imagery that suggests themes of cyclical regeneration, fertility, and natural beauty. Her simple but elegant depictions of the flitting butterfly and the graceful, white-breasted sparrow, for instance, amplify the young daughter's carefree childhood and foretell the coming loveliness of her womanhood. Even more strikingly, Mirikitani's likening of a youthful body to elegant and unyielding shoots of bamboo evokes an entire range of poetic connotations. This one image establishes simultaneously the beauty and the grace of the young woman, qualities not unnoticed by her legion of admirers, and her independence of mind and spirit.

The most central and poignant image of the poem, however, is rooted in human emotion rather than elemental majesty. The mother spins the red silk thread used in the slippers directly from her grieving heart and binds it to the finished product of her labors. At the end of "For a Daughter Who Leaves," the reader of the poem is confronted with the powerful visualization of the daughter walking away from her mother, each step spooling a blood-red length of thread from the chest of the woman who bore her.

Interior Monologue

Although the poem is related from an ethereal and detached third-person perspective, "For a Daughter Who Leaves" is an interior monologue of great power and poignancy. The entire poem is rooted in the recollections of a grieving mother and reflects her deep sadness and profound love for her soon-to-be-married offspring. Through the force of the poem, the reader shares in the old woman's imaginings and observes the passing of the years in an instant through her eyes. This allows for the unparalleled immersive quality of the poet's verse and renders each tug of the red silk thread spooling out from the mother's heart viscerally as well as visually compelling.

HISTORICAL CONTEXT

The history of Mirikitani's landmark poem is rooted in the traditions of ancient Japan and extends through the initial suppression and eventual flowering of Asian American culture and art in the New World. Mirikitani's parents, both second-generation Japanese Americans, or Nisei, were directly descended from the original Japanese immigrants who fled their homeland in the tens of thousands during the final decades of the nineteenth century and settled on the East Coast of the United States. Seeking new opportunity, political stability, and an easier life for their offspring, these first-generation Issei flocked first to Hawaii and later to California in search of an easier, less volatile existence for their children. From earliest days, these newcomers were forced to endure the distrust of their neighbors and fight an uphill battle against vicious anti-immigrant legislation. The Chinese Exclusion Act of 1882, effectively ending the flow of Chinese immigrants, who had previously made up the bulk of the East Coast workforce, made it possible for Isei to seek employment as farmers and laborers or in other physically demanding and generally underpaid professions.

With the infamous bombing of Pearl Harbor in 1941 and the outbreak of open hostilities between the nations of Japan and the United States, President Franklin D. Roosevelt approved the controversial order to evacuate over one hundred thousand Japanese Americans from Hawaii and the western states to be interned, under suspicion of disloyalty and treachery, in ten relocation centers across the nation. Mirikitani and her parents, held at the Rohwer relocation center in Arkansas, were among these wronged citizens. The trauma and staggering injustice of this dark chapter in American history informed much of Mirikitani's later poetry and continued activism.

In the wake of this troubled past and the growing influence and acceptance of those of Asian descent in American society, the Asian American Movement, in which Mirikitani was an outspoken participant, came to full fruition in the summer of 1968. Spearheaded by students at the University of California, Berkeley, the movement soon spread to Mirikitani's native San Francisco and across the East Coast. Members of the movement quickly differentiated themselves with a sweeping political and artistic

COMPARE
&
CONTRAST

- **Early 2000s:** At the turn of the twenty-first century and after more than three decades of serving the disenfranchised minorities of San Francisco on a local scale, the Glide Foundation garners national and even world recognition as a model organization of its kind.

  Today: Amidst increasing growth and success, Glide is active in helping to pass nationalized health care and is publicly praised by representatives of the government for its successful implementation of similar initiatives in the city of San Francisco.

- **Early 2000s:** In 2006, roughly half a century after the closing of the Japanese internment camps utilized during World War II, public money is devoted to their study, upkeep, and

reopening as historical and educational sites under the National Park Service.

Today: Presidential candidate Donald Trump publicly praises the earlier initiative of President Franklin D. Roosevelt in confining people of suspect ethnicities during wartime, putting forth a similar model as a proposed response to immigrants from the Middle East.

- **Early 2000s:** In 2000, Mirikitani is named the second poet laureate of San Francisco in recognition of her ample achievements within the arts and local activism.

  Today: Alejandro Murguia, the fifth San Francisco poet laureate and the first of Latino extraction, completed his second term in 2015.

---

agenda from preexisting cultural clubs, which sought largely to preserve tradition in a hostile land. By contrast, the new movement dedicated itself to the shaping of the future, making America a more hospitable home not just to Asian Americans but, indeed, to all ethnic minorities. They also sought to forge a new identity, in equal harmony with the present and the past, through the promulgation of the arts and renewed Asian American scholarship.

CRITICAL OVERVIEW

Critical discussions of Mirikitani's verse and literary achievements are often framed within the context of her personal magnetism, noted activism, and philanthropic contributions to the needy and disenfranchised of San Francisco. In her article for *AsianWeek* titled "Hearing the Muse: For Janice Mirikitani, Activism Feeds Poetry," reviewer Julie Shiroishi sheds light on the bold and uncompromising nature of Mirikitani's inspiration:

Mirikitani's is no gentle muse. And it is so inextricably intertwined with her mission to empower the disenfranchised that for Mirikitani to quell its ferocity would perhaps be more of a challenge than finding time to express its wails for justice.

In keeping with the fearless language of her review, the critic praises Mirikitani's open engagement with the folly of silence as well as the necessity of being heard as a rallying cry for those segments of American society who would otherwise remain voiceless. This "expansive and brash" quality of the poet's verse reflects an unapologetic strength of character and conviction bordering on the infectious. Despite its characteristic tone and style, however, Shiroishi asserts that Mirikitani's verse is far from stagnant or predictable. Rather, it ebbs and flows to keep pace with the necessities and realities of the times, evolving with the poet's ongoing journey of self and that of her many readers.

In a 1984 interview with Mirikitani, William Satake Blauvelt of the *International Examiner* echoes many of the sentiments expressed by other admirers of the poet's work, incorporating

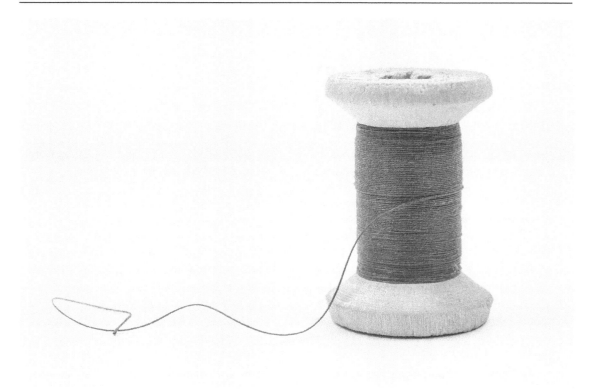

The thread unwinding from the spool is like the tie between the mother's heart and the daughter she loves
(©Olga Danylenko | Shutterstock.com)

her characteristic strength and fearlessness into a declaration of high praise. Blauvelt says of Mirikitani,

> For the past 15 years, she has been one of Asian America's strongest and most consistent voices, combining poetic expression with political and social activism into a force that is at once powerful and beautiful.

Blauvelt delves also into the foundational role of family in the work of Mirikitani and the care she takes in representing them with both sensitivity and accuracy, allowing them the freedom of their own voice even within the context of her poetry. In this way, the critic explains, Mirikitani expresses her own unwavering convictions in perfect harmony with empathy and respect for the equally viable viewpoints of others. Particularly when writing on the complex nature of her relationship with her own mother and grandmother, Mirikitani's verse is saturated with considerations of cultural tradition and historical precedent, mindful of what has come before and yet refusing to be imprisoned by it. In this way, Blauvelt maintains, Mirikitani's work is as delicate as it is bold, painstakingly

constructed to do justice to all, exclude no one, and evoke a wide array of emotions.

Whether writing about her family or political and social issues, Mirikitani's poetry reflects a deep-rooted commitment and compassion. Although she claims, as a medical student, to have "almost died in Chem 1A," the effect of her work on audiences is like the reaction certain chemicals have when they are mixed into the right combinations and come into contact with the air. Some explode, others can burn, while still others crystallize.

Although the overwhelming majority of critical dialogue and scholarship surrounding Mirikitani's body of poetry take broad views, encompassing the poet's life as well as her work, Tarisa Matsumoto, also of the *International Examiner*, authored a glowing review of *Love Works*, the collection containing "For a Daughter Who Leaves," in 2002. Matsumoto argues that this particular book of verse directs and intensifies one of the central obsessions of Mirikitani's literary career, namely, the ongoing triumphs and tribulations of countless Asian

Americans within the context of culture and of the family itself. Naming *Love Works* as the heart of Mirkitani's vast poetic body, "an intense synopsis of all her poetry thus far," the critic also praises the collection for contemporizing and universalizing these enduring themes and imbuing them with renewed relevance. *Love Works* is at once a recognition of incredible adversity and a celebration of triumph past, present, and future. Matsumoto continues:

> But there is something different about *Love Works.* Mirikitani's poems always seem to focus on not only where Japanese Americans find themselves in contemporary culture, but where Japanese American women in particular find themselves. They are the forgotten, the abused, and the impoverished. Still, no matter how bad a situation Mirikitani's female figures find themselves in, they are always triumphant by the poem's end. More so than her other collections of poetry, *Love Works* concentrates on this unrelenting strength of women, not just Japanese American women, but all women who find themselves objectified, vilified, or abused.

CRITICISM

Jeffrey Eugene Palmer

Palmer is a scholar, freelance writer, and teacher of high school English. In the following essay, he examines Mirikitani's treatment of the spoken and unspoken in her poems "For a Daughter Who Leaves" and "Breaking Tradition."

In analyzing the poetry of Mirikitani in a personal and societal context, much critical attention is paid to the poet's abhorrence of silence and her championing of bold utterance in its stead. Nowhere is this silence more damaging, the poet maintains, than when clung to by the wronged, the downtrodden, and, particularly in the context of her own work, the typified demure and voiceless Asian American woman. Although the poem is free from the vehemence that characterizes Mirikitani's poetry empowering women against the ravages of domestic and sexual abuse, "For a Daughter Who Leaves" is less divorced from her trademark themes of strife, silence, and subjugation than the casual reader might at first imagine. To more fully explore this assertion, and to understand the virtues and limitations of voice according to Mirikitani's sweeping poetic vision, it is helpful to first examine "For a

> THERE IS A POWER IN SILENCE AND ACCEPTANCE, THESE TWO POEMS SEEM TO AFFIRM, STRENGTH IN SUBMITTING TO THE INEVITABLE WILLINGLY AND WITH GRACE."

Daughter Who Leaves" on its own terms and then in comparison with one of the poet's more contemporary and vocal compositions.

The poetic, eighth-century elegy written by the Japanese noble woman Lady Otomo that prefaces the poem immediately establishes "For a Daughter Who Leaves" as a relic of a bygone era, still shackled by silence and by the dictates of custom. The poem is therefore emptied of all sound, every step silenced and every desperate lamentation left unheard. The vibrant imagery of the verse seems at odds with its mute characters and unexpressed thoughts and lends a subdued, almost furtive quality to the events it describes. The unassertive temperament of the weeping and dejected mother, in and of itself, seems strikingly out of character for a poet as committed to the ideal of strong and vocal femininity as Mirikitani.

The tragedy and strife inherent in "For a Daughter Who Leaves" are not immediately discernible in their entirety. The physical separation between a doting mother and a soon-to-be-married daughter is only the most evident manifestation of the poem's profound sense of loss. Subtle verbal clues suggest that the distance between these two characters is emotional as well as physical, however, and that the themes of struggle and confrontation so central to Mirikitani's work are alive and well in the otherwise deceptively tranquil poem. In a striking inversion of expectation, it becomes apparent that the conflict contained within the verse has little to do with the societal silencing of women or the harsh dictates of marital tradition in feudal Japan. Rather, it is represented through an ongoing war of wills between mother and daughter, which intensifies with the passing of the years and culminates in the decisive fragmentation of their once perfectly aligned identities and interests.

WHAT DO I READ NEXT?

- A landmark work of young-adult fiction published in 1977, Eleanor Coerr's *Sadako and the Thousand Paper Cranes* is a tragic and yet inspiring tale about the aftermath of nuclear destruction in Japan.

- Erika Lee's 2015 *The Making of Asian America: A History* is a comprehensive overview of the incredible stories and historical truths that make up the experience of Asian immigrants and their many descendants in the United States.

- *Remembering Manzanar: Life in a Japanese Relocation Camp* is a history book written by Michael L. Cooper in 2002 and intended for young-adult readers that documents the traumas and triumphs of thousands of Japanese Americans.

- *A Heartbreaking Work of Staggering Genius* is a semiautobiographical novel published in 2000 and written by world-renowned author Dave Egger, in which he recounts the details of a tragic yet inspiring childhood in San Francisco.

- Although he is better known for his works of science fiction, author J. G. Ballard wrote *Empire of the Sun* in 1984 as a fiction-infused memoir of his young adulthood spent in China as a prisoner of the Japanese during World War II.

- *The Naked and the Dead* is Norman Mailer's well-loved 1948 epic of camaraderie, cruelty, and compassion among a multicultural team of American soldiers fighting for their survival in the Pacific.

- A masterpiece of the footloose generation of American youth known as the Beat Generation, *On the Road* is a 1957 novel by author Jack Kerouac celebrating the city of San Francisco and the great expanse of America.

- Mirikitani's first volume of poetry, *Awake in the River*, was published in 1978 and reflects her early aspirations, anxieties, and artistic sentiments.

- Published in 2014 and engaging with contemporary world events from a mature artistic and humanitarian perspective, Mirikitani's *Out of the Dust* is her most recent collection of verse to date.

In this light, the bittersweet recollections of the mother assume a covetous and controlling quality. Although they are born purely of love and deep maternal attachment, the older woman nevertheless finds it difficult to relinquish ownership of that treasure which she holds most dear in her life, the daughter she brought into the world and raised with such tenderness. She laments the bygone ease and innocence of the girl's youth, her dependency on lovingly crafted articles of clothing and carefree dance across the flagstones of the courtyard. By contrast, the poet makes no mention of the daughter's corresponding sadness at leaving home or hesitation in beginning the next chapter of her life. The description of her willful, independent mind, strong and capable limbs, and bamboo-like durability all contribute to our understanding of the daughter's character as self-assured and unwavering in her plans for the future.

Faced with the strength of a daughter's determination to seize her own life, the grieving mother of the poem remains silent in expressing her worries and reservations. She hides even the shedding of her tears, refusing to be pitied or observed by others. While she is powerless or unwilling to voice her sorrow, the mother takes refuge in the only consolation available to her. Through the symbolic and literal act of weaving silk wedding slippers, she insinuates her presence in the married life of her daughter and every step she takes from that day forward. In this way, she relinquishes control over the young woman's life but reaffirms the far more important necessity of a continued connection, no matter how small, between her own heart and that of her daughter.

The outwardly demure and understated suffering of the mother, then, is tempered by an inner strength and shrewdness in her negotiation of reality. Mourning and dutiful acceptance do not prevent action in the context of the poem. This concept of silence and powerlessness as distinct in the context of Asian American literature is explored in some detail by Valerie Ooka Pang in her article "Intentional Silence and Communication in a Democratic Society: The Viewpoint of One Asian American." In her cultural examination, Pang not only combats the widely held Western alignment of voicelessness with weakness or passivity but also differentiates among the different varieties of silence and their origins and applications in a uniquely Asian American context. As she explains in her article:

> In mainstream society silence by particular ethnic groups and some women of color has been seen as passive acceptance of oppression or the trait of an "inscrutable" ethnic. This view, with an implicit valuing of speech, is part of the culturally hegemonic behavior of Western society. It shapes a view of speech as hierarchical, from verbal domination to silence from strength to weakness.... In contrast, some Asian Americans believe that silence does not show reticence, but rather denotes respectful and caring actions.

It is these selfsame qualities of respect and caring, more than cowed passivity or submission to cultural expectations, that best characterize the pointed silence of the mother in Mirikitani's poem, intent upon her solitary labor of love. Although she is saddened by her daughter's imminent departure, the woman hides the visible manifestations of her sadness out of regard for her daughter's individuality and right to exercise her own will. Without the necessity of uttering a word, she transmutes the emotions within to an external, practical expression of her enduring love. Growing up as she did, the virtue of this particular brand of silence, what Pang brands "dignified" silence, would not have been unknown to Mirikitani and, even if not personally favored, would have been accepted as a viable form of inarticulate communication. Pang briefly outlines the significance of this meaningful muteness within the cultural memory of Japanese Americans like the poet and her forbears. She explains the origin of this ethnic tendency by

writing: "Characteristic of many first generation Japanese American women, this type is the exhibition of great courage, as during the internment. As the women did not complain, they kept their sorrows to themselves."

An intriguing contrast to the "dignified" silence characterizing "For a Daughter Who Leaves" is laid out in Mirikitani's intimately related poem titled "Breaking Tradition" and written in recognition of the growing defiance of her own teenage daughter. Although it is entirely modern in tone and sprinkled with references to contemporary clothing styles, musical sensations, and steamy Latin dancing, the spirit of "Breaking Tradition" is consistent with her parallel composition set in a bygone age and written in a more traditional style.

Deceptively vocal and outspoken as an interior monologue, the poem is in actuality completely mute. Mirikitani dwells, not without some discomfort and regret, on an enduring and unbroken tradition of silence that frequently dominates interactions between the women in her family. In particular, she expresses difficulty in reconciling her own bold voice and love of expression with the silence she is at times forced to adopt toward her growingly independent, secretive daughter. This difficulty is neither unexpected nor unhealthy and entirely in keeping with Pang's analysis of the role of "intentional silence" in Eastern cultures. In her article, she openly affirms, "There is ample evidence that even though Asians have held tightly to the importance of dignified silence, they may feel ambivalence."

In grappling with this deeply ambivalent and personally distasteful issue, however, Mirikitani is characteristically empathic and evenhanded. She not only distinguishes among the degrees and varieties of silence but also refuses to equate an absence of voice with an absence of will. The skillful imagery that the poet assigns to her child is not altogether wholesome, evoking connotations of secrecy, irreconcilable differences, and even outright rebellion. In this way, Mirikitani's portrayal resonates with the form of inarticulate communication that Pang names "intentional silence" and likens to opposition to perceived oppression. "This form happens when a person does not want to give in to others and although she may feel that she cannot say anything, she is boldly silent," explains Pang in her

The birds and butterflies that surround the daughter represent the comparative freedom of her youth
(©Butterfly Hunter | Shutterstock.com)

article. "They see as oppressive to themselves specific demands or a general atmosphere."

Recognizing through her maternal instinct a form of silence fueled by teenage surliness and rebellion and the growing pains of dawning adulthood, Mirikitani responds in turn with her own, more mature variety of voiceless communication and love. Like the mother in her own creation "For a Daughter Who Leaves," the poet turns to "dignified" silence, recognizing and respecting the daughter's right to independence and to harbor her own secrets. It is out of measureless love and understanding that

Mirikitani keeps the utterances of her bold nature at bay, resisting the persistent itch of the unsaid and refusing to assert her dominance over the life of another. There is a power in silence and acceptance, these two poems seem to affirm, strength in submitting to the inevitable willingly and with grace. Where voice fails, both Mirikitani and her fictionalized protagonist come to realize, silence can sometimes be golden.

Source: Jeffrey Eugene Palmer, Critical Essay on "For a Daughter Who Leaves," in *Poetry for Students*, Gale, Cengage Learning, 2017.

Patricia Holt

In the following essay, Holt points out the strain of violence that threads through Mirikitani's poems.

Janice Mirikitani may be one of the most respected citizens in the Bay Area (see interview, Page 2), but when her poetic voice searches for signs of herself "in the pages of Time,/ ... (or) on the tube selling Colgate or Camay or Kotex or Crisco," what she finds is racial stigma, female alienation and cultural banishment.

(I) saw myself being shot by John Wayne, conquered by Stallone, out-karated by Norris, Van Damme, Carradine and Seagal. I found myself in a bar, dancing for a tip, cheong sam slit to my hip, or in a brothel, compliant and uncomplicated, high-heeled in bed, wiping some imperialist's lips with hot scented towels.

That's the Mirikitani many poetry fans know—unabashedly political, sexual, outraged and uncompliant. But the Mirikitani who emerges in *We, the Dangerous*, while never apologizing for the bitter invective, the slashing lashing-out of old, searches for a larger eloquence, a quieter, deeper stab, a less bitter resolve.

As before, many of the poems in this selection, which spans more than two decades, allow the poet an uncensored look at the once-taboo topic of childhood sexual abuse. In "Insect Collection," she describes an assignment for biology class ...

Refusing to be "kept ... in a jar/ of silence ... and muffled bedrooms," the poet finds solace, then liberation, in the heritage of survival of Asian women who have endured Hiroshima, Vietnam and the internment camp at Tule Lake, to which Japanese Americans were banished during World War II. Instead of remaining "locked ... in an airless vault of shame," Mirikitani seeks the greater freedom of the soul through "the quiet dignity" of spoken remembrance.

Indeed, one of the most moving poems is "Breaking Silence," the poet's restatement of her mother's testimony before the Commission on Wartime Relocation and Internment of Japanese American Civilians in 1981. ...

Thus the victim of history begins speaking for generations.

So when you tell me I must limit testimony, when you tell me my time is up, I tell you this: Pride has kept my lips pinned by nails my rage coffined. But I exhume my past to claim this

time ... Words are better than tears, so I spill them. I kill this, the silence ... "

Mirikitani has not minded using one-dimensional responses to cavalier racial cruelties. Her sheer poetic litany in "Yes, We Are Not Invisible" develops a rhythm and irony of its own. ...

Her directness is unsettling when she takes the voice of the Korean wife described in a news item who killed herself simply because she was late serving her husband's lunch. Could a woman be so programmed, so stupid, Mirikitani asks, or had she found a way ... to transcend a torment ... unseen by others ... yet witnessed all the same ...

Many of the poems take place in San Francisco's Tenderloin district, where routine violence dominates the landscape. ...

But it is at Glide Memorial Church, where Mirikitani is both president and executive director of programming, that the poet seems to find replenishment and renewal from the groups of women—many of them homeless, impoverished, addicted to drugs, just out of prison—who sit in circles, grappling with unspeakable obscenities and sometimes allowing for moments of hilarity, as when ...

It is in this "sanctuary," where her husband, the Rev. Cecil Williams, has said that "no secret is too shameful," that Mirikitani acknowledges that the true landscape for recovery is her own body, damaged for so many years from childhood abuse that she sees "like a burn victim/ ... cauterized shut." ...

Now, in her poem "for Cecil" called "War of the Body," she comes to believe his words, that "truth is not punished here," and that rebirth is possible ...

Source: Patricia Holt, Review of *We, the Dangerous*, in *SFGate*, February 25, 1996.

SOURCES

"Asian American Political Alliance 1968," Asian American Movement blog, http://aam1968.blogspot.com/2008/01/san-francisco-state-strike-1968-twlf.html (accessed September 5, 2016).

Blauvelt, William, "An Interview with Poet and Activist Janice Mirikitani," in *International Examiner*, July 4, 1984, p. 6.

"Janice Mirikitani," Poetry Foundation website, https://www.poetryfoundation.org/poems-and-poets/poets/detail/Janice-mirikitani (accessed September 5, 2016).

"Japanese Immigrants," Immigration to the United States website, http://www.immigrationtounitedstates.org/663-japanese-immigrants.html (accessed September 5, 2016).

"Immigration . . . Japanese," Library of Congress, http://loc.gov/teachers/classroommaterials/presentationsandactivities/presentations/immigration/japanese.html (accessed September 5, 2016).

Matsumoto, Tarisa, "Speaking for the Silent," in *International Examiner*, October 31, 2002, p. 31.

"Japanese-American Relocation," History.com, http://www.history.com/topics/world-war-ii/japanese-american-relocation (accessed September 5, 2016).

Mirikitani, Janice, "For a Daughter Who Leaves," in *Love Works*, City Lights Foundation Books, 2003.

———, *Shedding Silence: Poetry and Prose*, Celestial Arts, 1987.

"Our Story," GLIDE website, http://glide.org/story (accessed September 5, 2016).

Pang, Valerie O., "Intentional Silence and Communication in a Democratic Society: The Viewpoint of One Asian American," in *High School Journal*, Vol. 79, No. 3, 1996, pp. 183–90.

Sanchez, Yvonne W., and Dan Nowicki, "Donald Trump's Talk of World War II Internment Camps," in *AZ Central: The Arizona Republic*, http://www.azcentral.com/story/news/arizonpolitics/2015/12/12/donald-trump-world-war-ii-internment-camps/77106008/ (accessed September 5, 2016).

Shetterly, Robert, "Janice Mirikitani," Americans Who Tell the Truth website, http://www.americanswhotellthetruth.org/portraits/janice-mirikitani (accessed September 5, 2016).

Shiroishi, Julie, "Hearing the Muse: For Janice Mirikitani, Activism Feeds Poetry," in *AsianWeek*, March 22, 1996, p. 13.

"Timeline," in *Densho Encyclopedia*, http://encyclopedia.densho.org/timeline/ (accessed September 5, 2016).

Wakida, Patricia, "Janice Mirikitani," in *Densho Encyclopedia*, http://encyclopedia.densho.org/Janice_Mirikitani/ (accessed September 5, 2016).

FURTHER READING

Ferlinghetti, Lawrence, *San Francisco Poems*, City Lights Publishing, 1998.
    San Francisco Poems, a 1998 compilation of verse from the first poet laureate of the city and Mirikitani's immediate predecessor, Lawrence Ferlinghetti, provides beautifully rendered insight into the heart and soul of San Francisco's dynamic arts community.

Makoto, Ooka, *The Poetry and Poetics of Ancient Japan*, Katydid Books, 2006.
    The Poetry and Poetics of Ancient Japan is a collection of five seminal lectures assembled in 2006 and originally given by famed Japanese poet and intellectual Ooka Makoto.

Munro, Eleanor, *Wedding Readings: Centuries of Writing and Rituals on Love and Marriage*, Penguin Books, 1996.
    Wedding Readings: Centuries of Writing and Rituals on Love and Marriage is a font of traditional wisdom regarding the ancient rite across diverse eras, faiths, and cultures. This ambitious work was first released in 1996 under the editorship of Eleanor Munro.

Reeves, Richard, *Infamy: The Shocking Story of the Japanese American Internment in World War II*, Henry Holt, 2015.
    Critically praised and beautifully crafted from the newest research, *Infamy: The Shocking Story of the Japanese American Internment in World War II* is a 2015 history by Richard Reeves and an unflinching account of one of the nation's darkest chapters.

Williams, Cecil, *I'm Alive: An Autobiography*, Harper and Row, 1980.
    I'm Alive: An Autobiography is a personal account of the life and spiritual journey of Cecil Williams, Mirikitani's husband and cofounder of the renowned Glide Organization, providing support and opportunity to the people of San Francisco.

Williams, Cecil, and Janice Mirikitani, *Beyond the Possible: Fifty Years of Creating Radical Change in a Community Called Glide,*, HarperOne, 2013.
    A 2013 collaboration between Janice Mirikitani and her husband, Cecil Williams (with a foreword by Dave Eggers), *Beyond the Possible: Fifty Years of Creating Radical Change in a Community Called Glide* affords an intimate history of one of the most successful charitable organizations in San Francisco and in the world.

SUGGESTED SEARCH TERMS

Janice Mirikitani

Janice Mirikitani AND poetry

Janice Mirikitani AND Cecil Williams

Love Works AND Janice Mirikitani

"For a Daughter Who Leaves" AND Mirikitani

San Francisco poet laureates

Glide Foundation AND San Francisco

Japanese American internment AND World War II

Asian American Movement

Indigo

Chitra Banerjee Divakaruni's poem "Indigo," from her collection *Leaving Yuba City* (1997), describes the lives of Bengali peasant farmers, also known as *ryots*, who were forced to grow indigo, a plant used to make a blue dye, by British planters who were hungry for a piece of the East India Company's profit. Set just before the Nilbidroha—the Indigo Revolt of 1859—the poem is saturated with imagery of the color blue, mimicking the lives of the ryots whose hands and feet were discolored from their work with the indigo crop. The poem is narrated in the first-person-plural point of view, foreshadowing the coming unification and uprising of the peasants as they speak in one voice of the atrocities committed against them in the ruthless pursuit of indigo dye. *Leaving Yuba City* was awarded the Allen Ginsberg Poetry Prize, a Gerbode Foundation Award, and a Pushcart Prize.

CHITRA BANERJEE DIVAKARUNI

1997

AUTHOR BIOGRAPHY

Divakaruni was born in July 29, 1956, in Kolkata (formerly, Calcutta), India. She earned her bachelor's degree in English and Bengali literature from University of Calcutta in 1976, before moving to the United States at the age of nineteen. Her family allowed the move on the condition that she live close to her older brother in Ohio. Divakaruni enrolled in Wright State

The indigo dye is packed in chests to be shipped to England *(©Maksim Vivtsaruk | Shutterstock.com)*

University in Dayton, Ohio, where she earned her master's degree in English in 1978. She went on to earn her PhD from the University of California, Berkeley, in 1985.

In 1990, Divakaruni published her first poetry collection, *The Reason for Nasturtiums*, followed by *Black Candle: Poems about Women from India, Pakistan, and Bangladesh* in 1991. Her first short-story collection, *Arranged Marriage* (1994), explores gender roles within traditional Indian marriages, and it was awarded the 1996 Before Columbus Foundation American Book Award, the American Book Award, the PEN Josephine Miles Award, and the Bay Area Book Reviewers Award. In 1991, concerned with the lack of resources available to abused and threatened Indian women in the United States, she helped found a phone help line called Maitri in the San Francisco area, and she later founded a similar organization called Daya in Houston, Texas, serving victims of domestic violence. She serves on the board of Pratham, which helps provide education to impoverished children in India.

Leaving Yuba City (1997), in which "Indigo" was published, won the Allen Ginsberg Poetry Prize, a Gerbode Foundation Award, and a Pushcart Prize. The same year, Divakaruni turned her attention to fiction, publishing her best-selling novel *Mistress of Spices* in 1997, which was named best book of the year by the *Los Angeles Times* and the best paperback of 1998 by the *Seattle Times*; it was later turned into a film. She went on to publish many novels for adults and young adults, including *Sister of My Heart* (1999), which was also made into a film; *The Vine of Desire* (2002); *Neela: Victory Song* (2002); *Queen of Dreams* (2003); *The Brotherhood of the Conch: The Conch Bearer* (2003); *The Mirror of Fire and Dreaming* (2005); *Palace of Illusions* (2008); *One Amazing Thing* (2009); *Shadowland* (2009); and *Oleander Girl* (2013). Her children's book, *Grandma and the Great Gourd: A Bengali Folktale*, was published in 2013.

Her work has been translated into over twenty-nine languages and has been anthologized in *The Best American Short Stories*, the *O. Henry Prize Stories*, and the *Pushcart Prize Anthology*, as well as appearing in the *New*

Yorker, *Good Housekeeping*, and *Atlantic Monthly*. Divakaruni has served as a judge for the prestigious PEN Faulkner Award and National Book Award. Her awards include the South Asian Literary Association's Distinguished Author Award; a California Arts Council Award; International House Alumna of the Year from the University of California, Berkeley; the Light of India Award from the *Times* of India; the C. Y. Lee Creative Writing Award; and the Cultural Jewel Award from the Indian Culture Center in Houston, Texas. She is the Betty and Gene McDavid Professor of Creative Writing at the University of Houston.

POEM SUMMARY

The text used for this entry is from *Leaving Yuba City*, Anchor Books, 1997, pp. 54–55. A version of the poem can be found on the following website: https://www.poetryfoundation.org/poems-and-poets/poems/detail/57661.

"Indigo" begins with the setting of Bengal in the years 1779–1859. The speaker describes endless fields of the plant, looking like blue flame. The color resembles the venom of a cobra. Like poison it has entered the ryots' (farmers') bloodstreams, pulsing along with their heartbeats like nighttime. No other color exists. When the planter whips them, their faces bleed blue. Their lungs are dyed blue with each breath they take. Only their eyes stubbornly refuse to become blue; instead, they remember the color of the rice where it once pushed up from the fertile land before the rice crops were replaced with indigo crops. As the rice grew, first, the reeds were green, and then they turned a gold that rippled in the wind like waves in the Arhiyal Sea. With that memory comes another: the night the planters set the rice fields ablaze with torches. The wall of fire chased the ryots from their huts. Women were dragged away from their families, screaming.

In the present day, the peasants dip their blue-dyed hands into the bright dye, packing dried cakes of it into chests for the East India Company. Their ankles are blue from the chains they wear. Many of the women who were abducted the night of the fire had drowned themselves in the Arhiyal Sea to escape the memory of their rape, and their bodies are sometimes found later in the river. The ones they left behind

remember the red of their saris and the red marriage mark on their foreheads. They keep this memory hidden away inside their heads, which are otherwise dyed blue like the rest of them. The memory is like a spark of fire that a man cradles in his hands in the middle of winter, ignoring how the heat burns him. He clutches the flame close until he can set it down somewhere safe to watch the fire burst forth like the heart of a star. Then the fire becomes a blaze so bright and lovely that the viewers want it to never stop burning.

THEMES

Abduction

In "Indigo," countless abductions haunt the memories of the peasants. Invaders have abducted, or stolen away, their homeland, their culture, their economy, and their government. Under British control, their crops have changed. Instead of growing rice in their fields, as is traditional, they are forced to grow indigo for the British planters. The abduction of their fields is violent, with the planters torching the green and gold rice crops to make way for indigo. In the process, the peasants' huts are burned and the women are abducted and assaulted. The women never recover from the experience, and many drown themselves in the river.

The blue dye works its way into everything and stains, overpowering even the people's natural skin color. Memories of a time before their lives were taken over by indigo are precious to the ryots: anything unstained by blue is cherished as evidence that their lives were not always so painful. The violent takeover of the Bengali peasants' lives will be set right in the coming cleansing fire, which for now is held secret in the heart of each survivor who is stained blue and bears the scars of the planters' whips. The land belongs to the Indian people, not to the British planters. They may attempt to force their will on others through the abuse of their power, but each crime fans the secret flame of rebellion held by the ryots, waiting to erupt in an inferno and take back the fields, land, culture, and country that was stolen.

Community

The community of ryots has suffered major losses under British rule. Once rural farmers,

TOPICS FOR FURTHER STUDY

- Read Divakaruni's young-adult novel *The Conch Bearer* (2003), from her *Brotherhood of the Conch* series. How is poverty depicted in the novel? What insights into life in India did you gain while reading the work? How would you compare the lives of the peasants in "Indigo" to the lives of the characters Anand and Nisha? Organize your answers into an essay.

- Create a time line infographic of the history of Bengal from 1779 to 1859, the years during which "Indigo" is set. Your time line should end with the Indigo Revolt and include at least five other events along with explanations of the significance of these events to Indian history. Free infographics are available at http://www.easel.ly.

- Choose a different Indian American or Indian poet to study. Create a PowerPoint presentation about the author in which you provide a brief biography, a sample of his or her work (either a poem or a poem excerpt, which you will read aloud), an explanation of the themes and the style of the poem, and three quotations from reputable reviewers about the poet's work. Include a slide listing the sources cited at the end of your presentation.

- Write a poem in which you describe a memory from your childhood using a color motif, taking Divakaruni's use of the color blue in "Indigo" as your example.

they now serve an empire, packing crates of indigo for the powerful East India Company. They are a community in chains, recognized easily by their blue-dyed skin. Indigo arrived in their lives through fire, as the English planters set the fields of rice ablaze. Now, instead of growing food for themselves, the ryots grow a commodity crop for the global market. Instead of being happily married, many of the men have lost their wives to abduction, rape, and suicide. Their huts were burned along with the rice, marking indigo's entrance with the total collapse of the family and home. Yet the peasants maintain a sense of solidarity through that which oppresses them: the blue dye marks them as members of the same tragedy. Together they remember the women they have lost, the happiness they used to share, the colors they once knew. The poem is written in the first person plural ("we") to suggest this deep connectivity, which unites the ryots in a single voice even as their lives take on the blue of British control. The shared consciousness of the poem's peasants hints at the inevitability of uprising against the harsh planters. Stripped of dignity and humanity because of the planters' blind greed for profit, the peasants have reached the end of their endurance. Armed with their plural consciousness, the dear memory of those they have lost, and the stabilizing certainty that there is more than the color blue in the world, they approach rebellion. The peasants welcome the pain of this new fire, which reminds them of their agency—that they are alive and can take action—and prepares them for the upcoming clash. The planters, motivated by individualistic greed, cannot stand up to the united front of the peasants and their rage. Together, the peasants will burn the fields again on their own terms and grow a new life of color and freedom from the ashes.

Memory

Much of the poem is concerned with the memories of the peasants from the days before they farmed indigo. The act of remembering is an act of defiance as they lose their bodies and minds to the blue dye. Consumed by indigo, they hold on tightly to the memory of the color red in the women's saris and marriage marks so that they will not forget those who have drowned themselves in the Arhiyal. This memory will provide the spark of fire they will need to overthrow their oppressors. They remember the green and gold of the rice fields as well, from a time when they were free. It is this paradise that they will restore after their rebellion chases the invaders from their fields. Both the red of the sari and green-gold of the rice are tied to the horrific memory of the day the fields and huts were burned to the ground by the planters to make way for the indigo crop. That was the same day the women were abducted, the day all happiness in the peasants' lives came to an abrupt and violent end. That day, too, is kept safe in memory for later, when the ryots' fire will rise to answer the

The torches of the planter's men contrast with the fertile rice fields (©Rachelle Burnside | Shutterstock.com)

planters' flames, cleansing the earth of the British planters and their inedible crop, their chains, their rapes, and their whips. The coming rebellion will honor the memory of the women lost to the abductors and wash the blue from the skin of the ryots so they may live their lives unstained by imperial rule.

STYLE

First-Person-Plural Point of View

"Indigo" is written in the first-person-plural point of view, with the speaker referring not to "I" or "they" but to "we" when speaking about the farmers' experiences. The "we" of the poem is the peasant (or ryot) class, working under the harsh planters on the indigo fields to harvest dye. The peasants are whipped and raped, their huts are burned to the ground, and their skin is stained blue from working with the crop. Yet

they hold tight to the precious memories of their past life, when they were allowed to grow rice instead of indigo. The first person plural gives a united, powerful voice to a multitude—in this case the oppressed and powerless peasants—who speak out as one on the subject of their trauma and the trials they have endured at the hands of the planters.

Color Motif

In poetry, a motif is an image that repeats throughout the work. In "Indigo," for example, the color blue appears many times. The peasants' hands, skulls, ankles, blood, and lungs are described as dyed blue, and the fields in which they work are the same blue color as snake venom. Blue represents the indigo crops that the ryots are forced to raise by the British planters instead of rice. The blue-stained bodies of the peasants are representative of Britain's heavy hand in the lives of the poor Bengalis: their skin bears the mark of British rule through the permanent dye stains on their skin. Memories of other colors, such as red, green, and gold, are cherished and hidden away by the ryots against their blue reality. These colors represent traditional Indian life: the green and gold of rice fields, the red of saris and marriage marks on women's foreheads. The repeated blue imagery surrounds and suffocates these memories of happier times, as British rule dominates the land and fields of India.

HISTORICAL CONTEXT

Indigo Dye

Associated with religious figures such as the Hindu god Krishna and the Christian figure of the Virgin Mary, indigo is an ancient and powerful natural blue dye. The earliest evidence of the use of indigo dates to 2500 BCE, from an indigo-dyed garment discovered in an excavation of Thebes. In the town of Rojdi (present-day Gujarat) in the Harrappan civilization in the Indus Valley, archaeologists discovered a variety of *Indigofera* seeds dating from 2500–1700 BCE. Indigo has been a valuable export for centuries, with condensed blocks of the dye appearing in excavation sites across Europe, including sites from the Greek and Roman empires, in which indigo was a luxury item. Until Marco Polo returned to Europe in the late thirteenth century

COMPARE & CONTRAST

- **1859:** After a hundred years of the East India Company's rule of the Indian subcontinent, the British crown takes over the governance of India, beginning the period known as the British Raj, which will last from 1858 until 1947.

  1997: India celebrates fifty years of independence from British rule on August 15.

  Today: By population, India is the world's largest democracy, and it is the seventh-largest economy based on its nominal gross domestic product.

- **1859:** Indigo dye is known as Blue Gold—as highly sought after in international trade as salt, opium, and cotton. The East India Company profits heavily from the production of indigo dye from plantations in India, where the dye is extracted naturally from plants.

  1997: Rather than sourcing indigo dye from plants, the majority of indigo dye is produced through a synthetic process discovered by Adolf von Baeyer in 1878 and later perfected by Johannes Pfleger. Indigo dye is used most often in the manufacture of denim.

  Today: Over 18,500 tons of synthetic indigo dye is produced each year. The dye remains in high demand globally. Environmental concerns have led to a renewed interest in the natural production of indigo.

- **1859:** Neither British nor Indian men consider women to be their equals. Common practices in India include the killing of female newborns; child marriage, in which young girls would be married to significantly older men; and sati, the burning of a wife on her husband's funeral pyre.

  1997: Following Indian independence, women gain equal rights under the new constitution. Although great strides are made toward women's inclusion in education, business, government, and sports and although child marriage and the practice of sati are outlawed, female infanticide continues to occur, skewing the gender ratio in the country.

  Today: Fifty-two percent of Indian women report being victims of violence, while 60 percent of Indian men admit to having been violent against a woman in their lifetime. Some surveys indicate that the poorer the family, the more likely they are to prefer sons and practice strict gender roles, with the husband dominant in household decisions.

---

with firsthand experience of seeing the dye made, Europeans believed the blue rock-like cakes of pigment to be minerals. Once direct trade routes were established between Europe and Asia, demand for indigo grew rapidly beginning in 1498.

Spanish plantations in Central America began to grow indigo in the mid-sixteenth century. In Africa, indigo was used as currency in the slave trade, with one length of dyed cloth worth one slave. Once the crop was introduced to the British colonies in North America, it quickly outperformed both sugar and cotton as

an export. Hard cakes of indigo dye were used as currency during the American Revolution. Referred to as Blue Gold by traders, indigo was grown in India over a massive area of land (about 4,300 square miles at its peak) on plantations ruled over by planters working for the East India Company—until the Nilbidroha, or Indigo Revolt of 1859, in which the indigo plantations were destroyed.

As described in part in Divakaruni's "Indigo," the natural extraction of the dye from the plant is achieved through submerging the crop in a series of tubs of water until the concentrated, rich blue

Fields of rice, grown for food, were replaced by the cash crop of indigo plants (©Zvonimir Atletic / Shutterstock.com)

dye sinks to the bottom as sediment. This sediment is then dried into bricks and packed away for shipment. Natural indigo dye was all but replaced by synthetic dye toward the end of the nineteenth century as advances in the synthetic technology allowed manufacturers to meet the ever-growing worldwide demand that natural sources of the dye could no longer meet. The dye remains enormously popular today and is used to add color to denim clothing such as blue jeans.

Nilbidroha

The Nilbidroha, or Indigo Revolt, was a successful agrarian uprising in Bengal that lasted from 1859 until 1861. Rural Bengal peasant farmers, or ryots, were forced by British planters to cultivate indigo instead of their preferred crops of rice or tobacco. While ryots much preferred the higher profits and lessened labor of growing rice, not to mention the added benefits of raising an edible crop, the planters demanded the farming of indigo, which could be sold to the East India Company for a large profit. Ryots received little of the indigo profit, however, and resisted the planters' wishes as often as possible. Though at first relationships between ryots and planters were generally professional and allowed for

some negotiation between their conflicting desires, the passage of Act XI of 1860 made it illegal for ryots to refuse to grow exactly what the planters demanded. This resulted in the immediate abuse of power by the planters and the growing dissatisfaction of the ryots, as illustrated in "Indigo." V. B. Ganesan writes in "The Revolt That Foreshadowed Many Agrarian Uprisings" for the *Hindu*: "The planters took full advantage of this law and their oppression became severe.... The district officials also joined the planters in this oppression. But the ryots were determined."

The ryots began to rebel in 1859, burning down plantations and indigo storehouses, trying and hanging planters, and refusing to farm. The movement gained the support of the urban intellectual elite following the 1859 production of the play *Nil Darpan*, by Dinabandhu Mitra, which dramatized the abuse of the peasants by the planters and their brave fight against oppression. The *Hindoo Patriot*, a weekly Bengali paper popular among the middle class, remained firmly on the side of the besieged ryots. Though the revolt was brutally suppressed by a combination of local police and military forces, the movement was successful in inspiring the British government in India to establish the Indigo Commission of 1860, which examined the practices of indigo cultivation in order to find a solution to the issue. The revolt made a lasting impression in the minds of Indians as well, as Ganesan explains: "Historically, the Indigo Rebellion can be termed the first form [of] resistance of the countryside against the British in economic and social terms . . . a thread of dissent that lasted many decades thereafter."

CRITICAL OVERVIEW

Leaving Yuba City debuted to overwhelmingly positive reviews and was awarded an Allen Ginsberg Poetry Prize, a Gerbode Foundation Award, and the Pushcart Prize. In her review for the *Weber Journal*, Neila C. Seshachari writes about the wide range of the collection: "The topics of the poems range from a poet's growth to the social and political implications of immigrants' lives, the experience of growing up in colonial India, and the poet's reveries triggered by the works of artists."

In *Nirali* magazine, Ismat Sarah Mangla describes Divakaruni as an internationally famous novelist and a "compelling, lyrical writer whose bestselling works have garnered much praise." These works "often share the theme of the South Asian native or immigrant experience. . . . But Divakaruni recognizes that different readers will take different things from her work."

A review of *Leaving Yuba City* in *Publishers Weekly* states: "Divakaruni's persistent concern with women's experience often deepens as it is arrayed against varying cultural grounds." Her depiction of the suffering and suicide of the women peasants on the plantations in "Indigo" is one example of the depth of her portrayal of the struggle of women throughout the long history of India.

In an interview of Divakaruni in *Contemporary Women's Writing*, Metka Zupancic praises the inherent power of her writing to inspire others to find their own voices. This power, Zupancic comments, "comes from the connection to [her] heritage and to literature in general . . . As [her] writing triggers other people's emotions, other people's creativity, it helps them reconnect with their own source of what makes them better people."

In *Asian-American Poets: A Bio-Bibliographical Critical Sourcebook*, Purvi Shah comments on Divakaruni's devotion to both her subject matter and her craft as a poet. Although her early poems, Shah writes, display only an "engagement with history and immigrant experiences," her later work also displays a concern with generic play" and a focus on telling the individual stories of her characters. "In *Leaving Yuba City*," Shah continues, "this focus on telling particular stories is tied to experimentation with narration and prose formats."

CRITICISM

Amy L. Miller
Miller is a graduate of the University of Cincinnati. In the following essay, she explores the ways in which Divakaruni uses poetic devices to recreate the emotional atmosphere of a volatile moment in Bengali history in "Indigo."

Divakaruni's "Indigo" explores the toxic relationship between the peasant ryots and British planters leading up to the Indigo Revolt of 1859, yet rather than recount the important dates, famous names, or relevant legislation, she tells the true story of the peasants' struggles through poetry. With figurative language, bright imagery, color motifs, and an uncommon point of view, "Indigo" breathes life into history rather than letting it lie flat on the page. The poem is as overly saturated with the color blue as the lives of the ryots, who cannot wash the indigo stain from their skin or the memories of the planters' abuse from their minds. For them, the wind carries screams, the river carries bodies, and the rich dye they harvest reminds them of their own blood. "Indigo" illustrates the final days of the cruel planters, though they do not know their time has drawn to a close. The spark the peasant farmers have carried within them since their crops were burned, homes destroyed, and women abducted ignites in the final lines into a righteous fire that reclaims the fields and crops in the name of the local farmers.

Seshachari writes that Divakaruni's collection *Leaving Yuba City*, in which "Indigo" appears, is "divided into six sections, with five additional poems that raise their heads between the interstices of the sections, as if to announce that they breathe in their own nuclei and stand on their own." "Indigo" is one of these five independent poems: a world in five stanzas, separated from the works around it as if the dye that runs like water through the poem might otherwise bleed through into the neighboring pages. The dye has permeated not only the skin of the ryots but also their bodies, their organs, their senses, and their minds. Blue is the color of cobra poison, blood, veins, and—though it goes unsaid—the British flag beneath which the atrocities on the indigo plantations took place. The lungs, skulls, hands, and ankles of the ryots have been dyed to match the crop that enslaves them: a brand announcing indigo's ownership of their lives. The color symbolizes pain, poverty, and loss to the peasants forced to grow indigo. Before their lives became submerged in blue dye, they were happy. But the dye overpowers all other color, trapping the ryots in the planters' pursuit of East India Company profits.

Overcome by blue, the peasants take refuge in their memories of life before indigo. What makes Divakaruni's blue motif particularly powerful is the way in which she breaks it in the second and fifth stanzas with the introduction of colors other than blue. Though her speakers have made clear that there are no other colors, they soon reveal that this was not always the case. Colors live on in their memory: red, green, and gold. Green and gold represent the memory of rice—the ryots' favorite crop and a symbol of better times. Before the demand for indigo began to skyrocket internationally, the ryots were allowed to grow what they wanted, to earn profit for their work, and to rotate their crops with each new season. In an idyllic memory of this time before indigo, the waves of the Arhiyal Sea are gold rather than blue, a post-indigo adjustment to a happy memory to erase the hated color. The earth is fertile and the

harvest plentiful—at least, it would have been plentiful if not for the planter's fire that scorched the crops, the earth, and all life to dust in preparation for indigo.

The motif of fire begins, along with the motif of the color blue, in the poem's first line. Unlike the rice field, which rolled in beautiful golden waves like the Arhiyal, the indigo fields burn with a blue flame. The expected descriptions of colors of these natural phenomena would be of the endless waves of water as blue and the fire as gold. Instead, the flames burn blue and the waves crash golden against the shore. The natural is rendered unnatural by the presence of the hated dye, which arrives in the poem across an ocean of flame. The fire resembles a tidal wave as it crashes down from the field onto the huts. That night, the peasant women are abducted and dragged screaming to the plantations. The narration, spoken in first person plural, pauses here in the memory of the most horrific moment of the catastrophic night, in order to pack a chest full of the blue bricks for the East India Company. Then it resumes, to report that many of the women drowned themselves afterward, because that was the easiest way. Divakaruni ingenuously places the description of this human tragedy next to the blind greed that caused it. The story is interrupted, just as the ryots' lives were interrupted, by the East India Company's endless hunger for indigo. Ganesan writes: "The indigo planters forced the ryots to cultivate without remuneration, confined, beat, and compelled the villagers as well as corrupted their own servants." While indigo made slaves of the ryots, it made monsters of the planters, who destroyed lives in the name of profit.

The women are remembered by the color red, the lovely hue of their saris and the marriage marks they wore on their foreheads. Seshachari writes of the poems collected in *Leaving Yuba City*: "At the heart of these poems is the cold reality of women's experiences, their concerns and struggles, their unspoken influences and silent heroism." Without the women, the ryots are left freezing in an emotional winter. But through the memory of things represented by the color red, they find a spark with which to survive the cold. Unlike the poisonous blue fire of the planters, this spark is red and bright. The longer it is held, in secret, the brighter it glows. The poem's final stanza is devoted to the steadily

WHAT
DO I READ
NEXT?

- *Swami and Friends* (1983), a young-adult novel by R. K. Narayan, follows the adventures of Swami as he plays cricket with the Malguldi Cricket Club, struggles with school after being expelled twice in a row, and runs away from home after his simple life becomes entangled with the larger political forces at work in 1930s India on the brink of independence.

- Henry Freeman's *The East India Company: From Beginning to End* (2016) traces the history of the company and its role in establishing a global British Empire, including a detailed account of its role in China and India.

- Divakaruni's novel *The Palace of Illusions* (2008) retells the classic epic of Indian literature, the *Mahabharata*, from the perspective of its heroine, Panchaali, exiled along with her five husbands from their home. With help from her friend, the god Krishna, Panchaali prepares for a war of universal importance as she fights alongside her husbands for her right to rule.

- *The Complete Poems of Anna Akhmatova* (1990) collects the work of the famous Russian poet along with a biography, photographs, and notes on the poems and their translation. A voice of women's struggles amid poverty and war, Akhmatova's inspirational poetry has uplifted and inspired generations of artists and intellectuals to stand strong behind their values, unbending to the pressures of politics.

- In Bharati Mukherjee's *The Holder of the World* (1993), antique-hunter Beigh Masters discovers the story of a New England woman named Hannah Easton who traveled to India with her husband in the seventeenth century only to undergo a sudden transformation, abandoning her former identity to become the lover of a raja.

- Rita Dove's *Collected Poems: 1974–2004* (2016) collects the work of this Pulitzer

Prize–winning poet who served as the poet laureate of the United States. From childhood to the civil rights movement to retellings of Greek myth, Dove's lyrical and groundbreaking poetry explores the heart's capacity for pain, grief, forgiveness, and love.

- In Ved Mehta's *Walking the Indian Streets* (1960), the author writes of returning to India after a decade-long absence, observing the changes he finds as well as what has stayed the same. In reconnecting to his family and home, he reconnects with a past he left behind and an identity he had forgotten.

- Vikram Seth's novel *A Suitable Boy* (1993) is set in the chaotic years after India's independence from British rule. A family's struggle to find a suitable husband for their daughter, Lata, brings together the lives and fates of four families at a time of cultural upheaval and political uncertainty. Torn between love and duty to her family, Lata struggles to find a compromise that will leave her happily in the arms of the man she loves.

- Garrett Hongo's *Coral Road: Poems* (2011) reflects on the history of the author's Japanese ancestors, their arrival in Hawaii, and his great-grandparents' daring escape from the plantations. Through these threads of history he returns to his own life in Hawaii and California as a Japanese American with a better understanding of the mysteries of his existence and a firmer grasp on his place in the world.

- *The Collected Poems of A. K. Ramanujan* (1995) gathers the work of a beloved translator and poet of the finest talent who wrote Indian poetry in English. His immense knowledge of Indian folklore and love of language shines across the three volumes of poetry he published in his lifetime and a fourth published posthumously in this collection for the first time.

The final stanza makes it clear that the people hold on to their cultural traditions (©Natalia Yankelevich /
Shutterstock.com)

growing righteous flame of the ryots' revenge:
the spirit of their wives untouched by abductors,
reminding the peasants through its sting that
they are still alive. Instead of indigo, they begin
to grow the flame of their rage and indignation,
waiting for the right time and place to unleash
their fury in a red blaze. For once the fire will be
beautiful, like the rising of a star, bringing with it
revolution.

Though the poem stops short of the Indigo
Revolt, the planters' downfall has already
arrived in the hearts of the embattled ryots,
who simply will not take another day's abuse.
Joined together by the first-person-plural perspective, the peasants share a single, powerful
voice that has not yet been choked into silence
by their immersion in the dye. Speaking with
that communal voice, they remember the joys
of rice crops and marriage, the sorrows of fire
and loss; they share the secrets of their memories
and prepare to take action against their oppressors. The planters, their actions marked by self-
ishness and greed, stand little chance when so
outnumbered by those whom they have stripped

of all humanity, leaving behind only a desire for
vengeance. Divakaruni emphasizes the stubborn
personality of the peasants throughout the
poem: their eyes that refuse to forget, the way
they hold on to the color red as if it were the hand
of a lover, and the way they crouch around their
spark in the dead of winter, giving it their breath
and refusing to drop it even when it burns them.
Against such strength, the planters cannot hope
to prevail.

The indigo dye drips down from one stanza
to the next, smothering, staining, and stealing
life from its victims. Yet the red flame of the
final stanza works against this drip, burning all
mentions of blue from the poem's conclusion.
Like the gold waves and blue flame, the dye
and red fire work in opposition. As the author
notes at the end of the poem, the indigo plantations were destroyed in the Indigo Revolt. The
poem itself makes it clear that they were burned
to the ground. In order to escape the planters'
oppression, the peasants used their own tactics
against them: setting fire to the planters' crops
and destroying their homes. While the planters

> THE MYTHOLOGICAL LABYRINTH IN WHICH THE EPIC NARRATIVE IS WROUGHT RESTRICTS THE WRITER TO INTERPRET IT ALTERING THE VERY BASIS OF ITS CONSTRUCTION AND THUS, THE SIGNIFICANCE OF FATE WHICH MAY NOT APPEAR AS A GENUINE CAUSE OF LITERARY CONCERN CANNOT BE LEFT OUT OF DISCUSSION."

attempted to use fire as a means of control over the crops the peasants would grow, the peasants used fire to drive the planters away, to escape their control forever. This demonstrates, once again, how the planters' unnatural greed tainted their view of nature, for fire cannot be controlled. Fire, like the furious ryots, answers to no one. Throughout the poem, Divakaruni positions colors, images, and people on opposing sides of the conflict between ryots and planters, as if setting up a chessboard in preparation for a game. The poem may end before the battle begins, but a winner has already been named through the power of Divakaruni's poetic language.

Source: Amy L. Miller, Critical Essay on "Indigo," in *Poetry for Students*, Gale, Cengage Learning, 2017.

Sarannya V. Pillai

In the following excerpt, Pillai explains how Divakaruni redefines myths and legends in her work.

The Palace of Illusions by Chitra Banerjee Divakaruni is a text of great significance as the narrative unfolds the most criticized female character of Draupadi and the author's stance provides a broader view to reintrospect the epic. The book absolves Draupadi, wife of *Pandavas* in Indian epic *Mahabharata*, from the patriarchal shackles as well as the biased attitude toward her decisions and behavior which again beckons a need for reinterpreting the male-centric epics and legends from a woman's point of view.

Writers like Shashi Deshpande and Anita Desai are among the early Indian women writers who broke away from the age-old tradition of positioning women in the patriarchal construct and allowing their female characters to chase their dreams and fancies without making them lose their familial bonds. Divakaruni's protagonists exercise their freedom and are independent on their own terms. The key factor that one could find in these writings is that the protagonists would be iconoclasts and would be characterized in opposition to the other female characters, who are unable to evolve out of the social codes of conduct and discipline. The feminists worldwide demanded for the need of women writers to engage in writing about women to project the actual essence of womanhood which is in reality contradictory to those written by male writers.

Cixous revolutionized women's writing in "The Laugh of Medusa," asserting that,

> Woman must write her self, must write about women and bring women to writing, from which they have been driven away as violently as from their bodies—for the same reasons, by the same law, with the same fatal goal. Women must put herself into the text—as into the world and into history—by her own movement.

Divakaruni, in her fictional text *The Palace of Illusions* has carried forward Cixous' exhortations by reinterpreting the epic *The Mahabharata* from Draupadi's point of view—a woman rewriting a classic from a woman's perspective, deposing the male-centric narratives. Draupadi had been portrayed as the "harbinger of ill luck," throwing many women into the miserable fate of widowhood, causing many deaths that marked the end of an epoch. Divakaruni's writing has helped Draupadi to "liberate" herself from the dagger point of contempt and condescension. This chapter will look into the text from an angle that positions the women in the text as "figures that no authority can subjugate."

Divakaruni's text stands as a metaphor of the illusions or the assumptions on the characteristics of Draupadi in the epic *The Mahabharata*. The narrative unfolds the hidden levels of significations that had been overlooked as the absurdity of a woman's reasoning ability; in a more direct way, the "lack of reason" which is accepted as a woman's inherent nature; the text addresses and questions the manifold concerns of power, reason, gender and human temperament and predicament while confronting fate. The chapter focuses on Draupadi's dispositions as the narrative unfurls through her and the whole text purports a serious study of other male-centric epics and narratives from a feministic point of view so as to provide a holistic reflection, which otherwise is a partial or a blind-folded course of representation. The chapter discusses how the narrative draws parallel between the palace that has been constructed of magic to that of the illusion of existence called *maya* as propounded by Lord *Krishna* in the epic.

Lord *Krishna* explicates the concept of *maya* which means that the life on earth is an illusory phase and thus the human lives should be based on detachment from materialism. The epic, *The Mahabharata*, resonates with mystical occurrences and the episodes and events interrogate with our logical sense of belief. *Krishna* maintains throughout the narrative that the events entailed are nothing but a chain of reactions that would lead to the catastrophe which again is not the end but the beginning of another epoch. Divakaruni has employed *Krishna's* musings to justify the persona of Draupadi, who has been highly criticized for the reason that she became the unitary force behind the bloodshed. The text serves another purpose of regaining the lost dignity to the wronged women like Draupadi where the theological and oracular positions failed.

The illusory existence is established with the birth of Dhristadyumna and Draupadi from the fire. The king and his subjects welcomed Dhristadyumna just then they saw Draupadi emerging from the fire. The king's "initial rejection" of Draupadi for her being a girl and also a herald of change evinces how even a phenomenal birth could not cease the dichotomy of gender: "Only when Krishna insisted that the prophecy at my birth required me to get an education beyond what women were usually given.... Dhri, too, sometimes wondered if I wasn't learning the wrong things, ideas that would only confuse me as I took up a woman's life with its prescribed, restrictive laws."

Dhri, as she addressed Dhristadyumna, was the boon the King, Drupad, asked from the Gods to defeat Dhrona; however the Gods also gave Draupadi to the king and prophesied that "she will change the course of history." The privileges Draupadi had as a young princess were granted to her due to the prophesied magnitude of her life; yet she could not evade the phase of helplessness and misery irrespective of her class and uniqueness.

Draupadi, though, "hungered to know about the amazing, mysterious world...the world of the senses and of that which lay beyond them."

The male-oriented education signified culture, reason and sense and it was deemed as a dispensation for Draupadi whereas a forbidden mode of intellect for others that a woman engage herself in reasoning power. The concept of woman as representing the antithesis of "reason" so as to embody her as an image of ignorance has been the practice of the patriarchal society. The lack or absence of *logos* reinstates the "otherness" of woman in comparison to man and the attempt to bridge the difference comes in abject opposition to the dichotomies the male centric maintains. The phenomenal birth of Draupadi, and the prophecies related to it, earned her the otherwise outlawed learning that, as the epic is interpreted, takes the toll on the entire *Kaurava* and *Pandava* dynasty. However, the text suggests that the "prophecy" preceded the act of learning, and the deliberate effort of the interpreters to ignore this very fact of an insight that would have justified the women characters of the epic as being "pawns in the hands of Time." The epic *The Mahabharata* as explained and interpreted leaves no space for a woman who "has never her turn to speak." Whereas Divakaruni turns the plot into a fictional space where the women find expression to their thoughts and objectify their action that had been fashioned by the patriarchal norms and how their efforts to sustain their voice tarnished their stature in a world that is conditioned to look at things from a male-centered perspective.

The mythological labyrinth in which the epic narrative is wrought restricts the writer to interpret it altering the very basis of its construction and thus, the significance of fate which may not appear as a genuine cause of literary concern cannot be left out of discussion. Divakaruni has developed her narration based on the "prophecy" or the polyphonic predictions and pushed the culpability of catastrophe from a woman's shoulders to that of the materialization of fate. The patriarchal notions of reason and culture positioned on the gender itself define the destiny of a woman if she tries to come out of the cocoon and express her inner voice. Gandhari, Kunti, Madri, and the minor characters like Bhanumati. Subhadra, and so on, are seen as the epitome of womanhood as they evolved according to the expected dictum whereas Draupadi who was subjected to many embarrassing circumstances by men and because of men became the object of ridicule and detestation as she reacted against the oppression. *The*

Mahabharata and *The Ramayana* are the two greatest Indian epics that provide the basis of belief, standard of living, human qualities and so on. Sita's womanhood is celebrated to date and every woman character is compared in terms of similarities or dichotomies with respect to her. The text taken up for discussion also follows the same fashion of comparison. *The Palace of Illusions* uses the evaluation to draw the strength of Draupadi's character and explains why every woman should not be scrutinized in the image of Sita or another mythological female character who never raised a voice of retaliation but tolerated the shackles of oppression and dejection to their doom.

The woman who provides a sympathetic attitude to Draupadi is her *Dhai-Ma* (caretaker) who provides her with maternal care and concern whereas others maintain a distance from her due to her strange birth. *Krishna's* well-timed intervention facilitated the manifestation of the prophecy into a reality; the epic might suggest it to be a divine association. Divakaruni's text advocates this as a deliberate interference with a woman's selfhood defacing her reasoning power and, in this way, channeling the route through her toward destruction without her conscious effort. The text posits the question that how then could Draupadi be represented as a signifier for the war? The legends and epics were reduced to see that "women were the root cause of all the world's troubles" and the situation in which women became associated with a war or a temporal change in history were manipulated to suggest the disastrous outcome resulted due to their arrogance and misconduct. The text interrogates the existing norms and posits that a woman when made a pawn in a patriarchal structure is incapable of going against her conscience even when she knows that she is being directed toward a catastrophic path. . . .

Source: Sarannya V. Pillai, "Chitra Banerjee Divakaruni's *The Palace of Illusions*: An Écriture Féminine," in *Contemporary Women's Writing in India*, edited by Varun Gulati and Mythili Anoop, Lexington Books, 2014, pp. 161–64.

SOURCES

"Author Chitra Banerjee Divakaruni on Her New Book and Women's Empowerment," in *Hindustan Times*, April 28, 2016.

Bauer, Erika, "A Discussion with Chitra Divakaruni," ebStudios.com, March 1993, http://www.uni-saar land.de/fileadmin/user_upload/Professoren/fr43_ProfGhosh Schellhorn/Tas_Datenbank/South_Asia___Diasporas/ Divakaruni_Interview_Ebstudios.PDF (accessed August 15, 2016).

Beedy, Katrina, "Gender Roles in India," in *Borgen*, January 29, 2015, http://www.borgenmagazine.com/gender-roles-india/ (accessed August 16, 2016).

"Bio," Chitra Divakaruni website, http://www.chitradi vakaruni.com/about/bio/ (accessed August 15, 2016).

"Chitra Banerjee Divakaruni," Poetry Foundation website, https://www.poetryfoundation.org/poems-and-poets/poets/detail/chitra-banerjee-divakaruni (accessed August 15, 2016).

"Chitra Banerjee Divakaruni (1956–) Biography," Jrank.org, http://biography.jrank.org/pages/1589/Divakaruni-Chitra-Banerjee-1956.html (accessed August 15, 2016).

Divakaruni, Chitra Banerjee, "Indigo," in *Leaving Yuba City*, Anchor Books, 1997, pp. 54–55.

"1858: Beginning of the Raj," BBC website, March, 3, 2011, http://www.bbc.co.uk/history/british/modern/ independence1947_01.shtml (accessed August 16, 2016).

Ganesan, V. B., "The Revolt That Foreshadowed Many Agrarian Uprisings," in *Hindu*, June 23, 2014, http:// www.thehindu.com/books/books-reviews/the-revolt-that-foreshadowed-many-agrarian-uprisings/article6142637.ece (accessed August 15, 2016).

"History of Indigo and Indigo Dyeing," Wild Colours website, May 31, 2016, http://www.wildcolours.co.uk/ html/indigo_history.html (accessed August 16, 2016).

"Indigo: The Indelible Color That Ruled the World," NPR website, November 7, 2011, http://www.npr.org/ 2011/11/07/142094103/indigo-the-indelible-color-that-ruled-the-world (accessed August 16, 2016).

Mangla, Ismat Sarah, "Writing from Two Worlds," in *Nirali*, No. 20, April 2008, https://niralimagazine.com/ 2004/10/writing-from-two-worlds/ (accessed August 15, 2016).

Mattson, Anne, "Indigo in the Early Modern World," University of Minnesota Libraries website, https:// www.lib.umn.edu/bell/tradeproducts/indigo (accessed August 16, 2016).

Review of *Leaving Yuba City: Poems*, in *Publishers Weekly*, July 14, 1997, http://www.publishersweekly .com/978-0-385-48854-9 (accessed August 15, 2016).

Seshachari, Neila C., Review of *Leaving Yuba City*, in *Weber Journal*, Volume 15, No. 1, Winter 1998, http:// www.weber.edu/weberjournal/Journal_Archives/Archive _B/Vol_15_1/BookReviews.html (accessed August 15, 2016).

Shah, Purvi, "Chitra Banerjee Divakaruni (1956–)," in *Asian-American Poets: A Bio-Bibliographical Critical Sourcebook*, edited by Guiyou Huang, pp. 93–99.

Sofky, Elizabeth, "Cross-Cultural Understanding Spiced with the Indian Diaspora," in *Black Issues in Higher Education*, Vol. 14, No. 15, September 18, 1997.

"The Synthesis of Indigo," Ingenious.org, http://www.ingenious.org.uk/site.asp?s = RM&Param = 1&SubParam = 1&Content = 1&ArticleID = %7BCBDF1082-9F5C-498F-A769-B33A7DA83B30%7D&ArticleID2 = %7B3C4444FC-FC4D-4498-B0B4-8B8A47C5BA76%7D&MenuLinkID = %7BA54FA022-17E2-483C-B937-DEC8B8964C33%7D (accessed August 16, 2016).

"World Economic Outlook Database, October 2015: Report for Selected Countries and Subjects," International Monetary Fund website, October 2015, http://www.imf.org/external/pubs/ft/weo/2015/02/weodata/weorept.aspx?pr.x = 49&pr.y = 8&sy = 2013&ey = 2020&scsm = 1&ssd = 1&sort = country&ds = .&br = 1&c = 534&s = NGDPD%2CNGDPDPC%2CPPPGDP%2CPPPPC&grp = 0&a = (accessed August 15, 2016).

Zupancic, Metka, "The Power of Storytelling: An Interview with Chitra Banerjee Divakaruni," in *Contemporary Women's Writing*, Vol. 6, No. 2, August 7, 2011, http://cww.oxfordjournals.org/content/6/2/85.full (accessed August 15, 2016).

FURTHER READING

Divakaruni, Chitra Banerjee, *Before We Visit the Goddess*, Simon and Schuster, 2016.

Divakaruni's novel tells the story of three generations of women. Sabitri, a Bengali woman who desires an education, becomes the mother of Bela, who grows up and comes to the United States looking for a new life with her lover, a political refugee. Bela gives birth to Tara, an Indian American who knows only what her mother has taught her about her ancestral homeland. The novel explores family, choices, and the meaning of home as each woman strives to follow her dreams and make a life all her own.

Gooptu, Nandini, and Douglas M. Peers, *India and the British Empire*, Oxford University Press, 2012.

India and the British Empire studies the history of British imperialism in India and South Asia, with a focus on breaking down previously rigid binaries between those who ruled and those who were ruled to better examine the realities of the imperial power structure in India, its successes and failings, and its effect on Indian political and social culture. India's relationship to its neighbors and their experience of imperialism is studied as well, along with the power of Indian culture over its colonizers.

Hallisey, Charles, *Therigatha: Poems of the First Buddhist Women*, Harvard University Press, 2015.

This collection of poetry gathers the work of the first Buddhist women, composed more than two thousand years ago. Today, it is one of the oldest collections of poetry known, and it is the single oldest example of a collection of poetry exclusively written by women. The nuns' meditations on the path toward nirvana, their timeless wisdom, their strength of will, and their understanding of beauty make this a valuable document of both ancient Buddhism and the lives of women.

Mitra, Dinabandhu, *Nil Darpan*, Forgotten Books, 2012.

This drama, originally written in 1858 and produced in 1859, depicts the way in which the cultivation of indigo corrupted the planters and oppressed the ryots—two groups that had worked together in relative harmony before indigo became a treasured commodity. The play divides the responsibility for inciting the Indigo Revolt, as it tried to bring intellectuals to the side of the oppressed peasants, inspiring national sympathy for their plight.

SUGGESTED SEARCH TERMS

Chitra Banerjee Divakaruni

Divakaruni AND "Indigo"

Divakaruni AND Leaving Yuba City

India AND Indigo Dye

Bengal AND Indigo Revolt

Bengal AND Nilbidroha

Divakaruni AND Indian American poetry

East India Company AND Bengal

Inner Tube

MICHAEL ONDAATJE

1984

Canadian writer Michael Ondaatje's poem "Inner Tube" offers the reader a most relaxing, tranquil trip floating along on a river—and a sighting of a heron that seems to hold more than meets the eye. Ondaatje has a most worldly sensibility, having been born and raised in Ceylon—now Sri Lanka, matured in London, and grown into adulthood in Canada. "Inner Tube" demonstrates such a sensibility less in a cultural sense than in the sense of expanding the reader's consciousness in the context of the natural world. It is not easy to say where the poem takes place, with little hint of geographic location. In that "Inner Tube" is part of Ondaatje's multipart poem "Rock Bottom," which by and large treats the difficulties at the end of the author's first marriage, one may presume that it takes place in Canada. On the other hand, it might be reckoned a reminiscence of a moment in the writer's youth, as far back as in Ceylon. The impossibility of pinning down a place contributes to the universalizing sense of the poem, which draws on an inversion of perspective to consider the juxtaposition, and at times opposition, of humankind and nature.

"Rock Bottom" was published first in Ondaatje's collection *Secular Love* (1984) and then in his *The Cinnamon Peeler: Selected Poems* (1989). The multiple subparts within "Rock Bottom"—which are not listed in the tables of contents—are designated by asterisks,

Michael Ondaatje *(©Tony Moran / Shutterstock.com)*

occasionally as followed by an italicized subtitle enclosed in parentheses, as with "* *(Inner Tube)*" and the others.

AUTHOR BIOGRAPHY

Philip Michael Ondaatje was born on September 12, 1943, in Colombo, Ceylon (now Sri Lanka). With his paternal grandfather a wealthy planter—they were British colonists—his extended family was large and boisterous, and he would recall "a great childhood," as cited by *Dictionary of Literary Biography* writer Ann Mandel, with numerous aunts and uncles in different houses and much lively discourse and unique behavior. His father, in particular, he would lovingly single out in his writing as often engaging in over-the-top acts under the influence of alcohol. His parents separated in 1948, and after several years remaining in Colombo, Ondaatje in 1952 joined his mother, brother, and sister in London, England. There, he attended Dulwich College (a secondary school).

He grew disillusioned with the English school system, however, which obliged him to study mathematics when he wanted to focus on English. This led to his crossing the Atlantic to join his older brother in Montreal, Quebec, in 1962.

In Canada, Ondaatje attended Bishop's University, in Lennoxville, Quebec, studying English and history. He would finish his bachelor's degree in 1965 at the University of Toronto and added a master's in 1967 at Queen's University, both in Ontario. At Queen's, he was an editor of the university's literary magazine, *Quarry*, which had just achieved national circulation. In his personal life, Ondaatje married Kim Jones in 1964, and they had two children. Meanwhile, there was something of a cultural renaissance taking place in Canada in the 1960s, with poetry becoming a particular topic of interest, and Ondaatje found himself bolstered by the current. He would report, as cited by Douglas Barbour in *Michael Ondaatje*, that "meeting poets and having enthusiastic teachers brought things into focus for me and I began to write." Ondaatje came out with his first book of poetry, *The Dainty Monsters*, in the same year that he became an English instructor at the University of Western Ontario. He published several more volumes over the next several years, including *The Collected Works of Billy the Kid* (1970), a narrative mosaic that won Canada's most prestigious literary honor, the Governor General's Award—the first of four that Ondaatje would win. He also began directing films.

Moving to become a professor at Glendon College of Toronto's York University in 1971, Ondaatje sustained his trajectory of literary expansion and success, continuing in his established veins while also writing plays and editing collections. While he traveled for occasional visiting professorships—such as in Hawaii and Rhode Island—he did not return to Sri Lanka until 1978, some twenty-six years after he had left. Around 1980, he separated from his wife, and he would come to live with Linda Spalding. He dedicated to Spalding his collection *Secular Love* (1985), which includes "Inner Tube" as part of the longer poem "Rock Bottom." Ondaatje's biggest international success came with the novel *The English Patient* (1992), which was adapted into a film that won nine Academy Awards. He has continued to live, teach, and write in Toronto.

POEM SUMMARY

The text used for this summary is from *Secular Love*, W. W. Norton, 1985, p. 49. Versions of the poem can be found on the following web pages: http://www.poemhunter.com/best-poems/michael-ondaatje/inner-tube/ and http://www.poetry soup.com/famous/poems/best/michael_ondaatje.

Lines 1–9
The first line of "Inner Tube" sets the scene of a warm July river; it is not entirely clear whether this means a river in warm July or a warm river in July. Regardless, the scene is suggested to be one of relaxation, as someone (readily presumed the narrator) has his head tilted back, as if lounging—naturally, on the inner tube of the title.

Line 3 repeats the setting but now clarifies that the scene is upside down, such that it functions, as indicated in line 4, as an overhead shelter of sorts. The reader imagines, then, that the narrator's head is tilted so far back as to provide an inverted view of the scene, in which the river is at the top of his field of vision, the sky at the bottom.

The person (yet unspecified) is propelling himself along the river in a leisurely or deliberate way, as directed toward an *estuary*, an area where the outflow of the river meets the back-flow of the tides of the larger body of water into which it empties. This area is situated, whether from the narrator's point of view or an objective rendering of the scene, with trees on either side.

With line 7, the reader might momentarily conceive that the subject of the preceding actions is actually a dog, since no human subject has yet been presented; the line only affirms that a dog exists. However, in the ensuing line, the narrator finally makes his appearance by pronoun, clarifying that the dog is in the process of mastering the basic action of swimming not far from where the narrator floats along.

Lines 10–17
The fifth stanza is the longest, suggesting it may achieve the most topical depth. The narrator calls back to mind his head (and the position in which he is holding it), as it sinks into the water up to the level of his eyebrow. He thus now notes how he approximates, or how he (metaphorically) is, the projecting front of a seagoing ship from ages past. In this guise, on the afternoon of the present day, he will be heading to Peru, carrying his soul clenched in his teeth (perhaps the way a pirate might clench a knife there).

Lines 18–28
The scene as thus far portrayed is suddenly eclipsed by mention—by the sudden appearance or noticing—of a blue heron, a bird not seen to be especially graceful. It even has an awkward appearance with its back looking broken as it flaps its wings—and of course it is upside down (which may well be contributing to the perception of awkwardness).

Having reiterated, with just the two-word phrase itself in line 21, how something, another thing (along with the river), is *upside down*, the narrator is moved to assert that this upside-down-ness signifies a disjuncture: somebody, out of the individuals present, must be incorrect.

Stanza 8 describes the first of the potentially wrong individuals: the heron (specified as male), marked by the colors blue and grey as he (one imagines) makes a sound that might be called a

TOPICS FOR FURTHER STUDY

- Write two separate poems, each told from a first-person perspective, whereby a scene plays out in which the narrator sights or encounters a wild animal in nature, leading to the formation of a unique line of thought or questioning in the narrator's mind. The two poems should take place in different seasons.

- Ondaatje has been said to have written in the tradition of, among others, W. B. Yeats. Included in the Poetry for Young People series volume *William Butler Yeats* (2002), edited by Jonathan Allison, is "The Wild Swans at Coole," a famous poetic treatment involving waterbirds. Read that poem and consult at least one critical text discussing it in order to write an essay in which you first explicate Yeats's poem on its own and then focus on a comparison between "The Wild Swans at Coole" and Ondaatje's "Inner Tube."

- Critical reference has been made to earlier poems of Ondaatje's in which herons make appearances, but unfortunately the poems in question were not specified. Do extensive digital and printed-text research to find as many Ondaatje poems as you can in which a heron makes an appearance; you will likely benefit from a librarian's help. From there, refer to critical texts discussing these particular poems and write an essay in which you summarize the significance of the poet's earlier herons and what they suggest about the heron in "Inner Tube."

- Create a video presentation in which a deliberately paced reading of "Inner Tube" is provided through voice-over while the scene being described plays out. Note that as such, the actor playing the narrator would not perform the reading while acting (and the reader could be a different person entirely). There seem to be three obvious options (and perhaps others) for dealing with the heron: you could stake out an appropriate body of water for as long as necessary in order to film an actual heron (or similar bird) flying; you could suggest the action of the heron's flying indirectly, with sounds and the narrator's reactions to it; or you could splice in acquired or fabricated video of a heron flying.

---

thud each time he flaps his broad wings. As he flies, he seems to conceive that he is indeed correctly conscious of the way to emerge from the present situation. This escape route is described as being *blue*. The poem's final line indicates that the other potentially wrong individual is the narrator.

THEMES

Nature

The most prominent aspect of "Inner Tube" is the near-total immersion in nature that Ondaatje's narrator provides. Interestingly, the object of the title, on which the narrator is understood to be floating, is never mentioned in the body of the poem. (The title is also contained in parentheses in the original edition, which neatly suggests containment within something circular, but it should be recalled that all of the subtitles within Ondaatje's "Rock Bottom" are parenthetical.) This makes sense because the inner tube is not in the narrator's field of vision; he would not be floating on the river without it, but he has apparently fully adjusted to the novelty of the flotation it provides, because it is not on his mind at present. The restriction to the narrator's viewpoint also accounts for why even the means of his paddling is not stated; his hands, too, are not in his field of vision,

---

The speaker passes a summer afternoon floating on a river in an inner tube (©Epidote | Shutterstock.com)

allowing total visual immersion in the nature outside of himself.

Nature must certainly be seen to have a keen significance for the narrator, the way he has isolated this episode in which otherwise not much happens. He is simply out there, and he witnesses the flying of a heron. However, nature is precisely where one is enabled to dismiss rational, everyday concerns—bills to pay, jobs to fulfill, classes to attend, homework to complete—and be perfectly absorbed in the sense of the scene; the narrator gets so absorbed that he whimsically imagines himself an ancient ship sailing all the way to Peru. The one thing that might pull the narrator out of nature and his whimsical dream and back into his civilized mind would be his friends on the shore, but, thankfully, they seem to be so distant that they only get the briefest mention in line 9. After that quick glance, the human beings are perfectly absent from the narrator's thoughts.

Animals

The animals that the narrator sees out on the river play a special role in his achieving a sort of natural transcendence, one that ultimately spurs him to muse on a lightly philosophical question, whether either he or the heron might be wrong in discerning the way to exit the present scene: the heron with its awkward flight or the narrator in his imagined vessel. It is a whimsical question, to be sure, yet one with deep resonance.

Even before the narrator meets the heron, there is the dog. As a domesticated animal, the dog represents a link between humankind and civilization on the one hand and the wildness and purity of nature on the other. The dog itself is engaged in an act of self-education, learning how to swim, which might be seen to align it more with humanity. However, many animals do, at some point, learn how to swim, and, moreover, the dog's consciousness at such a moment, immersed in the water, is one fully engaged only with his immediate circumstances, which is widely understood to be the permanent mind-set of all animals. Some animals, of course, like beavers, do extensive planning and even calculation, but in general, animals simply are where they are and do what they do, in ways that humans often are not and do not.

The narrator transitions, then, after the sight of the dog, to that of the flying heron. This is a wild animal through and through, obedient to no humans, surviving precisely as its animal instincts dictate. For whatever reason, right now, it sees fit to fly—but its flight does not inspire much natural confidence in the narrator.

Right and Wrong

Most curiously in this poem, the narrator is inclined to conceive that one of them—the narrator or the heron—must be *wrong*. He has established how upside down the scene appears to be, and in particular how upside down the heron appears, which might suggest, from his perspective, that the heron must be "wrong" in the way he is going about things. Yet as the penultimate stanza unfolds, it is not clear that the heron's apparent orientation alone is what the narrator is talking about. Rather, he suggests that the heron is wrong in *thinking* a certain thing. Of note is that he ascribes conscious thought to the animal, which actually suggests a stronger link between humans and wild animals than some commentators would like to acknowledge. More to the point is what the heron is thinking: that he is conscious of a sure way to remove oneself from the current situation—to get *out of here*. Perhaps the narrator is suggesting that although the heron thinks it is flying up, the narrator can clearly see that the heron is flying down, which will not get him anywhere. This would again be a whimsical reading of what appears to be a rather whimsical moment in the narrator's life, floating on a river with nary a nagging thought in his mind—just a curious vision of sailing to Peru on his inner tube and a question that has popped up upon his sighting (upside down) a heron flying through the air.

The question is amusing. The reader is likely to answer it in a particular way: the narrator, of course, is the one who is actually upside down, so if anyone is *wrong* about their perspective on the current situation and how to emerge from it, the narrator would be the likeliest choice. Also, of course, sailing to Peru on an inner tube from anywhere at all in the world seems, realistically speaking, like a terrible idea. The reader must acknowledge, then, that the narrator might be referring to something else—perhaps a more colloquial sense of getting out of somewhere, out of an entanglement, a dilemma, an obligation, or a relationship. In this individual poem's

ambiguity, the specifics of narrator's situation may be beside the point. Regardless, he is the one viewing things upside down, whereas the heron may look awkward but quite clearly knows what it is doing. The poem functions, then, as a recognition of the delusional nature of human thought—how one is inclined to prioritize one's own perspective or point of view, even when undeniable clues suggest that perhaps one has the entire picture of things upside down. That is, one does this if one is a human—not so much if one is an animal. Human beings may be inclined to think themselves right all the time, but nature, in and of itself, has been around longer and should perhaps be acknowledged to know better.

STYLE

Sonority

While "Inner Tube" is a free-verse poem, with no standardized form in terms of rhyme and meter, the language Ondaatje uses is quite sonorous. The simplest means by which this is achieved is repetition, strategically used. Lines 1 and 3 both end with the same word, *river*, definitively setting the scene, after which the word is not repeated again. The two words of line 2 are repeated again in lines 10 and 12, where this time the distance between the repetitions lends the feel of a longer cycle within the poem, as if its content is swirling in both small and large eddies. The first mention of the narrator's head being back again sets the scene, positioning the narrator so that the reader understands his perspective; once the broader surroundings have been taken in, the second uses of the words *head* and *back* return the focus to the narrator himself and his state of mind. Again in line 3, the words will be repeated with strategic emphasis, just when the narrator posits the significance of things being *upside down*.

Consonance is also apparent. Lines 3 and 4 feature *d* and *r* sounds, and lines 5 and 6 continue both of these sounds while also adding multiple *l* and *t* sounds. The two last words of line 8 make for a double near rhyme with line 6. Lines 12 and 13 feature a more direct pair of rhymes, *eyebrow* and *prow*. Lines 15 and 16 present a pair of near rhymes, as *afternoon* meets resonance in *down* and *Peru*. Another line with particular resonance is 20, with pairs of *b*, *k*, and *a* sounds.

COMPARE
&
CONTRAST

- **1980s:** Taking office in 1984, Prime Minister Brian Mulroney gains admiration for his environmental priorities, signing the Acid Rain Accord with the United States, gaining passage of the Environmental Protection Act, and overseeing Toronto's hosting of the 1988 World Conference on the Changing Atmosphere, one of the earliest meetings on climate change.

  Today: The Conservative government of Stephen Harper, who holds office from 2006 to 2015, deals various blows to environmentalist causes through reductions in funding, the elimination of scientific agencies, and restrictions on communication between the scientific community and the press. Canada withdraws from the Kyoto Protocol, a landmark international accord aimed at reducing pollutants and emissions, in 2011.

- **1980s:** Bringing environmentalist concerns beyond the purview of nongovernmental organizations and more squarely into the realm of local and national politics, the Green Party of Canada is founded in 1983.

  Today: In 2011, leader Elizabeth May becomes the first Green Party candidate elected to Canada's House of Commons, the lower, popularly elected chamber in Canada's bicameral parliament.

- **1980s:** Ducks Unlimited Canada, a nonprofit devoted to preserving the nation's wetland habitats for ducks as well as other birds, launches the North American Waterfowl Management Plan in 1985, devoting $1.5 billion over fifteen years to conservation efforts.

  Today: Wetland protections were further expanded when World Wildlife Fund Canada launched a ten-year campaign in 1989 to establish an interconnected network of protected wildlife areas. By 2000, over one thousand new parks and reserves had been created, doubling the nation's total protected areas.

Form and Content

Beyond the language having its own inherent musicality, the sense of that musicality is readily seen to amplify the sense of the poem; that is, the form reflects the content, or the content is reflected in the form. The short lines with frequent stanza breaks lull the reader into a very slow, lazily paced reading, as if one is floating down the river alongside the narrator. The repeated words and sounds call to mind the recurrent splashes produced when paddling, as well as the way sound echoes over and around the water. When the bird has taken flight, the words *backed flap* evoke in sound the very flapping of its wings—while the word *back* appears now for the third time, as a second echo, verbally linking the heron and the narrator, with his head back.

HISTORICAL CONTEXT

Environmental Consciousness in Canada

With its vast stretches of plains and forests, much of which is cold enough to limit its desirability as habitat for humans, Canada has a popular image of a highly nature-friendly nation. In fact, Canada's vast tracts of wilderness remained pristine for so long, with relatively little encroachment by civilization, that Americans were the ones who took the lead in North American conservation efforts, such as with John Muir's founding of the Sierra Club in 1892. Canada did create its first national park, Banff National Park, in 1885—over a dozen years after the first US national park, Yellowstone—but this was primarily for economic reasons, to promote tourism along the Canadian Pacific Railway. Also, the

With his head tilted back, the speaker sees the heron upside-down *(©Joseph Scott Photography / Shutterstock.com)*

continent's first federal bird sanctuary was established in Saskatchewan in 1887.

However, it was the Canadian logging industry that first realized that efforts would need to be made to ensure sustainability—that is, to ensure that the industry did not harvest so many trees that the ecosystem was destroyed and rendered unfit for future forest growth. Thus, the Canadian Forestry Association was established in 1900. After being invited by Theodore Roosevelt, America's most renowned conservationist president, to the North American Conservation Conference in 1909, Canada went on to establish its own Commission of Conservation, which promoted limited logging, organic fertilizers, and recycling of suitable materials. Between 1907 and 1920, efforts were made to protect both bison and antelope in national parks. A pivotal moment came in 1930 with the passage of the Canadian National Parks Act, which ensured that national parks would not be exploited for resources.

After the conservation efforts of the first wave of Canadian environmentalism, second-wave efforts beginning in the 1960s focused on reducing pollution and the human impact on ecosystems. Air and water pollution, hazardous wastes, and pesticide use—brought to civilization's attention by American conservationist Rachel Carson in her 1962 exposé of DDT's harmful effects on bird populations, *Silent Spring*—all became major concerns. It was in Vancouver, British Columbia, that the famed nonprofit organization Greenpeace was founded in 1971, and several other environmental groups began Canadian operations over the next decade, including the World Wildlife Fund, the Sierra Club, and the Audubon Society. In the 1980s, nongovernmental organizations (NGOs) multiplied to focus on supplementing federal efforts to preserve the environment. It was in this context that Ondaatje wrote his poem "Inner Tube," in which the ability to appreciate the beauty of a pure natural environment can be taken for granted. Canada would still experience ecological ups and down over the course of the ensuing decades, largely in accord with the reigning prime minister's dedication to the environment, but the bureaucratic infrastructure was in place to allow successful conservation for decades to come.

CRITICAL OVERVIEW

Douglas Barbour, in his critical study *Michael Ondaatje*, calls his subject "a poet whose richly metaphoric prose texts have won him an international reputation" and whose "career demonstrates a consistent intent to enlarge the possibilities of his craft." In the *Dictionary of Literary Biography*, Ann Mandel indicates that Ondaatje "is one of the most brilliant and acclaimed of that impressive group of Canadian poets who first published in the 1960s," Margaret Atwood among them. Mandel affirms that Ondaatje's "widely praised books...have had wide popular appeal while at the same time occasioning considerable analysis by critics in Canada and elsewhere."

Reviewing *Secular Love* for the *New York Times*, Liz Rosenberg was not entirely enthusiastic about the specific enlargements evident in the poet's craft. For example, she found the drama a bit overdone—"Ondaatje tends to indulge in posturing and nonsense"—and disliked his forays into terrain in which gravity is all too apparently lacking: "His reliance on whimsy is even more unfortunate." Still, she recognizes that sometimes "what seems nonsense is another way of approaching sense, through surrealism and dream images of great beauty." She also expresses admiration for his "remarkable honesty," as evident in both "deep seriousness and sly humor." To sum up, she ambivalently declares, "Ondaatje is an oddity—a passionate intellect—and his book is alternatingly exasperating and beautiful."

In an *Essays on Canadian Writing* essay, Ken Norris cites Nell Waldman, author of *Michael Ondaatje and His Works*, as unreservedly praising the poet's 1984 collection: "*Secular Love*...is a raw, difficult, beautiful collection of poems. It cuts as close to the bone as anything Ondaatje has written. A remarkably personal series of lyrics." Sam Solecki, in a review in *Spider Blues*, similarly declares, "*Secular Love* is the ruthless and unembarrassed engagement with the self." He adds that the collection "shows a writer who has found a style and a form that allow openness without sacrificing the economy and selectivity necessary for art." Taking his cue from Ondaatje himself and considering the volume from an architectural perspective, Norris notes,

In completing a reading of *Secular Love*, one is left with the impression of a book whose materials have been shaped and managed. To label it simply a confessional work would be to sell it short. *Secular Love* is formally complex, and it employs the resources of a variety of literary genres.

"Inner Tube" has itself drawn a modicum of attention. In light of the acknowledged fact that *Secular Love* as a whole charts the course of Ondaatje's very difficult separation from his wife and the subsequent relief and fulfillment found in a new lover, the "Inner Tube" narrator's apparent desire to search for an escape of some kind has been read as signaling the author's desire to escape the confines of the situation created by his failing marriage. Barbour helpfully points out that "the implied intertext with Ondaatje's own earlier poems on herons poignantly emphasizes the desperation he identifies with in seeking to find 'the blue way / out of here' and out of the difficulties the affair has created." (Less helpfully, Barbour does not specify which earlier poems he means.) The scholar points out that the poems that follow "Inner Tube" indeed reveal "a man feeling ever more trapped in his present situation."

Solecki concludes that *Secular Love* is "a book rich in human experience, carefully structured and beautifully crafted. Almost every page shows evidence of Ondaatje's brilliant visual imagination and his auditory sensitivity to the musical possibilities of free verse."

CRITICISM

Michael Allen Holmes

Holmes is a writer with existential interests. In the following essay, he considers the resonance of the river, the bird, and the color blue in Ondaatje's "Inner Tube."

After floating down the river with the narrator of Ondaatje's poem "Inner Tube" and watching—upside down—an apparently not-so-graceful heron fly out into the blue, the reader may be left wondering what has just happened, or why. In a poem where almost nothing takes place, somehow either the narrator or the bird is wrong about how to exit the situation, how to escape, how to *get out of there*. The poem is explained easily enough if one wants to prioritize the autobiographical context of "Inner Tube," as

WHAT DO I READ NEXT?

- Perhaps Ondaatje's most admired collection of verse is *There's a Trick with a Knife I'm Learning to Do* (1979), which won him his second Governor General's Award. In this book, Ondaatje demonstrates evolution from a romantic poet into a more complex modernist one.

- Discussion of the manifold ways that humanity and water have interacted over the centuries, ranging from mythology to transportation to healing to religion, can be found in *Elixir: A History of Water and Humankind* (2011), by Brian Fagan.

- One of Ondaatje's compatriots in Canadian verse is Margaret Atwood, best known for her dystopian novel *The Handmaid's Tale* (1990). Her verse collection *The Circle Game* (1964), the revised edition of which won a Governor General's Award in 1966, treats themes familiar to readers of her fiction, including human behavior and the natural world.

- Another poet with whom Ondaatje is classed is the concrete poet Barrie Phillip Nichol, who styled his name "bpNichol." Nichol won a Governor General's Award for a set of four publications issued that

year: the poetry collection *Still Water*, the booklets *The True Eventual Story of Billy the Kidd* and *Beach Head*, and an anthology he edited, *The Cosmic Chef: An Evening of Concrete*.

- American poet Langston Hughes, perhaps the foremost figure of the Harlem Renaissance, professes an affiliation with rivers not unlike Ondaatje's in his famous poem "The Negro Speaks of Rivers" (1921), which can be found in *The Collected Poems of Langston Hughes* (1994).

- The middle-grade novel *Blue Heron* (1992), by Newbery Honor–winning author Avi Wortis, follows nearly thirteen-year-old Maggie as she copes with her parents' separation and the fact of her father's new family. At their lakeside cabin, she sights a blue heron and comes to visit it every morning, gaining inspiration—and also awareness of danger.

- Ondaatje served as editor for an acclaimed collection of short fiction by fellow Canadian practitioners, titled *From Ink Lake: Canadian Short Stories* (1990). He also edited *The Faber Book of Contemporary Canadian Short Stories* (1990).

---

both a subsection of "Rock Bottom" and within the greater trajectory of its collection, *Secular Love*. Ondaatje's acknowledged poetic orientation around the breakup of his first marriage and later union with another makes clear that the time when he hit "rock bottom" is what is being treated in the serial poem of that title, and, naturally, one then conceives that the situation the narrator of "Inner Tube" is at wit's end about extricating himself from is the deteriorating marriage, including his own emotional response to it.

This is convincing enough, but it fails to account for the fact that when someone writes and publishes a poem, putting the verse out into the world for people to read and appreciate, the

verse is given life of its own; in and of itself it means something, it creates meaning in the minds of those who read or hear it, and that meaning is just as important as—perhaps even more important than—the biographical circumstances that played into the poem's creation. When one reads a poem in isolation, one reads precisely and only what one reads, and the resulting meaning may be different from the poet's original conception but remains perfectly valid. Looking more closely at "Inner Tube" with such thoughts in mind, it seems that the way the objects and images come together indeed suggests a more universal sense to the poem.

> IT IS CERTAINLY POSSIBLE FOR PEOPLE TO FIND THEMSELVES IN CIRCUMSTANCES FROM WHICH THERE IS NO ESCAPE—AT LEAST FOR THE TIME BEING."

The poem opens easily enough, setting a lazy midsummer scene in which little seems to matter but the warmth, the narrator's sense of relaxation of both body and mind, and the river. In fact, "Inner Tube" is such a casual poem that it might be read as verse with little meaning tossed off by the poet in a moment of verbal indulgence. Ondaatje himself, after all, humorously notes in the dedication that while the whole collection is "for Linda" (his new love) and the serial poem "Tin Roof" is for fellow poet Phyllis Webb, "Rock Bottom" is "for any hound dog's sake." The dog in "Inner Tube" may be one he has in mind, but to return to the poem, one might observe that the poetic mind often sees poetry without rationally grasping exactly why a poem must be written or, to give it some agency, as many poets do, why it *wants* to be written. In "Inner Tube," there is surely something more profound than just a lazy summer float going on.

Likely part of what lulled Ondaatje into writing the poem about this summer moment was the river itself. Rivers, which give life to human beings especially by nurturing crops in fertile and well-watered river valley lands, have long been worshipped by human civilizations, and this sense of the sacred can play out in the mind of the individual, not just the collective social mind. That is, rivers, as much of both history and literature attest, can be transcendental places. Mark Twain's *Life on the Mississippi* may be the American masterpiece of riverine philosophizing, not only in the concepts expounded by the author but in how it reveals that the great river played an instrumental role in making Samuel Clemens, onetime steamboat pilot, into someone who would write such profoundly important texts to American literature and history; no one who has read it can forget Huck and Jim's own trip along the Mississippi in *Adventures of Huckleberry Finn*. While fictional texts long and short have used rivers as instrumental to plots, one relatively obscure story,

Brazilian author João Guimarães Rosa's "The Third Bank of the River," uniquely reveals the transcendent possibilities of the setting: it depicts a man who devotes himself to a river much as a monk devotes himself to his religious way of life, going out on a canoe and living permanently on the flowing waters, exposed to the elements, ever hovering near enough to his family's village but never allowing contact with anyone again— like an exhaustive, all-absorbing quest for nirvana. Nobel Prize–winner Hermann Hesse, in *Siddhartha*, a fictionalization of the life of the man who became the Buddha, situates the title character precisely on a riverside for his final achievement of a sustained transcendent state.

The narrator of "Inner Tube" may not be on a quest for nirvana, but he is clearly affected by the inherently transcendental sense of the river— its constant flux speaks to the Buddhist conception that life and the world are always changing and that acceptance of change is at the heart of spiritual fulfillment—to the extent that he engages in an apparently whimsical and yet strikingly profound vision of himself as an age-old ship making its way to Peru, of all places. The country in question may not carry too much significance; it was perhaps chosen because it resonates so well with *-noon* and sustains the flow of the stanza in just the way Ondaatje's ear wanted it to. However, Peru was home to one of history's most storied ancient cultures, the Incas, and has a bit of a sense of old-time existential magic to it. When the narrator speaks of being at the fore of an *ancient vessel*, one perhaps thinks not just of a ship, but of the very body he inhabits. The sense of the body as a sort of sacred vessel is especially strong in the sacrificial cultures of Latin America, where the sacrificed individual is like a vessel carrying the people's devotion to the gods.

Leaving this ultimately unpleasant sense aside, one also finds in pacific religions like Buddhism notions of humans being vessels, particularly a vessel for the soul. This conception is especially strong in accord with reincarnation, where souls pass from body to body somewhat in the way water can be poured from pitcher to pitcher. The narrator, then, may not just be having a frivolous vision but be experiencing a sense that he is somehow beside, or outside of, his ordinary self at this moment—he is transcending his ordinary self—in conceiving of his body as the vessel of a soul that has been living for ages and ages, that knows everything from the cavemen to the Incas to the Orient. This is not just the narrator's personal soul; rather the idea carries the Hindu sense of the *Atman*, the universal soul that all beings share, which is equivalent to the *Over-soul* that Ralph Waldo Emerson conceived as such. With the soul in mind, the dipping of the narrator's brow into the water is especially intriguing because it signals the water's meeting the third eye, a point of meditative focus in yoga that is understood to be a center of cosmic energy and wisdom. A person's partially immersing their head—not unlike being dipped in Christian baptismal waters, though inverted—can thus be seen to focus and activate that cosmic energy.

Thereupon appears the heron. Ondaatje has been aligned with Wallace Stevens in part for his favoring of symbolist approaches, and early in his career especially he deliberately manipulated symbols. The heron carries a lengthy history as a bird of symbolic significance. A primary reason for this is the bird's demonstration of extraordinary patience in standing perched in shallow water potentially for hours on end in order to suddenly snatch its beak into the water for a fish that swims too close. As explained in *The Continuum Encyclopedia of Animal Symbolism in Art*, this mode of subsistence resonates especially well with Buddhism: "The heron is…a symbol of Buddhist meditation from its habit of standing absolutely still with eyes closed." That the heron should be seen to signify something to Ondaatje's narrator is suggested by J. C. Cooper in *Symbolic and Mythological Animals* in his relating that in Greek myth, the heron is "a messenger bird, sent…as a favourable omen." Egyptian myth lends the bird especially strong signification, figuring the heron

> as the first transformer of the soul after death; it also symbolizes the rising sun.… It is regeneration as the bird of the flooding of the Nile and the renewal of life; the bird then leaves the river and flies over the fields.

In this light, the heron might readily be interpreted as a good omen for the narrator—a sign of a new beginning, and indeed a capacity to depart the river whose catastrophic flooding must bring about that new beginning. Christian symbolism, too, suggests an important role for the sighted bird, as related in *The Continuum Encyclopedia of Animal Symbolism in Art*: "The heron sometimes appeared in allegories of Christians rising above the storms of life, as herons rise above rain clouds." The narrator, of course,

precisely seems to be going through a storm of life. Thus, beyond raising him up out of his own troubles, the heron with its spiritual associations signifies achievement of a higher plane, some kind of elevation or even apotheosis of the soul. During the Middle Ages, because of its capacity for devouring serpents, the heron was a symbol of Christ himself.

And what about the color blue? It appears three times between lines 18 and 26, more than any other significant word; *river* and *upside down* appear only twice, while otherwise only the more constitutive words *down* and *back* appear three times. The heron, of course, is blue, which accounts for the first mention. The second mention is more curious because it seems to be describing the noise of the heron's flight as blue, in a sort of synesthesia suggesting the transcendent power of the color to present itself even to senses other than sight. The third mention of the word is equally curious, in that now an undefined *way*, something with no material existence, is being described as blue. This blueness is inaccessible to any of the senses, seeming to be purely abstract. Of course, as the narrator looks upside down at the world, the blue sky and the reflectively blue water necessarily dominate his field of vision. The heron's way out is blue simply because its background is blue. But the usage seems to carry more significance than this, as if this blue is no ordinary color but indeed a sparkling *azure*—a word derived from the Persian name for lapis lazuli, a gem—a transcendent blue. This is the color connoted by Herman Melville, in *Moby-Dick*, when a young man on watch, mesmerized by the apparently infinite water around him, "takes the mystic ocean at his feet for the visible image of that deep, blue, bottomless soul, pervading mankind and nature." Blue is also the color connoted by Emily Dickinson, in "I heard a Fly buzz when I died," a poem apparently about death but readable as the record of a moment of nirvana, which, after all, means "extinguishment." The narrator lies on a bed with a supreme stillness in the air. She fully detaches herself from her material existence, and then as a fly produces a *Blue uncertain stumbling buzz*, the narrator's vision fails, in an ambiguous sense, and she slips beyond her earthly existence. It seems as though the *blue way* toward which the heron is pointing the narrator is precisely Melville's blue and Dickinson's blue, a universally transportive blue.

The speaker imagines himself as the figurehead of a ship *(©AVN Photo Lab | Shutterstock.com)*

The narrator's sense of all this is, perhaps, vague at best, no matter how well read he is, but it is often precisely when one becomes unconscious of the particulars of one's mind-set and the rational significance of a situation that the irrational part of the mind, the faithful and spiritual part, takes over. The way the narrator asks his question at the end certainly leaves the answer open; it is not self-evident whether the narrator or the heron should be considered "wrong" or even what one must be wrong about. The narrator, after all, is only human, and he can control his own actions but no one else's. It is certainly possible for people to find themselves in circumstances from which there is no escape—at least for the time being. Perhaps the narrator's only means of escape in his present life is precisely either fantasy, getting lost in imaginary notions of sailing overseas on an inner tube—a means not so promising in the long term—or an escape that, being internal, is possible no matter what one's external circumstances might be. He may have no choice but to resort to a quest for transcendence, and this is precisely what the heron is signaling.

The narrator can perhaps be seen to register a degree of self-consciousness just sufficient to allow an awareness that the heron, after all, is the one who is right. Indeed, his consciousness of the heron's apparent wrongness in lines 19–21 is so acute as to suggest that he knows that the heron's "wrongness" is *only* apparent; he is actually right. The structure of lines 22–28 adds to this implication. The heron gets more press, a full five-line stanza, in addressing the question of who is wrong, focusing attention on it. However, the repetition of *blue* in those lines, with the connotations elaborated in earlier literature and in the minds of many who appreciate open seas and skies, signals a rightness that cannot be denied. It is as if, in dwelling on the heron's knowledge, the narrator comes to the slow realization of the answer to his own question. Lines 24–27 point to that answer by tapering down, getting shorter and shorter, leading to the two tiny words of the final line: *or me*. The answer to the question of who is *wrong* is the final word; the narrator has pointed to himself with his text, and with the heron's help, one day, he will find his own blue way out of there.

> PARATAXIS BECOMES THE OPERATING
> MODE OF THE WHOLE SEQUENCE, EACH SECTION
> FRAGMENTING NARRATIVE AND PRONOMINAL
> REFERENCE, ALTHOUGH SOME TENTATIVE
> CONNECTIONS OF IMAGE AND MOOD EMERGE
> BY IMPLICATION."

Source: Michael Allen Holmes, Critical Essay on "Inner Tube," in *Poetry for Students*, Gale, Cengage Learning, 2017.

Douglas Barbour

In the following excerpt, Barbour provides an overview of the collection Secular Love.

Ondaatje's acknowledgments page to *Secular Love*, with its laconic "Thanks to friends in the clutch" and "Bellrock-Toronto-Honolulu-Colombo-Blyth-Collingwood-Madoc 1978–1983," reveals that its poems and poem sequences were a major part of his writing life while he worked on *Running in the Family*. It also invites speculation about their autobiographical content, which the individual poems also feed. Nevertheless, the subject of all these speculations is a written one, and to that extent a creature of invention. This is not to deny that there are strong autobiographical elements in these poems; it is to argue that they succeed or fail as poems and not as gossip.

Ondaatje sees *Secular Love* as "'a novel.' ... its structure and plot are novelistic ... [yet its figures) are drawn in a lyric, perceived by a lyric eye" (Solecki 1984, 324). Patricia J. Eberle argues that *Secular Love* seeks "a new kind of coherence as it follows the course of the current of feelings involved in a personal breakdown and the end of a marriage." The "novelistic" structure and plot do render a complex story of the destruction of a marriage and the rediscovery of love with another, but the assumption that the first section "describes *Ondaatje's* feelings during a party at his house one evening when everything seemed to be 'slipping away'"(Eberle, 75; emphasis added) seems a bit simplistic. In fact, in all the sections of the book, the writer is very

careful not to name any of the central actors in the drama, granting them the fictional freedom implied by his choice of the term *novel*.

Secular Love is divided into four sections. "Claude Glass" and "Tin Roof" are single medium-length poems; "Rock Bottom" is a sequence of linked lyrics; and "Skin Boat" is a collection of separately titled poems that are nevertheless carefully ordered into a larger unit that brings the collection as a whole to a satisfying, if open, conclusion. The main sequence of narrative events is carefully kept at the level of implication while other, smaller, narratives occupy the foreground and complicate the obvious "plot" with implied connections among characters and their changing environments. Even as a novel, the book fragments and deconstructs conventional narrative, substituting intense lyric moments of perception for the gradual construction of insight that story allows and seeks. As in all his other longer works, Ondaatje invokes generic distinctions here only to confuse them in the actual writing. The borders are blurred, as usual.

I always read the title "Claude Glass" as an odd name. But no, the epigraph explains that it's a special kind of dark mirror "used to concentrate the features of the landscape in subdued tones" (*SL*). The third-person protagonist of the poem is himself a kind of dark mirror, reflecting and distorting the features of his personal surroundings, including both landscape and people. Immediately establishing a distance between narrator and narratee reinforces the generic breakdown between fiction and autobiography that will be maintained in various ways throughout the book. The poem begins after its action is complete, setting up the rest of it as a complex series of analepses: "He is told about / the previous evening's behaviour" (*SL*). This sounds like a singular situation, but the series of present participles suggests that neither the party nor the behavior are one-time-only events. The behavior is drunken, mean, excited, possibly desperate, certainly angry, and also blackly comic at times. Throughout, the syntax creates ambiguities that raise questions without answering them and make it quite unclear at times who is doing what.

Even if we read the first verse paragraph as referring to a single night, within that time there are other conditional possibilities, and the tense shifts mime a drunken slipperiness of focus as they move from "he has always loved that ancient darkness...where he can remove clothes" to "as he moves in back fields...and then stands to watch the house" (*SL*). Beyond the ambiguity of tense there are other syntactical slippages, as in the image of him lying "with moonlight on the day's heat / hardened in stone, drowning / in this star blanket this sky / like a giant trout" (*SL*). The modulations of the text here—in which moonlight or heat or "he" could be "hardened in stone," while all three or the stone could be drowning, and then whoever is drowning or the sky might be "like a giant trout"—thoroughly dissipate any possibility of a single meaning. The text resists interpretive analysis, as such.

It also continually sets up echoes and reiterations that maintain a sense of narrative, however dislocated. Yet the sense of disintegration exceeds the poem's power to hold things together: "And he knows something is happening there to him / solitary while he spreads his arms / and holds everything that is slipping away together" (*SL*). Is he holding everything together as he desires or only holding on to everything that together is slipping away? The apparent statement of power dissolves into an admission of none. A similar attempt at bravado falls apart in the following stanza, where he once again enters the continuing world of the present participle, "slouching towards women, revolving / round one unhappy shadow," which may be his or that of the friend waving from "the darkest place." Again, the insistence that "[h]e is not a lost drunk / like his father or his friend, can, / he says, stop on a dime, and he can / he could" stumbles on that slip from "can" to "could," implying at least the possibility that the "could" of the past is no longer the asserted "can" of the present.

For readers of *Running in the Family*, the references to son and daughter, to a drunken father, imply that the "he" is an autobiographical subject. But the writing subject is displaying the written subject as a figure of invention as much as of memory. The linguistic echoes, the sudden shifts of point of view and tone, and the various intertexts, including Salinger's Glass family stories, Yeats's poem, and Phyllis Webb's "Naked Poems," as well as the darker tales in *Running in the Family*, all recall us to the poem as written performance rather than transparent rendering of a given autobiographical history.

The poem is something of an emotional roller coaster, leaping up to highs as soon as it hits lows. In "this brilliant darkness," at least the protagonist knows "the hour of magic / which no matter what sadness / leaves him grinning." The world refuses to let anyone with perception escape fully into depression or self-pity. Yet within that magic, the animal night of species warfare continues while his desires go unassuaged. Returning to narrative, the poem presents more images of self-destructive behavior at the party and further examples of what he lacks and wants (*SL*). The tone keeps sliding from humor to anger to pain, with no single emotion allowed to dominate, as the man keeps struggling over and over again out of the house and into nature. But he cannot escape the human and technological, no matter where he goes or what he desires, as the simile of "blood like a cassette through the body" (*SL*) suggests. He may remove his clothes, but the inner man is implicated in civilization even to the way he images the circulation of his blood.

In a parallel action, his "desire to be riverman," makes him remember "his drunk invitation to the river," an invitation only made possible because he "steered the awesome car" to its banks. A contained flashback, this stanza makes the by-now expected gesture of escaping the party only to return. A complex image of an outdoor slide show follows, but the sheet collapses and the "pictures fly without target / and howl their colours over Southern Ontario" (*SL*), giving him the slip, like everything else in his purview. Despite his loss of coherence, the exhilaration of "[l]andscapes and stories / flung into branches" and across animals and birds has a transformative energy. By its shifts of tone and image, the poem continues to invoke contradictory feelings from stanza to stanza, line to line. Bleak desperation is not allowed to be the only, and somehow "true," mood of the poem.

"Rivers of the world meet" and local waters become foreign when Asia is projected onto them. The poem shifts direction once again, to deal with a specific time, as "he wakes in the sheet / that earlier held tropics in its whiteness" (*SL*). By metaphoric overlap, the sheet and the invited river have become one, and when that river "flows through the house" and "he awakens" again "and moves within it," the second waking renders moot any judgment as to whether the vision is "real" or a dream. It is textual, and recalls earlier texts (the "river he has walked elsewhere" is the Depot Creek of "Walking to Bellrock," as the list of places where the poems of *Secular Love* were written implies). The image of the river washes everything in the house clean, but even inside the image "he" can only *wish* "to swim / to each of his family and gaze / at their underwater dreaming." The desire expressed in "wants" and "wishes" negates itself, but even if he got his wish he would remain apart from those he loves, because "for hours / there has been no conversation" (*SL*), no connection with them.

Read that way, the poem seems once again to present a figure cut off from friends and family, in fact "a lost drunk" (*SL*). But imagination refused defeat, and the text insists he is "the sentinel, / shambling back and forth, his anger / and desire against the dark" (*SL*). This image of the undaunted warrior, the protector of the hearth, cannot sustain itself, possibly because anger and desire mix contradictorily in the effort that contains its own defeat: he has closed his eyes, and, given one waking within another, how are we to know that he is awake, eyes open, even now? Each sentence within the text makes sense, but together they create contradictions and enigmas. Even in its final few lines, the poem continues to alter all it touches, gathering an image of its own process into the aural pun of "[c]reak and echo" as it moves to an apparent conclusion that resolves nothing: "With absolute clarity / he knows where he is." But the only clarity of this poem is that of its fragmented vision, not of its overall insight, and we cannot decide even if he is awake or asleep, let alone where precisely he might be.

As the title's dictionary meaning suggests, "Claude Glass" offers a richly chiaroscuro vision, full of contrasts, dark brooding, crazy laughter, and, more than likely, distortions. Its subject is not so much lost as at a loss, cut off from former connections, however much he desires to maintain them, yet without any new ones to hold on to. This poem leaves him in limbo, but it is only the first of four parts; later ones will take him out of that lonely place in one direction or another. Despite its period, the ending is an open door.

Ondaatje reveals his gift for finding exactly the right epigraph throughout *Secular Love*. A wryly comic quotation from Elmore Leonard

prepares us for the homage to and subversion of romantic tough guys in "Tin Roof," while suggesting that it will *try* "to tell you how I feel without exposing myself" (*SL*). Feelings will be important here, but also ploys of self-protection; and the first of these is once again to project subjectivity onto some other pronoun than the first person: "You stand still for three days / for a piece of wisdom / and everything falls to the right place // or wrong place" (*SL*). This "you" appears to represent the "I" who appears later, but it is also the generalized "one" who is everybody, and it might even be the other whom the poem comes to address more and more as it proceeds. Neither figure nor ground is fixed in this passage, which thus pulls the rug out from under the final assertion of "Claude Glass." Both the identity of the subject and "where he is" are suddenly unclear, and as the next stanza emphasizes, "you" may speak, but you "don't know" anything, let alone "whether / seraph or bitch / flutters at your heart." The poem begins in complete uncertainty.

Parataxis interrupts rather than adds to any sense of unified flow, while the sudden intrusion of the first person underlines the sense of interruption and fragmentation, even as it offers an apparently sincere confession: "This last year I was sure / I was going to die." We can but do not have to read this final couplet as a comment on the previous poem. Connections are hinted at but never made absolute. Parataxis becomes the operating mode of the whole sequence, each section fragmenting narrative and pronominal reference, although some tentative connections of image and mood emerge by implication.

The second section is a first-person description of the writer's cabin at night, but the third section throws the subject into the third person. These continual pronominal shifts signal a profound uncertainty in the text as to the autobiographical agenda of the poem. Equally indeterminate is the way the poem attends with great care to the specifics of perception and action in each small fragment while refusing to tie them up in a single narrative knot. Questions go unanswered, deictic pointers fail to clarify the situations they apparently point to, everything remains in flux like the ocean, which figures throughout as a kind of symbol of uncontrollable change, "the unknown magic he loves / throws himself into // the blue heart" (*SL*).

Each section seems self-sufficient and works as a separate gesture, yet none can really stand alone. "Tin Roof" comes closer to matching the definition of a serial poem than anything else Ondaatje has written, for its unity depends upon an implicit narrative of the writing rather than any explicit narrative, which is at best only hinted at, of the written story of some part of one person's "life." And perhaps the pronominal shifts are one way it seeks to avoid the conventional egotism of the speaker in traditional lyrics. As in his earlier long poems about other figures, Ondaatje has created a forum for various voices in "Tin Roof," achieving a dialogic heteroglossia that is "novelized" in the Bakhtinian sense (Balchtin, 324–31). The various deliberately prosaic passages, let alone the tone of questions like "Do you want / to be happy and write?" (*SL*), implicate language "as a social phenomenon that is becoming in history, socially stratified and weathered in this process of becoming" (Baktin, 326). . . .

Source: Douglas Barbour, "Secular Love," in *Michael Ondaatje*, Twayne Publishers, 1993, pp. 161–66.

Richard Eder

In the following review, Eder explains that Ondaatje's best work focuses on details.

Michael Ondaatje is a Canadian poet from a Ceylonese family; a Pacific sensibility tackling an Atlantic destiny. He invokes Rilke with reverence, and Yeats with exasperation, but his talent is not for the grand line, the racking emotion or the metaphysical bear-trap. His North Woods landscapes come out dark and rigid, as if his light values were set for dazzlement and tended to underexpose anything more subdued. Many of his poems are love poems, yet he is least successful when he most directly presses a passion.

What he excels at is the flash of color transmuted by his particular prism; the large mystery seen not directly but by some suspicious detail, as if Providence had hidden all its tracks except for one tiny toenail-scraping visible only to Ondaatje's bifocal sensitivity.

His hallucinations are better than his visions. And so, of the four groups of poems in this collection, the most successful is the first. It expresses middle-aged anguish using a narrator who drinks at a party past the point of despair. He wanders outdoors; nature suddenly appears uncoded. . . .

He wakes later, at 4 a.m., in the solitude of the drinker. His house, it seems, is under water, and he swims from room to room. . . .

In the second section, "Tin Roof," the poet is living in a cabin somewhere on the Pacific coast. . . .

The third section, "Rock Bottom," is an array of personal fragments, some of them splendid. Floating on an inner tube on a river, he tilts his head so far back that the heron he spots seems upside down. . . .

Insomnia is a commoner poetic theme nowadays than passion, but Ondaatje has his own: . . .

This is Ondaatje at his best, fractioned but magical. When he becomes vehement, more philosophical, more of a wooer, his voice goes off pitch. A poem to a daughter is emotional and commonplace. Poems celebrating the Ontario countryside have a forced pastoral quality; he carpenters dryads for his trees. The style does not hold; he seems to be trying out voices.

When he remains still, poetry comes to him. When he pursues it, he pursues it uphill. He is a poetic Archimedes, seeking a place to set his lever, and shifting restlessly from spot to spot.

Source: Richard Eder, "Poetry from Keeping Still," in *LA Times*, June 5, 1985.

SOURCES

Barbour, Douglas, *Michael Ondaatje*, Twayne's World Authors Series No. 835, Twayne Publishers, 1993, pp. ix, 1–9, 170–71.

Becker, Udo, "Heron," in *The Continuum Encyclopedia of Symbols*, A&C Black, 2000, p. 142.

"Brian Mulroney," in *The Canadian Encyclopedia*, http://www.thecanadianencyclopedia.ca/en/article/brian-mulroney/ (accessed September 13, 2016).

Cooper, J. C., "Heron," in *Symbolic and Mythological Animals*, Aquarian/Thorsons, 1992, pp. 127–8.

Dickinson, Emily, "I heard a Fly buzz when I died," in *Final Harvest*, Back Bay Books, 1964, p. 111.

Emerson, Ralph Waldo, "The Over-soul," in *Selected Writings of Ralph Waldo Emerson*, Signet Classic, 1983, p. 286.

"Environmental and Conservation Movements," in *The Canadian Encyclopedia*, http://www.thecanadianencyclopedia.ca/en/article/environmental-and-conservation-movements/ (accessed September 13, 2016).

Mandel, Ann, "Michael Ondaatje," in *Dictionary of Literary Biography*, Vol. 60, *Canadian Writers since 1960: Second Series*, edited by William H. New, Gale Research, 1987.

Melville, Herman, *Moby-Dick; or, The Whale*, Penguin Books, 1992, pp. 172–73.

Norris, Ken, "The Architecture of *Secular Love*: Michael Ondaatje's Journey into the Confessional," in *Essays on Canadian Writing*, No. 53, Summer 1994, pp. 43–50.

Ondaatje, Michael, "Inner Tube," in *Secular Love*, W. W. Norton, 1985, p. 49.

Rosenberg, Liz, "Geckos, Porch Lights and Sighing Gardens," in *New York Times*, December 22, 1985.

Solecki, Sam, *Ragas of Longing: The Poetry of Michael Ondaatje*, University of Toronto Press, 2003, pp. 150–54.

———, ed., "Coming Through: A Review of *Secular Love*," in *Spider Blues: Essays on Michael Ondaatje*, Véhicule Press, 1985, pp. 125–31.

Venefica, Avia, "Symbolic Meaning of the Heron," Whats-Your-Sign website, http://www.whats-your-sign .com/meaning-of-the-heron.html (accessed September 14, 2016).

Werness, Hope B., "Heron," in *The Continuum Encyclopedia of Animal Symbolism in Art*, Continuum, 2006, pp. 213–14.

for attaining a life free of civil strife; migrant crossings of the Mediterranean have only increased in the twenty-first century with the warfare in Iraq, Syria, Sudan, and elsewhere. King explores the effects that such migration has on the people on the move as well as those they meet on the other side.

Ondaatje, Michael, *Vintage Ondaatje*, Vintage, 2004.
    Those curious about the diverse manifestations of Ondaatje's style would do well to consult this reader, which samples his poetry as well as his short and long fiction.

Wright, James, *Shall We Gather at the River*, Wesleyan University Press, 1968.
    Wright is a major poetic American voice of the twentieth century, and this collection shares verse that touches often on scenes from nature, such as in the poems "Living by the Red River," "The Small Blue Heron," and "The River down Home."

FURTHER READING

Baker, Lisa, *Built on Water: Floating Architecture + Design*, Braun, 2014.
    In the twenty-first century, estuaries and shorelines are the sights of increasing concern as floodwaters from rising high tides threaten to swamp urban infrastructures. Baker explores ways that modern architects and corporations have designed structures so that people can permanently and safely inhabit the waterfront.

King, Russell, *The Mediterranean Passage: Migration and New Cultural Encounters in Southern Europe*, Liverpool University Press, 2001.
    For some, floating out toward land beyond the horizon is not just a daydream but a last hope

SUGGESTED SEARCH TERMS

Michael Ondaatje AND "Inner Tube"

Ondaatje AND Rock Bottom

Ondaatje AND Secular Love OR "The Cinnamon Peeler"

Ondaatje AND poetry AND herons OR rivers

herons AND literature

herons AND symbolism

Canada AND nature

Canada AND environmentalism

global warming AND river flooding

inner tubes AND safety

Patterns

AMY LOWELL

1915

"Patterns" is a dramatic monologue written by American poet Amy Lowell. Written in 1915, the poem was first published in the August 1915 issue of the periodical *Little Review*. She then included it as the lead poem in her 1916 collection, *Men, Women and Ghosts* as part of a grouping of poems called "Figurines in Old Saxe."

Particularly in the United States, Lowell emerged as the spiritual leader of a movement in American and English poetry called imagism. The movement was launched in England in 1912 by Ezra Pound, H. D. (Hilda Doolittle), Richard Aldington, and F. S. Flint, whose work, along with that of other imagists, was published in various imagist anthologies and in literary journals such as *Little Review* and *Poetry*. Imagism marked a new course for Anglo American poetry, with its emphasis on concrete language, precise figures of speech, and metrical freedom. Imagist verse tends to be succinct, with an emphasis—as the name of the movement might suggest—on a sharply defined and precise visual image. While "Patterns" is more of a monologue—spoken by an eighteenth-century woman who is bound by the conventions, or "patterns," of her aristocratic life and who learns that her lover has been killed in war—it incorporates many of the features of imagism, particularly in its use of *vers libre*, or free verse.

Amy Lowell *(©Bettmann / Getty Images)*

AUTHOR BIOGRAPHY

Lowell was born on February 9, 1874, in the Boston suburb of Brookline, Massachusetts, the youngest of five surviving children of Augustus Lowell and Katherine Lawrence Lowell, who named their home "Sevenels" ("seven L's") because it housed seven Lowells. Lowell came from a long line of Boston Brahmins, members of a New England aristocracy who played prominent roles in the educational and cultural affairs of New England: her great-grandfather was a cofounder of the Boston Athenaeum. Her grandfather was a trustee of the Lowell Institute, and his cousin was the American poet James Russell Lowell. Four Lowells served as trustees of Harvard College, and one of Amy's brothers became president of the college. Another became a noted astronomer, and a descendant of the family, Robert Lowell, would become a major modern American poet.

As a child, Lowell was a bit of a tomboy who enjoyed physical activities. She also enjoyed reading the English classics and composing poetry and stories. She attended various private schools but was not a particularly good student, and she gained a reputation for being a spoiled, willful troublemaker. She was a debutante in the fall of 1891, and in the years that followed, she enjoyed the life of a respectable, well-off scion of a dynastic family who traveled extensively and took an active part in community affairs. Her creative powers began to emerge in the years after 1902: that year she saw in Boston a stage performance given by the Italian actress Eleonora Duse and in response wrote an eponymous poem about her, Lowell's first serious effort at poetry. Her first published poems appeared in the *Atlantic Monthly* magazine in 1910, and her first collection of poetry, *A Dome of Many-Coloured Glass*, was released in 1912.

At this point, Lowell's life underwent a profound transformation. The first half of her life, centered on home, family, and community, had not been marked by any particular public accomplishments. However, from 1912 until her death, her life was a whirlwind of readings, overseas travel, lecture tours, and publications, not only of her own poetry but also of book reviews, anthologies, works of criticism, and responses to her critics. She became something of a flamboyant, even bombastic, public figure because of her position at the forefront of an American literary renaissance. Her public wrangling with other poets; critics, and editors; her inveterate cigar smoking; her oft-times masculine clothing; her habit of sleeping into the afternoon and working through the night; and her practice of delivering her poetry to editors in person rather than through the mail so that she could read it to them (based on her conviction that poetry is an oral medium)—all would foster her reputation as an iconoclast, if not an eccentric. She quipped that while God made her a businesswoman, she made herself into a poet.

It was in 1912 that Lowell began living with actress Ada Dwyer Russell, who supported her and organized the poet's hectic life until her death. Lowell was so pleased with "Patterns," which she wrote when Russell was absent, that she rushed to meet Russell at the door on the latter's return to read the poem to her. Some biographers maintain that the relationship may have been a largely platonic one based on friendship and mutual esteem, but most believe that the two had a lesbian relationship and that their bond fostered a strain of eroticism in Lowell's poetry. Either way, the two were said to have entered into a "Boston marriage" (sometimes called a "Wellesley marriage" to reflect an emphasis on women's education), a term used in New England at the time to refer to romantic friendships or life partnerships between two women who lived together without support from a man.

In 1913, Lowell read a volume of poetry by H.D. (Hilda Doolittle), which sparked her interest in imagism. That year in London, Lowell met important figures in the imagist movement, including Ezra Pound, who edited the first imagist anthology, *Des Imagistes* (1914). After quarreling with the dictatorial Pound (largely because of her refusal to help fund a journal that he would edit and for challenging him as the leading voice in the imagist movement), she returned to the United States and decided to compile an imagist anthology, making her the American impresario of imagism, to Pound's resentment. She realized her goal in 1915, when she published the first of three annual anthologies, which appeared under the title *Some Imagist Poets*, all three of which contained the work of the same six poets: Richard Aldington, H.D., John Gould Fletcher, F. S. Flint, D. H. Lawrence, and Lowell herself. Meanwhile, her feud with Pound amused observers as he threatened to sue her and dismissed her role in the imagist movement by referring to "Amygism."

In 1914, Lowell published another collection of her own poetry, *Sword Blades and Poppy Seed*, which included the earliest of what she called "polyphonic prose poems." The following year, she published a work of literary criticism, *Six French Poets*, began to engage in polemics and debates about the future of American poetry, and wrote "Patterns," the lead poem in her 1916 collection, *Men, Women and Ghosts*. She published another work of criticism in 1917, *Some Tendencies in Modern American Poetry*, in which she examined the work of Edgar Arlington Robinson, Robert Frost, Edgar Lee Masters, Fletcher, and H.D. Later volumes of poetry include *Can Grande's Castle* (1918), *Pictures of the Floating World* (1919), *Legends* and *Fir-Flower Tablets* (1921), and *A Critical Fable* (1922; a long humorous poem commenting on contemporary poets, including herself). In 1919, she was the first woman ever to give a lecture at Harvard. A lifelong admirer of the poetry of English romantic John Keats, she published a well-received two-volume biography of the poet in 1925.

From her childhood, Lowell was chronically overweight as a result of a glandular condition. During the last seven or eight years of her life, she suffered from a number of health problems that greatly impaired her. Among the worst were abdominal hernias, which probably originated with torn muscles resulting from a buggy accident in 1916. She had her first hernia surgery in 1918, followed by two more surgeries in 1920 and a fourth in 1921. In early April 1925, she suffered a major hernia attack that left her in acute pain. On May 12, 1925, the day before scheduled surgery, she suffered a stroke and died at Sevenels in Brookline. After her death, her collections *What's O'Clock* (1925), *East Wind* (1926), and *Ballads for Sale* (1927) were published. In 1926, *What's O'Clock* was awarded the Pulitzer Prize for poetry.

POEM TEXT

I WALK down the garden paths,
And all the daffodils
Are blowing, and the bright blue squills.
I walk down the patterned garden-paths
In my stiff, brocaded gown.   5
With my powdered hair and jewelled fan,
I too am a rare
Pattern. As I wander down
The garden paths.

My dress is richly figured,   10
And the train
Makes a pink and silver stain
On the gravel, and the thrift
Of the borders.
Just, a plate of current fashion,   15
Tripping by in high-heeled, ribboned shoes.
Not a softness anywhere about me,
Only whalebone and brocade.
And I sink on a seat in the shade
Of a lime tree. For my passion   20
Wars against the stiff brocade.
The daffodils and squills
Flutter in the breeze
As they please.
And I weep;   25
For the lime-tree is in blossom
And one small flower has dropped upon my
    bosom.

And the plashing of waterdrops
In the marble fountain
Comes down the garden-paths.   30
The dripping never stops.
Underneath my stiffened gown
Is the softness of a woman bathing in a marble
    basin,

A basin in the midst of hedges grown
So thick, she cannot see her lover hiding,   35
But she guesses he is near,
And the sliding of the water
Seems the stroking of a dear
Hand upon her.
What is Summer in a fine brocaded gown!   40
I should like to see it lying in a heap upon the
    ground.
All the pink and silver crumpled up on the
    ground.

I would be the pink and silver as I ran along the
    paths,
And he would stumble after,
Bewildered by my laughter.   45
I should see the sun flashing from his sword-
    hilt and the buckles on his shoes.
I would choose
To lead him in a maze along the patterned
    paths,
A bright and laughing maze for my heavy-
    booted lover.

POEM SUMMARY

The text used for this summary is from *Amy Lowell: Complete Poetical Works and Selected Writings*, Vol. 2, edited by Naoki Onishi, Eureka Press, 2007, pp. 3–9. A version of the poem can be found on the following web page: https://www.poetryfoundation.org/poems-and-poets/poems/detail/42987.

"Patterns" consists of seven unrhymed stanzas of irregular length.

Stanza 1

As the poem opens, the speaker envisions herself walking down a garden path surrounded by daffodils blowing in the wind and by blue squills (an herbaceous plant belonging to the lily family). The speaker describes the paths as patterned and herself also as a pattern in her formal brocade dress, her powder-covered hairstyle, and her fan studded with gems.

Stanza 2

The speaker describes her gown as richly figured and observes that its pink and silver train makes a stain on the gravel and the thrift (low-growing evergreen herbs) along the paths' borders. She describes herself as the image of current fashion trends, down to her feet, which are clad in shoes with high heels, decorated with ribbons. Nothing about her is soft, including the whale-bone used to stiffen her corset, or bodice. She sits under the shade of a lime tree, but her passion contends with her constraining fabric of her dress. She watches the daffodils and squills, which have more freedom than she does to flutter as they wish. She cries because the lime tree has dropped a blossom on her bosom.

Stanza 3

The speaker hears the continuous splashing of water in a nearby marble fountain. She envisions beneath her gown the softness of a woman bathing in the fountain, which is set among thick hedges that hide her lover. She guesses that he is nearby, and the splash of the water on her body is like the stroking of his hand. To the speaker, summer is spoiled by a fine brocaded gown, which she would like to see crumpled untidily on the ground.

Stanza 4

The speaker entertains a fantasy: she would like to see herself as pink and silver (that is, nude) as she runs, laughing, along the paths, her lover stumbling after her. She imagines the sunlight glancing off the hilt of his sword and his boot buckles. She imagines leading him through the maze of garden paths until he catches her. As he clasped her in an embrace, his coat buttons would bruise her. She imagines herself swooning as she is surrounded by the sunlight, the shadows of leaves, and the water drops from the fountain but also weighed down by the brocaded gown.

Stanza 5

The speaker returns to the here and now and to a letter she has hidden in the bodice of her gown. The letter, delivered by a messenger from the duke, informs her that her lover, Lord Hartwell, was killed in battle just over a week before. As she reads the letter, the writing on the paper moves like writhing serpents. The footman who had handed her the letter asked if she had any answer. She responded that she did not and told the footman to provide the messenger with refreshment. She then walked up and down the garden paths in her stiff gown, trying to stand upright like the flowers in the sun.

Stanza 6

The speaker reflects that she and Lord Hartwell would have been married in a month. The wedding would have taken place under the lime tree, and it would have broken the pattern of their lives. He, the colonel, would have given himself to her; she, the lady, would have given herself to him.

He made the marriage proposal sitting under the lime tree. She accepted, but now he is dead.

Stanza 7

In the final stanza, the speaker predicts that she will walk up and down the garden paths in summer and winter, always wearing the brocade dress; the daffodils and squills will yield their places to roses, asters, and snow. She will continue to walk up and down the garden paths, wearing her gorgeous gown, along with her whalebone and stiff corsets. Her softness will be guarded from embraces, for her lover, who would have released her from them, has died fighting with the duke in Flanders in another pattern, war. The poem concludes with the speaker asking what purpose patterns serve.

THEMES

Love

"Patterns" is in large measure a love poem. The lines of the poem are spoken by an aristocratic woman who is engaged to be married to a colonel in the army. As she walks up and down the paths of her garden, she thinks about her lover. The atmosphere that surrounds her—the flowers, the sunshine, the splashing of the water in a fountain—leads her to engage in a fantasy about her lover. She imagines herself bathing nude in the fountain with her lover nearby. She also imagines herself leading him along the garden paths, with him rushing after until he catches her and wraps her in an embrace. She imagines that his uniform buttons bruise her body. The scene is an erotic evocation of heterosexual desire, which might surprise some readers given that Lowell is generally believed to have been a lesbian. Despite her own leanings, she wrote about heterosexual love and, as she did in "Patterns," often channeled her eroticism in a way that would more likely have been acceptable to readers at the time.

War

"Patterns" is also a poem about the impact of war on love ones who are left behind. The poem is set in the Queen Anne period, referring to the early years of the eighteenth century in England. (Queen Anne reigned in England from 1702 to 1714.) During those years, England was entangled in the War of Spanish Succession, a conflict that engulfed most of Europe and that reached North America, the Caribbean, and India. The speaker's fiancé, Lord Hartwell, was a colonel in the army, fighting under the command of an unnamed duke. The speaker has received a letter from the duke informing her that Lord Hartwell died in action just over a week before. The speaker has secreted this letter in the bodice of her gown, but as she sits under a lime tree, she pulls the letter out and reads it again. It is her grief at the loss of her fiancé in war that prompts her recollections and fantasies. Late in the poem, the reader learns that the scene of the battle was Flanders, a region that included at the time portions of modern-day Belgium, France, and the Netherlands. Readers in 1915 and 1916 would have responded emotionally to the very word *Flanders*, for Flanders, specifically the commune of Ypres, was the scene of some of the fiercest fighting of World War I in 1914 and again in 1915, the year in which "Patterns" was written and first published. The British sustained heavy losses during the First and Second Battles of Ypres, and many women, like the speaker of the poem, would have been grief stricken after receiving notification that their husbands or lovers had lost their lives. War then becomes its own "pattern" that disrupts the lives of the people it affects.

Confinement

Perhaps the chief theme of "Patterns" has to do with confinement, boundaries, and limitations. The speaker of the poem is confined by the conventions of the society in which she lives. In particular, she is confined by her heavily brocaded gown, which is stiff and limits her movements. In common with other women at the time, she wears corsets and bodices that are stiffened with whalebone. Additionally, she powders her hair and carries a jeweled fan, suggesting that she is an aristocrat. She walks about in a neoclassical garden, with paths, borders, and geometric designs that form patterns that tame nature and that emphasize a sense of restriction. Because of these details, the speaker describes herself as a pattern, as a person whose passions war against the limits and boundaries that define and shape her life. In contrast to these stiff, confining patterns, she sees herself as a soft, vibrant woman, one who longs to cast off the constraints of her life, just as she fantasizes about shedding her gown and leaving it in a heap on the ground so that she can bathe freely

TOPICS FOR FURTHER STUDY

- In the March 1913 issue of *Poetry* magazine, the poet F. S. Flint published a manifesto of imagism under the title "Imagisme." His brief article was followed by a set of observations by Ezra Pound that further laid out the goals of the movement. The articles can be found on the Modern Journals website at http://library.brown.edu/pdfs/1201897921671875.pdf. Read the poets' prescriptions, then write an essay assessing the extent to which Lowell conformed to them in "Patterns."

- Select another imagist poet. Possibilities include H.D., Richard Aldington, D. H. Lawrence, F. S. Flint, and others. Assemble a montage of readings from that author's work and present your program to your classmates. Invite them to comment on the characteristics of that author's work.

- Write your own poem in the imagist style, keeping in mind the movement's emphasis on precision, brevity, and polish, particularly in creating a visual image. Your poem could tackle any subject: a blade of grass, a dewdrop, a sunset, a flower bud, a cloud, a firefly. Post your poem on your social networking site and invite your classmates to comment. Consider posting your poem on the Protagonize website at http://www.protagonize.com/category/poetry/teen_or_young_adult.

- In the early decades of the twentieth century, small literary journals such as *Poetry* and *Little Review* published the work of important poets. Investigate the history of these journals. Who founded them? Whose work did they publish? What types of poetry (and other forms of literature) did they favor? How influential were they? Present the results of your findings in a research essay.

- Locate another poem that relies on a garden setting. Among the many possibilities are "The Garden," by Andrew Marvell; "This Lime Tree Bower My Prison," by Samuel Taylor Coleridge; "Ode to Silence," by Edna St. Vincent Millay; and "The Deserted Garden," by Elizabeth Barrett Browning. Read your poem to your classmates, and invite a discussion about how the poet uses the garden to create an image or illustrate a theme.

- American poet Maya Angelou is best known for *I Know Why the Caged Bird Sings*. The image of that title is used in her poem "Caged Bird." Locate the poem, available in *Maya Angelou: The Complete Poetry* (Random House, 2015) and write a brief review of it as you think Amy Lowell might have responded. In particular, comment on themes the poems share.

- *Poetry for Young People: Robert Frost* (Sterling, 1994) contains twenty-five poems with nature themes by Frost, who wrote some of his most famous poems ("Mending Wall," "Birches," and "The Road Not Taken") contemporaneously with Lowell. The poems are presented in an illustrated format for younger readers. Select one or more poems from the collection and read your selection(s) aloud to your classmates. Be prepared to comment on what you believe Lowell might have thought about the Frost poems.

---

and spontaneously in the marble fountain. Even the brief reference to the footman who brings her the letter informing her of Lord Harwell's death contributes to the theme, for good manners and high breeding—a need to be correct in her behavior—demand that rather than giving expression to her grief, she must bottle it up as she instructs the footman to see to it that the messenger from the duke is given refreshment. Her erotic fantasy about her fiancé allows her momentarily to escape from the social conventions of dress and manners that restrict her.

The speaker strolls the paths of a formal garden (©jennyt | Shutterstock.com)

STYLE

Narrator

"Patterns" is a dramatic monologue. With this type of poem, the poet creates an identifiable speaker who delivers the lines of the poem. Very often, the speaker is caught in some sort of dramatic situation that gives rise to the poem: Put differently, the dramatic monologue is in a sense like a speech lifted out of a play. In the case of "Patterns," the narrator is an eighteenth-century woman who is engaged to marry a colonel in the army. The colonel, however, has lost his life in battle, prompting the unnamed woman to reflect on relationship with him. The reader is invited to envision the woman pacing her garden, then sitting under a tree to read again the letter informing her of her fiancé's death.

Setting

The setting of "Patterns" is a key element of the poem. The poem is set in a neoclassical garden of the early eighteenth century. This type of garden would have been characterized by balanced and symmetrical geometrical patterns, clearly defined paths and borders, and formal arrangements of flowers, shrubbery, and trees, along with such features as benches and, in particular, fountains. The patterned nature of the garden in which the speaker walks becomes a metaphor for the restrictions and limitations that her life imposes on her, the borders that surround and confine her. Just as the daffodils, squills, and other flowers in the garden bloom, flutter, and reach toward the sun, the speaker wants to escape her confining circumstances and live in a way that is freer and more spontaneous and that allows her to express her longings as a woman. The cool, smooth marble fountain that occupies center stage in the garden becomes the focal point for her fantasies about her absent lover. If the garden tames nature, the speaker wishes to unleash her passions.

Meter

Lowell was at the forefront of efforts in the early twentieth century to free poetry from traditional forms. In particular, she was an advocate of *vers libre*, or free verse, which the poet T. S. Eliot, in

COMPARE
&
CONTRAST

- **Early eighteenth century:** Europe is engulfed in the War of Spanish Succession.

  1915: Europe is again embroiled in armed conflict as World War I rages.

  Today: Europe is facing a new kind of warfare as terrorist strikes take place in Paris and Nice, France; Brussels, Belgium; and Ankara and Istanbul, Turkey.

- **Early eighteenth century:** Flanders is the site of major military campaigns in 1708 during the War of Spanish Succession.

  1915: Flanders again is the scene of intense fighting during the First and Second Battles of Ypres.

  Today: Ypres in Flanders pays tribute to those killed or listed as missing during World War I through the Flanders Fields Museum, the Menin Gate Memorial to the Missing, and war cemeteries.

- **Early eighteenth century:** During the neo-classical period in Britain, gardens were highly formal, with an emphasis on balance and symmetry and on geometric patterns.

  1915: The "cottage garden," with old-fashioned flowers, trellises, plantings that cascade into pathways, and an informal design, is a favored style among avid New England gardeners such as Lowell. During her career she will write "The Garden by Moonlight," "In a Garden," "A Tulip Garden," "Patterns," "A Roxbury Garden," "The Little Garden," "The Emperor's Garden," "The Fruit Garden Path," and "The Statue in the Garden."

  Today: Many gardeners prefer natural garden spaces, with native plants, grasses, and an emphasis on free-flowing layouts rather than formality; gardeners in arid regions often prefer xeriscaping, which preserves moisture with stones, gravel, mulch, and drought-resistant plants.

---

an article in *New Statesman* titled "Reflections on Vers Libre," defined as the absence of patterns, the absence of rhyme, and the absence of meter (the pattern of stressed and unstressed syllables). Free verse originated with the French poets of the nineteenth century, who wanted to liberate poetry from what they saw as the encumbrances of traditional forms, with their strict metrical patterns, rigid rhyme schemes, fixed stanzaic forms, and the like. It was their belief that free verse was more natural because it reflects the sound patterns and rhythms of speech. Thus, "Patterns" does not conform to the traditional metrical and other techniques often associated with poetry. The poem consists of seven stanzas of irregular lengths. Although the poem uses some end rhymes, for the most part, its lines do not rhyme. The lengths of lines vary from as few as three syllables to as many as eighteen, and there is no fixed metrical pattern,

such as iambic pentameter. The poem, however, is not without a sense of form and structure. In particular, Lowell makes considerable use of alliteration (repetition of the initial sounds of words), assonance (repetition of vowel sounds), consonance (repetition of consonant sounds), and the repetition of words to give the poem a cadence and sonorousness that elevate the speaker's outpouring of emotion and longing to the level of poetry.

HISTORICAL CONTEXT

"Patterns" makes reference to the speaker's lover, Lord Hartwell, a fictional colonel who is said to have died fighting while under the command of an unnamed duke in Flanders, a region that corresponds with portions of modern-day

Belgium but that historically has encompassed portions of modern-day Holland and France as well. The poem does not specify the conflict, but the details of the poem suggest that it is set in the early eighteenth century. This in turn suggests that the conflict Lowell most likely had in mind was the War of Spanish Succession (1701–1714), one in a long series of conflicts that engulfed much of Europe.

King Louis XIV was determined to expand France's frontiers and to dominate Europe. A step toward that end would be to bring Spain under French domination by placing a member of the French royal family on the Spanish throne. Matters reached a crisis when the king of Spain, Charles II, died in 1700. Charles was childless, so he left his domains to Philip, Duc d'Anjou, Louis's grandson and the great-grandson of Philip IV, who had been king of Spain. Alarmed by this formidable alliance of the two nations and by the fact that Louis had the largest army in Europe, King William III of the United Provinces (Holland) and Holy Roman Emperor Leopold formed an alliance to keep Louis in check. England, whose forces were led by John Churchill, the first Duke of Marlborough, joined the fight against France, largely because Louis favored the restoration of the Stuart (hence, Catholic) line of succession to the British throne.

What ensued was the War of Spanish Succession, which included major campaigns in Flanders in 1708. The war turned out to be futile. The alliance won key victories, but Louis retained his grip on France and preserved the throne of Spain for his grandson, who reigned as Philip V. Meanwhile, several other kingdoms in Europe entered the fray, pursuing territorial and other aims of their own. Even North America served as one of the theaters of war: from 1702 to 1713 France and England contended for control of the continent in a conflict called Queen Anne's War, referring to the monarch who had assumed the throne of England in 1702. (As a side note, it should be noted that it was not until 1707 that the nations of England and Scotland, under the Acts of Union, formed the state of Great Britain.) The war ended in 1714 with the signing of various treaties, particularly the Treaty of Utrecht.

"Patterns" was written and first published in 1915, as World War I was raging

The speaker is confined by her stiff, formal clothes (©Damian Palus | Shutterstock.com)

on the European continent, and many thousands of people, like the speaker of the poem, received word that their husbands, sons, brothers, and lovers had been killed or were missing in action. The commune of Ypres, located in West Flanders, stood in the way of the German advance through Belgium. It therefore became a focal point for some of the war's bloodiest and most protracted battles, and "Flanders" would have resonated strongly with most readers at the time because of crushing losses suffered both by the Allied Powers (which included Great Britain) and by the Central Powers, particularly Germany. The First Battle of Ypres took place in late 1914; the Second Battle of Ypres, during which the Germans violated the Hague Convention by using poison gas, was fought in the spring of 1915. A Third Battle of Ypres would be fought in 1917. The large number of red poppies that grow in the fields of Flanders remain a metaphor for the many lives that were lost during these campaigns.

CRITICAL OVERVIEW

In a letter to Lowell dated October 13, 1915, the poet Sara Teasdale writes from her hospital bed: "I think that the wonderful 'Patterns' in 'The Little Review' has given me the most delight." Teasdale compares the poem to "an exquisitely enameled old French snuff-box—so fresh and undaunted in the clear color, and the design so firm and so delicate." Teasdale knew Harriet Monroe, the editor of *Poetry* magazine, who in a review of *Men, Women and Ghosts* for the magazine singles out "Patterns" for praise, writing that the poet "lifts the poem to a higher plane with [the heroine's] poignant cry, 'What are patterns for!'" Monroe continues, observing that "'Patterns' is, indeed, not only the most effective of the *Figurines* in decorative quality, but the most human and convincing as well."

The headline of a *Boston Evening Transcript* review of *Men, Women and Ghosts*, the volume in which "Patterns" appeared, reads "Amy Lowell Again Assails Tradition." The review was written by William Stanley Braithwaite, who refers to Lowell's "courageous use of new poetical forms" and her recognition that to bring "a new force into the world," she had to "begin by killing, or at least wounding a tradition." In *Modern American Poetry*, Louis Untermeyer writes that the volume

> brims with . . . contagious vitality; it is richer in variety than its predecessors, swifter in movement, surer in artistry. It is, in common with all of Miss Lowell's work, best in its portrayal of colors and sounds, of physical rather than the reactions of emotional experience. She is, preeminently, the poet of the external world; her visual effects are as "hard and clear" as the most uncompromising Imagist could desire.

James W. Tupper, in "The Poetry of Amy Lowell," an article in *Sewanee Review*, writes that "Patterns" "in many ways is one of the most remarkable in the collection." Tupper remarks that the poem

> is symbolic of the modern woman's fierce rebellion against the conventions or patterns that deny her freedom to express herself. She is hemmed in by the conventions of society, symbolized by her "stiff brocaded gown," the formal garden, the well-trained servants, when all the time she wants to have her lover break the patterns.

S. Foster Damon, in *Amy Lowell: A Chronicle*, comments:

"Patterns," the first poem in the book, and the first of her poems to become very popular, remains as great as it seemed on first reading. A dramatic monologue expressing the tragedy of woman in wartime, it transcends both war and love, and is ultimately an expression of the repressed rebellion against the conventions and laws of life that bind the heart of every living soul.

Among modern critics, Jean Gould, in *Amy: The World of Amy Lowell and the Imagist Movement*, writes that Lowell was

> shrewd enough to place "Patterns," which had been an instant success when it appeared in the *Little Review*, in front, as an "opener," and she was confident it would mean surefire success for the book as well. It was the perfect lead-off for a volume of poems on themes of love-and-war, and it could be interpreted in any number of ways.

Melissa Bradshaw, in *Amy Lowell, Diva Poet*, sounds the same theme:

> The poem was so closely associated with the poet during her lifetime that she initially resisted including it in the second volume of the anthology *Some Imagist Poets*, wanting instead to showcase less popular work. She relented because she knew that its popularity would draw readers. . . . The poem remains popular today. Often used as an audition piece by aspiring actresses, it is the Lowell poem most likely to appear in high school textbooks and in college introductory literature courses.

Glenn Richard Ruihley, in *The Thorn of the Rose*, commenting on the theme of the poem, refers to "the rebellion of the heart against external constraints." He goes on to remark: "This attitude was given its classic expression in 'Patterns,' one of the best known recent American poems." Richard Benvenuto, in *Amy Lowell*, called "Patterns" one of the author's "undoubted masterpieces." The speaker of the poem, in Benvenuto's view, is a "vividly realized and timeless, tragic figure," and the poem as a whole is "an expertly constructed monologue," with "the subtle tonal and musical effects that Lowell argued free verse was capable of."

Not all critics admire "Patterns." In an essay titled "'Which, Being Interpreted, Is as May Be, or Otherwise': Ada Dwyer Russell in Amy Lowell's Life and Work," Lillian Faderman, taking a feminist view of Lowell's poetry and highlighting her place as a lesbian poet, dismisses "Patterns" for what she saw as "its clichéd heterosexual fantasy scene of a pink and silver female surrendering her soft and willing body to a heavy-booted man in a dashing uniform."

CRITICISM

Michael J. O'Neal

O'Neal holds a PhD in English. In the following essay, he examines the language patterns in "Patterns."

In discussing Lowell's "Patterns," it seems nearly impossible to avoid the use of the word *patterns*, thus inviting accusations of lame word-play. Yet the poem, while written in free verse, with stanzas of irregular lengths, lines of widely varying lengths, and only intermittent rhyming, relies on a number of other types of patterns that give the poem unity and allow it to coalesce as a thematic whole. Some of these patterns have to do with the diction and grammar of the poem, others with the use of sounds.

With regard to the poem's diction: *diction* refers to the selection of words in a literary work. An author's thematic concerns can frequently dictate, perhaps unconsciously, a pattern of word choices that in turn buttress his or her treatment of the theme. Alternatively, diction can be thought of as a major determinant of style: formal or informal, Latinate or Anglo-Saxon, simple or complex, abstract or concrete.

One of the first observations a reader might make about "Patterns" is the simplicity and directness of its diction. The nouns are concrete and almost entirely of one or two syllables: *paths, squills, gown, dress, gravel, shoes, tree, flower, fountain*—a reader could proceed through the poem making a list of the nouns and not come across a single one that needs defining (other than perhaps "squills" and "thrift," plants that might be unfamiliar). Nor would the reader find one that represents an abstraction or a concept; about the closest the poem comes to an abstraction is the word *blessing*. The same could be said of its verbs and verb forms: *walk, wander, tripping, sink, flutter, dropped, comes, see, guesses, sliding*—again, commonplace words of one or two syllables representing specific actions that require no explanation and that are unambiguous in their significance.

Along the same lines, the reader is likely to notice the utter simplicity of the sentence structure. Virtually all the sentences of "Patterns" are built around a noun + verb + modifier structure. The speaker walks down garden paths. The daffodils are blowing. The speaker sinks on a seat. A flower drops on her bosom. The dripping

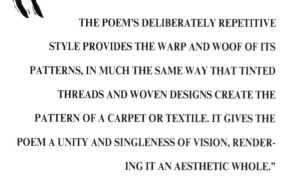

THE POEM'S DELIBERATELY REPETITIVE STYLE PROVIDES THE WARP AND WOOF OF ITS PATTERNS, IN MUCH THE SAME WAY THAT TINTED THREADS AND WOVEN DESIGNS CREATE THE PATTERN OF A CARPET OR TEXTILE. IT GIVES THE POEM A UNITY AND SINGLENESS OF VISION, RENDERING IT AN AESTHETIC WHOLE."

of the fountain never stops. A number of these elemental sentences correspond with a single line. Many of the remaining sentences consist of just two or three lines, and even those consisting of more than three lines are still brief and simple, making the sentences clear and readily understood. It is also worth noting that the poem contains very few figures of speech—that it is a remarkably literal record of the speaker's activities, recollections, and fantasies. The few figures of speech to be found in the poem—the speaker's passion *warring* against the stiff brocade of her gown, the flowers in the garden *standing*—are so commonplace that they hardly even qualify as figures of speech. Of course, this is not to deny that the poem taken as a whole is an elaborate metaphor, for the material circumstances of the speaker function metaphorically to represent the repression against which she is bent on rebelling.

Yet another feature of the poem's diction has to do with the lexical sets from which the words of the poem are selected. A lexical set is simply a group of words that share similar features by belonging to the same class. Thus, for example, the lexical set "pets" would contain such words as *dog, cat, parrot, gerbil,* and the like. A lexical set that features prominently in "Patterns" has to do with the notion of "down." The speaker walks *down* a path (in several lines). She *sinks* on a seat. A flower from the lime tree *drops* on her bosom. The sound of the water from the fountain comes *down* the path. The water *drips*. The speaker wants to see her gown lying in a heap on the *ground*. This emphasis on "down-ness" subtly hints at the speaker's sense of restriction and limitation, as she feels tethered to a life and a set of patterns that she wants desperately to break.

WHAT DO I READ NEXT?

- Lowell's "The Garden by Moonlight" originally appeared in her 1919 collection *Pictures of a Floating World* (Nabu Press, 2012).

- On May 3, 1915, during the second Battle of Ypres, Lt. Colonel John D. McCrae of the Canadian army composed a famous poem about World War I, "In Flanders Fields." The poem is available in *In Flanders Field and Other Poems*, at Project Gutenberg (http://www.gutenberg.org/files/353/353-h/353-h.htm).

- One of the most famous and poignant poems about the futility of World War I, first published in 1920, is "Anthem for Doomed Youth," by Wilfred Owen, available in *The Collected Poems of Wilfred Owen*, edited by C. Day Lewis (New Directions, 1963).

- *The Return of the Soldier*, by Rebecca West (Modern Library, 2004), was originally published in 1918 and tells the story of a shell-shocked army officer who, in 1916, during World War I, returns home from the trenches to England and the women who have shaped his life.

- *Amy Lowell in Her Own Words: A One-Woman Play* was created by Carolyn Gage. The piece weaves together selections of Lowell's poetry, along with diary entries, observations about the art of poetry, and reactions to her critics. The text is available as a Kindle download.

- *Love Speaks Its Name: Gay and Lesbian Love Poems*, edited by J. D. McClatchy (Everyman's Library, 2001) is a compact collection of 144 poems by and about gays and lesbians from the ancient world to modern times.

- *America in the 1900s and 1910s* (Facts on File, 2005), by Jim Callan, part of the publisher's Decades in American History series, provides young-adult readers with an overview of the history, politics, and culture of the decade when Lowell was publishing much of her work, including "Patterns."

- The imagists, including Lowell, were strongly influenced by the visual quality of Chinese poetry, which is written in characters, and Lowell produced a number of her own translations or adaptations of Chinese poetry, including that of eighth-century poet Tu Fu. *Carrying Over* (Copper Canyon Press, 1988) is a collection of poems translated by Carolyn Kizer. It includes poems by Tu Fu, along with those by Rachel Korn (contemporary Yiddish), M. Safdar Mir (Pakistan, translated from Urdu), Bogomil Gjuzel (Yugoslavia, translated from Macedonian), Edouard Maunick (French African, from Madagascar), and Shu Ting (contemporary China).

In contrast, however, the flowers reach upward toward the sun, and in the bathing idyll midway through the poem, this lexical set is replaced by one expressing vibrant activity. Now the speaker *runs*. Her lover *stumbles*. The sun *flashes*. The maze, like the speaker, is *laughing*. The lover *catches* the speaker and *clasps* her. The water drops *plop*. The sun *sifts* through the shade. However, in the portions of the poem that precede and follow this idyll, the verbs are static, or at least colorless. The speaker *is*. Her gown *is*.

She *walks*. She *goes*. Again, these lexical selections subtly but effectively reinforce the message of the poem.

In connection with diction, it is noteworthy that Lowell repeats words with some frequency. Thus, the word *pattern* and its derived forms *patterns* and *patterned* are used at least eight times. The word *path* appears multiple times, as do the words *garden*, *brocaded*, *stiff/stiffness*, *sun/sunlight/sundrops* (along with the repetition of *drop* in *sundrops/waterdrops/dropped*), *walk*,

After the speaker receives news that her lover has been killed in battle, she feels she will be trapped forever in her restricted life (©Billion Photos | Shutterstock.com)

up and *down, pink* and *silver, gown, whale-bone/boned, laughter/laughing,* and others.

The sense that the speaker is caught in a fixed, rigid, static set of circumstances is reinforced by the poem's reliance on past participle verb forms, that is, the *–ed* (or *–en*) form of a verb, as with *walk/walked* or *eat/eaten.* (Note that irregular past participles, such as *swum* and *drunk,* do not have the ending.) The past participle form is used when verbs are turned into adjectives that define nouns. Thus, the garden is twice said to be *patterned.* The speaker's gown is *brocaded* and richly *figured.* Her hair is *powdered,* her fan is *jewelled,* and her shoes are *ribboned* and *high-heeled.* The speaker describes herself as *arrayed, boned,* and *stayed* (the latter two words referring to the whalebone and stays used to stiffen her gown and corset). This reliance on past participle forms creates a sense of static fixity. Things are as they are; they do not change, nor are they in motion. In contrast, present participles—the *–ing* forms of verbs—are verbs in motion. They suggest activity and change. Thus, during the nude bathing idyll, the

sun is *flashing,* the maze is *laughing,* the speaker is *aching* and *melting.* The water drops are *plopping.* Thus, the very grammar of the poem helps to further its thematic concerns by highlighting the contrast between stasis and motion.

Although "Patterns" does not incorporate traditional metrics or stanzaic forms, it relies heavily on other poetic devices commonly associated with poetry, including alliteration, consonance, assonance, and repetition. These devices give the poem a kind of musical quality that, as one critic has pointed out, has made it a widely used audition piece for actresses. Alliteration, for example—the repetition of initial sounds—helps to link the lines and clauses of the poem: *down/daffodils, bright/blue/brocaded, path/patterned/powdered, silver/stain/softness/sink/seat/squills,* and *breeze/blossom/bosom.* Later, alliteration figures prominently in the sequences *swoon/sun/sifts/shade, sink/seat/shade,* and *sliding/seems/stroking/summer.*

Similarly, *consonance* adds to the musical quality of the poem. Strictly speaking, consonance refers to the repetition of consonant sounds in accented syllables, particularly the final syllables of words. More loosely, the term refers to any pattern of repeated consonant sounds in neighboring words. Thus, for example, the reader finds repetition of the *w* sound in *down/blowing/powdered/wander*. Repeated *r* sounds in the second stanza are found in *dress/richly/figured/train/gravel/thrift/borders/current/tripping*. These types of consonant patterns continue throughout the poem.

So, too, do patterns of assonance, or repeated vowel sounds. Accordingly, in the third stanza, the reader hears repeated *a* sounds (pronounced as in the word *ash*) in *splashing/paths*, followed by the *a* (as in *ate*) in *bathing/basin/brocaded*. Later, the same sound pattern appears in *maze/shade*. Similar instances of assonance appear in *figured/pink/silver/thrift* and *stain/plate/whale/brocade/shade*. Sometimes patterns of assonance overlap with the author's intermittent use of rhyme, as in the fourth stanza, with *shoes/choose/booted/bruised/noon/swoon*.

All of these characteristics can be subsumed under the word *repetition*. "Patterns," as a poem about patterns, relies heavily on various sorts of patterns created by repeated lexical and grammatical choices and by repeated patterns of sound that echo and re-echo throughout. The poem's deliberately repetitive style provides the warp and woof of its patterns, in much the same way that tinted threads and woven designs create the pattern of a carpet or textile. It gives the poem a unity and singleness of vision, rendering it an aesthetic whole.

Source: Michael J. O'Neal, Critical Essay on "Patterns," in *Poetry for Students*, Gale, Cengage Learning, 2017.

Adrienne Munich and Melissa Bradshaw
In the following excerpt, Munich and Bradshaw characterize Lowell as an early modernist poet.

"Amy Lowell Again Assails Tradition" reads the headline of William Stanley Braithwaite's review of Lowell's third volume of poetry, *Men, Women and Ghosts*, in the October 21, 1916 edition of the *Boston Evening Transcript*. Braithwaite applauds the poet's courageous use of new poetical forms, her comprehension that in "bringing a new force into the world," she must "begin by killing, or at least wounding a tradition, even if that tradition once had all the virtues." The accompanying photograph of the poet, her head

> THE BATTLE OVER THE PACKAGING AND PROMOTION OF IMAGIST POETRY, HOWEVER, ONLY SCRATCHES THE SURFACE OF POUND AND LOWELL'S IDEOLOGICAL DIFFERENCES."

cocked slightly to the side under a jaunty, feathered hat, staring straight into the camera with expressive, even mischievous eyes, her mouth set in a firm line with a trace of a smile at the corners, shows a woman secure in her role as one of the most powerful and popular poets of the day, confident of her ability to lure readers away from the safety of conventional verse and into the experimental forms, unrhymed lines, and uneven meters of modern poetry Her look is defiant and self-assured, a challenge to those who would question her right to assail tradition and a promise of reward to those willing to risk their own deeply ingrained ideas of what poetry should be.

The Amy Lowell whose unflinching gaze stares out from the middle of Braithwaite's review was at the top of her game. Her second volume of poetry, *Sword Blades and Poppy Seed* (1914), had established her as one of America's premier poetic innovators; the following year, with the critical and popular success of her first volume of literary criticism, *Six French Poets* (1915), she earned a reputation as a literary critic. *Men, Women, and Ghosts* (1916) would establish her as a popular poet, almost selling out before it was published. That same year saw the publication of the second of three imagist anthologies edited by Lowell. The next few years would prove just as productive: in addition to a steady stream of reviews and critical essays, Lowell published five more volumes of poetry, another volume of literary criticism, *Tendencies in Modern American Poetry* (1917), and a two-volume biography of John Keats before her sudden death from a stroke at the age of fifty-one in 1925. She left behind enough material for three more volumes of poetry, the first of which, *What's O'Clock*, won the 1926 Pulitzer Prize for poetry.

The many memorial tributes at Lowell's death unanimously sounded a note of grief and surprise, not only for the loss of a woman many called friend, but for the loss of a vital presence in American letters. In their shock and disbelief Lowell's peers, many of whom had long-standing feuds with the poet, expressed their confidence that the legacy of Lowell's brief but intensely productive career—her unwavering belief in a poetics both modem and inimitably American, her conviction that anyone "with a spark of poetry in them, be they blacksmiths or millionaires" could find pleasure in poetry—would leave a lasting mark on twentieth-century literary history.

They were apparently, if temporarily, mistaken. In the intervening years Amy Lowell has been reduced to a footnote, sometimes a derisory one, in the history of modern poetry. There is no single explanation for the neglect of Lowell in current debates and discussions about American poetry and modernism. Literary historians agree that her contribution to the consciousness of both the self-described New Poetry movement in American letters and to international modernism was central to ways of defining and understanding the period. For poetry readers from 1912 through the 1920s, Lowell's imposing presence dominated the scene. It would not be overstatement to claim that Lowell *was* modem poetry to the majority of readers: her opinions about other poets, her views about literary history, her popular and well-attended lectures reading her own poems and those of her contemporaries definitively reshaped conceptions of the literary scene.

Today Amy Lowell is best remembered as the self-appointed leader of the imagist poets. The imagists, writing in vers libre, strove to capture the sounds, colors, and textures of the sensory world. They aimed for conciseness of image, not the evocation of sentiment or the imputation of morality. As Lowell explained, "the modem poet has a passionate desire for truth, and a dispassionate attitude towards whatever his search for truth may bring him. He records; he does not moralize. He holds no brief for or against, he merely portrays." But what the poet attempts to portray—the hard, clear image of an instant's perception—is at once objective and subjective. That is to say, the poem strives for the objective presentation of the artist's subjectivity, as in Ezra Pound's 1913 "In a Station of a Metro" ("The apparition of these faces in the crowd; Petals on a wet, black

bough."), which uses only fourteen words to convey Pound's experience of stepping out of a subway car into a pressing crowd of people. The poem's energy comes from a flash of recognition as the reader, however briefly, shares the poet's visualization. For this reason Michael Levenson has described imagism as a "radical literary individualism."

Few poems in the imagist canon so purely illustrate the tenets of imagism as Pound's haiku. Amy Lowell imitated many such haiku, such as "Nuance" (1919: "Even the iris bends When a butterfly lights upon it"). More typical of Lowell's short lyrics is her 1922 "Vespers," with its subtle interplay of sound and image:

> Last night, at sunset,
> The foxgloves were like tall altar candles.
> Could I have lifted you to the roof of the green-
>   house, my Dear
> I should have understood their, burning.

In a manner characteristic of Lowell, the poem moves from images to powerful personal emotion, the cadences set up by a gathering of the rhymes "could," "should," and "understood" that deftly brings together other echoing vowels. Many of Lowell's longer poems aim for a direct impression of the sensory world, imitating musical sounds, loading the poem with color images, trying to force language beyond conventional boundaries. The issues swirling around the concept of modernism are not so much about these matters; they have more to do with egos than with images.

Lowell's well-known schism with Pound over the use of the term *imagism* and leadership of the movement is the stuff of modernist legend. Whether she is remembered as the interloper who used money and family connections to wrest the term away from Pound, water it down, and sell it to the masses; or whether she is remembered as pivotal in introducing modern poetics to American audiences through her clever deployment and marketing of the term depends on who is telling the story. Certainly, the drama of her dispute with Pound, and her subsequent, infamously vociferous promotion of imagist poetry obscures Lowell's other accomplishments, but the feud is worth briefly revisiting here inasmuch as it underscores where Lowell and Pound's aesthetic principles differed, and where their aims diverged.

Initially, Lowell and Pound enjoyed a cordial relationship. When she traveled to England in the summer of 1913 to meet the enigmatic *Imagiste* poets whose poems and critical writings had appeared in several issues of Harriet Monroe's *Poetry* magazine, Pound arranged her introductions, read her work, and offered editorial suggestions, and included her poem "In a Garden" in his anthology *Des Imagistes* (1914). Their brief alliance quickly collapsed when Lowell announced plans to publish a yearly imagist anthology, to be brought out by a major U.S. publishing house, with each poet receiving an equal allotment of poems and sharing editorial responsibilities. Pound argued that such a project would dilute the concept of imagism, conflating it with any poem written in vers libre. Having nominally acceded to Pound's wishes by dropping the final *e* in *imagiste*. Lowell went on to edit three anthologies of *Some Imagist Poets* (1915, 1916, and 1917).

In addition to the struggle for dominance between two immense egos, the battle between Lowell and Pound centered on the very concept of an avantgarde. Whereas they both agreed that modern poetry should "make it new" and strip the line of any Victorian excess, Pound imagined poetry as an elite enterprise and accused Lowell of trying to turn imagism into "an uncritical democracy with you as intermediary between it and the printers." Three years later, he was still hectoring her. "My dear Amy," he wrote, "You tried to stampede me into accepting as my artistic equals various people whom it would have been rank hypocrisy for me to accept in any such manner. There is no democracy in the arts." Amy would agree about standards, but not about elites. Aiming for a far-sighted and inclusive canon in poetry, Lowell wanted to admit as much quality of as varied a kind as possible, and, unlike Pound, she was interested in representing the immense energies of American voices. Although certainly not free of the ethnic and racial prejudices of her time and class, she espoused a democracy of letters, celebrating a wide range of poets, wildly different from herself, In a lecture introducing such poets to an audience avid for enlightenment. Lowell encouraged literary patriotism and the development of a uniquely American brand of modern letters: "the New Poetry is blazing a trail toward Nationality far more subtle and intense than any settlement houses and waving the American flag in schools can ever achieve." Pound disparaged Lowell for encouraging a wide audience and betrayed to Margaret Anderson, editor of the *Little Review*, a fear of spawning inferior American women poets in a literary democracy of equal suffrage: "Do you honestly think that a serious writer OUGHT to be reminded of the United States??...Ought one to be distracted, ought one to be asked to address that perpetual mother's meeting, that chaste Chitaqua [*sic*]; that cradle of on-coming Amys???" Pound resisted an imaginary army of hugely menacing Lowells, as if their sheer numbers (or her single threat) would squelch, silence, overpower him. His disparagement of Lowell can be understood in part as a defense against her.

The battle over the packaging and promotion of imagist poetry, however, only scratches the surface of Pound and Lowell's ideological differences. With the beginning of Pound's friendship and poetic alliance with T. S. Eliot in the autumn of 1914 came a dramatic reversal in his methods and a return to the classical models and forms he had studied and practiced earlier in his career; Lowell's aesthetic, meanwhile, remained closely tied to the early modernism of T. E. Hulme, Ford Madox Ford, and Pound himself, focusing on freedom of form, revolt from tradition, and above all, the presentation of "an intellectual and emotional complex in an instant of time." This divergence is telling on a number of levels. A primarily self-educated woman, Lowell had a sturdy knowledge of traditional poetic forms and of classical literature (albeit through translations), but she approached them as a common reader. A life-long, voracious student, first in her father's library, later in the Boston Athenaeum, she enthusiastically but haphazardly studied those authors and topics that most excited her, without a set curriculum, and without a sense of obligation to tradition. This has to do, in part, with the restrictions of gender: as a woman raised in the nineteenth century she was not allowed the education in Greek and Latin that would have granted her access to this kind of elite knowledge. But it has to do as well with Lowell's background as a New Englander—and as a Boston Brahmin—raised in a post-Emersonian age: hers was a confident relationship to her American cultural inheritance that goes back to the flowering of the American Renaissance. The questions and anxieties that inform later modernism were not hers....

Source: Adrienne Munich and Melissa Bradshaw, Introduction to *Amy Lowell, American Modern*, edited by

Adrienne Munich and Melissa Bradshaw, Rutgers University Press, 2004, pp. xi–xv.

Richard Benvenuto

In the following excerpt, Benvenuto explores the theme of relations between men and women in "Patterns."

... "Patterns" is almost certainly Lowell's best-known poem, as well as one of her undoubted masterpieces. First published in the August 1915 issue of the *Little Review*, it has appeared frequently in anthologies and textbooks since, and its speaker—an eighteenth-century English woman whose fiancé has just been killed fighting with the duke in Flanders—is one of the familiar characters in American poetry. Her passionate outcry against her personal loss and against such universal evils as war and artificial restraint makes her a vividly realized and timeless, tragic figure.

An expertly constructed monologue, "Patterns" contains the subtle tonal and musical effects that Lowell argued free verse was capable of. The poem is both too long and too familiar to be quoted in its entirety, but the first stanza illustrates the artistry of Lowell's word sounds, rhythm, and design:

> I walk down the garden paths,
> And all the daffodils
> Are blowing, and the bright blue squills.
> I walk down the patterned garden-paths
> In my stiff, brocaded gown
> With my powdered hair and jewelled fan,
> I too am a rare
> Pattern. As I wander down
> The garden paths.
> (*C.*)

Besides the internal and the end rhymes, assonance threads through and links the lines: w*a*lk, g*a*rden, *a*ll; p*a*ths, d*a*ffodils, p*a*tterned, f*a*n; daff*o*dils, bl*o*wing, br*o*caded; squ*i*lls, st*i*ff; g*o*wn, p*o*wdered. Alliteration occurs in "blowing. . . bright blue" and "patterned garden- paths"; and consonance or near rhyme in "gown" and "fan." Such interweaving sound patterns, of course, are appropriate in a poem about the social patterns that enmesh human life. The circular figure of the stanza—from "I walk down the garden paths" to "I wander down / The garden paths"—emphasizes the trapped, circular movement of the speaker, who will walk in her garden the rest of her life as one pacing a prison cell.

Rhythmically, 'Patterns' ranks with the best free-verse poems of Lowell's era. The cadence, as well as the diction, is that of unaffected but impassioned human speech—Lowell's ideal for poetry as it had been Wordsworth's more than a hundred years earlier. Though it is the language of prose, it is cadenced, not chopped up arbitrarily but designed to fall into rhythmic units. The lines quoted are essentially iambic and have from two to four accents per line, with varying numbers of syllables....

As we have seen, in her preface for *Some Imagist Poets*, 1916 Lowell compared the writer of free verse to someone who had the task of walking round a circle in two minutes, his only requirement being to complete each half circle in exactly a minute. Otherwise, he is free to increase or slacken his pace, go fast or slow. In "Patterns," she balances the rapidly moving third line, with its three unstressed syllables in a row, with the slower and heavier fifth line—thus contrasting the light, breeze-blown flowers of the one with the stiff gown of the other. The jammed accents and the dead stop of the period slow the movement even more two lines later: ... The slowing down suggests the speaker's hesitation to admit what she must about herself, while the line break is like a catch in her thought, for she is not what one might expect her to call herself—not a rare flower or thing of beauty—but a pattern walking a pattern. In thus integrating rhythm with self-discovery, accent with insight, Lowell simply demonstrates her command of the poetic craft.

But there is likeness as well as difference between the woman and the flowers she walks among. Both represent civilization's notion of beauty. The garden is nature pruned and arranged by man; the woman likewise is gorgeously arrayed and socially correct in whalebone and brocade. Her dress makes a pink and silver stain on the edge of the garden, as if she were one of the flowers. But whereas she suffers under the restraints and stiffness of society's patterns, the flowers do not. With more freedom than she has, the flowers can flutter "in the breeze / As they please." They touch and feel the air with their bodies. The speaker's body is imprisoned, and she can release herself only in dream and wishful thinking, in which she imagines herself naked and leading her lover in a maze. She wants to be her own "pink and silver" signaling to her lover, and she would press her body, not against his naked body, but against the signs of the pattern that restrains and encases him—his sword hilt, the buttons of his waistcoat that would bruise her body as he clasped her. Her dream is to be free herself and, by exposing and opposing her flesh to his uniform, liberate him as well.

In effect, she is a modern Eve who dreams of tempting her lover back to *the* garden, to a state of innocence before the fall and the necessity of the stiff clothes that conceal them from each other and the patterns that separate them. But whereas Adam awoke to find his dream of Eve to be true, her dream only taunts her. For the woman's garden, the product of civilization, is already fallen and contains a serpent sent from civilization—the letters that "squirmed like snakes" on the missive informing her of her lover's death. Rather than showing her the forbidden fruit, the serpent—death—denies it to her. Yet, though she is Eve without Adam and without the chance to sin, she is penalized—not expelled from the garden as her prototype was, but forced to remain in it. In a month, she says, "We would have broken the pattern"; now, she cannot even express her emotions as she feels them:

> The blue and yellow flowers stood up proudly in
> the sun,
> Each one.
> I stood upright too,
> Held rigid to the pattern
> By the stiffness of my gown.
> (*C*)

She will not feel the water of the fountain stroking her body like a dear hand—will not be reborn. In summer and in winter she will walk the garden paths, while the squills and daffodils "give place to pillared roses, and to asters, and to snow." In the natural pattern of generation and decay, however, the flowers and trees at least send forth their blossoms before they die. She will remain rigid and unchanging. The explosive last—"Christ! What are patterns for?"—is thus the poignant protest of one sacrificed figure to another, a barren Eve to the second Adam.

"Appuldurcombe Park," a dramatic monologue included in the mostly lyrical *Pictures of the Floating World*, deals even more explicitly with frustrated passion and sexual needs: . . .

Again it is the eighteenth century and the principal setting is a garden, but the Appuldurcombe flowers are more sensuous and vibrant than those in "Patterns," while the woman's emotions rage more intensely: . . .

Symbolizing the passionate needs that her invalid and presumably impotent husband cannot satisfy, the flowers both arouse her desires and threaten her with them, for she can be cured of her sickness only by adultery. Then, in an effective use of cinematic dissolve, the flashing red flowers become the scarlet coat of her "Cousin-Captain," who makes illicit love to her in the garden at night . . . .

This time the woman sins. Her heart blossoms like the sensuous toucan-colored flowers that hurt her with their loveliness, and identifies itself not with the purity of the lily, but with the passion of the rose . . . .

But the sinning woman meets the same sterile and unfulfilling fate as the unfallen Eve of "Patterns." The Cousin-Captain proves false and does not return when she sends for him after her husband's death. He had wanted her only for sex. "Your coat lied," she realizes. "Only your white sword spoke the truth." And she realizes too that the husband she wronged at least needed her. Stricken with guilt and now more sick than before, she imagines she hears her dead husband calling her; his voice mixes and blends with the snow that now covers all the flowers, just as winter descended on the garden in "Patterns." Betrayed by passion and the man in scarlet, still wedded in her widowhood to the cold, sterile man whom she betrayed, she apparently goes insane and prepares a "little dish of posset" for her husband, as she used to do when he was alive. "Do the dead eat?" she wonders. "I have done it so long, / So strangely long." The snow-covered tower-clock strikes eleven over the barren waste of her life—the same hour it struck when she parted from her lover in the garden to take posset to her husband.

In effect, she has not moved forward; the pattern she hoped to break with her sin still controls her.

... In the preceding poems about the sexes, we have seen the woman's passion having to contend with social restraints and with the frustrations caused by an absent or imperceptive male. "New Heavens for Old" celebrates the sexual vitality and freedom of the man. As they "bare ... their lusts," the young men become a raw masculine force, roaring and exploding upon the "dead houses like new, sharp fire." Unashamed of their instincts, but rather Whitmanesque in their love of their bodies and acceptance of physical appetites, "They call for women and the women come" (*C*).

The speaker, however, remains in her room, a lonely voyeur. The scene and her situation are almost certainly derived from section 11 of Whitman's "Song of Myself," Whitman describes a lonely woman looking through the windows of her house at twenty-eight young men bathing by the shore. As in Lowell, the sensual exuberance and freedom of the men contrasts with the barren, sheltered life of the woman. But in Whitman, the woman imaginatively joins the men to become the twenty-ninth bather and their unseen lover, passing her invisible hand over their bodies and seizing fast to them without their knowing it. Lowell's speaker, though drawn to the masculine energy she so forcefully describes, holds back even from imaginative participation in it. The spectacle astonishes and excites her, and of course it is because she has suppressed her own instincts that she sees the men in strong sexual terms. But when they call for women, and "bare the whiteness of their lusts" to the house she gazes from, she resists and instead of joining them arranges three roses in a Chinese vase: ...

She turns from the passion displayed in the streets to a life of patterns, arranging and fussing over the flowers that will die in their vase, just as she endures, or has chosen, a living death in her room. She mixes poison with her wine and thinks of winter. Having held herself back from passion, she is mentally in the sterile, dead world that descended on the passionate, struggling women of "Patterns," "Appuldurcombe Park," and "Pickthorn Manor." But whereas they reached for and were denied a "new heaven," she denies it to herself—not, however, without a sense of regret and a tragic self-awareness of her desolation as strong as in any of those who gambled and lost. In fact, what Lowell suggests in these poems is the tragedy of "Patterns" repeating itself

and becoming more harrowing and more difficult to overcome, as the patterns, the system of customs and restraints, become more and more internalized ....

Source: Richard Benvenuto, "Narrative Poetry I. Lowell's Different Voices," in *Amy Lowell*, Twayne Publishers, 1985, pp. 72–85.

SOURCES

Benvenuto, Richard, *Amy Lowell*, Twayne Publishers, 1985, pp. 1–30, 72.

Bradshaw, Melissa, *Amy Lowell, Diva Poet*, Ashgate Publishing, 2011, pp. 81–82.

Braithwaite, William Stanley, "Amy Lowell Again Assails Tradition," Review of *Men, Women and Ghosts* in *Boston Evening Transcript*, October 21, 1916; quoted in "Introduction" to *Amy Lowell, American Modern*, edited by Adrienne Munich and Melissa Bradshaw, Rutgers University Press, 2004, p. xi.

Chambers, Mortimer, et al., *The Western Experience*, 7th edition, McGraw-Hill Education, 1999, pp. 585–86, 955–57.

Damon, S. Foster, *Amy Lowell: A Chronicle*, Houghton Mifflin, 1935, p. 375.

Dinneen, Marcia B. "Amy Lowell," in *American National Biography Online*, Oxford University Press, 2000, http://www.anb.org/articles/16/16-01028.html (accessed August 3, 2016).

Eliot, T. S., "Reflections on Vers Libre," *New Statesman*, March 3, 1917, pp. 518–19.

Faderman, Lillian, "'Which, Being Interpreted, Is as May Be, or Otherwise': Ada Dwyer Russell in Amy Lowell's Life and Work," in *Amy Lowell: American Modern*, edited by Adrienne Munich and Melissa Bradshaw, Rutgers University Press, 2004, p. 66.

Gardner, Carol Brooks, "Boston Marriages," in *Encyclopedia of Gender and Society*, Vol. 1, edited by Jodi O'Brien, Sage Publications, 2009, pp. 87–88.

Gould, Jean, *Amy: The World of Amy Lowell and the Imagist Movement*, Dodd, Mead, 1975, p. 206.

Lowell, Amy, "Patterns," in *Amy Lowell: Complete Poetical Works and Selected Writings*, Vol. 2, edited by Naoki Onishi, Eureka Press, 2007, pp. 3–9.

Monroe, Harriet, Review of *Men, Women and Ghosts*, in *Poetry: A Magazine of Verse*, Vol. 9, No. 4, January 1917, p. 208.

Ruihley, Glenn Richard, *The Thorn of the Rose: Amy Lowell Reconsidered*, Archon Books, 1975, p. 40.

Teasdale, Sara, letter to Amy Lowell, October 13, 1915, quoted in *Amy Lowell: A Chronicle*, by S. Foster Damon, Houghton Mifflin, 1935, p. 318.

Tupper, James W., "The Poetry of Amy Lowell," in *Sewanee Review*, Vol. 28, January 1920, p. 47.

Untermeyer, Louis, ed., *Modern American Poetry*, rev. ed., Harcourt, Brace, 1921, p. 164.

"Vers libre," in *Merriam-Webster's Encyclopedia of Literature*, Merriam-Webster, 1995, p. 1164.

FURTHER READING

Blaisdell, Bob, ed., *Imagist Poetry: An Anthology*, Dover, 2011.
> This volume provides the reader with a compact collection of poetry by imagists and those who were greatly influenced by the imagist movement. Among the poets represented, in addition to Lowell, are H.D., Richard Aldington, John Gould Fletcher, James Joyce, and a number of lesser known poets.

Carr, Helen, *The Verse Revolutionaries: Ezra Pound, H.D. and the Imagists*, Jonathan Cape, 2009.
> This immense study is not a work of literary criticism per se. Rather, it chronicles in detail the history of the imagist movement, providing information about the intersections between the lives of the poets, their cultural milieu, and their material circumstances.

Gioia, Dana, David Mason, and Meg Schoerke, eds., *Twentieth-Century American Poetics: Poets on the Art of Poetry*, McGraw-Hill Education, 2003.
> The anthology comprises fifty-eight essays by fifty-three poets, including Lowell. It includes observations on the art of poetry by early

figures such as James Weldon Johnson and Robert Frost along with those from later poets such as Rhina Espaillat, Anne Stevenson, Ron Silliman, William Logan, Alice Fulton, and Christian Wiman.

Rollyson, Carl, *Amy Lowell Anew: A Biography*, Rowman & Littlefield, 2013.
> Rollyson relies on newly discovered documents to chronicle the development of the poet. He gives attention to her performances at readings and lectures and her interest in Asian culture. He also provides insight into Lowell's biography of Keats and traces the sources of negative views of her.

SUGGESTED SEARCH TERMS

Amy Lowell

Amy Lowell AND "Patterns"

Boston Brahmin

Boston marriage

Ezra Pound

Flanders

free verse OR vers libre

imagism

Lowell AND Men, Women and Ghosts

War of Spanish Succession

Persimmons

LI-YOUNG LEE

1981

"Persimmons" was first published in the *American Poetry Review* in 1981 and then collected in Li-Young Lee's first book, *Rose*, in 1986. *Rose* won the Delmore Schwartz Memorial Poetry Award from New York University and set the stage for Lee's career.

The collection contains a foreword by Gerald Stern, a professor of Lee's at the University of Pittsburgh, who outlines Lee's central poetic project as a "search for wisdom and understanding," as well as being characterized by "a devotion to language, a belief in its holiness," and "a willingness to let the sublime enter his field of concentration and take over." In the mid-1980s, as theoretical frameworks were being laid for poststructural and postmodernist projects like language poetry, Lee's making so explicit his belief that language, and in particular poetic language, was a doorway to the divine was deeply unfashionable. It is a testament to the power of his work that he continued to both publish and win awards.

The themes of *Rose*, in particular the extraordinary story of the Lee family's flight from the center of Chinese government power and influence to exile in Indonesia, fame in Hong Kong, and exile again in the backwaters of rural Pennsylvania, continue to inform his next two books, *The City in Which I Love You* (1990), and *The Winged Seed: A Remembrance* (1995). After *The Winged Seed* Lee took a long break, and his

Rummaging in his parents' basement, the speaker finds several scrolls on which his father painted images from memory *(©photosync / Shutterstock.com)*

poetry in both *Book of My Nights* (2001) and *Behind My Eyes* (2008) moves away from his family story and explores his deep conviction that poetry is an expression of the divine. Lee is one of America's most crucial poets, a man working from the depths of his own soul and expressing something essential about people's lives as multicultural citizens of the world.

AUTHOR BIOGRAPHY

Lee was born in Jakarta, Indonesia, on August 19, 1957, to Chinese parents. Lee's great-grand-father on his mother's side was Yuan Shikai, the first president of the Republic of China, whose tenure from 1912 to 1915 ended in disgrace after he declared himself emperor. Lee's father trained as a doctor and for a short time was the personal physician to Mao Zedong. The Lee family fled to Indonesia in the early 1950s, where Dr. Lee helped to found Gamaliel University, a Christian university where he taught English and

philosophy. As anti-Chinese as well as anti-Western sentiment grew in Indonesia, Dr. Lee was arrested and imprisoned for almost two years. When he was released, the family moved to Hong Kong, where Dr. Lee became a hugely popular evangelist, and then to the United States, where he attended divinity school and became a Presbyterian minister in rural Pennsylvania.

Lee was seven when the family came to America, and he was then raised in the small town of Vandergrift, where they were the only Asian family for miles. Dr. Lee taught his children English by reading to them from the King James Bible, and Lee counts the Psalms, along with the classic Sung and Tang dynasty Chinese poets his father loved, as his biggest poetic influences. Lee attended the University of Pittsburgh, and it was there he began to write poetry.

"Persimmons" was first published in 1981 in the *American Poetry Review* and appears in his first book, *Rose*, published in 1986. *Rose* won the Delmore Schwartz Memorial Poetry Award from New York University. His second collection, *The City in Which I Love You*, published in 1990, won the Laughlin Award, a poetry prize specifically designated for a second book. In 1995 Lee published *The Winged Seed*, a prose memoir of his family's history and journey from Indonesia to small-town Pennsylvania. While the book is prose, it is a deeply lyrical and associative prose that interweaves dreams and memories in a distinctively nonlinear fashion. Published in 2001, *Book of My Nights* is a poetic exploration of Lee's lifelong insomnia, taking on the very nature of the self for its subject matter. He continues this examination of the nature of self and identity in *Behind My Eyes*, published in 2008.

In a number of interviews, Lee has rejected the notion that his poetry is "Chinese American" or "Asian American." In an interview with Tod Marshall in the *Kenyon Review*, he noted, "I have no interest in that. I have an interest in spiritual lineage connected to poetry—through Eliot, Donne, Lorca, Tu Fu, Neruda, David the Psalmist." However, he adds that the job of the artist is "to discover a dialogue that is so essential to his being, to his self, that it is no longer cultural or canonical, but a dialogue with his truest self. His most naked spirit."

POEM SUMMARY

The text used for this summary is from *Rose*, BOA Editions, 1986, pp. 17–19. A version of the poem can be found on the following web page: https://www.poetryfoundation.org/poems-and-poets/poems/detail/43011.

Lines 1–6

"Persimmons" opens with the poet's memory of being physically abused and punished by his sixth-grade teacher, who slapped him on the head and made him stand in the corner for confusing two words. Even for a child in grade school in the 1960s, this is an excessive and humiliating punishment, as by that time, corporal punishment was generally frowned upon. The crime for which the child was punished was confusing two English words that sound alike but have very different meanings, *persimmon* and *precision*. While it is understandable that any child might make this mistake, that Lee is attending the sixth grade in his third language makes it more clear that his teacher's

punishment is probably race related. (With its details, the poem readily lends itself to autobiographical interpretation.) He is the Chinese child, the strange child, odd in his small, isolated Pennsylvania town.

Lines 7–17

The first stanza turns on the question of how to choose, leaving open for a moment, in that gap between stanzas, the object of that choice. As the second stanza begins, the poet notes that it takes precision to choose a good persimmon, and by so doing he demonstrates that he can tell the words apart—and probably could all along but simply got them confused, as one does, especially when working in a second or third language. It takes precision to find a good persimmon, to sniff out a ripe one, smelling the base of the fruit to see if it is fragrant. It takes precision, too, to eat a persimmon, as a truly ripe persimmon is a messy and delicious fruit, necessitating the spreading out of newspaper to protect the table. First, Lee notes, you do not cut a persimmon with a knife, for it is a delicate fruit, one you want to peel with your fingers, taking the time to suck the sweetness from the skin before swallowing. Only then does the precise eater of persimmons move on to the body of the fruit itself, eating the sweetness down to the core, to the fruit's heart.

This stanza demonstrates a deep and visceral knowledge of persimmons, as well as Lee's precise skill with language, and therefore stands as a direct contradiction to the small-minded teacher's punishment.

Lines 18–28

In the third stanza, the poet seems to be older, a teenager or young adult who lies naked in the darkness of the backyard with his girlfriend, named Donna. Not only does Donna have a name typical of a white girl of their generation, but Lee notes that her stomach is white. They are different, and yet not so different, and as they lie in the chill and dewy yard, Lee teaches her Chinese. The word for crickets he remembers; the words for dew and naked, he has forgotten; the words for you and me, he remembers. He remembers, too, to tell her that she is beautiful, as beautiful as the moon, an eternal symbol of beauty in both Chinese and Western poetry.

While this stanza explores young sexuality, it also addresses the similarities and differences between any two lovers, from the naming that comes with sexual exploration to the way life and intimacy can make one forget even words one once knew.

Lines 29–39

The fourth stanza returns to the idea that words can lead a person to get into trouble, both by mispronouncing them and by mistaking their meanings. Chinese is a tonal language in which many words are pronounced using the same phonemes but with different emphases, whereas English is a language in which emphasis has only connotative meaning; that is, one's tone can be sarcastic or humorous, but the tone does not change the denotative, or literal, meaning of the word. This difference is just one obstacle between Chinese becoming fluent speakers of English and vice versa. Here, *fight* and *fright*, separated by just one consonant, small but difficult for native Chinese speakers to pronounce, have related yet separate meanings. Lee recalls fighting when frightened and being frightened when fighting, thereby linking the words in a sort of circle of meaning.

Meanwhile, *wren* and *yarn* are also linked, not through the same sort of circle of denotation but by a personal connotative meaning. To the poet the two words sound similar and are forever linked because one word, *wren*, describes a small, soft bird, the kind of bird his mother used to fashion from the other word, *yarn*. She made little toys for the children, birds, rabbits, and tiny dolls, out of yarn, which the poet links to the ideas of things that are soft and comforting, like mothers and blankets. This, too, is a demonstration of the precision of language the poet evinces throughout the poem—as indeed throughout his career—further demonstrating the unfairness of the punishment meted out to him in the first stanza.

Lines 40–45

The poet returns to the scene of his punishment in the fifth stanza, where he reintroduces the teacher, Mrs. Walker, a woman who, while correct in identifying the fruit in her hand as a persimmon, is imprecise in both calling it a "Chinese apple" and in feeding it to the children in its unripe, bitter state. The persimmon in this stanza becomes something of a metaphor for the teacher, a sour woman, a woman who humiliates a child in one stanza and then forever links his ethnicity to something strange and unpalatable in another.

Lines 46–48

The poet's mother, however, who is linked to images of softness and resourcefulness, rescues the poor persimmon in the sixth stanza, giving her son a happy memory to hold in his heart in place of the sour persimmon of the classroom. At home, in a place of safety where people properly understand these things, a persimmon, Lee is told, contains the golden warmth of the sun, a heart that glows as warm as his face, as warm as a boy's face held in his mother's loving hands.

Lines 49–53

The seventh stanza begins with a descent into the cellar, where the boy finds two persimmons, carefully wrapped in newspaper to preserve them. Wrapping unripe fruits like apples or tomatoes in newspaper and then storing them in a cool cellar is an old way of preserving them for winter. The poet brings the persimmons upstairs and sets them on his windowsill to ripen. Outside, a cardinal, a bird whose bright red plumage sets him off against nature's background—perhaps the gray and brown days of late winter, early spring—calls every morning, a call the boy connects to the idea of the sun, coming up in the morning, coming back in force after the winter.

Lines 54–60

The eighth stanza introduces the poet's father, who is going blind. When he realized it, he stayed up all night in prayer, hoping for a sign. To comfort him for that which cannot be changed, the poet gives him the persimmons he has been ripening on his windowsill, heavy and sweet.

Lines 61–69

The ninth stanza brings the reader back to the cellar of the seventh, as the poet, a grown man now, has returned to visit his parents. He is looking for something stored in the cellar, something he has lost, while his father sits on the stairs above him. Distracted, the poet asks his father about his eyesight, at once realizing that it is a thoughtless question. His father, sitting on stairs the poet describes as tired, with his cane between his knees, effectively waves the question away, simply noting that his sight is all gone. In this stanza, Lee uses the cellar as an image of the past, of his childhood, the place where forgotten things are stored away, while his father, old and blind, now watches over him from above.

Lines 70–76

The tenth stanza describes what the poet finds in the cellar of forgotten items, a box containing scrolled brush paintings. There are three: one of two cats, one of a hibiscus leaf and flower, and one of two persimmons. The painting of persimmons speaks to the poet, the fruit seeming so full of sweetness, so ripe that it appears ready to drop right off the canvas.

Lines 77–88

The poem ends, in stanzas 11 to 13, with the father raising his hands to touch the cloth upon which the persimmons are painted, asking which painting he touches. The poet tells him it is the persimmons, and then his father, remembering, tells his son about painting them. He remembers the feel of the brush, the proper alignment and tension of the wrist that one must use to paint a Chinese brush painting. Even when he could see, the father tells his son, he painted persimmons with his eyes shut, painted the ideal persimmon he saw in his mind's eye. Over the years, his father—and in life Lee's father was a properly educated Chinese scholar—has painted hundreds of persimmons, and these ones before him, the ones his son just admired for being so beautiful, so clearly an expression of the essence of persimmon, he painted after losing his sight. Some things, he tells his son, you never lose, even if you lose your sight, among them the feel of a ripe persimmon in your hand, the weight of its sweetness.

"Persimmons" is a poem in which a central image is used as a device to contain an experience and by which to demonstrate the ways in which that experience has meaning for the poet. In this poem the reader sees how persimmons become a means of estrangement from the outer society, while remaining an image of love and harmony within the inner society of the family.

THEMES

Cultural Identity

"Persimmons" begins with a moment of cultural confusion. The boy hears two words that sound alike to him, *persimmon* and *precision*, and he confuses their meanings. The teacher, confronted with her only student from a different culture, mistakes the confusion for stupidity, or perhaps defiance, and punishes him with physical violence and public humiliation.

The poem turns here at the end of the first stanza, as Lee notes that to choose a persimmon takes a certain precision; that a sweet, ripe persimmon is not the pretty persimmon but the soft one, the one with brown spots, the one that appears on the verge of rot. In the small-town United States of the 1960s, when the poem is set, fruit was shiny and hard, spotless and uniform. It was the era when processed and commodity foods took over the American supermarket, replacing the more interesting and local fruits, which might have spots and which might nonetheless taste delicious.

To the teacher and to Lee's classmates, a persimmon remains a hard, bitter, crunchy thing, forever linked to Lee's identity as the Chinese stranger when his teacher, in a moment of startling imprecision, tells the children that the unripe persimmon she gives them to taste is a "Chinese apple." Like Lee, the fruit is a stranger.

Inside the Lee family, however, the persimmon is not a bitter taste, but a sweet one. From inside the family, from inside a culture that knows and values the fruit, it is something that bears the sun inside its heart, a sweet and tender fruit to be saved, wrapped in newspaper in the basement, and then carefully tended on a windowsill until fully ripe. It is a messy fruit to eat, requiring that newspapers be spread out, but the waiting, the tending, the messiness all add to the sensual beauty of the fruit itself.

Persimmons also take on a third level of cultural meaning in the poem when Lee introduces his father, the product of the finest classical Chinese education, a man who not only knows and preaches the King James Bible and Christianity but who also practices classical Chinese brush painting. The scrolls Lee finds in the basement depict three typical scenes from Chinese art, a hibiscus leaf and flower, two cats preening, and two persimmons, painted so that they look ripe enough to drop off the painting itself into his hand. The point of Chinese brush painting is not to have the most original take on a subject but to capture the essence of that subject by perfecting the ancient form by which the subject has always been painted. That Lee's father has painted persimmons hundreds of times over the years, practicing with his eyes closed even before he lost

TOPICS FOR FURTHER STUDY

- The father in "Persimmons" practices Chinese brush painting even as he is losing his sight. The goal of a good Chinese brush painting is the perfect representation of one's subject as it has been portrayed in the medium over the centuries, a pleasure that Lee's father recalls even through the paintings he can no longer see. Research Chinese brush-painting techniques and create a series of lessons for other students in your classroom. Topics should include how to correctly hold a brush, inking techniques, how to correctly paint a persimmon, and how to correctly paint one other subject. Teach at least one of these lessons to your fellow classmates.

- Lee's poetry often begins by describing the world around him. One way to work towards such a poem yourself is to write a list. Go to a place that you find interesting—it could be a store, a place in nature, your school cafeteria, or even your classroom. Start with the five senses: taste, touch, smell, hearing, and sight—then make a list of five observations for each of the five senses. Print them out in a list, cut the list into strips so that each observation stands alone, and arrange them and tape them down as the outline of a poem. Complete the assignment by writing a poem of at least twenty lines, and read it to your class.

- In a group of four or five students, brainstorm ideas for visually representing and interpreting "Persimmons" through the medium of film. Then storyboard your movie, containing at least ten scenes, with a title screen and credits listed in proper MLA citations. Using the Internet, find images and short clips that express your storyboard or create your own images and video clips and compile them into a movie to visually represent the poem. Record the poem over these images, and present the movie to your class along with a short written explanation about how you chose these images and scenes.

- After the Chinese revolution, Lee's family was exiled to Indonesia. Two years later, his father was imprisoned, and then, as they were being exiled yet again to Macao, they were rescued in dramatic fashion by one of Dr. Lee's former students, who pulled up alongside the ship carrying them to exile and saved them. Dr. Lee subsequently had a very successful career in Hong Kong, where he was an evangelical leader of enormous popularity and charisma, but he left abruptly after an argument and took the family to America. Team up with several classmates and write a play in which you imagine and dramatize the experience of being exiled. Where is your protagonist when he or she is exiled? Why does the government declare that this person can never return home? What loved ones does your character leave behind? Your play should have at least three scenes, and when it is complete, perform it for your class.

- Gene Luen Yang's *American Born Chinese* (2008), a graphic novel for young adults, is the story of Jin Wang, a lonely Taiwanese American boy navigating the challenges of middle school. The novel filters Jin Wang's feelings of displacement through the story of a Chinese folk hero, the Monkey King, and through the figure of Chin-kee, an amalgamation of every ugly Chinese American stereotype. Imagine an encounter between Jin Wang and Lee as he portrays himself in "Persimmons" and tell the story of that encounter in a graphic story of your own. The story should have a beginning, a middle, and an end, and something significant needs to occur between the characters.

As a child learning English, the speaker confuses words that sound similar, such as 'persimmon' and 'precision' *(©Ohm2499 | Shutterstock.com)*

his sight, seeking to perfect the form of the persimmon painting, is demonstrated in the beauty of this scroll Lee has found in the basement, a scroll painted after his father lost his eyesight.

"Persimmons" is a poem that quietly demonstrates the gap between Chinese and American cultures, between that of Lee's family and that of the country in which they have ended up. The family values language and art and education, but they find safety after a lifetime of exile and escape in a town of such isolation and closed-mindedness that the teacher, a figure who in the Chinese tradition should embody wisdom and refinement, cannot even recognize an unripe persimmon when confronted with one.

Transcendence

While "Persimmons" demonstrates the imprecision of the teacher's evaluation of Lee's intelligence and perception, it also demonstrates the poet's belief that words are never just words, that they contain endless references to images and ideas and carry cultural weight, which ultimately leads the reader back to the ideas of the eternal

and the divine. Lee has always been a poet who seeks out the transcendental, who is driven to use words to express a reality that lies beyond them.

In the foreword to *Rose*, the collection in which "Persimmons" was published, the poet Gerald Stern, who had been Lee's professor at the University of Pittsburgh, notes that Lee's poetry is characterized by "a willingness to let the sublime enter his field of concentration and take over, a devotion to language, a belief in its holiness." And while it is true that Lee was raised in a deeply religious home, as his father was a famous evangelist before they left Hong Kong and spent the last decades of his life as a Presbyterian minister in Pennsylvania, Lee's poetry is never in the service of any denominational religion. Rather, as he told Marie Jordan in an interview in the *Writer's Chronicle*, he feels that poetry is one of the key ways to access the silence that reveals the presence of God. He commented:

> The deepest possible silence is the silence of God. I feel a poem ultimately imparts silence. That way it's again disillusioning. It disillusions

us of our own small presence in order to reveal the presence of this deeper silence. . . . I don't know another form of language where this is possible except in poetry.

This is a somewhat inverse understanding of the transcendental, which normally indicates rising above reality, rather than sinking into it, but it hews to the core meaning of the term, which is to reveal an eternal meaning that is obscured by the surface meaning. In another interview, with Tod Marshall of the *Kenyon Review*, Lee tried to explain it like this:

> When I read poetry, I feel I'm in the presence of universe mind; that is, a mind I would describe as a 360-degree seeing; it is manifold in consciousness, so that a line of poetry says one thing, but it also says many other things.

In "Persimmons" the reaching for transcendence is manifest through the progression the poet makes, examining first the word, then the thing, then the representation of the thing. He begins with the word in English, with its tricky phonemes that together can be confused with another, also interesting word. The word in English is necessarily different from the word in Chinese, and both differ from the thing itself, the sweet fruit one eats at a table covered in newspaper. As the poem progresses, Lee goes deeper, ending not only with an image of the eternal persimmon of classical art but also with his father's memories, his insistence that there are some things one never forgets, like the people one loves or the weight of a ripe persimmon in the hand. The persimmon has transcended all of these meanings, while still remaining the thing itself. This exploration, striving for the eternal essence of the thing itself, characterizes not only "Persimmons" but Lee's later work as well.

STYLE

Lyric

The ancient meaning of *lyric* poetry is the song form—in ancient Greece these were poetic songs accompanied by a lyre and often sung by a chorus, and in China they were represented by the short song-form poems of the Tang dynasty. In modern usage, a lyric poem is usually fairly short and has a single speaker (who may represent either the poet or a persona) and reflects upon a personal experience, mood, or feeling. "Persimmons" falls into this category; it is a reasonably short poem in which the poet reflects upon

the nearly unbridgeable gap between the internal experience of being a member of his Chinese family and the manner in which they remain foreign and "other" in the small town where they have ended their long journey. The poem relies upon a single image, the persimmon, to tie together these different experiences. In the beginning of the poem, that the word is a near homonym for *precision* and that the speaker gets them confused cause him to be punished and humiliated by his teacher, a woman so ignorant of the nature of persimmons that she feeds the children a bitter, unripe one while telling them that this bitter fruit is what "the Chinese," including Lee's family, understand as an apple. This parable of misunderstanding is offset by Lee's meditation upon what the persimmon means inside his family, the sweetness that glows within its heart, a sweetness that Lee links both to his mother's love and to his father's ability to express the best of classical Chinese artistic expression.

Metaphor

Metaphor is one of the central stylistic hallmarks of poetry. Most poems seek to use figurative language in order to evoke new ways of thinking, whether the shift is in the way readers think about a particular subject or about the nature of language itself. The work of the poet is to expand the ordinary meaning of words and expressions in order to illuminate new ways of thinking and feeling. There are two primary forms of metaphor: comparative metaphors, which rely on the formula "A is B," and substitution metaphors, in which the poet uses term A in place of term B. The second type of metaphor is the one that Lee is using in "Persimmons" when he meditates upon the nature of the fruit as a means of exploring questions about culture, family, and the relationships of words to their objects and of those objects to art. Lee starts with the word, describing a moment of confusion between words that sound similar in English. He stumbles over *persimmon* and *precision*, *fight* and *fright*, *wren* and *yarn*, in turn moving through the literal meanings of those words to speculate about the relationship between words and their meanings, the way meanings are so often personal, interior. Although students often misunderstand metaphor as a sort of a puzzle, as if an author is saying something other than what he or she means, it is important to remember that by creating metaphors the poet is expanding the reader's understanding beyond the boundaries of ordinary thought. That is, by working with language in a metaphoric manner, the poet creates new ways of imagining language and the world.

Image

"Persimmons" is an example of a poem that uses a central image of domestic life to carry the weight of the familial experience, to serve as a sort of emblem of the value of that experience. This kind of poem grows out of the imagism movement of the early twentieth century, a moment now represented by the poetry of William Carlos Williams and Ezra Pound, although in the intervening century this stylistic approach has become somewhat synonymous with the lyric poem itself. In this poem, the central image is the persimmon, an ordinary object inside the Lee family, yet one that remains exotic to the American culture in which the family has been embedded. That the poet as a child is punished for confusing the word for this homely object with a near homonym becomes the starting point for the poem. Lee begins with the word and with the difficulty of distinguishing the words for things and feelings from their objects. *Persimmon* and *precision* are linked forever in his mind because of the time he was punished for confusing them. *Wren* and *yarn* sound alike to him, and both bring to mind the image of his mother, making toys from yarn, yarn that is soft like the bird it represents.

But the poem moves beyond a meditation on words as it becomes about the notion of imagery itself. As Lee takes on the task of being precise about the nature of the persimmon, as he describes the ripe sweetness of the fruit, how the fruit reminds him of the woman who (again, according the poem with real life) became his wife, of his family, and finally of his father and his Chinese heritage, the thing itself takes on a life beyond the word that represents it. This is characteristic of Lee's work.

In an interview with Tod Marshall in the *Kenyon Review*, Lee noted his opposition to the theory that meaning bears only an arbitrary relationship to language: "Language's mystery doesn't come from the notion that it doesn't refer to anything. What I find mysterious in language is that it's involved in a state of infinite referral." "Persimmons" is one of Lee's earliest poems, and this notion of a chain of referral is

evident even here. The persimmon is misunderstood by the teacher but known intimately inside the Lee family. It is literally a sweet and delicious fruit, one to be treasured and ripened carefully, and yet it is also a classic image from Chinese art, one that Lee's father, a man he revered, paints gloriously, even after he has lost his sight. In the same interview, Lee noted, "The whole universe keeps referring infinitely back. That's the way I experience it."

HISTORICAL CONTEXT

Yuan Shikai, First President of Republican China

Yuan Shikai, the first president of the Republic of China, was Lee's great-grandfather. A warlord and a nobleman from northern China, he made his name leading troops against Korea in the late nineteenth century. Upon his return, he undertook reform of the Chinese army and became a part of the Emperess Dowager Cixi's court. When she died in 1908, he retired to his family compound in northern China, the one Lee describes in *The Winged Seed* as his mother's childhood home. It was a walled compound with nine houses, one for the family of each of his wives. In 1911, Yuan returned to political life, leading forces in a rebellion against what remained of the Manchu Qing monarchy, and helped establish a Chinese government. The child emperor Pu Yi was forced to abdicate, and after a brief power struggle Yuan Shikai was elected the first president over Sun Yat-sen. In part, this was because Yuan had a large private army at his command, while Sun did not. The provisional constitution of 1912 called for the establishment of a democratically elected parliament, but this body never attained any real power. There was an abortive Second Revolution in 1913, after which Yuan Shikai dissolved the parliament, reinstated the monarchy, and had himself declared emperor. Yuan's death in 1916 marked the end of the monarchy and the beginning of what has come to be known as the "warlord period." During this time, China was divided among many local rulers, each of whom hosted his own private army.

Chinese Communist Revolution

The Chinese civil war between the Nationalist and Communist forces began in 1927 when

COMPARE & CONTRAST

- **1960s:** Political unrest in early 1960s Indonesia causes President Sukarno to scapegoat ethnic Chinese populations, imprisoning successful Chinese immigrants like Lee's father, and many of them, like the Lee family, flee the country.

  1980s: The mid-1980s sees liberalization of China's hard-line Communism as central planners seek out Western investment. Students and political dissidents agitate for political freedom of expression. The death of reformer and deposed secretary-general Hu Yaobang in 1989 is the catalyst for thousands of students to gather in Tiananmen Square, demanding democratic reform. In early June, central party leader Deng Xiaoping gives the order to clear the square with tanks. Many reformers, intellectuals, and poets flee the country, just as the Lee family had done two decades before.

  Today: While Lee, who has spent his adolescent and adult life in the United States, has fully assimilated into American society and the English-language poetic tradition, the ongoing persecution of poets and artists in China demonstrates the wisdom his parents showed in emigrating when they did. While Chinese dissident poetry and art is still vital, the government continues to prosecute artists, often under false charges of corruption.

- **1960s:** The Immigration and Nationality Act of 1965 reforms the quota-based immigration policies of the United States. While previous immigration policy had barred Asian immigrants, the 1965 act opens immigration preference to all with family ties as well as to those who can demonstrate professional competencies in areas where the United States is lacking.

  1980s: As it becomes clear that the People's Republic of China will demand the return of Hong Kong when the protectorate agreement expires in 1997, many wealthy and middle-class Chinese make arrangements to emigrate to protect their political and financial

  freedoms. The influx of Hong Kong Chinese immigrants to the United States, especially to the West Coast, differs from earlier waves of immigration in that these immigrants are wealthier and settle in suburbs rather than urban cores. Many also travel back and forth between the United States and Hong Kong, maintaining investments in both places.

  Today: In the early twenty-first century, as China's economy booms, many American young adults move to China for reasons of economic opportunity. While most do not stay permanently, spending a few years in China becomes an expected part of rising through the ranks of many multinational corporations.

- **1960s:** The "domino theory" is used by the US government to justify war in Southeast Asia. The theory holds that the institution of a Communist government in any nation will inevitably result in the spread of Communism to nations around it. Thus, the United States backs President Sukarto's suppression of political dissidents in Indonesia as part of its foreign policy of opposing Communism.

  1980s: In 1985, the Cold War with the West begins to thaw. The Soviet Union experiences increasing shortages of food and consumer goods and is increasingly unable to fund its satellite nations. In late 1989, thousands of people physically destroy the wall that has divided the city since 1961. Within a year the Soviet Union is disbanded, and the totalitarian Communist experiment is considered a failure.

  Today: The globalization of industry, banking, and economic activity has intensified in the post–Cold War period. Opened to economic investment in the 1980s, China in the intervening decades has become a driver of world economic growth. In the wake of the fall of the Soviet Union, proponents of unrestricted free markets have gained political power. In the early decades of the twenty-first century, the gap between rich and poor widens in almost every economy.

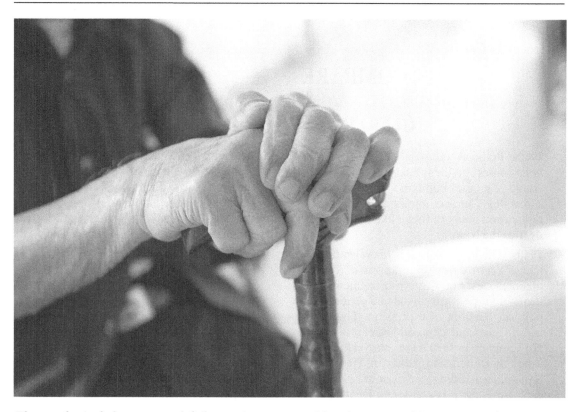

The speaker's father ages and fades, as is represented by the image of him gripping his cane
(©hxdbzxy | Shutterstock.com)

Chiang Kai-shek's armies began their northern campaign in order to unite China in the wake of the warlord period. It was during this time that Chiang purged leftists from his party, the Kuomintang, and began his program of fighting to defeat the Communist forces led by Mao Zedong. After a series of Nationalist victories, the Communist forces retreated to the countryside and reorganized into numerous small cells in order to fight a guerrilla war. In 1935 Mao began his famous Long March, in which the Communist forces withdrew from the populous southeast of the country and retreated to the arid far northwest. Over one hundred thousand Communists began the arduous six-thousand-mile march, during which they were attacked by the Nationalists and forced to cross several mountain ranges and large rivers. Nine months later, Mao arrived in the northern city of Yan'an with six thousand survivors; by the time other groups joined them, they numbered about twenty thousand. For the next decade, Yan'an was their stronghold, from which they waited out World War II. After that war ended, the Nationalist

forces sought to eliminate the Communists once and for all, even taking Yan'an; however, by the end of 1947 a successful Communist counteroffensive was under way. By November 1948, the Communists had taken Manchuria at the cost of one hundred thousand Nationalist troops and in 1949 the Communists took Beijing, Nanjing, and Shanghai. The Nationalist Kuomintang retreated to Taiwan, where they declared the island the Republic of China, a designation disputed to this day by the government of the mainland People's Republic of China.

During the prolonged revolution, Lee's father was originally attached to a Nationalist general, for whom he served as personal physician. After this general switched sides, Dr. Lee found himself, for a time, personal physician to Mao himself. After the war, in part because the Communist government disapproved of Lee's parents' marriage, since his mother was the granddaughter of the now-disgraced first president, and in part because of Dr. Lee's growing evangelical faith, the couple fled to Indonesia, which had always had a large ethnic Chinese population and where Dr. Lee helped found a Christian university.

Tang Dynasty Poets

In his interview with Marie Jordan, Lee noted that his mother does not think much of his poetry. "Once in a while I translate a poem for her," he said. "Her idea of what a poet is would be the classic Chinese poet like Laotzu or Li Po." He continued by noting, "My mother looks at me and says, 'You're not enlightened.' Those poets were enlightened."

The Tang dynasty is generally considered the golden age in the three-thousand-year history of Chinese poetry and is characterized by the work of the great poets Li Po, Du Fu, and Wang Wei. During the Tang, the Chinese imperial civil system was established, including the all-important imperial examinations, by which all bureaucratic positions were determined. Poetry was a crucial element of these examinations, and poems were judged not on their originality of expression or content but rather on the rigor with which they fulfilled the expectations of that particular form. Poetic forms were determined by elements such as the number of characters per line, the tonal patterns (Chinese is a tonal language, thus one character might have several meanings depending on the tone in which it is spoken), the use of parallel imagery, and restraint from repetition (for instance, if there is a tree in the first line, there should not be another tree in the poem).

The importance of these poets to Chinese culture is such that Lee could tell Jordan that in his mother's family, literature is invoked when "they sit at a table and eat. One of them will start reciting some passage of Laotzu, Li Bai, Wang Wei, or the philosophers." The classic poets are still so well known and such a part of Chinese culture that, as Lee says, "when that person stops reciting in the middle of the poem, the person to the right completes the poem." While Lee is adamant that he is as influenced by Western poets like Theodore Roethke, Wallace Stevens, and T. S. Eliot and by the Psalms, he readily acknowledges that the classical Chinese poets are in his blood.

CRITICAL OVERVIEW

"Persimmons" is Lee's most anthologized poem and appears in his first book, *Rose*, published in 1986, which won the Delmore

Schwartz Memorial Poetry Award from New York University.

In the foreword, the poet Gerald Stern, who had been Lee's professor when he was an undergraduate, claims that "what characterizes Lee's poetry is a certain humility, a kind of cunning, a love of plain speech." He goes on to note that what set Lee apart from his other students, and perhaps set the stage for his later career, was "a willingness to let the sublime enter his field of concentration and take over." Despite extending such praise, Stern also sets the stage for decades of ethnocentric readings of Lee's poetry when he states that Lee demonstrates "a pursuit of certain Chinese ideas, or Chinese memories, without any self-conscious ethnocentricity."

This question of ethnocentricity, of Lee's identity as a Chinese American poet, is one that has dogged him throughout his career, and one he explicitly rejects. In the interview with Marshall for the *Kenyon Review*, Lee claims that the question about where he stands as an Asian American writer is meaningless to him, because this is a question about dialogue with culture, a question in which he is entirely disinterested. "I have no interest in that," he replied to Marshall. "I have an interest in spiritual lineage connected to poetry—through Eliot, Donne, Lorca, Tu Fu, Neruda, David the Psalmist." He continued in the same interview by claiming, "Somehow an artist has to discover a dialogue that is so essential to his being, to his self, that it is no longer cultural or canonical, but a dialogue with his truest self. His most naked spirit."

Critic Zhou Xiaojing notes that critics who read Lee's ethnicity as the defining feature of his work are "not only misleading, but also reductive of the rich cross-cultural sources of influence on Lee's work and of the creative experiment in his poetry." Zhou continues by noting that "Li-Young Lee's poems cannot be fully understood or appreciated by tracing his heritage, which is mistakenly categorized as exclusively Chinese." What Zhou means here is that while Lee's parents were Chinese and while he "learned to recite classical Chinese poems from his father, who had a classical Chinese education and used to recite poems from the Tang Dynasty to his children," what is too often overlooked is that Lee's father not only taught his children English by reading to them from the King James Bible, as a man of deep and complicated Christian faith, but also wrestled with that beautiful and allegorical text on a daily and public basis.

For Lee, then, who came to the writing of poetry through the English language and the American school system, the central tension in his work is not one between Chinese and American culture, but rather a struggle with the nature of being and the divine. In the interview with Jordan, Lee claimed that while all poems are projections, they are projections that people study "to begin to understand the projector, the mind, or ground, of the projection." He goes on to note that "a poem is an image of the maker, as a human being is an image of God. But a poem doesn't simply transpose being. It also proposes possibilities of being."

Lee's volume *The City in Which I Love You* was the 1990 Lamont Poetry Selection of the Academy of American Poets. His other collections of poetry include *Book of My Nights*, published in 2001, and *Behind My Eyes*, published in 2008. His prose remembrance *The Winged Seed* was published in 1995. Lee's other honors include grants from the Illinois Arts Council, the Commonwealth of Pennsylvania, the Pennsylvania Council on the Arts, and the National Endowment for the Arts; a fellowship from the John Simon Guggenheim Memorial Foundation; and a Writer's Award from the Mrs. Giles Whiting Foundation.

CRITICISM

Charlotte M. Freeman

Freeman is a writer, editor, and former academic living in small-town Montana. In the following essay, she examines the poem "Persimmons" and explores the ways that Lee uses the persimmon to build an extended metaphor about the nature of the relationship between words and the divine.

"Persimmons" is a poem that begins in confusion and humiliation but which redeems the humiliation by turning the terms of confusion inside out, through close examination of the object of misapprehension. Lee is a poet who has always written in English, although it is his third language, one he did not grow up speaking at home. His family is Chinese, descended from nobility on his mother's side, while his father not only received a classical Chinese education but also became a medical doctor and a Christian minister, founded a university, was exiled, and

IN 'PERSIMMONS' LEE SEEKS OUT TRANSCENDENT MEANING BEYOND LITERAL UNDERSTANDING. HE REACHES FOR TRANSCENDENCE FROM A POSITION OF HUMAN FAILURE, THE KIND OF FAILURE WE ARE ALL PRONE TO WHEN WE CONFUSE EXTERNAL DIFFERENCE WITH ESSENTIAL DIFFERENCE."

after a successful career as an evangelist in Hong Kong fled to the United States, where he spent his last decades as a Presbyterian minister in a backwater town in Pennsylvania. Lee's educational background was similarly manifold—his parents taught him to read, write, and speak Chinese as well as English, while his childhood was steeped in both the classical Chinese poets and the beauty of the King James Bible. He cites as influences not only the Tang and Sung poets of China but also the psalmist David, Roethke, Williams, and John Keats. Lee is a poet who constantly seeks to use poetry to discover the reality beyond words, which for him is always the reality of God.

In the foreword to *Rose*, the collection in which "Persimmons" was published, the poet Gerald Stern, who had been Lee's professor at the University of Pittsburgh, notes that Lee's poetry is characterized by "a willingness to let the sublime enter his field of concentration and take over, a devotion to language, a belief in its holiness." The sublime, the transcendental, the eternal—these are all terms we use to describe this quest to uncover the holy in the everyday. Lee is well aware of the paradoxical nature of this quest. How do we use words to express or uncover that which is beyond words? In an interview with Marie Jordan published in the *Writer's Chronicle*, he says that poetry is one of the key ways to access the silence that reveals the presence of God. He stated:

> The deepest possible silence is the silence of God. I feel a poem ultimately imparts silence. That way it's again disillusioning. It disillusions us of our own small presence in order to reveal the presence of this deeper silence.... I don't know another form of language where this is possible except in poetry.

WHAT DO I READ NEXT?

- The American poet Gary Snyder has been deeply influenced by Chinese poetry, and in 1996 he published *Mountains and Rivers without End*, a collection inspired by a classical work of Chinese scroll art by the same name.

- Zong-qi Cai's *How to Read Chinese Poetry: A Guided Anthology* (2008) is both an anthology of classical Chinese verse and an attempt to bridge the gap between English and Chinese language systems. Compiled by a professor of Chinese and comparative literature, the volume comprises six chronological sections covering the entirety of Chinese poetry. Sound recordings of the poems are also available online for free.

- Yangsze Choo's novel *The Ghost Bride* (2013), tells the story of Li Lan, the daughter of a respectable yet impoverished Chinese family in colonial Malaysia in the 1890s. Because her father has lost his fortune, she has few marriage prospects, until the fabulously wealthy Lim family offers to make her a ghost bride to their recently deceased son. Li Lan finds herself drawn into a shadowy world of intrigue in the big house as well as an ill-advised attraction to the surviving son and heir.

- Lee's memoir *The Winged Seed: A Remembrance* (1995) is a lyrical meditation on identity, love, and exile. It is a book of sleeplessness and memory in which Lee ruminates on his father's life and several exiles as well as the different personalities he seemed to have in his American church and during annual retreats with other Chinese preachers. Lee also examines the distances between people and those they love, as his wife, Donna, sleeps beside him during his night of lyrical reminiscence and exploration of what it means to be a person in this world.

- Jeanette Winterson won the Whitbread Prize for a first novel for *Oranges Are Not the Only Fruit* (1985). This coming-of-age novel is narrated by a character also named Jeanette, who struggles to escape her overbearing and repressive evangelical mother. Convinced from an early age that she is indeed one of God's chosen, Jeanette must come to terms with her growing realization that she is not attracted to boys or men. Written with the same astonishing attention to image and sentence that characterizes Winterson's later work, this is a stunning and poetic novel.

- In *The Kidney Hypothetical: Or How to Ruin Your Life in Seven Days* (2015), Lisa Yee tells the story of Higgs Boson Bing, a Chinese American high-school student, named after the famous "God particle." Higgs is a superachiever, who has excelled through high school and has been admitted to Harvard and whose life comes to "ruin" in just seven days after his girlfriend poses a hypothetical question, asking him whether he would give her a kidney if she really needed it. His answer and her reaction start a spiral in which Higgs is forced to examine everything he thought he knew about life, high school, and his future plans.

- Lee's *Book of My Nights* (2001) picks up in poetry the same thread of insomnia and lyrical late-night thinking that he first wove in *The Winged Seed*. In these poems he explores the dark interrogative pathways, such as regarding who one is and why one exists, that confront all thoughtful people in those late-night moments when one's humanity renders one most vulnerable. Lee's poetic search for the nature of being and existence is expressed in this book in the simple yet powerful language for which he is known.

In "Persimmons" Lee seeks out transcendent meaning beyond literal understanding. He reaches for transcendence from a position of human failure, the kind of failure we are all prone to when we confuse external difference with essential difference. The poem begins with a humiliating misunderstanding. The poet recalls being punished as a boy for confusing two English words with similar phonemes, *persimmon* and *precision*. He is physically punished by his teacher for the error, then humiliated by being made to stand in a corner in front of the whole class. The error is treated not as an understandable mistake of translation but as a critical failure to comprehend that these are different words, with different meanings. As we all know, different languages have different words for the same things—in Chinese, there will be two different terms for persimmon and precision, words that may not sound at all alike, as they do in English, but which express the same concepts. As the boy stands in the corner, his thoughts turn slyly to the meanings of the words he confused. Of course, he understands the difference between them, which he demonstrates by meditating on the precision it takes to distinguish a sweet, ripe persimmon from a bitter, unripe one.

It is here that Lee makes the first turn in the poem, a turn away from the words themselves to an exploration of the nature of what those words signify. The poem turns to a very precise description of what a ripe persimmon is, how to eat it, what pleasure it holds. And in the following stanza he seems to call up the biblical Song of Songs when he compares the pleasures of the ripe fruit to the naked body of his beloved Donna. This third stanza sets words and their referents in contrast to one another. The poet knows some of the things in Chinese—*crickets*, *you*, and *me*—and some things he knows only in English—*dew* and *naked*. And some things, including the sweetness of the naked body of his beloved, are known beyond words.

Lee's interest in portraying the ways our experiences exceed language is something he has wrestled with throughout his career. In an interview with Tod Marshall published in the *Kenyon Review*, Lee attempted to explain. "Language's mystery doesn't come from the notion that it doesn't refer to anything," Lee began, raising the poststructuralist idea that language and meaning are only coincidentally linked to

each other. He continued: "What I find mysterious in language is that it's involved in a state of infinite referral. A flower isn't even a flower; it's a referent for something else." As the poem progresses, we see Lee examine the way words refer to something else; a *wren*, for example, sounds to him like the word *yarn*, and they both are soft, sweet items. And yarn takes Lee to the memory of his mother making little dolls, birds, and other animals with yarn, to amuse her children. So for him, *wren* and *yarn* are always going to be linked; they refer to each other, even if that reference is not universal for everyone. He went on to note in the interview that "the whole universe keeps referring infinitely back. That's the way I experience it."

Lee begins the poem with a confusion of words, then spends several stanzas examining the slippery ways that words refer to their objects. Sometimes the reference is *denotative*, that is, something we all understand as the literal definition of the word, and sometimes the reference is *connotative*, or associative, perhaps personal, and dependent on the context. But Lee is not a poet primarily interested in self-expression; for him, poetry is a means of accessing the eternal and the divine. In the interview with Marshall, Lee stated: "When I read poetry, I feel I'm in the presence of universe mind: that is, a mind I would describe as a 360-degree seeing; it is manifold in consciousness, so that a line of poetry says one thing, but it also says many other things."

In "Persimmons," this notion of universe mind is represented by Lee's father, who is losing his sight. Lee's father is a man of great faith, a man who believes not only in universe mind but also in the Christian story of personal salvation, and so, when he realizes he is losing his sight, he stays up all night. He waits for a sign, a song, a visitation—but receives none. His son gives him the only comfort he can, the two persimmons he has been ripening on his windowsill, persimmons rescued from the darkness of the basement, brought up into the light to gather the golden warmth of the distant sun and grow heavy and sweet. Sometimes, the poem posits, a fruit is more than a fruit: it is an offering of love, an emblem of the sweetness with which we all wish we could replace the sorrows of our loved ones.

In the interview with Marshall, Lee continued his discussion of the relationship between universe mind and poetry. He remarked:

When somebody writes a poem, when he opens himself up to universe mind and that universe mind is suddenly present in the visible world, the poet isn't the only one that gets the benefits of that. Universe mind comes down and that whole mind is a little more pure, a little more habitable.

He goes on to note that this is what Percy Bysshe Shelley meant when he claimed that poets are "the unacknowledged legislators of the world. I never understood that until recently. We keep the world from falling apart. . . . If we stop writing poems, you'll see this world go into such darkness." In this, Lee clearly believes that art, including poetry, is the means by which people access the divine and by doing so keep the pathways to the eternal open.

In "Persimmons" one can read the final stanzas as an expression of Lee's belief that art accesses this universe mind and in so doing benefits us all. The poem closes with the son returning home. Like all grown children, he is trying to be patient with his father, to be gentle with his father's happiness at having his son home again, albeit only temporarily. Family life has been portrayed throughout the poem as the haven, the safe space in which the poet can be himself, can be understood, in contrast to the outside world, represented by the school, where he is considered a stranger, a foreigner, someone from a culture that would prize a hard, bitter fruit over a sweet crunchy apple. However, the son has grown up and gone out into the world, and he is being patient with his father's happiness, even as he rummages in the basement for something he has forgotten.

As his father sits on the stair above, he is elevated over the son, not only literally but figuratively. He is the fountain of wisdom, the pastor who is officially in touch with the divine, the one responsible for transmitting not only the faith of the Christian Bible to his son but also the entire cultural history of Chinese tradition. And yet he has gone blind. He is the seer who cannot see. As the poet rummages among the forgotten items, he unearths a box that contains three scrolled paintings. He sits beside his father on the step, unscrolling the art. The third painting is of two persimmons, painted so beautifully that they express the essential nature of the persimmon. They appear so ripe, so sweet, that the poet notes they could almost drop from the silk the scroll is painted on into his hands, like the actual persimmons with which he tried to comfort his father in the past.

The father asks which painting they are looking at. When the poet tells him, the father, as though he is holding a brush in his hand, notes that he painted those persimmons so many times that he can feel the brush, feel the exact angle of the wrist with which one paints. While for a Western painter, the goal is to express one's individuality and unique perception in a painting, in Chinese brush painting the goal is to so completely fulfill the ancient formal definition that you express the eternal nature of the object you portray. The Chinese brush painter seeks to express, as Lee would call it, universe mind through the perfection of his persimmons. Lee's father in this moment notes that with these persimmons, the ones Lee is admiring, these he painted blind, the expression was not of what he could see in the external world, a world now lost to his sight, but of what he sees in his internal sight, the sight where we contact "universe mind."

For Lee, it is this contact with the eternal and the longing to contact the eternal that save us from the kind of closed-mindedness that characterizes the teacher who humiliates him at the beginning of the poem. In the interview with Marshall, Lee noted, "Cruelty is possible only when we are ignorant of who we are and who the other person is." And that cruelty arises when "I mistake you for something other than God. Or I mistake myself for someone other than God." The solution, Lee claims, is to "practice our mutual divinity," to remember that we are all manifestations of the universe mind. And it is, he would argue, the job of the poet to do this for society. It is the job of the poet to keep painting, even if he is painting blind.

Source: Charlotte M. Freeman, Critical Essay on "Persimmons," in *Poetry for Students*, Gale, Cengage Learning, 2017.

Matt McCarter

In the following review, McCarter points out Lee's use of symbolism.

Li-Young Lee's poetry in the book, *Rose*, has a depth of sadness and reflection that makes it meaningful and thought provoking to the reader. Lee draws on his own life experience in such a way that readers will wonder if he is trying to exorcize those experiences from his inner self. While these poems are deeply personal, they are also universal in their appeal.

The crickets bring to the reader's mind the sounds of a summer evening (©encikAn | Shutterstock.com)

Lee uses a simple and uncomplicated voice to render complex themes that are held together by the threads of his memory. His work is filled with vivid images of nature that take the reader on a journey through flowers and trees in Lee's imagined garden of experience.

The central theme in Lee's work is how the past and the present are interconnected. Lee not only suggests that the past affects the present, but also suggests that there is a great deal of past alive and well in the present. Lee seems to linger on the memories of his father. His father, both in life and in death, is omnipresent throughout Lee's offerings in *Rose*. For example, Lee writes his "hair spills/ through my dream, sprouts/from my stomach, thickens my heart, and tangles in the brain." The threads of the memories of his father and the threads of the thoughts that Lee has about his own life are weaved into an elegant tapestry of verse in *Rose*.

Lee's use of symbolism is very interesting in *Rose*. For example, in the poem, "Water," Lee explains that water is the way his father was destined to die according to the zodiac. As a result, water becomes the symbol for the

inevitable and timeless qualities of death. For Lee, "the sac of water we live in" is death itself. In "Falling: The Code," Lee uses apples falling to the ground in the middle of the night as an allegory for death. When Lee considers their "bruised bodies," he decides to locate them the next day only to find "they all look alike lying there." Wanting to know the "syncopated code" of the falling apples—of death—Lee sleeps outside the next night only to hear "each dull/ thud of unseen apple-/ body, the earth/ falling to earth/ once and forever, over/ and over."

Lee uses symbolism throughout the work and does so often in contrasting ways. For example, in "Dreaming of Hair," the hair is the ominous thread of death. This symbol can be juxtaposed with the use of hair in "Early in the Morning." In this poem, Lee uses the simple image of his father braiding his mother's hair. In the more sensual poem, "Irises," Lee writes "the memory of hair/ lingers on their sweet tongues." Lee's work is filled with these varying symbolic representations of the ordinary. This is one of the things that make his work so unique and interesting.

THIS POEM SHOWS VERY CLEARLY HOW THE SPEAKER IS HAUNTED BY THE EXTERNAL AND VISIBLE SIGNS OF HIS RACIAL IDENTITY, AND THUS HIS PERCEIVED STATUS AS A PERPETUAL FOREIGNER, AND ALSO HOW HE WORKS TO CHALLENGE, RESIST, EVEN SUBVERT THE TERMS OF SUCH RACIALIZATION."

The poetry of Li-Young Lee consists of simple forms that create a natural and earthy feel for the reader. The symbolism and imagery in his work comes from the deep well of experience and Lee writes in a style that gives the reader a sense of his urgency—almost as if Lee is trying to purge himself from what lies within him. Because of this, *Rose* is a very interesting and thought provoking read.

Source: Matt McCarter, Review of *Rose*, in *Ascent Aspiration*, Vol. 18, Nos. 11–12, November/December 2014.

Donna T. Tong
In the following excerpt, Tong characterizes Lee's work as "minor literature."

Li-Young Lee opens his collection of poems in *Rose* with "Epistle," splitting the voice of the speaker in the poem by alternating between first-person singular and the third-person figure of an unnamed boy ... These questions indicate that the two figures, the first-person speaker and third-person figure of an anonymous boy, are not actually the same despite the claim made earlier in the poem. This ambivalence and contradiction establish an abstract and abstracted tone and define a poetics which pervades and characterizes Lee's poetry ...

I begin with Lee's "Epistle" not only because it is the starting point of his *Rose* but also because in, through, and alongside the abstract and abstracted ambivalence and contradiction which characterize this poem specifically, as well as Lee's poetry in general, one is able to discern a poetics that plays on and with language itself, a poetics that Gilles Deleuze and Felix Guattari's concept of a minor literature may help to illuminate. Here I intend to look closely at Lee's well-known poem "Persimmons" and at

its condensation of various counter-hegemonic strategies characteristic of his poetics in *Rose*, strategies closely tied to the central thematic concern with family, memory, and language. Alongside and through this matrix, Lee's poetics, as "Persimmons" demonstrates, defamiliarizes English as a language, drawing attention to its constructedness and thereby exposing the inherently political interconnections of language teaching, language usage, and racial hegemony to expose its inherently political interconnections. Moreover, these tactics and concerns are broadly resonant with, and also critique, the ways in which Asians in America are imagined as Asian Americans; they provide us with a lens which focuses on this hybrid category *qua* category and refracts it.

MINOR POETICS
To begin with, I wish to show how Lee's poetics in *Rose* in general, and "Persimmons" in particular, defamiliarizes English. To do so, I propose to analyze his writing as a form of "minor literature." In *Kafka: Toward a Minor Literature*, Deleuze and Guattari claim that "[t]he three characteristics of minor literature are the deterritorialization of language, the connection of the individual to a political immediacy, and the collective assemblage of enunciation" (18). But what does it mean to "deterritorialize" a language? In its ordinary sense "deterritorialization" is the action or condition of removing, separating, or negating the jurisdiction of a governmental authority or country or otherwise the boundaries of an area delineated by an animal or group of animals as its or their nesting and/or denning site. Additionally, an affective element may underlie this process. Thus, the "deterritorialization" of a language involves the removal or negation of its boundedness or boundaries, a practice potentially affectively disturbing.

Deleuze and Guattari further explain this process through their analysis of deterritorialization in Kafka's writing. For them, when Kafka deterritorializes German, "What interests Kafka is a pure and intense sonorous material that is always connected to *its own abolition*—a deterritorialized musical sound, a cry that escapes signification, composition, song, words" (6; emphasis in original). Moreover, "the first characteristic of minor literature in any case is that in it language is affected with a high coefficient of deterritorialization," and "[i]n this sense, Kafka marks the impasse that bars access to writing for the Jews of Prague and turns their literature into something impossible— the impossibility of not writing, the impossibility of writing in German, the impossibility of writing otherwise" (16). Not writing is impossible "because national consciousness, uncertain or oppressed, necessarily exists by means of literature"; writing in German is impossible because "for the Prague Jews" there is an inevitable "feeling of an irreducible distance from their primitive Czech territoriality"; yet "writing otherwise" is also impossible because "writing in German" expresses "the deterritoralization of the German population itself" and the fact that the Jewish minority "speaks a language cut off from the masses, like a 'paper language' or an artificial language" (16).

Deleuze and Guattari thus claim that Kafka's "Prague German is a deterritorialized language, appropriate for strange and minor uses." They note parenthetically that "[t]his can be compared in another context to what blacks in America today are able to do with the English language" (17). In the words of Réda Bensmaïa in his "Foreword" to Deleuze and Guattari's text, the deterritorialization of language has to do with the way in which a given form of literary, or poetic speech or writing "affects the language in which it is effected" (xvi). We can also see, then, as deterritorialization encapsulates the defamiliarizing estrangement of sound from sense, it is a defamiliarization that nonetheless paradoxically "enables imagination, even as it produces alienation" (Kaplan 188).

Here I will contend that Lee's poetics in *Rose* is imbued with these impossibilities that Deleuze and Guattari assign to Kafka, for if writing in German is both necessary and impossible for Kafka, then so is writing in English both necessary and impossible for Lee. This Chinese American poet defamiliarizes English to create a hybrid language that generates out of itself, as its own *effect*, alienation and exile but also sensuousness and love...

We are told here that there is "no precision in a persimmons," where "precision" might suggest western logic or rationality and "persimmon" may symbolize, as becomes clear later in the poem, the aesthetics of traditional Chinese culture, and yet the "precision" of the poet's moves with and *within* the English of his text, which also deterritorialize this English, are also

"beautiful." In various ways the poet's Chinese "persimmons" (or "Chinese apples" as they are called later in the poem) are reterritorialized.

Here then Lee inverts traditional patterns of language learning not only to draw attention to the arbitrary nature of distinctions in language but also to show, that is, to *perform* the way in which those very patterns, used initially to establish the authority of the pedagogue over her pupil, can be retooled by the pupil in order to demonstrate his or her own authority and expertise in English. That is, Lee defamiliarizes English, showing a command of the language that affects it and also appears (in Deleuze-Guattarian terms) as an effect of it. Beginning with the seemingly nostalgic scene of a teacher-student interaction in primary school, where the student mistakes "precision" for "persimmon," the poet goes on to demonstrate his own precise understanding of the differences and similarities between these two words linguistically, semantically, and culturally. In this way he draws the reader's attention to the arbitrary and *artificial* constructedness of English as a language and reservoir of culture and history, as if perhaps this or any language were a vast manmade maze (or persimmon) within which we all become lost or alienated. Yet we also have here the "finding" or reintegration or reterritorialization of the Asian- American poet's own authoritatively Asian voice.

Indeed all languages are often taught as being something neutral and ahistorical, detached from the immediate context and in this sense artificial. Yet Lee's inversion works here by moving from the cold, mechanical rationality of "precision" to the living nature, beauty, and sensuousness of the "persimmon," where the latter is correlated with his family, his childhood memories, and traditional Chinese culture. This move also implies an active questioning, critiquing, and deconstructing of the cultural and linguistic constructions embedded in the English language. Here then I will look at Lee's poetry primarily as a medium of expression that resonates with the ways in which Asians in America are imagined as Asian Americans, that is, as part of a larger racial and linguistic order.

To read Lee's poetics in the context of "minor literature" is to foreground one of the underlying concerns in Asian American studies and literature. In *Imagining the Nation*, David

Leiwei Li comments on the uncritical acceptance of English as the *lingua franca* of Asian Americans and Asian American literature. He points out that "[i]t is ironic that the formation of a separate canon, with all its subversive energy against the nation that has historically suppressed it, actually works to supplement the national tradition" (29) through this uncritical assumption. Moreover, "[i]n this sense, English as the mode of expression for an Asian American cultural body speaks of the language of minor literature, which, according to Deleuze and Guattari, 'doesn't come from a minor language' but rather 'constructs itself within a major language'" (29). Li argues that deterritorialization occurs "in [that] inheriting a language not their own, Asian Americans have so appropriated, challenged, and colored English that it is made into a minority literary agency in the redefinition of the nation" (29). Yet the acceptance of "a monolingual English tradition is at sharp odds with the reality of a bilingual, multidialectal Asian American constituency" and "also fails to reflect the reading habits of a significant proportion of the Asian American community, whose subjective interests it intends to incorporate" (29). For Li, there has not been a clear literary theory of Asian American literature and/or aesthetics, beyond David Wand's rather tepid and somewhat Orientalist idea of a dual cultural heritage. Here I am not attempting to theorize an Asian American literary theory or aesthetics. Rather, I am concerned with investigating the manner in which Lee's poetry demonstrates how, in Li's own words, "by inhabiting the nation as a space of contradiction, the Asian American also constitutes a critique of the national community and proposes an alternative reconstruction" (12).

In other words I am interested in the negotiations involved in the paradoxical situation whereby a language used to hail the subject, to use Louis Althusser's terms, as subordinate is also the same language employed by that subordinated subject to contest his or her subordination. Deleuze and Guattari gesture towards this complication in their summation of the "impossibilities" that they claim Kafka faced and which his writings confront. While many of the poems in *Rose* are concerned with these problematics of language, culture, and politics, I consider Lee's poem "Persimmons" to concentrate in the most overt fashion on the complex relationship of an Asian American to the English

language. I will focus upon this poem in my analysis of Lee's poetics, due both to its exemplary status within the collection and for the sake of space. This poem shows very clearly how the speaker is haunted by the external and visible signs of his racial identity, and thus his perceived status as a perpetual foreigner, and also how he works to challenge, resist, even subvert the terms of such racialization.

Many Asian Americanists have written about the long-standing stereotype of Asians in America as being perpetually alien and foreign, as never fully belonging to the American majority, and of the particular historical circumstances and racial projects which perpetuate this image. However, as Kandice Chuh has proposed, conceiving of "Asian American" as an analytic may enable us to go beyond the surface of these projections (124–25). This is a crucial point with Lee's poetry, which is not about propagating this stereotype or others like it. This is no doubt in part because of his own complicated history of dislocation. Lee immigrated to the U.S. at six years of age, having been born in Indonesia and lived in Japan, Malaysia, Macao, and Hong Kong (Duesing 306). Even upon entering the United States, Lee and his family still had a peripatetic life, residing variously in Seattle, Pittsburg, and Chicago (Duesing 306).

Indeed, because of his engagement with English as the language through which Asians in America are imagined and represented, Lee in his poetry exhibits a "political immediacy," another integral aspect of minor literature in Deleuze and Guattari's formulation. In fact, the parenthetical comment about Black English in Deleuze and Guattari's *Kafka* calls to mind Fanon's conceptualization of the intersection of race, colonialism, and language, and both Deleuze-Guattari and Fanon can shed light on Lee's political immediacy in *Rose*. As Fanon writes in *Black Skin, White Masks*, "[t]o speak means to be in a position to use a certain syntax, to grasp the morphology of this or that language, but it means above all to assume a culture, to support the weight of a civilization" (17–18). In this way the first two characteristics of minor literature are interwoven. To deterritorialize English is for Lee an inherently political act since English is itself already heavily politicized. For any speaker of English assumes "a certain syntax . . . [and] culture," and in the context of the United States this is a culture steeped in a history of white privilege and of asymmetrical relations of power across categories of race, ethnicity, nationality, sexuality, and gender. As Lee shows us in "Persimmons," for Asian Americans the cultural context of English-language monolingualism in the USA disdains and penalizes non-native speakers of English.

Furthermore, as Deleuze and Guattari explain, Kafka's political immediacy is necessarily integral to his writing. For them, "[t]he second characteristic of minor literatures is that everything in them is political" (17). Deleuze and Guattari explain that "[i]n major literatures, in contrast, the individual concern (familial, marital, and so on) joins with other no less individual concerns, the social milieu serving as a mere environment or a background; this is so much the case that none of these Oedipal intrigues are specifically indispensable or absolutely necessary but all become as one in a large space.... Minor literature is completely different; its cramped space forces each individual intrigue to connect immediately to politics" (17)....

Source: Donna T. Tong, "Troubling English: Reading Li-Young Lee's Rose as Minor Literature," in *Concentric: Literary and Cultural Studies*, Vol. 39, No. 2, September 2013.

SOURCES

"Chinese Civil War," "Chinese Communist Party," "Chinese Revolution of 1911," "Kuomintang," "Long March," "Suharto," "Warlords," and "Yuan Shikai," in *Oxford Dictionary of World History*, 2nd ed., Oxford University Press, 2006, pp. 130–31, 358, 381, 614–15, 682, 705.

"Domino Theory," in *Encyclopædia Britannica*, https:// www.britannica.com/topic/domino-theory (accessed September 12, 2016).

Fischer, Hannah, "Lee, Li-Young," Postcolonial Studies @ Emory, July 2012, https://scholarblogs.emory.edu/ postcolonialstudies/2014/06/11/lee-li-young/ (accessed September 12, 2016).

Hewitt, Duncan, "China Cracks Down on Poet Li Bifeng and Dissident Writer Li Yuanlong," in *Daily Beast*, November 23, 2012, http://www.thedailybeast.com/ articles/2012/11/23/china-cracks-down-on-poet-li-bifeng-and-dissident-writer-li-yuanlong.html (accessed September 12, 2016).

"Hong Kong Immigrants," Immigration to the United States, http://immigrationtounitedstates.org/556-hong-kong-immigrants.html (accessed September 2, 2016).

Jordan, Marie, "An Interview with Li-Young Lee," in *Writer's Chronicle*, May/Summer 2002, https://www .awpwriter.org/magazine_media/writers_chronicle_view/ 2134/an_interview_with_li-young_lee (accessed September 2, 2016).

Lee, Li-Young, "Persimmons," in *Rose*, BOA Editions, 1986, pp. 17–19.

"Li-Young Lee," Poetry Foundation website, https:// www.poetryfoundation.org/poems-and-poets/poets/detail/ li-young-lee (accessed September 2, 2016).

Logan, Liz, "An Interview with Poet Li-Young Lee," in *Poets and Writers Magazine*, February 11, 2008, http:// www.pw.org/content/interview_poet_liyoung_lee (accessed September 12, 2016).

Marshall, Tod, "To Witness the Invisible: A Talk with Li-Young Lee," in *Kenyon Review*, Vol. 22, No. 1, Winter 2000, pp. 129–47.

Stern, Gerald, Foreword to *Rose*, BOA Editions, 1986, pp. 8–10.

Troyano, Joan Fragaszy, "Immigration and the Hart-Celler Act, 50 Years Later," National Museum of American History website, September 24, 2015, http:// americanhistory.si.edu/blog/immigration-and-hart-celler-act-50-years-later (accessed September 12, 2016).

Xiaojing, Zhou, "Inheritance and Invention in Li-Young Lee's Poetry," in *MELUS*, Vol. 21, No. 1, Spring 1996, pp. 113–32.

Zheng, Anjie, "Twice as Many Expatriates Leaving China Than Arriving, Moving Company Says," in *Wall Street Journal*, February 9, 2015, http://blogs.wsj.com/ chinarealtime/2015/02/09/twice-as-many-expatriates-leaving-china-than-arriving-moving-company-says/ (accessed September 12, 2016).

FURTHER READING

Bei Dao, *The Rose of Time: New and Selected Poems*, edited by Eliot Weinberger, translated by Yanbing Chen, et al., New Directions, 2010.

> Bei Dao is a Chinese poet who is about ten years older than Lee. He was active in the Democracy Wall protests of the late 1970s and has lived in exile since the Tiananmen Square rebellion of 1989. This bilingual volume presents poems from each of Bei Dao's books published in English—*The August Sleepwalker, Old Snow, Forms of Distance, Landscape over Zero*, and *Unlock*—as well as fifteen new poems. The poems are presented *en face* with the original Chinese versions, and the book includes a preface by the poet and an afterword by Weinberger, a highly respected literary critic and translator.

Ingersoll, Earl G., *Breaking the Alabaster Jar: Conversations with Li-Young Lee*, BOA Editions, 2006.

This volume is a collection of more than a dozen interviews with Lee over a twenty-year span. In these interviews he discusses his family's flight from political oppression in both China and Indonesia as well as the effects of being raised as an outsider in small-town America. He discusses his faith in God and how it is influenced by Christianity, Buddhism, and the Daoist poets of ancient China. He also discusses his poetics, particularly the influence of Roethke, Stevens, Keats, and the King James Bible.

Lee, Li-Young, *Behind My Eyes*, W. W. Norton, 2009. Lee told an interviewer for *Poets & Writers* magazine that he hoped *Behind My Eyes* is "clearer than *Book of My Nights*," a book he described as a sort of wilderness he had to traverse in order "to get to this book. I hope it's deeper and simpler."

———, *Book of My Nights*, BOA Editions, 2001. In his third collection of poetry, Lee extends the metaphor of sleeplessness that informed *The Winged Seed* as a means of exploring the nature of the self and the relation of that self to the cosmos and to God. In an interview with *Poets & Writers* magazine, Lee described the collection as a "real wilderness, tangled vines and trees and being lost...confusion about who I am and what's going on, and what is language, what's a poem, why am I writing."

———, *The City in Which I Love You*, BOA Editions, 1990. Lee's second collection was chosen as the Lamont Poetry Selection, now known as the Laughlin Award, by the Academy of American Letters. In this collection Lee continues to interrogate his childhood memories and his father's influence.

———, *The Winged Seed: A Remembrance*, Simon & Schuster, 1995. Lee's third book is a nonfiction prose memoir set over the course of a single night of insomnia, as Lee thinks through his family's history and their journey from China to Indonesia, to Hong Kong, and finally to the United States. It is an act of allusive storytelling that depends more on imagistic linking than on narrative progression.

Watson, Burton, ed., *The Columbia Book of Chinese Poetry: From Early Times to the Thirteenth Century*, Columbia University Press, 1984. This anthology contains over four hundred poems by ninety-six of China's great classical poets. Each of the greatest is represented by a chapter containing a generous selection of the poet's most iconic verse, while minor poets are grouped by time period and poetic school. Watson is one of the most respected translators of ancient Chinese, and many of his translations have come to be considered the standard English versions against which all others are judged.

SUGGESTED SEARCH TERMS

Poetry AND Chinese Tang dynasty

Poetry AND imagism

Li-Young Lee AND biography

Li-Young Lee AND sacred

Li-Young Lee AND William Carlos Williams

Chinese immigration AND Immigration and Nationality Act of 1965

Chinese AND Christian evangelism

Chinese history AND Yuan Shikai

Rite of Passage

SHARON OLDS

1984

The poem "Rite of Passage" first appeared in *The Dead and the Living*, the second collection of poetry by American poet Sharon Olds. *The Dead and the Living*, published in 1984, won the National Book Critics Circle Award and is considered a best seller of modern poetry. "Rite of Passage" was later included in *Strike Sparks: Selected Poems 1980–2002*, which was published in 2004 and also won the National Book Critics Circle Award.

The recurring theme in Olds's poetry is family: the poet has never shied away from depicting scenes of marital bliss or parental abuse, sexual love or the journey of parenthood. Her graphic revelations of a dysfunctional family have led to Olds's labeling as a confessional poet; however, Olds herself denies the label and maintains there is a separation between her life and her art. In keeping with her familiar theme and style, Olds's poem "Rite of Passage" shares from a first-person perspective a family event, the birthday of a young son. While the birthday boy, his guests, and their childlike bickering will not seem out of the ordinary to readers accustomed to small children, the extraordinary metaphor Olds creates from a boys' game of war will give the reader a laugh and then a grimace.

AUTHOR BIOGRAPHY

Olds was born as Sharon Stuart Cobb in San Francisco on November 19, 1942, and was raised

Sharon Olds *(©Jim Spellman / WireImage / Getty Images)*

in nearby Berkeley, California, in the Calvinist faith. With an alcoholic father and unhappily married parents, Olds and her siblings suffered physical, mental, and emotional abuse through their childhood. A tumultuous upbringing followed by a turn to atheism influenced Olds's focus on religion, free will, and family in her writing, which is typically classified in the confessional genre. According to an interview in *Salon*, Olds prefers to call her work "apparently very personal" in an attempt to protect the private lives of her family, Olds has remained reluctant throughout her years of writing to name her parents, husband, and children as the complex characters in her works.

After earning degrees from both Stanford University (BA) and Columbia University (PhD), Olds turned from her study of literature to begin writing her own. Her first collection of poems, *Satan Says* (1980), was published when she was thirty-seven, and it has been followed by a dozen more collections, including the award-winning *The Dead and the Living*, in which the poem "Rite of Passage" was first printed.

Among her most recognized and notable works are Olds's *The Father* (1992), which detailed the evolution of Olds's relationship with her father up until his death, and *Stag's Leap* (2012), similarly documenting the dissolution of the writer's marriage to her husband of thirty-two years and the father of her children. Olds's work consistently receives critical attention and praise: she held the position of New York State poet laureate between 1998 and 2000, and she has been awarded the National Book Critics Circle Award, the Pulitzer Prize, and the T. S. Eliot Prize and has enjoyed fellowships from both the Guggenheim and the National Endowment for the Arts. Olds divides her time between New Hampshire, where she resides with partner Carl Wallman, and New York, where she teaches in the Creative Writing Program at New York University and leads creative writing workshops at Goldwater Hospital.

POEM SUMMARY

The text used for this summary is from *Strike Sparks: Selected Poems 1980–2002*, Knopf, 2004, p. 27. Versions of the poem can be found on the following web pages: https://www.poetry foundation.org/poems-and-poets/poems/detail/ 47055 and http://www.ducts.org/12_00/poetry/ poetry_olds.html.

"Rite of Passage" opens on a living room where party guests gather for a boy's birthday. Lines 1–4 of the poem not only reveal the setting and speaker of the poem but also present details that serve to characterize the speaker and establish themes. The speaker is the birthday boy's parent and the party host, and as the speaker describes the guests, the reader learns that the birthday boy is a young child. The parent describes the guests as "men" who are in the first grade, so the reader may assume that the guests are friends of the same age as the son. Further details about the children attending the party include descriptions of immature yet masculine features such as beardless faces and small stature. The speaker's presentation of children as not-yet-grown men establishes a theme of masculinity.

Lines 5–10 burst with activity from the pack of small men party guests who assert traditionally masculine traits in their childish ways.

Alternating between passive monitoring and aggressive questioning, the boys mimic older men's words and actions. The boys use their elbows to shift and shove one another, and occasionally they tussle. The speaker notices how the boys maneuver their bodies and hears them question each other's ages in an effort to establish a pecking order according to age, strength, and influence.

The words of lines 5–10 portray these little fights as simultaneously serious yet insignificant. In the first two words of line 6 are alliteration, repetition of beginning consonant sounds in nearby words; assonance, repetition of vowel sounds within nearby words; and internal rhyme, rhyming words within the middle of a line or lines. These two words grab attention and jar the reader, drawing from the poem an atmosphere of tension. However, the next words reassure the reader that the little fights are resolved almost as soon as they begin. Yet again, the alliterative *s* sound and the one- and two-syllable words through line 8 are percussive, and the question mark at the end of line 8 punctuates with contempt. The reader is caught in the midst of a dubious battle. In lines 9 and 10, the boys seem to back off, eyeing each other defiantly.

In lines 10–15, a theme of militarism emerges as the boys' show of masculinity escalates. The speaker notes the boys' folded arms and furrowed brows, thinking they look like bankers, as they shrewdly evaluate each other as potential combatants. Appealing to the sense of hearing, the boys' clearing their throats is reminiscent of engines revving, a warm-up before the performance. The conversation turns to violence, as one boy boasts that he could beat another, younger boy in a fight, and the little men seem ready for battle. The military theme is emphasized by the presence of a large, dark cake shaped like a turret, a tower or protected stand meant for discharging weapons, which looms in the background.

A change in tone occurs in lines 15–21 as the speaker's son acquires the focus of his guests and of the reader. The hard masculinity and nervous energy of pending battle is gone with the parent's soft description of the son. He is freckled like nutmeg, a simile engendering warmth, and his small body is likened to a model boat, the crafting of which requires gentleness and patience.

The boy has long, thin hands, not a warrior's large calloused palms. In lines 19 and 20, the reader learns that the parent speaking is the boy's mother, as she remembers the day her son entered the world outside her body. Through the mother's memory and her tender depiction of the birthday boy, the poem's tone becomes decidedly feminine rather than masculine.

A third theme of the cycles of life is born in the mother's flashback. At her six- or seven-year old son's birthday party, she observes the young boys who are her son's guests rile each other with taunts and jabs. The children act like older men, soldiers or warriors ready to battle, and in this moment the mother is reminded of the day of her son's birth. She is transported in memory, and the specificity of her remarks about the day signifies that she feels that her son's birth was not long ago. In lines 20 and 21, the son acts as a leader of the group, and this mature action on his part likely causes his mother to reflect on how her little boy has grown, from the day of his birth to this birthday.

Lines 22–26 weave together the three themes of masculinity, militarism, and cycles of life. The son's words to his party guests are shocking in their clear conciseness. The mother's beloved boy, speaking to unite the group of party guests, assures his fellow men that, together, the six- and seven-year-olds could defeat a two-year-old. While the young men may be entirely sincere in their militaristic fervor, the reader is assured that there is no real threat of murder or harm. The reader can practically sense the mother's surprise at her son's declaration, yet she is wise in the ways of socializing children, and she makes no move to address or stop the boys. The children have come to the conclusion that, because they are potentially lethal as a group toward a younger, more vulnerable child, they may proceed to enjoy one another's company without any suspicion or jealousy of each other's masculinity.

The cycles of life continue: the mother realizes her son's maturation, the boys test each other, and the threat of war and violence is forgotten for the allure of play. The paradox of death within the life cycle is poignant in the last few lines of the poem. As the guests again clear throats like older men, the mother likens them to "Generals." This simile speaks of another level, globally and politically. These are not only boys arguing at a birthday party; they are the future men who will participate in confrontations as bankers or generals. The sardonic tone of the poem's ending, with small boys celebrating a birthday by pretending to be at war, also draws a simile between real warriors and children. The fantasy of war as a part of the life cycle is played out by men and boys alike.

THEMES

Rites of Passage

Though the titular phrase *rite of passage* does not appear anywhere in the poem, it is a key theme. *Encyclopædia Britannica* defines a rite of passage as a "ceremonial event . . . that marks the passage from one social or religious status to another." It also notes that, most often, "rites of passage are connected with the biological crises, or milestones, of life . . . that bring changes in social status and, therefore, in the social relations of the people concerned." Within Olds's poem, the prominent rite of passage is the birthday party. The celebration of birthdays often consists of a gathering of family and friends who share food, often a cake or dessert, and gifts in a ritual that marks the passing of years and joyously rings in the new year. Elements of this celebration can be spotted throughout the poem, and while the passage of another year is not an uncommon occurrence, it is treated as a special occasion that even warrants its own poem.

Life Cycles

Birth, maturation, and death are parts of the cycle of life, and the presence of these life stages in the poem contribute to the cyclical theme. The stages do not develop chronologically, as the poem opens on a birthday party, an event that marks an individual's annual maturation, and then flashes back to the birthday boy's entry into the world. The boy's mother, who is also the poem's speaker, reflects on her son's birth and growth as she observes the celebration of life playing out before her. Party guests who are feisty young men prepared to fight one another over a perceived pecking order taunt with the possibility of death. The absurdity of the mention of death and defeat from the mouths of small children underscores the paradigm of death in life. Boys who have not yet reached

TOPICS FOR FURTHER STUDY

- Research at least three rites of passage from a culture other than yours and make a PowerPoint presentation detailing how significant events are celebrated and why they are important to that culture. Consider rites of passage that accompany births, the arrival of a significant age, puberty, marriage, and death.

- Read William Golding's 1954 novel *Lord of the Flies* and write a short essay of comparison or contrast between the book and the poem "Rite of Passage." Respond to this prompt: Is there any difference between the boys' war in the poem and the boys' war in the book?

- Research Michael McClure's instructions for creating a Personal Universe Deck, a list of one hundred words that capture the essence of your existence. Generate your own deck of cards and then use it to write a confessional-style poem of at least six lines.

- Explore the sensation that is Mortified, a project that aims to make diverting the drama of teen angst through sharing embarrassing diary entries, home videos, poems, and artwork on stage, over podcasts, in documentaries and TV shows, in print anthologies, and online. Then conduct an interview with an adult willing to share his or her own mortifying story from teenagehood; discover and record how the shame has (or has not) given way to amusement.

the primes of their lives seem obsessed with dying rather than living, yet the older and wiser mother recognizes that this phase is simply a part of the natural order of the life cycle.

Masculinity

A writer who often focuses her creative lens on aspects of sex and gender, especially within

The poem is set at a five-year-old boy's birthday party (©udra11 | Shutterstock.com)

familial relationships, Olds remarks with not a small amount of humor on the masculine complex of very small men. The party guests in the poem are boys of six and seven years old, but they are described as though they are senior men. Their conversation and gestures are simultaneously true to their boyhood while signaling heightened levels of testosterone. These boys elbow, struggle, roughhouse, challenge, and grimace until they have mutually agreed, without really knowing why, that they do not pose any actual threat to one another's masculinity. The theme of masculinity is opposed by a glimmer of femininity from the mother's flashback to her son's birth. In contrast to the vivid action and tension from the excess masculinity in the room, the mother's tone in remembering a tender moment is soft and steady. The masculine tone returns with the end of the poem, heightened by the prior contrast, as the boys get back to their game of war.

Militarism

Traditional masculinity is marked by traits like strength and competitiveness, which are aspects seen throughout the poem's theme of masculinity; yet when strength and competition turn into aggression and battle, a theme of militarism emerges. When the boy party guests gather, they engage in fights that alternately break out and then cool down again; they view each other suspiciously as one views an enemy. These boys are called "Generals," and with a cake like a turret behind them, the scene is set for battle. The boys play pretend war and talk of killing one another or killing a mutual foe, and while the reader is aware that these children will not actually harm anyone, the militaristic undertone is clear.

This theme of militarism builds off and complements the themes of masculinity, life cycle, and rites of passage. As children age in cultures where war is a necessary aspect of living, traits of masculinity may become toxic, especially if they are encouraged through outdated rites of passage. In Olds's poem, the children are not dangerous because they are not evil warmongers themselves; they merely imitate what they have learned from tradition and culture.

STYLE

Free Verse

"Rite of Passage" is a single-stanza poem written in Olds's typical free verse, poetry unconstrained by rigid rhyme or meter. In her guide to poetry, *Thirteen Ways of Looking for a Poem*, Wendy Bishop writes that

> free verse is not simply free and easy writing. Instead, it is lined verse that works against the ghosts and memory of fixed forms, that plays with jazz, song, and other popular forms, that works into and out of stanzas and with and against a variety of conventional expectations.

This made-to-look-easy essence is especially true of Olds's poetry, in which metaphor, abstract comparison through image, and motif, repeating elements that connect to a theme, dance through lines and stanzas.

Confessional Poetry

While Olds has been classified as a confessional poet, she gives her work another title: apparently very personal poetry. Confessional poetry, which came into style in the mid-twentieth century, reveals, sometimes startlingly, truths about the poet or speaker. Personal truths revealed in confessional poetry are often secrets, histories, or flaws that the poet-speaker shares as if in a church confessional. Olds has declined the label and is reticent regarding the reality that seems to inform her work. In an interview with Marianne Macdonald for the *Guardian*, Olds demures,

> What I'm nervous about is making explicit and "part of the record" connections between poems and actual people.... I've never talked about actual biography—it just seems to me like the right thing to do when you look at the poems I write.

In "Rite of Passage," Olds could easily be the mother narrator speaking of her son's birthday party. However, since the poet has vocalized her wish that readers not assume her poems perfectly reflect reality, the reader should consider "Rite of Passage" to be a poem about any parent, not specifically about Olds.

Point of View

The point of view is first person peripheral, which means that the speaker tells the story of another character or characters and is not involved in the plot of the story or is only marginally involved. In "Rite of Passage," the speaker shares with the reader the story of the birthday party, acting as the observer and recorder who does not interfere with the action of the story. In this poem, the peripheral perspective enhances the children's portrayals as small adults; the speaker is present to supervise the children but at enough of a distance to allow the boys a sense of independence and control. The first-person-peripheral point of view complements the subject and themes of the poem.

HISTORICAL CONTEXT

From the time Olds was born in 1942 until the publication of her first poetry collection in 1980, the United States had been involved in innumerable foreign conflicts. With the presidency of Ronald Reagan, US foreign policy became even more militaristic. As both the United States and the Soviet Union raced toward new technologies of armament, including the possibility of a "space-based missile defense program" that would, according to the U.S. Department of State's "Timeline of U.S. Diplomatic History," "protect the country from a large-scale nuclear attack," the United States stepped into its role as world superpower. Throughout Reagan's presidency, the Strategic Defense Initiative was a sore spot in arms negotiations between the United States and the Soviet Union, and it was criticized by skeptics of the technology and by peaceniks opposed to war—cold, nuclear, or otherwise. There is an implication in one of the more subtle themes of "Rite of Passage" that Olds did not support such wide-scale US involvement in war efforts. The comparison she draws between the children faux-battling and capital-G Generals points, or rather wags, a maternal finger at the US leaders responsible for bringing the nation into one conflict after another.

As a working mother of school-age children during the 1980s, Olds likely would have taken interest in a 1986 article by George Guilder in the *Atlantic* titled "Women in the Work Force." The article cites a variety of studies and polls focused on the numbers of women both flocking to and successfully avoiding the workplace in the twentieth century. The author shares statistics such as these: "Half of all 1985 College graduates were women," "21 percent of married men declared that they would prefer to stay home and care for the children if they could," and "As of 1984 only 29 percent of married women held full-time year-

COMPARE
&
CONTRAST

- **1980s:** The primary goal for the earliest supporters of the women's rights movement, or first-wave feminists, is women's suffrage. Second-wave feminists lobby throughout the mid- to late 1900s for government protection from discrimination against women in both the private and public spheres. In 1982, the Equal Rights Amendment (ERA) fails to gain sufficient state ratification by its extended deadline, despite an outpouring of local and national support.

  Today: Supporters of the women's rights movement are called third-wave feminists. Along with championing women's issues such as reproductive rights, military service roles, and paid family leave for new parents, the movement focuses on intersectionality, the concept that supporters of the movement experience discrimination in multifaceted ways. Now more than ever, the movement is for women of any age, race, religion, region, and sexuality. Advocates for the amendment continue to raise awareness and support in the fifteen states where the amendment was not ratified, as they lobby Congress for another extension.

- **1980s:** Although Jimmy Carter's presidency through 1980 has focused on more peaceful international relations, President Ronald Reagan's foreign policy from 1981 to 1989 sees the United States involved in global conflicts, specifically in fighting the existence and spread of communism in such places as Lebanon and Libya. In a speech given in 1983, Reagan terms the Soviet Union an "evil empire" and voices concern over the threat of nuclear war. He calls for a 7 percent increase in military spending by the middle of the decade and deploys nuclear missiles to Germany, Britain, and Italy. Arms talks in Geneva set the stage for later arms-control treaties.

  Today: In his 2016 statement before the Committee on Foreign Relations, former national security adviser Thomas E. Donilon characterizes the world as "unusally ... unstable and volatile." Among the current serious problems are the "breakdown of state authority" in the Arab Middle East, from Syria to Yemen, leaving room for the growth and expansion of terrorist groups like ISIS. Competition for power between the United States and Russia returns to the international stage, as Russia flexes its military muscles by invading Ukraine and taking control of Crimea.

- **1980s:** Mid-century American poets begin to focus on confessional poetry, addressing subjects previously thought to be too personal, among them, love, sex, depression, divorce, and death. By the 1980s, such subjects are no longer considered radical. The *Cambridge Introduction to Twentieth-Century American Poetry* affirms that "the postconfessional lyric" has entered the mainstream. Critics are divided in their reception of the confessional as commonplace; it is simultaneously praised as daring and rejected as self-indulgent.

  Today: Outside the proliferation of the confessional in the literary sphere, social media platforms springing up throughout the 2000s gain massive popularity. These platforms allow anyone to document and share personal details of daily life; reality television and online blogs also capitalize on a cultural hunger for the confessional. In this atmosphere, confessional poetry requires, in the words of poet Lavinia Greenlaw, "extraordinary judgement, detachment, and control."

round jobs." Yet Guilder believes that the statistics may not be as clear regarding the choices women make to work part-time or leave their jobs. He cites married women's unlikeliness to

After the grim conversation, the boys return to the party and their play *(©Sean Locke Photography | Shutterstock.com)*

fully "exploit…their 'earnings capacity'," "basic differences between the sexes in attitudes toward work," and women's views of "their own employment as less important than their husband's" as possible explanations for his interpretation of statistics indicating women's "discriminating against the job 'rat race' and in favor of their families." As is apparent from Guilder's article, issues of gender roles in the home and the workplace were an important topic of conversation among men and women of 1980s America.

A 1991 article in the *New York Times* by Roberto Suro concerning the reality of changing family demographics and needs also addresses gender roles in the home in 1980s America. Suro quotes research psychologist Arlene Skolnick, who identifies a reason for the nation's "tremendous amount of ambivalence" as being a reluctance or an inability to return to the familial norms of yesterday. The psychologist assures Suro that changes are part of "a century of steady evolution in sexual mores and family structures…a historical continuum." Social, cultural, political, and economic factors were working with and against one another as "the

challenge to male dominance and the definition of new female roles" contributed to the march forward, from the sexually free 1960s through the family-oriented 1980s. Olds and her husband, married in the 1960s and divorced in the 1990s, certainly lived through the progression of changes to the American family structure, and the poet's work of writing her personal experience reflects the truth of that continuum of history.

CRITICAL OVERVIEW

"Rite of Passage" was first published in Olds's 1984 collection *The Dead and the Living*, which won the National Book Critics Circle Award and was a Lamont Poetry Selection. From her first publication, Olds and her poetry have collected both accolades and censure in response to her subject matter, her candor, and her craftsmanship. As a woman writing unabashedly about matters of love, sex, marriage, parenthood, and childhood, Olds's most constant criticism has been for being too transparent, especially because her poems are apparently about her (and her family members') lived experiences. Conversely, Olds has been extolled through the years for her courage and creativity in writing on taboo topics.

Responding in *Poetry* magazine to *The Dead and the Living*, Linda Gregerson honors Olds's "connoisseur's way with the sensuous image, an unabashed advocacy of the flesh," while citing "insufficient guidance" in the first section—the "Public" poems dedicated to social and political issues of the day. Gregerson names these poems a "self-serving project," less sincere than "poems to the living family, where Olds is willing to anatomize the workings of power and principle and partisanship before our eyes." Gregerson argues, and other critics echo, that Olds's "clear-eyed powers of transcription" are best focused on "the body . . . her credo and her inexhaustible source of metaphor."

In Carolyne Wright's review of *The Dead and the Living*, Olds's family portraiture is both colorful and condemning; those meant to be exposed are drawn into the light, and those who should be celebrated are. Some readers and critics may predict that Olds inflicts her childhood suffering on her own children, in the scrutiny to which her family is exposed through these intimate poems. Yet Wright points out that amid the suffering depicted there is a kindness and generosity; she says, "Olds does not stand outside or above the people in her poems; . . . she is part of the same emotive fabric as they are, and this identification lends the work much compassion."

CRITICISM

Sara Noelle Stancliffe

Stancliffe is a freelance writer and practicing poet. In the following essay, she studies how, in their reviewing the poet's body of work, including The Dead and the Living, *in which the poem "Rite of Passage" was first printed, Olds and her critics see harm or benefit in "apparently personal" or confessional poetry.*

Christina Patterson, writer for the *Independent*, has interviewed Olds on more than one occasion. When the two women get together, their conversations revolve around what Patterson calls the "fascinating and complicated relationship . . . between life and art." In her 2006

> OLDS WOULD HAVE US BELIEVE THAT SHE WRITES ABOUT BOTH AN ABUSIVE FATHER AND HER CHILDREN'S BODIES, NOT BECAUSE SHE IS DISLOYAL OR ESPECIALLY BRAVE BUT BECAUSE SHE MUST BE TRUE TO HER ART."

article, Patterson does not explicitly question Olds on the connection between reality and art, significant because Olds and her husband of thirty-two years had recently divorced. Early in Olds's career, the poet had promised to keep her family separate from her writing, a promise that could be difficult for a poet whose typical subjects include romantic and familial relationships.

When Patterson inquires about the "comparisons with the so-called 'confessional' poets—Sylvia Plath, Anne Sexton and Robert Lowell," Olds refers to "a different group of poets—people like Muriel Rukeyser, Gwendolyn Brooks and Galway Kinnell—who had a greater influence on her work. 'Those were the poets,' she says, 'whose lives I loved and whose work I loved.'" She tells Patterson that she calls her work "apparently personal" because it "is so different from life."

Patterson interviewed Olds again for the *Independent* in 2013, upon the release of *Stag's Leap*, the poetic product of Olds's divorce many years earlier. Patterson returns to the idea of confession, quoting in her article a conversation with poetry professor Lavinia Greenlaw, who said, "No one wants to be called a confessional poet. . . . It suggests all you do is blurt your feelings." Greenlaw, however, had conceded, "To work explicitly with the self requires extraordinary judgement, detachment and control. Sharon Olds, like Plath, has these qualities." Patterson notes the discipline required of a poet who writes, apparently, about the self, "with the pain and the shame . . . under such tight control." She refers in her article to a line from *Stag's Leap* where Olds writes, "My job is to eat the whole car / of my anger, part by part, some parts / ground down to steel-dust."

WHAT DO I READ NEXT?

- Originally published in 2003 by Nigerian author Chimamanda Ngozi Adichie, the novel *Purple Hibiscus* tells teenage Kambili's coming-of-age story in the midst of Nigeria's political upheaval. The narrator achieves profound growth through her experience of clashing loyalties regarding family, religion, politics, and love.

- Maxine Kumin's book *Bringing Together: Uncollected Early Poems 1958–1989*, published in 2003, showcases a frankness similar to Olds's and an understanding of place like Robert Frost's, but it is the precision of her poetry that is most widely praised. Another female poet like Olds whose work exists outside a specific classification, Kumin was a highly celebrated author whose poems depict New England farm life and the landscape of human connections with nature.

- Olds's 2012 collection *Stag's Leap: Poems* was published fifteen years after the imploded marriage it documents, as Olds promised her family this time to process the event. The winner of both the Pulitzer Prize and the T. S. Eliot prize, *Stag's Leap* has accumulated critical praise for its graceful yet poignant depiction of love before, during, and after divorce.

- Considered one of the most influential confessional poets, Sylvia Plath was a pioneer for women exploring the genre of profoundly personal writing during the mid-twentieth century. While Olds's verse sings of both the silly and the solemn, Plath's is regarded for its relentless depth; readers will gain insight to a mind enlightened and disturbed in reading *The Journals of Sylvia Plath*, edited by Plath's husband, Ted Hughes, and published in 1998.

- Winner of the Newbery Medal, Virginia Sorensen's 1956 novel *Miracles on Maple Hill* follows a family that moves from the city to the quiet country for the sake of the father, a recently returned prisoner of war. Through hard work restoring a dilapidated farm, the power of pristine nature, and old-fashioned togetherness, the family finds the miracle of healing.

- Published in 1997, Susan Goldsmith Wooldridge's instructional book *Poemcrazy: Freeing Your Life with Words*, takes its readers on a journey of introspection and redemption through poetry. For both accomplished and amateur poets, this guide to writing poetry intertwines tips for writing with concepts of self-awareness.

The discipline required to rein in and express complicated emotions has not always been so apparent in Olds's work. In her 1981 review of Olds's first collection of "uncompromisingly autobiographical" poetry, *Satan Says*, Lisel Mueller remarks on the insincerity of poems in which Olds is "using a voice so vehement, a language so hyperbolic, as to incur disbelief." Yet Mueller goes on to say, "By far the greater number of her poems are believable and touching, and their intensity does not interfere with craftsmanship. Listening to Olds, we hear a proud, urgent, human voice." However, in spite of her willingness to accept the poet's intensity, Mueller has not

been the only critic in Olds's decades-long career to notice the poet's tendencies toward oversized, overdramatized metaphor.

In his 1997 review for *Poetry* magazine, David Baker appraises "the recent Romantic lyric," whose "fundamental method is the plain style, its frequent mode the personal anecdote." Included among Baker's lyricists is Olds, whose collection *The Wellspring* failed to impress the critic. Baker does not take issue with Olds's confessional style; rather, he questions her authenticity and its impact on her audience. The critic says Olds's poems offer up "a combination of sentimentality and exaggeration, even falsification," what he believes is the poet's "most serious short-coming." In Baker's opinion, Olds takes on topics too lofty for her "unchanging and inculpable sense of self, the same in the womb as in middle-age." Olds, he writes, speaks of her parents' and her children's wrongs, but "she herself bears little sense of guilt or wrongdoing and undergoes surprisingly little change." Referencing her popular collection *The Dead and the Living*, Baker surmises "that much of Olds's influence and power draw precisely from the widespread sense of victimization that permeates our culture." When the critic acknowledges that Olds's "poetry often articulates our lonely silences," he does so begrudgingly, loath to accept the popularity of a poet whose message, to him at least, does not ring true.

If we listen to Baker, pretense is the worst we can expect from Olds, but the best is, according to Tony Hoagland in his 2009 critique for *American Poetry Review*, her "complexity of metaphor." Defending Olds against critics aiming to degrade her for "prurient" subject matter or uninspiring craftsmanship, Hoagland says of Olds's work that these are "poems which plumb the range of family dynamics and intimate physicality with a precision and metaphorical resourcefulness greater than may have ever before been applied to those subjects." Quoting in his review a portion of Olds's poem "Prayer," Hoagland agrees with the poet that experiences like first sexual encounters and labor of childbirth are "central meanings" to the lives of many. The critic champions "the poetry of the everyday," saying that "contemporary high-concept verse and domestic poetry coexist comfortably." Olds, as Hoagland affirms, is carrying out the work of the poet, whose job it is "to imagine his way vividly into the unfashionable nooks and crannies of experience." Yes, the critic does acknowledge the poet's "temperamental proclivity for shock, a somewhat insatiable drive for seeking and finding the taboo, the off-color, off-the-record, unsayable urges, sins and behaviors of the human." However, it is clear to the critic and to the poet's audience that Olds "doesn't seem to care about not repeating herself or about impressing critics." To Hoagland, Olds is writing "the real human story."

According to a 1996 interview with Dwight Garner for *Salon*, when writing about her own real story, the control Olds exerts in her poems is due to a device she calls "the spectrum of loyalty and betrayal." When Garner inquires after her children's responses to their mother's poetry, Olds mentions the spectrum by which she judges what may or may not be a mistake. She says,

> I've worked out this thing I've called "the spectrum of loyalty and betrayal." Which is also the spectrum of silence and song. And at either end, we're in a dangerous state, either to the self, or to others. We all try to fall in the right place in the middle.

In the opinions of some critics, Olds veers dangerously close to betrayal when her poems discuss her children. Olds's eye is fixed on the physical, and while her description in *The Dead and the Living* of play-fighting five-year-old boys seems innocuous, her close, almost obsessive detailing of a daughter's head-turning figure at an all-boy pool party might make some squirm. Certainly, there are more brazen poems on less subtle subjects in any one of Olds's collections, yet the slightly Freudian undertones of a mother depicting her children's bodily attributes, changes, and experiences from youth to adulthood are likely lost on few.

Carolyne Wright, in her 1985 review of *The Dead and the Living*, calls these undertones "the complexity of nuance and interrelation of characters" which "[remind] us of a good collection of short fiction . . . accessible and believable in the same way that fiction is." While she acknowledges the possibility but asserts the absence of neither "pre-Freudian awe nor post-Freudian resentment" in Olds's work, Wright praises the poet for her graciousness in discussing her familial dysfunction. She says that Olds "provides us with a sympathetic view of human love persisting in spite of cruelty and emotional trauma." According to Wright, Olds's poetry is cleansing and redemptive as much as it is a necessary evil. For readers who may identify with the pain Olds experienced, these verses show how to live, thrive, and possibly forgive after enormous hurt. And for readers who question what harm has been inflicted upon the Olds family, Wright hints at the notion of justice that Olds takes very (apparently) personally.

During her 1996 interview with Amy Hempel for *BOMB*, Olds speaks more on the subject of loyalty and how it might be learned, especially by those who must protect those most vulnerable. Those devoted to Olds have called her brave, daring, a pioneer for speaking so openly about a woman's life as a wife, lover, and mother. Yet Olds is not above second-guessing herself, and she uses the spectrum in determining whether she has been brave or simply disloyal. As a human fulfilling roles that may overlap messily, especially as a confessional-style writer, Olds must remain loyal to her own identity. She says to Hempel:

> It's almost like a spectrum of identity, who one is in relation to other people.... There's loyalty to the other and none to the self. But then, at the other end, if you tell secrets, and names, then other people are in danger the way you're in danger if you have to be silent. It could be a kind of spiritual murder. I mean—where on the spectrum of loyalty and betrayal does song begin? And where does it end?

In considering her loyalties to self and to those dear to her, Olds has come to see that those with "a passionate sense of loyalties" may have had to learn to consider others' feelings. The spectrum Olds has created helps here. When Hempel reminds the poet that many admire Olds for saying what most will not, the poet acknowledges her compulsion to write what she does. She refers to the "need and pleasure" and asserts that, in her view, "being brave means that you do something that you don't want to do, because you have to—for someone else, probably." Olds would have us believe that she writes about both an abusive father and her children's bodies, not because she is disloyal or especially brave but because she must be true to her art.

The list of readers, writers, and critics who are grateful to Olds for her candor is long: Alicia Ostriker places herself on the list with her 1987 review of Olds's *Gold Cell* for *Poetry* magazine. Ostriker applauds those she calls "poets of moral urgency," those who "affirm and undermine our lives simultaneously" through poetry that "exists to support and celebrate the life we live and the society we live in... [and] to subvert and transform what we already know and feel into... a further consciousness." Olds is one of these agents of subversion. In Ostriker's view, "some of her most haunting poems," "many... no less than breathtaking," cement Olds as a powerful American poet. With "clear unsentimental compassion," "the rich and precise tactility of her imagery," and "stunningly awful details," Olds lays bare her familial melodrama in a way that "make[s] anger impossible." Ostriker argues that, through writing clear-eyed narratives of daily and dysfunctional family occurrences, Olds teaches her audience how dear a life truly is. The poet "neither philosophizes nor moralizes explicitly," yet "Olds's refusal to establish any conventional poetic distance from her subjects amounts to a tacit moral imperative." Somehow, Ostriker says, Olds's particular, sometimes peculiarly personal poetry inspires us to "affirm as intensely as possible our biological existence and the attachments to others it implies." In stark contrast to Baker's dismay for the societal implications of Olds's popularity, Ostriker rejoices at the notion that poets such as Olds exist and thrive on the platform of love—familial, sexual, or otherwise.

Regarding her own popularity, Olds is not unaware of her following or her opposition. In her customarily gracious manner, Olds responded to Garner's *Salon* interview question regarding harsh reviews and disappointment by simply acknowledging her detractors. She believes that it is only fair that those who see little or no value in her work should say as much. Unfavorable criticism of her own work does not affect her faith in literary criticism. She says she reminds herself "of the great things I have read, great stuff describing other people's work that a critic likes or loves. Criticism can be so enriching, it can add to the pleasure we take in the poetry."

Whether the response to Olds's poetry is shock, shame, appreciation, or conviviality, it cannot be said that her poetry leaves any room for apathy. As Mueller says of Olds's poetic necessity, "She moves (and usually persuades) us by the very passion, even need, of her utterance." The poetry is fiery, and though Olds, her admirers, and her detractors may be consumed or scarred in the process, it is impossible to ignore the spark of a life ablaze in Olds's confessions.

Source: Sara Noelle Stancliffe, Critical Essay on "Rite of Passage," in *Poetry for Students*, Gale, Cengage Learning, 2017.

William Ames

In the following essay, Ames provides an overview of Olds's work.

Sharon Olds is a relatively modern poet. Born in 1942 in San Francisco, she attended Stanford and Columbia Universities. Little has been written about Olds, since she has only been published since 1980. She teaches at New York University and runs their workshop program for the Goldwater Hospital in New York, and she

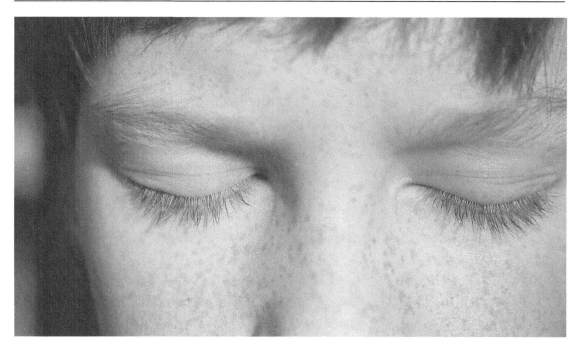

The speaker notes aspects of her son that emphasize his youth: his freckled face and slim body
(©Nyrelle Hawkins | Shutterstock.com)

has enjoyed acclaim in her short career. Olds has won the San Francisco Poetry Center Award for *Satan Says* (1980), the Lamont Poetry Selection and National Book Critics Circle Award for *The Dead and the Living* (1984), and the T. S. Eliot Prize for *The Father* (1992). (Olds, *Wellspring*) Sharon Olds has been the recipient of endowments from the National Endowment for the Arts, a fellowship from the Guggenheim Foundation, and she has published widely in periodicals such as the *New Yorker*, *Poetry*, the *Atlantic Monthly* and others. (Olds, *Living*) Since little is known about Olds' life, she presents opportunity to be read without the encumbrance or baggage of other critics opinions or predilections. Fortunately, Olds' speakers are intensely personal, and much can be inferred about the author through them.

Sharon Olds' body of work is dominated by her relationships with her family, especially her father. Although only sparse biographical evidence is available, the tenacious grasp her relationships have on her writing is undeniable. In her early poems, Olds clearly defines her work as very personal and outspoken. Using a dispassionate yet intimate voice, she details lurid experiences with an eerie, yet calm, distance.

(Schultz, 777) As an example, the first poem in her first book, *Satan Says*, shows immediately that she is unafraid of expletives and even vulgarity....

With this introduction, Olds prepares her reader for something a little unique and highly personal. Going further into *Satan Says*, Olds becomes more narrative in her work, and this is typical of her style. She seems to be simply chronicling events that have taken place in her life with the eye of a reporter. Still, her words are poetic, and never does the reader feel that another form would be more appropriate. Susan Schultz states in her review of Olds in the *Virginia Quarterly Review* that, "Olds holds to arch-realism, and tries to find plenitude in plain speech." She goes further to state that, "Olds does have a voice: it does not seem difficult to match her poems to her picture on the cover of the *APR*," hinting that Olds may "look the part." (777) Perhaps it is her voice that has brought such sensation to her modest collection of works, for it is quite new and daring, even in an age that knows e. e. cummings and Allen Ginsberg.

The motif of Olds' speaker's brutal relationships becomes much stronger as her works progress, perhaps this is Olds' response to her father's protracted death. In *The Dead and Living* and *The Gold Cell*, Olds seems to be focused on her relationships with her children, and on remembering herself as a child. In *The Takers*, her speaker describes her grotesque experiences with her older sister . . . .

It is with numerous scenes like this, repeated again and again, that Olds uses to create her style. Her fascination with the dark side of family life forces the reader to inquire the source of her inspiration. Is Olds the speaker of her poems? It seems natural that they would be, since they take on an almost "confessional" sound. Olds has written on these subjects nearly to the exclusion of all else. There seems to be very little of love and beauty in the world of Sharon Olds. Still, it is difficult to know if the works are autobiographical without more information on her life and personal relationships. The imagination of the poet can run wild with shocking images that are only partially based on reality. It is possible that Olds' poems are pure fantasy or complete reality, but it may be some time before an analysis of her life can reveal those answers. Regardless of their source, with poems like *The Pope's Penis*, (*The Cold Cell*, 19) her compositions linger and leave an indelible image with any reader.

Olds' latest books are dominated by her father, indeed, *The Father* is based entirely on her attempt to cope with his death. The voice of this memorial volume ranges from the bizarre to the beautiful. Overall, she keeps up her image of her father as some kind of monster, calling back images from some of her earlier books, but one poem defies the logic of the rest. *The Race* seems to be elevated from Olds' usual inclination towards the disgusting and bizarre, hinting that, perhaps, she may have felt some kindness for him. *The Race* depicts her frenzied dash to catch the airplane that will take her to her father's deathbed. Atypical of the rest of her works on her father, this poem seems to look on him reverently as she details her desperate journey through the airport . . . .

The poem ends equivocally, though, and it is difficult to be sure if Olds' speaker has shown a last bit of pity or of love or of nothing. (Dillon, 116) It is difficult to believe that any person can so totally and undeniably hate and detest their father so much that they are incapable of pity.

In her latest book, *The Wellspring*, Olds' speaker continues her unabashed abhorrence of her father, but it is interspersed with other, more vital poems that tell of her family—especially her children—and she seems to have taken a large step toward conciliating her past. Overall, Sharon Olds seems to have matured as she has written over the last sixteen years, and she will undoubtedly continue well into the future.

Source: William Ames, "An Introduction to Sharon Olds," in *Poet's Forum*, 2016.

SOURCES

Alexander, Bobby C., and Edward Norbeck, "Rite of Passage," in *Encyclopædia Britannica*, 2016, https://www.britannica.com/topic/rite-of-passage (accessed August 23, 2016).

Baker, David, "Romantic Melancholy, Romantic Excess," in *Poetry*, Vol. 170, No. 5, August 1997, pp. 288–301.

Beach, Christopher, "The Confessional Moment," in *The Cambridge Introduction to Twentieth-Century American Poetry*, Cambridge University Press, 2003, pp. 154–72.

Bishop, Wendy, *Thirteen Ways of Looking for a Poem: A Guide to Writing Poetry*, Addison Wesley Longman, 2000, p. 408.

"A Brief Guide to Confessional Poetry," Academy of American Poets website, 2014, https://www.poets.org/poetsorg/text/brief-guide-confessional-poetry (accessed August 31, 2016).

Donilon, Thomas E., "Examining America's Role in the World," Council on Foreign Relations website, May 12, 2016, http://www.cfr.org/united-states/examining-americas-role-world/p37857 (accessed October 18, 2016).

Eisenberg, Bonnie, and Mary Ruthsdotter, "History of the Women's Rights Movement," National Women's History Project website, 1998, http://www.nwhp.org/resources/womens-rights-movement/history-of-the-womens-rights-movement/ (accessed September 14, 2016).

Frances, Roberta W., "The Equal Rights Amendment," Equal Rights Amendment website, http://equalrightsamendment.org/index.htm (accessed October 7, 2016).

Garner, Dwight, "Sharon Olds," in *Salon*, 1996, http://www.salon.com/1996/07/01/interview_19/ (accessed August 30, 2016).

Gregerson, Linda, "Short Reviews" in *Poetry*, October 1984, pp. 36–37.

Guilder, George, "Women in the Work Force," *Atlantic*, September 1986, http://www.theatlantic.com/magazine/archive/1986/09/women-in-the-work-force/304924/ (accessed October 24, 2016).

Hempel, Amy, "Sharon Olds," in *Bomb*, 1996, http://bombmagazine.org/article/1927/sharon-olds (accessed August 30, 2016).

Hoagland, Tony, "The Unarrestable Development of Sharon Olds," in *American Poetry Review*, Vol. 38, No. 1, January–February 2009, pp. 7–9.

Lewis, Daniel, "Galway Kinnell, Plain-Spoken Poet, Is Dead at 87," in *New York Times*, October 29, 2014, http://www.nytimes.com/2014/10/30/books/galway-kinnell-poet-who-went-his-own-way-dies-at-87.html (accessed September 24, 2016).

Macdonald, Marianne, "Olds' Worlds," in *Guardian*, July 25, 2008, https://www.theguardian.com/books/2008/jul/26/poetry (accessed September 8, 2016).

Mueller, Lisel, "Three Poets," in *Poetry*, June 1981, pp. 171–72.

Olds, Sharon, "Rite of Passage" in *Strike Sparks: Selected Poems 1980–2002*, Knopf, 2004, p. 27.

Ostriker, Alicia, "The Tune of Crisis," in *Poetry*, Vol. 149, No. 6, January 1987, pp. 231–36.

Patterson, Christina, "Me, Myself, and I: How Easy Is It to Write Confessional Poetry?," in *Independent*, January 23, 2013, http://www.independent.co.uk/arts-entertainment/books/features/me-myself-and-i-how-easy-is-it-to-write-confessional-poetry-8463999.html (accessed August 31, 2016).

———, "Sharon Olds: Blood, Sweat and Fears," in *Independent*, October 26, 2006, http://www.independent.co.uk/arts-entertainment/books/features/sharon-olds-blood-sweat-and-fears-421691.html (accessed September 5, 2016).

"Poetry," Pulitzer Prizes website, http://www.pulitzer.org/prize-winners-by-category/224 (accessed September 24, 2016).

"Ronald Reagan: Foreign Affairs," Miller Center, http://millercenter.org/president/biography/reagan-foreign-affairs (accessed October 21, 2016).

Saxon, Wolfgang, "Donald Justice, 78, a Poet Admired for Precise Beauty," in *New York Times*, August 10, 2004, http://www.nytimes.com/2004/08/10/arts/donald-justice-78-a-poet-admired-for-precise-beauty.html?_r=0 (accessed September 24, 2016).

"Sharon Olds," Poetry Foundation website, 2012, https://www.poetryfoundation.org/poems-and-poets/poets/detail/sharon-olds (accessed July 14, 2016).

Suro, Roberto, "The New American Family: Reality Is Wearing the Pants," in *New York Times*, December 29, 1991, http://www.nytimes.com/1991/12/29/weekinreview/the-nation-the-new-american-family-reality-is-wearing-the-pants.html (accessed October 24, 2016).

"Timeline of U.S Diplomatic History," U.S. Department of State website, https://2001-2009.state.gov/r/pa/ho/time/ (accessed September 14, 2016).

Wright, Carolyne, Review of *The Dead and The Living*, in *Iowa Review*, Vol. 15, No. 1, 1985, pp. 151–61, http://ir.uiowa.edu/iowareview/vol15/iss1/54 (accessed September 8, 2016).

FURTHER READING

Linden, David J., *The Accidental Mind: How Brain Evolution Has Given Us Love, Memory, Dreams, and God*, Belknap Press, 2007.

> Brain researcher David J. Linden translates into simple, accessible terms the way that the human brain functions in line with or in spite of evolutionary biology. Readers may be particularly interested in illuminating chapters that explain the neuroscience behind emotions, memory, love, sex, and individuality.

Minot, Stephen, *Three Genres: The Writing of Fiction/Literary Nonfiction, Poetry, and Drama*, Pearson Education, 2003.

> For students interested in pursuing writing, either privately or professionally, this guide serves as a treasured resource. Minot refers to the book as a "process text," which aids learning through doing, in this case, practicing the craft of writing under the tutelage of an accomplished author.

Sussman, Ellen, *Bad Girls: 26 Writers Misbehave*, W. W. Norton, 2007.

> This variety of essays is an homage to the modern woman's naughty escapades. Readers should approach with caution, as the essays are blunt, biting, and sometimes unapologetically crude. For the reader who finds Olds's candor refreshing, these essays may allow the enjoyment of vicarious misconduct or serve as inspiration for one's own antics.

Swenson, Karen, *A Daughter's Latitude*, Copper Canyon Press, 1999.

> Admirers of Olds's keen eye for observation will appreciate this collection of poems by Swenson, an experienced international traveler and journalist who documents the dignity of ordinary humans from the American West to Southeast Asia. Like Olds, Swenson writes of what it is to be a woman; unlike Olds, Swenson marries political and social contexts to her uniquely female perspective.

SUGGESTED SEARCH TERMS

Sharon Olds

"Rite of Passage" AND Olds

The Dead and the Living AND Olds

American confessional poetry

cycles of life AND poetry

American free verse

masculinity AND militarism

third-wave feminism

gender roles AND 1980s America

The Ruined Maid

THOMAS HARDY

1902

On the surface, Thomas Hardy's poem "The Ruined Maid" (written in 1866, published in 1902) is a comic criticism of Victorian sexual hypocrisy. Two young women from a small farming town both come to work in the big city and happen to run into each other; one is filled with envy at the beauty, fashion, and sophistication of the other. The difference, the more polished one says, is that she's been *ruined*, having become the mistress of a rich man. She's obtained everything society tells her she should have but at the cost of becoming the one thing society tells her she should not be.

A thoughtful analysis of the poem suggests that Hardy has a more serious purpose and wants the reader to ask about the social inequalities that make the ruined girl feel that she is better off in her fallen state. Hardy also explores another casualty of the Industrial Revolution: regional identity. Hardy took great pride in his origins in Dorsetshire, but once the Dorset girl comes to London, part of her ruin is to become merely English and leave the language, culture, and identity of Dorset behind. Thus she is also ruined in the sense of losing her cultural heritage.

AUTHOR BIOGRAPHY

Hardy was born in Higher Bockhampton in Dorsetshire on June 2, 1840. His father, also Thomas, was a stonecutter who started a business as a

Thomas Hardy *(©Bettmann | Getty Images)*

builder. Hardy attended a free school in Dorchester run by the British and Foreign School Society. The education was based on the English public (really, exclusive private) schools. Hardy would have learned and intensively studied poetry in Latin and only at the end of his education might have read English poets like William Shakespeare or John Milton (probably nothing more recent). Hardy's parents' home was close enough to Dorchester to allow him to walk to school; nevertheless, one of the key ideas of his later literary career was the isolation from the modern world in a village like Higher Bockhampton. The physical barrier was only a few miles, but it was a different world from a city or even a town. Hardy's parents could not afford to send him to university. He considered the idea of becoming an Anglican priest, but by 1856 he was apprenticed to the Dorsetshire architect John Hicks, who specialized in restoring medieval churches. He also began to write poetry in this period, under the influence of his former headmaster, William Barnes, who was a poet writing in the Dorset dialect.

In his early twenties, Hardy took a job as a draftsman with the prominent London architect Arthur Blomfield, where he stayed from 1862 to 1867. In Blomfeld's office, Hardy found a sophomoric atmosphere of other young unmarried men his own age whose talk was dominated at times by sex and particularly gossip about the mistresses of prominent members of the London elite. Many of the men would pick up prostitutes at London dance halls, but Hardy seems to have refrained from the practice. It was in this atmosphere that he wrote "The Ruined Maid" in 1866. At the time, he had no thought of publishing it, although the previous year he had had a short story, "How I Built Myself a House," published in the popular *Chambers's Journal*. The story is unlike any of his later work, a satire of middle-class urban sprawl that would have seemed more in tune with the 1960s. Hardy wrote several volumes' worth of poetry in the 1860s and early 1870s, but none of it would see publication until later in his life, after he had won fame as a novelist. Disappointed with London, Hardy returned to Dorsetshire and continued to work as an architect.

Hardy also undertook to write a novel, "The Poor Man and the Lady," since a novelist could make a living out of writing, as a poet could not. The book was rejected by publishers in 1868, however, as too politically radical in its social criticism, and Hardy later destroyed the manuscript. In 1871, Hardy was to anonymously publish his new novel *Desperate Remedies*, closely imitating the work of the popular novelist Wilkie Collins. The next summer, Hardy began to publish a novel called *A Pair of Blue Eyes* in the form of a magazine serial, then a common practice. His next novel was *Far from the Madding Crowd* (1874), whose popularity finally freed Hardy of the need to work other than as an author. With success, Hardy had returned to London, but in 1883 he again moved back to Dorchester and built a house, Max Gate, of his own design.

Hardy's last two novels were *Tess of the d'Urbervilles* (serialized in 1891 and published as a book in 1892) and *Jude the Obscure* (serialized in 1894 and published as a book in 1895), both of them attacks on the hypocrisy of Victorian morality. *Tess*'s plot focuses on the life of a young peasant girl who becomes *ruined* after bearing an illegitimate child when she is raped by her aristocratic landlord's son. During his career as a novelist, Hardy made no further attempt to publish poetry, but beginning in 1898 he brought out his lifetime's accumulation of poetry in *Wessex Poems* (1898) and, in 1901,

Poems of the Past and the Present, which saw the first publication of "The Ruined Maid," although this version of the poem is slightly different from the original. Hardy would continue to publish new volumes of poetry periodically over the next two decades and, between 1903 and 1908, published the three volumes of the enormous verse drama (not intended for performance) *The Dynasts*, about the Napoleonic Wars.

For each of the last dozen years of his life, Hardy was nominated for the Nobel Prize in Literature but was never awarded it. On January 11, 1928, Hardy died, after a long illness and decline, of a heart attack at home in Dorset. In what might be termed a prophecy of literary celebrity in the media-conscious twentieth century, Sydney Cockerell, Hardy's executor and effectively his business manager, rushed an announcement of Hardy's death to the British Broadcasting Corporation, so notice of it would make it into the evening news. Hardy himself had already made arrangements for the republication of his collected works as well as of a new collection of poems, *Winter Words* (1928), as soon as he died, to take advantage of the publicity that would then be focused on him, to the profit of his heirs.

POEM TEXT

"Omelia, my dear, this does everything crown
Who could have supposed I should meet you in
    Town?
And whence such fair garments, such prosperi-
    ty ?"—
"O didn't you know I'd been ruined?" said she.

—You left us in tatters, without shoes or socks,   5
Tired of digging potatoes, and spudding up
    docks;
And now you've gay bracelets and bright feath-
    ers three!"—
"Yes : that's how we dress when we're ruined,"
    said she.

—"At home in the barton you said 'thee' and
    'thou,'
And 'thik oon' and 'theäs oon,' and 't'
    other'; but now   10
Your talking quite fits 'ee for high compa-
    ny"—
"Some polish is gained with one's ruin," said
    she.

—"Your hands were like paws then, your face
    blue and bleak,

But now I'm bewitched by your delicate cheek,
And your little gloves fit as on any la-dy!"—   15
"We never do work when we're ruined," said
    she

—"You used to call home-life a hag-ridden
    dream,
And you'd sigh, and you'd sock; but at present
    you seem
To know not of megrims or melancho-ly"—
"True. There's an advantage in ruin," said she.   20

—"I wish I had feathers, a fine sweeping gown,
And a delicate face, and could strut about
    Town!"—
"My dear—a raw country girl, such as you be,
Isn't equal to that. You ain't ruined," said she.

POEM SUMMARY

The text used for this summary is from *Poems of the Past and Present*, 2nd ed., Harper & Brothers, 1902, pp. 192–94. A version of the text can be found on the following web page: https://www.poetryfoundation.org/poems-and-poets/poems/detail/44332.

"The Ruined Maid" is written in twenty-four lines divided into six four-line stanzas. The poem consists almost entirely of dialogue between two characters, the ruined maid and an old acquaintance of hers from her village. In most of the stanzas, the first three lines are the acquaintance speaking with the fourth being the reply of the ruined maid, marked in each case by "said she." In the sixth stanza only, the ruined maid speaks the last two lines.

Lines 1–4

The acquaintance, who is never named, addresses the ruined maid by her first name, 'Melia, which is obviously short for "Amelia." The two women meet by chance on the street in a large city. It is most likely London but could be any industrial city, like Birmingham, Manchester, or Liverpool. They both had lived in the same village. At some point, however, Amelia must have left the village to look for opportunity in the city, as millions of English peasants did in the Victorian period. Presumably, the acquaintance has now followed her. She is surprised to see Amelia dressed in clothes that are more expensive than she would have expected. In modern America, Steve Jobs, the founder of Apple, famously dressed in blue jeans and a nondescript black turtleneck, precisely to erase class

MEDIA ADAPTATIONS

- Brief as it is, "The Ruined Maid" has been dramatized a few times on various BBC television shows, most accessibly in 2006 (episode 4) on the series *Arrows of Desire*. While the BBC does not maintain a public archive of the show, "The Ruined Maid" clip from the show can be found posted at various Internet sites.

- In 1981 Seymour Barab wrote a twenty-minute chamber operetta titled "The Ruined Maid" only loosely based on Hardy's poem. It is occasionally performed but has never been recorded.

consciousness, but in Victorian society, class stratification was strongly marked by dress. If Amelia is dressed according to aristocratic style, she would be wearing a long dress with a bustle, a hat, and gloves, and her figure would be artificially shaped by a corset. This kind of dress was meant as a display of wealth and to signal the fact that the position of a husband meant his wives and daughters did not have to work.

A woman in Amelia's position would simply be imitating the fashion to give the appearance of being aristocratic. Accordingly, the acquaintance infers from her clothes that Amelia has raised herself up to a higher class. By way of explanation, Amelia says, however, that she has been "ruined." The polyvalent social resonance of this term is the point of the poem. On the one hand, Victorian women were meant to follow a strict moral code based on Christianity. This means that they had to remain celibate except with their husbands. Any other kind of behavior meant that a woman would become ruined or fallen, as if her intrinsic worth and even her intrinsic personhood were damaged or corrupted.

While men were supposedly under the same social strictures, in practice they were not, particularly middle- and upper-class men. The age of marriage for middle-class men was likely to be closer to thirty than twenty (while women married much younger), so celibacy before marriage would have been much more difficult. It is not surprising, therefore, that a demimonde of ruined maids—mistresses and prostitutes—existed to cater to middle- and upper-class men. In practice, middle-class men, both before and after marriage, were free to make any associations they wished with a mistress or with visits to prostitutes without much in the way of social, and especially not legal, sanction. When Amelia says she is ruined, she means that rather than working in a factory or finding marriage with a man of her own class, she has found a place for herself in the demimonde.

Lines 5–8

The acquaintance recalls Amelia's departure from whatever agricultural town the two women came from. As a peasant girl, Amelia had found seasonal work harvesting potatoes: digging them out of the ground and lugging the heavy bags of potatoes to the platform of the railway station, where she had to pile them for their eventual transport to the city. As an unmarried girl, all of her wages would have gone to her father, and she would also have owed all of her domestic labor to her parents' household. Amelia was so poor she had to dress in worn-out clothes in need of mending and could not afford shoes. In contrast now, her acquaintance notes, Amelia's clothing is decorated with expensive feathers and jewelry. To Amelia, this seems a perfectly normal part of her ruined life.

Lines 9–12

The acquaintance recalls their life in the village using the term *barton*. Originally a feudal term, by the nineteenth century, the word had come to mean land owned by a landlord and worked by laborers paid a wage (probably figured by the amount of work produced—in this case weight of potatoes—rather than time)—rather than rented to workers. Even in the countryside, the traditional network of rights and obligations between landlords and tenants had been transformed into wage labor to the advantage of the landlords, all of whose obligations had been transferred into a cash payment of considerably lesser value than the duties a feudal landlord would have had to fulfill towards his tenants. The acquaintance further observes that Amelia, like the acquaintance herself, had spoken in the regional dialect of their village, but now she speaks in a more standard English. Amelia's reply suggests that, since in the demimonde she associates with higher classes than she ever would have in the village, her manner of speech has changed accordingly.

Lines 13–16

The acquaintance again recalls that in the village Amelia's body and appearance had been rough and degraded by hard physical labor (and probably by poor nutrition as well), but now the softness of her body corresponds to traditional standards of beauty. This means, in effect, that she looks like an aristocratic woman, not only in her dress but in her very person. Amelia replies that, being ruined, she no longer has to do physical work.

Lines 17–20

Back in the village, Amelia used to constantly complain about the physical circumstances of her life, comparing it to a nightmare. As it seems to her acquaintance from Amelia's outward appearance, however, she must now know neither physical discomfort nor unhappiness. Amelia suggests that her acquaintance has found the advantage in being ruined.

Lines 21–24

Her acquaintance expresses her envy of Amelia's beautiful appearance and her beautiful clothes. Amelia assures her that these things are quite beyond a girl just come from the country to the city, because she is not ruined.

THEMES

Language

Hardy's teacher, William Barnes, wrote poetry in the Dorset dialect rather than standard English. This was part of a tendency of poets from across Britain to write in local dialects as an attempt to valorize and save them as it became apparent that the new forms of communication and transportation devised in the Industrial Revolution threatened to swallow up regional variation in the standard dialect (eventually known as BBC English precisely because of the leveling effect of the new medium of radio). There are still native speakers of the dialect—as there are for most British dialects—but the trend to standardization will doubtless continue.

Hardy was concerned with regionalism and set his novels in a somewhat fictionalized part of England he called *Wessex*, reviving the name of the early medieval kingdom that had included Dorset, Devon, and Somerset. One subject of "The Ruined Maid" is Amelia's change of accent. She used to speak in the Dorset dialect, but after her ruin in London allowed her to move in aristocratic circles, she adopted a more standard form of English. Hardy himself went through the same transformation in his education, shifting from dialect to standard English; the few recordings he made in his lifetime reveal him speaking in a flawless aristocratic accent.

Amelia's unnamed friend notes the change in her accent, observing in the third stanza that she no longer uses such Dorset pronunciations as *thik oon* ("this one"), *theäs oon* ("these ones") or *t'other* ("the other"). The doubled *o* means the short *o* sound is to be pronounced for a longer than usual time, while the mark of diaresis over the *a* indicates the word has two syllables and the preceding *e* is long. The list looks more as if it came from a handbook of comparative grammar than being a normal subject of speech, but Hardy, a Dorset man himself, would certainly have known the dialect firsthand. Hardy also uses two Dorset dialect words, glossing both of them with the standard English equivalent to avoid confusing the reader. In the second stanza, he uses *spudding* to mean "potato digging" (which Americans might miss as dialectical, since *spud* is standard American English), while in the fifth stanza he uses *sock* for "sigh." Although *barton* is often identified as a dialectical word like *sock*, it would appear rather to be simply archaic like *thee* and *thou*; the term *barton* occurs in place names throughout England and Scotland.

Pastoral

The pastoral is a genre of poetry that goes back to Greek and Roman antiquity. Its audience was aristocratic city dwellers whose lives would have been tied to the business and institutions of the city, although they may have owned rural estates, which they would occasionally visit as a forerunner of the vacation. Pastoral poetry celebrated the virtues and beauties of country life, in an unspoken contrast to the pressures and annoyances of living in a city. The pastoral presents farm life as simple and natural and points out the uncomplicated pleasures of shepherds, who would spend their time in poetry

TOPICS FOR FURTHER STUDY

- Make a presentation to your class illustrating "The Ruined Maid" as it would have been conceived when it was first written in 1866. Contrast images of aristocratic women's fashion of the late Victorian period with working women's clothes. Images can be readily found by searching the Internet. Be sure to use the search term "Gibson girl," since the drawings of Charles Gibson generally supplied the popular idea of women's fashion in that period.

- *Lyddie* (1995), by Katherine Paterson, is a young-adult novel set during the Industrial Revolution. The protagonist is a young girl whose family is dispossessed of its Vermont farm and who eventually becomes a Lowell Mill girl and attempts to improve her life through education. Write a paper comparing her responses to the new industrial economy with those of Amelia in "The Ruined Maid."

- The Yetties were a popular English folk music band that performed songs written in the Dorset dialect. The band was so named because all of its members came from Yetminster in Dorset. The Yetties retired after giving a final concert in 2011; however, they have a large number of music recordings and videos of their performances. Edit together a presentation from the Yetties material for your class, highlighting their use of the Dorset dialect.

- In the decade prior to World War I, the Japanese economy was rapidly industrializing, resulting in many of the same social dislocations that occurred in Europe and America generations before. These events were chronicled in a lively literature of short stories written by young working-class Japanese who were attuned to the international labor movement. A sample of these stories was recently edited and translated by Norma Field and Heather Bowen-Struyk in *For Dignity, Justice, and Revolution: An Anthology of Japanese Proletarian Literature* (University of Chicago Press, 2016). One of these stories is "The Prostitute," by Hayama Yoshiki. Write a paper comparing this story with Hardy's "The Ruined Maid," paying particular attention to the role of the industrial economy, class, and traditional morality in both works.

---

contests directed toward seducing shepherdesses or nymphs. Other themes included the beauty of the rural landscape and the innate virtue of country people. It presented an escapist fantasy, an idyll (originally a technical term meaning "pastoral poetry"), for the sophisticated, even jaded, urban audience.

"The Ruined Maid" is a satire of pastoral. In Hardy's poem, a woman from a rural village has left her town to escape the harsh realities of country life, which is presented as filled with backbreaking labor that nevertheless leaves the farmworkers in dire poverty. In contrast, the ruined maid has found a life of ease and plenty and apparent happiness, among the demimonde of prostitutes and mistresses, supposedly the most corrupt, but nevertheless most characteristic part of urban life, so horrible it was not even to be mentioned in polite society.

When moralists of the period talked about the wickedness of cities, it was precisely the demimonde they referred to in coded language. In Hardy's poem, it is the city, and the supposedly most corrupt part of the city, that gives rest from the bare struggle of existence of the farm laborer. Hardy presents the demimonde as a means of escape from the physical degradation and poverty of village life, exactly reversing the conventional wisdom of his time. Through satire, he exposes the hypocrisy that, in different ways,

The poem features two acquaintances meeting in London (©*Andrea Visconti | Shutterstock.com*)

oppressed rural and urban workers alike. In both the country and the city, the rich have a life of ease. It is the fluidity of the demimonde that has allowed the ruined maiden to rise to what in all but name is a higher social status. If Amelia attempted, for instance, to attend the church in her original village and the congregation knew that she was ruined, she might be shunned or worse, yet in every other respect her position is envied by another woman from her village. Perhaps Hardy is wondering how it is that the only way a poor woman can get ahead in Victorian society is by becoming ruined?

STYLE

Irony

Irony is a rhetorical device in which a supposed statement of the truth is made that is really the opposite of the truth, leaving readers to realize the actual situation for themselves. An everyday example is to comment *what a beautiful day* when it is raining. The obvious irony of "The

Ruined Maid" is that Amelia seems anything but ruined. Her unnamed friend is envious of her good fortune. Moreover, every attribute of Amelia's that her friend praises—her clothes, her health, and so on—Amelia ironically attributes to her ruin, but she might more literally have said she was saved from poverty and degradation. The poem contains a larger irony that is meant as a criticism of Victorian society.

Stanley Renner, in his "William Acton, the Truth about Prostitution, and Hardy's Not-So-Ruined Maid," observes, "Hardy exploits the great well of moral and sexual feeling bound up with the idealization of female purity and the shock he could evoke merely by mentioning the word 'ruin.'" Hardy is suggesting that it is Victorian culture that is confused about ruin and salvation. It is society that makes the judgement that Amelia is ruined, but it is obvious to Amelia herself that she has been saved by the choices she made. Her friend's observations act as an objective viewpoint to verify the tremendous improvement in Amelia's circumstances. It seems to Hardy that Victorian England is

COMPARE
&
CONTRAST

- **1860s:** Social status is strongly marked by clothing and manner of dress.

  Today: Dress is more egalitarian; denim pants may be worn equally by a workman and a billionaire.

- **1860s:** Regional dialects and cultures in English counties like Dorset are rapidly disappearing because of the standardization of culture.

  Today: One can still find young people in rural English counties who speak with the

regional accent, but their numbers are dwindling rapidly now—not only because of standardized education and population mobility but especially because of the standardizing effect of mass media.

- **1860s:** Prostitution is not only reflexively considered a sin by Christian morality but is also illegal.

  Today: Since 2009, prostitution has not been a crime in Britain.

---

privileging a legalistic concept of virtue over human happiness, a real irony.

Poetics

Hardy's verse looks old-fashioned compared with his contemporaries like Ezra Pound or William Butler Yeats. There is not much doubt that Hardy had the technical skill to write in modern verse, then called free verse, but he seems to have had an innate sense of orderliness that did not make it attractive to him, the same impulse that led him to seriously consider becoming a priest and to actually work for many years as an architect. "The Ruined Maid" is therefore completely traditional in its prosody.

The poem is in a rather unusual meter for an English poem, anapestic quadrameters. (This a perfectly natural meter, however, for someone who learned poetry by reading the Latin dramatists Terence and Plautus.) This means that each line is composed of four metrical units or feet: an iamb followed by three anapests, creating a dancing, almost walking rhythm used in the choral songs of ancient drama and similar to a waltz. The metrics of the poems are very tight and regular, with little substitution, while the first foot of each line is regularly an iamb in place of an anapest.

The stanzas of the poem rhyme *aabb*, meaning that the first two and last two lines of each stanza rhyme with each other. Moreover, the *bb*

portion of the stanzas makes the same rhyme throughout the poem. The overall effect of the meter and the rhyme scheme is to make the poem appear as if it were a traditional ballad. The repeated rhyme at the end of each stanza, the semantic equivalence of each final line, and the repeated "said she," in particular, resembles the refrain of a folk song. Hardy makes adept use of alliteration throughout the poem. The plosive *b*'s and *p*'s in the first line of the fourth stanza evoke the blows and buffeting of fortune Amelia has suffered. In the fifth stanza, the sibilant *s*'s of the second line suggest the exasperated release of air being described, while in the next line the nasal humming of the *m*'s and the sharp velar *g*'s mark her physical suffering.

HISTORICAL CONTEXT

Old English was directly descended from the closely related Germanic languages, such as Saxon, spoken by the invaders of Britain at the end of late antiquity. (*Beowulf* and similar works represent a privileged literary dialect, but there was considerable regional variation in language even in the early Middle Ages.) In the tenth and eleventh centuries, Britain suffered a new wave of invasion from speakers of Old Norse and the closely related Old Danish. The result of this was villages and even families with mixed populations, some of whom spoke Old English and others Old Norse. Both are closely related Germanic languages and shared many linguistic roots, but communication was difficult because the systems of word endings that governed grammar and syntax in both languages were quite different. People found a new way to communicate with one another by dropping the grammatical endings of the words, keeping only the shared roots, and expressing grammar through a strictly enforced word order. (Indeed, this gave raise to one of the common techniques of marking poetic language in English: the word order can be changed in poetry, so what would in prose have to be *she said*, can become *said she*.) This is technically a pidgin, an artificial language created to communicate between groups speaking different languages, but it became Middle English and is still the basis of modern English.

The process of creating the pidgin, however, went on simultaneously village by village, so the result was different in each region. Another factor was that lack of mobility in the Middle Ages meant that each region of England was isolated from the others, so that the natural process of change and development tended to create regional dialects. Each region had a certain way of pronouncing shared words (an accent) and also unique vocabulary. What we think of as standard English was originally the Oxfordshire dialect, which was adopted by the royal court and also enjoyed the prestige of the major universities (Oxford and Cambridge) in Britain, being located in its language area.

Regional dialects eventually made their way across the Atlantic. The Boston accent, for instance, is descended from the dialect of East Anglia. However, the second-most-common form of English in America, the southern accent, and the closely related dialect often identified as Black English, is descended from the dialect of Dorset, the same dialect that Hardy grew up speaking (though he would have been trained out of it at school) and which Amelia in "The Ruined Maid" has also given up in favor of a more standard, aristocratic English.

The main features of the Dorset accent are a lengthening and slowing of the pronunciation of vowels (resulting in the frequent description of American southern dialect being *slower* than standard English, the so-called southern drawl) and the pronunciation of the letter *r* following vowels. (The suppression of this feature is a

Now Amelia seems to be a fine society lady
(©Sandra Scramm / Shutterstock.com)

distinct characteristic of the East Anglian/Boston accent, resulting, for example, in the word *car* being pronounced *ca*.) Indeed, a post-vocalic *r* is often inserted so that a word like *wash* comes out *warsh*. Other features include dropping the final *g* from the present participle and prefacing the participle in the participial present with the prefix *a-*, so that *I'm going* becomes *I'm a-goin'* (with the *oi* pronounced nearly as a diphthong but certainly not shortened in duration of pronunciation).

CRITICAL OVERVIEW

Hardy's poetry was not as well received in his lifetime as his novels. His verse underwent a revival under the influence of the school that referred to itself as the Movement in the 1950s, which included Philip Larkin and Kingsley Amis. They admired and imitated his social realism in contrast to the literary experimentation that dominated other poets of that era. "The Ruined Maid," as an early and minor poem, did not begin to receive much attention until twenty years later; its reputation no doubt benefited from the intervening cultural upheaval of the 1960s.

David Holbrook, in his *Lost Bearings in English Poetry*, compares poems from the beginning of *The Oxford Book of Twentieth Century Verse* (citing "The Ruined Maid" as his example) with those at the end at the time of his writing (about 1970). Holbrook considers Hardy's poem to be simply frivolous, but the women in the poem, he admits, at least have personal agency, and their lives have a meaning, in contrast to the depiction of women he finds in the poetry of his own era. U. C. Knoepflmacher, in "Hardy Ruins," draws attention to the fact that the idea of ruin must have a special significance for Hardy as an architect and especially as a restorer of medieval churches. Dominique Costa's "Language through Poetry" gives a remarkably full stylistic analysis of the poem, covering its lexical, syntactic, and phonological and metrical features.

Stanley Renner's "William Acton, the Truth about Prostitution, and Hardy's Not-So-Ruined Maid" is probably the most important study of the poem, placing it in the context of the slight remnants of Hardy's biography as well as William Acton's important Victorian book on prostitution (*Prostitution, Considered in Its Moral, Social, and Sanitary Aspects in London*). In particular, he points out that the Contagious Diseases Act (a legislative response to Acton's book) was promulgated in 1866, the year of the poem's composition. It was becoming clear in Britain by that time that moral condemnation was not a sufficient response to the existence of prostitution. Renner observes that Victorian received wisdom about prostitution held that

> the evil regulated itself through a built-in system of retribution through which those who indulged in it—particularly women, who, by putting temptation in the way of men, were, after all, most to blame—would inexorably sink into disease and death.

Renner's ironic comment on Victorian patriarchal attitudes aside, Acton book's made it clear that this was not the case and that the material condition of prostitutes did tend to prosper over those of, for example, factory workers or farmworkers, a fact that one can even say is celebrated in "The Ruined Maid."

THE ELEGANCE OF THE RUINED MAID'S COUTURE FILLS HER FRIEND WITH ENVY BUT IN NO SENSE REFLECTS HER SOFT, WOMANISH DESIRE FOR LUXURY; IT IS HER WORK UNIFORM."

"Deftly," Renner observes, "the poem ironically questions which maid is actually ruined, the sinful or the virtuous."

Rachel G. Fuchs, in her *Gender and Poverty in Nineteenth-Century Europe*, takes a historical and generally a social realist attitude toward her subject matter. In the case of prostitution, however, she cannot entirely escape some ideological coloring of her analysis, for which she cites "The Ruined Maid" as a proof text. "Although Hardy does not indicate how she became a prostitute, he presents a picture of a woman who escapes from poverty into a world of finery and does not appear to regret it," as though luxury, rather than survival, was the lure.

CRITICISM

Rita M. Brown

Brown is an English professor. In the following essay, she examines Hardy's "The Ruined Maid" in the context of the social history and industrial reform that especially concerned the young Hardy.

Prostitution is as old as human civilization. The practice must have developed alongside the first accumulation of wealth. Writing developed much later, but if one could single out an individual literary work as the first, it would be the Epic of Gilgamesh, which dates to the third millennium BCE. In this work, the countryside around the city of Uruk is being ravaged by a wild man, known as Enkidu, a half-human, half-animal monster. The people call on their king, Gilgamesh, for help, but rather than going out of the city to fight the monster, he goes out with the prostitute Shamhat, who proceeds to have relations with Enkidu. Each time, the monster becomes less and less savage until, after the seventh sexual encounter, Enkidu is fully human and becomes Gilgamesh's friend and greatest companion in the rest of the epic.

WHAT DO I READ NEXT?

- Norman Ware's *The Industrial Worker, 1840–1860: The Reaction of American Industrial Society to the Advance of the Industrial Revolution* (originally published in 1924 but frequently reprinted) was the first important historical study of a labor movement. The book focuses on the writings of labor activists concerning the dehumanizing effects of wage labor. The work also brought serious attention for the first time to the important role of female workers displaced from the agricultural economy, the so-called Lowell Mill girls.

- In traditional Asian society, the mistresses of court nobles were expected to be at least as culturally sophisticated as their lovers and their lover's legal wives. In Korea, mistresses at the Korean royal court during the sixteenth and seventeenth centuries produced an important body of poetry reflecting on their lives and situations. A sample of this work has been translated by Constantine Contogenis in *Songs of the Kisaeng: Courtesan Poetry of the Last Korean Dynasty* (1997).

- *Howards End* is a 1910 novel by E. M. Forster. One feature of the novel is an examination of the social repercussions when a middle-aged millionaire is confronted at the reception of his second wedding by one of the guests whose services as a prostitute he had used in Burma and whose chances for a respectable life (along with those of her husband) he had unwittingly destroyed.

- Marc W. Steinberg's *Fighting Words: Working-Class Formation, Collective Action, and Discourse in Early Nineteenth-Century England* (1999) demonstrates how women were exploited by industrialists to attack and undercut the efforts of groups of male workers to organize for collective action. Moreover, women going into industrial work, while they were not considered ruined, were generally seen as having dishonored themselves by crossing over into the male sphere.

- *Through the Fray: A Tale of the Luddite Riots* (1886) is a novel by the pioneering young-adult novelist G. A. Henty. It is set during the Luddite movement, an early organized and violent resistance by workers to the capitalist transformation of the economy.

- Hardy was a compulsive diarist and note taker throughout his life, and he just as compulsively and systematically destroyed his lifetime's accumulation of paper records before he died. Nevertheless, after his death, Hardy's family was able to scrape together a few diary entries, letters, significant newspaper clippings, and other documents, along with reminiscences of people who knew him, the mass of which was published in 1928 (and since then frequently reprinted) as *The Early Life of Thomas Hardy, 1840–1891*.

The story suggests that prostitution is an inherent part of sophisticated civilized culture, compared with the rude countryside. At least it must have been so regarded by the aristocrats of Sumerian civilization. Later, when Enkidu is dying, he curses Shamhat because, if he had remained a savage wild man, he would never have died in the quest Gilgagmesh had involved him in. Gilgamesh reminds Enkidu that in that

case he would never have known the pleasures of civilization, and Enkidu agrees that was worth the cost of his life and takes back his curse. Shamhat's achievement in the story suggests that there are other ways to read a Victorian poem about prostitution like Hardy's "The Ruined Maid" than as a moral scandal, as most of his contemporaries would have considered it (a fact that accounts for Hardy's holding it back from publication for more than thirty years and offering it only after his literary position was impregnable).

The book that dominated historical understanding of prostitution in Victorian England is William Acton's *Prostitution, Considered in Its Moral, Social, and Sanitary Aspects*, originally published in 1857 with a second edition in 1870. Acton was a medical doctor, a fact that allowed him to publish respectably on such a controversial topic thanks to the nearly priestly aura that the medical profession was gathering in the nineteenth century. He wanted to give an objective view of prostitution so that the social problem it presented could be considered dispassionately and dealt with scientifically. Acton pointed out that the stereotype of the prostitute as a woman obviously ruined in her body (through alcoholism or drug addiction, which were effectively anesthetics used by prostitutes in the worst circumstances) and liable to effect a comically horrible exaggeration of sexually alluring attire and makeup was a rarity (probably more in his experience than in absolute number of lower-class prostitutes in London). Such women would not be encountered by the sons of his middle- and upper-class readers. Rather, he suggested that prostitutes worked to appear more sophisticated and fashionable than other women:

> The Gorgon of the present day against whom we should arm our children should be a woman who, whether sound or diseased, is generally pretty and elegant—oftener painted by Nature than by art—...and on whose backs...the ministers of fashion exhibit the results of their most egregious experiments.

This description recalls the clothes that Amelia wears in "The Ruined Maid." The elegance of the ruined maid's couture fills her friend with envy but in no sense reflects her soft, womanish desire for luxury; it is her work uniform. The man or men who pay her salary expect her to dress that way. Her own desires or tastes have nothing to do with the matter.

Acton also explains the social background out of which Hardy's Amelia emerges. Prostitutes often left their villages to find work in a city in some other field, either in domestic service or in an industrial workshop. In her private life, the woman would be seduced, often by a man of a higher class and not infrequently by an employer. After such a woman becomes pregnant, her lover (who may well have been married) repudiates her, and the young woman finds

herself the object of public shame, fired from her job, and unable to obtain another one because she has been *ruined*. In this case, the woman has little hope of supporting herself and her child except by turning to prostitution, since she was no longer marriageable. (The idea that a poor woman would sue a middle-class man for child support would have been a fantasy in Victorian England.) Arranging her working life around the duties of child care was also an obstacle to any profession.

The real problem that underlies prostitution, in Acton's view, is the inability of women workers to make a wage sufficient for their needs in any other way, particularly if they are already raising a child alone. Another consideration is that the availability of industrial work varied according to the boom-and-bust cycle created by an unregulated capitalist economy. In addition, the efficiency of industrial production had so far outstripped demand that factory machines would be left idle for up to weeks at a time until new orders came in, and workers were neither provided with an income during the hiatus nor paid enough even at peak work periods to permit savings to accumulate. Many women filled in the gap with sex work.

Realizing that the economy played a role in creating prostitution, Acton preferred the decriminalization and toleration of prostitution, since in that case the practice could be more easily regulated from the point of public health (his main interest in the book being the control of venereal disease) as well as the protection of the women from violence and theft by their employers and clients. Nevertheless, Acton expressed moral disapproval of prostitution and prostitutes. He was unable, as hardly any Victorian would have been, to separate sex work from an excessive love of ease, luxury, and pleasure; in other words, sin:

> They are in the majority of cases servants or workwomen, who have gradually brought themselves to prefer the easy and sometimes voluptuous wages of prostitution—the seductions of coquetry, gluttony and dancing, and the attractions of a lazy and dissipated life, to small wages and the interminable privations of an honest and laborious existence.

It takes a truly Victorian level of cognitive dissonance to say this after explaining how the need for prostitution was generated by economic factors.

Acton observed that in the conditions of employment typical in industrial Britain,

the rights of man are remembered, the duties of man forgotten, each man getting for himself all he can, and giving only what he must, till willing service and kindly rule have almost passed away.

As the Industrial Revolution progressed, democracy and the rights of the poor and of workers also progressed, but Acton saw this as paradoxically the cause of their worsening situation. Once the feudal ties between the aristocratic class and their workers were broken, then the responsibility of employers to protect their employers was also eroded. One could object that capitalism had hardly been created by workers. One impetus to capitalism was precisely its promise to free the elite from feudal obligations: land enclosure laws, which stripped peasants of their traditional feudal rights and converted what had been public land to private property, proceeded at the same pace as industrialization. Acton's solution seems to reverse the process and shift what little power workers had away from them, as though economic security in a rapidly expanding economy need only come at the cost of social dependence.

Acton seems strangely incurious about why "an honest and laborious existence" inevitably led "to small wages and ... interminable privations." Why were women working twelve or even eighteen hours a day, six days a week, not able to make enough money to render sex work unattractive? That question, and it is a question of economic justice not sexual morality, is the real subtext of Hardy's poem, as it must have been of his novel "The Poor Man and the Lady," unpublishable because of its political radicalism. "The Ruined Maid" shows that the reward for the poor in exchange for honest labor is poverty. In the face of that fact, imposed by society, why should social structures such as those that condemn prostitution be considered valid?

Noam Chomsky, in *Understanding Power*, shows that the answer to these questions is that women were vulnerable to capitalist exploitation because of their unequal legal and social positions compared with men. He talks about "young women who came off the farms to work in factories." Chomsky points out:

In fact, a good deal of the labor organizing in the nineteenth century in the United States was done by women, because just like today in the Third World, it was assumed that the most

docile and controllable segment of the workforce was women—so therefore they were the most exploited.

This is the position that Amelia must have found herself in when she came to London, with no hope of securing her own present or future because of systemic inequalities imposed on the poor and doubly so on poor women. We possess an insight into the lives and thoughts of women like Amelia in the form of newspapers published by young working women. Chomsky again points out that

some of the main labor journals at the time were edited by women, and they were young women mostly. And they were people who wanted to read, they wanted to learn, they wanted to study—that was just considered normal by working people back then. And they wanted to have free lives.

He is referring to a group of newspapers that were published by female workers in Lowell, Massachusetts (then one of the leading industrial cities in the world), where circumstances were not significantly different than they were in England. At the time, they were called Lowell Mill girls. These newspapers include the *Offering* and the more radical *Voice of Industry*, edited by the millworker Sarah Bagley from 1845 to 1848. The very adept political analysis presented in these magazines gets even closer to the social hypocrisy that Hardy is aiming at in "The Ruined Maid." An anonymous (the author must have been a factory worker who would certainly have been fired if her authorship became known) article in the *Voice of Industry* suggests: "But those who have given the subject a careful and candid investigation, are perfectly convinced that the present organization of society is at war with the better and higher feeling of man's nature." It is the economic system of capitalism as it existed in the mid-nineteenth century that forced women like Amelia to turn to prostitution, but an equally integral part of that society, Christian morality, then tainted the same women with the label *ruined* and blamed the women's own sinful nature for their situation. Hardy must have felt that what violates Christian doctrines of love and equality is the system that exploits women and the poor in this way. In "The Ruined Maid" the disconnect between reality and ideals is presented as laughable. For the workers on the receiving end of the hypocrisy who wrote in the *Voice of Industry*, it was criminal.

Amelia used to have a hard life, digging potatoes while barefoot (©*Garsya | Shutterstock.com*)

Source: Rita M. Brown, Critical Essay on "The Ruined Maid," in *Poetry for Students*, Gale, Cengage Learning, 2017.

Peter Widdowson

In the following excerpt, Widdowson describes Hardy's transition from prose to poetry.

With the publication of *Jude* and *The Well-Beloved*, then, Hardy gave up writing prose fiction. The reasons for this may be summed up as follows. First, partly financial: when he could afford to stop producing novels, he did so; secondly, partly personal: the scandalized response of the late-Victorian moralizing lobby to *Tess* and *Jude* had seriously depressed him; thirdly, partly aesthetic: as the preceding chapter has sought to show, Hardy's fictional writing was increasingly pressing against the limits of nineteenth-century realist conventions, challenging and subverting them, and he seems to have reached a formal *impasse* in giving expression to his world-view. *The Life*, of course, as we saw earlier, invariably denigrates his novel-writing career and presents him as *always* primarily a poet, so to suggest that he was first a

novelist and then a poet is to misrepresent him—A at least in his own estimation; and on his shift of genre in the 1890s, it comments that, "if he wished to retain any shadow of self-respect," he must abandon fiction and "resume openly that form of [literary art] which had always been instinctive with him... the change, after all, [being] not so great as it seemed. It was not as if he had been a writer of *novels proper...*" (*Life*, 291, emphasis added). That final loaded phrase is further amplified by a memorandum of March 1886 reflecting on the future of prose fiction:

> novel-writing cannot go backward. Having reached the analytic stage it must transcend it by going still further in the same direction. Why not by rendering as visible essences, spectres, etc., the abstract thoughts of the analytic school?... Abstract realisms to be in the form of Spirits, Spectral figures, etc.... The Realities to be the true realities of life, hitherto called abstractions. The old material realities to be placed behind the former as shadowy accessories. (*Life*, 177)

In itself, this is an indicative statement about Hardy's attitude to fiction in the year he published *The Mayor of Casterbridge* and was

> ALMOST EVERY LYRIC IS DIFFERENT IN
> RHYTHM AND RHYME; AND RATHER THAN ANY
> LONGER BEING PRAISED AS THE PRODUCT OF AN
> EXCELLENT BUT 'UNTRAINED' EAR, THEY ARE NOW
> RECOGNIZED TO BE THE RESULT OF SUPREME
> PROFESSIONAL CRAFT."

writing *The Woodlanders*—one which leads him four years later to decide that "'realism' is not Art" (*Life*, 229)—but his retrospective comment on it is even more revealing: "This notion was approximately carried out, *not in a novel*, but through *the much more appropriate medium of poetry*, in the supernatural framework of *The Dynasts* as also in smaller poems" (*Life*, 177; emphases added). The hundreds of "smaller poems" were to follow in the succeeding volumes of poetry, but it is not without point that the single major work Hardy undertook after completing the novels was the non-realist epic verse-drama, *The Dynasts*.

Space prevents discussion of this work here, but we may note in passing both that it was long planned—*The Life* characteristically implying, throughout the years dealing with his novel-writing, that it would be Hardy's truly major achievement—and that the first mention of it is in May 1875, when he was engaged in writing his uncompromisingly anti-realist novel, *The Hand of Ethelberta*. If there is any longer any doubt about ironic self-reflexivity in Hardy's work, the reader should turn to the final chapter of that novel, where Ethelberta—financially freed from the need to be a "professional romancer"—is described as living "'mostly in the library. And, O, what do you think? She is writing an epic poem, and employs Emmeline as her reader'" (*HE* 409). That Hardy's first wife was called Emma is only a secondary cypher here. *The Dynasts*—an enormous poetic drama of the Napoleonic wars never intended for performance in its entirety—combines detailed historical research (and "real" historical figures) with an ironic cosmology which sees the ruling spiritual presence of the universe as an indifferent

"Immanent Will" and the human beings as essentially will-less: however (self-)important they may be, they are nevertheless depicted as insignificant figures trapped in the toils of Time and Fate. Various choruses of "Phantom Intelligence" (e.g. the "Pities" and the "Spirits Sinister and Ironic") help to articulate this cosmic "satire," which also involves many modes of writing. Some of these—especially those which ironically intercut disparate short scenes, or the high panoramic "shots" of large historical events in the wars—have been seen as cinematic in technique (before film was widely developed as an art form), and hence proto-modernist in tendency. The "much more appropriate medium" of *The Dynasts* thus remains at once a comment on Hardy's uneasy relation to realist fiction and an indication that prose "Satires of Circumstance" would transmogrify into poetic—if wry and mordant—"Moments of Vision."

As observed in Chapter 3, it is the vast bulk of Hardy's shorter poetry which always makes it difficult to deal with, despite the existence now of a tacit critical consensus about the canonic core of his "finest" poems. My intention here is briefly to try and bring together this familiar Hardy and the less well-known figure represented by some of those poems seldom—if ever—selected, anthologized or critically acclaimed, and which must, therefore, be among that mass of "bad," or "not 'good'," poetry we heard the critics identifying earlier. To do this, I will first consider Hardy's perceived achievement as a poet in general—with brief illustrations along the way—then assess what different emphases and inflexions are given to that achievement by returning some of the "bad" poetry to the recognized *œuvre*—especially that about women and sexuality. Finally, I will compare in a little more detail cognate poems which nevertheless sit markedly on either side of the evaluative line drawn by critical discrimination of the "true," "finest," "great," "most characteristic" instances of Hardy's poetic work.

If we turn back to T. R. M. Creighton's unintentionally self-parodic statement quoted earlier: that "my broad classifications—Nature, Love, Memory and Reflection, Dramatic and Personative, and Narrative—can claim almost canonical authority," we may begin to see the shape the familiar canon takes. Four "classifications" here draw attention to major themes in Hardy's work, and three to important modes of writing in it. To make two large generalizations in reverse order: first, much of the admiration for Hardy's poetry—leaving aside some (mainly earlier) cavils at "awkwardness," "clumsiness," "irregularity," etc.—has increasingly pointed to his range, innovativeness—and technical skill in prosody. Almost every lyric is different in rhythm and rhyme; and rather than any longer being praised as the product of an excellent but "untrained" ear, they are now recognized to be the result of supreme professional craft. Equally, his style—especially the clotted syntax and eclectic vocabulary—is now seen, not as the flawed "primitive" poetic discourse of a self-educated rural genius, but as evidence of complex control and dedicated precision in the use of language. Secondly, there is an "almost canonical" consensus as to what Hardy's "finest" poems are about. If we add "Death and the Dead" to Creighton's list, assume that "Memory" includes Time, and "Reflection" Hardy's religio-philosophical poetry, then most people would concur that these themes are indeed what we read him for. His most admired poems are those which deal with the sights, sounds, and rhythms of the countryside; with dead lovers, friends, and relatives; with time—especially what Samuel Hynes has called his "sense of the tragic nature of "all" human existence: the failure of hopes, the inevitability of loss, the destructiveness of time" and with love—pre-eminently in the famous sequence of elegies to his first wife, Emma, "Poems of 1912–13" in *Satires of Circumstance, Lyrics and Reveries* (1914).

Grouping the poems by theme is, of course, too exclusive and schematic, as Hardy's most characteristic topics interpenetrate widely, but a rough taxonomy would show the following. There are, very obviously, those poems in which he celebrates natural phenomena by way both of sharply precise denotative description and of connotative anthropomorphic empathy: "An August Midnight" (*PPP*), "At Day-Close in November" (*SC*), "At Middle-Field Gate in February" (*MV*), "Weathers" (*LLE*), "Snow in the Suburbs" (*HS*) "Proud Songsters," "Throwing a Tree" (both *WW*)—with "Afterwards" (*MV*) as the classic text. Linked, are poems like "She Hears the Storm" (*TL*), "A Sheep Fair" and "Shortening Days at the Homestead" (both *HS*), which combine vivid rural images with a melancholic recognition of time passing and the transitoriness of living things; and related again are those famous poems which descry a rather more metaphysical significance in the counterpoint of

natural and human events: "Neutral Tones," "Nature's Questioning" (both *WP*), "The Darkling Thrush," "In Tenebris I" (both *PPP*), "The Convergence of the Twain," "Wessex Heights" (both *SC*), "In Time of The Breaking of Nations" (*MV*). Then there are the lyrically evocative elegies which memorialize the personal and familial past—again, usually involving a celebratory imagery drawn from natural and homely things: "Thoughts of Phena" (*WP*), "The Self-Unseeing" (*PPP*), "The House of Hospitalities," "Former Beauties," "A Church Romance," "The Roman Road," "One We Knew" (all *TL*), "The Oxen," "Great Things," "Old Furniture," "Logs on the Heart," "During Wind and Rain" (all *MV*). Most familiar, too, are the many poems which, in diverse ways, deal with ageing, death, and the dead: from the more astringent ones to do with the tensions of becoming old—"I Look Into My Glass" (*WP*), "Shut Out That Moon," "Reminiscences of a Dancing Man" (both *TL*), "An Ancient to Ancients" (*LLE*), "Nobody Comes" (*HS*), "He Never Expected Much" (*WW*)—through the variously witty or mournful reflections on a beloved's or his own death—"In Death Divided" (*SC*), "On a Midsummer Eve," "Something Tapped," "Who's in the Next Room?" (all *MV*), "I am the One," "Lying Awake"(both *WW*)—to those most "characteristic" poems which, in effect, resurrect the known local dead: "Friends Beyond" (*WP*), "Transformations," "Paying Calls" (both *MV*), "Voices from Things Growing in a Churchyard" (*LLE*). There are also three smaller categories— although, as we shall see, these become significantly larger when we restore some of the lesser known poetry: first, the poems which centre on female sexuality, often dramatizing the woman's "voice"—"She at his Funeral" (*WP*), "To Lizbie Brown," "The Ruined Maid" (both *PPP*), "A Trampwoman's Tragedy" (*TL*), "The Sunshade" (*MV*); secondly, poems which display humanistic social observation—"Midnight on the Great Western" (*MV*), "No Buyers" (*HS*); and, thirdly, Hardy's much anthologized war poems—which again display his de-heroicizing humanism: "Drummer Hodge" (*PPP*), "The Man He Killed" (*TL*), "Channel Firing" (*SC*), "In Time of 'The Breaking of Nations'" (*MV*), "Christmas: 1924" (*WW*). Finally, there are the poems to and about Emma—all, in one way or another, refashionings of a lost love—which lie at the very heart of Hardy's poetic canon: "When I Set Out for Lyonnesse," "Under the Waterfall"

❝ THESE ARE HARSH WORDS, BUT IT MAY BE
THAT HARSHNESS IS WHAT IS CALLED FOR. FOR IT
BEGINS TO LOOK AS IF HARDY'S ENGAGING MODESTY
AND HIS DECENT LIBERALISM REPRESENT A CRUCIAL
SELLING SHORT OF THE POETIC VOCATION, FOR
HIMSELF AND HIS SUCCESSORS"

(both *SC*), "At the Word 'Farewell,'" "The Musical Box," *The Wind's Prophecy* (all *MV*), and of course the "Poems of 1912–13...."

Source: Peter Widdowson, "Hardy the Poet," in *Thomas Hardy*, Northcote House, 1996, pp. 76–80.

Donald Davie

In the following excerpt, Davie characterizes Hardy's poetry as somewhat baffling.

Hardy's poetry is a body of writing before which one honest critic after another has by his own confession retired, baffled and defeated. It is nothing short of comical that a criticism which can make shift to come to terms with Ezra Pound or Apollinaire, Charles Olson or René Char, should have to confess itself unable to appraise with confidence a body of verse writing like Hardy's, which at first glance offers so much less of a challenge to tested assumptions and time-honored procedures. Irving Howe's confession is admirably explicit:

Any critic can, and often does, see all that is wrong with Hardy's poetry, but whatever it was that makes for his strange greatness is much harder to describe. Can there ever have been a critic of Hardy who, before poems like "The Going" and "During Wind and Rain," did not feel the grating inadequacy of verbal analysis, and the need to resort to such treacherous terms as "honesty," "sincerity," and even "wisdom"?

Unless he has felt as Irving Howe describes, no critic of Hardy's poetry is qualified to speak. Equally, for the mere honor of the critical vocation, no one has the right to publish yet another essay on Hardy unless he thinks he can transpose the discussion into other terms than those which Howe rightly calls "treacherous." I write in that hope, or under that delusion.

Yvor Winters declared that Hardy was, "like Emily Dickinson, essentially a naif, a primitive, but one of remarkable genius." Yet neither "naive" nor "primitive" is the word that comes first to mind to characterize the most elaborate and considered of Hardy's few statements about his understanding of his own art. The statement is made in the third person because it comes from the very reticent autobiography which Hardy "ghosted" through his second wife:

In the reception of this [Wessex Poems] and later volumes of Hardy's poems there was, he said, as regards form, the inevitable ascription to ignorance of what was really choice after full knowledge. That the author loved the art of concealing art was undiscerned. For instance, as to rhythm. Years earlier he had decided that too regular a beat was bad art. He had fortified himself in his opinion by thinking of the analogy of architecture, between which art and that of poetry he had discovered, to use his own words, that there existed a close and curious parallel, both arts, unlike some others, having to carry a rational content inside their artistic form. He knew that in architecture cunning irregularity is of enormous worth, and it is obvious that he carried on into his verse, perhaps in part unconsciously, the Gothic art-principle in which he had been trained—the principle of spontaneity, found in mouldings, tracery, and such like—resulting in the "unforeseen" (as it has been called) character of his metres and stanzas, that of stress rather than of syllable, poetic texture rather than poetic veneer; the latter kind of thing, under the name of "constructed ornament," being what he, in common with every Gothic student, had been taught to avoid as the plague. He shaped his poetry accordingly, introducing metrical pauses, and reversed beats; and found for his trouble that some particular line of a poem exemplifying this principle was greeted with a would-be jocular remark that such a line "did not make for immortality."

One may believe that this is a wrongheaded or foolish way of considering poetry, as is (so some think) any consideration of one art by analogy with another or with others. But in that case, surely, one regards it as oversophisticated, not "primitive." And right or wrong, this way of looking at the arts was not an eccentric quirk in Hardy, but was shared by his contemporaries, including those, like Pater and Hopkins and Patmore, whose education had been both extensive and orthodox. Too much has been made of Hardy's provincialism, and his being self-educated; people still treat him with a sort of patronizing indulgence on these false grounds, very much in the way that Hardy himself resented when he looked through the eyes of Jude Fawley. If Hardy was self-educated, the education that he gave himself was in the end enviably thorough; and if for instance we cannot make much use of the distinction Hardy made in the passage just quoted, it is because our education has been neglected, and has not included those texts of Pugin and Ruskin which Hardy and Patmore took for granted when they talked about the aesthetic of Gothic architecture. Nor is this the only field in which Hardy shames our ignorance; as a prosodist, for instance, he was immensely learned, with a learning that seems to be lost beyond recovery.

All the same, we should not fly to the other extreme. The autodidact *does* suffer, when set beside the man whose education has come to him without struggle against circumstance. My guess is that the autodidact suffers most from having had to discipline himself to depend too heavily on his own will, his own resolve to outwit circumstance and overcome it. And this is a very important element in Hardy's personality. Though he struck those who met him as a gentle and retiring man, the facts of his literary career speak for themselves: it is a Victorian success story, a model career on the lines of Samuel Smiles's self-help, with all that that involves of driving oneself hard with grim and clenched determination. And sometimes this is what offends us in Hardy's poetry—its form mirrors a cruel self-driving, a shape *imposed* on the material, as it were with gritted teeth. Edmund Blunden says something like this when he remarks: "The faults of Hardy's verse are seldom those of the mediocre man, with his apparently easy measures, never quite full measures; they are those of a zealous experimenter, whose materials do not always obey the purpose or yield a restful completeness." An example is "Lines to a Movement in Mozart's E-Flat Symphony."

... Accordingly, in most of the senses of "great" as we apply it to poets, Hardy is not a great poet at all. He is not "great" because, except in *The Dynasts*, he does not choose to be, does not enter himself in that competition. This is the burden of R. P. Blackmur's essay of 1940, "The Shorter Poems of Thomas Hardy." Blackmur insists that, tot up as we may the sum of admirable poems by Hardy, what stops him short of greatness is something in the quality of his attention to experience and to the poetic rendering of it. It is not a matter of his having only so many admirable poems to plead his case

for him, but of something that is built into his poems even at their most admirable. If we say that even at his best Hardy was not enough the craftsman, we certainly do not mean what Yeats meant when he said (incredibly) that Hardy's work "lacked technical accomplishment." (In sheer *accomplishment*, especially of prosody, Hardy beats Yeats hands down.) We mean that Hardy failed to be a craftsman to just the degree that he insisted on being the triumphant technician. As Blackmur put it, "what Hardy really lacked was the craft of his profession—technique in the wide sense." Hardy too often lacked craft, to just the extent that he had expertise; he lacked technique "in the wide sense," to just the degree that he exulted in possessing it in its narrower senses. The honesty of the honest journeyman may be dishonest in his master.

It may not be clear how Hardy the technician is related to Hardy the scientific humanist and Hardy the "liberal." But the relation is one that is familiar enough, though we seldom encounter it, or any analogue of it, in poetry. It is the relation between pure science and applied science, a crucial relation for any advanced technological logical culture, and one which throws up in many aspects of that culture—for instance, in its politics—precisely the contradiction that I am struggling to define in Hardy's attitude to his art, and his practice of it. For we accuse the corporate enterprise of science and technology of being insufferably and perilously arrogant in the way that it manipulates and conditions us and our environment. And yet the individual scientist or engineer often sees himself, quite sincerely, as very modest, merely an honest worker at specific tasks and problems. It is not he, but the literary man or the philosopher, who has the presumption to question the whole cultural design, and offer to set the whole world to rights! In just the same way the liberal in politics usually contends that he addresses himself to each question "on its merits"; and he rejects as intolerably presumptuous the radical's contention that each and every question—for instance, whether a university should harbor an officers' training corps—must be related to the ultimate issues of how, if at all, mankind is to survive on this planet. At the scientist in his laboratory, as at the earnest liberal in his committee, the radical throws the angry word "cop-out"—meaning by that precisely that the individual's modesty is what makes possible the corporate presumption. And Hardy in his poetry is this sort of cop-out, a modest (though proudly expert) workman in a corporate enterprise which from time to time publishes a balance-sheet called *The Golden Treasury* or *The Oxford Book of English Verse*.

These are harsh words, but it may be that harshness is what is called for. For it begins to look as if Hardy's engaging modesty and his decent liberalism represent a crucial selling short of the poetic vocation, for himself and his successors. For surely the poet, if any one, has a duty to be radical, to go to the roots. So much at least all poets have assumed through the centuries. Hardy, perhaps without knowing it, questions that assumption, and appears to reject it. Some of his successors in England, and a few out of England, seem to have agreed with him.

Source: Donald Davie, "Hardy as Technician," in *Thomas Hardy and British Poetry*, Oxford University Press, 1972, pp. 13–16, 39–40.

SOURCES

Acton, William, *Prostitution, Considered in Its Moral, Social, and Sanitary Aspects in London and Other Large Cities and Garrison Towns, with Proposals for the Control and Prevention of Its Attendant Evils*, 2nd ed., John Churchill and Sons, 1870, pp. 28–29, 100, 291.

Chomsky, Noam, *Understanding Power: The Indispensable Chomsky*, New Press, 2002, p. 248.

Costa, Dominique, "Language through Poetry: A Stylistic Analysis of Thomas Hardy's 'The Ruined Maid,'" in *Actas do 4 encontro nacional do ensino das línguas vivas no ensino superior em Portugal*, 1999, pp. 215–22.

Dalley, Stephanie, *Myths from Mesopotamia, Creation, the Flood, Gilgamesh and Others*, revised edition, Oxford University Press, 2000, p. 137.

Dabhoiwala, Faramerz, *The Origins of Sex: A History of the First Sexual Revolution*, Oxford University Press, 2012, pp. 37–78, 234–81.

Fuchs, Rachel G., *Gender and Poverty in Nineteenth-Century Europe*, Cambridge University Press, 2005, pp. 144–51.

Hardy, Thomas, "The Ruined Maid," in *Poems of the Past and Present*, 2nd ed., Harper & Brothers, 1902, pp. 192–94.

Holbrook, David, *Lost Bearings in English Poetry*, Vision, 1977, p. 175.

"Importance of Radical Reform," in *Voice of Industry*, March 5, 1847, http://industrialrevolution.org/true-spirit-of-reform.html#importanceofradicalreform (accessed Aug 31, 2016).

Knoepflmacher, U. C., "Hardy Ruins: Female Spaces and Male Designs," in *Proceedings of the Modern Language Association*, Vol. 105, No. 5, October 1990, pp. 1055–70.

Millgate, Michael, *Thomas Hardy: His Career as a Novelist*, Palgrave Macmillan, 1994, pp. 17–18.

Renner, Stanley, "William Acton, the Truth about Prostitution, and Hardy's Not-So-Ruined Maid," in *Victorian Poetry*, Vol. 30, No. 1, Spring 1992, pp. 19–28.

FURTHER READING

Carpenter, Richard, *Thomas Hardy*, Twayne Publishers, 1964.
  Carpenter's book is a standard introduction to Hardy aimed at students.

Mitchell, Rebecca N., *Victorian Lessons in Empathy and Difference*, Ohio State University Press, 2011.
  Mitchell examines what may be termed the personal or emotional aspects of the class concerns expressed in "The Ruined Maid" but focuses on novels, including Hardy's.

Montgomery, David, *The Fall of the House of Labor: The Workplace, the State, and American Labor Activism, 1865–1925*, Cambridge University Press, 1989.
  Montgomery investigates how the form of the modern industrial economy was created by the industrialist class over the protests of organized labor movements.

Stevenson, Robert Louis, *Strange Case of Dr. Jekyll and Mr. Hyde*, Longmans, Green, 1886.
  The premise of this famous novel is that its protagonist, Jekyll, has an ordinary professional life as a research physician and a separate life spent in the demimonde of ruined and fallen women. He finds himself torn between his two lives: whenever he is indulging in one life, he is distracted by his desire to return to the other. He wants therefore to find a drug that would enable him to indulge fully in whichever life he finds himself without distraction from the other, although his experiment goes horribly wrong. The larger point of the novel concerns the unacknowledged divide in Victorian society that Hardy also toys with in "The Ruined Maid."

SUGGESTED SEARCH TERMS

Thomas Hardy

"The Ruined Maid"

Victorian morality

social realism AND literature

Industrial Revolution AND women

pastoral AND literature

Dorset dialect

Lowell Mill girls

They Flee From Me

THOMAS WYATT

1557

"They Flee from Me" is a poem by sixteenth-century English poet Sir Thomas Wyatt. It exists in two versions. The first is a manuscript known as the Egerton manuscript in the British library, which contains the poem in Wyatt's own hand; the second is a slightly amended version that was published in a collection of English poetry titled *Songs and Sonnets*, also known as *Tottel's Miscellany*, published in 1557, fifteen years after Wyatt's death. The date the poem was written is not known. Most modern editions of the poem modernize the spelling. As a prominent poet during the Tudor period in England, Wyatt wrote many lyrics and sonnets, and "They Flee from Me" is usually regarded as one of his most successful lyrics. It is a poem about love and the disappointment and disillusionment love can produce when the feelings of the people involved change. The poem is also somewhat mysterious, because it alludes to a romantic episode (or episodes) without giving many details about it.

AUTHOR BIOGRAPHY

Wyatt led a colorful and sometimes dramatic life as an English courtier and diplomat. He was born in 1503, at Allington Castle, near Maidstone, Kent, England, the son of Sir Henry Wyatt and Anne Skinner Wyatt. Henry Wyatt was a powerful figure in the court of King Henry

Sir Thomas Wyatt (©*Everett Historical / Shutterstock.com*)

VII, the first monarch of the Tudor period, and retained that power after Henry VIII ascended the throne in 1509. Wyatt was therefore an aristocrat who grew up at the royal court. He may have been educated at Cambridge, though no definite record exists. In 1520, he married Elizabeth Brooke, daughter of Thomas, Lord Cobham, and the couple had a son, Thomas, in 1521.

Wyatt pursued his career in the court of Henry VIII. In 1524, he was appointed esquire of the king's body and clerk of the king's jewels, a position he occupied until 1530. By 1525, Wyatt had become estranged from his wife, accusing her of adultery. The following year, Wyatt accompanied Sir Thomas Cheney on a diplomatic mission to France, and in 1527, he was also part of a mission to the papal court in Rome. During this time, he was captured by Spanish forces but freed after a ransom was paid.

Wyatt also had literary interests. He translated works from Italian and was also an innovator, introducing the sonnet to English literature based on Italian models. He also wrote lyric poems, although little of his work was published in his lifetime. A few poems may have been published in *The Court of Venus*, an anthology that appeared around 1538. His poems did, however, circulate in manuscript form in aristocratic circles.

From about 1529 to 1530, Wyatt was high marshal of Calais—a port city in northern France that was possessed by England from 1347 to 1558—and in 1532, he was appointed justice of the peace in Essex. In spite of a brief imprisonment in 1534 for his part in a brawl in which a man was killed, Wyatt's career flourished. He was granted a license to have twenty men in his livery and also the ability to raise and command men for war throughout the county of Kent. He was knighted in 1535, the same year he was appointed high steward of the abbey of West Malling, Kent. About a year later he formed a relationship with Elizabeth Durrell, who was to become his mistress for the rest of his life. In spite of this new attachment, he was suspected of having an affair with Anne Boleyn, Henry VIII's second wife. In 1536, he was imprisoned and was charged with adultery with Queen Anne but was released in June following his father's intervention. The unfortunate Anne had been beheaded (along with five of her alleged lovers) just one month prior.

Wyatt soon regained the favor of Henry VIII and in 1537 went on a diplomatic mission to the court of Emperor Charles V, returning in 1538. After the execution of his patron Sir Thomas Cromwell in 1540, however, Wyatt's position became vulnerable, and in 1541, he was arrested for treason and imprisoned in the Tower of London. The charge dated back to an allegation made in 1538, accusing him of meeting with a known traitor. He had been cleared of the charge at the time. In the Tower, Wyatt declared his innocence and was then released without trial. In 1542, Wyatt was named vice admiral of the fleet, but he collapsed and died on October 11, 1542, in Sherborne, Dorset, on his way to meet the Spanish envoy.

In 1557, ninety-seven of Wyatt's poems were published in *Songs and Sonnets*, also known as *Tottel's Miscellany*, a collection of 271 poems by English authors, so named because it was issued by the painter Richard Tottel. Included in the volume was "They Flee from Me."

POEM TEXT

They flee from me, that sometime did me seek
With naked foot stalking within my chamber.
Once have I seen them gentle, tame, and meek

That now are wild, and do not once remember
That sometime they have put themselves in danger 5
To take bread at my hand, and now they range,
Busily seeking in continual change.

Thankèd be fortune, it hath been otherwise,
Twenty times better; but once especial,
In thin array, after a pleasant guise, 10
When loose gown did from her shoulders fall,
And she me caught in her arms long and small,
And therewithal, so sweetly did me kiss
And softly said, "Dear heart, how like you this?"

It was no dream, for I lay broad awaking. 15
But all is turned now, through my gentleness,
Into a bitter fashion of forsaking.
And I have leave to go, of her goodness.
And she also to use newfangleness.
But since that I unkindly so am servèd, 20
How like you this, what hath she now deservèd?

POEM SUMMARY

The text used for this summary is from *The Norton Anthology of English Literature*, 5th ed., Vol. 1, W. W. Norton, 1986, pp. 467–68. Versions of the poem can be found on the following web pages: https://www.poetryfoundation.org/poems-and-poets/poems/detail/45589 and https://www.poets.org/poetsorg/poem/they-flee-me. (Both versions vary very slightly from the version published in the Norton anthology.)

Stanza 1

The poem consists of three stanzas of seven lines each. In the first stanza, the first-person speaker offers the view that people who formerly sought him out in his chamber (likely somewhere in the royal household) are now running away from him. In former times, these unnamed and unidentified people, referred to only as "they," were "gentle" and "tame," but now they are "wild," in the sense that they cannot be controlled. The language may suggest animals, perhaps wild animals that have been tamed but have reverted to their original condition, but that is only metaphorical, since it is likely that people are meant—the speaker's friends and lovers. Lines 5–7 repeat the same sentiment. In line 5, the speaker states that in the past, these people have been willing to put themselves in his power (the meaning of the phrase "in danger") in order to "take bread" from him, but now they "range" freely, continually seeking to find what they want. The word "range" might apply both to wild animals seeking food and to fickle women.

MEDIA ADAPTATIONS

- An audio reading of the poem, read by Jim Clark, can be found at https://www.youtube.com/watch?v = -wPv1HNCRzQ.

Stanza 2

The poet is a little more explicit, because this stanza clearly refers to women. Again, he looks back to former times and offers his thanks to "fortune" that those days were different from the situation as it exists in the present. He even offers the view that the former situation was "twenty" times better than it is for him now. Then he offers a specific recollection of an incident involving a woman. The woman was dressed in a pleasing, perhaps fashionable manner. In line 4, the poet recalls how she allowed her garment to fall from her shoulders and then took him in her arms, which were slender and attractive in appearance. She kissed him and spoke softly to him, inquiring how he liked what she was doing.

Stanza 3

The speaker clarifies the memory he has just had of the amorous woman in his chamber. He was not dreaming, he says, but wide awake. However, everything has changed now, he continues in line 2, because of his "gentleness." In other words, whatever happened between the woman (or women) and himself is not his fault, since he has behaved well. Line 3 suggests the acrimony that now exists between them, now they have parted, but in line 4 he refers to her as if she is someone high-born, since it appears that it is she who grants him permission to leave, as a result of her "goodness," perhaps meaning graciousness. Line 5 suggests that she herself has in a sense given herself permission to act in a changeable or fickle manner, which the speaker dislikes.

In line 6, the speaker begins the question with which the poem ends. He refers the notion that he is not to blame for the situation; on the contrary, he is the one who has been treated "unkindly," a word that carries the meaning of

TOPICS FOR FURTHER STUDY

- Write a poem from the point of view of a male speaker, presenting his feelings about a failed love affair. The poem can be in free verse, but those who wish for a challenge might enjoy writing a poem in rhyme royal, the *ababbcc* rhyme scheme found in "They Flee from Me." Such an exercise is extremely useful because it can show the aspiring poet how difficult it is to write such verse well and also instill a respect for those poets over the centuries (and still today) who wrote in traditional rhyme and meter.

- Wyatt was alleged to have had an illicit affair with Anne Boleyn. Who was Anne Boleyn, and what happened to her? After doing Internet research, give a class presentation, including illustrations, that tells the story of her life.

- Read a few more poems by Wyatt, then select one you like and write an essay in which you compare and contrast it to "They Flee from Me." A selection of Wyatt's poems is available at the Poetry Foundation website: https://www.poetryfoundation.org.

- Read "Avising the Bright Beams" (https://www.poetryfoundation.org/poems-and-poets/poems/detail/45574) and "Farewell Love and All Thy Laws Forever" (https://www.poetryfoundation.org/poems-and-poets/poems/detail/45575), both of which are sonnets by Wyatt. Give a class presentation in which you analyze these sonnets and compare them to the sonnet form developed by Henry Howard, Earl of Surrey and used by William Shakespeare.

- Read *Partly Cloudy: Poems of Love and Longing*, by Gary Soto (2012), which is a collection of poems for young adults about love and relationships told from the point of view of both boys and girls. Choose a poem you like and compare it to "They Flee from Me." What are the similarities and differences between the two poems? Even though the poems are separated in time by nearly five hundred years, are the emotions they express similar? Write a blog post and invite comments from your classmates.

unnaturally and inconsiderately as well as elements of the modern meaning. In the last line, he repeats the phrase the woman used in speaking to him in stanza 2 and concludes by asking, in the light of her behavior, what does she deserve? The question may carry a negative charge, perhaps obliquely suggesting that she deserves to suffer some unhappiness—since he himself appears also to have been made unhappy.

THEMES

Love

The poem presents the joys and sorrows associated with love between a man and woman. It emphasizes the changeability of love and looks back regretfully from the present, in which former lovers—one in particular—have deserted the speaker, to a happier time in the past (in stanza 2), in which love had been fulfilling and apparently happy. Written nearly five hundred years ago, the language used and the situation depicted in the poem might seem strange and hard to penetrate for a modern reader, but to put it simply, the poet is reflecting on a romantic relationship that did not last.

The pattern of the relationship is simple to follow. At first there was great trust on the part of the woman. (Although the first stanza refers to more than one person, it seems that the poet has one woman in particular in mind.) She came to his chamber barefoot, he states in the first stanza, which implies trust and openness to intimacy; the woman must have been more than ready to step out of a more formal social relationship and enter into something closer and more sensual and sexual in nature. In this stanza, the male speaker is clearly in the stronger position. He is inviting a woman into his own chamber, where, presumably, his own rules and ways of doing things will apply. The woman is a guest, and her meekness is emphasized. She willingly puts herself in a vulnerable position with a man who has a high position at the court. The first stanza thus presents a situation of trust between the people involved, as conveyed by the image of the woman (although again, more than one person is referenced) eating out of his hand, like a tame animal. Most people would agree that trust is a strong and necessary element in any romantic relationship if it is to succeed.

The incident recalled in stanza 2 also suggests trust between two people, as the woman disrobes and is obviously in an amorous mood, kissing the man. The memory is no doubt a sweet one for the speaker, as he recalls it in such detail, down to the very words the lady spoke. However, the last stanza reveals that there is likely also some bitterness involved, or at least some regret, because the relationship turned sour at some point. The speaker, like many lovers after a breakup, likely feels hard done by, and there is some sarcasm and anger in his tone, although it is still couched in diplomatic, restrained language.

This romance recalls the tradition of courtly love that was widespread in the Middle Ages. According to D. S. Brewer and L. Elisabeth Brewer, in their introduction to Chaucer's *Troilus and Criseyde*, courtly love is close to what Chaucer, writing perhaps a century and a half before Wyatt, called "the law of love," which the Brewers define as "the obligation to remain faithful to one's promises of love" and "the art and craft of fine loving" (Chaucer's phrase again), which according to the Brewers, "is the art of pleasing the beloved by behaving well in all respects, from personal cleanliness through good manners to complete moral integrity." It is perhaps this code of love that the speaker and his love in "They Flee from Me" were ostensibly devoted to and that the speaker feels was violated by the woman: she was not faithful to him.

Memory

The poem is also about memory, recollection, and forgetting. Alternating between a pleasurable past and a problematic or sorrowful present, it shows how love can be both remembered and

The poem's speaker is a young man puzzled over his lack of success with women (©Kiselev Andrey Valerevich | Shutterstock.com)

forgotten over time. The first stanza starts in the present and then looks back to a former, contrasting situation, and then returns at the end of the stanza to the present. In that stanza, the speaker's former friends and lovers are not only avoiding him and seeking their pleasures elsewhere; they have even forgotten (or so the poet states) that they used to visit him in his chambers for what may have been intimate encounters. It is as if the passage of time can obliterate all memory of past love, although that is not so for the poet: he is able to recall at least one of those encounters in exact detail, and it is the presence of memory that creates the distress he feels in the present. This detailed memory is recorded in stanza 2. The poet even goes to the trouble of stressing that he recounts the details of something that actually happened, affirming in the first line of stanza 3 that his recollection of that erotic interlude was not a dream. His former companions may have the capacity to forget, but he is doomed to remember.

STYLE

Metaphor

The first stanza contains an extended metaphor in which the visitors to the poet's chamber are presented in terms that might suggest wild animals that have been tamed. The descriptions, however, are metaphors that present certain qualities that are being applied to women, and the male speaker therefore casts himself in the role of the hunter. It is possible also that describing women in these terms suggests the poet is thinking of them in terms of their lower or more animalistic nature, which would hardly be very flattering to them. Some critics have also noted that the word "stalking" in line 2, applied to the visitors, creates a certain ambiguity, since that would suggest that they, rather than the speaker, are the hunters and the speaker the prey.

Meter

The poem is written in iambic pentameter, which is the most common foot in English poetry. An iamb is a poetic foot consisting of two syllables, the first unstressed and the second stressed. Pentameter consists of five feet.

To avoid monotony, the poet makes a number of variations to the basic iambic rhythm. This has the effect of emphasizing certain words, which stand out because they represent deviations from the standard rhythm that the reader or listener expects to hear. One example occurs in line 2 of the first stanza, in which the third foot is a trochee rather than an iamb. A trochee is the opposite of an iamb, consisting of a stressed syllable followed by an unstressed syllable. A trochee is substituted for an iamb again later in the same stanza, in the second foot.

Also, on occasion the line contains an extra, unstressed syllable at the end of the line. This is known as a feminine ending. Examples include the last two lines of the third stanza as well as the first line of that stanza.

Rhyme

The rhyme scheme in "They Flee from Me" is *ababbcc*. In other words, lines 1 and 3 contain end rhymes, as do lines 2 and 4, which also rhyme with line 5. Lines 6 and 7 also rhyme. This rhyme scheme in a seven-line stanza was first used by Chaucer in his long poem *Troilus*

and Criseyde and some of *The Canterbury Tales*. It is referred to as rhyme royal and was popular in medieval literature and was also used by many Tudor poets.

HISTORICAL CONTEXT

Early Tudor Literature

The early Tudor age extends from the reign of Henry VII, the first Tudor monarch (reigned 1485–1509) until 1558, when the ascension of Elizabeth I to the throne inaugurated the Elizabethan age. During Henry VII's reign, the most prominent poet was John Skelton (1460–1529). Although little of his work was published in his lifetime, it circulated widely in manuscript form. Skelton was also a cleric and scholar who at one point was tutor to the future Henry VIII. His most well-known poem is "Philip Sparrow" (1508), an elegy in which the speaker is a young girl who laments the death of her pet sparrow, eaten by a cat. The poem is notable for its use of colloquial speech. Skelton's reputation, however, did not long outlast his death, and even a couple of decades before that, change was in the air as far as poetry was concerned. In *The English Renaissance: 1510–1688*, V. de Sola Pinto states that "poetry...awoke as from a long sleep at the court of Henry VIII....The time was now ripe for poetry of a less medieval and a more definitely humanistic kind." As a result, the lengthy allegories that characterized the medieval period were no longer popular, and in their place arose a new breed of courtier-poets who wrote "short poems of a more subjective kind dealing particularly with love."

One of these poets was Wyatt, a new voice in English literature who introduced Italian styles and also new subject matter. He was influenced largely by the Italian poet Petrarch (1304–1374), who is famous for his love sonnets, some of which Wyatt translated or adapted. According to Murray Roston in *Sixteenth-Century English Literature*, Wyatt's "introspective focus upon the emotional state of the speaker, and even its validation of love as an absorbing theme for poetry had little precedence in the English poetic tradition." Up to this point, Roston states, poets had occupied themselves writing ballads, satire, and rural scenes and narratives.

COMPARE
&
CONTRAST

- **1530s–1550s:** Wyatt and Surrey give new impetus to English literature in the 1530s and 1540s with their lyrics and sonnets, which are first published in the 1550s.

  Today: The lyric poem written according to a definite rhyme scheme has become more rare, and free verse rules the day. Although the sonnet is no longer a popular form for contemporary poets, it is still used. The anthology *TheReality Street Book of Sonnets* (2008), edited by Jeff Hilson, contains work by British poets such as Tom Raworth, Peter Riley, Tony Lopez, and Geraldine Monkas, all of whom have successfully used the form. In the United States, poet Karen Volkman (b. 1967) has written sonnets, as did Wanda Coleman (1946–2013).

- **1530s–1550s:** This period includes the reigns of four English monarchs in the Tudor dynasty: Henry VIII (1509–1547), Edward VI (1547–1553), Mary (1553–1558), and Elizabeth I (1558–1603).

  Today: The monarchy continues to exist in England, which along with Scotland, Wales, and Northern Ireland, forms the United Kingdom. The reigning monarch is Elizabeth II, who has been on the throne since 1952. She is the longest-reigning British monarch.

- **1530s–1550s:** In 1533, the English church separates from the Roman Catholic Church. In 1534, King Henry VIII issues the Act of Supremacy and becomes head of the Church of England. In the later years of this decade, Catholic monasteries and convents in England, Wales, and Ireland are disbanded.

  Today: The Church of England remains the established church in England. Roman Catholicism also has a presence in the country, with an estimated four million Catholics in England and Wales. This is much lower than the estimated twenty-six million people who have been baptized in the Church of England.

Henry Howard, Earl of Surrey (1517–1547), was another notable figure who contributed to this new direction in poetry. Surrey, who was a friend of Wyatt's, also wrote sonnets. He developed the form known as the English or Shakespearean sonnet, divided into three quatrains with a concluding couplet. Surrey also introduced blank verse to English literature, in an English verse translation of sections of Virgil's epic poem *Aeneid* in unrhymed iambic pentameter. This type of blank verse would later be adopted by Elizabethan dramatists, including William Shakespeare. Surrey had the misfortune to be beheaded in 1547, shortly before the death of Henry VIII, after his political rivals conspired to have him charged with treason.

Another new development in literature was the poetry anthology, which helped to shape poetic taste. One such was *The Court of Venus*, published in the 1530s and containing a few of Wyatt's poems. *Tottel's Miscellany* (1557), which went through nine editions in thirty years, offered a variety of poetic forms, including sonnets, ottava rima, heroic couplets, blank verse, and rhyme royal. "In an age when poetry-writing was becoming a fashion at court," writes Roston of the *Miscellany*, "it offered a broadened range of models, and confirmed that the continental Renaissance had entered the poetry of England." Other anthologies published later in the century included *The Paradise of Dainty Devices* (1576) and *The Bower of Delights* (1591). Another significant work during this period was *A Mirror for Magistrates* (1559), a long verse narrative by several poets, led by William Baldwin, that focused on English history.

The speaker fondly remembers a romantic kiss
(©Serg Zastavkin | Shutterstock.com)

CRITICAL OVERVIEW

Wyatt's poetry was neglected for some centuries after his death, but by the mid-twentieth century, his reputation was fully established, according to J. W. Lever in his book *The Elizabethan Love Sonnet*. Wyatt's "lighter lyrics" drew the following comment from Lever, writing in 1956: "Their attractive rythms, their pure diction, above all, their blend of grace and forthrightness, make immediate appeal to modern taste." Lever also comments that Wyatt's "best love poetry was really out-of-love poetry," a rather apt comment when applied to "They Flee from Me."

Murray Roston, in *Sixteenth-Century English Literature*, praises "They Flee from Me" for its combination of "sharply etched actuality with dream-like meditation, of idealised love with scorn for the changeability of women, of melodious tone broken by direct colloquialism" and comments that Wyatt's poems "deserve to be classed among the finest of his era."

According to Kenneth Muir in *Life and Letters of Sir Thomas Wyatt*, the success of "They Flee from Me" rests on

> its rhythmical subtlety...on the effective image in the first stanza, on the particularity of the second stanza which carries immediate

conviction, on the perfection of phrasing, and on the way Wyatt walks the tight-trope of acceptable tone. He avoids sentimentality, sensuality, exaggeration, and bitterness.

For Patricia Thomson, in *Sir Thomas Wyatt and His Background*, the poem is "courtly and traditional in its terms and ideas" and "combines the effects typical of the moaning complaint and of the satirical attack. His self-pity, decidedly that of the melancholy prototype, takes a sarcastic turn."

Susan Brigden, in *Thomas Wyatt: The Heart's Forest*, comments on the fact that the people the poet refers to, who are fleeing from him, are identified only by the pronoun "they":

> Whoever they are, they are also in flight from us, forever fugitive, anonymous in the dark, inner world of the poem, though intensely known to the narrator, and perhaps even recognisable to those for whom it was written, to whom it was first read.

Brigden regards the poem's conclusion as a negative one in which the poet gives expression to "bitter sarcasm":

> These are not the raptures of romantic love. The poem ends with the narrator vengeful, bespeaking his disillusionment and pain, and posing a question which is hardly rhetorical: her false faith deserves betrayal in return.

For Ellen C. Caldwell, in *Dictionary of Literary Biography*, the poem is one "of betrayal and remembrance" that "may be the definitive expression of Wyatt's attitude toward courtly love: it is a game that can cause real pain, and one in which the players are only half-aware of their own complicity."

CRITICISM

Bryan Aubrey

Aubrey holds a PhD in English. In the following essay, he discusses Wyatt's "They Flee from Me" in terms of the tradition of courtly love.

In terms of its subject matter and theme, the basic outline of Wyatt's "They Flee from Me," despite its somewhat opaque use of language, is not difficult for the modern reader to discern. It is obviously a poem about love and its disappointments, and it tells a rather universal story: everything started well, with intimate encounters in private rooms in which both parties took pleasure. One such incident is recalled in detail

WHAT DO I READ NEXT?

- "And Wilt Thou Leave Me Thus?" is one of Wyatt's best-known lyrics. Like "They Flee from Me," it presents the unhappy outcome of a romantic relationship. The male speaker laments the loss of his love and appeals directly to her. He loved her faithfully, he says, and yet now she is leaving him. The poem can be found in Wyatt's *Complete Poems* (1989).

- Henry Howard, Earl of Surrey (1517–1547) was an aristocratic English poet who was born just fourteen years after Wyatt. Their names are often linked, and Surrey's poetry was first published, like Wyatt's, in *Tottel's Miscellany* in 1557. Surrey developed the sonnet form that had been introduced into English literature by Wyatt and created the form of the sonnet that was used by Shakespeare. Surrey's sonnet "Alas, Now All Things Do Hold Their Peace" is an adaptation of a sonnet by the Italian poet Petrarch: nature is calm, but the poet feels the joys and sorrows of love. The poem can be found in *Selected Poems of Henry Howard, Earl of Surrey* (2003) edited by Dennis Keane.

- "Song: Go, and Catch a Falling Star" is a poem by English poet John Donne (1572–1631), who began writing around a half-century after Wyatt's death. This poem is one of Donne's many love poems, although it takes a very cynical view of love. The speaker claims it is not possible to find a chaste woman anywhere in the world. Donne's unusual images, his wit, and his sudden turns of thought make it a typical Donne poem, although many of his poems present a more idealistic view of love.

- A half-century after Wyatt's death, William Shakespeare began making a name for himself as dramatist and poet. The 154 sonnets he wrote, which were published in 1609, give expression to many different aspects of love. One of the most famous is sonnet no. 116, "Let me not to the marriage of true minds," which describes the nature of true love, which is always constant, not subject to change. The poem can be found in *Shakespeare's Sonnets*, published by the Folger Shakespeare Library, in 2004.

- *Graven with Diamonds: The Many Lives of Thomas Wyatt, Poet, Lover, Statesman and Spy in the Court of Henry VIII*, by Nicola Shulman (2011), focuses on the life and poetry of Wyatt while also giving insight into the court of Henry VIII, where to fall out of royal favor could cost a courtier his life. Shulman discusses Wyatt's alleged affair with Anne Boleyn but, like most scholars who have tackled the subject, does not reach a definite conclusion about whether the rumors of their adulterous relationship had any basis in fact.

- *New Songs from a Jade Terrace: An Anthology of Early Chinese Love Poetry* edited by J. H. Prynne and translated by Anne Birrell was published in the Penguin Classics series in 1987. Chinese literature began much earlier than English literature, and this anthology is a selection of love poems that were written between the second century BCE and the sixth century CE.

- *The Crescent Moon Book of Elizabethan Love Poetry* (second, revised edition 2014) edited by Carol Appleby is an anthology of Elizabethan love poetry that includes selections from the works of Christopher Marlowe, Edmund Spenser, Michael Drayton, Thomas Campion, Sir Walter Raleigh, Samuel Daniel, William Shakespeare, and others.

- *Henry VIII: Royal Beheader* (2009) by Sean Stewart Price, a volume in the Wicked History series, is a lively account of the turbulent reign of England's King Henry VIII written for young adults.

> THE FINAL LINE OF THE POEM STRONGLY
> SUGGESTS THAT HE THINKS HIS FORMER LOVER,
> HIS ONCE ADORED AND PRESUMABLY ADORING
> MISTRESS, DESERVES TO SUFFER TOO, FOR HER
> UNFAITHFULNESS."

(in stanza 2), but then everything went wrong. The man now feels betrayed and expresses resentment or anger about the end of the affair and the way the woman behaved.

Universal the story may be, but it is couched in language that shows the influence of the concept of courtly love that was popular in western Europe in medieval times. M. H. Abrams, in *A Glossary of Literary Terms*, describes courtly love as "an elaborate code governing the relations of aristocratic lovers.... The courtly lover idealizes and idolizes his beloved, and subjects himself entirely to her every whim." She may be capricious, but he stays true to her, adhering "to a rigorous code of behavior, both in knightly battles and in the complex ceremonies of courtly speech and conduct."

In English literature, courtly love is exemplified in Chaucer's long narrative poem *Troilus and Criseyde* (which was undoubtedly known to Wyatt). The poem tells the story of the love between the Trojan warrior Troilus, son of King Priam, and Criseyde, a Trojan woman who ultimately betrays him. In their introduction to Chaucer's poem, D. S. Brewer and L. Elisabeth Brewer note that courtly love is close to what was called in medieval France *fine amour* or "refined love." The Brewers identify a number of elements that made up *fine amour*: it is up to the man to take the initiative; the love is based on sexual desire, although "the beloved becomes a symbol of inexpressible and almost transcendental longings." The man regards his beloved as superior to him and therefore adopts a posture of humility. The love fundamentally affects the lover in the sense that it refines his personality for the better, and the love is not displayed in public. Rather it is enacted in private and kept secret, being considered too precious for disclosure.

A courtier poet like Wyatt, moving in aristocratic circles and wanting to explore themes of love, would undoubtedly have been influenced by the courtly love and *fine amour* traditions, and such influences are discernible in "They Flee from Me." Indeed, the speaker seems to present himself as having been too much the courtly lover, which somehow caused his lady to reject him.

The very first line of the poem sounds its theme of the betrayal of love, because the women who had formerly come to his private chamber are now running in the opposite direction. In this first stanza, the poet refers to more than one mistress—it seems as if he has had many of them. They all used to come discreetly to his chamber, and he was very much in the traditional masculine position of holding all the power. The women had, it seems, willingly given themselves up to him, but now they have forgotten all that, and like formerly tame animals that have reverted to the wild, the women roam around doing, it would appear, whatever they want. The first stanza then, sounds the theme of the fickleness, the changeability of women— which would seem to be something of a departure from the idealization of women that formed the basis of the courtly love tradition, although, of course, in Chaucer's poem that is underpinned by courtly love, Criseyde also proved unfaithful to Troilus.

From this point on, however, the speaker in "They Flee from Me" refers to just one woman, rather than a whole cluster of them, who seems to have caused him particular emotional pain. The second stanza strikes a wholly different note from the first one. As he recalls a particular moment in their relationship, it seems rather unlike the kind of seduction that, based on the first stanza, one might have been expecting. It is not the man who takes the lead but the woman. Rather than the man confidently making yet another sexual conquest, he seems to be entirely passive. It is the woman who lets her garment fall from her. It is she who initiates the embrace, and it is the man who is caught in her arms, not the other way around. Finally, it is she who initiates the kiss and then asks him how he likes it. He seems to have done precisely nothing in this little scenario other than go along with what was happening.

Perhaps this is a hint of the courtly lover who is so adoring of his lady, so humble in his feelings regarding this superior being, that he willingly cedes the power in their relationship

Whereas he used to be sought after by women, the speaker now fears they avoid him
(©maradon 333 | Shutterstock.com)

to her. Nor is this something he feels he has to hide. Indeed, at the beginning of stanza 3, he feels compelled to insist on the accuracy of his memory of an actual incident; it was not a dream or a fantasy, he says. One wonders why he inserts this line: Does he know and intend that his poem will be circulating among others in the court of Henry VIII, who may actually know who he is referring to, unlike the modern reader who is completely in the dark about who these people are?

It is stanza 3 that perhaps reveals most fully the underlying courtly love philosophy. The speaker states in the second line that everything has changed in that relationship because of his "gentleness." Today, the word *gentle* means kind and mild, but in former times, it also carried the meaning of honorable, noble, and chivalrous—exactly the qualities that the courtly lover liked to display. However, it seems that in the speaker's mind, the lady took advantage of him. By being too chivalrous, he laid himself open, became vulnerable, and ultimately suffered an emotional wound at her hands. She proved unworthy of his devotion, at least in his eyes. Line 4 of stanza 3 also shows quite clearly a courtly love theme, although the poet alludes to it with sarcasm. Ironically, he puts her in the position of being his superior, like royalty perhaps, with the power to dismiss him from her presence; she is graciously allowing him to leave. Lying behind the courtly language lies a spirit of anger and recrimination on the part of the speaker, who feels badly let down. The final line of the poem strongly suggests that he thinks his former lover, his once adored and presumably adoring mistress, deserves to suffer too, for her unfaithfulness.

The poem thus succeeds in conveying what one suspects are authentic feelings that a man experienced following the breakup of an intimate relationship. These feelings are partly expressed through the highly stylized or artificial language of courtly love. In this sense, the poem veers between sincerity and artifice, between honesty of feeling and the code that seeks to manage such turbulent feelings under a smooth surface of prescribed attitudes and conduct. This

> BY MAKING HIS *PERSONA* CONSPICUOUSLY PASSIVE ALL THROUGH THE POEM, WYATT MAKES AN OBJECT OUT OF HIM, AN OBJECT OF DESIRE."

coexistence of sincerity and artifice raises an interesting question: to what extent was the tradition of courtly love ever a lived reality in medieval times? As Abrams puts it:

> There has long been a debate as to whether medieval courtly love was merely a literary convention and a topic for elegant conversation at courts, or whether to some degree it reflected the actual conditions of aristocratic life at the time.

The question is probably unanswerable, but the literary influence of the philosophy was undoubtedly long-lasting and profound, and from Petrarch to Chaucer and others, it found its way to Wyatt, an innovative poet and aristocrat who made effective use of it as he sought to create new forms of expression in the developing body of English literature.

Source: Bryan Aubrey, Critical Essay on "They Flee From Me," in *Poetry for Students*, Gale, Cengage Learning, 2017.

Krisztina Szalay

In the following excerpt, Szalay examines how Wyatt's real-life experiences with women may have influenced his poetry.

. . . The poem comes from the Egerton MS. and Wyatt's authorship is unquestioned. No immediate source has been identified, though there are critics who claim that Wyatt's text owes something to Ovid, *Amores*, III.7. (Muir and Thomson 299).

Whether Wyatt was familiar with Charles d'Orleans' ballad beginning, in French, with the same words "they flee from me" is also uncertain (ibid). Regarding stanzaic form and language in "They fle from me . . ." Kay has convincingly demonstrated that they "derive from and participate in that specifically English version of *fin amor*, which flourished at the court of Henry VIII and whose primary inspiration and model was Chaucer's *Troilus*" (215). Kay also highlights other Chaucerian elements in

the poem, such as the epithet of female beauty in line 12 ("armes long and small") or "new fanglines" in line 19, both of which were frequently used by the fourteenth century master. He also observes that the stanzaic form, the rhyme royal, might derive from Chaucer (215). Ferry points out the similarities between Wyatt's sonnets and this ballad insofar as the latter " . . . does not catalogue the lover's experiences in an additive structure . . . but develops dramatically, and by means of ambiguities of language also associated with Wyatt's sonnets" (101).

Indeed, "They fle from me . . . " is a dramatic poem. It not only dramatises the gap between courtly love conventions and Wyatt's actual love experience, but it also portrays the gap between traditional ideas of male and female roles. In the drama happening between him and women Wyatt makes them protagonists and himself an episodist.

It is perhaps in this poem that the gap between "them" and the poetic *persona* is the most markedly represented. Inscrutable in their moves, unpredictable in their choices, women are described here as free, autonomous and somewhat ruthless creatures, pursuing the "manly" role of choosing, courting, seducing and abandoning their lovers, one of whom—one among many, as the poem suggests—is the *persona* himself. We do not know how other men would have responded to such treatment, for here, quite exceptionally, the *persona* is "alone" with these ladies. Perhaps it is this very feature of the poem which gives it a moving, personal touch by which the reader is initiated into what Harding has called "direct handling of real experience" (37).

By making his *persona* conspicuously passive all through the poem, Wyatt makes an object out of him, an object of desire. The many personal pronouns in the oblique case together with the lack of active verbs on the *persona*'s side speak for this. Wyatt's poetic ego is represented as an onlooker in his own life, not necessarily because this is the position which appeals to him, but more probably because this is the role he is allowed to inhabit in these relationships. All the initiatives are taken by women, even in that nostalgically recalled, intimate episode, where the *persona* experiences real gentleness and affection from the woman: "Therewithall swetely did my kysse,/And softly said 'dere hert, how like you this?'" (lines 13–14). The episode might seem so unreal and, perhaps, untypical, for the *persona* that he hastens to add: "It was no dreme: I lay brode waking" (line 15).

The *persona's* only choice now, it seems, is to admit defeat. He does this in general, voicing the melancholy complaint of an ageing, no longer popular or sexually attractive man when he says: "They fle from me that sometyme did me seke." But defeat is being admitted in a more concrete instance as well, and this is what really hurts by its immediacy: "And I have leve to go of her goodeness" (line 18). The same woman is turning him out now, who "ons in speciall" had been especially kind to him. Were it not for her decision to end the relationship he, in all likelihood, would not be able to leave. So positioned, the *persona* is made to be unable to perform that last gesture of face-saving we use when, sweeping up fragments of broken love, we finally say: enough is enough.

I am deliberately using the generic and genderless "we" in this case because through the reversal of traditional gender roles, the underlying sentiment of the poem somehow becomes genderless. Disappointment is disappointment, sorrow is sorrow whoever might feel them. And the same holds for aggression as well, the note on which the poem ends: "But syns that I so kyndely ame serued, /I would fain knowe what she hath deserued" (lines 20–21). Frustration over both our own and our partner's behaviour often results in ill will and in a compulsive, self-destructive curiosity.

Bespeaking, over again, great knowledge of human psychology, the poem thus hovers between subjugation and self-preservation. I see the latter manifested in the opening stanza where Wyatt speaks of women through metaphorical allusions to wild animals (deer, probably), giving himself a chance to pun on the contrast between "tame and meke" and "wyld." Also, it is through these metaphors that he can allude beautifully to consummated sexual relationships, as "To take bred at my hand" in line 6 stands for feeding both hunger and sexual appetite. The metaphors here express, though very subtly, a momentary rise in status since the *persona* sees himself as one in command: "they put theimself in daunger" (line 5) when visiting him in his bedchamber. The slight disgust one feels reading "Besely seking with a continuell chaunge" in line 7 also adds to this effect. Another attempt at self-preservation lies in the somewhat childish boasting: "Thanceked be fortune, it hath been othrewise/Twenty tymes

better" in lines 8–9. But perhaps the most effective of these attempts is Wyatt's irony when he puns on the double meaning of "gentilnes" in line 16, and of "kyndely" in line 20. "Gentilnes" standing for "gentleness," "gentility" (i.e. "being a gentleman") and also for "weakness" offers an inexhaustible source of self-irony. "Kyndely" meaning "with kindness" is ironic, but if read as "naturally," (i.e. "keeping with the law of kind?") it gives a stoic touch to the line.

In conclusion I would like to caution against reading Wyatt's love poems through nineteenth century lenses, a century where, whether we like it or not, most of our expectations and prejudices derive from. Our traditional views concerning courtship, being in love, gender roles or power-relations in love have repeatedly proved irrelevant or misleading, concerning early-Tudor poetry. What Ferry said about Wyatt may be true of Surrey or Raleigh "the character of court poetry in some sense mirrors its actual circumstances, even by its very artificiality. Love's games, as they are rendered in verse, were actually played at court, and in the same style" (71). Wyatt, in my opinion, in the overwhelming majority of his poems refused to play just these games and refused the style as well in which those games were represented. But this, I emphasise, does not make him into a good feminist or a misogynist either. He was what he was, a man of exceptional sensitivity and of melancholy disposition, capable of differentiating between individuals, and reacting to them as such. He would appreciate steadfastness just as much as he would acknowledge the contrary.

There are three paintings that keep coming to my mind whenever I read Wyatt's love lyrics. One is by an unknown fifteenth century Italian master, and is entitled *Lady With Unicorn*. I sense some kinship between this painting and "Who so list to hounte . . . ." Reclining in the depth of a forest, far away from civilisation and guarded by a gentle, attentive unicorn, this lady is just as self-assured and chaste as is Wyatt's mysterious lady. "They fle from me . . . ," on the other hand, calls into my mind Paolo Uccello's *St. George and the Dragon*. I consider Uccello's painting an archetypal iconographic representation of women being inscrutable, having bonds to the "dragon," which men only too often fail to notice or notice when it is already too late. This is why St. George, the saviour of virgins, is portrayed as an intruder who only makes trouble disturbing the homely companionship of the lady and the dragon. Does he see that there is a leash in the lady's hand and that the leash ends in a collar around the dragon's neck? I doubt that, since St. George in this painting is very, very young. The third painting is by Botticelli, his famous *Venus and Mars*. It has been interpreted in a hundred different ways. My "reading" of it coincides with my general impression of Wyatt's love poems. Both artists represent women as "knowers," who keep some knowledge solely for themselves and thus gain power over men. Power-relations in *Venus and Mars* are exquisitely depicted by visual means: Venus is sitting up, awake and fully dressed, while Mars is lying naked, fast asleep. Much as the viewer would like to have a share in Venus's power, that is impossible: the goddess casts her calm glance over one's head and into some distance she only can see....

Source: Krisztina Szalay, "Wyatt and Women: 'Who So List to Hounte...' and 'They Fle from Me...' Revisited," in *The Obstinate Muse of Freedom: On the Poetry of Sir Thomas Wyatt*, Akadémiai Kiadó, 2000, pp. 5–79.

SOURCES

Abrams, M. H., *A Glossary of Literary Terms*, 4th ed., Holt Rinehart and Winston, 1981, pp. 34–35.

Brewer, D. S., and L. Elisabeth Brewer, Introduction to *Troilus and Criseyde*, by Geoffrey Chaucer, Routledge and Kegan Paul, 1970, pp. xxxii, xxxiii.

Brigden, Susan, *Thomas Wyatt: The Heart's Forest*, Faber and Faber, 2012, pp. 24–25.

Caldwell, Ellen C., "Thomas Wyatt," in *Sixteenth-Century Nondramatic Writers: First Series*, edited by David A. Richardson, *Dictionary of Literary Biography*, Vol. 132, Gale Research, 1993.

de Sola Pinto, V., *The English Renaissance: 1510–1688*, Cresset Press, 1966, p. 10.

"How Many Catholics Are There in Britain?" BBC News, September 10, 2010, http://www.bbc.com/news/11297461 (accessed September 8, 2016).

Lever, J. W., *The Elizabethan Love Sonnet*, Methuen, 1956, pp. 14, 31.

Muir, Kenneth, *Life and Letters of Sir Thomas Wyatt*, Liverpool University Press, 1963, p. 245.

Roston, Murray, *Sixteenth-Century English Literature*, Schocken Books, 1982, pp. 41, 47, 49.

Thomson, Patricia, *Sir Thomas Wyatt and His Background*, Stanford University Press, 1964, p. 142.

FURTHER READING

Foley, Stephen Merriam, *Sir Thomas Wyatt*, Twayne Publishers, 1990.

This study of Wyatt examines the conditions in Tudor culture that allowed Wyatt's work to emerge and offers readings through the lens of that historical culture.

Friedman, Donald M., "The Mind in the Poem: Wyatt's 'They Fle from Me,'" *Studies in English Literature, 1500–1900*, Vol. 7, No. 1, 1967, pp. 1–13.

According to Friedman's reading of the poem, the speaker is not Wyatt himself, recording a personal experience, but a fictional or imagined figure who is trying to work out his feelings regarding the unfaithfulness of his lady. With this interpretation, the poem becomes a dramatization rather than a personal revelation.

Kay, Dennis, "Wyatt and Chaucer: 'They Fle from Me'," in *Huntingdon Quarterly*, Vol. 47, No. 3, Summer 1984, pp. 211–25.

Kay traces the influence of Chaucer on Wyatt's poem.

Mason, H. A., *Sir Thomas Wyatt: A Literary Portrait, Selected Poems, with Full Notes, Commentaries and a Critical Introduction*, Bristol Classical Press, 1986.

This is an edition of Wyatt's poems that also includes notes and commentary on individual poems, as well as information about the Tudor world in which Wyatt lived.

Rex, Richard, *The Tudors*, Amberley, rev. ed., 2013.

This is a critically acclaimed, well-illustrated, and entertaining account of England's Tudor dynasty, providing valuable information about the cultural context in which Wyatt wrote his poetry.

SUGGESTED SEARCH TERMS

Sir Thomas Wyatt

"They Flee from Me" AND Wyatt

Anne Boleyn

courtly love

Wyatt AND Chaucer

Wyatt AND Tudor period

rhyme royal

iambic pentameter

Petrarch AND courtly love

a total stranger one black day

E. E. CUMMINGS

1958

As is often the case, given E. E. Cummings's irregular pattern of giving his poems titles (when he gave titles at all), locating the origins of a specific work proves a challenge. Most sources agree that "a total stranger one black day" was copyrighted originally in 1923, although it first appeared in his collection *95 Poems* in 1958. While a typical Cummings poem is known for its challenge to traditions of grammar and punctuation, this one does take a slightly more philosophic turn than much of his writing. Not focused on sex or death (two of his more common themes), "a total stranger one black day" explores how an individual understands himself and how this sense of self is, in fact, a multiplicity of selves compressed into a single life.

AUTHOR BIOGRAPHY

Edward Estlin Cummings was born on October 14, 1894, to Edward Cummings and Rebecca Haswell Clarke. Cummings's mother came from a well-known family in Cambridge, Massachusetts, and his father was both a sociology professor at Harvard University and a nationally known Unitarian minister. His mother took it upon herself to nurture the creativity of her children, and the young Edward wrote poems from an early age.

E.E. Cummings *(©Library of Congress, Prints & Photographs Division, Reproduction number LC-USZ62-116342)*

Cummings graduated from Harvard in 1915, adding an advanced degree in 1916. Following graduation, he enlisted in the Norton-Harjes Ambulance Corps, along with friend and fellow writer John Dos Passos, despite the fact that both men openly expressed antiwar sentiments. In September 1917, Cummings and his friend William Slater Brown were arrested by the French military on suspicion of espionage. Cummings was held in a military detention camp for three and a half months, eventually released in part because of his father's diplomatic lobbying behind the scenes.

Cummings returned to the United States on New Year's Day 1918, only to be drafted into the army. He served until November 1918, when he left the army, and, as Adam Kirsch notes, "like so many of his fellow Modernists...made the pilgrimage to Paris" in 1921, "finding it a liberation and a revelation." He returned to New York City two years later, settling in Greenwich Village. Cummings established himself as an avant-garde poet with the publication of two books: *Tulips and Chimneys* (1923) and *XLI*

Poems (1925). These were followed by such collections as *no thanks* (1935), *Collected Poems* (1938), *50 Poems* (1940), and *95 Poems* (1958), which included "a total stranger one black day."

Cummings was also a frequent traveler in the early part of his career, visiting most of Europe, the Soviet Union, North Africa, and Mexico. For part of this period (1924–1927) he earned his living, in part, as an essayist and portrait artist for *Vanity Fair* magazine. Overall, Cummings had a remarkably prolific career, producing nearly three thousand poems, two novels, four plays, and a remarkable number of sketches, paintings, and portraits. During his writing life, Cummings was recognized with numerous awards, including a pair of Guggenheim Fellowships (1933, 1951), an American Academy of American Poets fellowship (1950), and the Bollingen Prize in Poetry (1957).

Cummings led a somewhat tumultuous personal life. He married Elaine Orr in 1924, but the couple divorced within a year. Their relationship produced a daughter, Nancy (1919–2006), who was estranged from her father until 1946, when they reconnected. Cummings married his second wife, Anne Minnerly Barton, in May of 1929, but the couple divorced three years later. He met fashion model and photographer Marion Morehouse in 1934, with whom he lived in a common-law marriage until his death. Awarded an honorary professorship at Harvard in 1952, Cummings spent the final decades of his life traveling, enjoying speaking engagements, and spending time at his summer home in Silver Lake, New Hampshire. Cummings died of a stroke on September 3, 1962. He was sixty-seven.

POEM SUMMARY

The text used for this summary is from *E. E. Cummings: Selected Poems*, Liveright, 1994, p. 165. Versions of the poem can be found on the following web pages: http://www.best-poems.net/e_e_cummings/a_total_stranger_one_black_day.html, http://www.artvilla.com/a-total-stranger-one-black-day-poem-by-ee-cummings/, http://www.poetrysoup.com/famous/poem/408/a_total_stranger_one_black_day, and http://www.poemsandpoets.net/E-E-Cummings/total-stranger-one-black-day.html.

Written as a series of three nonrhyming, noninterlocking free-verse couplets, this poem is very typical of Cummings's writing in its open rhythms, creative punctuation and spelling, and power to evoke impact through misdirection and metaphor. The opening line begins with Cummings's trademark lowercase letter. It goes on to join nouns and adjectives by way of setting a tone (the day is dark) and a somewhat unsettling sense of strangeness that is underscored by the absence of a verb. The sentence is grammatically incomplete (no verb), as is the experience of the opening sentence, which functions as a statement of a stranger's presence.

The second sentence answers the mystery of the missing verb with its first word. The action described in the verb itself is violent and sudden and comes with the implication of the speaker's being struck with a hard, unexpected blow. This implicit violence is reinforced in the subsequent words of the sentence but only after a typical Cummings-esque twist of wording that reconfigures the familiar phrase "the living hell" into something far less clichéd and far more interesting. An attentive reader pauses at this unexpected twist and reflects: What has been knocked out of the speaker? And how does this knocking relate to the speaker's living? Has the speaker actually had "living the hell" knocked out of his worldview? In this case, what does that phrase actually mean?

The second sentence (and first stanza) ends with what is technically called an *em dash*, rather than a more common element of punctuation like a comma, period, or even a hyphen. The em dash signals an abrupt transition between parts of a thought that are either related tangentially or not really related at all. A reader is asked to bridge the logical gap marked by the em dash and to carry the reading of these two lines across the white space on the page in order to discover a connection with the opening words of the second stanza.

Cummings, however, does not allow for clear connections, opening the second stanza with a pronoun that might refer to the newly introduced stranger but also might refer to the speaker who has been knocked about by this same stranger. With a single word, the poem bifurcates (splits in two), as a reader ponders which of the two referents (the stranger or the speaker) found it hard to secure forgiveness for his or her actions. The alliterative *f* sound joining the second and third word of the sentence create a soft spot in what to this point has been a poem of roughness and harshness. Forgiveness exists in this sentence in

a pause, and slowing down from the short bursts of energy that has filled the poem to this point. This brief respite is underscored by the appearance of another solid, almost resistant word following immediately after.

The fourth line ends the second stanza with a melange (mixture) of classic Cummings twirls of language. The first word (the reflexive pronoun *myself*) is interrupted by a parenthetical aside that effectively turns it into two words: the possessive (*my*) and a significant noun of identification (*self*). This play on words is significant, underscoring the complacency with which culture tends to use one form (*myself*) without ever thinking through the complexities and contours of what exactly the word means (*my self*).

It is into this space of overly simplified usage that Cummings takes readers in the final two words of the second stanza. The sense of identity that was split apart only one sentence earlier snaps back together suddenly when the speaker states, almost casually, that he and the stranger are the same person. What opened as a poem about an encounter with a stranger on a black day becomes a poem about a speaker's coming to a deep realization about the nature of his own self, acknowledging that he is not a singular self but an amalgam (intricate mixture) of various aspects of himself. Whether a reader wants to see this "stranger" as the dark side of himself, the mortal version of himself (liable to death), or an embodiment of death itself is not the driver of this poem. What shapes the poem is the speaker's recognition of the complexity of his sense of self and the multiple facets of his identity. More specifically, as the third stanza opens behind the second em dash of the poem, the speaker comes to recognize the duplicity, or doubleness, of his sense of self as part of who he is. It is important to note that the two sides of himself recognized in the poem (one good, one fiendish) are an everlasting and undeniably connected union that defines his identity. The poem moves from an unexpected meeting through a moment of recognition to an acceptance of the complexity of his own being and the multiplicity of sense of self.

THEMES

Aging
Aging is a natural and unavoidable part of life and one that all individuals come to accept to varying degrees as they go through the inevitable

TOPICS FOR FURTHER STUDY

- Cummings was influenced by such modernist notables as Gertrude Stein and Ezra Pound. Select a poem from either Stein or Pound and write a well-structured essay in which you compare it (focusing on the similarities only) to "a total stranger one black day." Feel free to focus on shared themes, tone, word choice, or imagery, but do be certain to highlight the elements that the two poems have in common.

- Cummings loved phonetic spellings, invented words, and unconventional word ordering. Create a colorful poster in which you take some common words and phrases and give them a twist in the same way Cummings would.

- Cummings's poems have been adapted or set directly to music by an eclectic range of musicians, including Björk. Using any of the dozens of available apps (Garageband or Metallic Spheres as examples) for making music, create a musical adaptation of "a total stranger one black day" that you can share with your class. Feel free to use (or not use) voice as one of the instruments of choice. Prepare a statement of your artistic vision for the interpretation. Why did you choose the instruments you did? How did you determine the basic rhythm and pacing of your interpretation?

- Cummings was an accomplished artist whose estate included over sixteen hundred oils and watercolors. As Paul Muldoon suggests, "When he went to Harvard . . . Cummings was at least as interested in visual art as in poetry, and later considered pursuing a career as a painter." Create a painting that interprets "a total stranger one black day." Prepare it to be displayed in your classroom, including a one-paragraph statement of your vision for the painting.

- Known for what Susan Cheever remembers as "an electrifying and acrobatic way to give poetry readings," Cummings was really one of the first of American rock-star poets. As Billy Collins notes, Cummings's "contracts for public readings—usually sellouts—even included 'rules of engagement' meant to protect him from the throng of his fans." Taking "a total stranger one black day" as your lead, create an audio performance of six poems by Cummings.

- Read JonArno Lawson's *The Hobo's Crowbar* (2016), a collection full of wordplay, quick and unexpected rhymes, and powerful rhythms. Write a thoughtful and well-structured essay in which you either compare (mark similarities) or contrast (mark differences) Lawson's style with Cummings's style as represented in "a total stranger one black day."

process. With aging, as Cummings suggests, comes the opportunity for a growing awareness of oneself and the identity that each person takes forward into the world. Some people, like the speaker in "a total stranger one black day" resist the opportunities that come with aging through humor and an irascible defiance. Regardless of the degree or tone of resistance, insight finds a way to make itself known, as a kind of stranger appearing suddenly in a life. With a couple of lines, the speaker goes from sudden confrontation to recognition and acceptance of the various sides of himself that are presenting themselves throughout the aging process.

Conformity

Arguably the most consistently satirical aspect of Cummings's poetry is aimed at the powerful and persistent social pressures that the poet saw as driving the unquestioned compliance with rules and standards of behavior (implicit and explicit). More specifically, Cummings believed strongly that the complacency of social thinking, the expanding influence of commercialism, and any restrictions on freedom of expression are conspiring to deaden the creativity of the American mind. As Kirsch notes, Cummings's

> poems are constantly exhorting [readers] to be original, independent, self-reliant. And he is scornful of everyone who takes refuge in received ideas and conventional standards— all the cumbersome traditions that parents pass on to their children.

As Cummings himself explained: "I envisaged the future of so called mankind as a permanent pastlessness, prenatally enveloping semi identical supersubmorons in perpetual nonunhappiness."

Although it is satirical in nature, "a total stranger one black day" is a poem that sets out to puncture conformity (and its near cousin complacency) by inviting a reader to reflect upon what most people take for granted: a sense of identity. Having his speaker acknowledge that he has parts of himself that are strangers to him is a provocation to readers to think, even momentarily, about the multiple sides that each of us carries into the world everyday. As Susan Cheever suggests of Cummings, he is determined "to slow down the seemingly inexorable rush of the world, to force people to notice their own lives."

Modernism

Arising in the late nineteenth and early twentieth centuries, the movement known as modernism was shaped in large part by the emergence of industrial cities, rapid urban growth, and weakening of traditional religions in social and cultural values. Modernism reached its peak of influence when the horrors of World War I undercut the certainties (in faith, in humanity) that had expressed for generations such endeavors as art, architecture, literature, social organizations, and even the sciences. Perhaps the most famous and succinct statement of the modernist vision was Ezra Pound's 1934 challenge to "Make it new!" from the essay collection *Make It New*.

Susan Cheever summarizes Cummings's relationship with modernism and its emphasis on making it new this way:

> Modernism as Cummings...embraced it had three parts. The first was the method of using sounds instead of meanings to connect words

Cummings was also an artist, as can be seen in this self-portrait (© *Library of Congress, Prints & Photographs Division, Reproduction number LC-USZ62-108318*)

to the reader's feelings. The second was the idea of stripping away all unnecessary things to bring attention to form and structure: the formerly hidden skeleton of a work would now be exuberantly visible. The third facet of modernism was an embrace of adversity.

STYLE

Language

Like many of the writers of his generation, Cummings was concerned with the limitations of traditional language to convey the depth of subjective experiences in a world that had just recovered from world war and that was beginning to become aware of such transcendent opportunities as meditation, Buddhism, and even consciousness-altering drugs. In "a total stranger one black day," for instance, he looks to develop what Marcello Pagnini calls "a kind of compression of ideas, of images, of sensations" through manipulation of traditional word order, punctuation, and grammar. As Kirsch notes,

Cummings was not the first poet to use a type-writer, but as [his poems show], he was the first to take advantage of its power to control the exact spacing and shape of every line, and thus to make a poem's visual appearance as important as its musical rhythms.

"No American poet of his generation so fractured the surfaces of poetry," states Kirsch. As Muldoon put it, no poet was as exuberant in "typographical high jinks" as Cummings.

Punctuation

Punctuation creates both rhythm and meaning in poetry, allowing lines to become distinct units of thought and sound (each ending with a period or terminal point) or allowing ideas to flow across lines in order to connect and build gradually as the poem develops (known as run-on lines). Cummings uses punctuation very creatively in "a total stranger one black day" in order to allow ideas to flow and unfold almost organically while others are framed as powerful, almost definitive statements of fact. The use of em dashes, for instance, set sections of the poem off in a kind of punctuating frame that underscores the movement of the poem from disruption to merger of the concept of self-identity.

HISTORICAL CONTEXT

The 1950s saw a postwar boom that redefined in many ways how Americans saw themselves, their communities, and their place in the world. Consumerism, spreading suburbanism, and economic optimism came to define the decade in which Cummings was most prolific as a poet and was often the source for his satires on conformity, middle-class mores (the characteristic customs and conventions of a community), and what he perceived as a dwindling creativity in American culture generally. In 1955, for instance, over eight million cars were sold (to a population of 168 million), with 70 percent of American families now owning an automobile. The first McDonald's restaurant was built in 1955 in response, in part, to the rapidly expanding middle-class market for fast food and TV dinners. The American cultural experience was increasingly being defined by an emphasis on entertainment and enhanced consumer experience. Disneyland opened in California in 1955, the same year that Coca-Cola moved to include cans alongside its trademark bottles. Music was dominated by the first wave of domestic rock and roll, with such iconic artists as Elvis Presley, Bill Haley and the Comets, Chuck Berry, and the Platters rising through the charts.

On a darker note, and one that resonated with Cummings and many poet colleagues, the US involvement in the Vietnam War began in 1955, while in Montgomery, Alabama, that same year, a young African American woman named Rosa Parks refused to obey a bus driver's demand that she give up her seat to a white passenger. Parks's refusal and subsequent arrest formed the catalyst needed to set the American civil rights movement in motion.

The motion created in the mid-1950s fueled an at times deeply divisive debate about American education. In 1954 the US Supreme Court had ruled unanimously that state laws establishing separate schools for blacks and whites were unconstitutional. Integration of previously all-white schools in the cities of the South was met with resistance—Little Rock, Arkansas, being a prime example. The crisis, involving a lawsuit by the National Association for the Advancement of Colored People and the calling out of the National Guard to support the segregationists, was finally resolved when President Dwight Eisenhower sent in the US Army's 101st Airborne Division to end the stalemate. As the decade progressed and living standards improved, a revitalization of postsecondary education took place. It is estimated that by mid-decade, 30 percent of American high school graduates were heading to pursue a college degree.

The year 1958 saw a dip in the economy, causing the United States to slip into a mild recession, with a large increase in unemployment to over 7 percent. Despite this downturn, automobiles continued to get larger, more powerful, and heavier. At the same time, the importation of cars from Japan began to grow, as Datsun and Toyota made inroads into American markets.

Technologies of all types began to figure more and more prominently as the decade unfolded. Cape Canaveral saw America's first satellite launch, and Russia launched the first of its *Sputnik* projects. The first microchips were in development, and television (now expanding into color) made such shows as *Rawhide*, *Bonanza*, and *The Twilight Zone* extremely popular. At movie theaters, patrons were drawn to such titles as *Some Like It Hot* (1959), *Ben-Hur* (1959), and *North by Northwest* (1959). Barbie dolls became

COMPARE
&
CONTRAST

- **1950s:** The economy of the United States in the 1950s is relatively active, sparked in part by two periods of inflation and a swing toward increased consumerism. Following the removal of price controls after World War II, housing construction takes off, with families flocking to newly minted suburbs. The outward migration from traditional urban homes spreads through the economy both directly (through an increase in car sales) and less obviously (a flourishing of life insurance companies, for instance).

  Today: The United States is one of the world's largest economic engines when measured by real gross domestic product (the financial value of all the finished goods and services that are produced by a country annually). The domestic economy has benefited from the use of natural resources as well as the productivity from its large workforce.

- **1950s:** Environmentalism is emerging as a deeply held and political belief in the responsibility of individuals to protect and improve the land for future generations. Specific issues that are addressed under the umbrella of the movement include pollution, protection of indigenous plant and animal life, and the concept of a minimal footprint of human development. Environmentalism begins to emphasize the deep connection of humans and land as well as the need to maintain a balanced relationship between humans and the land's natural systems. By 1950, Aldo Leopold publishes one of the seminal environmentalist books of a generation, *A Sand County Almanac*. Immediately influential, the book articulates Leopold's philosophy that humans should have a moral respect for the environment and that it is unethical to hurt or harm the land in any way. Leopold's writing sparks a new awareness of environmental issues, which leads, in turn, to a surge in membership in organizations like the Sierra Club.

  Today: Environmental concerns are a major concern, from oil spills through impacts on global climate and weather patterns. Activism and science continue to focus on such issues as the impact of the extraction and consumption of fossil fuels, the growing list of extinct or endangered plant and animal species, and the dramatic rate of reduction that is being seen in polar ice caps and glacier areas around the world.

- **1950s:** Cummings is openly and aggressively exploratory of sexual attitudes and activities. The terms *sex* (referring to biological determinants) and *gender* (sociocultural determinants) are seen commonly as closely related concepts. In the later part of the decade and into the 1960s, however, this changes as an increased interest in homosexuality, transsexuality, and other sexual orientations and preferences come into focus. Although homosexuality is still considered illegal in many parts of the United States, attitudes and assumptions are undergoing seismic changes.

  Today: Today scientists are increasingly curious about how and why a person might develop a particular sexual orientation. Many scientists believe that it is a combination of nature and nurture, meaning it is a montage of genetic, hormonal, and familial influences. However, scientists today do favor biologically based theories that center on what happens during early development.

popular, Fidel Castro came to power in Cuba, and the birth control pill was introduced, albeit in limited ways, into the American market. By the end of the 1950s, all the pieces were in place for the counterculture energies of the 1960s to find fertile soil and for a questioning, irreverent poet

At first, the reader might think the collision with the stranger is a literal one, as if on a crowded street

(©connel | Shutterstock.com)

like Cummings to make his mark on American literature and culture.

CRITICAL OVERVIEW

Critics of Cummings tend to celebrate his creativity but also his position within the canon of modern American poetry as what Kirsch describes as "the most notorious and beloved child" of his era. John Cheever is more direct and specific in his comparison, calling Cummings his "generation's beloved heretic, a Henry David Thoreau for the 20th century."

Most naturally, critics focus on Cummings's trademark creativity as he builds a "blizzard of punctuation, the words running together or suddenly breaking part, the type spilling like a liquid from one line to the next" (Kirsch). As Pagnini observes:

> The poetry of Cummings . . . is characterized by an extreme poverty of content, and by as insistent a repetition of themes as one can find in a lyrical production worthy of historical

attention, while his concern for the physicality of the linguistic means and for the effects produced by his idiosyncratic treatment of them is immense.

Former American poet laureate Billy Collins notes that Cummings "could be childlike," "bitterly satiric," and "political," none of which harmed his reputation in any way. Collins observes that "no poet was more flamboyant or more recognizable in his iconoclasm." By

> erasing the sacred left margin, breaking down words into syllables and letters, employing eccentric punctuation, and indulging in all kinds of print-based shenanigans, Cummings brought into question some of our basic assumptions about poetry, grammar, sign, and language itself, and he also succeeded in giving many a typesetter a headache. . . . No American poet compares to him, for he slipped Houdini-like out of the locked box of the stanza, then leaped from the platform of the poetic line into an unheard-of-way of writing poetry.

Collins concludes, with evident sadness, that "these days Cummings is rarely mentioned. He has become the inhabitant of the ghost houses of anthologies and claustrophobic seminar room discussions" rather than "in the light of the window or the reading lamp."

HE AIMED, IN THE END, TO CREATE A GREAT POEM OF SELF-DISCOVERY IN WHICH SOUND IS MEANING AND MEANING IS SOUND."

CRITICISM

Klay Dyer

Dyer is a freelance writer specializing in topics relating to literature, popular culture, and the relationship between creativity and technology. In the following essay, he views Cummings's short poem "a total stranger one black day" as an exploration of the concept of self as a stable, knowable entity.

The relationship between Cummings's poetry and his love of music has always been an intimate and mutually influential one. Building on his understanding of medieval minstrels, who set tales to the sounds of music in order to convey complex social messages, Cummings was always a poet very much aware of the power of poetry to align itself with contemporary music, most notably with the rising power of jazz. Cummings's interest was timely, as he came to maturity at a time in American cultural history when the overlap of the worlds of poetry and music was particularly vibrant, fueled in part by the self-proclaimed Beat poets as well as by such modernist writers as T. S. Eliot, William Carlos Williams, Wallace Stevens, and the controversial Ezra Pound. What this diverse collection of writers produced, both on the page and in performance, would go on to change the contours (and sound) of poetry for generations to follow.

Around the time that Cummings was rising to prominence from his home in Greenwich Village, New York City was clearly and deeply under the influence of such jazz pioneers as Charlie Parker (1920–1955), Miles Davis (1926–1991), and Chet Baker (1929–1988), all of whom were moving what was then known as bebop toward a new horizon of cool. It was a horizon that would see more improvisation and experimentation, an emphasis on relaxed and fluid tempos, and a new freedom to borrow openly and creatively from classical and non-jazz antecedents. Significantly, this new coolness also allowed musicians to adopt more intimate postures in their music, turning away from the physicality of earlier iterations of musical expression to allow more expressive elements to be highlighted.

For a poet like Cummings, the rawness of bebop combined with the increasingly technical musicality of cool jazz was seen as a potentially engaging platform through which he could explore and articulate the emotional and sexual energies of the day. Rising out of the increasingly industrialized and urban centers of the United States, cool jazz was charged with racial overtones and freed into improvisation in a time of formal conservatism. Like its modernist cousins in poetry, jazz musicians broke with the sociocultural pressures of established musical forms (vocal-driven pop, traditional country and western) in an attempt to find a new language and new poetic forms that could articulate the realities of a world still reeling from the inhumanities that punctuated years of brutal war. Radical in virtually every aspect, jazz proved a natural attraction for the always-curious, intensely creative Cummings.

Cummings and other modernist poets saw in jazz what can best be described as a spontaneous interconnectedness between expression (of emotion, of concept) and form; more particularly for Cummings, this interconnectedness was tied to pushing the limits of language, grammar, and typography in order to bring his writing closer to the real experience of the moment. Just as skilled jazz musicians were asked to play off each other with no specific direction or form, responding only to the organic flow of the notes and the directions set by the other players, Cummings pushed his poems to a new level of spontaneity and creativity that would begin to break down the distance between experience and expression. Thought of another way, Cummings was determined to find a way that would allow him to transform free thought into equally free writing that would capture authentically the rhythms and meanings of what he felt in the moment.

WHAT DO I READ NEXT?

- Mati McDonough produced a wonderfully illustrated children's interpretation of the poem "i carry your heart with me" in 1991. The poem explores the adventures of a mother who carries her young daughter with her everywhere in order to introduce her to the world in its full range of seasons and storms.

- Edna St. Vincent Millay is often cited as a predecessor of Cummings in terms of her exploration of self and identity. Peruse her *Collected Poems* (1949) to gain a sense of context for Cummings's work.

- Irish writer James Joyce was a writer with whom Cummings was very familiar and from whom Cummings "learned how to present a verbal equivalent of the mind's wanderings between past and present, and so a fleeting triumph over linear time" according to Muldoon. Joyce's *A Portrait of the Artist as a Young Man* (1916) is an excellent (and accessible) example of what would have inspired Cummings to continue his poetic explorations of time and consciousness.

- Cummings often spoke of his appreciation of the poetry of the English romantic poet John Keats, especially for his powerful lyric poems and sonnets. Peruse any of Keats's sonnets in the collection *The Complete Poems of John Keats* (1994) to see how the two poets used language and form to explore the complexities of human emotions and connections.

- Like Cummings, Wallace Stevens was a Harvard-educated modernist poet who lived and wrote in New York City. Of his many poems, "Not Ideas about the Thing but the Thing Itself" captures most elegantly a philosophy of reality and identity similar to that found in "a total stranger one black day." You can find the poem in *Wallace Stevens: The Collected Poems* (2015).

- Any of Shel Silverstein's books of poetry, including *Falling Up* (1996), are in many ways a tame, but nonetheless relevant contemporary homage to the open creativity of the avant-garde writers through his blending of sketch and verse.

- Carol Kimball's *Art Song: Linking Music and Poetry* (2013) is a readable study of the specific ways that the art of song and the production of powerful lyric poetry are intimately related. Establishing a balance between the practical and artistic aspects of creativity, Kimball explains the key connections based on such elements as preparation and building of a poem and song, the intersection of word and rhythm, and the power of performance in both cases.

What Cummings and the modernists were striving for was by no means new. Ralph Waldo Emerson (1803–1882) had already spoken in his famous essay "Nature" (1836) about his desire to move poetry beyond the limits of language, which he saw as limiting artistic expression and, more important, an individual's ability to connect with his truest self. It was this determined experiment that Cummings brought to "a total stranger one black day," which works to realize two interdependent goals: how to express the deepest realization of self within the speaker and to do so in a language that, Cummings believed, traditionally worked against (not in support of) such deep self-discovery. He aimed, in the end, to create a great poem of self-discovery in which sound is meaning and meaning is sound.

The short, rhythmic lines that build in layers across Cummings's poem are far more aligned with jazz than with traditional poetics (of the lyric, the sonnet, the ballad) that stress metrical beats, rhyme schemes, and definable rhythms.

Structure and form are submerged in the poem in support of a tightly compressed stream of consciousness (the flow of thoughts in the conscious mind) that drives the lines forward across breaks that resist traditional markers of enjambment (the continuation of a line of verse without a pause beyond the end of a line, couplet, or stanza). Meaning carries across lines, which are, in turn, held together in a perceptual thread that is based more in sound than traditional grammar. Moving the poem from page to performance (reading aloud), which is always a valuable exercise when approaching a modernist poem, breathing underscores what Cummings is trying to achieve, allowing pauses to come organically through the lines without the need to look for the usual markers of hesitation or break (commas and periods).

In this movement toward a poetry that resists the traditional restrictions of language, Cummings also pushes "a total stranger one black day" toward a poem that becomes in its experience a moment *of* self-discovery, as distinct from a poem *about* self-discovery. For while a simple, common word and concept ("i," to stay true to Cummings's lowercase) can be stabilized to mean one thing, that same word and concept is never fully locked into a stable semantic relationship with reality within a Cummings poem. Put another way, the "i" is never *only* linked to the concept of self within "a total stranger one black day" but is freed to collide with the presence of stranger-ness but also to cascade and spiral so as to include a plethora of meanings, shifts, and identities. The line itself becomes a multitude of potential meanings, each of which is held in the "i" symbol and each opening to the improvisation/interpretation of the reader/performer. The poem is about identity, to be sure, but it is also about so much more. It is about the multiplicity that each reader carries within, about the pressures to conform to the long tradition of a singular and stabilized sense of self and the freedoms that come with moving beyond these same restrictions. Like a great work of cool jazz, Cummings's poem spins around this word in order to evoke an impression and, through that impression, to spin away into a free fall through the labyrinthine maze of self-identity.

It is not merely the improvisational aspect of jazz that appealed to Cummings and the modernists. Jazz brought with it a powerful and often rebellious sociopolitical impact that flew in the face of mainstream American preoccupations with postwar consumerism and the perceived value of living a suburban life. It was considered, to borrow Cummings's words, an antidote to the black days that many poets of this generation had seen as overtaking an increasingly suburbanized American society. Jazz was distinctly urban, predominately the venue of African American musicians—with trumpet player Baker and pianist Dave Brubeck (1920–2012) being notable exceptions—and was aligned openly, though not always accurately, with a type of open, creative lifestyle. Not surprisingly, jazz culture was seen as intense, edgy, exponentially creative, and engagingly dangerous. By the early 1950s, in other words, jazz already was what the iconoclastic Cummings had hoped to become: a groundbreaking creative force that tossed social norms aside with fervor, embraced creativity with passion, and tested limits (both psychological and sexual) with fearlessness.

Cummings, while he was more tame than fellow modernist Pound, embraced the opportunity to challenge American ideals of the day through his poetry. His less-than-subtle challenges to one of the cornerstone concepts of American culture (a stable, knowable identity) is at the same time an open challenge to a broader and deeply held perception of long-term economic prosperity that was apparently preordained to define America in the postwar era. To Cummings and his fellow modernists, all prosperity came with a corresponding cost, and to see an almost blind faith in industrialization take hold of the country was akin in their eyes to a descent into the depths of a cultural hell.

As in the finest jazz improvisation, "a total stranger one black day" spins further and faster as the poem unfolds. By the time the poet-speaker turns to peruse himself as a newly recognized union of self and stranger (or angel and fiend), the poem has found its own rhythm, one no longer tied to words but to phonetic representations, punctuation twists and turns that move beyond meaning by creating meaning. As the final line of the poem underscores, in the end it is understanding through the rhythms and sounds of language that mattered most to Cummings and that rendered the experience of the poem powerful and within reach.

Source: Klay Dyer, Critical Essay on "a total stranger one black day," in *Poetry for Students*, Gale, Cengage Learning, 2017.

As the reader progresses through the poem, it becomes clear that the meeting described is some kind of new self-awareness (*©InnervisionArt | Shutterstock.com*)

Richard S. Kennedy

In the following excerpt, Kennedy discusses some of Cummings's problematic beliefs, which appear more often in his later poetry.

The remaining years of Cummings' life were attended by health problems. As early as 1941 arthritis had begun to trouble his back and legs. Soon he was wearing a metal-braced corset that he dubbed "The Iron Maiden." Although this brought some relief his pains increased as the years went by and his journals are filled with details about his difficulties in sleeping, standing, and traveling by automobile or airplane for any extended period. In the late 1940s he began to have heart fibrillations, which caused intermittent alarm. He tried to stop smoking but usually relapsed after a short period of ill-tempered restraint. His journal entries show him full of crochets and complaints—and occasionally giving in to irrational fulminations. Cummings was beginning to feel his years.

His next collection of poems, *Xaipe* (1950), which means "rejoice" in Greek, does not have the exuberant spirit of its title. In addition to two elegies for dead friends, Paul Rosenfeld and Peter Munro Jack, the reader will find a number of poems on old age, including a tribute to the sculptor Aristide Maillol at age eighty, and other poems on death and immortality. Beyond that, one might say that the seventy-one poems offer "the mixture as before," to use Somerset Maugham's phrase. Even so, a few additional features should be singled out.

Many of the satires in the book seem overly fierce. His attack on President Franklin Roosevelt five years after the president's death seems unusually mean-spirited: "F is for foetus(a punk-slapping/ mobsucking/ gravypissing poppa" (*CP*). Yet we should be aware, I suppose, that Cummings' opposition to authority was so unceasing that he was hostile to all of the presidents of his adult lifetime, from Wilson to Kennedy, even though there is no evidence that he ever voted in any election.

His antiwar poems seem out of date, especially "o to be in finland/ now that Russia's

> BUT THE EXPLORATION OF THE POSSIBILITIES
> OF LINGUISTIC EXPRESSION WAS HIS SPECIAL
> CONTRIBUTION. HIS LEGACY TO LATER WRITERS
> WAS THE SPECTACLE OF HIS PUSHING LANGUAGE
> TO ITS EXTREMES."

here," which denounced "uncle shylock" for not coming to the rescue of Finland in World War II. That poem actually ran counter to Cummings' pronounced objection to the United States' entry into the War, a position he maintained throughout the entire four-year period. But the real folly of this publication is an epigram that brought upon him charges of anti-Semitism....

(*CP*)

This piece would have caused even more of an uproar if he had published the last line as he had originally written it, "it comes both pricked and cunted," but he changed it when publication problems arose as early, as 1945, the year he sent it to the *Quarterly Review of Literature*. Cummings defended himself in explanations to his friends by saying that what he meant was that a Jew who had been corrupted by American wealth was no longer a Jew but just someone worthy of the derogatory term "kike."

No matter what he maintained about his intentions the word "kike" used in this blunt attack carried connotations to a civilized reader, aghast at the recent revelations of Hitler's death camps, of hate and persecution. Quite understandably his epigram met widespread denunciation and also became the focus of a symposium in a special issue of *Congress Weekly* on the question of his anti-Semitism. Moreover Cummings had brought the controversy upon himself knowingly for before publication he had been warned by two friends, the poet Lloyd Frankenberg and the artist Evelyn Buff Segal, that this little rhyme was deeply insulting to Jews and would cause outrage among a wide range of readers. They urged him to withdraw it. But Cummings stubbornly refused this advice, even indicating that he would enjoy riling the public. He was carrying out, it seems, a frequent practice

of the paranoid personality: doing something to enrage people so that he could complain that everyone was ganging up on him.

Actually Cummings was revealing an attitude that he had harbored for some time. His anti-Semitism seems to have been awakened during the summer that he spent in Los Angeles trying to land a job as a script writer, for the journals and letters describing his experiences at that time show a series of offensive remarks about Hollywood Jews. This prejudice against Jews is not an isolated instance in his life. Cummings grew up at a time and in a community of people that, however enlightened, looked upon the recent immigrants to America in general as an inferior lot. In the Boston area it was the Irish who had swarmed in, and young Estlin and his friends despised the "Somerville Micks" who were their neighborhood enemies (and who put rocks in their snowballs). In later years, as New York increased its rich ethnic mix, Cummings regarded the recently arrived Italians, Irish, Poles, and East European Jews as a servant class. He felt benignly patronizing if they carried out their jobs and haughtily critical if they presumed above what he considered their station. These were, however, attitudes toward groups; he made exceptions for his friends. Indeed, always intensely loyal to friends, he would have gone to the guillotine for Jewish friends such as Paul Rosenfeld, Jere Knight, or Dr. Fritz Wittels, his psychoanalyst.

Even so, as years went by and he became increasingly touchy and irritable toward everyone his journals show frequent derogatory comments about Jews ("les choisis," as he mockingly called them) and other ethnic groups, comments that seem ironically out of keeping with the persona of his poems who frequently exhibits so much love and joy. Yet sometimes in his journals he chastises himself for these feelings and acknowledges an evil streak within that is a part of his being. "What is the 'problem of evil,'," he wrote in March 1946, "except a failure to recognize *in myself* the Hawk the Spider and the Cat—those opposites of the Thrush, the Butterfly, and the Mouse, whom in myself, i not merely recognize but cherish with a jealous love?" He goes on to admire Thoreau's declaration "I never met a man worse than myself." Once in a while a poem will reveal that he perceives the many selves that jostle within his own psyche.

III

...He is more than remembered. The poetry of E. E. Cummings has made a lasting impact upon twentieth-century literature. For one thing he taught his ever-increasing audience how to read him. To date four editions of his *Complete Poems*, each with an expanded number of items, have been published, and many of his earlier volumes have been reissued. His poems continue to appear in anthologies, particularly those for literary study in college courses. The persona that the poems project has a special appeal for young, sensitive readers who are aware of the overwhelming forces, social and political, that surround them and whose emotions surge as they grope for ways to adjust to their world. Cummings' self-characterization as "i," the "nonhero," expresses for them their joy in life, their conflicts of desire, their push against authority, and their desire to grow.

For the poets who followed him Cummings' creative endeavors constituted an important example. As some have testified, he represented a predecessor whose play with language and form had loosened up poetry. Louis Zukofsky was simply grateful that Cummings had abolished the convention of beginning each line of poetry with a capital letter. For Theodore Weiss, Cummings "renewed our language, tickled it wide awake, to its surprise, in its sleepiest corners, mainly its adverbs, prepositions, articles, and adjectives. These words—mostly regarded as lowly and anonymous menials—in the dancing democracy of his discourse kicked up their heels and proved themselves lovely shining Cinderellas.... His work encouraged me to a larger freedom and at the same time to an appreciation for the look of a poem, its comely shape, upon the page...He showed me how...to convert writing's normal temporality to the spatial." Robert Creeley has said that *The Enormous Room* "probably was the work that had the most impact upon me." But for him Cummings' influence as a poet was more subtle and pervasive: "Cummings' authority has so permeated the conditions of poetry in this country for the so-called modern poets of my generation that it is very hard to say, 'Here is particularly what he did or here particularly is how I related to him.' Yet it is just impossible for me to imagine a poetry of my tune without this poet as the context, as one of the determining fact ors of that context which literally led me to it or even made it possible."

In addition Cummings showed the way in which he could choose ordinary scenes and experiences and make them become little myths of twentieth-century life whether they were the childhood activities of Cambridge, the street happenings of New York, or encounters with the features of rural life in New Hampshire.

As for his love poems and his treatments of natural phenomena, he was continuing the Romantic tradition in a time when the harsh realities of urbanization and the pervasive intrusions of technology were bruising the sensibilities of modern human beings and blunting the awareness of the essential self and the consciousness of individual feelings.

But the exploration of the possibilities of linguistic expression was his special contribution. His legacy to later writers was the spectacle of his pushing language to its extremes. Joyce, Eliot, Pound, Dos Passos, and Faulkner were the major innovators of his time, but Cummings did not imitate them. He responded in spirit to their work but he made his own innovations, inspired especially by the modern movements in the visual arts: Impressionism and Postimpressionism, Cubism and Futurism, Dada and Surrealism. His poetic practice shows continuing experiment and growth over a stretch of forty-five years so that like Eliot and Yeats he was a poet of two generations. Not all of his attempts were aesthetic successes, nor was he critically stringent in what he allowed himself to publish. But an extensive selection of his poetic output would yield a huge body of permanently valuable work.

Cummings' creativity was so inexhaustible that he reached into other genres as well. As in his poetry these excursions had mixed results. Yet even though *Him* was dramatically disappointing, [No Title] was only a shaggy-dog joke, anci *Tom* was never given its chance to be part of the American ballet repertoire, still *The Enormous Room* and *Eimi* are lasting monuments, each of them unique.

This is not the place for an assessment of his extensive work in drawing and painting. Nevertheless we should be aware that Cummings' creative personality expressed itself continually in more than just the literary mode of art. His success in the visual arts was limited and he never became recognized as an important practitioner. But we should not forget that these extra talents gave him a perspective on language that allowed him to present his poems in new ways.

This innovative direction is the principal reason E. E. Cummings will always be remembered as one of the leading figures of the literary revolution of the early twentieth century and that his work will never disappear from the anthologies of American literature. For individual readers, moreover, his place is secure as a "Household Poet" in the way that the chief nineteenth-century poets of America were cherished. For these readers his poems will continue to amuse, awaken, instruct, inspire and, at times, to provide the deep satisfaction that attends aesthetic experience.

Source: Richard S. Kennedy, "Aches and Pains and Daffodils," in *E.E. Cummings Revisited*, Twayne, 1994, pp. 125–28, 137–40.

Iaian Landkes

In the following excerpt, Landles faults earlier critics for often seeing Cummings's early poems as somehow unformed or immature in comparison with his later work, rather than purposefully different.

The aim of this investigation has been to show how Cummings has been effectively marginalized due to the misreading of his work by critics whose interpretations have been closed ones. The critics have, as we have seen, "read" Cummings through later interpretations that the critics themselves have arrived at They have taken little, if no account of either the textual evidence or the contextual situation of Cummings' life—both personal and artistic. Thus, instead of being read in the open and expansive ways that many poets of his generation have been, the vast majority of analyses of Cummings' work are restricted. New attics have thus seen little in the field of Cummingsian criticism left to do—a direct result of misreading since critics have generally read the work in the same way and either implicitly or explicitly supported one another's readings. Hence, Cummings' work has become "fixed"—the case, effectively closed. What needs to be said has been said.

This investigation has set out to read Cummings' early work deliberately seeking the "cracks" in the so-called "established" critical position of Cummings. It has attempted to show how Cummings in the 1920s was not the finished product that most critics have misread

him to be. Thus, this investigation has shown Cummings exploring, searching, experimenting both technically and philosophically. By doing so a different Cummings emerges. Instead of the romantic individualist, we find a poet who has very clear social interests. This poet emerges in the filth and outrage that was La Ferté-Macé. His bonding with his fellow prisoners becomes a social stance that Cummings was to lose in his later years. However, for the purposes of this investigation, the early Cummings was socially orientated and aware.

For the poet accused of celebrating sex, the demimonde, vulgarity of all types and low-life figures and scenarios, we read a poet disgusted at this subject matter—especially sex, which he seemed to view with repulsion mixed with a slight tone of moral repugnance, so much so that it begs a question: what actually formed Cummings' opinion about sex? Thus, we have seen in this investigation how Cummings' opinions developed because of a highly unsatisfactory sex life, dominated by the squalid world of prostitutes; tainted by the amoral affair with Elaine Orr which eventually turned into a bizarre *ménage-à-trios*; even this affair, which became a marriage, was sullied by Elaine's unfaithfulness and lead Cummings almost to a nervous breakdown.

Forever stamped on Cummings' work will be the critic's traditional opinion that Cummings was a positive, childish, *joie de vivre* type poet, yet the readings presented here show a negative, scathing, satirical Cummings who seems to be lashing out at all concerned. It is not surprising that Cummings became so negative. We have seen how his treatment in La Ferté-Macé formed his opinions about governments and controlling institutions; add to this the acrimonious divorce and the fight for custody over Nancy, Cummings' child with Elaine, and one can understandably see Cummings' negativity emerge.

Yet, the Cummings who is the lyrical love poet also appears in this investigation. This investigation reveals the split in *is 5*—a split that occurred during the writing of the collection in 1925: the year Cummings met Anne Barton. Anne turned Cummings' life around—he recovered from his near-breakdown, he began to work again in a positive light, and he accepted the divorce and the loss of Nancy. The love Cummings had for Anne is seen in every one of the love poems in *is 5*. Also his transcendent vision—

which the critics had tried so hard in vain to find in the early work—begins to emerge if only at a primitive level. Sex is now celebrated and accorded a place in Cummings' view about love and gradually the parts which would make up Cummings philosophical vision begin to form.

Indeed, the main focus on sex, the female, art, and the "I", coalesced in Cummings' first play, *Him*. This play becomes a site of debate for Cummings as he tries to work out his artistic vision, and one sees the realisation that the selfish "i" and tough guy Cummings is dropped in light of his discovery of the sensitive, feminine side of Cummings—enacted in this play by the evolution (forty years before Cixous) of *écriture féminine*. Cummings realises, through his love for Anne, that to achieve transcendence he has to give/share—something Him in the play can't do. Cummings acknowledged this thirty years later during his *six nonlectures*

> But supposing Him to exemplify that mythical entity "the artist,"we should go hugely astray in assuming that art was the only selftranscendence. Art is a mystery, all mysteries have their source in a mystery-of-mysteries who is love: and if lovers may reach eternity directly through love herself, their mystery remains essentially that of the loving artist whose way must lie through his art, and of the loving worshipper whose aim is oneness with his god.

This is Cummings' final journey—the realisation that art, and the artists' selfish love for art, is not the only way to transcendence—it is a mixture of these things. 0) This philosophy was to be honed in the twenty-seven years between *Him* and *i: six nonlectures* but this investigation makes plain that Cummings at this point in his life had not fully attained such a philosophy.

The deliberate targeting of only using Cummings' work in the 1920s is a reaction to the critics misreading. Since the contention of this investigation has been to show that critics misread the work because they had established Cummings' artistic, and personal, vision via the later work, and then read those conclusions back into the earlier work and attempted to make the facts "fit." This becomes a misreading since, although they reach insightful conclusions, their working methodologies did not help them each those conclusions.

Rather, they made insightful "leaps" that had little to do with their investigations—ignoring contextual evidence is another aspect of their misreading, since often they would, as we have seen, presume some fact or totally ignore it if it didn't "fit." Thus, to re-read in more open and expansive ways, this investigation has had to go back to the source of the original misreading and review the evidence once more—hence, the 1920s. It was with this period that the critics have taken the most liberties since, as we have seen, Cummings began his artistic and personal journey during *is 5* and *Him*.

What, then, is the point of this investigation other than call into question critical misreading? In short, this investigation calls for a revaluing of Cummings in the light of new and developing critical theories. For too long now, Cummings has languished in the "minor" status of modernist poetry—that is, a poet deemed not that worthy of analysis. Everyone seems to have heard of Cummings (could the same be said of Pound, for example?); his poetry books and *The Enormous Room* have been in print since they were first published; Cummings was praised by all the major figures of the 1920s and 1930s—among them: Eliot, Pound, Williams, Hemingway, Fitgereld, Stein, Moore, Barnes, and Crane. The fact that at least half of the critics were virulently opposed to Cummings, itself is an indicator that something special was going on in the work. He was an accomplished painter, essay writer, playwright, novelist, travel writer, as well as a poet. His poems challenge traditional modes of thinking by using letters and words as visual icons in their own right to aid (obscure?) meaning and communication. Punctuation takes on new functions, grammar bent and distorted, even the poems on the page look completely different to the "norm." Perhaps the meta-language was not in place to aid Cummingsian criticism, yet now is precisely the time to review Cummings' work, for, as this investigation has shown, certain theories of post-structuralism can be helpful in deciphering his work—a meta-language of sorts which is new to Cummings at least. To bring Cummings back into the mainstream is almost an evangelical task—but it should not be shied away from. Cummings is a great poet; he is worth looking at; the field of Cummings is not closed, and there is still so much to learn. This then, is the first step in the case for Cummings.

Source: Iain Landles, "Conclusion: Taken Thy Last Applause," in *The Case for Cummings: A Reaction to the Critical Misreading of E.E. Cummings*, VDM Verlag, 2008, pp. 342–47.

SOURCES

Cheever, Susan, "The Prince of Patchin Place," in *Vanity Fair*, March 2014, http://www.vanityfair.com/culture/2014/02/e-e-cummings-susan-cheever-biography (accessed July 17, 2016).

Collins, Billy, "Is That a Poem? The Case for E.E. Cummings," in *Slate*, April 20, 2005, http://www.slate.com/articles/arts/culturebox/2005/04/is_that_a_poem.html (accessed July 17, 2016).

Cummings, E. E., "a total stranger one black day," in *E. E. Cummings: Selected Poems*, Liveright, 1994, p. 165.

——, "e e cummings Tries to Answer the Question "Who Am I?" in This Delightful Lecture," in *New Republic*, November 2, 1953, https://newrepublic.com/article/119831/ee-cummings-lectures-about-his-parents-and-poetry (accessed July 17, 2016).

Cureton, Richard D., "E.E. Cummings: A Study of the Poetic Use of Deviant Morphology," in *Poetics Today*, Vol. 1, Nos. 1–2, 1979, pp. 213–44.

Kennedy, Richard S., Introduction to *E. E. Cummings: Selected Poems*, Liveright, 1994, pp. xv–xvii.

Kirsch, Adam, "The Rebellion of E.E. Cummings," in *Harvard Magazine*, March–April 2005, http://harvardmagazine.com/2005/03/the-rebellion-of-ee-cumm.html (accessed July 17, 2016).

Muldoon, Paul, "Capital Case: The Poetry of E. E. Cummings," in *New Yorker*, March 3, 2014, http://www.newyorker.com/magazine/2014/03/03/capital-case (accessed July 17, 2016).

Pagnini, Marcello, "The Case of Cummings," in *Poetics Today*, translated by Keir Elam, Vol. 6, No. 3. 1985, pp. 357–73.

Popova, Maria, "Enormous Smallness: The Sweet Illustrated Story of E. E. Cummings and His Creative Bravery," in *Brainpickings*, https://www.brainpickings.org/2015/03/30/enormous-smallness-e-e-cummings-matthew-burgess/ (accessed July 17, 2016).

Pound, Ezra, *Make It New: Essays*, Faber & Faber, 1934.

Simon, John, "The Theatre of E. E. Cummings," in *New Criterion*, April 2013, http://www.newcriterion.com/articles.cfm/The-theatre-of-E–E–Cummings-7619 (accessed July 17, 2016).

"Unravelling a Life," in *Economist*, February 22, 2014, http://www.economist.com/news/books-and-arts/21596912-tricky-poet-becomes-easier-understand-unravelling-life (accessed July 17, 2016).

FURTHER READING

Burgess, Matthew, *Enormous Smallness: A Story of E. E. Cummings*, illustrated by Kris Di Giacomo, Enchanted Lion Books, 2015.

Enormous Smallness is a wonderfully illustrated nonfiction picture book about the life and work of Cummings that carries insight for adult and youth readers alike. Given Cummings's own love of art and play, it is appropriate that illustrations are used to complement a discussion of what led him to play with language and how he saw the world through a unique lens of music, spirituality, and joy.

Cheever, Susan, *E. E. Cummings: A Life*, Pantheon, 2014.
The daughter of the famous American writer John Cheever, Susan Cheever spent many hours around Cummings, which gives this exploration of his life and influences a more intimate and detailed feel compared with more standard biographies.

James, William, *The Principles of Psychology*, Henry Holt, 1890.
Cummings, like many writers of his generation, was intrigued by James's ideas, especially as they related to the influence of the unconscious on an individual's sense of the world and of reality. This book is foundational reading for anyone wanting to understand this connection more completely.

Sawyer-Laucanno, Christopher, *E. E. Cummings: A Biography*, Metheun, 2006.
A well-written, relatively standard look at the life and work of one of the first poets of the twentieth century to successfully unite poetic tradition with avant-garde experimentation and play. Sawyer-Laucanno takes full advantage of what was, to this point, an unprecedented level of access to Cummings's personal papers to create a colorful picture of the man and the poet.

SUGGESTED SEARCH TERMS

E. E. Cummings

"a total stranger one black day"

E. E. Cummings AND self-identity

E. E. Cummings AND modernism

E. E. Cummings AND psychology

American poetry AND free verse

American modernist poetry

American poetry AND identity

American poetry AND self-analysis

American poetry AND avant-garde

To the Lady

MITSUYE YAMADA

1976

In Mitsuye Yamada's poem "To the Lady," first published in *Camp Notes and Other Poems* in 1976, a woman in San Francisco has asked the speaker why Japanese Americans did not protest when the government interned them during World War II. The speaker responds sarcastically with a list of subversive, violent, and outrageous actions she ostensibly should have taken against the government instead of allowing herself to be interned. The speaker then suggests that, if only she had gone to these extremes, the lady would have found the courage to join her in protest. But neither the speaker nor the lady fought back. Written years after Yamada herself was interned in the Minidoka Relocation Center in Idaho as a young woman, "To the Lady" and the other poems of *Camp Notes* illustrate the lasting emotional trauma of internment and the continued misrepresentation and misunderstanding of the plight of innocent Japanese Americans forced to sacrifice nearly everything in the name of loyalty during World War II.

AUTHOR BIOGRAPHY

Yamada was born on July 5, 1923, in Fukuoka, Japan. In 1926 her family moved to Seattle, Washington, where her father founded a poetry society and worked as an interpreter for the US Immigration and Naturalization Service. At the

The speaker and her family were sent to an internment camp during World War II *(©Everett Historical /*
Shutterstock.com)

age of eleven Yamada returned to Japan to live with her grandparents for a year. There she experienced the same isolation from her peers as an American that she felt in America as a Japanese immigrant. She returned to Seattle, where she attended Cleveland High School, participating in the debate club and school magazine. Following the Japanese attack on Pearl Harbor on December 7, 1941, Yamada's father was arrested on the false suspicion that he was a spy and taken to prison.

Nineteen-year-old Yamada, her three brothers, and their mother were forced to leave their home and move into the Minidoka Relocation Center in Hunt, Idaho. After eighteen months of internment, by renouncing her loyalty to the Japanese emperor, Yamada was allowed to leave the camp in order to pursue her education. She enrolled in the University of Cincinnati and went on to earn her bachelor's degree from New York University in 1947 and a master's degree from the University of Chicago in 1953. In 1950 she married Yoshikazu Yamada; the couple had

four children. In 1955, Yamada became a naturalized US citizen.

Her collection *Camp Notes and Other Poems*, in which "To the Lady" appears, was first published in 1976. The poems, written during and after her internment, center on racism against Japanese Americans and the ordeal of relocation and confinement inside the camps. In 1988 she published a second collection, titled *Desert Run: Poems and Stories*. Both works were combined in the 1992 collection *Camp Notes and Other Poems*.

In addition to her poetry, Yamada is the author of "Teaching Human Rights Awareness through Poetry," an essay published in a volume of *The Literary Encyclopedia* in 1999, and a coauthor of *Three Asian American Writers Speak Out on Feminism*, published in 2003. Deeply concerned with the visibility of Asian American women artists, she cofounded the Multicultural Women Writers of Orange County and coedited an anthology of their work, *Sowing Ti Leaves: Writings by Multicultural Women*, in 1990.

Yamada serves on the boards of *MELUS* and Amnesty International. Additionally, she is a member of the International Women's Writing Guild, the Pacific Asian American Center, the American Civil Liberties Union, and the National Women's Political Caucus. Alongside Nellie Wong, Yamada is the subject of *Mitsuye and Nellie: Asian American Poets*, a Women Make Movies documentary produced in 1981. Yamada has received the Vista Award from the Woman's Building of Los Angeles in 1982, a writer's residency from Yaddo in 1984, and an honorary doctorate of humane letters from Simmons College in 2009. She has taught English at Cypress College and Fullerton College, both in California. As of the early 2010s, Yamada was living in Orange County, California, with her husband.

POEM TEXT

The one in San Francisco who asked
Why did the Japanese Americans let
the government put them in
those camps without protest?

Come to think of it I   5

should've run off to Canada
should've hijacked a plane to Algeria
should've pulled myself up from my
bra straps
and kicked'm in the groin   10
should've bombed a bank
should've tried self-immolation
should've holed myself up in a
woodframe house
and let you watch me   15
burn up on the six o'clock news
should've run howling down the street
naked and assaulted you at breakfast
by AP wirephoto
should've screamed bloody murderd   20
like Kitty Genovese

Then
YOU would've

come to my aid in shining armor
laid yourself across the railroad track   25
marched on Washington
tattooed a Star of David on your arm
written six million enraged
letters to Congress

But we didn't draw the line   30
anywhere
law and order Executive Order 9066
social order moral order internal order

YOU let'm
I let'm   35
All are punished.

POEM SUMMARY

The text used for this summary is from *Camp Notes and Other Writings*, Rutgers University Press, 1998.

"To the Lady" begins with an address to the lady in San Francisco who asked the speaker why Japanese Americans allowed the US government to detain them in internment camps during World War II. Why, the lady asked, did they not protest? The speaker answers sarcastically that, now that she is thinking of it, she indeed should have protested somehow. She should have fled to Canada. She should have hijacked a plane and flown to Algeria. She should have pulled herself up by her bra straps and fought dirty against the powers that had her interned. She should have bombed a bank. She should have set herself on fire. She should have locked herself inside a house, burned it down, and dominated the six o'clock news. She should have run naked and shouting down the street, to assault the lady at breakfast with Associated Press (AP) photos of her detainment. She should have screamed out for help like Kitty Genovese, who was infamously murdered while numerous neighbors who partially saw or overheard the attack failed to come to her aid.

If only the speaker had done these things, then the lady surely would have come to her rescue like a knight in shining armor. The lady would have laid herself on the railroad tracks in a spectacular protest. She would have marched on Washington, DC. She would have gotten the Star of David tattooed on her arm in solidarity. She would have written six million letters to Congress explaining her rage at the government's treatment of the Japanese Americans.

But neither the speaker nor the lady drew the line at any point in the shameful proceedings. Instead they each followed the law in the form of Executive Order 9066, which called for the removal of Japanese Americans from their homes on the West Coast and their subsequent internment in the camps. They followed the social, moral, and internal order of the day instead of breaking the law. The lady let the government do it. The speaker let the government do it. And everyone suffers punishment as a result.

MEDIA ADAPTATIONS

Yamada is the subject of the documentary film *Mitsuye and Nellie: Asian American Poets*, directed by Allie Light and Irving Saraf and produced by Light-Saraf Films in 1981, with a running time of fifty-eight minutes.

THEMES

Ignorance

The ignorance of the lady is exemplified in the ignorance of her question. She asks why the Japanese Americans did nothing to stop the government from putting them in camps but fails to see her own guilt in the matter through inaction. The lady asks the speaker her question from a position of privilege: she was not interned during the war after enduring discrimination and prejudice; she was not forced to give up her job, car, home, and personal possessions in order to prove her loyalty; and she did not endure these hardships only to face the ongoing misinterpretation and silencing of her experience once she was free. Yet, because of her privilege, she feels she has the right to ask the speaker such an ignorant question—one that perhaps implies that Japanese Americans were partly at fault for failing to stand up for themselves.

The speaker, rightly offended, frames her response in sarcasm. Yes, if only she had made a gigantic fuss, the speaker says, then surely the lady would have come to the Japanese Americans' rescue. In this way the speaker implies that the lady could have protested herself instead of letting the government take Japanese Americans away from their homes. The lady has effectively blamed the Japanese Americans for their own incarceration without seeing how she and other non-Japanese Americans could be found at fault just as easily. The blame lies not with one part of the population or the other, but with everyone. Just because the lady was not personally involved in internment does not excuse her from blame. The imprisonment of innocent civilians without trial is a dark mark in American history as a human rights violation of inexcusable and enormous proportions, a lesson to all citizens against the kind of ignorance that draws divisions based on arbitrary differences and not on the reality of shared human existence. The lady's ignorance renders her at once baffled by interment, yet eager to blame its innocent victims.

Obedience

The lady wonders why Japanese Americans were obedient to the government's mandate that they be interned in camps during World War II. Her question perhaps implies that, if she were told to give up her life and enter prison, she would have protested. The speaker sarcastically agrees, pretending the thought of protesting her internment had simply never crossed her mind. Now that she considers it, she can think of many actions to have taken against Executive Order 9066. The speaker plays off the lady's own misconception of the stereotypically obedient Japanese person, mocking her ignorance by acting as if the lady has inspired a revelation in her by suggesting protest. The truth is that of course the Japanese Americans protested, of course they dreamt up fantastic scenarios in which they freed their people or scandalized the authorities with brazen defiance, and of course they resented their imprisonment without trial.

However, the same fears that kept them obedient kept non-Japanese Americans like the lady obedient: wartime panic and paranoia. Japanese Americans followed the rules to prove they were not the enemy the government claimed they were. They followed the rules because the future was frightening and uncertain and they saw no other way out. They followed the rules because they were not the enemy but normal, law-abiding citizens of the United States with a (misplaced) trust in the government's interest in protecting them from harm. The lady may believe that she would have acted differently, but having never been placed in such a scenario, she has no way of knowing how she would respond. The government has not betrayed her the way it betrayed the

TOPICS FOR FURTHER STUDY

- Read Yoshiko Uchida's *The Invisible Thread* (1987), a memoir for young adults. What choices were given to Uchida during her internment? What did she have control over and what was out of her hands? Take notes as you read, marking pages in which Uchida has agency over her decisions versus when she is forced to obey commands or accept what is given to her. Write a few paragraphs in preparation for a class discussion in which you compare the realities of camp life to the assumption of the lady in "To the Lady" that Japanese Americans simply allowed internment to happen.

- Watch actor and activist George Takei's 2014 TED Talk on his family's internment during World War II, titled "Why I Love a Country That Once Betrayed Me" and available online. In an essay, summarize Takei's experience and the ways in which internment shaped his identity. Compare the tone of Takei's TED Talk to that of "To the Lady." How do Takei's and Yamada's tones toward their subject matter differ? How are their tones each suited toward their subject and audience? What effect does an author's tone have on an audience's reaction to the work?

- Create a blog about the internment of Japanese Americans in the United States during World War II. Your blog may focus on one of the following topics: the legislative history of internment; the daily lives of the interned citizens; the literature, art, and music produced by interned Japanese Americans; the reactions of non-Japanese Americans to internment and the propaganda to which they were exposed; or the history of redress and apology by the US government since the end of internment. Explore your chosen topic in a minimum of five blog posts and include relevant photographs, maps, and links to reputable sources. When you have completed your assignment, visit one blog of your classmates' on each of the other subjects, and leave a thoughtful comment on the post you found most informative for each topic. Free blogspace is available at Blogger.

- Read a different poem collected in *Camp Notes*. What aspect of internment does this poem illustrate? What are the main themes of the poem? Is there anything unique or unusual about the poem's structure or style? Answer these questions in an essay in which you compare and contrast the representation of internment in the poem you chose and "To the Lady."

Japanese Americans, but through their internment it failed the nation as a whole.

Social Protest

In "To the Lady," Yamada lists numerous forms of social protest as sarcastic alternatives to accepting Japanese American internment, for both the poet and the lady being addressed. The speaker proposes self-immolation, a tactic used in the past especially by Buddhist monks, in which protesters burned themselves alive. She suggests bombing a bank or hijacking a plane, forms of violent terrorism. She suggests a peaceful letter-writing campaign, as commonly used by grassroots political organizations to make their voices heard by elected officials. Tying oneself to the train tracks would be an act of self-sacrifice, while getting a tattoo of the Star of David would show solidarity with the Allied cause in World War II, specifically the saving of the Jews. Running away to Canada has long been a common response to political unrest and injustice in America. Solving internment through running naked through the streets or physically assaulting the authorities

The speaker comes up with drastic things she might have done to protest the internment, like hijacking a plane *(©manzrussali | Shutterstock.com)*

would only lead to a longer imprisonment. Also unlikely to help is the suggestion that non-Japanese Americans could have ridden to the rescue like a white knight toward a captured princess.

The speaker dismisses these forms of protest because the question itself is ill informed and insulting to the intelligence of those who were interned. The speaker emphasizes this through the fact that there are two lists of possible protests—the first for the speaker, the second for the lady. To be truly effective, the speaker suggests, any protest on the part of Japanese Americans would have needed to be accompanied by the support of non-Japanese Americans. Instead, non-Japanese Americans let their fellow citizens be imprisoned, following the rules of the day as obediently as the lady implicitly accuses the Japanese Americans of acting. As a result, all Americans share the guilt for not standing up for their own. No matter what form social protest takes, it is always more effective with more participants involved in the fight.

STYLE

Hyperbole

Hyperbole is a device through which a writer or speaker uses exaggerated language and imagery in order to emphasize her point. "To the Lady" features two series of hyperbolic imagery. The first is a list of the extreme measures the speaker should have gone to in order to avoid her internment as a Japanese American. The second is a list of what heroic and selfless actions the speaker's protest would have inspired in the lady. The two lists are equally unlikely. The speaker, who is—despite being a Japanese American and thus labeled an enemy of the state during wartime—an average citizen, is not likely to blow up a bank in protest. Likewise, the lady would not have tied herself to railroad tracks in solidarity with Japanese Americans, especially since she probably was not acquainted with any. The hyperbole adds dark humor to the poem: the actions listed are humorous in their extremity, but the truth behind the exaggerations is sobering. Because of the obedience of the wartime population, no such grand protest occurred, and the government acted out a truly hyperbolic atrocity in the veritable destruction of the lives of over one hundred thousand innocent, loyal American citizens.

Tone

The tone of a poem is what reflects the poet's feelings toward her subject matter, which can be read in the syntax, structure, and mood of the work. In "To the Lady," the speaker's sarcasm toward the lady's question reveals Yamada's tone of anger and sadness. The use of all capitals in the speaker's "YOU" serves to accuse not only the lady but also the reader of the same complacency. Thus every party involved in the poem—the speaker/Yamada, the lady, and the reader—are blamed for what happened to Japanese Americans during World War II, and all share the punishment of the final line. Through her sarcasm Yamada suggests that the lady's question is not only offensive and tone-deaf but ridiculous, and she illustrates just how ridiculous she finds it through the list of outrageous responses to internment and outrageous acts of sympathetic protest that the lady would have performed to help her endangered fellow citizens. The anger and sadness Yamada feels toward the ongoing misunderstanding of the cost of internment not only to Japanese Americans but to all American people is portrayed through her implication, through the capitalized "YOU," that the reader shares in the same complicity as the lady.

HISTORICAL CONTEXT

Executive Order 9066

On February 19, 1942, President Franklin D. Roosevelt signed into law Executive Order 9066. In response to the Japanese attack on Pearl Harbor on December 7, 1941, and in conjunction with the growing resentment and suspicion of the public toward Japanese immigrants and Japanese Americans, the order allowed the removal of people from a military area as deemed necessary by the US government. The area in question was soon defined as the West Coast and the people in question the Japanese Americans who lived there.

Immediately after the Pearl Harbor attack, over one thousand men of Japanese ancestry were arrested and held, many without trial, on suspicion of criminal activity such as spying. Yamada's father was imprisoned during this initial sweep of community leaders and prominent businessmen. On March 1, 1942, Public Proclamation No. 1 placed a curfew on Japanese Americans and began the process of their removal: first to assembly centers and then to the internment camps. Failure to comply with Executive Order 9066 resulted in imprisonment and fines.

Over one hundred thousand people of Japanese ancestry, two-thirds of whom were American citizens, were forced to take only what possessions they could carry and submit to relocation. Those interned in the camps could escape only through military service, college enrollment (like Yamada), or sponsored work. Those who could not leave lived in internment for up to four years. Conditions were poor, but the government censored any photographs of the camps showing evidence of low morale, dissension, and prison-like conditions. Additionally, the government claimed that internment served to protect the Japanese Americans from racist attacks following Pearl Harbor, when internment was motivated by racist fear and prejudice.

On December 18, 1944, after the Supreme Court ruled in favor of Mitsuye Endo's charge that she could not be detained against her will in the case *Ex parte Endo*, Public Proclamation No. 21 announced that internees could return home beginning on January 2, 1945. Japanese Americans arrived home to find their houses destroyed, belongings looted, and anti-Japanese sentiment still high among the general public. Though initially given only twenty-five dollars and a train ticket home by the government, in 1988, following years of agitation by human rights activists, survivors of internment received $20,000 each and an official apology from the US government.

Kitty Genovese

On March 13, 1964, Kitty Genovese, a twenty-eight-year-old bar manager, was stabbed to death outside of her apartment building in New York City by Winston Mosley. Her murder became infamous after the *New York Times*

COMPARE
&
CONTRAST

- **1946:** Japanese Americans released from the internment camps return home to find their houses vandalized, their personal property stolen or destroyed, and their former jobs reassigned.

  1976: Japanese immigrants and their Japanese American children begin to feel the long-lasting and potentially devastating health effects from their time in internment. They have been given no government education on potential risks to their physical and mental health or encouragement to seek out medical and psychological care to ameliorate the damage of their imprisonment.

  Today: The long-term negative health effects of internment have become gravely apparent, as former internees have exhibited greater chances of developing heart disease; lasting psychological trauma, including flashbacks to their internment experience; and a higher risk of premature death.

- **1946:** Interned Japanese Americans are released from the camps into a national atmosphere still hostile toward them. Given twenty-five dollars and a train ticket home, they are left to their own devices in rebuilding their shattered lives.

  1976: The Japanese American Citizens League begins to agitate in the late 1970s for redress payments to those interned and imprisoned during World War II. They request an apology from Congress, an educational trust fund, and restitution payments of $25,000 per victim for damages caused to their lives as a result of the wrongful imprisonment. By 1980, the Commission on Wartime Relocation and Internment of Civilians is formed to address the concerns of Japanese Americans.

  Today: The Civil Liberties Act of 1988 ordered that $20,000 be paid to every survivor of internment. The ten internment camps were named national historical landmarks in 2001, to preserve the memory of the United States' failure to protect its own citizens and to honor the Japanese Americans whose lives were uprooted and permanently altered by that failure.

- **1946:** On March 20, Tule Lake is the last of the ten internment camps to close.

  1976: Though President Franklin D. Roosevelt unofficially rescinded Executive Order 9066 in December 1944, the order is not officially rescinded until 1976 by President Gerald Ford, who calls the internment a mistake and a national embarrassment.

  Today: Fred Komatsu, who was arrested for defying Executive Order 9066, is awarded the Presidential Medal of Honor. In California in 2011, January 30 is declared Fred Komatsu Day of Civil Liberties and the Constitution in honor of his protest. In 2015, the state of Virginia passes legislation to officially recognize Fred Komatsu Day as well.

---

published an article by Martin Gansberg under the headline "Thirty-Eight Who Saw Murder Didn't Call the Police," alleging that Genovese died as a result of her neighbors' failing to act after she called out for help. Gansberg wrote: "For more than half an hour 38 respectable, law-abiding citizens in Queens watched a killer stalk and stab a woman in three separate attacks in Kew Gardens." Though the truth of the allegations of inaction against Genovese's neighbors has since been questioned and in many cases debunked, the murder became a symbol of communal apathy in the United States. The term *Genovese syndrome*, or *bystander effect*, was coined following Genovese's murder, describing the lack of responsibility felt by individual witnesses in proportion to the number of witnesses present.

The speaker also imagines bombing a bank to draw attention to her peril (©*Fer Gregory | Shutterstock.com*)

CRITICAL OVERVIEW

Camp Notes and Other Poems received widespread critical acclaim and established Yamada as an important new voice in American poetry. Di Gan Blackburn writes in *Asian-American Poets: A Bio-bibliographical Critical Sourcebook*: "Yamada's poetry gives voice to her experience as a woman and as a Japanese American. . . . Ethnicity, gender, language, identity, and community—all issues of considerable personal relevance—provide the focus for much of her writing."

In Anita Haya Patterson's "Resistance to Images of the Internment: Mitsuye Yamada's *Camp Notes*," she praises the complexity of Yamada's depiction of Japanese American obedience and obligation during the internment: "Yamada shows us that acts of obedience on the part of the internees were neither voluntarily consented to nor precisely involuntary . . . because they were simply performed."

Kim Whitehead, in *The Feminist Poetry Movement*, examines the way in which Yamada

subverts dominant male narratives of war with her language and experimental poetic forms: "This was the only way, Yamada began to understand, that women were going to bring their lives into view and confront the oppressive literary establishment that had previously stolen *their* words."

In "'You Should Not Be Invisible': An Interview with Mitsuye Yamada," Caroline Kyungah Hong, Shirley Geok-Lin Lim, and Sharon Tang-Quan describe the unique perspective Yamada brought to American poetry when she first appeared on the literary scene: "Though much of Yamada's work predates the current 'transnational turn' in American and Asian American studies, she exemplifies a critical global awareness that has long been present in Asian American culture and politics."

Susan Schweik, in her essay "A Needle with Mama's Voice: Mitsuye Yamada's *Camp Notes* and the American Canon of War Poetry," admires the way in which the poems of *Camp Notes* reflect the disconnect between the heinous truth of Japanese internment and the common cultural depiction of American's victory in World War II as one of good over evil: "Permanently marginal, perpetually in opposition to dominant versions of its events, energized by its interruptions, *Camp Notes* reaches toward the construction of a discourse of discontinuity."

In her book section "Mitsuye Yamada: The Relocation of Identity," Traise Yamamoto finds the locus of all Yamada's work on the subject of internment: "At their most basic level, these poems witness moments of national and personal history, often locating themselves in the space where the two histories collide." Yamada's poetry serves as a powerful and invaluable illustration of the ways in which large-scale national events affect the lives of individual citizens.

CRITICISM

Amy L. Miller

Miller is a graduate of the University of Cincinnati. In the following essay, she examines the relationship between the speaker of Yamada's "To the Lady" and the lady being addressed, as enemies, as women, and as Americans.

In Yamada's "To the Lady," the speaker answers an ignorant white woman's question with sarcastic humor, defying the stereotype of the obedient Japanese American that the woman attempts to force on her. In her list of solutions to the problem of Japanese American obedience, the speaker suggests that the lady would have come to her rescue like a knight in shining armor, cleverly subverting the expectation of a male knight so that the Caucasian lady assumes the dominant, masculine role of rescuer over the weaker, feminine role of meek Asian. This reversal, leading into a series that places blame for internment squarely on the lady and people like her, strikes directly at the heart of the misunderstanding between the two women. Yamada's speaker finds the lady's question foolish and the ease with which she asks such a thing offensive. Speaking from a privileged position as a white American, the lady takes for granted that she was not betrayed by her own government, forced to abandon her freedom, and imprisoned in a desert camp. She is uninformed, assuming that the Japanese Americans did not protest, as well as blind to her own guilt. Instead, the lady implicitly blames the victims of internment for letting it happen, since she presumably believes

> SPEAKING FROM A PRIVILEGED POSITION AS A WHITE AMERICAN, THE LADY TAKES FOR GRANTED THAT SHE WAS NOT BETRAYED BY HER OWN GOVERNMENT, FORCED TO ABANDON HER FREEDOM, AND IMPRISONED IN A DESERT CAMP."

that—in the same situation—she would not have. Faced with the lady's ignorance, the speaker gives her a demonstration of the power of Japanese American protest, revealing the lady's culpability in the internment with devastating wit. The poem's conclusion reaches out to include the lady in the tragedy of the Japanese Americans, suggesting that the speaker and lady are united as Americans in their shared grief for freedom lost.

The speaker has survived internment and World War II but finds herself yet again singled out by the lady in San Francisco. This lady is readily presumed to have been a conscientious adult citizen during World War II, given the nature of the poet's response to her. Armed with the misinformation actively spread by the government to keep citizens from understanding the truth behind the camps, the lady feels justified in asking why the Japanese Americans allowed the camps to happen. This question, as the speaker wryly points out, would be better asked of the lady herself, but, Schweik writes, "the disturbing fact of the concentration camps, and the realities of the Japanese-American population the camps contained, threatened dominant representations of a nation 'all in it together.'" The lady, having never lost faith in her government, cannot comprehend its heinous act of imprisoning innocent civilians. She is aided in this ignorance by propaganda that promised that the Japanese Americans were happy and safe. Though she has come to understand internment as distasteful and wrong, she has not yet made the connection between the obligatory smiles of interned Japanese Americans and the lack of outrage she felt toward internment when the war was on. Instead, she believes that Japanese Americans must have allowed themselves to be imprisoned and

WHAT DO I READ NEXT?

- Jerry Stanley's young-adult volume *I Am an American: A True Story of Japanese Internment* (1994) tells the story of Shi Nomura, a high-school senior who was sent to the Manzanar internment camp during World War II. Using maps and photographs, and with a special focus on the prejudice and racism that led to Executive Order 9066, Stanley paints a vivid portrait of Japanese American internment and its devastating costs.

- Mary Matsuda Gruenewald's *Looking like the Enemy: My Story of Imprisonment in Japanese American Internment Camps* (2005) is the story of the author's internment at the age of sixteen, told from her perspective as an eighty-year-old survivor.

- Yamada's second collection, *Desert Run: Poems and Stories* (1988), continues her exploration of self and nation following her internment during World War II. These stories and poems focus on survival, lingering emotional scars, and the power of breaking silences rather than letting oneself remain unheard and invisible.

- In the young-adult novel *Aleutian Sparrow* (2003), by Karen Hesse, the Japanese invasion of the Aleutian Islands leads to Vera and her family's being rounded up and transported to an Alaskan relocation center. The native Aleut people struggle to survive under harsh conditions, fighting to maintain a sense of their cultural heritage despite their dislocation and effective detainment far from home.

- John Okada's *No-No Boy* (1957) is considered the first Japanese American novel. Ichiro Yamada is ostracized by his community following his imprisonment for answering no on a survey asking if he was loyal to the United States and willing to serve in the nation's army. Yet he cannot bring himself to forgive the country that interned him during World War II. Ignored by the public when it was first published but revived in the 1970s, the novel shatters Japanese American stereotypes and presents a dark portrait of the effects of internment.

- John Yau's *Borrowed Love Poems* (2002) presents surrealist, postmodern poetry in which dark and light humor, ingenious wordplay, and issues of identity mingle to blur the line between reality and fiction.

- In Marilyn Chin's *Rhapsody in Plain Yellow: Poems* (2002), the personal and political spheres collide as Chin mourns the death of her mother and grandmother while tracing the history and meaning of her Chinese American identity as well as the unsolved mysteries of her family's journey across cultures.

- Li-Young Lee's poetry collection *Behind My Eyes* (2008) examines modern immigrant life, the struggles and victories of love, the inevitability of familial joy and obligations, and observations on religion and mundane life. The collection includes a CD of Lee reading his work, giving each word its perfect nuance and moment in the spotlight.

- Julie Otsuka's *The Buddha in the Attic* (2011) tells a story of Japanese immigration to the United States through a group of picture brides, married to husbands they have never met. Though they are unpleasantly surprised by the life and men who await them in America, the women set down roots and grow stronger each year, until Executive Order 9066 abruptly ends their American dreams.

---

demands to know why. She is caught up completely in the national myth of World War II victory of the good over the bad, incapable of recognizing the bad in her own country. Victim blaming allows her to escape the cognitive dissonance such a realization would cause: the

Japanese Americans must have, through some strange impulse, wanted to be interned. Having thought this through on her own, the lady asks a Japanese American for confirmation.

The speaker does not react to the question how the lady might expect. Patterson writes: "The lyric speaker (like the poet herself) is . . . burdened by popular racist attitudes and propagandistic, stereotyped images of Japanese-Americans that impede her efforts to recognize and imagine herself." The question causes an explosion of outrage, sparking a virtuoso protest performance piece in response as the speaker takes back the selfhood the lady attempted to rip from her hands. The lady, who wants to know why Japanese Americans did not protest, finds herself the sudden subject of a protest by a Japanese American. The speaker employs sarcasm, hyperbole, and historical references and—as exemplified in the reversal of the image of the knight in shining armor—demonstrates her knowledge of and mastery over the English language and American popular culture. Attacked by the lady for not fighting back against the system, the speaker fights back against the system that speaks through the lady, a woman who is exactly as misinformed by propaganda as the government could hope. Stripped of her home, her livelihood, her personal property, and years of her life, the speaker flatly refuses to give up her identity. Her sarcastic list of potential protests against the government is a protest itself, in which she strips herself bare of society's image of what she could or should be and dresses herself instead in personal rage.

Tellingly, at the end of the speaker's list of actions she could have taken in order to impress the lady with her protest, the speaker names Kitty Genovese. By referring to the infamous murder of a woman before dozens of witnesses as she cried for help, the speaker suggests that her protests, no matter how violent or spectacular, would have fallen on deaf ears. Blackburn writes: "Believing that the principal survival concern of Asian American women has been to 'redefine oneself' from the misrepresentations of others, Yamada reacts sharply against culturally imposed silence." Yamada's speaker, in an effort to reclaim herself from the lady's attempt to label her as an obedient Japanese American, suggests she bomb a bank in acceptance of the villainous role in which she has been cast, pull

herself up by her bra straps in a feminist play on the concept of roughshod American self-reliance, or self-immolate with the calm composure of a Buddhist monk. Each of these protests reflects an aspect of the speaker's personality, but—by ending the list with the Genovese murder—the speaker makes clear that these acts would have achieved nothing.

But "YOU," the speaker says, could have made a difference. She is careful to note that the lady would have been spurred to action only by the Japanese Americans' protest, ironically protecting the woman's false sense of separation from the events of Japanese American internment by placing the responsibility of protest on those stripped of their rights. Of course, the speaker suggests, it would be irrational to expect the woman to act on her own for the benefit of Japanese Americans. Yamamoto writes: "Yamada employs a tone of heavy sarcasm to highlight the woman's ignorance on two counts: many white Americans do not realize that, in fact, Japanese Americans did protest their incarceration . . . ; second, sixties-style forms of activist protest cannot be retroactively prescribed." The speaker suggests that the lady would have written six million letters and gotten a tattoo of the Star of David, references to the Holocaust that draw the connection between Nazi and American concentration camps, and thus between German citizens and Americans tricked into complacency through wartime fear and propaganda. The speaker's own protest would have been a good start, she teases darkly, but it would have taken heroic white Americans like the lady to truly get the job done. Through her unexpected inclusion of the lady in the protests, the speaker begins to draw together their fates as American citizens exposed to the same climate of fear.

Particularly difficult to comprehend for the lady and others exposed to the propaganda of the time was the double jeopardy in which Japanese Americans were placed following the attack on Pearl Harbor. Patterson writes: "Paradoxically, the same act of internment or exclusion that marked them as enemies to the State also stood as an affirmation of their identity as American citizens." Thus, to prove they were loyal, Japanese Americans were forced to give up the freedom they were guaranteed as citizens. To protest in the paranoid atmosphere following Japan's attack would have been to announce

*The poem concludes that everyone suffers when
no one speaks out against injustice* (©Vladimir Volodin /
Shutterstock.com)

oneself as an enemy. Through their imprisonment, the Japanese Americans proved their loyalty in the national consciousness in a grotesque reversal of all American values. Yet, after all this, the speaker is asked why she did not protest her internment, with the heavy implication that allowing her freedom to be stripped from her was an un-American act.

The speaker responds that the internment of Japanese Americans was itself an un-American act, as is the thought process that leads one race to view another's struggles as separate from its own. The lady asks why the Japanese Americans did not protest as if this is an expected action, yet she did not protest their internment herself. Yamamoto writes: "The structure of these closing lines insists on an understanding of domination, oppression, collusion and implication that goes beyond reductive assignations of who is 'good' and therefore innocent, and who is 'bad' and therefore responsible." The speaker includes

the lady in her struggle in the final lines of the poem by including her in her guilt. If the Japanese Americans let the government take away their rights, then so did non-Japanese Americans through their complacency. It is not solely the Japanese Americans who suffered, but all Americans, who now must doubt their own national myths and peer with skepticism at photographed smiles.

Source: Amy L. Miller, Critical Essay on "To the Lady," in *Poetry for Students*, Gale, Cengage Learning, 2017.

SOURCES

"About the Incarceration," in *Densho Encyclopedia*, http://encyclopedia.densho.org/history/ (accessed August 16, 2016).

Blackburn, Di Gan, "Mitsuye (May) Yamada (1923–)," in *Asian-American Poets: A Bio-bibliographical Critical Sourcebook*, edited by Guiyou Huang, Greenwood Press, pp. 331–37.

Darley, John M., and Bibb Latané, "Bystander Intervention in Emergencies: Diffusion of Responsibility," *Journal of Personality and Social Psychology*, Vol. 8, pp. 377–83, http://www.wadsworth.com/psychology_d/templates/student_resources/0155060678_rathus/ps/ps19.html (accessed August 20, 2016).

"February 19, 1942: Roosevelt Signs Executive Order 9066," History.com, 2010, http://www.history.com/this-day-in-history/roosevelt-signs-executive-order-9066 (accessed August 16, 2016).

Gansberg, Martin, "Thirty-Eight Who Saw Murder Didn't Call the Police," in *New York Times*, March 27, 1964, http://www2.southeastern.edu/Academics/Faculty/scraig/gansberg.html (accessed August 20, 2016).

"Health Impact," in *Children of the Camps*, PBS website, 1999, http://www.pbs.org/childofcamp/history/health.html (accessed August 20, 2016).

Hong, Caroline Kyungah, Shirley Geok-Lin Lim, and Sharon Tang-Quan, "'You Should Not Be Invisible': An Interview with Mitsuye Yamada," in *Contemporary Women's Writing*, Vol. 8, No. 1, 2014, pp. 1–16, http://cww.oxfordjournals.org/content/8/1/1.full?sid=e9f9c39a-5670-4d88-b288-60e45221ef16 (accessed August 16, 2016).

"Mitsuye Yamada," in *Densho Encyclopedia*, http://encyclopedia.densho.org/print/Mitsuye%20Yamada/ (accessed August 16, 2016).

"Mitsuye Yamada," Poetry Foundation website, https://www.poetryfoundation.org/poems-and-poets/poets/detail/mitsuye-yamada (accessed August 16, 2016).

"Mitsuye Yamada," in *Voices from the Gaps*, University of Minnesota website, 2009, https://conservancy.umn.edu/bitstream/handle/11299/166364/Yamada,%20Mit

suye.pdf?sequence = 1&isAllowed = y (accessed August 16, 2016).

Patterson, Anita Haya, "Resistance to Images of the Internment: Mitsuye Yamada's *Camp Notes*," in *MELUS*, Vol. 23, No. 3, Fall 1998.

"Relocation and Incarceration of Japanese Americans during World War II," Calisphere, 2005, https://calisphere.org/exhibitions/essay/8/relocation/ (accessed August 16, 2016).

Schweik, Susan, "A Needle with Mama's Voice: Mitsuye Yamada's *Camp Notes* and the American Canon of War Poetry," in *Arms and the Woman: War, Gender, and Literary Representation*, edited by Helen M. Cooper, Adrienne Auslander Munich, and Susan Merrill Squier, University of North Carolina Press, 1989, pp. 225–43.

Taylor, Ella, "'The Witness' Looks Back at Those Accused of Ignoring a Murder," NPR website, June 2, 2016, http://www.npr.org/2016/06/02/480442769/the-witness-looks-back-at-those-accused-of-ignoring-a-murder (accessed August 20, 2016).

"Timeline," in *Densho Encyclopedia*, http://encyclopedia.densho.org/timeline/ (accessed August 16, 2016).

"Transcript of Executive Order 9066: Resulting in the Relocation of Japanese (1942)," Our Documents, http://www.ourdocuments.gov/doc.php?flash = false&doc = 74&page = transcript (accessed August 16, 2016).

Whitehead, Kim, *The Feminist Poetry Movement*, University Press of Mississippi, 1996, pp. 28, 41–43.

Yamada, Mitsuye, "To the Lady," in *Camp Notes and Other Writings*, Rutgers University Press, 1998, pp. 40–41.

Yamamoto, Traise, *Masking Selves, Making Subjects: Japanese American Women, Identity, and the Body*, University of California Press, 1999, pp. 203–20.

Yoshino, William, and John Tateishi, "The Japanese American Incarceration: The Journey to Redress," Japanese American Citizens League website, https://jacl.org/redress/ (accessed August 16, 2016).

FURTHER READING

Gordon, Linda, and Gary Y. Okihiro, *Impounded: Dorothea Lange and the Censored Images of Japanese American Internment*, photographs by Dorothea Lange, W. W. Norton, 2006.

Hired to photograph interned Japanese Americans under the stipulation that she avoid the watchtowers, armed guards, barbed wire, and protests, Dorothea Lange nevertheless captured images of internment at once too grim and humanizing for the tastes of the American War Relocation Authority, which kept the images from the public. Historians Gordon and Okihiro, providing context and personal anecdotes, collect 119 never-before-seen images of Japanese internment in this volume, along with notations.

Inada, Lawson Fusao, ed., *Only What We Could Carry: The Japanese American Internment Experience*, Heyday Books, 2000.

This anthology brings together newspaper articles, photographs, personal essays, biographies, poetry, short stories, and government documents and propaganda to paint a portrait of internment during World War II and the innocent lives crushed beneath wartime panic, capturing a moment in time in which the American people turned against their own in a fit of racism and fear.

Reeves, Richard, *Infamy: The Shocking Story of the Japanese American Internment in World War II*, Henry Holt, 2015.

Reeves recounts the internment of Japanese Americans from its racist and irrational origins as a toxic idea in Washington, DC, through the legislation that made it possible to detain American citizens without due trial, to the realities of the arrests, evacuation, and camp lives of over one hundred thousand innocent people. He also examines the methods by which Japanese Americans attempted to escape this unjust punishment through litigation and enlistment in the US Army—to fight for the country that had labeled them the enemy.

Yamada, Mitsuye, Merle Woo, and Nellie Wong, *Three Asian American Writers Speak Out on Feminism*, Radical Women Publications, 2003.

Yamada, Woo, and Wong discuss literature, feminism, and the role of Asian American women in both, including expectations of their behavior as members of a model minority versus the reality of their daily lives, the differences between white feminism and that of women of color, and the challenge of making their voices heard in a society disinclined to listen.

SUGGESTED SEARCH TERMS

Mitsuye Yamada

Yamada AND "To the Lady"

Yamada AND Camp Notes

Executive Order 9066

Yamada AND Japanese American poetry

Japanese American internment AND poetry

Japanese American internment AND social protest

Japanese Americans AND World War II

Woodchucks

MAXINE KUMIN

1972

"Woodchucks" is a poem from Maxine Kumin's Pulitzer Prize–winning collection *Up Country: Poems of New England* (1972). At first reading, the poem might seem satirical, exploring the poet's existential crisis at having to exterminate a colony of woodchucks in the garden of her New Hampshire farm. The poem certainly has an inviting comic tone. However, a closer reading reveals it has more serious concerns. Kumin views the extermination of the woodchucks as a symbol for the destruction of the Jews by the Nazis during the Holocaust. Kumin ultimately wants to interrogate how people can summon the inner resources to commit senseless murder and find out what happens to them after they do.

AUTHOR BIOGRAPHY

Kumin (née Winokur) was born in Philadelphia on June 6, 1925. Her father, Peter Winokur, was a pawnbroker. The family was Jewish. They lived near a convent school, and Kumin was enrolled there, but in third grade she was switched to the public schools because her father wanted her to have a secular education. She attended Radcliffe, the women's college at Harvard, during World War II when the college's classes were integrated with the general university because of lack of male enrollment. She met Victor Kumin in the closing days of the war, and

Maxine Kumin (©*Bettmann* / *Getty Images*)

they were married once he was discharged and started working as an engineer in 1946. His career would be spent in Boston. During the next two years, Kumin took a master's degree in literature from Radcliffe and between 1948 and 1953 had three children. Kumin published her first poem in 1953 in the *Christian Science Monitor*.

In 1957, she started attending poetry workshops at the Boston Center for Adult Education and met Anne Sexton and Sylvia Plath, who would soon become prominent poets themselves. She remained friends with Sexton and had lunch with her on the day of Sexton's suicide in 1974, probably being the last person to see her. In 1958, Kumin began to teach as an adjunct at Tufts University and would hold increasingly prestigious teaching positions over the next twenty years. Kumin continued to publish and in 1960 brought out a children's book, *Sebastian and the Dragon*. Her first poetry collection, *Halfway*, was published in 1961. In 1965, she

published her first novel, the autobiographical *Through Dooms of Love*, a book about a teenage girl's relationship with her father. Kumin's fifth poetry collection, *Up Country: Poems of New England* (1972), won the Pulitzer Prize for Poetry in 1973 and included the original publication of "Woodchucks." In 1963, the Kumins bought a small farm in Warner, New Hampshire (close enough Boston to commute), and moved there permanently in 1976 once their children were grown. Much of Kumin's writing would concern the rural life of the New Hampshire countryside. Her poetry also offers a progressive critique of American politics. On their farm, the Kumins bred thoroughbred race and show horses.

Kumin served as US poet laureate in 1981–1982 (when the post was still called the consultant in poetry to the Library of Congress). She would use her position to support and encourage female poets. Kumin was also poet laureate of New Hampshire from 1989 to 1994. Kumin served on the board of the Academy of American Poets (a post called a chancellor), but in 1998 she and Carolyn Kizer resigned from the prestigious body in protest over the academy's lack of women and minority members and officials. Later that year, Kumin was training a horse for a carriage show when the animal was startled by a passing truck and overturned the carriage Kumin was driving, breaking Kumin's neck in addition to causing other serious injuries. Her chances for survival were slim, and immediately after the accident her arms and legs were paralyzed. However, she responded well to the arduous physical therapy she underwent and within a few years was restored to normal function. She wrote a memoir about the experience, *Inside the Halo and Beyond: The Anatomy of a Recovery* (2000). Kumin died in her sleep on February 6, 2014. Two books were published posthumously—her second volume of memoirs, which cover her early life, *The Pawnbroker's Daughter* (2015), and a last collection of poetry, *And Short the Season* (2014).

POEM SUMMARY

The text used for this summary is from Kumin's *Our Ground Time Here Will Be Brief*, Viking, 1982, p. 155. A version of the text can be found on the following web page: https://www.poets.org/poetsorg/poem/woodchucks.

Kumin lived on a working farm with her family in rural Pennsylvania. That provides the setting for "Woodchucks." While the theme of the poem no doubt relates to the lived conditions of Kumin's life, no poem, which is essentially a work of fiction, can be simply equated to an autobiographical narrative, nor can the speaker of the poem be assumed to represent Kumin herself in any uncomplicated way. The poem consists of thirty lines divided into five six-line stanzas.

Lines 1–6
Kumin begins the narrative of the poem in media res, after the failure of the first attempt to kill the woodchucks with poison gas. These animals had invaded and were in the process of destroying the speaker's flower and vegetable gardens, so she had determined to exterminate them as pests. The speaker of the poem describes the first attempt to kill them in a mixture of commercial, legal, and military metaphors. First, she refers to the gas canister she bought at the rural supply store, the packaging of which had advertising matter that claimed it would kill the animals quickly and painlessly. Next, she says she had an airtight case against the woodchucks, as if there had been a legal verdict justifying their execution. Really she is making a pun, meaning that the woodchucks' tunnels had been sealed before the poison was applied; the gassing had failed, however, because the burrows went deeper than expected, leaving the woodchucks out of range, as if she were firing artillery at them. So the woodchucks survived this first attempt to kill them.

Lines 7–12
The next morning, it becomes clear that the woodchucks, which she will presently reveal constitute a family, survived despite being gassed with what Kumin significantly describes as cyanide. Just as the woodchucks survived poisoning, Kumin and her family had survived the night despite poisoning themselves with tobacco and alcohol, neither family being worse for the wear. Although the speaker of the poem, in her role as a farmer, does not hesitate to exterminate vermin, she acknowledges here her own moral failing in drinking and smoking. Perhaps she is not sure of her moral justification in her actions. The comparison is certainly humorous, however, reflecting the general tone of the poem. The humor is used to deflect any obvious moral

meaning the poem might have. Her tone is more inviting than a more didactic treatment would be. The woodchucks, for their part, proceed to attack her flowers and then turn to the vegetables in the garden. Being animals, they eat enough of each plant to kill it—from the human perspective ruining it, destroying far more than they would strictly need to eat to sustain themselves.

Lines 13–18
Now the speaker turns to other means to exterminate the woodchucks, namely, shooting them. The beginning of this stanza is a quotation from a half-mumbled justification for her actions that she speaks to herself, that the animals' depredations are taking food from her and her family's mouths. She feels triumphant in the actual act of shooting, completely assured that she is in the right. Moreover, she feels a natural excitement attached to hunting. She luxuriates in the feel of the bullets as she loads her rifle. She is conflicted, however, and it seems to her that the act of extermination is making her fall away from her innate pacifism and indeed making her fall from grace—as though she considers killing them a sin. She has to manufacture new justifications for her acts, placing them in what she describes as a Darwinian context, replacing religious piety with a pseudoscientific justification. She aims her rifle at the baby woodchuck. She does not describe firing, but the animal dies among the roses, either where it was shot or perhaps scampering a short distance. The speaker of the poem does not hesitate to control the pests in her garden, but at the same time she has to discipline a strong urge to not harm the animals that, looked at in another way, are cute and endearing. No doubt the poem would be very different if the animals being killed were rats or snakes.

Lines 19–24
The speaker of the poem continues to watch for woodchucks and after a few minutes shoots the mother. She was knocked over by the impact of the bullet and fell with a half-eaten leaf of Swiss chard still clutched in her mouth. Next, the speaker kills another baby woodchuck. Her counting in the second half of line 22 enumerates the dead woodchucks but is also like a child's version of an incantation, summoning up within the speaker the power to kill. The killer that lurks inside her is taking over her actions, as if,

in a play, a new character might come on stage and take over the action.

Lines 25–30

There is one woodchuck left, the father of the family. He proves far more adept at staying alive than the others, clever in the way he avoids her. She has to keep watch for him for days and hunt him through the night. Even when she sleeps, she dreams about shooting the last woodchuck. She wishes the poison gas had worked and that they had all died in their burrows, where she could not see what was happening or have to face her own responsibility—just as had been the case in Nazi Germany during World War II.

THEMES

Murder

Particularly in the third stanza of Kumin's "Woodchucks," the speaker of the poem considers her own role in killing the animals. As a pacifist, she thinks she ought not to have been able to do it. In any event, she found it all too easy to pull the trigger. She is able to kill them, she finds, because she is able to think about them as vermin. Killing vermin as vermin would be nothing to write a poem about. What she is really concerned about is how the act of killing has changed her. Is she morally damaged by the act because she excuses it by dismissing the animals as vermin? After she has exercised whatever instinct she used to kill, will it become stronger? She finds, much to her surprise, that she has a killer inside her, which the act of pulling the trigger sets free. Killing woodchucks is one thing, but the Nazis killed men. What happened to those killers?

Kumin hints at the question several times, but naturally it is something the Nazis thought about themselves. Heinrich Himmler was the head of Adolf Hitler's paramilitary SS, an organization in Nazi Germany that competed with the armed forces, supplying its own small, but elite private army to the fighting as well as administering the Holocaust. By 1943, at the time he addressed a group of his officers in the occupied Polish city of Poznan on October 4, Himmler was the second most powerful man in Germany. In the speech (quoted in David Livingstone Smith's *Less Than Human*), Himmler is concerned about the effect that the millions of

TOPICS FOR FURTHER STUDY

- Make a presentation to your class comparing "Woodchucks" and Sylvia Plath's "Daddy" as Holocaust poems. Provide a background for the Holocaust using original sources such as the young-adult classic *The Diary of Anne Frank* as well as important studies of the Holocaust such as Erich Fromm's *Anatomy of Human Destructiveness* (1973), which particularly deals with the psychological themes that interest Kumin.

- The woodchuck, or groundhog, is native to North America. As such, it often appears in Native American myths and legends. Although his sourcing is somewhat confused, the well-known figure of Nokomis in Henry Wadsworth Longfellow's epic poem *Hiawatha* (1855) is a woodchuck (or woodchuck woman, that is, a spirit animal in human disguise). Research woodchucks in Native American myth, using the Internet and sources like Fred Ramen's *Native American Mythology* (2008), and make a presentation on the topic to your class.

- Kumin's "Woodchucks" begins in medias res, rather than at the beginning of the story. Make a time line of the story in its chronological order and display it next to an outline of Kumin's arrangements. Make your result into a class poster at a site like https://www.easel.ly/.

- On one level, "Woodchucks" is about the interaction of human beings and wild animals as humans encroach on wild lands. Woodchucks become garden pests because their natural habitat is the border between woods and fields. In an urban landscape, that habitat expands rather than contracts. An animal in a similar position is the Japanese raccoon dog (*tanuki*). A treatment of their role in a landscape reshaped by human expansion is given in Isao Takahata's film *Pom Poko* (1994). Write a paper comparing the film with Kumin's poem.

The woodchucks are tearing up the speaker's vegetable garden *(©Aygul Bulte / Shutterstock.com)*

murders they had already carried out might be having on the murderers. He said,

> I am referring to...the extermination of the Jewish people.... Most of you men know what it is like to see 100 corpses lying side by side, or 500 or 1,000. To have stood fast through this and—except for cases of human weakness—to have stayed decent, that has made us hard.

Amazingly, Himmler is convinced that his murderers have not been morally degraded. They have not, in Kumin's terms, unleashed the killers inside themselves that cannot be put back. They remain decent human beings, if hardened by the unpleasantness of their work. He can say this because, as he tells them, they have been fighting a war against the infectious bacteria of the Jews. Himmler is confident that

> all in all...we can say that we have carried out this most difficult of tasks in a spirit of love for our people. And we have suffered no harm to our inner being, our soul, our character.

In other words, Himmler is arguing that the SS men can stay sane only by interpreting their actions as protecting civilization from a plague. Kumin implicitly mocks Himmler and the Nazis by showing his arguments in miniature. The truth she uses to justify her killing (that woodchucks really are vermin in a garden) is the lie the Nazis used to justify human murder.

Feminism

Alicia Ostriker, in her essay "Making the Connection: The Nature Poetry of Maxine Kumin," characterizes Kumin as a feminist, and this is certainly a standard interpretation of her. It is hard to imagine a prominent female poet of her generation who would not have been read that way. Nevertheless, Ostriker notes some particularities in Kumin's feminism. "Kumin," Ostriker states, "differs from other feminists in her capacity to locate strength in normality." Kumin accepts the routine of farm life as the normal pattern of life rather than seeing it as an oppressive patriarchal structure. Moreover, Ostriker asks, what other feminist poet creates positive masculine characters who are "a bit like and a bit unlike herself, highlighting continuities and distinctions across gender and other boundaries?" One of Kumin's achievements in "Woodchucks" is to meet the second-wave feminist goal of moving beyond gender.

To the degree the poem is autobiographical, its speaker nevertheless acts in a way that would have been seen as stereotypically male in the 1970s but without apology or explanation, as it is simply how she is. It must be noted, however, that since the speaker of the poem is not to be directly identified with the author, there is, in fact, no way of determining the speaker's gender. Kumin's poem is postgender and therefore postfeminist, the feminist goal of full self-actualization having been met.

STYLE

In Medias Res

The term *in medias res* (in the middle of things) refers to a literary rule that Aristotle discovered through his examination of Greek tragedy. The idea is that a story should begin at the last possible moment within the narrative, that is, as close to the ending as possible, so as to create dramatic tension for the audience. It is a rule that Kumin observes in "Woodchucks." If the narrative were presented in chronological order, it would proceed along these lines: I noticed something was eating the flowers and vegetables in my garden. I discovered that it was a family of woodchucks. I searched and found the entrances to their tunnels. I went to the feed store and bought poison gas. And so it would continue. Instead, in the very first line of the poem, Kumin begins by describing the failure of the gas attack on the woodchucks. This engages readers by making them want to find out what happened. Readers become eager for the details of the story, such as the trip to the feed store, which, presented in chronological order, would have been tedious and off-putting.

Poetics

In the late nineteenth and early twentieth centuries, poets reexamined the art of poetry. They wanted to reduce language to its essence and concluded that that essence was figurative language, language that elicits meaning from the reader beyond what is possible in prose. The traditional form of poetry, meter and rhyme, was judged to be a secondary consideration that could be abandoned or modified as the poet wished. As a result, poetry changed in form, so modern poetry is for the most part distinguishable from traditional poetry at a

simple reading, if not at sight. Given that background, "Woodchucks" is, for a poem of the 1970s, highly conservative in its poetic form. Its language is basically iambic, although it does not follow a tight metrical scheme as does a Shakespearean sonnet. An iamb is an unstressed syllable followed by a stressed syllable; it is the basic metrical unit in English verse. Kumin feels free, however, to abandon iambic rhythm when she thinks it would interfere with the clear presentation of her ideas and language.

Kumin's use of rhyme is similar. The lines of the poem do rhyme, but not in an expected scheme. In stanzaic poetry, each stanza should ideally have the same rhyme scheme, so that, for instance, the first and third lines would rhyme and likewise the second and fourth, giving *abab* in the notation used to represent rhyme. What Kumin actually does with the rhyme is quite interesting. Each stanza does follow the same rhyme scheme (*abcacb*), but it is an asymmetrical one (*abcabc* or *abccba* would be expected) that at first suggests the poem is more chaotic and *modern* than it really is, destabilizing the reader. In the last stanza, however, she cannot keep it up, and the *c* elements do not rhyme. That is a forgivable lapse even in traditional poetry. Kumin also plays with some other poetic conventions. The last line of the third stanza is a satire of epic language; the final two words are an epithet of the same form as might have been used to describe the death of a hero in the *Iliad* or *Beowulf*. Applying the language to a dead baby woodchuck makes it comic.

HISTORICAL CONTEXT

In "Woodchucks" Kumin creates an analogy between her extermination of the woodchucks in her garden as vermin and the Holocaust. This may seem frivolous, but it is all too apt. In the last line of the poem, she likens her attempt to gas the animals to the use of gas chambers in the Nazi Holocaust. Earlier in the poem (line 8) she mentions cyanide as the gas used to kill the woodchucks, but the gas used to exterminate vermin like woodchucks and moles is methyl bromide, not cyanide, which is far too dangerous. This *mistake* signals that Kumin is really already talking about the Holocaust.

In the single Nazi death camp of Auschwitz, over one million Jews were killed on an industrial

COMPARE
&
CONTRAST

- **1970s:** Second-wave feminism wants to find equality between the sexes in literature as well as other areas, so that gender differences would no longer matter.

  Today: Third-wave feminism, as it touches upon literature, is concerned with the control and policing of language to suppress differences of gender, which are seen as part of an oppressive structure of patriarchal power.

- **1970s:** Although Kumin clearly does so, few would think that there was any moral component in the decision to exterminate woodchucks from a garden.

- **Today:** Animal rights activism has gained a broader social footprint thanks to the Internet and become more militant, criticizing routine rural activities such as Kumin engaged in, including the extermination (as opposed, perhaps, to trapping and relocating) of animals like woodchucks and also vealing and even the domestication of animals itself.

- **1970s:** Kumin buys the poison she uses against the woodchucks at an independently owned local store.

  Today: The rural economy is dominated by a small number of national chains.

---

scale in gas chambers that the Nazi planners had calculated to be the most efficient means of execution. The agent used was a compound of cyanide developed by the chemical works I. G. Farben, with the brand name Zyklon B. They had earlier developed the similar compound Zyklon A, but since this compound had been tested during World War I as a means of gas warfare, its manufacture was prohibited after Germany's defeat. Before World War II, Zyklon B was mostly used as a pesticide, and its largest purchaser was the US government. When Mexican migrant laborers entered the United States for temporary work (at the time a perfectly legal arrangement), customs agents would strip them and delouse them by covering their bodies in powdered DDT while their clothes were put in a gas chamber and exposed to Zyklon B. The Nazis considered the Jews themselves to be vermin and so exposed them directly to the more poisonous gas.

The analogy between Jews and vermin is one made not by Kumin, who reverses it for the sake of a very dark humor, but in all seriousness by the Nazis. How could such an analogy be made? Gregory H. Stanton, in his article "The Ten Stages of Genocide," explains that in the preparation for genocide, "one group denies the humanity of the other group. Members of it are equated with animals, vermin, insects or diseases. Dehumanization overcomes the normal human revulsion against murder." The intellectual work to justify the Holocaust was mostly done by the German medical profession, and so it was natural for them to describe Jews as disease organisms or carriers of disease.

This became a theme in German mass culture in the 1940 Nazi propaganda film *The Eternal Jew*. The film intercuts scenes of rats attacking bags of grain in a warehouse (similarly to how Kumin speaks of the woodchucks taking the food in the vegetable garden from her family's mouths) with street scenes filmed in the ghettos of Polish cities. The accompanying narration is quoted in David Livingstone Smith's *Less Than Human*:

> Wherever rats appear they bring ruin, by destroying mankind's goods and foodstuffs. In this way, they spread disease, plague, leprosy, typhoid fever, cholera, dysentery, and so on. They are cunning, cowardly, and cruel, and are found mostly in large packs. Among the animals, they represent the rudiment of an insidious and underground destruction, just like the Jews among human beings.

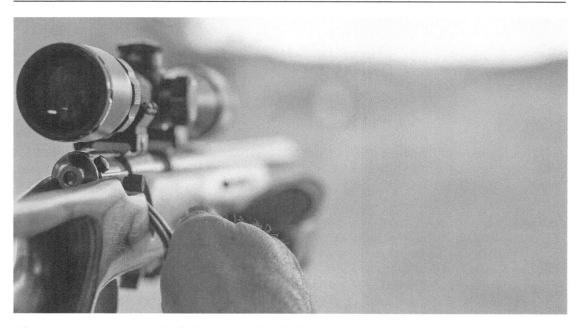

The speaker is surprised by the killer instinct that she feels with a gun in her hands (©jfwalker / Shutterstock.com)

Earlier, during the Ottoman government's Armenian genocide in the early nineteenth century, Mehmed Resid, a professor at the Istanbul Medical School, who helped to plan that atrocity, said (quoted by Smith in *Less Than Human*) that Turks needed to "rid ourselves of these Armenian parasites." He asked, referring to the Armenians, "Isn't it the duty of a doctor to destroy these microbes?" Kumin, one may say, is reminded of this kind of dehumanization by having to exterminate actual vermin.

CRITICAL OVERVIEW

Living or recently dead poets (and Kumin died only in 2014) tend to be underserved by critical scholarship, and that is certainly true in Kumin's case. "Woodchucks" is a Holocaust poem that deserves to be seen alongside Kumin's colleague Sylvia Plath's "Daddy," but it is barely acknowledged in the literature. An important collection of criticism about Kumin is *Telling the Barn Swallow*, edited by Emily Grosholz. In this, several poets analyze Kumin's work. Alicia Ostriker, in her article, "Making the Connection," deals with Kumin's nature poetry. Ostriker situates Kumin within a feminist criticism of the tradition of nature poetry. This view sees nature as feminine (the Latin *natura*

being a feminine noun) in nature poetry written by men, making women and nature both something inherently disordered and wild, to be conquered and overcome. She sees this stereotype as a hindrance to the acceptance of female poets in the nineteenth and early twentieth centuries. According to Ostriker, however, Kumin breaks this paradigm by producing an ungendered poetry. Ostriker views "Woodchucks" as Kumin's recognition of hidden brutality in her own nature and points out that Kumin would develop the theme in her later poem "The Vealers," in which she describes her own farmwork in immobilization and force-feeding calves for veal, a practice that is increasingly coming under moral scrutiny.

Ostriker also places Kumin in the tradition of bucolic or pastoral poetry stretching back to Hesiod's *Works and Days* at the beginning of Western civilization, though Kumin's poetry often seems disconnected from that tradition and connected instead to the actual lived experience of farm life.

In the same collection, Wesley McNair, in "Kumin's Animal Confederates," discusses how the darkness of human nature clouds any vision of a pastoral ideal Kumin hopes to achieve. Still in the Grosholz collection, Carole Simmons Oles, in "Max's Garden: For Present and Future Consumption," contrasts the woodchucks (in the poem "Encounter in August") who are to be exterminated for eating chard from the garden with a bear who devours beans but is let live in exchange for the wonder of standing close to a bear. This is because the bear is valorized as being part of wild nature, whereas the woodchucks represent merely horticultural nature. Enid Dame, in her obituary of Kumin on the Jewish Women's Archive, reads the poem in its true context as a Holocaust poem, saying that "in 'Woodchucks,' the speaker compares her own escalating determination to exterminate the garden pests to the Nazi's mad social Darwinism. Violence against a demonized enemy, the poet implies, is regrettably a universal human trait." Perhaps like Kumin herself, Dame misrepresents the relationship between the Nazis and Darwin. It should be noted that one of the last things Kumin wrote was a brief memoir (published in *American Scholar* in 2014) in which she explains the real life inspiration of "Woodchucks." She notes that she herself had never learned to shoot and so did not kill the woodchucks, but a string of handymen and other visitors to the farms slowly picked the animals off over time with a rifle the Kumin family owned.

CRITICISM

Bradley A. Skeen

Skeen is a classicist. In the following essay, he explores Kumin's "Woodchucks" as a Holocaust poem.

Kumin clearly signals that the true subject matter—or one subject matter—of the seemingly innocuous poem "Woodchucks" is the crisis of racism in the twentieth century. She openly refers to the Nazis and also speaks of them in a more recondite reference that forces one to think of the awful history that provides the context for her mention of cyanide. Kumin's invocation of Charles Darwin exactly halfway through the poem (line 16) is also connected to her larger concern. She says that Darwin's ideas can be used to justify killing.

The statement is certainly not true, as Kumin is well aware ("pieties" in this case being used sarcastically), but it nevertheless has a long and important political history. In the early twentieth century, Darwin's theory of evolution was misinterpreted to make it appear to

THE GARDENER DOES NOT CHOOSE THE STRONGEST; HE PROTECTS THE WEAKEST."

support the then-popular movement of eugenics. In more recent times, opponents of Darwin and science, who do not want the theory of evolution taught in American schools, have similarly misrepresented evolution to make it appear as if its use by eugenicists was justified and consonant with the theory itself, in order to discredit science using the odious doctrines of the eugenics movement. Kumin is doubtless speaking ironically in "Woodchucks," as if it were possible to use evolution as a justification for extermination, and she certainly intends to draw the reader's attention to the issue.

The speaker of "Woodchucks" realizes that as a gardener, she has to exterminate the woodchucks that are destroying her garden. She describes herself as a pacifist and shows some reluctance to kill, especially cute animals like woodchucks. At the same time she is able to utilize her basic instincts to kill efficiently and mercilessly. The self-criticism in the poem is concerned not so much with the act of killing as with her capacity for killing. She is uncomfortable with the part of herself that she is able to use to do it. If the woodchucks had just died from the gas in the way the Nazis' victims had, then she would never have had to encounter her own feelings, the feelings that let her pull the trigger of her rifle. On one hand, she criticizes those instincts as related to the instincts that allowed, even drove, the Nazis to slaughter innocents, but, on the other hand, she also tries to find some justification for having those feelings, to lessen her shame. She turns to evolution to justify those same feelings; this cannot be entirely successful, since what she is doing is not analogous to evolution but precisely the opposite.

In his 1974 commencement address at Caltech, the physicist Richard Feynman defined pseudoscience as cargo-cult science, by which he meant that it aped all of the outward forms of science and even appropriated as much of science as it could but stopped short of actually using the scientific method to reach valid

WHAT DO I READ NEXT?

- *Lizzie!* (2014) is a young-adult novel written by Kumin. Its story about an eleven-year-old girl left partially paralyzed and in a wheelchair after an accident reflects the experience of Kumins' own crippling accident and rehabilitation.

- Kumin's *The Pawnbroker's Daughter* (2015) is her second volume of memoirs, covering the period though her childhood to her maturity as a poet.

- *Tanuki's Gift* (2002), by Tim Myers, was given an honorable mention for the Asian Pacific American Award for Literature. It draws on the folklore of the Japanese raccoon dog, or *tanuki*, an animal that occupies a niche similar to that of the American woodchuck in the rural/urban landscape.

- *To Make a Prairie: Essays on Poets, Poetry and Country Living* (1979) is Kumin's first collection of essays, in which she discusses how her work was changed by moving from an urban to a rural environment.

- Mary A. Hood's *Walking Seasonal Roads* (2012) is a memoir/essay about the experience of rural life in New Hampshire that at many points engages Kumin's poetry.

- Kumin's *Where I Live: New and Selected Poems 1999–2010* (2010), republishes the poems of the period Kumin considers her most important and includes twenty-three new poems devoted to her rural life and environment.

conclusions. Rather, it attempted to justify its presuppositions by dressing them up to look like science. It is essentially an attempt to borrow the social authority of science as a rhetorical device to justify nonscientific claims. The pseudoscience of eugenics began to use the theory of evolution in this way already in the late nineteenth century and throughout the early twentieth century. The idea was that

Darwin had discovered the principle of the survival of the fittest, with organisms in a bloody competition for survival. The way natural selection actually works, however, is that each new generation in a given species contains more individuals than their environment can support, so only those most fitted by some slight variation to their particular environment will survive to pass their genes (as we now know) on to the next generation.

Proponents of the eugenics movement, founded by Darwin's cousin Francis Galton, thought that they understood natural selection and that it no longer operated on human beings. They reasoned that in at least the developed countries of Europe and North America, natural selection no longer affected the human population and that unfit as well as fit variations would have an equal chance to pass on their genes, thus *degrading* the human gene pool. The solution eugenics offered was to artificially take over the role of natural selection and prevent less fit humans from breeding, generally through voluntary or compulsory sterilization.

Thomas Huxley, known as Darwin's bulldog and the most vociferous promoter of evolutionary science in the nineteenth century, already explained at the beginning of the eugenics movement why it was mistaken and had created a pseudoscientific program. In the first place, how could the eugenicist know what was most or least fit and fit for what purpose, since fitness functioned only in respect of natural selection? In practice, eugenics answered these questions by a blind adherence to then-prevalent racial stereotypes and really served to give a scientific veneer to quite unscientific racism. More fundamentally, what the eugenicists claimed they wanted to do was impossible. Huxley explained the error of their reasoning by a comparison of gardening and natural selection:

> The tendency of the cosmic process [evolution] is to bring about the adjustment of the forms of plant life to the current conditions; the tendency of the horticultural process is the adjustment of the conditions to the needs of the forms of plant life which the gardener desires to raise.

In the wild, only the organisms most suited to their environment survive because of natural selection, but what the gardener does is exactly the opposite. He takes a flower he considers beautiful or a vegetable he likes to eat and creates an artificial environment that allows it to flourish. He does this by systematically destroying any other organism that might compete with it. This is weeding. The weeds are the plants that are naturally fitted to the environment of the garden, but the gardener kills the weeds so that they cannot compete with the flowers that are themselves naturally unfit. If a rose garden is left untended, it does not take very long for all the roses to die without reproducing and be replaced by weeds. which naturally outcompete them. The gardener does not choose the strongest; he protects the weakest. While the eugenicist claims to be acting according to natural selection and allowing the strongest to survive, he is actually acting like the gardener. He arbitrarily chooses some characteristic (like race, which does not have any real existence in the human population from a genetic viewpoint) and protects it on the premise that it is too weak to survive and would be outcompeted by the *common* varieties unless eugenicists artificially prevented their breeding. In her role as a gardener, this is exactly what the speaker of Kumin's poem is doing—protecting her flowers and vegetables from the woodchucks by destroying the animals that would otherwise overwhelm the weak, but by her favored, flowers and vegetables.

In "Woodchucks," Kumin draws a parallel between pseudo-Darwinian eugenics and Nazism. She wishes that the woodchucks had succumbed to the gas so she would not have had to experience the more direct and disturbing act of shooting the animals, which she justifies to herself with "Darwinian pieties." It is clear enough that she is referring not to the theory of evolution but instead to the eugenic pseudoscience that tried to claim Darwin's name. Far from embracing this eugenic thinking, it is clear that Kumin is wrestling with an idea she does not want to be true. It is less certain how the reader is to associate Nazism and pseudo-Darwinism. It is not surprising that Kumin is unclear here, since the two concepts are often connected in the popular imagination, though imprecisely so.

How pervasive the idea of such a connection is can be seen in the case of Andrew Marr, a prominent British journalist who was the editor of the newspaper *Independent* and of the BBC News Service and very much a figure of the political mainstream. In 2009, he wrote an article in the *Daily Mail* in which he confidently asserted that Nazi eugenics was based on their twisting of Darwinian evolution. It is easy to see

how such confusion could arise, because Nazi race policies and ultimately the Holocaust were justified in eugenic terms and they could hardly have been carried out without the widespread acceptance of eugenics among German intellectuals, especially in the medical profession, quite apart from the Nazis. Nazi eugenics was, in fact, anything except Darwinian (or pseudo-Darwinian) in nature. This is a vital distinction, since even today, opponents of evolution, for example, creationists who want to exclude the teaching of evolution from public schools, use this confusion as one of their chief arguments against science.

In a typical example, Jerry Bergman, in an article published on the website of the prominent creationist organization, Answers in Genesis, correctly points out that eugenics is a pseudoscientific corruption of the theory of evolution but nevertheless argues that it is evolution itself, whether misunderstood or not, that led directly to Nazis and ought to be opposed for that reason on the ground that acceptance of the theory might have similar effects in the future. Specifically he states that "the belief that evolution can be directed by scientists to produce a 'superior race' was the central leitmotif of Nazism." He goes on to say that "Hitler elaborated his Darwinian views by comparing the strong killing the weak to a cat devouring a mouse," but the truth is precisely the opposite. Nazi race theory was eugenic in nature, but it strictly and absolutely rejected any idea that their form of eugenics could have anything to do with evolution or Darwin. The books of Darwin were among those prominently burned at Nazi rallies, and the teaching of evolution in German schools was made illegal by the Nazis.

In his manifesto, *Mein Kampf*, Hitler himself asserted his belief that God had made all of life in the form of fixed kinds:

> Even a superficial glance is sufficient to show that all the innumerable forms in which the life-urge of Nature manifests itself are subject to a fundamental law—one may call it an iron law of Nature—which compels the various species to keep within the definite limits of their own life-forms when propagating and multiplying their kind.

Note that he uses the biblical word *kind* instead of a scientific term like *genus* or *species*. He means that evolution is impossible and does not exist. If animals can never change out of their kind, then no new species can arise, and

The speaker is frustrated by the infestation of woodchucks in her yard *(©zixian | Shutterstock.com)*

evolution could never take place. Hitler believed similarly that the individual human races had been created separately by God and while they might degenerate (hence the beginning of the Holocaust with the murder of tens of thousands of disabled German children), they could not change. Rather, Hitler believed the races had an equally fixed order between them, with the Aryans as the master race; since the Jews disputed this, they had to be destroyed to protect the Aryans, in the same way that Kumin had to destroy the woodchucks to protect her Swiss chard. How horrible the Nazis were is often a bar to seeing how ridiculous they were, but Kumin is perfectly clear in that regard.

In "Woodchucks," Kumin is, of course, not advocating eugenics. She is, after all, an actual gardener who is merely tending her garden. Rather, the poem is a call to be on guard. Feynman was keenly aware how easy it is for even trained scientists to fall into cargo-cult science. There is no worse example of pseudoscience than eugenics because of the disaster it led to, not only in the case of the Nazis but also in the many thousands of individuals who underwent forced

sterilization in the United States and other Western countries because of it. Kumin is really on guard against the impulse to kill (in this case to protect her garden), the danger that a person can be seduced by a pseudoscience like eugenics to support atrocities like those of the Nazis. If she did not know better, she might be able to kill people as easily as she does woodchucks. She wants to be a pacifist but is appalled when she finds she is not.

Source: Bradley A. Skeen, Critical Essay on "Woodchucks," in *Poetry for Students*, Gale, Cengage Learning, 2017.

Maxine Kumin

In the following transcribed lecture, Kumin explains how to determine a poet's intent when reading a poem.

How do poems begin? Who really knows? "How do I love you, let me count the ways" is probably as good an answer as any. The impulse to build a poem may be something amorphous, inchoate, vague yet persistent as a floating sense of unease. It may be an emotion as specific as anger, as explicit as the sex drive, as necessary as

> **FOR ME A POEM MUST GO BEYOND ITS SETTING OR ITS PARTICULAR TO SAY OUTRIGHT OR BY SUBTLE SUGGESTION SOMETHING ABOUT MAN'S UNIVERSAL CONDITION."**

food. The poet may start with a fact or feeling. He may be the kind of writer who knows from the outset what he is aiming at, or he may be the kind who at the moment of particularly heightened tension in a peculiar aura seizes his chaos or prickly perception and seeks to interpret it, make some sort of order out of it, never knowing really where the muse will lead him.

I think most poets have had both kinds of experience—the immediate palpable need to get a poem down whole, and the other, formless but equally valid urge to follow wherever the words and feelings lead. Once in a great while the "given" poem comes along, the *don*, the gift, a poem that flows easily. It proceeds onto the page as if it had been shaped by the seraphim up there on the golden pavement and lightly handed down to the poet simply to record. It is like admitting to having had an earthly visitation to get such a poem—three times in ten years this has happened to me—and each time I was totally unprepared for the event. Much more often there is the sweat and wrestle of tearing the poem out of experience and struggling to get it into being. Barry Spacks has immortalized this process in a little poem . . . .

Spacks here is describing ironically and in a delightful self-mocking tone the visitation that doesn't quite come off. The muse comes, all right, and she is an Amazon of a lady before whom the poet quails, filled with feelings of unworthiness or inadequacy. Is he up to the necessary courtship? Will she stay? She is redolent of elemental drives: she smells "like flame, like starch on sweat, / like sperm, like shame, like a launderette"—and he is the poor fish who is expected to give voice, give life to these basic and vital items. Then, when the lady speaks, the mask falls away and she does so in the querulous tone of an unsatisfied woman. No one, she says, has loved me right. Day and night, day and

night. The muse's statement, indeed the whole poem, becomes then a metaphor for the inability of the poet ever quite to fulfill his inspiration. No one ever realizes his highest potential. Man, that pseudoperfectible being, never quite attains his godhood.

How can we ever live up to our muse, that demanding, petulant Junoesque creature who comes, pulling off her gown? The honest and obvious answer is simply that we can't, or at least that we rarely can. The dissatisfied poet ought to take some comfort, though, from the very fact of his dissatisfaction. The worst sin is complacency. We can't afford to be smug about what we write. We need always to ask ourselves of a poem, yes, but does it work? Does it do what we wanted it to do, excite sympathy, anger, lift the reader out of his chair? Does it *come across*? What is the intent of the poem and how is it established?

Let's look at a poem by Randall Jarrell, titled "Eighth Air Force." The poem is very open-faced. It describes in detail a group of World War II soldiers at rest between flying their bombing missions. There is the eternal puppy, that in other instances is a kitten, or sometimes a war waif, who has been adopted as company mascot. There are the flowers, a domestic touch, a hankering after beauty. There is the idle game being played, the ablution—shaving—being performed. There is the forgetfulness of booze, there is the terrible memory of missions past and the dread of missions to come, all of them adding up to the present one, one, one. All this is told through the voice of the speaker, one of the company, and it is told flatly, directly, resolutely. But what is Jarrell's intent? Is it simply to describe men at their leisure between air strikes, men who "play, before they die, / Like puppies with their puppy"?

It seems to me that the poem's intent becomes clear the minute we fall onto the allusion, *ecce homo*—behold the man. *Ecce homo* evokes Pontius Pilate pointing in all those paintings, Pontius Pilate who pleaded for Jesus's life, but not forcefully enough. We are induced by these details to remember the dream out of the Apocrypha, although it was Pontius's wife who dreamed it and then she harassed him further, poor man. It was Peter who lied three times before the cock crowed, but everything now coalesces in the poem to raise goosebumps on the arms of the reader. "Men wash their hands in blood, as best they can./I find no fault in this just man." It is all déjà vu—we have been here before, surely, at this washing of the hands. Now even the game of pitching pennies takes on a more sinister meaning, suggesting the Roman soldiers gambling under the cross. Here we all are playing this game of war, but like Pilate too weak to dissent from the general will or habit. Jarrell expresses an intense revulsion against war as a form of legal murder, of which he, the speaker, is as guilty as the rest of the soldiers. The poem is prophetic with Jarrell now dead; it speaks to the Vietnam war as vividly as any contemporary poem might. It is a poem that means to persuade and polemicize. It doesn't specifically say, "War is evil" or "War is hell" or "Just men will refuse to go forth and kill any longer" but that is the message the reader receives.

The effect is doubly powerful because it is implied rather than so stated. The poet shows, rather than tells. The shock of revulsion is intensified because the poet moves away from the direct recording of experience, poignant though that is, into an honorable literary (or more accurately, biblical) allusion and that allusion swoops down on us, bearing the full freight of our spiritual history. Notice I am speaking only of intent and tone, not of meter, rhyme, and language, though these are all germane to the topic and add to the coming across.

Lastly, a poem in the simplest possible, quiet, understated diction of Linda Pastan. It is called "Consolations." . . .

This poem is written in free verse; it has no regular meter, although there is a stanzaic pattern. Most of the sentences are simple declarative statements—"I speak," "the dog whines," "Afternoons smell of burning," and so on. A contrast is being drawn between the sounds of language, language even with all its limitations, and what the poet calls "the consolations of silence." In silence, communications are conveyed in other, visual, tactile, olfactory ways, but conveyed nonetheless. She lists these, very quietly and quite obliquely, but with telling effect.

The intent of the poem and its emotive power depend heavily on what I will call the elegiac underlay. This poem, in common with virtually every lasting love lyric down the ages, casts before it the premonitory shadow of our mortality. The poignancy of the setting with its autumnal trees, of the participants, that man and woman and "the child lent us awhile" is contained wholly in the small capsule that is a lifetime. It is the presence of death that makes the moment meaningful, the knowledge of finite time that sharpens the edge of each image.

The intent, then, as I read it, parallels Matthew Arnold's anguished cry for solidarity between the lovers in "Dover Beach": "let us be true / To one another!" for " . . . we are here as on a darkling plain." But when Pastan says "Our griefs / are almost one" and goes on to turn that handsome simile of the child on loan, we are both caught up in the aptness of the image and arrested by the chilling, qualifying word *almost*. She has taken a frank and unsentimental look at the human condition. She is telling us that we are locked up in our individual autonomy, that we cannot, despite all manner of close bonds, go undifferentiated. Although touch functions as "another language," although the child between them "holds one hand of yours / and one of mine" the *I* of the poem acknowledges that neither language nor the consolations of silence can bridge entirely the gap that separates the lovers. They and their child must move inexorably "down the dark stem / of evening"; the coming on of darkness seems quite plainly here to serve as an archetypal image for the final closure of death.

Intent, as I read it, is something larger than the simple event or plot of the poem. I have a lot of narrow prejudices in this connection. I'm not very often satisfied with a straight imagist poem. For me a poem must go beyond its setting or its particular to say outright or by subtle suggestion something about man's universal condition. If the gift without the giver is bare, the poem without the concept is emaciated, merely a skeleton. I want, I am hungry for something elusive I can only call *realization*. I don't know another word for it except maybe to say that what I want of a poem is that it arouse in me a sympathetic response to its authenticity.

Source: Maxine Kumin, "Coming Across: Establishing the Intent of a Poem," in *To Make a Prairie: Essays on Poets, Poetry, and Country Living*, University of Michigan Press, 1979, pp. 140–46.

SOURCES

Bergman, Jerry, "Darwinism and the Nazi Race Holocaust," Answers in Genesis website, https://answersingenesis.org/charles-darwin/racism/darwinism-and-the-nazi-race-holocaust/ (accessed August 18, 2016).

Christianson, Scott, *The Last Gasp: The Rise and Fall of the American Gas Chamber*, University of California Press, 2010, p. 92.

Dame, Enid, "Maxine Kumin 1925–2014," Jewish Women's Archive, http://jwa.org/encyclopedia/article/kumin-maxine (accessed August 17, 2016).

Feynman, Richard, "Cargo Cult Science," http://calteches.library.caltech.edu/51/2/CargoCult.htm (accessed August 18, 2016).

Hitler, Adolf, *Mein Kampf*, Hurst and Blackwell, 1939, p. 222.

Huxley, Thomas H., *Evolution and Ethics and Other Essays*, Macmillan, 1894, pp. 1–45.

Kumin, Maxine, "Woodchucks," in *Our Ground Time Here Will Be Brief*, Viking, 1982, p. 155.

———, "Our Farm, My Inspiration," in *American Scholar*, Vol. 83, No. 1, Winter 2014, pp. 64–79.

Marr, Andrew, "I Revere This Man (and His Book on Earthworms)," February 21, 2009, in *Daily Mail*, http://www.dailymail.co.uk/sciencetech/article-1151579/I-revere-man-book-earthworms—Andrew-Marr-real-legacy-Darwin.html (accessed August 18, 2016).

McNair, Wesley, "Kumin's Animal Confederates," in *Telling the Barn Swallow: Poets on the Poetry of Maxine Kumin*, edited by Emily Grosholz, University Press of New England, 1997, pp. 122–34.

Oles, Carole Simmons, "Max's Garden: For Present and Future Consumption," in *Telling the Barn Swallow: Poets on the Poetry of Maxine Kumin*, edited by Emily Grosholz, University Press of New England, 1997, pp. 154–74.

Ostriker, Alicia, "Making the Connection: The Nature Poetry of Maxine Kumin," in *Telling the Barn Swallow: Poets on the Poetry of Maxine Kumin*, edited by Emily Grosholz, University Press of New England, 1997, pp. 74–91.

Smith, David Livingstone, *Less Than Human: Why We Demean, Enslave, and Exterminate Others*, St. Martin's, 2011, pp. 139–45.

Stanton, Gregory H., "The Ten Stages of Genocide," Genocide Watch website, http://www.genocidewatch.org/genocide/tenstagesofgenocide.html (accessed August 15, 2016).

FURTHER READING

Kumin, Maxine, *Inside the Halo and Beyond: The Anatomy of a Recovery*, W. W. Norton, 1999.
Kumin's first volume of memoirs deals with her recovery from her spinal cord injury.

———, *Quit Monks or Die*, Story Line, 1999.
Kumin is better known as a poet than a novelist, but this is her fifth novel. It marks her radicalization on the issue of animal rights and criticizes the use of animals in laboratory experiments. It takes the form of a conventional murder mystery.

Plath, Sylvia, *The Collected Poems*, Harper, 2008.
Plath was a contemporary and colleague of Kumin's, but because of the publicity generated by her suicide, she has become nearly a cult figure, far surpassing her fellow Pulitzer Prize winner Kumin in popularity. She is also considered one of the most important Holocaust poets because of her works like "Daddy" and "Lady Lazarus."

Sexton, Ann, *The Complete Poems*, Mariner, 1999.
Sexton was a close friend of Kumin's and, like Plath, has been glamorized by her suicide. Kumin wrote the introduction to this edition.

SUGGESTED SEARCH TERMS

Maxine Kumin

"Woodchucks" AND Kumin

Holocaust poetry

eugenics AND pseudoscience

Darwin AND theory of evolution

Zyklon B

pastoral AND satire

worldwide racism AND twentieth century

Glossary of Literary Terms

A

Abstract: Used as a noun, the term refers to a short summary or outline of a longer work. As an adjective applied to writing or literary works, abstract refers to words or phrases that name things not knowable through the five senses.

Accent: The emphasis or stress placed on a syllable in poetry. Traditional poetry commonly uses patterns of accented and unaccented syllables (known as feet) that create distinct rhythms. Much modern poetry uses less formal arrangements that create a sense of freedom and spontaneity.

Aestheticism: A literary and artistic movement of the nineteenth century. Followers of the movement believed that art should not be mixed with social, political, or moral teaching. The statement "art for art's sake" is a good summary of aestheticism. The movement had its roots in France, but it gained widespread importance in England in the last half of the nineteenth century, where it helped change the Victorian practice of including moral lessons in literature.

Affective Fallacy: An error in judging the merits or faults of a work of literature. The "error" results from stressing the importance of the work's effect upon the reader—that is, how it makes a reader "feel" emotionally, what it does as a literary work—instead of stressing its inner qualities as a created object, or what it "is."

Age of Johnson: The period in English literature between 1750 and 1798, named after the most prominent literary figure of the age, Samuel Johnson. Works written during this time are noted for their emphasis on "sensibility," or emotional quality. These works formed a transition between the rational works of the Age of Reason, or Neoclassical period, and the emphasis on individual feelings and responses of the Romantic period.

Age of Reason: See *Neoclassicism*

Age of Sensibility: See *Age of Johnson*

Agrarians: A group of Southern American writers of the 1930s and 1940s who fostered an economic and cultural program for the South based on agriculture, in opposition to the industrial society of the North. The term can refer to any group that promotes the value of farm life and agricultural society.

Alexandrine Meter: See *Meter*

Allegory: A narrative technique in which characters representing things or abstract ideas are used to convey a message or teach a lesson. Allegory is typically used to teach moral, ethical, or religious lessons but is sometimes used for satiric or political purposes.

Alliteration: A poetic device where the first consonant sounds or any vowel sounds in words or syllables are repeated.

Allusion: A reference to a familiar literary or historical person or event, used to make an idea more easily understood.

Amerind Literature: The writing and oral traditions of Native Americans. Native American literature was originally passed on by word of mouth, so it consisted largely of stories and events that were easily memorized. Amerind prose is often rhythmic like poetry because it was recited to the beat of a ceremonial drum.

Analogy: A comparison of two things made to explain something unfamiliar through its similarities to something familiar, or to prove one point based on the acceptedness of another. Similes and metaphors are types of analogies.

Anapest: See *Foot*

Angry Young Men: A group of British writers of the 1950s whose work expressed bitterness and disillusionment with society. Common to their work is an anti-hero who rebels against a corrupt social order and strives for personal integrity.

Anthropomorphism: The presentation of animals or objects in human shape or with human characteristics. The term is derived from the Greek word for "human form."

Antimasque: See *Masque*

Antithesis: The antithesis of something is its direct opposite. In literature, the use of antithesis as a figure of speech results in two statements that show a contrast through the balancing of two opposite ideas. Technically, it is the second portion of the statement that is defined as the "antithesis"; the first portion is the "thesis."

Apocrypha: Writings tentatively attributed to an author but not proven or universally accepted to be their works. The term was originally applied to certain books of the Bible that were not considered inspired and so were not included in the "sacred canon."

Apollonian and Dionysian: The two impulses believed to guide authors of dramatic tragedy. The Apollonian impulse is named after Apollo, the Greek god of light and beauty and the symbol of intellectual order. The Dionysian impulse is named after Dionysus, the Greek god of wine and the symbol of the unrestrained forces of nature. The Apollonian impulse is to create a rational, harmonious world, while the Dionysian is to express the irrational forces of personality.

Apostrophe: A statement, question, or request addressed to an inanimate object or concept or to a nonexistent or absent person.

Archetype: The word archetype is commonly used to describe an original pattern or model from which all other things of the same kind are made. This term was introduced to literary criticism from the psychology of Carl Jung. It expresses Jung's theory that behind every person's "unconscious," or repressed memories of the past, lies the "collective unconscious" of the human race: memories of the countless typical experiences of our ancestors. These memories are said to prompt illogical associations that trigger powerful emotions in the reader. Often, the emotional process is primitive, even primordial. Archetypes are the literary images that grow out of the "collective unconscious." They appear in literature as incidents and plots that repeat basic patterns of life. They may also appear as stereotyped characters.

Argument: The argument of a work is the author's subject matter or principal idea.

Art for Art's Sake: See *Aestheticism*

Assonance: The repetition of similar vowel sounds in poetry.

Audience: The people for whom a piece of literature is written. Authors usually write with a certain audience in mind, for example, children, members of a religious or ethnic group, or colleagues in a professional field. The term "audience" also applies to the people who gather to see or hear any performance, including plays, poetry readings, speeches, and concerts.

Automatic Writing: Writing carried out without a preconceived plan in an effort to capture every random thought. Authors who engage in automatic writing typically do not revise their work, preferring instead to preserve the revealed truth and beauty of spontaneous expression.

Avant-garde: A French term meaning "vanguard." It is used in literary criticism to describe new writing that rejects traditional approaches to literature in favor of innovations in style or content.

B

Ballad: A short poem that tells a simple story and has a repeated refrain. Ballads were originally intended to be sung. Early ballads, known as folk ballads, were passed down through generations, so their authors are often unknown. Later ballads composed by known authors are called literary ballads.

Baroque: A term used in literary criticism to describe literature that is complex or ornate in style or diction. Baroque works typically express tension, anxiety, and violent emotion. The term "Baroque Age" designates a period in Western European literature beginning in the late sixteenth century and ending about one hundred years later. Works of this period often mirror the qualities of works more generally associated with the label "baroque" and sometimes feature elaborate conceits.

Baroque Age: See *Baroque*

Baroque Period: See *Baroque*

Beat Generation: See *Beat Movement*

Beat Movement: A period featuring a group of American poets and novelists of the 1950s and 1960s—including Jack Kerouac, Allen Ginsberg, Gregory Corso, William S. Burroughs, and Lawrence Ferlinghetti—who rejected established social and literary values. Using such techniques as stream of consciousness writing and jazz-influenced free verse and focusing on unusual or abnormal states of mind—generated by religious ecstasy or the use of drugs—the Beat writers aimed to create works that were unconventional in both form and subject matter.

Beat Poets: See *Beat Movement*

Beats, The: See *Beat Movement*

Belles-lettres: A French term meaning "fine letters" or "beautiful writing." It is often used as a synonym for literature, typically referring to imaginative and artistic rather than scientific or expository writing. Current usage sometimes restricts the meaning to light or humorous writing and appreciative essays about literature.

Black Aesthetic Movement: A period of artistic and literary development among African Americans in the 1960s and early 1970s. This was the first major African-American artistic movement since the Harlem Renaissance and was closely paralleled by the civil rights and black power movements. The black aesthetic writers attempted to produce works of art that would be meaningful to the black masses. Key figures in black aesthetics included one of its founders, poet and playwright Amiri Baraka, formerly known as LeRoi Jones; poet and essayist Haki R. Madhubuti, formerly Don L. Lee; poet and playwright Sonia Sanchez; and dramatist Ed Bullins.

Black Arts Movement: See *Black Aesthetic Movement*

Black Comedy: See *Black Humor*

Black Humor: Writing that places grotesque elements side by side with humorous ones in an attempt to shock the reader, forcing him or her to laugh at the horrifying reality of a disordered world.

Black Mountain School: Black Mountain College and three of its instructors—Robert Creeley, Robert Duncan, and Charles Olson—were all influential in projective verse, so poets working in projective verse are now referred as members of the Black Mountain school.

Blank Verse: Loosely, any unrhymed poetry, but more generally, unrhymed iambic pentameter verse (composed of lines of five two-syllable feet with the first syllable accented, the second unaccented). Blank verse has been used by poets since the Renaissance for its flexibility and its graceful, dignified tone.

Bloomsbury Group: A group of English writers, artists, and intellectuals who held informal artistic and philosophical discussions in Bloomsbury, a district of London, from around 1907 to the early 1930s. The Bloomsbury Group held no uniform philosophical beliefs but did commonly express an aversion to moral prudery and a desire for greater social tolerance.

Bon Mot: A French term meaning "good word." A *bon mot* is a witty remark or clever observation.

Breath Verse: See *Projective Verse*

Burlesque: Any literary work that uses exaggeration to make its subject appear ridiculous, either by treating a trivial subject with profound seriousness or by treating a dignified subject frivolously. The word "burlesque" may also be used as an adjective, as in "burlesque show," to mean "striptease act."

C

Cadence: The natural rhythm of language caused by the alternation of accented and unaccented syllables. Much modern poetry—notably free verse—deliberately manipulates cadence to create complex rhythmic effects.

Caesura: A pause in a line of poetry, usually occurring near the middle. It typically corresponds to a break in the natural rhythm or sense of the line but is sometimes shifted to create special meanings or rhythmic effects.

Canzone: A short Italian or Provencal lyric poem, commonly about love and often set to music. The *canzone* has no set form but typically contains five or six stanzas made up of seven to twenty lines of eleven syllables each. A shorter, five- to ten-line "envoy," or concluding stanza, completes the poem.

Carpe Diem: A Latin term meaning "seize the day." This is a traditional theme of poetry, especially lyrics. A *carpe diem* poem advises the reader or the person it addresses to live for today and enjoy the pleasures of the moment.

Catharsis: The release or purging of unwanted emotions—specifically fear and pity—brought about by exposure to art. The term was first used by the Greek philosopher Aristotle in his *Poetics* to refer to the desired effect of tragedy on spectators.

Celtic Renaissance: A period of Irish literary and cultural history at the end of the nineteenth century. Followers of the movement aimed to create a romantic vision of Celtic myth and legend. The most significant works of the Celtic Renaissance typically present a dreamy, unreal world, usually in reaction against the reality of contemporary problems.

Celtic Twilight: See *Celtic Renaissance*

Character: Broadly speaking, a person in a literary work. The actions of characters are what constitute the plot of a story, novel, or poem. There are numerous types of characters, ranging from simple, stereotypical figures to intricate, multifaceted ones. In the techniques of anthropomorphism and personification, animals—and even places or things—can assume aspects of character. "Characterization" is the process by which an author creates vivid, believable characters in a work of art. This may be done in a variety of ways, including (1) direct description of the character by the narrator; (2) the direct presentation of the speech, thoughts, or actions of the character; and (3) the

responses of other characters to the character. The term "character" also refers to a form originated by the ancient Greek writer Theophrastus that later became popular in the seventeenth and eighteenth centuries. It is a short essay or sketch of a person who prominently displays a specific attribute or quality, such as miserliness or ambition.

Characterization: See *Character*

Classical: In its strictest definition in literary criticism, classicism refers to works of ancient Greek or Roman literature. The term may also be used to describe a literary work of recognized importance (a "classic") from any time period or literature that exhibits the traits of classicism.

Classicism: A term used in literary criticism to describe critical doctrines that have their roots in ancient Greek and Roman literature, philosophy, and art. Works associated with classicism typically exhibit restraint on the part of the author, unity of design and purpose, clarity, simplicity, logical organization, and respect for tradition.

Colloquialism: A word, phrase, or form of pronunciation that is acceptable in casual conversation but not in formal, written communication. It is considered more acceptable than slang.

Complaint: A lyric poem, popular in the Renaissance, in which the speaker expresses sorrow about his or her condition. Typically, the speaker's sadness is caused by an unresponsive lover, but some complaints cite other sources of unhappiness, such as poverty or fate.

Conceit: A clever and fanciful metaphor, usually expressed through elaborate and extended comparison, that presents a striking parallel between two seemingly dissimilar things—for example, elaborately comparing a beautiful woman to an object like a garden or the sun. The conceit was a popular device throughout the Elizabethan Age and Baroque Age and was the principal technique of the seventeenth-century English metaphysical poets. This usage of the word conceit is unrelated to the best-known definition of conceit as an arrogant attitude or behavior.

Concrete: Concrete is the opposite of abstract, and refers to a thing that actually exists or a description that allows the reader to experience an object or concept with the senses.

Concrete Poetry: Poetry in which visual elements play a large part in the poetic effect. Punctuation marks, letters, or words are arranged on a page to form a visual design: a cross, for example, or a bumblebee.

Confessional Poetry: A form of poetry in which the poet reveals very personal, intimate, sometimes shocking information about himself or herself.

Connotation: The impression that a word gives beyond its defined meaning. Connotations may be universally understood or may be significant only to a certain group.

Consonance: Consonance occurs in poetry when words appearing at the ends of two or more verses have similar final consonant sounds but have final vowel sounds that differ, as with "stuff" and "off."

Convention: Any widely accepted literary device, style, or form.

Corrido: A Mexican ballad.

Couplet: Two lines of poetry with the same rhyme and meter, often expressing a complete and self-contained thought.

Criticism: The systematic study and evaluation of literary works, usually based on a specific method or set of principles. An important part of literary studies since ancient times, the practice of criticism has given rise to numerous theories, methods, and "schools," sometimes producing conflicting, even contradictory, interpretations of literature in general as well as of individual works. Even such basic issues as what constitutes a poem or a novel have been the subject of much criticism over the centuries.

D

Dactyl: See *Foot*

Dadaism: A protest movement in art and literature founded by Tristan Tzara in 1916. Followers of the movement expressed their outrage at the destruction brought about by World War I by revolting against numerous forms of social convention. The Dadaists presented works marked by calculated madness and flamboyant nonsense. They stressed total freedom of expression, commonly through primitive displays of emotion and illogical, often senseless, poetry. The movement ended shortly after the war, when it was replaced by surrealism.

Decadent: See *Decadents*

Decadents: The followers of a nineteenth-century literary movement that had its beginnings in French aestheticism. Decadent literature displays a fascination with perverse and morbid states; a search for novelty and sensation—the "new thrill"; a preoccupation with mysticism; and a belief in the senselessness of human existence. The movement is closely associated with the doctrine Art for Art's Sake. The term "decadence" is sometimes used to denote a decline in the quality of art or literature following a period of greatness.

Deconstruction: A method of literary criticism developed by Jacques Derrida and characterized by multiple conflicting interpretations of a given work. Deconstructionists consider the impact of the language of a work and suggest that the true meaning of the work is not necessarily the meaning that the author intended.

Deduction: The process of reaching a conclusion through reasoning from general premises to a specific premise.

Denotation: The definition of a word, apart from the impressions or feelings it creates in the reader.

Diction: The selection and arrangement of words in a literary work. Either or both may vary depending on the desired effect. There are four general types of diction: "formal," used in scholarly or lofty writing; "informal," used in relaxed but educated conversation; "colloquial," used in everyday speech; and "slang," containing newly coined words and other terms not accepted in formal usage.

Didactic: A term used to describe works of literature that aim to teach some moral, religious, political, or practical lesson. Although didactic elements are often found in artistically pleasing works, the term "didactic" usually refers to literature in which the message is more important than the form. The term may also be used to criticize a work that the critic finds "overly didactic," that is, heavy-handed in its delivery of a lesson.

Dimeter: See *Meter*

Dionysian: See *Apollonian and Dionysian*

Discordia concours: A Latin phrase meaning "discord in harmony." The term was coined by the eighteenth-century English writer Samuel Johnson to describe "a combination of dissimilar images or discovery of occult resemblances in things apparently unlike." Johnson created the expression by reversing a phrase by the Latin poet Horace.

Dissonance: A combination of harsh or jarring sounds, especially in poetry. Although such combinations may be accidental, poets sometimes intentionally make them to achieve particular effects. Dissonance is also sometimes used to refer to close but not identical rhymes. When this is the case, the word functions as a synonym for consonance.

Double Entendre: A corruption of a French phrase meaning "double meaning." The term is used to indicate a word or phrase that is deliberately ambiguous, especially when one of the meanings is risque or improper.

Draft: Any preliminary version of a written work. An author may write dozens of drafts which are revised to form the final work, or he or she may write only one, with few or no revisions.

Dramatic Monologue: See *Monologue*

Dramatic Poetry: Any lyric work that employs elements of drama such as dialogue, conflict, or characterization, but excluding works that are intended for stage presentation.

Dream Allegory: See *Dream Vision*

Dream Vision: A literary convention, chiefly of the Middle Ages. In a dream vision a story is presented as a literal dream of the narrator. This device was commonly used to teach moral and religious lessons.

E

Eclogue: In classical literature, a poem featuring rural themes and structured as a dialogue among shepherds. Eclogues often took specific poetic forms, such as elegies or love poems. Some were written as the soliloquy of a shepherd. In later centuries, "eclogue" came to refer to any poem that was in the pastoral tradition or that had a dialogue or monologue structure.

Edwardian: Describes cultural conventions identified with the period of the reign of Edward VII of England (1901-1910). Writers of the Edwardian Age typically displayed a strong reaction against the propriety and conservatism of the Victorian Age. Their work often exhibits distrust of authority in religion, politics, and art and expresses strong doubts about the soundness of conventional values.

Edwardian Age: See *Edwardian*

Electra Complex: A daughter's amorous obsession with her father.

Elegy: A lyric poem that laments the death of a person or the eventual death of all people. In a conventional elegy, set in a classical world, the poet and subject are spoken of as shepherds. In modern criticism, the word elegy is often used to refer to a poem that is melancholy or mournfully contemplative.

Elizabethan Age: A period of great economic growth, religious controversy, and nationalism closely associated with the reign of Elizabeth I of England (1558-1603). The Elizabethan Age is considered a part of the general renaissance—that is, the flowering of arts and literature—that took place in Europe during the fourteenth through sixteenth centuries. The era is considered the golden age of English literature. The most important dramas in English and a great deal of lyric poetry were produced during this period, and modern English criticism began around this time.

Empathy: A sense of shared experience, including emotional and physical feelings, with someone or something other than oneself. Empathy is often used to describe the response of a reader to a literary character.

English Sonnet: See *Sonnet*

Enjambment: The running over of the sense and structure of a line of verse or a couplet into the following verse or couplet.

Enlightenment, The: An eighteenth-century philosophical movement. It began in France but had a wide impact throughout Europe and America. Thinkers of the Enlightenment valued reason and believed that both the individual and society could achieve a state of perfection. Corresponding to this essentially humanist vision was a resistance to religious authority.

Epic: A long narrative poem about the adventures of a hero of great historic or legendary importance. The setting is vast and the action is often given cosmic significance through the intervention of supernatural forces such as gods, angels, or demons. Epics are typically written in a classical style of grand simplicity with elaborate metaphors and allusions that enhance the symbolic importance of a hero's adventures.

Epic Simile: See *Homeric Simile*

Epigram: A saying that makes the speaker's point quickly and concisely.

Epilogue: A concluding statement or section of a literary work. In dramas, particularly those of the seventeenth and eighteenth centuries, the epilogue is a closing speech, often in verse, delivered by an actor at the end of a play and spoken directly to the audience.

Epiphany: A sudden revelation of truth inspired by a seemingly trivial incident.

Epitaph: An inscription on a tomb or tombstone, or a verse written on the occasion of a person's death. Epitaphs may be serious or humorous.

Epithalamion: A song or poem written to honor and commemorate a marriage ceremony.

Epithalamium: See *Epithalamion*

Epithet: A word or phrase, often disparaging or abusive, that expresses a character trait of someone or something.

Erziehungsroman: See *Bildungsroman*

Essay: A prose composition with a focused subject of discussion. The term was coined by Michel de Montaigne to describe his 1580 collection of brief, informal reflections on himself and on various topics relating to human nature. An essay can also be a long, systematic discourse.

Existentialism: A predominantly twentieth-century philosophy concerned with the nature and perception of human existence. There are two major strains of existentialist thought: atheistic and Christian. Followers of atheistic existentialism believe that the individual is alone in a godless universe and that the basic human condition is one of suffering and loneliness. Nevertheless, because there are no fixed values, individuals can create their own characters—indeed, they can shape themselves—through the exercise of free will. The atheistic strain culminates in and is popularly associated with the works of Jean-Paul Sartre. The Christian existentialists, on the other hand, believe that only in God may people find freedom from life's anguish. The two strains hold certain beliefs in common: that existence cannot be fully understood or described through empirical effort; that

anguish is a universal element of life; that individuals must bear responsibility for their actions; and that there is no common standard of behavior or perception for religious and ethical matters.

Expatriates: See *Expatriatism*

Expatriatism: The practice of leaving one's country to live for an extended period in another country.

Exposition: Writing intended to explain the nature of an idea, thing, or theme. Expository writing is often combined with description, narration, or argument. In dramatic writing, the exposition is the introductory material which presents the characters, setting, and tone of the play.

Expressionism: An indistinct literary term, originally used to describe an early twentieth-century school of German painting. The term applies to almost any mode of unconventional, highly subjective writing that distorts reality in some way.

Extended Monologue: See *Monologue*

F

Feet: See *Foot*

Feminine Rhyme: See *Rhyme*

Fiction: Any story that is the product of imagination rather than a documentation of fact. Characters and events in such narratives may be based in real life but their ultimate form and configuration is a creation of the author.

Figurative Language: A technique in writing in which the author temporarily interrupts the order, construction, or meaning of the writing for a particular effect. This interruption takes the form of one or more figures of speech such as hyperbole, irony, or simile. Figurative language is the opposite of literal language, in which every word is truthful, accurate, and free of exaggeration or embellishment.

Figures of Speech: Writing that differs from customary conventions for construction, meaning, order, or significance for the purpose of a special meaning or effect. There are two major types of figures of speech: rhetorical figures, which do not make changes in the meaning of the words, and tropes, which do.

Fin de siecle: A French term meaning "end of the century." The term is used to denote the last decade of the nineteenth century, a transition period when writers and other artists abandoned old conventions and looked for new techniques and objectives.

First Person: See *Point of View*

Folk Ballad: See *Ballad*

Folklore: Traditions and myths preserved in a culture or group of people. Typically, these are passed on by word of mouth in various forms—such as legends, songs, and proverbs—or preserved in customs and ceremonies. This term was first used by W. J. Thoms in 1846.

Folktale: A story originating in oral tradition. Folktales fall into a variety of categories, including legends, ghost stories, fairy tales, fables, and anecdotes based on historical figures and events.

Foot: The smallest unit of rhythm in a line of poetry. In English-language poetry, a foot is typically one accented syllable combined with one or two unaccented syllables.

Form: The pattern or construction of a work which identifies its genre and distinguishes it from other genres.

Formalism: In literary criticism, the belief that literature should follow prescribed rules of construction, such as those that govern the sonnet form.

Fourteener Meter: See *Meter*

Free Verse: Poetry that lacks regular metrical and rhyme patterns but that tries to capture the cadences of everyday speech. The form allows a poet to exploit a variety of rhythmical effects within a single poem.

Futurism: A flamboyant literary and artistic movement that developed in France, Italy, and Russia from 1908 through the 1920s. Futurist theater and poetry abandoned traditional literary forms. In their place, followers of the movement attempted to achieve total freedom of expression through bizarre imagery and deformed or newly invented words. The Futurists were self-consciously modern artists who attempted to incorporate the appearances and sounds of modern life into their work.

G

Genre: A category of literary work. In critical theory, genre may refer to both the content of a given work—tragedy, comedy, pastoral— and to its form, such as poetry, novel, or drama.

Genteel Tradition: A term coined by critic George Santayana to describe the literary practice of certain late nineteenth-century American writers, especially New Englanders. Followers of the Genteel Tradition emphasized conventionality in social, religious, moral, and literary standards.

Georgian Age: See *Georgian Poets*

Georgian Period: See *Georgian Poets*

Georgian Poets: A loose grouping of English poets during the years 1912-1922. The Georgians reacted against certain literary schools and practices, especially Victorian wordiness, turn-of-the-century aestheticism, and contemporary urban realism. In their place, the Georgians embraced the nineteenth-century poetic practices of William Wordsworth and the other Lake Poets.

Georgic: A poem about farming and the farmer's way of life, named from Virgil's *Georgics*.

Gilded Age: A period in American history during the 1870s characterized by political corruption and materialism. A number of important novels of social and political criticism were written during this time.

Gothic: See *Gothicism*

Gothicism: In literary criticism, works characterized by a taste for the medieval or morbidly attractive. A gothic novel prominently features elements of horror, the supernatural, gloom, and violence: clanking chains, terror, charnel houses, ghosts, medieval castles, and mysteriously slamming doors. The term "gothic novel" is also applied to novels that lack elements of the traditional Gothic setting but that create a similar atmosphere of terror or dread.

Graveyard School: A group of eighteenth-century English poets who wrote long, picturesque meditations on death. Their works were designed to cause the reader to ponder immortality.

Great Chain of Being: The belief that all things and creatures in nature are organized in a hierarchy from inanimate objects at the bottom to God at the top. This system of belief was popular in the seventeenth and eighteenth centuries.

Grotesque: In literary criticism, the subject matter of a work or a style of expression characterized by exaggeration, deformity, freakishness, and disorder. The grotesque often includes an element of comic absurdity.

H

Haiku: The shortest form of Japanese poetry, constructed in three lines of five, seven, and five syllables respectively. The message of a *haiku* poem usually centers on some aspect of spirituality and provokes an emotional response in the reader.

Half Rhyme: See *Consonance*

Harlem Renaissance: The Harlem Renaissance of the 1920s is generally considered the first significant movement of black writers and artists in the United States. During this period, new and established black writers published more fiction and poetry than ever before, the first influential black literary journals were established, and black authors and artists received their first widespread recognition and serious critical appraisal. Among the major writers associated with this period are Claude McKay, Jean Toomer, Countee Cullen, Langston Hughes, Arna Bontemps, Nella Larsen, and Zora Neale Hurston.

Hellenism: Imitation of ancient Greek thought or styles. Also, an approach to life that focuses on the growth and development of the intellect. "Hellenism" is sometimes used to refer to the belief that reason can be applied to examine all human experience.

Heptameter: See *Meter*

Hero/Heroine: The principal sympathetic character (male or female) in a literary work. Heroes and heroines typically exhibit admirable traits: idealism, courage, and integrity, for example.

Heroic Couplet: A rhyming couplet written in iambic pentameter (a verse with five iambic feet).

Heroic Line: The meter and length of a line of verse in epic or heroic poetry. This varies by language and time period.

Heroine: See *Hero/Heroine*

Hexameter: See *Meter*

Historical Criticism: The study of a work based on its impact on the world of the time period in which it was written.

Hokku: See *Haiku*

Holocaust: See *Holocaust Literature*

Holocaust Literature: Literature influenced by or written about the Holocaust of World War II. Such literature includes true stories of survival in concentration camps, escape, and life after the war, as well as fictional works and poetry.

Homeric Simile: An elaborate, detailed comparison written as a simile many lines in length.

Horatian Satire: See *Satire*

Humanism: A philosophy that places faith in the dignity of humankind and rejects the medieval perception of the individual as a weak, fallen creature. "Humanists" typically believe in the perfectibility of human nature and view reason and education as the means to that end.

Humors: Mentions of the humors refer to the ancient Greek theory that a person's health and personality were determined by the balance of four basic fluids in the body: blood, phlegm, yellow bile, and black bile. A dominance of any fluid would cause extremes in behavior. An excess of blood created a sanguine person who was joyful, aggressive, and passionate; a phlegmatic person was shy, fearful, and sluggish; too much yellow bile led to a choleric temperament characterized by impatience, anger, bitterness, and stubbornness; and excessive black bile created melancholy, a state of laziness, gluttony, and lack of motivation.

Humours: See *Humors*

Hyperbole: In literary criticism, deliberate exaggeration used to achieve an effect.

I

Iamb: See *Foot*

Idiom: A word construction or verbal expression closely associated with a given language.

Image: A concrete representation of an object or sensory experience. Typically, such a representation helps evoke the feelings associated with the object or experience itself. Images are either "literal" or "figurative." Literal images are especially concrete and involve little or no extension of the obvious meaning of the words used to express them. Figurative images do not follow the literal meaning of the words exactly. Images in literature are usually visual, but the term "image" can also refer to the representation of any sensory experience.

Imagery: The array of images in a literary work. Also, figurative language.

Imagism: An English and American poetry movement that flourished between 1908 and 1917. The Imagists used precise, clearly presented images in their works. They also used common, everyday speech and aimed for conciseness, concrete imagery, and the creation of new rhythms.

In medias res: A Latin term meaning "in the middle of things." It refers to the technique of beginning a story at its midpoint and then using various flashback devices to reveal previous action.

Induction: The process of reaching a conclusion by reasoning from specific premises to form a general premise. Also, an introductory portion of a work of literature, especially a play.

Intentional Fallacy: The belief that judgments of a literary work based solely on an author's stated or implied intentions are false and misleading. Critics who believe in the concept of the intentional fallacy typically argue that the work itself is sufficient matter for interpretation, even though they may concede that an author's statement of purpose can be useful.

Interior Monologue: A narrative technique in which characters' thoughts are revealed in a way that appears to be uncontrolled by the author. The interior monologue typically aims to reveal the inner self of a character. It portrays emotional experiences as they occur at both a conscious and unconscious level. Images are often used to represent sensations or emotions.

Internal Rhyme: Rhyme that occurs within a single line of verse.

Irish Literary Renaissance: A late nineteenth- and early twentieth-century movement in Irish literature. Members of the movement aimed to reduce the influence of British culture in Ireland and create an Irish national literature.

Irony: In literary criticism, the effect of language in which the intended meaning is the opposite of what is stated.

Italian Sonnet: See *Sonnet*

J

Jacobean Age: The period of the reign of James I of England (1603-1625). The early literature of this period reflected the worldview of the Elizabethan Age, but a darker, more cynical attitude steadily grew in the art and literature of the Jacobean Age. This was an important time for English drama and poetry.

Jargon: Language that is used or understood only by a select group of people. Jargon may refer to terminology used in a certain profession, such as computer jargon, or it may refer to any nonsensical language that is not understood by most people.

Journalism: Writing intended for publication in a newspaper or magazine, or for broadcast on a radio or television program featuring news, sports, entertainment, or other timely material.

K

Knickerbocker Group: A somewhat indistinct group of New York writers of the first half of the nineteenth century. Members of the group were linked only by location and a common theme: New York life.

Kunstlerroman: See *Bildungsroman*

L

Lais: See *Lay*

Lake Poets: See *Lake School*

Lake School: These poets all lived in the Lake District of England at the turn of the nineteenth century. As a group, they followed no single "school" of thought or literary practice, although their works were uniformly disparaged by the *Edinburgh Review*.

Lay: A song or simple narrative poem. The form originated in medieval France. Early French *lais* were often based on the Celtic legends and other tales sung by Breton minstrels—thus the name of the "Breton lay." In fourteenth-century England, the term "lay" was used to describe short narratives written in imitation of the Breton lays.

Leitmotiv: See *Motif*

Literal Language: An author uses literal language when he or she writes without exaggerating or embellishing the subject matter and without any tools of figurative language.

Literary Ballad: See *Ballad*

Literature: Literature is broadly defined as any written or spoken material, but the term most often refers to creative works.

Lost Generation: A term first used by Gertrude Stein to describe the post-World War I generation of American writers: men and women haunted by a sense of betrayal and emptiness brought about by the destructiveness of the war.

Lyric Poetry: A poem expressing the subjective feelings and personal emotions of the poet. Such poetry is melodic, since it was originally accompanied by a lyre in recitals. Most Western poetry in the twentieth century may be classified as lyrical.

M

Mannerism: Exaggerated, artificial adherence to a literary manner or style. Also, a popular style of the visual arts of late sixteenth-century Europe that was marked by elongation of the human form and by intentional spatial distortion. Literary works that are self-consciously high-toned and artistic are often said to be "mannered."

Masculine Rhyme: See *Rhyme*

Measure: The foot, verse, or time sequence used in a literary work, especially a poem. Measure is often used somewhat incorrectly as a synonym for meter.

Metaphor: A figure of speech that expresses an idea through the image of another object. Metaphors suggest the essence of the first object by identifying it with certain qualities of the second object.

Metaphysical Conceit: See *Conceit*

Metaphysical Poetry: The body of poetry produced by a group of seventeenth-century English writers called the "Metaphysical Poets." The group includes John Donne and Andrew Marvell. The Metaphysical Poets made use of everyday speech, intellectual analysis, and unique imagery. They aimed to portray the ordinary conflicts and contradictions of life. Their poems often took the form of an argument, and many of them emphasize physical and religious love as well as the fleeting nature of life. Elaborate conceits are typical in metaphysical poetry.

Metaphysical Poets: See *Metaphysical Poetry*

Meter: In literary criticism, the repetition of sound patterns that creates a rhythm in poetry. The patterns are based on the number of syllables and the presence and absence of accents. The unit of rhythm in a line is called a foot. Types of meter are classified according to the number of feet in a line. These are the standard English lines: Monometer, one foot; Dimeter, two feet; Trimeter, three feet; Tetrameter, four feet; Pentameter, five feet; Hexameter, six feet (also called the Alexandrine); Heptameter, seven feet (also called the "Fourteener" when the feet are iambic).

Modernism: Modern literary practices. Also, the principles of a literary school that lasted from roughly the beginning of the twentieth century until the end of World War II. Modernism is defined by its rejection of the literary conventions of the nineteenth century and by its opposition to conventional morality, taste, traditions, and economic values.

Monologue: A composition, written or oral, by a single individual. More specifically, a speech given by a single individual in a drama or other public entertainment. It has no set length, although it is usually several or more lines long.

Monometer: See *Meter*

Mood: The prevailing emotions of a work or of the author in his or her creation of the work. The mood of a work is not always what might be expected based on its subject matter.

Motif: A theme, character type, image, metaphor, or other verbal element that recurs throughout a single work of literature or occurs in a number of different works over a period of time.

Motiv: See *Motif*

Muckrakers: An early twentieth-century group of American writers. Typically, their works exposed the wrongdoings of big business and government in the United States.

Muses: Nine Greek mythological goddesses, the daughters of Zeus and Mnemosyne (Memory). Each muse patronized a specific area of the liberal arts and sciences. Calliope presided over epic poetry, Clio over history, Erato over love poetry, Euterpe over music or lyric poetry, Melpomene over tragedy, Polyhymnia over hymns to the gods, Terpsichore over dance, Thalia over comedy, and

Urania over astronomy. Poets and writers traditionally made appeals to the Muses for inspiration in their work.

Myth: An anonymous tale emerging from the traditional beliefs of a culture or social unit. Myths use supernatural explanations for natural phenomena. They may also explain cosmic issues like creation and death. Collections of myths, known as mythologies, are common to all cultures and nations, but the best-known myths belong to the Norse, Roman, and Greek mythologies.

N

Narration: The telling of a series of events, real or invented. A narration may be either a simple narrative, in which the events are recounted chronologically, or a narrative with a plot, in which the account is given in a style reflecting the author's artistic concept of the story. Narration is sometimes used as a synonym for "storyline."

Narrative: A verse or prose accounting of an event or sequence of events, real or invented. The term is also used as an adjective in the sense "method of narration." For example, in literary criticism, the expression "narrative technique" usually refers to the way the author structures and presents his or her story.

Narrative Poetry: A nondramatic poem in which the author tells a story. Such poems may be of any length or level of complexity.

Narrator: The teller of a story. The narrator may be the author or a character in the story through whom the author speaks.

Naturalism: A literary movement of the late nineteenth and early twentieth centuries. The movement's major theorist, French novelist Emile Zola, envisioned a type of fiction that would examine human life with the objectivity of scientific inquiry. The Naturalists typically viewed human beings as either the products of "biological determinism," ruled by hereditary instincts and engaged in an endless struggle for survival, or as the products of "socioeconomic determinism," ruled by social and economic forces beyond their control. In their works, the Naturalists generally ignored the highest levels of society and focused on degradation: poverty, alcoholism, prostitution, insanity, and disease.

Negritude: A literary movement based on the concept of a shared cultural bond on the part of black Africans, wherever they may be in the world. It traces its origins to the former French colonies of Africa and the Caribbean. Negritude poets, novelists, and essayists generally stress four points in their writings: One, black alienation from traditional African culture can lead to feelings of inferiority. Two, European colonialism and Western education should be resisted. Three, black Africans should seek to affirm and define their own identity. Four, African culture can and should be reclaimed. Many Negritude writers also claim that blacks can make unique contributions to the world, based on a heightened appreciation of nature, rhythm, and human emotions—aspects of life they say are not so highly valued in the materialistic and rationalistic West.

Negro Renaissance: See *Harlem Renaissance*

Neoclassical Period: See *Neoclassicism*

Neoclassicism: In literary criticism, this term refers to the revival of the attitudes and styles of expression of classical literature. It is generally used to describe a period in European history beginning in the late seventeenth century and lasting until about 1800. In its purest form, Neoclassicism marked a return to order, proportion, restraint, logic, accuracy, and decorum. In England, where Neoclassicism perhaps was most popular, it reflected the influence of seventeenth-century French writers, especially dramatists. Neoclassical writers typically reacted against the intensity and enthusiasm of the Renaissance period. They wrote works that appealed to the intellect, using elevated language and classical literary forms such as satire and the ode. Neoclassical works were often governed by the classical goal of instruction.

Neoclassicists: See *Neoclassicism*

New Criticism: A movement in literary criticism, dating from the late 1920s, that stressed close textual analysis in the interpretation of works of literature. The New Critics saw little merit in historical and biographical analysis. Rather, they aimed to examine the text alone, free from the question of how external events—biographical or otherwise—may have helped shape it.

New Journalism: A type of writing in which the journalist presents factual information in a form usually used in fiction. New journalism emphasizes description, narration, and character development to bring readers closer to the human element of the story, and is often used in personality profiles and in-depth feature articles. It is not compatible with "straight" or "hard" newswriting, which is generally composed in a brief, fact-based style.

New Journalists: See *New Journalism*

New Negro Movement: See *Harlem Renaissance*

Noble Savage: The idea that primitive man is noble and good but becomes evil and corrupted as he becomes civilized. The concept of the noble savage originated in the Renaissance period but is more closely identified with such later writers as Jean-Jacques Rousseau and Aphra Behn.

O

Objective Correlative: An outward set of objects, a situation, or a chain of events corresponding to an inward experience and evoking this experience in the reader. The term frequently appears in modern criticism in discussions of authors' intended effects on the emotional responses of readers.

Objectivity: A quality in writing characterized by the absence of the author's opinion or feeling about the subject matter. Objectivity is an important factor in criticism.

Occasional Verse: Poetry written on the occasion of a significant historical or personal event. *Vers de societe* is sometimes called occasional verse although it is of a less serious nature.

Octave: A poem or stanza composed of eight lines. The term octave most often represents the first eight lines of a Petrarchan sonnet.

Ode: Name given to an extended lyric poem characterized by exalted emotion and dignified style. An ode usually concerns a single, serious theme. Most odes, but not all, are addressed to an object or individual. Odes are distinguished from other lyric poetic forms by their complex rhythmic and stanzaic patterns.

Oedipus Complex: A son's amorous obsession with his mother. The phrase is derived from the story of the ancient Theban hero Oedipus, who unknowingly killed his father and married his mother.

Omniscience: See *Point of View*

Onomatopoeia: The use of words whose sounds express or suggest their meaning. In its simplest sense, onomatopoeia may be represented by words that mimic the sounds they denote such as "hiss" or "meow." At a more subtle level, the pattern and rhythm of sounds and rhymes of a line or poem may be onomatopoeic.

Oral Tradition: See *Oral Transmission*

Oral Transmission: A process by which songs, ballads, folklore, and other material are transmitted by word of mouth. The tradition of oral transmission predates the written record systems of literate society. Oral transmission preserves material sometimes over generations, although often with variations. Memory plays a large part in the recitation and preservation of orally transmitted material.

Ottava Rima: An eight-line stanza of poetry composed in iambic pentameter (a five-foot line in which each foot consists of an unaccented syllable followed by an accented syllable), following the abababcc rhyme scheme.

Oxymoron: A phrase combining two contradictory terms. Oxymorons may be intentional or unintentional.

P

Pantheism: The idea that all things are both a manifestation or revelation of God and a part of God at the same time. Pantheism was a common attitude in the early societies of Egypt, India, and Greece—the term derives from the Greek *pan* meaning "all" and *theos* meaning "deity." It later became a significant part of the Christian faith.

Parable: A story intended to teach a moral lesson or answer an ethical question.

Paradox: A statement that appears illogical or contradictory at first, but may actually point to an underlying truth.

Parallelism: A method of comparison of two ideas in which each is developed in the same grammatical structure.

Parnassianism: A mid nineteenth-century movement in French literature. Followers of the movement stressed adherence to well-defined artistic forms as a reaction against the often chaotic expression of the artist's ego that dominated the work of the Romantics. The Parnassians also rejected the moral, ethical, and social themes exhibited in the works of French Romantics such as Victor Hugo. The aesthetic doctrines of the Parnassians strongly influenced the later symbolist and decadent movements.

Parody: In literary criticism, this term refers to an imitation of a serious literary work or the signature style of a particular author in a ridiculous manner. A typical parody adopts the style of the original and applies it to an inappropriate subject for humorous effect. Parody is a form of satire and could be considered the literary equivalent of a caricature or cartoon.

Pastoral: A term derived from the Latin word "pastor," meaning shepherd. A pastoral is a literary composition on a rural theme. The conventions of the pastoral were originated by the third-century Greek poet Theocritus, who wrote about the experiences, love affairs, and pastimes of Sicilian shepherds. In a pastoral, characters and language of a courtly nature are often placed in a simple setting. The term pastoral is also used to classify dramas, elegies, and lyrics that exhibit the use of country settings and shepherd characters.

Pathetic Fallacy: A term coined by English critic John Ruskin to identify writing that falsely endows nonhuman things with human intentions and feelings, such as "angry clouds" and "sad trees."

Pen Name: See *Pseudonym*

Pentameter: See *Meter*

Persona: A Latin term meaning "mask." *Personae* are the characters in a fictional work of literature. The *persona* generally functions as a mask through which the author tells a story in a voice other than his or her own. A *persona* is usually either a character in a story who acts as a narrator or an "implied author," a voice created by the author to act as the narrator for himself or herself.

Personae: See *Persona*

Personal Point of View: See *Point of View*

Personification: A figure of speech that gives human qualities to abstract ideas, animals, and inanimate objects.

Petrarchan Sonnet: See *Sonnet*

Phenomenology: A method of literary criticism based on the belief that things have no existence outside of human consciousness or awareness. Proponents of this theory believe that art is a process that takes place in the mind of the observer as he or she contemplates an object rather than a quality of the object itself.

Plagiarism: Claiming another person's written material as one's own. Plagiarism can take the form of direct, word-for-word copying or the theft of the substance or idea of the work.

Platonic Criticism: A form of criticism that stresses an artistic work's usefulness as an agent of social engineering rather than any quality or value of the work itself.

Platonism: The embracing of the doctrines of the philosopher Plato, popular among the poets of the Renaissance and the Romantic period. Platonism is more flexible than Aristotelian Criticism and places more emphasis on the supernatural and unknown aspects of life.

Plot: In literary criticism, this term refers to the pattern of events in a narrative or drama. In its simplest sense, the plot guides the author in composing the work and helps the reader follow the work. Typically, plots exhibit causality and unity and have a beginning, a middle, and an end. Sometimes, however, a plot may consist of a series of disconnected events, in which case it is known as an "episodic plot."

Poem: In its broadest sense, a composition utilizing rhyme, meter, concrete detail, and expressive language to create a literary experience with emotional and aesthetic appeal.

Poet: An author who writes poetry or verse. The term is also used to refer to an artist or writer who has an exceptional gift for expression, imagination, and energy in the making of art in any form.

Poete maudit: A term derived from Paul Verlaine's *Les poetes maudits* (*The Accursed Poets*), a collection of essays on the French symbolist writers Stephane Mallarme, Arthur Rimbaud, and Tristan Corbiere. In the sense intended by Verlaine, the poet is "accursed" for choosing to explore extremes of human experience outside of middle-class society.

Poetic Fallacy: See *Pathetic Fallacy*

Poetic Justice: An outcome in a literary work, not necessarily a poem, in which the good are rewarded and the evil are punished, especially in ways that particularly fit their virtues or crimes.

Poetic License: Distortions of fact and literary convention made by a writer—not always a poet—for the sake of the effect gained. Poetic license is closely related to the concept of "artistic freedom."

Poetics: This term has two closely related meanings. It denotes (1) an aesthetic theory in literary criticism about the essence of poetry or (2) rules prescribing the proper methods, content, style, or diction of poetry. The term poetics may also refer to theories about literature in general, not just poetry.

Poetry: In its broadest sense, writing that aims to present ideas and evoke an emotional experience in the reader through the use of meter, imagery, connotative and concrete words, and a carefully constructed structure based on rhythmic patterns. Poetry typically relies on words and expressions that have several layers of meaning. It also makes use of the effects of regular rhythm on the ear and may make a strong appeal to the senses through the use of imagery.

Point of View: The narrative perspective from which a literary work is presented to the reader. There are four traditional points of view. The "third person omniscient" gives the reader a "godlike" perspective, unrestricted by time or place, from which to see actions and look into the minds of characters. This allows the author to comment openly on characters and events in the work. The "third person" point of view presents the events of the story from outside of any single character's perception, much like the omniscient point of view, but the reader must understand the action as it takes place and without any special insight into characters' minds or motivations. The "first person" or "personal" point of view relates events as they are perceived by a single character. The main character "tells" the story and may offer opinions about the action and characters which differ from those of the author. Much less common than omniscient, third person, and first person is the "second person" point of view, wherein the author tells the story as if it is happening to the reader.

Polemic: A work in which the author takes a stand on a controversial subject, such as abortion or religion. Such works are often extremely argumentative or provocative.

Pornography: Writing intended to provoke feelings of lust in the reader. Such works are often condemned by critics and teachers, but those which can be shown to have literary value are viewed less harshly.

Post-Aesthetic Movement: An artistic response made by African Americans to the black aesthetic movement of the 1960s and early '70s. Writers since that time have adopted a somewhat different tone in their work, with less emphasis placed on the disparity between black and white in the United States. In the words of post-aesthetic authors such as Toni Morrison, John Edgar Wideman, and Kristin Hunter, African Americans are portrayed as looking inward for answers to their own questions, rather than always looking to the outside world.

Postmodernism: Writing from the 1960s forward characterized by experimentation and continuing to apply some of the fundamentals of modernism, which included existentialism and alienation. Postmodernists have gone a step further in the rejection of tradition begun with the modernists by also rejecting traditional forms, preferring the anti-novel over the novel and the anti-hero over the hero.

Pre-Raphaelites: A circle of writers and artists in mid nineteenth-century England. Valuing the pre-Renaissance artistic qualities of religious symbolism, lavish pictorialism, and natural sensuousness, the Pre-Raphaelites cultivated a sense of mystery and melancholy that influenced later writers associated with the Symbolist and Decadent movements.

Primitivism: The belief that primitive peoples were nobler and less flawed than civilized peoples because they had not been subjected to the tainting influence of society.

Projective Verse: A form of free verse in which the poet's breathing pattern determines the lines of the poem. Poets who advocate projective verse are against all formal structures in writing, including meter and form.

Prologue: An introductory section of a literary work. It often contains information establishing the situation of the characters or presents information about the setting, time period, or action. In drama, the prologue is spoken by a chorus or by one of the principal characters.

Prose: A literary medium that attempts to mirror the language of everyday speech. It is distinguished from poetry by its use of unmetered, unrhymed language consisting of logically related sentences. Prose is usually grouped into paragraphs that form a cohesive whole such as an essay or a novel.

Prosopopoeia: See *Personification*

Protagonist: The central character of a story who serves as a focus for its themes and incidents and as the principal rationale for its development. The protagonist is sometimes referred to in discussions of modern literature as the hero or anti-hero.

Proverb: A brief, sage saying that expresses a truth about life in a striking manner.

Pseudonym: A name assumed by a writer, most often intended to prevent his or her identification as the author of a work. Two or more authors may work together under one pseudonym, or an author may use a different name for each genre he or she publishes in. Some publishing companies maintain "house pseudonyms," under which any number of authors may write installations in a series. Some authors also choose a pseudonym over their real names the way an actor may use a stage name.

Pun: A play on words that have similar sounds but different meanings.

Pure Poetry: Poetry written without instructional intent or moral purpose that aims only to please a reader by its imagery or musical flow. The term pure poetry is used as the antonym of the term "didacticism."

Q

Quatrain: A four-line stanza of a poem or an entire poem consisting of four lines.

R

Realism: A nineteenth-century European literary movement that sought to portray familiar characters, situations, and settings in a realistic manner. This was done primarily by using an objective narrative point of view and through the buildup of accurate detail. The standard for success of any realistic

work depends on how faithfully it transfers common experience into fictional forms. The realistic method may be altered or extended, as in stream of consciousness writing, to record highly subjective experience.

Refrain: A phrase repeated at intervals throughout a poem. A refrain may appear at the end of each stanza or at less regular intervals. It may be altered slightly at each appearance.

Renaissance: The period in European history that marked the end of the Middle Ages. It began in Italy in the late fourteenth century. In broad terms, it is usually seen as spanning the fourteenth, fifteenth, and sixteenth centuries, although it did not reach Great Britain, for example, until the 1480s or so. The Renaissance saw an awakening in almost every sphere of human activity, especially science, philosophy, and the arts. The period is best defined by the emergence of a general philosophy that emphasized the importance of the intellect, the individual, and world affairs. It contrasts strongly with the medieval worldview, characterized by the dominant concerns of faith, the social collective, and spiritual salvation.

Repartee: Conversation featuring snappy retorts and witticisms.

Restoration: See *Restoration Age*

Restoration Age: A period in English literature beginning with the crowning of Charles II in 1660 and running to about 1700. The era, which was characterized by a reaction against Puritanism, was the first great age of the comedy of manners. The finest literature of the era is typically witty and urbane, and often lewd.

Rhetoric: In literary criticism, this term denotes the art of ethical persuasion. In its strictest sense, rhetoric adheres to various principles developed since classical times for arranging facts and ideas in a clear, persuasive, appealing manner. The term is also used to refer to effective prose in general and theories of or methods for composing effective prose.

Rhetorical Question: A question intended to provoke thought, but not an expressed answer, in the reader. It is most commonly used in oratory and other persuasive genres.

Rhyme: When used as a noun in literary criticism, this term generally refers to a poem in which words sound identical or very similar and appear in parallel positions in two or more lines. Rhymes are classified into different types according to where they fall in a line or stanza or according to the degree of similarity they exhibit in their spellings and sounds. Some major types of rhyme are "masculine" rhyme, "feminine" rhyme, and "triple" rhyme. In a masculine rhyme, the rhyming sound falls in a single accented syllable, as with "heat" and "eat." Feminine rhyme is a rhyme of two syllables, one stressed and one unstressed, as with "merry" and "tarry." Triple rhyme matches the sound of the accented syllable and the two unaccented syllables that follow: "narrative" and "declarative."

Rhyme Royal: A stanza of seven lines composed in iambic pentameter and rhymed *ababbcc*. The name is said to be a tribute to King James I of Scotland, who made much use of the form in his poetry.

Rhyme Scheme: See *Rhyme*

Rhythm: A regular pattern of sound, time intervals, or events occurring in writing, most often and most discernably in poetry. Regular, reliable rhythm is known to be soothing to humans, while interrupted, unpredictable, or rapidly changing rhythm is disturbing. These effects are known to authors, who use them to produce a desired reaction in the reader.

Rococo: A style of European architecture that flourished in the eighteenth century, especially in France. The most notable features of *rococo* are its extensive use of ornamentation and its themes of lightness, gaiety, and intimacy. In literary criticism, the term is often used disparagingly to refer to a decadent or over-ornamental style.

Romance: A broad term, usually denoting a narrative with exotic, exaggerated, often idealized characters, scenes, and themes.

Romantic Age: See *Romanticism*

Romanticism: This term has two widely accepted meanings. In historical criticism, it refers to a European intellectual and artistic movement of the late eighteenth and early nineteenth centuries that sought greater freedom of personal expression than that allowed by the strict rules of literary form and logic of the eighteenth-century neoclassicists. The Romantics preferred emotional and imaginative expression to rational analysis.

They considered the individual to be at the center of all experience and so placed him or her at the center of their art. The Romantics believed that the creative imagination reveals nobler truths—unique feelings and attitudes—than those that could be discovered by logic or by scientific examination. Both the natural world and the state of childhood were important sources for revelations of "eternal truths." "Romanticism" is also used as a general term to refer to a type of sensibility found in all periods of literary history and usually considered to be in opposition to the principles of classicism. In this sense, Romanticism signifies any work or philosophy in which the exotic or dreamlike figure strongly, or that is devoted to individualistic expression, self-analysis, or a pursuit of a higher realm of knowledge than can be discovered by human reason.

Romantics: See *Romanticism*

Russian Symbolism: A Russian poetic movement, derived from French symbolism, that flourished between 1894 and 1910. While some Russian Symbolists continued in the French tradition, stressing aestheticism and the importance of suggestion above didactic intent, others saw their craft as a form of mystical worship, and themselves as mediators between the supernatural and the mundane.

S

Satire: A work that uses ridicule, humor, and wit to criticize and provoke change in human nature and institutions. There are two major types of satire: "formal" or "direct" satire speaks directly to the reader or to a character in the work; "indirect" satire relies upon the ridiculous behavior of its characters to make its point. Formal satire is further divided into two manners: the "Horatian," which ridicules gently, and the "Juvenalian," which derides its subjects harshly and bitterly.

Scansion: The analysis or "scanning" of a poem to determine its meter and often its rhyme scheme. The most common system of scansion uses accents (slanted lines drawn above syllables) to show stressed syllables, breves (curved lines drawn above syllables) to show unstressed syllables, and vertical lines to separate each foot.

Second Person: See *Point of View*

Semiotics: The study of how literary forms and conventions affect the meaning of language.

Sestet: Any six-line poem or stanza.

Setting: The time, place, and culture in which the action of a narrative takes place. The elements of setting may include geographic location, characters' physical and mental environments, prevailing cultural attitudes, or the historical time in which the action takes place.

Shakespearean Sonnet: See *Sonnet*

Signifying Monkey: A popular trickster figure in black folklore, with hundreds of tales about this character documented since the 19th century.

Simile: A comparison, usually using "like" or "as," of two essentially dissimilar things, as in "coffee as cold as ice" or "He sounded like a broken record."

Slang: A type of informal verbal communication that is generally unacceptable for formal writing. Slang words and phrases are often colorful exaggerations used to emphasize the speaker's point; they may also be shortened versions of an often-used word or phrase.

Slant Rhyme: See *Consonance*

Slave Narrative: Autobiographical accounts of American slave life as told by escaped slaves. These works first appeared during the abolition movement of the 1830s through the 1850s.

Social Realism: See *Socialist Realism*

Socialist Realism: The Socialist Realism school of literary theory was proposed by Maxim Gorky and established as a dogma by the first Soviet Congress of Writers. It demanded adherence to a communist worldview in works of literature. Its doctrines required an objective viewpoint comprehensible to the working classes and themes of social struggle featuring strong proletarian heroes.

Soliloquy: A monologue in a drama used to give the audience information and to develop the speaker's character. It is typically a projection of the speaker's innermost thoughts. Usually delivered while the speaker is alone on stage, a soliloquy is intended to present an illusion of unspoken reflection.

Sonnet: A fourteen-line poem, usually composed in iambic pentameter, employing one of several rhyme schemes. There are three major types of sonnets, upon which all other variations of the form are based: the "Petrarchan" or "Italian" sonnet, the "Shakespearean" or "English" sonnet, and the "Spenserian" sonnet. A Petrarchan sonnet consists of an octave rhymed *abbaabba* and a "sestet" rhymed either *cdecde, cdccdc,* or *cdedce.* The octave poses a question or problem, relates a narrative, or puts forth a proposition; the sestet presents a solution to the problem, comments upon the narrative, or applies the proposition put forth in the octave. The Shakespearean sonnet is divided into three quatrains and a couplet rhymed *abab cdcd efef gg.* The couplet provides an epigrammatic comment on the narrative or problem put forth in the quatrains. The Spenserian sonnet uses three quatrains and a couplet like the Shakespearean, but links their three rhyme schemes in this way: *abab bcbc cdcd ee.* The Spenserian sonnet develops its theme in two parts like the Petrarchan, its final six lines resolving a problem, analyzing a narrative, or applying a proposition put forth in its first eight lines.

Spenserian Sonnet: See *Sonnet*

Spenserian Stanza: A nine-line stanza having eight verses in iambic pentameter, its ninth verse in iambic hexameter, and the rhyme scheme ababbcbcc.

Spondee: In poetry meter, a foot consisting of two long or stressed syllables occurring together. This form is quite rare in English verse, and is usually composed of two monosyllabic words.

Sprung Rhythm: Versification using a specific number of accented syllables per line but disregarding the number of unaccented syllables that fall in each line, producing an irregular rhythm in the poem.

Stanza: A subdivision of a poem consisting of lines grouped together, often in recurring patterns of rhyme, line length, and meter. Stanzas may also serve as units of thought in a poem much like paragraphs in prose.

Stereotype: A stereotype was originally the name for a duplication made during the printing process; this led to its modern definition as a person or thing that is (or is assumed to be) the same as all others of its type.

Stream of Consciousness: A narrative technique for rendering the inward experience of a character. This technique is designed to give the impression of an ever-changing series of thoughts, emotions, images, and memories in the spontaneous and seemingly illogical order that they occur in life.

Structuralism: A twentieth-century movement in literary criticism that examines how literary texts arrive at their meanings, rather than the meanings themselves. There are two major types of structuralist analysis: one examines the way patterns of linguistic structures unify a specific text and emphasize certain elements of that text, and the other interprets the way literary forms and conventions affect the meaning of language itself.

Structure: The form taken by a piece of literature. The structure may be made obvious for ease of understanding, as in nonfiction works, or may obscured for artistic purposes, as in some poetry or seemingly "unstructured" prose.

Sturm und Drang: A German term meaning "storm and stress." It refers to a German literary movement of the 1770s and 1780s that reacted against the order and rationalism of the enlightenment, focusing instead on the intense experience of extraordinary individuals.

Style: A writer's distinctive manner of arranging words to suit his or her ideas and purpose in writing. The unique imprint of the author's personality upon his or her writing, style is the product of an author's way of arranging ideas and his or her use of diction, different sentence structures, rhythm, figures of speech, rhetorical principles, and other elements of composition.

Subject: The person, event, or theme at the center of a work of literature. A work may have one or more subjects of each type, with shorter works tending to have fewer and longer works tending to have more.

Subjectivity: Writing that expresses the author's personal feelings about his subject, and which may or may not include factual information about the subject.

Surrealism: A term introduced to criticism by Guillaume Apollinaire and later adopted by Andre Breton. It refers to a French literary and artistic movement founded in the 1920s. The Surrealists sought to express unconscious thoughts and feelings in their works. The best-known technique used for achieving this aim was automatic writing—transcriptions of spontaneous outpourings from the unconscious. The Surrealists proposed to unify the contrary levels of conscious and unconscious, dream and reality, objectivity and subjectivity into a new level of "super-realism."

Suspense: A literary device in which the author maintains the audience's attention through the buildup of events, the outcome of which will soon be revealed.

Syllogism: A method of presenting a logical argument. In its most basic form, the syllogism consists of a major premise, a minor premise, and a conclusion.

Symbol: Something that suggests or stands for something else without losing its original identity. In literature, symbols combine their literal meaning with the suggestion of an abstract concept. Literary symbols are of two types: those that carry complex associations of meaning no matter what their contexts, and those that derive their suggestive meaning from their functions in specific literary works.

Symbolism: This term has two widely accepted meanings. In historical criticism, it denotes an early modernist literary movement initiated in France during the nineteenth century that reacted against the prevailing standards of realism. Writers in this movement aimed to evoke, indirectly and symbolically, an order of being beyond the material world of the five senses. Poetic expression of personal emotion figured strongly in the movement, typically by means of a private set of symbols uniquely identifiable with the individual poet. The principal aim of the Symbolists was to express in words the highly complex feelings that grew out of everyday contact with the world. In a broader sense, the term "symbolism" refers to the use of one object to represent another.

Symbolist: See *Symbolism*

Symbolist Movement: See *Symbolism*

Sympathetic Fallacy: See *Affective Fallacy*

T

Tanka: A form of Japanese poetry similar to *haiku*. A *tanka* is five lines long, with the lines containing five, seven, five, seven, and seven syllables respectively.

Terza Rima: A three-line stanza form in poetry in which the rhymes are made on the last word of each line in the following manner: the first and third lines of the first stanza, then the second line of the first stanza and the first and third lines of the second stanza, and so on with the middle line of any stanza rhyming with the first and third lines of the following stanza.

Tetrameter: See *Meter*

Textual Criticism: A branch of literary criticism that seeks to establish the authoritative text of a literary work. Textual critics typically compare all known manuscripts or printings of a single work in order to assess the meanings of differences and revisions. This procedure allows them to arrive at a definitive version that (supposedly) corresponds to the author's original intention.

Theme: The main point of a work of literature. The term is used interchangeably with thesis.

Thesis: A thesis is both an essay and the point argued in the essay. Thesis novels and thesis plays share the quality of containing a thesis which is supported through the action of the story.

Third Person: See *Point of View*

Tone: The author's attitude toward his or her audience may be deduced from the tone of the work. A formal tone may create distance or convey politeness, while an informal tone may encourage a friendly, intimate, or intrusive feeling in the reader. The author's attitude toward his or her subject matter may also be deduced from the tone of the words he or she uses in discussing it.

Tragedy: A drama in prose or poetry about a noble, courageous hero of excellent character who, because of some tragic character flaw or *hamartia*, brings ruin upon him- or herself. Tragedy treats its subjects in a dignified and serious manner, using poetic language to help evoke pity and fear and bring about catharsis, a purging of these emotions. The tragic form was practiced extensively by the ancient Greeks. In the Middle Ages, when classical works were virtually unknown, tragedy came to denote any works about the fall of persons from exalted to low conditions due to any reason: fate, vice, weakness, etc. According to the classical definition of tragedy, such works present the "pathetic"— that which evokes pity—rather than the tragic. The classical form of tragedy was revived in the sixteenth century; it flourished especially on the Elizabethan stage. In modern times, dramatists have attempted to adapt the form to the needs of modern society by drawing their heroes from the ranks of ordinary men and women and defining the nobility of these heroes in terms of spirit rather than exalted social standing.

Tragic Flaw: In a tragedy, the quality within the hero or heroine which leads to his or her downfall.

Transcendentalism: An American philosophical and religious movement, based in New England from around 1835 until the Civil War. Transcendentalism was a form of American romanticism that had its roots abroad in the works of Thomas Carlyle, Samuel Coleridge, and Johann Wolfgang von Goethe. The Transcendentalists stressed the importance of intuition and subjective experience in communication with God. They rejected religious dogma and texts in favor of mysticism and scientific naturalism. They pursued truths that lie beyond the "colorless" realms perceived by reason and the senses and were active social reformers in public education, women's rights, and the abolition of slavery.

Trickster: A character or figure common in Native American and African literature who uses his ingenuity to defeat enemies and escape difficult situations. Tricksters are most often animals, such as the spider, hare, or coyote, although they may take the form of humans as well.

Trimeter: See *Meter*

Triple Rhyme: See *Rhyme*

Trochee: See *Foot*

U

Understatement: See *Irony*

Unities: Strict rules of dramatic structure, formulated by Italian and French critics of the Renaissance and based loosely on the principles of drama discussed by Aristotle in his *Poetics*. Foremost among these rules were the three unities of action, time, and place that compelled a dramatist to: (1) construct a single plot with a beginning, middle, and end that details the causal relationships of action and character; (2) restrict the action to the events of a single day; and (3) limit the scene to a single place or city. The unities were observed faithfully by continental European writers until the Romantic Age, but they were never regularly observed in English drama. Modern dramatists are typically more concerned with a unity of impression or emotional effect than with any of the classical unities.

Urban Realism: A branch of realist writing that attempts to accurately reflect the often harsh facts of modern urban existence.

Utopia: A fictional perfect place, such as "paradise" or "heaven."

Utopian: See *Utopia*

Utopianism: See *Utopia*

V

Verisimilitude: Literally, the appearance of truth. In literary criticism, the term refers to aspects of a work of literature that seem true to the reader.

Vers de societe: See *Occasional Verse*

Vers libre: See *Free Verse*

Verse: A line of metered language, a line of a poem, or any work written in verse.

Versification: The writing of verse. Versification may also refer to the meter, rhyme, and other mechanical components of a poem.

Victorian: Refers broadly to the reign of Queen Victoria of England (1837-1901) and to anything with qualities typical of that era.

For example, the qualities of smug narrow-mindedness, bourgeois materialism, faith in social progress, and priggish morality are often considered Victorian. This stereotype is contradicted by such dramatic intellectual developments as the theories of Charles Darwin, Karl Marx, and Sigmund Freud (which stirred strong debates in England) and the critical attitudes of serious Victorian writers like Charles Dickens and George Eliot. In literature, the Victorian Period was the great age of the English novel, and the latter part of the era saw the rise of movements such as decadence and symbolism.

Victorian Age: See *Victorian*

Victorian Period: See *Victorian*

W

Weltanschauung: A German term referring to a person's worldview or philosophy.

Weltschmerz: A German term meaning "world pain." It describes a sense of anguish about the nature of existence, usually associated with a melancholy, pessimistic attitude.

Z

Zarzuela: A type of Spanish operetta.

Zeitgeist: A German term meaning "spirit of the time." It refers to the moral and intellectual trends of a given era.

Cumulative
Author/Title Index

Cumulative
Nationality/Ethnicity Index

Subject/Theme Index

Cumulative Index of First Lines

Some say a host of cavalry, others of infantry, (Fragment 16) V38:62

Some say it's in the reptilian dance (The Greatest Grandeur) V18:119

Some say the world will end in fire (Fire and Ice) V7:57

Something there is that doesn't love a wall (Mending Wall) V5:231

Sometimes walking late at night (Butcher Shop) V7:43

Sometimes, a lion with a prophet's beard (For An Assyrian Frieze) V9:120

Sometimes, in the middle of the lesson (Music Lessons) V8:117

somewhere i have never travelled,gladly beyond (somewhere i have never travelled,gladly beyond) V19:265

South of the bridge on Seventeenth (Fifteen) V2:78

Stiff and immaculate (My Father in the Navy) V46:87

Stop all the clocks, cut off the telephone, (Funeral Blues) V10:139

Strong Men, riding horses. In the West (Strong Men, Riding Horses) V4:209

Such places are too still for history, (Deep Woods) V14:138

Sundays too my father got up early (Those Winter Sundays) V1:300

Sunset and evening star, (Crossing the Bar) V44:3

Sweet day, so cool, so calm, so bright, (Virtue) V25:263

Swing low sweet chariot (Swing Low Sweet Chariot) V1:283

T

Taped to the wall of my cell are 47 pictures: 47 black (The Idea of Ancestry) V36:138

Take heart, monsieur, four-fifths of this province (For Jean Vincent D'abbadie, Baron St.-Castin) V12:78

Take sheds and stalls from Billingsgate, (The War Correspondent) V26:235

Take this kiss upon the brow! (A Dream within a Dream) V42:80

Talent is what they say (For the Young Who Want To) V40:49

Tears, idle tears, I know not what they mean (Tears, Idle Tears) V4:220

Tell all the Truth but tell it slant— (Tell all the Truth but tell it slant) V42:240

Tell me not, in mournful numbers (A Psalm of Life) V7:165

Tell me not, Sweet, I am unkind, (To Lucasta, Going to the Wars) V32:291

Temple bells die out. (Temple Bells Die Out) V18:210

That is no country for old men. The young (Sailing to Byzantium) V2:207

That negligible bit of sand which slides (Variations on Nothing) V20:234

That time of drought the embered air (Drought Year) V8:78

That's my last Duchess painted on the wall (My Last Duchess) V1:165

The apparition of these faces in the crowd (In a Station of the Metro) V2:116

The Assyrian came down like the wolf on the fold (The Destruction of Sennacherib) V1:38

The bored child at the auction (The Wings) V28:242

The brief secrets are still here, (Words Are the Diminution of All Things) V35:316

The bright moon lifts from the Mountain of (The Moon at the Fortified Pass) V40:180

The broken pillar of the wing jags from the clotted shoulder (Hurt Hawks) V3:138

The bud (Saint Francis and the Sow) V9:222

The Bustle in a House (The Bustle in a House) V10:62

The buzz saw snarled and rattled in the yard (Out, Out—) V10:212

The couple on the left of me (Walk Your Body Down) V26:219

The courage that my mother had (The Courage that My Mother Had) V3:79

The Curfew tolls the knell of parting day (Elegy Written in a Country Churchyard) V9:73

The day? Memorial. (Grape Sherbet) V37:109

The fiddler crab fiddles, glides and dithers, (Fiddler Crab) V23:111–112

The fog comes (Fog) V50:110

The force that through the green fuse drives the flower (The Force That Through the Green Fuse Drives the Flower) V8:101

The Frost performs its secret ministry, (Frost at Midnight) V39:75

The ghosts swarm (Unbidden) V55:190

The grains shall be collected (All Shall Be Restored) V36:2

The grasses are light brown (September) V23:258–259

The green lamp flares on the table (This Life) V1:293

The grey sea and the long black land; (Meeting at Night) V45:137

THE GUN full swing the swimmer catapults (400-Meter Freestyle) V38:2

The house is crammed: tier beyond tier they grin ("Blighters") V28:3

The ills I sorrow at (Any Human to Another) V3:2

The instructor said (Theme for English B) V6:194

The jaunty crop-haired graying (Poem about People) V44:174

The king sits in Dumferling toune (Sir Patrick Spens) V4:177

The land was overmuch like scenery (Beowulf) V11:2

The last time I saw it was 1968. (The Hiding Place) V10:152

The Lord is my shepherd; I shall not want (Psalm 23) V4:103

The man who sold his lawn to standard oil (The War Against the Trees) V11:215

The moon glows the same (The Moon Glows the Same) V7:152

The old man (Birdfoot's Grampa) V36:21

The old South Boston Aquarium stands (For the Union Dead) V7:67

The one in San Francisco who asked (To the Lady) V56:243

The others bent their heads and started in ("Trouble with Math in a One-Room Country School") V9:238

The pale nuns of St. Joseph are here (Island of Three Marias) V11:79

The Phoenix comes of flame and dust (The Phoenix) V10:226

The plants of the lake (Two Poems for T.) V20:218

The poetry of earth is never dead: (On the Grasshopper and the Cricket) V32:161

The rain set early in to-night: (Porphyria's Lover) V15:151

The river brought down (How We Heard the Name) V10:167

The room is full (My Mother Combs My Hair) V34:132

The rusty spigot (Onomatopoeia) V6:133

The sea is calm tonight (Dover Beach) V2:52

The sea sounds insincere (The Milkfish Gatherers) V11:111

The shattered water made a misty din. (Once by the Pacific) V47:195–196

The slow overture of rain, (Mind) V17:145

The snow is knee-deep in the courtyard (The Cucumber) V41:81

The Soul selects her own Society— (The Soul Selects Her Own Society) V1:259

The summer that I was ten— (The Centaur) V30:20

The sun that brief December day (Snow-Bound) V36:248–254

"The sun was shining on the sea, (The Walrus and the Carpenter) V30:258–259

The surface of the pond was mostly green— (The Lotus Flowers) V33:107

The tide rises, the tide falls, (The Tide Rises, the Tide Falls) V39:280

The time you won your town the race (To an Athlete Dying Young) V7:230

The trees are in their autumn beauty, (The Wild Swans at Coole) V42:286

The way sorrow enters the bone (The Blue Rim of Memory) V17:38

The whiskey on your breath (My Papa's Waltz) V3:191

The white ocean in which birds swim (Morning Walk) V21:167

The wind was a torrent of darkness among the gusty trees (The Highwayman) V4:66

The windows were open and the morning air was, by the smell of lilac and some darker flowering shrub, filled with the brown and chirping trills of birds. (Yet we insist that life is full of happy chance) V27:291

The woman wore a floral apron around her neck, (The Floral Apron) V41:140

the world is not a pleasant place (The World Is Not a Pleasant Place to Be) V42:303

The world is too much with us, late and soon, (The World Is Too Much with Us) V38:300

There are blows in life, so hard . . . I just don't know! (The Black Heralds) V26:47

There are strange things done in the midnight sun (The Cremation of Sam McGee) V10:75

There have been rooms for such a short time (The Horizons of Rooms) V15:79

There is a hunger for order, (A Thirst Against) V20:205

There is a pleasure in the pathless woods (Childe Harold's Pilgrimage, Canto IV, stanzas 178–184) V35:46

There is no way not to be excited (Paradiso) V20:190–191

There is the one song everyone (Siren Song) V7:196

There will come soft rains and the smell of the ground, (There Will Come Soft Rains) V14:301

There you are, in all your innocence, (Perfect Light) V19:187

There's a Certain Slant of Light (There's a Certain Slant of Light) V6:211

There's no way out. (In the Suburbs) V14:201

These open years, the river (For Jennifer, 6, on the Teton) V17:86

These shriveled seeds we plant, (Daily) V47:63

These unprepossessing sunsets (Art Thou the Thing I Wanted) V25:2–3

They choke cities like snowstorms. (Blonde White Women) V56:21

They eat beans mostly, this old yellow pair (The Bean Eaters) V2:16

They flee from me, that sometime did me seek (They Flee From Me) V56:211

They left my hands like a printer's (Blackberries) V55:34

They said, "Wait." Well, I waited. (Alabama Centennial) V10:2

They say a child with two mouths is no good. (Pantoun for Chinese Women) V29:241

They turn the water off, so I live without water, (Who Understands Me But Me) V40:277

they were just meant as covers (My Mother Pieced Quilts) V12:169

This girlchild was: born as usual (Barbie Doll) V9:33

This is a litany of lost things, (The Litany) V24:101–102

This is my letter to the World (This Is My Letter to the World) V4:233

This is the Arsenal. From floor to ceiling, (The Arsenal at Springfield) V17:2

This is the black sea-brute bulling through wave-wrack (Leviathan) V5:203

This is the hall of broken limbs. (Guide to the Other Gallery) V48:102

This is the ship of pearl, which, poets feign, (The Chambered Nautilus) V24:52–53

This poem is concerned with language on a very plain level (Paradoxes and Oxymorons) V11:162

This tale is true, and mine. It tells (The Seafarer) V8:177

Thou ill-formed offspring of my feeble brain, (The Author to Her Book) V42:42

Thou still unravish'd bride of quietness (Ode on a Grecian Urn) V1:179

Three days Natasha'd been astray, (The Bridegroom) V34:26

Three times my life has opened. (Three Times My Life Has Opened) V16:213

Time in school drags along with so much worry, (Childhood) V19:29

to fold the clothes. No matter who lives (I Stop Writing the Poem) V16:58

To him who in the love of Nature holds (Thanatopsis) V30:232–233

To pray you open your whole self (Eagle Poem) V56:72

To replay errors (Daughter-Mother-Maya-Seeta) V25:83

To weep unbidden, to wake (Practice) V23:240

Toni Morrison despises (The Toni Morrison Dreams) V22:202–203

Tonight I can write the saddest lines (Tonight I Can Write) V11:187

tonite, *thriller* was (Beware: Do Not Read This Poem) V6:3

True ease in writing comes from art, not chance, (Sound and Sense) V45:201

Truth be told, I do not want to forget (Native Guard) V29:183

Trying to protect his students' innocence (The History Teacher) V42:100

Turning and turning in the widening gyre (The Second Coming) V7:179

Cumulative Index of Last Lines

I take it you are he? (Incident in a Rose Garden) V14:191

I the late madonna of barren lands. (Jamaica 1980) V48:131

I, too, am America. (I, Too) V30:99

I turned aside and bowed my head and wept (The Tropics in New York) V4:255

I would like to tell, but lack the words. (I Built My Hut beside a Traveled Road) V36:119

I'd understand it all— (Nebraska) V52:147–148

If Winter comes, can Spring be far behind? (Ode to the West Wind) V2:163

I'll be gone from here. (The Cobweb) V17:51

I'll dig with it (Digging) V5:71

Imagine! (Autobiographia Literaria) V34:2

In a convulsive misery (The Milkfish Gatherers) V11:112

In a heavy light like yellow onions. (Yellow Light) V55:255

In an empty sky (Two Bodies) V38:251

In balance with this life, this death (An Irish Airman Foresees His Death) V1:76

In beauty. (Eagle Poem) V56:72

in earth's gasp, ocean's yawn. (Lake) V23:158

In Flanders fields (In Flanders Fields) V5:155

In ghostlier demarcations, keener sounds. (The Idea of Order at Key West) V13:164

In hearts at peace, under an English heaven (The Soldier) V7:218

In her tomb by the side of the sea (Annabel Lee) V9:14

in the family of things. (Wild Geese) V15:208

in the grit gray light of day. (Daylights) V13:102

In the rear-view mirrors of the passing cars (The War Against the Trees) V11:216

In these Chicago avenues. (A Thirst Against) V20:205

in this bastion of culture. (To an Unknown Poet) V18:221

In this old house. (Sadie and Maud) V53:195

in winter. (Ode to My Socks) V47:173–174

in your unsteady, opening hand. (What the Poets Could Have Been) V26:262

Inns are not residences. (Silence) V47:231

iness (l(a) V1:85

Into blossom (A Blessing) V7:24

Is breaking in despair. (The Slave Mother) V44:213

Is Come, my love is come to me. (A Birthday) V10:34

is love—that's all. (Two Poems for T.) V20:218

is safe is what you said. (Practice) V23:240

is going too fast; your hands sweat. (Another Feeling) V40:3

is still warm (Lament for the Dorsets) V5:191

Isn't equal to that. You ain't ruined," said she. (The Ruined Maid) V56:193

It asked a crumb—of Me ("Hope" Is the Thing with Feathers) V3:123

It had no mirrors. I no longer needed mirrors. (I, I, I) V26:97

It hasn't let up all morning. (The Cucumber) V41:81

It is always brimming May. (A Golden Day) V49:129

It is Margaret you mourn for. (Spring and Fall: To a Young Girl) V40:236

It is our god. (Fiddler Crab) V23:111–112

it is the bell to awaken God that we've heard ringing. (The Garden Shukkei-en) V18:107

it over my face and mouth. (An Anthem) V26:34

It rains as I write this. Mad heart, be brave. (The Country Without a Post Office) V18:64

It takes life to love life. (Lucinda Matlock) V37:172

It was your resting place." (Ah, Are You Digging on My Grave?) V4:2

it's always ourselves we find in the sea (maggie & milly & molly & may) V12:150

its bright, unequivocal eye. (Having it Out with Melancholy) V17:99

It's funny how things blow loose like that. (Snapping Beans) V50:244–245

It's the fall through wind lifting white leaves. (Rapture) V21:181

its youth. The sea grows old in it. (The Fish) V14:172

J

Judge tenderly—of Me (This Is My Letter to the World) V4:233

Just imagine it (Inventors) V7:97

K

kisses you (Grandmother) V34:95

L

Laughing the stormy, husky, brawling laughter of Youth, half-naked, sweating, proud to be Hog Butcher, Tool Maker, Stacker of Wheat, Player with Railroads and Freight Handler to the Nation (Chicago) V3:61

Learn to labor and to wait (A Psalm of Life) V7:165

Leashed in my throat (Midnight) V2:131

Leaving thine outgrown shell by life's un-resting sea (The Chambered Nautilus) V24:52–53

Let my people go (Go Down, Moses) V11:43

Let the water come. (America, America) V29:4

life, our life and its forgetting. (For a New Citizen of These United States) V15:55

Life to Victory (Always) V24:15

like a bird in the sky … (Ego-Tripping) V28:113

like a shadow or a friend. *Colombia.* (Kindness) V24:84–85

like it better than being loved. (For the Young Who Want To) V40:50

Like nothing else in Tennessee. (Anecdote of the Jar) V41:3

Like Stone— (The Soul Selects Her Own Society) V1:259

like the evening prayer. (My Father in the Navy) V46:87

Little Lamb, God bless thee. (The Lamb) V12:135

Look'd up in perfect silence at the stars. (When I Heard the Learn'd Astronomer) V22:244

love (The Toni Morrison Dreams) V22:202–203

Love is best! (Love Among the Ruins) V41:248

Loved I not Honour more. (To Lucasta, Going to the Wars) V32:291

Luck was rid of its clover. (Yet we insist that life is full of happy chance) V27:292

M

'Make a wish, Tom, make a wish.' (Drifters) V10: 98

make it seem to change (The Moon Glows the Same) V7:152

Or whistling, I am not a little boy.
(The Ball Poem) V47:24
ORANGE forever. (Ballad of
Orange and Grape) V10:18
our every corpuscle become an elf.
(Moreover, the Moon) V20:153
Our love shall live, and later life
renew." (Sonnet 75) V32:215
outside. (it was New York and
beautifully, snowing . . . (i was
sitting in mcsorley's) V13:152
owing old (old age sticks) V3:246

P

patient in mind remembers the time.
(Fading Light) V21:49
Penelope, who really cried. (An
Ancient Gesture) V31:3
Perhaps he will fall. (Wilderness
Gothic) V12:242
Petals on a wet, black bough (In a
Station of the Metro) V2:116
*Plaiting a dark red love-knot into her
long black hair* (The
Highwayman) V4:68
plunges into the heart and is gone.
(The Panther) V48:147
Powerless, I drown. (Maternity)
V21:142–143
Práise him. (Pied Beauty) V26:161
Pressed to the wall, dying, but
fighting back! (If We Must Die)
V50:145
Pro patria mori. (Dulce et Decorum
Est) V10:110

Q

Quietly shining to the quiet Moon.
(Frost at Midnight) V39:75

R

Rage, rage against the dying of the
light (Do Not Go Gentle into
that Good Night) V1:51
Raise it again, man. We still believe
what we hear. (The Singer's
House) V17:206
Remember. (Remember) V32:185
Remember the Giver fading off the lip
(A Drink of Water) V8:66
Ride me. (Witness) V26:285
rise & walk away like a panther. (Ode
to a Drum) V20:172–173
Rises toward her day after day, like a
terrible fish (Mirror) V1:116

S

Sans teeth, sans eyes, sans taste, sans
everything. (Seven Ages of
Man) V35:213

Shall be lifted—nevermore! (The
Raven) V1:202
shall be lost. (All Shall Be Restored)
V36:2
Shall you be overcome.
(Conscientious Objector)
V34:46
Shantih shantih shantih (The Waste
Land) V20:248–252
share my shivering bed. (Chorale)
V25:51
she'd miss me. (In Response to
Executive Order 9066: All
Americans of Japanese Descent
Must Report to Relocation
Centers) V32:129
Show an affirming flame.
(September 1, 1939) V27:235
Shuddering with rain, coming down
around me. (Omen) V22:107
Simply melted into the perfect light.
(Perfect Light) V19:187
Singing of him what they could
understand (Beowulf) V11:3
Singing with open mouths their
strong melodious songs (I Hear
America Singing) V3:152
Sister, one of those who never
married. (My Grandmother's
Plot in the Family Cemetery)
V27:155
Sleep, fly, rest: even the sea dies!
(Lament for Ignacio Sánchez
Mejías) V31:128–30
slides by on grease (For the Union
Dead) V7:67
Slouches towards Bethlehem to be
born? (The Second Coming)
V7:179
so like the smaller stars we rowed
among. (The Lotus Flowers)
V33:108
So long lives this, and this gives life
to thee (Sonnet 18) V2:222
So prick my skin. (Pine) V23:223–224
so that everything can learn the
reason for my song. (Sonnet
LXXXIX) V35:260
Somebody loves us all. (Filling
Station) V12:57
someone (The World Is Not a
Pleasant Place to Be) V42:303
Speak through my words and my
blood. (The Heights of Macchu
Picchu) V28:141
spill darker kissmarks on that dark.
(Ten Years after Your
Deliberate Drowning) V21:240
Stand still, yet we will make him run
(To His Coy Mistress) V5:277
startled into eternity (Four
Mountain Wolves) V9:132

still be alive. (Hope) V43:81
Still clinging to your shirt (My
Papa's Waltz) V3:192
Stood up, coiled above his head,
transforming all. (A Tall Man
Executes a Jig) V12:229
strangers ask. *Originally?* And I
hesitate. (Originally)
V25:146–147
Surely goodness and mercy shall
follow me all the days of my life:
and I will dwell in the house of
the Lord for ever (Psalm 23)
V4:103
sweet land. (You and I) V49:274
sweet on the tongue. (Maestro)
V47:153
sweet things. (Problems with
Hurricanes) V46:157
switch sides with every jump.
(Flounder) V39:59
syllables of an old order. (A Grafted
Tongue) V12:93

T

Take any streetful of people buying
clothes and groceries, cheering
a hero or throwing confetti and
blowing tin horns . . . tell me if
the lovers are losers . . . tell me
if any get more than the
lovers . . . in the dust . . . in the
cool tombs (Cool Tombs)
V6:46
Take it, no one will know. (My Heart
Is Heavy) V50:204
Than from everything else life
promised that you could do?
(Paradiso) V20:190–191
Than that you should remember and
be sad. (Remember) V14:255
Than the two hearts beating each to
each! (Meeting at Night)
V45:137
that does not see you. You must
change your life. (Archaic
Torso of Apollo) V27:3
that dying is what, to live, each has to
do. (Curiosity) V47:43–44
that floral apron. (The Floral Apron)
V41:141
that might have been sweet in
Grudnow. (Grudnow) V32:74
That story. (Cinderella) V41:43
That then I scorn to change my state
with Kings (Sonnet 29) V8:198
that there is more to know, that one
day you will know it.
(Knowledge) V25:113
That watches and receives. (The
Tables Turned) V54:237

To be a queen! (Fear) V37:71

To beat real iron out, to work the bellows. (The Forge) V41:158

To every woman a happy ending (Barbie Doll) V9:33

To find they have flown away? (The Wild Swans at Coole) V42:287

To find out what it really means. (Introduction to Poetry) V50:167

to float in the space between. (The Idea of Ancestry) V36:138

to glow at midnight. (The Blue Rim of Memory) V17:39

to its owner or what horror has befallen the other shoe (A Pied) V3:16

To live with thee and be thy love. (The Nymph's Reply to the Shepherd) V14:241

To mock the riddled corpses round Bapaume. ("Blighters") V28:3

To perfume the sleep of the dead. (In the Bazaars of Hyderabad) V55:118

To see the cherry hung with snow. (Loveliest of Trees, the Cherry Now) V40:160

To strengthen whilst one stands." (Goblin Market) V27:96

To strive, to seek, to find, and not to yield (Ulysses) V2:279

To the moaning and the groaning of the bells (The Bells) V3:47

To the temple, singing. (In the Suburbs) V14:201

To wound myself upon the sharp edges of the night? (The Taxi) V30:211–212

too. (Birdfoot's Grampa) V36:21

torn from a wedding brocade. (My Mother Combs My Hair) V34:133

Tread softly because you tread on my dreams. (He Wishes for the Cloths of Heaven) V51:125–126

True to our God, true to our Native Land. (Lift Every Voice and Sing) V54:136

Turned to that dirt from whence he sprung. (A Satirical Elegy on the Death of a Late Famous General) V27:216

U

Undeniable selves, into your days, and beyond. (The Continuous Life) V18:51

under each man's eyelid. (Camouflaging the Chimera) V37:21

unexpectedly. (Fragment 16) V38:62

until at last I lift you up and wrap you within me. (It's like This) V23:138–139

Until Eternity. (The Bustle in a House) V10:62

unusual conservation (Chocolates) V11:17

Uttering cries that are almost human (American Poetry) V7:2

W

Walt Whitman shakes. This game belongs to him (Defending Walt Whitman) V45:42

War is kind (War Is Kind) V9:253

watching to see how it's done. (I Stop Writing the Poem) V16:58

water. (Poem in Which My Legs Are Accepted) V29:262

We are satisfied, if you are; but why did I die?" (Losses) V31:167–68

we tread upon, forgetting. Truth be told. (Native Guard) V29:185

We wear the mask! (We Wear the Mask) V40:256

wedding slippers (For a Daughter Who Leaves) V56:88

Went home and put a bullet through his head (Richard Cory) V4:117

Were not the one dead, turned to their affairs. (Out, Out—) V10:213

Were toward Eternity— (Because I Could Not Stop for Death) V2:27

What will survive of us is love. (An Arundel Tomb) V12:18

When I died they washed me out of the turret with a hose (The Death of the Ball Turret Gunner) V2:41

When I have crost the bar. (Crossing the Bar) V44:3

When locked up, bear down. (Fable for When There's No Way Out) V38:43

When the plunging hoofs were gone. (The Listeners) V39:136

when they untie them in the evening. (Early in the Morning) V17:75

when you are at a party. (Social Life) V19:251

When you have both (Toads) V4:244

Where deep in the night I hear a voice (Butcher Shop) V7:43

Where ignorant armies clash by night (Dover Beach) V2:52

where it's been. (Unbidden) V55:190

Where things began to happen and I knew it. (Ground Swell) V49:149

Which caused her thus to send thee out of door. (The Author to Her Book) V42:42

Which Claus of Innsbruck cast in bronze for me! (My Last Duchess) V1:166

Which for all you know is the life you've chosen. (The God Who Loves You) V20:88

which is not going to go wasted on me which is why I'm telling you about it (Having a Coke with You) V12:106

which only looks like an *l*, and is silent. (Trompe l'Oeil) V22:216

whirring into her raw skin like stars (Uncoiling) V35:277

white ash amid funereal cypresses (Helen) V6:92

White-tipped but dark underneath, racing out (Saturday at the Canal) V52:197–198

Who may revel with the rest? (In the Orchard) V45:105

Who toss and sigh and cannot rest. (The Moon at the Fortified Pass) V40:180

who understands me when I say this is beautiful? (Who Understands Me But Me) V40:278

Why am I not as they? (Lineage) V31:145–46

Wi' the Scots lords at his feit (Sir Patrick Spens) V4:177

Will always be ready to bless the day (Morning Walk) V21:167

will be easy, my rancor less bitter . . . (On the Threshold) V22:128

Will hear of as a god." (How we Heard the Name) V10:167

Wind, like the dodo's (Bedtime Story) V8:33

windowpanes. (View) V25:246–247

With courage to endure! (Old Stoic) V33:144

With gold unfading, WASHINGTON! be thine. (To His Excellency General Washington) V13:213